THE COMPLETE PC AT AND COMPATIBLES REFERENCE MANUAL

COVERS 286, 386, AND 486 SYSTEMS

Gilbert Held

John Wiley & Sons, Inc.

New York   Chichester   Brisbane   Toronto   Singapore

IBM PC AT® is a registered trademark of International Business Machines Corp.

Library of Congress Cataloging-in-Publication Data

Held, Gilbert, 1943–
    The complete PC AT and compatibles reference manual :
covers 286, 386, and 486 systems / Gilbert Held.
        p.   cm.
    Includes index.
    ISBN 0-471-53315-7 (paper)
    1. IBM Personal Computer AT.   2. IBM compatible computers.
I. Title.
QA76.8.I2595H44   1991
004.165—dc20   91-15937

Printed in the United States of America

10 9 8 7 6 5 4 3 2 1

Preface

The introduction of the IBM PC AT in 1984 helped to spawn an industry of manufacturers producing compatible computers that use the same bus design. Based on the user of the Intel 80286 microprocessor, the PC AT design—including random-access memory, read-only memory, and expansion slots—was used in modified form for the development of compatible personal computers using faster-operating Intel 80286 microprocessors as well as the Intel 80386 and 80486 chips.

Today, such computers as the AST Bravo and Premium, Compaq Deskpro, NEC PowerMate, and personal computers from Dell, Gateway, and over 100 other vendors that are based on various Intel microprocessors can trace a common heritage to IBM's PC AT. In fact, many components originally manufactured by IBM and other vendors for use with the PC AT can be used with personal computers manufactured a decade later. Even IBM recognized the viability of the PC AT design in its family of PS/2 computers, introducing the PS/2 Model 30 286, whose design is based on the architecture of the PC AT. This computer as well as more recently introduced PS/2 models can use almost all of the adapter cards and peripheral devices manufactured by IBM and other vendors for use in the original PC AT.

Regardless of whether you have an original IBM PC AT or a compatible computer or anticipate the purchase of this type of computer, this book will help you use the computer effectively. The book first examines the hardware components that make up an IBM PC AT and compatible computers, including proper setup. Information presented in the first two chapters will enable you to understand the differences between the IBM PC AT and 286, 386, and 486 based compatible computers manufactured by over a hundred vendors as well as the options you can consider to install and expand your computer. This information is followed by several chapters that will provide an in-depth examination of the use of the commands of the most popular versions of the Disk Operating System—DOS 3.3, 4.0, and 5.0. The series of chapters devoted to DOS will show you how to use DOS commands as well as how to automate different operations through the construction of a variety of practical batch files.

Because almost all versions of DOS include a copy of a BASIC language interpreter, most IBM PC AT and compatible computer users have a readily available programming language at no additional cost. To facilitate its use this book devotes several chapters to a step-by-step coverage of both BASICA contained on PC-DOS diskettes sold by IBM and GW-BASIC included on the MS-DOS diskette furnished with most compatible computers. In addition to coverage of the two most popular versions of interpretive BASIC and the recently introduced QBASIC bundled with DOS Version 5.0, this book also examines the statements unique to Microsoft's popular QuickBASIC compiler, providing readers with the ability to rapidly and effectively develop programs in BASICA, GW-BASIC, QBASIC, and QuickBASIC. After examining the operation and use of BASIC language statements and functions, you will develop several practical programs you can tailor to your specific requirements and use instead of purchasing costly application programs. Some of the programs build databases and retrieve records, generate charts, and sort data and perform other valuable functions. You may wish to incorporate these into your larger applications.

As a professional author, I realize the importance of reader feedback and actively solicit your comments and suggestions. Readers can contact me through John Wiley & Sons, Inc., at the address printed on the back cover of this book.

Gilbert Held
Macon, Georgia

Acknowledgments

The preparation of a book in many respects is like an orchestra—it requires many players working in harmony to be effective. This book is no exception as it required the fine efforts of many persons to convert my notes into the book you are reading.

First and foremost I would like to thank my family for their patience and understanding as I literally took over a portion of our home to write this book. I would like to again thank Mrs. Carol Ferrell for converting my notes into a manuscript suitable for submission to my publisher. Concerning my publisher, I would be remiss if I did not thank Therese Zak and Katherine Schowalter at John Wiley & Sons, Inc., for their encouragement and support. Last but not least, once again Lynn Brown has made a substantial contribution to another book, which I wish to acknowledge.

Trademark Acknowledgments

Contents

Chapter 5   FIXED DISK ORGANIZATION   148

Chapter 6   BATCH FILE OPERATIONS   172

Chapter 9   BASIC OPERATIONS IN BASIC   270

1 // Hardware Overview

Unveiled during 1984 on the third anniversary of the introduction of the IBM PC, the IBM PC AT (Advanced Technology) represented the latest generation of personal computer technology at that time. Although advances in technology have resulted in the development of display adapters, monitors, diskette drives, fixed disks, and other components that provide a considerably improved performance over original PC AT components, that computer provided a platform for personal computing that will last through this century. In fact, although IBM discontinued manufacturing its PC AT in April 1987 with the release of the PS/2 family of computers, that company rectified its mistake and satisfied consumer demand for "AT" type systems by introducing its PS/2 Model 30 286 computer during 1988. Today the PS/2 Model 30 286 accounts for a substantial portion of PS/2 sales.

The popularity of PC AT type systems is best noted by the fact that over 100 companies currently market "AT-compatible" personal computers. Although most of these computers use a more powerful microprocessor than that used in the original PC AT, most computers retain both software and hardware compatibility with programs and equipment designed for use with the IBM PC AT.

This chapter first focuses on the "true blue" PC AT manufactured by IBM, including different types of components used inside or attached to the system unit of that computer. This examination will help you gain a firm understanding of the basic components of the IBM PC AT. Note that most of the components that were used to provide the PC AT with its functionality, although no longer marketed by IBM, are today available from over 100 different vendors. Keyboards, video displays, diskette drives, fixed disks, and a variety of adapter boards can be used in both the IBM PC AT and compatible computers based on the use of the Intel 80286, 80386, and 80486 microprocessors.

Thus, when you obtain a detailed understanding of the different types of PC AT components and their operation, you will also appreciate their operation and use in compatible computers. Next, the chapter focuses on compatible PC AT computers manufactured by IBM and other vendors, discussing the similarities and differences between those computers and the original PC AT. In concluding, this chapter reviews the use of several third-party hardware products that you can use to expand the functionality and capability of the PC AT and compatible personal computers.

The IBM PC AT

Although there is no such item as a typical PC AT system, each PC AT system will include a minimum of four major components—a keyboard unit, a system unit containing space for the installation of a variety of adapter boards and storage devices, a monitor, and a printer. Figure 1.1 illustrates a common IBM PC AT system configuration showing the installation of one diskette drive in its system unit.

Basic and Enhanced Models

When originally announced, two models of the PC AT were offered. The basic PC AT includes 256K (K representing 1024 units) bytes of random access memory (RAM) and a single 5¼-inch, half-height, double-sided floppy diskette drive capable of storing 1.2 megabytes (M representing one thousand 1024 units) of information on a diskette, as well as a dual floppy diskette and fixed disk controller installed in the system unit. The enhanced PC AT includes 512K bytes of RAM, a 1.2-megabyte floppy disk drive, a serial/parallel adapter card, and a 20-megabyte fixed disk. Both the basic and the enhanced PC AT models include a keyboard; to display and print information, however, you must obtain a variety of optional equipment: a monitor, a printer, and appropriate adapter cards that must be installed inside the PC AT's system unit.

Although every IBM PC AT has a keyboard and system unit, the wide variety of equipment available from both IBM and other manufacturers that can be interfaced to the PC AT may cause some systems not to resemble the one shown in Figure 1.1. In fact, even the system unit may look slightly different if it has two diskette drives or two fixed disks. If the second diskette drive is not included in the system unit, a beige

Figure 1.1   IBM Personal Computer AT System. The major components include a keyboard, a system unit, a 25-line by 80-column display, and a printer (not shown). (*Courtesy of IBM Corporation.*)

backing plate will be installed to cover the slot where the second diskette drive or a second fixed disk can be inserted, as illustrated in Figure 1.1.

The remaining portions of this section examine the two components that are common to all IBM PC ATs—the keyboard and system unit—and take a look at some of the optional equipment available from both IBM and non-IBM sources.

Keyboard

The keyboard supplied with the original IBM PC AT had 84 keys as well as a row of 3 green indicator lights to show you when the Caps Lock, Num Lock, and Scroll Lock keys are active. This keyboard was later replaced by the 101-key IBM Enhanced PC Keyboard, which is illustrated in Figure 1.2.

The enhanced keyboard contains 12 function keys, labeled F1 through F12, located in a row across the top of the keyboard. In comparison, the original PC AT keyboard, which resembled keyboards used with the PC and PC XT, had 10 function keys, labeled F1 through F10, arranged in two rows that were 5 keys high and 2 keys wide located at the left side of the keyboard. These keys are called *function keys*, because they can initiate special functions, such as bringing a menu or help information to the screen. Because each function key emits a unique (but nonprintable) code when you press it, an application program can assign special meanings to these keys, such as commands to load a data file or to terminate the program and return to the disk operating system (DOS) command level. With the help of special utility programs, you can assign your own definitions to these keys; for example, you could make a single keystroke initiate some complex command sequence that you use often.

IBM assigned predefined functions to the function keys for editing DOS command-line entries and for generating BASIC language commands. For DOS command-line editing, only the first 6 function keys have a predefined meaning. In BASIC, the first 10 keys are initially assigned meanings in the form of BASIC commands that are generated when each key is pressed. You can change the meaning of one or more function keys in BASIC to correspond to a function or sequence of operations you more commonly perform; hence, the use of these keys can be viewed as a labor-saving device,

Figure 1.2   The PC AT Keyboard. The 101-key keyboard contains a row of three green LED indicator lights that illuminate when the Caps Lock, Num Lock, and Scroll Lock keys are activated. (*Courtesy of IBM Corporation.*)

because they reduce a sequence of keystrokes to a single keystroke. Table 1.1 lists the BASIC commands initially assigned to each function key.

At the right-hand side of the keyboard is the numeric keypad, which is useful for the rapid entry of numeric data. Because most keys in this area have dual meanings, you must enable their numeric usage by pressing the Num Lock key, which is above the 7/Home key. Note that there is an indicator directly above the numeric keypad on the keyboard to denote whether the numeric function is enabled or disabled. Similarly, the Caps Lock and Scroll Lock keys have indicators to inform you of the current state of these keys.

In the upper left portion of the keyboard, to the right of the F1 key, is the Esc or escape key. As its name implies, this key is typically used by application programs as a request to escape from a current activity. However, because it's so close to F1, you can easily press Esc when you mean to press F1, with possible disastrous results to your work.

Between the typewriter area located in the left portion of the keyboard and the numeric keypad is a four-key keypad. These keys are labeled with arrows indicating four directions and are used for screen and cursor control movements.

Although the keyboard may not appear from outside to be a sophisticated device, it in fact contains an Intel 8048 microcontroller that provides a significant degree of intelligence. The microcontroller supervises all keystrokes, generates a unique code for each key, and transmits these codes to the microprocessor located inside the system unit to which the keyboard is cabled. Other tasks performed by the 8048 include a diagnostic test of the keyboard when power is applied to the system unit; preventing one keystroke from being interpreted as two, which is more formally known as *debouncing*; and checking the keyboard for stuck keys.

When you press a key, it generates an identifying number known as the *scan code*. For the keys on the keyboard illustrated in Figure 1.2, the scan codes are numbered 1 through 101 to correspond to the number of keys on the keyboard. When you press a key, the 8048 transmits the scan code of the key to the system unit. Similarly, when you release the key, the 8048 transmits the key release code to the system unit; the release code is the regular scan code of the key plus 128.

When a key is pressed, released, or repeated by holding it down, its action is recorded into a 20-character buffer inside the keyboard. The microcontroller chip in the keyboard generates an interrupt to the system unit, in effect requesting the servicing of the key action. In response to the interrupt, part of the operating system code, known as the Basic Input Output System (BIOS)—which is contained on a read-only memory (ROM) chip in the system unit—reads the scan code from the keyboard microcontroller and sends instructions back to the keyboard. These instructions tell the 8048 microprocessor in the keyboard to remove the key action from the keyboard's buffer.

The ROM BIOS routines in the system unit are responsible for monitoring all keyboard activity. That is, they keep track of the scan codes and release codes to determine

Table 1.1	Key	Command		Key	Command
Initial Function Key					
Assignment in BASIC	F1	LIST		F6	LPT1
	F2	RUN		F7	TRON
	F3	LOAD		F8	TROFF
	F4	SAVE		F9	KEY
	F5	CONT		F10	SCREEN

whether you pressed a sequence of alphanumeric keys; held down one key to make it repeat the character; or held down the Alt, or Ctrl, or Shift key while you pressed other key(s) in order to initiate some special function. The routines also keep track of the current status of the toggle keys (Caps Lock, Num Lock, and Scroll Lock). In the light of all this information, the BIOS routines are able to translate your keystrokes into the appropriate ASCII codes for processing.

System Unit

The heart of the IBM PC AT is its system unit. When viewed from the front, the window to the right of the IBM logo contains a keylock and two indicators. The first indicator is a power-on light indicator, while the second LED denotes when the fixed disk, if installed, is in use. The keylock accepts a hard-to-duplicate "tubular" key, similar to ones used in many home security systems. When the PC AT is placed in a locked position and the key is removed, an operating machine will not accept keystroke input, so you can leave your system powered on and perform a desired activity without having to worry that someone could accidentally interrupt the activity. In addition, if the system unit is locked and not powered on, although an unauthorized user could turn the power switch on, he or she could not perform any operations on the AT. Due to the critical importance of the key, you should place it in an appropriate location when the key is not required and record its serial number.

Under the nameplate on the left and extending toward the diskette and optional fixed disk drive housing area is a ventilation grille. Take care to keep this grille uncovered during operation, because it permits an airflow through the interior of the system unit and serves to prevent heat buildup that could cause the electronics inside the system unit to fail.

The diskette and optional fixed disk housing area permit the installation of two half-height devices into the system unit. Standard equipment for both the basic and enhanced PC AT is a half-height, dual-sided, 1.2-megabyte (M byte) floppy diskette drive that is mounted in the upper portion of that location. Under the 1.2M-byte high-density floppy diskette drive, you can install another 1.2M-byte floppy diskette drive, a second fixed disk (if you purchased an enhanced PC AT), or a conventional 360K-byte half-height diskette drive. Although diskettes created on a PC, XT, or Portable PC can be read by the high-capacity 1.2M-byte diskette drive, do not write to those diskettes when they are in the high-capacity drive, because doing so will make them unreadable by a conventional 360K-byte drive. Thus, if you anticipate creating diskettes to be used on the PC, XT, or PPC, obtain and install a conventional 360K-byte diskette drive for your PC AT.

On the right rear of the system unit is the power switch. Similar to the switch on the original PC, when it is pushed upward the system is powered on.

System Unit Interior

Figure 1.3 presents, in diagrammatic form, the layout of the interior of the PC AT's system unit. In the upper right-hand portion of that illustration is the power supply and cooling fan. The power supply converts alternating current (ac) to the direct current (dc) required to operate the various components installed in the system unit. This power supply can be switched for 115- or 230-volt operation and thus permits the PC AT to be used worldwide. You can select either voltage by toggling a recessed switch on the back panel of the system unit. The cooling fan expels excess heat generated by the electrical operation of the components in the system unit and prevents a heat buildup that could adversely affect your computer.

In the lower right portion of Figure 1.3 is the housing for the 1.2M-byte floppy diskette drive and an optional 20M-byte fixed disk, another 1.2M-byte floppy diskette drive, or a 360K-byte floppy diskette drive. With the latter optional device, you can create diskettes that can be read by the diskette drives installed in the IBM PC, XT, and PPC. A high-capacity 1.2M-byte floppy diskette drive is installed in the top part of the housing in both the basic and enhanced models of the PC AT, and any of the three optional devices previously mentioned can be installed in the lower part of this housing area.

In the enhanced model of the PC AT, a 20M-byte fixed disk is installed to the left of the previously discussed housing area. This device is also illustrated in Figure 1.3. Later versions of both the basic and enhanced PC AT were marketed by IBM with a 30M-byte fixed disk.

RAM

The lower left portion of the system unit contains the Intel 80286 microprocessor, read-only memory (ROM), and random access or read/write memory (RAM). Probably due to unavailability in sufficient quantities or the cost of 128K RAM chips, IBM used a piggyback arrangement of two 64K-bit chips for RAM in the initial versions of the basic and enhanced models of the PC AT.

RAM is obtained by filling up to four rows of sockets with memory chips, with each row referred to as a *memory bank*. Memory banks are numbered from 0 for the top row to 3 for the bottom row. In the basic model, only banks 0 and 1 were populated, yielding 256K bytes of RAM. In the enhanced model, all four rows were populated with piggybacked 64K-bit chips to obtain a total of 512K bytes of RAM on the system board. As in the PC and PC XT, each bank consists of nine chip sockets to enable memory parity checking. Later models of the PC AT used 256K-bit memory chips in banks 0

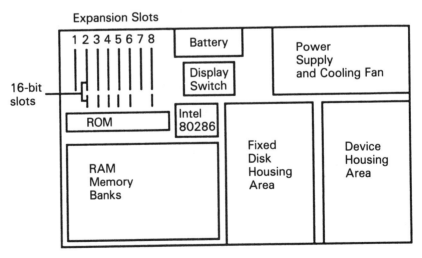

Figure 1.3 IBM PC AT System Unit Interior. Expansion slots 2 through 6 and slot 8 can be used for either 16-bit or 8-bit data transfer adapter cards, containing either one or two edge connectors, as long as the card does not contain a skirt.

and 1 and 64K-bit chips in banks 2 and 3 to obtain a total of 640K bytes of on-board storage.

Eight of the nine chips in each row hold a byte of data; the ninth is a parity bit that provides a means of error detection. When the computer stores a byte into memory, it counts the number of bits that are set to 1, then sets the parity bit so that the total number of 1s is even (for even parity) or odd (for odd parity). For example, a capital A, whose ASCII code is decimal 65, would have bit positions 0 and 6 set to 1. This is an even number, so for an odd-parity scheme, the computer would also set the parity bit, as follows:

Bit position:	P	7	6	5	4	3	2	1	0	
Weight:	256	128	64	32	16	8	4	2	1	
Contents:	1	0	1	0	0	0	0	0	1	$(64 + 1 = 65)$

When the computer next reads that location, it checks the parity bit, finds a 1, and therefore expects to find an even number of 1s in positions 0 through 7. If the computer in fact finds an odd number of 1s, it knows that an error has occurred in reading or writing the data and executes an error-handling routine that is part of the operating system to determine what action to take. On IBM systems, this action terminates the use of the computer by shutting it down.

When you power up the PC AT, a BIOS routine initiates what is known as a *power-on self-test (POST)*. During POST, the PC AT writes data into each memory location, computing the proper parity-bit state, and checks the parity bit to determine whether a parity error occurred. If so, a memory chip is considered to be defective, and the PC AT displays a code in the upper left corner of the screen to denote that a parity error occurred. The code defines the bank and chip in the bank that caused the error. You can use this information to locate and replace the failed chip.

ROM

Above the RAM chips are the ROM chips that contain built-in instructions that govern the initial POST of the AT that occurs when you power on the system. In addition, these ROM chips contain a built-in version of the BASIC programming language and other specialized diagnostic and control information. Even though the AT has no cassette interface, Cassette BASIC is included in ROM, because it is included in the nucleus of the IBM's BASIC language. You add features to this nucleus by loading different BASIC interpreters from diskette into RAM.

Intel 80286 Microprocessor

Above the ROM chips is a large square chip, which is the brain of the PC AT. This chip is the Intel 80286 microprocessor.

The Intel 80286 is a true 16-bit microprocessor that has both internal and external data buses that are 16 bits wide. This enables data to be manipulated in 16-bit units as well as sent to and received from expansion slots and memory in 16-bit units. In comparison, the 8088 microprocessor in the PC and PC XT manipulates data in 16-bit units but uses an 8-bit data bus to send and receive data in 8-bit units.

Other differences between the 80286 and 8088 concern the operating rate of each microprocessor and the level of integration of auxiliary chips on each device. The 80286 receives clocking directly from a crystal that can easily be replaced. Initial versions of the PC AT used a 6-megahertz (MHz) crystal that was faster than the 4.77-MHz operating rate of the 8088 used in the PC and PC XT. Later models of the PC AT use an 8-MHz crystal, which provides the 80286 with a clock speed almost twice that of the 8088.

The level of integration in the 80286 is approximately six times that of the 8088. The 80286 contains over 120,000 transistors on one chip, eliminating several separate chips that were required by the 8088. When taken together, the PC AT 80286's 16-bit data bus, its faster operating rate, and the higher level of chip integration permit software to operate between four and five times faster than on an 8088-based PC or PC XT.

Real Versus Protected Mode Operation

The 80286 can be operated in either real or protected modes. When the microprocessor operates in its real mode, in essence it functions as an 8088 with respect to memory address capability. In this mode the 80286—like the earlier microprocessor—can only address 1024K bytes (1 megabyte) of memory directly, because it uses a 20-bit address to access memory. The 80286 uses a 20-bit address to provide compatibility with the IBM PC and PC XT, which use the 8088 microprocessor. The design of the 80286's real mode addressing is related to the design of the 8088. The Intel 8088 is a microprocessor that has 16-bit internal data paths and for each memory operation generates a 20-bit address that can access 2^{20} (1,048,576) memory locations. However, the microprocessor has only eight pins for data, so it has to perform two memory operations to fetch or store a 16-bit data word, 1 byte at a time. Further, because it's desirable to be able to keep program code, data, and the stack in separate blocks of memory, the microprocessor computes every memory address in two parts, known as the *segment* and the *offset*.

The segment is an area of contiguous memory, and the offset is the number of bytes from the start of the segment. Because the segment is limited to 64K bytes in length, you can represent any offset by a 16-bit number. The segment must start on a 16-byte boundary within the physical memory. The 8088 has four 16-bit segment registers, each of which points to the base of one of the four possible segments (which may overlap each other). To calculate a physical address, the 8088 multiplies the value in a segment register by 16 and then adds the logical (offset) address; the result is always a 20-bit address. Thus, the 20-bit address used by the 80286 in its real mode provides address compatibility with the 8088 microprocessor.

In the second mode of the 80286, the protected mode, the microprocessor uses a 24-bit address bus, permitting direct addressing of 16M bytes of memory. In addition, in the protected mode of operation the microprocessor becomes capable of safely running several applications at one time, a process more formally known as *multitasking*.

Bus

The *bus* is the path along which data moves from the microprocessor to each of the system expansion slots into which various types of adapter cards can be inserted. The lines that are visible between system expansion slots are known as *trace lines* and are part of the bus. These lines contain three types of data paths or circuits—addressing, control, and data. The control circuits direct the flow of information to and from the expansion slots, whereas the addressing circuits enable data to reach its appropriate destination or to be read from a specific destination. The data circuits carry information to or from the microprocessor.

The key differences between the 80286 bus and the 8088 bus used in the PC and PC XT are in the physical number of data and address lines.

The 80286 data bus has 16 lines instead of the 8 lines used in the 8088-based PC and PC XT. This enables the 80286 to transfer data in 16-bit chunks in comparison to the 8-bit chunks used by the 8088 to transfer data. Concerning the addressing lines, the 80286 contains 24, permitting the direct addressing of 2^{24} or 16M bytes of memory. In comparison, the 8088 uses 20 address lines, permitting 1M byte of RAM to be addressed.

Expansion Slots

To enable many of the large number of 8-bit adapter cards designed for operation in the PC and PC XT to work with the PC AT, IBM provided two control signals on the bus and structured the physical layout of the expansion slots to accommodate 8-bit adapter cards.

As indicated in Figure 1.3, there are eight system expansion slots in the PC AT. Expansion slots 2 through 6 and slot 8 have two edge connectors, whereas slots 1 and 7 each have only one edge connector. The edge connector closer to the rear of the system unit is the standard 62-pin IBM PC expansion slot connector used in the PC and PC XT. The second slot connector included in expansion slots 2 through 6 and slot 8 is a 36-pin connector designed to support the additional data and address lines used by the PC AT's 80286 microprocessor.

Cards specifically designed for 16-bit data transfers have two edge connectors and have to be inserted into expansion slots 2 through 6 or slot 8. Older adapter cards designed for use in the PC and PC XT can usually work in the PC AT; however, using them may significantly reduce the performance of the computer, depending on the type of 8-bit adapter used. One example of performance degradation is the use of an 8-bit memory adapter designed for use in the PC or PC XT. This adapter has a single 62-pin edge connector and lacks a skirt, enabling it to be installed in any PC AT expansion slot. If you install this 8-bit memory card in any of the expansion slots 2 through 6 or slot 8, its lack of a second 36-pin edge connector results in two control lines on the 36-pin expansion slot connector not being activated, in effect informing the AT that an 8-bit card is installed in that expansion slot. Thereafter, data transfers to and from that expansion slot only occur 8 bits at a time.

If an 8-bit adapter card has a skirt, it is physically restricted to use in expansion slot 1 or 7. If you try to install it in any of the expansion slots 2 through 6 and slot 8, the skirt bumps against the second connector of these slots and prevents the edge connector of the card from being inserted into the 62-pin connector, as Figure 1.4 illustrates. The graphics card illustrated in Figure 1.5 is a prime example of an adapter card with a skirt that is physically restricted to installation in expansion slot 1 or 7 in the PC AT.

Battery

Located between expansion slot 8 and the power supply is a lithium battery that is used to supply power to a clock/calendar and 64K bytes of complementary metallic oxide semiconductor (CMOS) RAM. The 64K-byte CMOS RAM is a low-power memory area that stores the system configuration data initially entered during the installation process. This memory area is set via software and replaces the inaccessible configuration switches found on the PC and PC XT.

Because the CMOS RAM contains information about the PC AT's configuration, if the battery should fail you not only lose the clock and calendar settings but also such important information as the number of disk drives and amount of RAM installed. When

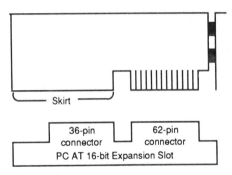

Figure 1.4   Physical Incompatibility. The skirt on some 8-bit adapter cards physically precludes their insertion into a 16-bit expansion slot on the PC AT.

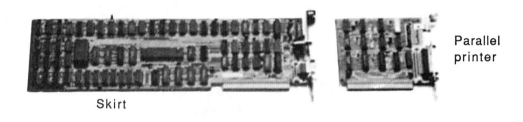

Figure 1.5   Color Graphics Card. Because of the skirt behind the connector edge, the color graphics card must be installed in either expansion slot 1 or expansion slot 7. (*Courtesy of IBM Corporation.*)

this information is lost, you have to reconfigure the system every time it is turned on—a time-consuming and tedious task until you replace the battery.

Figure 1.6 illustrates perhaps the most important replacement part you will require. The lithium battery illustrated is manufactured by Tadiran, which supplied over 80 percent of the batteries used in the IBM PC ATs. This battery is exclusively marketed by IBC of Reseda, California, as a replacement for the original battery supplied with the AT, which can be expected to last approximately 3 years. The Tadiran battery can be expected to last for about 10 years.

As previously noted, if battery power is lost, configuration information is lost. A simple procedure can help you reset the system parameters if the need arises. To guide you in selecting the appropriate options in the Setup program contained on the diagnostic diskette included with each PC AT, use Setup to display and print your system's configuration prior to a battery failure. The following illustrates the type of screen display you see as you use the Setup program, which you should print and save. Once you save the program results, the replacement of a battery that results in the loss of configuration data becomes a simple procedure to correct by rerunning Setup.

```
Your system may have other options
installed.  They are not required for
Setup and are not displayed.
```

```
The following options have been set:
Diskette Drive A - High Capacity
Diskette Drive B - Double Sided
Fixed Disk Drive C - Type 2
Fixed Disk Drive D - Not installed
Base memory size - 640KB
Expansion memory size - 1024KB
Primary display is:
- Color Display (80 columns)

Are these options correct (Y/N)?
```

Display Switch

The only switch contained in the PC AT system unit is located slightly below the area where the battery is located. This switch sets the default for the type of display you want to use when the computer is powered on. When you position the switch toward the rear of the system unit, it selects the monochrome display as the primary display. If you position the switch toward the front of the system unit, a color graphics display becomes the default.

Expansion/Adapter Cards

A variety of expansion/adapter cards are available from IBM and other manufacturers and provide the ability to enhance the functionality of your PC AT. Take care, however, to ascertain which expansion slots an adapter card can be inserted into, because many cards cannot operate effectively in expansion slots 2 through 6 and 8 even if they do not have skirts and can be inserted into those slots.

Performance Constraints

For AT users and owners who have access to earlier PC systems, Table 1.2 will serve as a compatibility guide indicating which IBM PC, XT, and PPC adapters can be used

Figure 1.6   IBM Replacement Battery. Because the life of the battery originally installed in the PC AT is approximately three years, many users will have to replace it one or more times during the life of their computer. (*Courtesy of IBC.*)

Table 1.2
PC Adapter
Compatibility Guide

Adapter Cards	Compatibility with PC AT
Monochrome display and parallel printer	Works in expansion slot 1 or 7
Color/graphics	Works in expansion slot 1 or 7
Parallel printer	Not recommended for use in PC AT
64K to 256K memory	Not recommended for use in PC AT
Asynchronous communications	Not recommended for use in PC AT
5¼-inch diskette drive	Not recommended for use in PC AT
Game control	Works in expansion slot 1 or 7

with the PC AT and which are not recommended for use in that computer. The adapters listed in Table 1.2 that are not recommended for use in the PC AT are incapable of appropriate performance because they are designed to operate with the 8-bit data transfer used with the 8088 microprocessor that powers the PC, XT, and PPC, rather than the 16-bit rate the Intel 80286 microprocessor addresses.

As an example, consider the 5¼-inch diskette drive adapter that controls the floppy diskette drives on the PC and PC XT. This diskette drive adapter is designed to work with the 8088 microprocessor that receives data from a diskette drive 8 bits at a time, processes it internally in a 16-bit register, and then sends the result back to the drive in an 8-bit form. Because the 80286 is capable of performing input and output operations using a 16-bit bus containing 16 wires, this diskette drive adapter cannot work efficiently with the 80286. Figure 1.7 illustrates the eight most common IBM PC adapter cards and can be used as a visual reference in conjunction with the data contained in Table 1.2 to ascertain which adapters that operate with the PC or PC XT can be efficiently used with the AT.

AT Adapter Cards and Other Options

Table 1.3 lists the adapter cards and options originally marketed by IBM for use with the PC AT. Adapter cards provide memory expansion, serial and parallel ports, and monitor functions. Options include a memory expansion module to increase on-board system unit memory, as well as a special cable that converts a 9-pin connector on the serial portion of the serial/parallel adapter card to the more common 25-pin connector. Similar to most adapter cards designed for use in the PC and PC XT, the PC AT adapter cards listed in Table 1.3 are no longer manufactured by IBM. However, numerous third-party vendors continue to manufacture compatible adapter cards for use in the PC AT and PC AT compatible computers. These vendors provide a viable source of personal computer components to build or expand your system.

Memory Kits

If you want to expand the 256K-byte memory of a basic PC AT, you can obtain a 256K-byte memory expansion kit that consists of 18 single 128K-bit chips. You insert these chips into the sockets of memory banks 2 and 3, bringing the total memory on the system board to 512K bytes. PC-DOS supports as many as 640K bytes of RAM, so you can bring the memory up to full capacity by adding a 128K-byte memory adapter card in one of the expansion slots.

Serial and Parallel Adapters

The serial and parallel ports on the serial/parallel adapter card and the parallel port on the monochrome display and parallel printer adapter provide two of the more popular methods by which personal computers can communicate with devices cabled to their system units. The parallel port on the serial/parallel card and the parallel printer interface on the monochrome display and parallel printer card transmit data from your computer in parallel, 8 bits at a time. Each parallel port can be identified by a 25-pin female (socket) connector at the rear of the card that, for an installed card, is at the rear of the system unit. The 25-pin connector includes eight data lines, as well as control lines, and the connector is formally referred to as a DB-25S connector by cabling companies, where the S stands for socket. On the IBM monochrome display and parallel printer card illustrated in Figure 1.7, the parallel printer port is located directly below a smaller 9-pin video output port used to connect the adapter card to a monochrome display.

Parallel Ports

Up to three parallel ports can be installed in an IBM PC AT. These ports are designated LPT1 through LPT3, which are their DOS device names. Due to the high data transfer rate at which data is sent through the parallel port, the width of the data bits is very narrow, making them susceptible to interference. Because of this, parallel cables are usually no longer than 15 feet.

Serial Ports

The second popular method by which personal computers communicate with external devices is through serial ports. The serial/parallel card includes electronics that convert

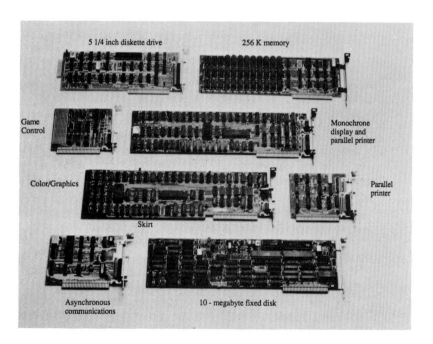

Figure 1.7   Common Adapter Cards Used in the PC, XT, and PPC. From top to bottom, left to right, the following adapter cards are illustrated: 5¼-inch diskette drive, 256K-byte memory, game control, monochrome display and parallel printer, color graphics, parallel printer, asynchronous communications, and 10-megabyte fixed disk. (*Courtesy of IBM Corporation.*)

Adapter Card/Option	Function
128K-byte memory adapter card	Increases system unit memory by 128K bytes after on-board memory totals 512K bytes
256K-byte memory expansion module	Increases on-board system unit memory by 256K
512K-byte expansion adapter card	Increases system unit memory by 512K bytes after on-board memory totals 512K bytes
1M-byte expansion adapter	Increases system unit memory by 1M byte after on-board memory totals 512K bytes
Serial/parallel adapter card	Contains the interface for one serial and one parallel device
Serial adapter connector	A short cable that converts the DB-9 connector on the serial interface of the serial/parallel adapter card to a more common DB-25 connector
1.2M-byte floppy diskette drive	Reads diskettes in 160/180K-byte, 320/360K-byte, and 1.2M-byte mode; writes to diskettes in 1.2M-byte mode
320/360K-byte diskette drive	Reads and writes 5¼-inch diskettes in 160/180K-byte and 320/360K-byte modes
3½-inch diskette drive	Reads and writes 3½-inch diskettes in 720K-byte mode
Diskette drive and hard disk adapter	Provides signal interfacing for up to four devices, but only three can be installed within the system unit
Monochrome display and parallel printer adapter	Has dual function of providing a parallel printer interface and the interface necessary to drive the IBM monochrome display
Color/graphics monitor adapter	Permits attachment of a wide variety of TV frequency monitors and TV sets via a user-supplied RF modulator (including a light pen interface); must be installed in expansion slot 1 or 7
Enhanced graphics adapter	Can be used with both the IBM monochrome display and the color display: provides the monochrome display with graphics capability that is unattainable with the monochrome display and parallel printer adapter; improves the resolution on the color screen when used with a color display.
Video graphics array adapter	Generates analog video signals that must be displayed on an analog monitor.

8-bit bytes that your computer operates on into a serial stream of 8 bits that flows over a single wire in the serial connector at the rear of the card. You can install up to four serial ports in your computer. Serial ports are designated COM1 through COM4, which are their DOS device names. These ports are also referred to as EIA RS-232 ports, which is the method by which the Electronics Industries Association (EIA) denoted a standard for this interface. In this instance, RS stands for *recommended standard*, and 232 is the identification number of the standard.

Most standard serial ports can be identified by a 25-pin male (plug) connector, formally referred to as a DP-25P, which is the reverse of the connector on a parallel port. This should prevent you from plugging a serial cable into a parallel interface or a parallel cable into a serial interface.

A second type of serial port is represented by the use of a 9-pin connector on the serial/parallel adapter card. The use of a smaller 9-pin connector enables both a serial and a parallel port connector to be mounted on one card.

Common data rates supported by serial communications range from 110 to 19200 bits per second when BIOS serial routines are used. However, many vendors bypass BIOS to obtain a serial rate up to approximately 100 Kbps, which enables two computers to rapidly transfer data when they are directly cabled. In addition to supporting data transmission via a modem, serial ports can be used to operate serial interface printers, plotters, and scanners, as well as some mice. With a serial interface, your cable connecting the serial port to a serial device can be up to 50 feet long.

A combination serial/parallel adapter card contains a serial and parallel interface that can be used to transfer data to serial or parallel devices. Serial devices that can be connected to this card include modems and acoustic couplers, as well as serial printers and other serial interfaced devices. Your typical use of the parallel interface on this card would be to drive a parallel printer.

The parallel interface on this card is a DB-25 connector, which is the same as that used in the parallel interface card on the original PC. The serial interface on this card uses a male-headed DB-9 connector that requires one to purchase a special DB-9/DB-25 serial adapter connector in order to use a standard cable to connect the serial interface to a serial device.

Diskette Drives

The IBM PC AT supports the use of four types of diskette drives—the 1.2M-byte 5¼-inch high-capacity diskette drive, the 5¼-inch 360K-byte diskette drive, and the 3½-inch 720K-byte and 1.44M-byte diskette drives.

1.2M-byte Floppy Diskette Drive

Although the 1.2M-byte high-capacity diskette drive can read 5¼-inch diskettes created on the PC and PC XT, when the drive writes on a diskette using a 360K-byte format, the data is placed on tracks that are thinner than those created on conventional 5¼-inch diskettes. Thus, PC and PC XT diskette drives will more often than not be unable to read diskettes created on the 1.2M-byte high-capacity diskette.

360K-byte Floppy Diskette Drive

The 360K-byte floppy diskette drive permits data to be recorded onto diskettes in a format compatible with other members of the IBM PC family. This drive is mounted in the lower portion of the disk housing area inside the system unit and has a star in its lower right corner to distinguish it from the 1.2M-byte floppy diskette drive.

720K/1.44M-byte Diskette Drives

The first 3½-inch diskette drive marketed by IBM for use with the PC AT had a storage capacity of 720K bytes. Later, IBM introduced a high-capacity 3½-inch diskette drive that can record and read data in both 720K-byte and 1.44M-byte storage formats. Although the 1.44M-byte diskette can read a diskette recorded in a 720K-byte drive, the 720K-byte drive cannot read a diskette recorded in the high-density recording mode used in a 1.44M-byte drive.

Both 3½-inch diskette drives require special mounting brackets for installation in the device housing area of a PC AT, because the device housing area of the PC AT was constructed to house the larger 5¼-inch devices.

Diskette Drive and Hard Disk Adapter

This adapter card provides the signal interface to attach up to three diskette drives and fixed disks. Although many AT users will attach one fixed disk and a 1.2M-byte floppy diskette drive and a conventional 360K-byte drive to this card, a total of 61.2M-bytes of on-line storage can be supported by this device using IBM fixed disks. This is accomplished by installing two fixed disks, each with a storage capacity of 30M bytes, and one 1.2M-byte high-capacity diskette drive in the PC AT and connecting the three devices to the diskette drive and hard disk adapter card. This device is standard on both versions of the AT, although the enhanced version only permits one additional device to be attached to the card, because two storage devices are standard with that model.

Monitors

Four IBM monitors were originally available for use with the PC AT—the IBM 5151 monochrome display, the IBM 5153 color display, the IBM 5175 PC professional graphics display and controller, and the IBM 5154 color display.

After the PC AT was manufactured, IBM developed the Enhanced Graphics adapter (EGA) and EGA monitor and the video graphics array (VGA) adapter and VGA monitor that became more common than the original monochrome display adapter (MDA). Both the EGA and VGA adapter cards and the EGA and VGA monitors can be used with the PC AT.

IBM 5151 Monochrome Display

The IBM 5151 monochrome display illustrated in Figure 1.1 is a high-resolution, green phosphor display. The screen of the display features an 11½-inch-wide surface with an anti-glare coating and displays 25 lines of 80 characters. Each character is displayed as a 7-by-9-dot text image within a 9-by-14-dot box, and the total resolution when the monitor is used in a graphics mode is 720 horizontal by 348 vertical picture elements (pixels).

To use the IBM monochrome display, you install the monochrome display and printer adapter option or the Enhanced Graphics Adapter into one of the expansion slots in the system unit. The monochrome display and parallel printer adapter card was previously illustrated in Figure 1.7. The end of the adapter card that fits into one end of the system expansion slot facing the rear of the system unit contains two connectors. The upper connector on the adapter card is a 9-pin video connector to which the cable from the monochrome display will be attached. The lower connector is a 25-pin printer connector that can be used to connect the system unit to a printer that has a parallel interface and uses the device address LPT1.

Note that the monochrome display can obtain power from the system unit by connecting the display's power plug to the electrical receptacle at the left rear part of the system unit. In addition to reducing the requirements for wall outlets to power the entire computer system, it allows the system unit's power on/off switch to control the display unit. Unfortunately, this is not the case with other types of monitors.

IBM 5153 Color Display

The IBM 5153 color display is used to display text and graphics output on a 13-inch-diagonal high-resolution color monitor. The display format is 25 lines by 80 characters and permits 16 colors (two shades of gray, red, green, blue, magenta, and cyan; and one shade of yellow, white, brown, and black) to be displayed at any one time. This display must be connected to a color/graphics monitor adapter card or an EGA card installed in the system unit of the PC AT.

Color/Graphics Monitor Adapter

The color/graphics monitor adapter card is shown in Figure 1.5. It has several video interfaces as well as a light pen connector. Both a 9-pin D-type shell RGB connector and a composite phono jack hookup are available to directly interface a monitor. To the rear of the retaining bracket of the adapter card is a 4-pin Berg strip that you can use to connect the adapter card to a radio frequency (RF) modulator. The RF modulator, in turn, can be connected to a standard TV. Normally, the output from the RF modulator is connected to a switch box, which in turn is connected to the TV's antenna connector. The slide switch on the switch box can be placed in one of two positions. In the position labeled "TV," the TV set is connected via the switch box to its antenna or perhaps a cable TV hookup. When the switch is moved to the position marked "game" (on some switch boxes the position is marked "computer"), the TV will be directly connected to the PC AT. Neither the 4-pin Berg strip for the radio frequency (RF) modulator nor a similar 6-pin strip connection to a light pen uses pin 2, which is missing its prong on both pin strips.

The key differences between using the IBM monochrome display and a TV set or monitor are in the areas of data output representation and display color. The IBM monochrome display can only operate in a noncolor text mode of 25 lines of 80 characters per line or a noncolor graphics mode when the monitor is used with an EGA. TVs and monitors can operate in color and both text mode and two graphics modes—medium-resolution graphics of 320 by 200 pixels and high-resolution graphics of 640 by 200 pixels.

The lower resolution and bandwidth display clarity of standard TVs in comparison to monitors normally limit the former to displaying 40 characters per line in text mode and medium-resolution graphics. Because high-resolution graphics appear in black and white, if you wanted to use this capability of the AT exclusively, a black-and-white monitor would suffice. For color text display and medium-resolution graphics, you can use either a color TV or color monitor; however, a color monitor would provide greater clarity as well as the ability to clearly display 80 characters of text per line. Both the number of characters displayed per line as well as the graphics mode one is operating in are controlled via software.

The use of the color/graphics monitor adapter permits black-and-white or color operation. The two basic modes of operation of the adapter card are alphanumeric (A/N) and all points addressable (APA) graphics. Within each mode, several display character widths or pixel sizes are available for selection.

In the A/N mode, the display can be operated in a 40-character by 25-line mode if you are using a low-resolution monitor or TV. The AT can be operated in an 80-character by 25-line mode if you have a high-resolution monitor attached to the color/graphics monitor adapter card. Character blinking and highlighting as well as reverse video are available for display under program control when your PC is in the black-and-white mode of operation. In the color mode of operation, a total of 16 foreground colors and 8 background colors can be selected for each displayed character. In addition, under program control, individual characters can be blinked.

IBM 5154 Enhanced Color Display

The IBM 5154 enhanced color display is similar in size to the 5153 monitor but includes circuitry that allows a greater resolution. The 5154 can display data with a resolution of 640 by 350 pixels as well as operate in the lower resolutions of 320 by 200 and 640 by 200 that the 5153 display uses. When the unit is operating in the enhanced color display mode, it can display 16 colors at one time from a palette of 64 colors. To operate the monitor in this mode, you must install an EGA in an expansion slot in the PC AT system unit. When used with a CGA card, the 5154 functions as if it were a 5153 display. Table 1.4 compares the major parameters of three of the IBM monitors pre-

Table 1.4
IBM Monitor
Parameters

	Monitor		
Parameter	**Monochrome**	**Color/Enhanced (TV Frequency)**	**Enhanced (High Resolution)**
Horizontal Scan Frequency	18.43 KHz	15.75 KHz	21.85 KHz
Vertical Scan Rate	50 Hz	60 Hz	60 Hz
Displayable Colors	4	16	64
Normal Character Size	7 by 9 pixels	7 by 7 pixels	7 by 9 pixels
Character Box Size	9 by 14 pixels	8 by 8 pixels	8 by 14 pixels
Maximum Resolution (Scan Lines)	720 by 350	640 by 200	640 by 350

viously discussed. Refer to Monitor Selection Considerations later in this chapter for a description of many of the terms contained in Table 1.4 related to scan rates.

IBM 5175 PC Professional Graphics Display and Controller

The IBM 5175 graphics display and professional graphics controller enable engineers, scientists, technicians, and designers to use the PC AT as an integrated workstation. The display and controller offer a variety of advanced graphics functions to include computer-aided design (CAD), computer-aided manufacturing (CAM), computer-aided engineering (CAE), and business presentation graphics.

The graphics display is attached to a controller, which occupies two adjacent expansion slots. The controller—a set of cards that includes an Intel 8088 microprocessor, 320K bytes of memory, and 64K ROM—provides many graphics functions that reduce the need to load software subroutines for most graphics activities. The controller provides for the following key functions:

- Two- and three-dimensional capabilities for drawing, rotating, translating, and scaling
- Moving and drawing with absolute or relative coordinates
- User-selectable character sizes
- User-redefinable color selection
- User-programmable character set
- Vector and polygon drawing and polygon fill

The IBM PC professional graphics display has the same physical dimensions as the IBM 5153 color display but has a darkened screen to enhance contrast. Up to 256 colors can be displayed simultaneously, with the colors selected from a palette of 4,096 colors, and the bit-mapped display provides a resolution of 640 by 480 pixels.

Due to the high cost of the professional graphics controller, the PC professional graphics display and controller never captured more than a fraction of a percent of the video graphics market. Because the high resolution provided by that controller was favorably received by personal computer users, IBM developed two additional video displays that provide an equivalent degree of screen resolution at a lower cost—the EGA and VGA display adapters.

Matching the Graphics Adapter to Your Monitor

EGA Card

The enhanced graphics adapter can be considered as three display adapters on one card, because it can be used with the IBM monochrome display, the 5153 color display, and the 5154 enhanced color display. Unlike the CGA adapter, the EGA does not support television receivers or composite monitors. Like the CGA, the EGA does not include a built-in parallel printer adapter such as that of the IBM monochrome display and parallel printer adapter card.

The IBM EGA card consists of three modules that were originally sold separately. The EGA full-slot board included 64K bytes of RAM. A graphics memory expansion card (GMEC) piggybacks onto the EGA, adding 64K bytes. A graphics memory module kit consists of 128K bytes of memory chips that fill out the GMEC for a total of 256K bytes of memory.

The EGA not only provides all of the display modes of the MDA and CGA but also adds several new modes. If you have a 5154 display unit (or equivalent), the EGA will provide a 16-color, 320-by-200-pixel image; and on a monochrome display unit, the EGA will provide 640-by-350-pixel, 4-color graphics, and a 43-line upper- and lowercase text display with 40 or 80 characters per line.

You may wonder how a monochrome monitor can provide four colors. In fact, blinking and high intensity are each considered a "color," and these, together with black and white, provide four distinct ways of representing any part of an image. A 43-row text display is also unusual. If you generate characters in a 9-by-14-pixel box, dividing the 350 scan lines by the 14-pixel-box height yields 25 rows of characters. However, if you reduce the size of the character box to 8 by 8 pixels—which is the standard size for the color graphics mode—you get $350 \div 8 = 43.75$ rows. Of course, you can't use three-quarters of a row, so you end up with 43 rows.

VGA Card and Analog Monitors

With the introduction of the PS/2 series, IBM incorporated the new VGA video standard into all systems except the PS/2 Model 25 and Model 30. In actuality, the video circuits are built into the PS/2 system board and do not require the use of a separate adapter card. To provide an upgrade path for PC series users, IBM marketed a VGA adapter board for use in that series of personal computers, including the PC AT.

Unlike earlier adapter cards that generate discrete digital signals, the VGA adapter generates analog output signals and cannot be used with earlier monitors that were designed to accept digital signals. Using analog signals, the intensity information required to drive the red, green, and blue color guns of a display is encoded as variable- rather than fixed-level signal amplitudes. This enables a VGA adapter to display a much wider range of colors than an EGA or other digital video cards.

In its maximum color mode of operation, the VGA uses three color registers, each 6 bits wide. Each color register can produce 64 intensity levels for each primary color, so a total of $64 \times 64 \times 64$ or 262,144 different color combinations are selectable.

IBM Analog Monitors

IBM offers four types of monitors for use with its PS/2 series of computers that can be used with a PC AT once a VGA adapter card is installed in that computer. All four monitors share a number of attributes, including the ability to accept analog input at the scan rate associated with VGA.

8503 Monochrome Display

The IBM 8503 monochrome display has a 12-inch diagonal screen. This display is capable of generating up to 64 shades of gray on a paper-white background. The 8503 weighs 19 pounds and is encased in a pearl-white housing that matches the color of the PS/2's system unit. The monitor is approximately 12 inches square, resulting in a 144-square-inch footprint, and it supports a maximum resolution of 640 by 480 pixels.

8512 Color Display

The IBM 8512 color display has a 14-inch diagonal screen. This display weighs approximately 33 pounds, including a tilt-and-swivel base. Like the 8503 monochrome display, the maximum resolution of the 8512 is 640 by 480 pixels. The 8512 has a coarse dot pitch of 0.41 mm that produces only marginally legible characters. Because of this, the 8512 should probably be restricted to moderate daily use.

8513 Color Display

The IBM 8513 color display uses a 0.28-mm dot pitch, creating a clearer image than you can obtain from the 8512. The 8513 has the same maximum resolution as the 8503 and 8512 monitors. However, because of its better dot pitch than the 8512 for a retail price difference of less than $100, the 8513 is more suitable for frequent use.

8514 Color Display

At the top of the line of IBM monitors is the firm's 40-pound 8514. Unlike the other IBM monitors, which are compatible only with the MCGA and VGA scan rates, the 8514 is a multiscan monitor that you can use with MDA, CGA, and EGA in addition to the VGA adapter.

Monitor Selection Considerations

To select an appropriate monitor for your computer, you should examine its dot pitch, horizontal and vertical scan frequencies, and adapter or video chip compatibility. The dot pitch is measured in millimeters and indicates the spacing of the pixels from one another. In general, the smaller the dot pitch, the sharper the characters will appear on a display.

The display capability of a monitor results from an electron beam that is passed from right to left over each line of the screen. This beam's intensity is varied in proportion to the intensity of the image to be displayed on the screen. A memory buffer in the video display adapter or video chips stores a bit pattern of the image to be displayed. Thus, the data in the buffer tells the monitor when to turn the electron beam on or off.

The rate at which the video adapter reads the contents of the display buffer and translates them into a screen display corresponds to the scan rate of the adapter. This scan rate actually consists of horizontal and vertical scan components. The rate at which the electron beam sweeps from right to left across the screen is known as the *horizontal scan frequency*, whereas the rate at which the beam moves from the top to the bottom of the screen is known as its *vertical scan rate*. In general, the faster the vertical scan rate, the lower the amount of screen flicker, because a high scan rate allows a screen to be refreshed in a shorter amount of time.

The VGA's horizontal scanning frequency is 31.5 kilohertz (KHz), which is approximately double the CGA's 15.75-KHz rate, almost double the MDA's 18.4-KHz rate, and almost 50 percent above the EGA's 21.85-KHz rate. The VGA's vertical scan rate is 60 Hz using a 640 by 480 resolution and 70 Hz when emulating a CGA or EGA, in comparison to the 60-Hz rate of the CGA and EGA and the 50-Hz rate of the MDA.

Compatible Computers

The success of the IBM PC AT created an Industry Standard Architecture (ISA) that will continue in use for the foreseeable future. In fact, after IBM discontinued the manufacture of the PC AT, over 100 vendors marketed compatible personal computers whose sales currently represent a significant percentage of all personal computers sold. Although many compatible PC AT computers have a processing and data storage capability that significantly exceeds that offered with the IBM PC AT, each computer has two features that make it compatible with the PC AT. These features include the ability to use adapter cards manufactured for use in the PC AT and the ability to execute almost every program designed for use on the IBM PC series of personal computers, including the PC, PC XT, and PC AT.

This section examines two PC AT compatible personal computers. It discusses the similarities and differences between the PC AT and the various compatible personal computers with respect to their system units because that major component provides the ability to develop the functionality and operational capability of the personal computer.

AST Premium 386 SX/16

Figure 1.8 shows the AST Premium 386 SX/16 computer. This personal computer uses the Intel 80386SX microprocessor, which is a 32-bit processor that uses a 16-bit input/output bus. The /16 in the nomenclature of the computer references the fact that the microprocessor operates at a clock rate of 16 MHz. Later, this section examines the different types of Intel microprocessors used in PC AT compatible personal computers and their clock rates.

Figure 1.8   The AST Premium 386 SX/16 Computer. (*Courtesy of AST Research, Inc.*)

In Figure 1.8 note that, like the PC AT, one device housing area is visible. This device housing area comes equipped from the factory with one 5¼- or one 3½-inch diskette drive mounted in the top bay. Two additional bays in the visible device housing area allow two additional on-line storage devices to be installed. A second device housing area located behind the front panel control of the system unit contains two additional bays, so you can mount up to five on-line storage devices in this computer. In comparison, the PC AT can have a maximum of three on-line storage devices mounted in its system unit.

Like the PC AT, AST Premium 386 SX/16 owners usually mount removable storage devices, such as diskette drives and tape backup units, in the bays in the visible device housing area, because such a setup makes access to the drives easy. Similarly, fixed disks that do not require media access are normally mounted in the bays of the hidden device housing area.

Three additional differences between the IBM PC AT and the AST Premium 386 SX/16 are in the areas of expansion slots, on-board memory, and built-in ports. The AST Premium 386 SX/16 contains seven full-length expansion slots. Six of those slots support 8- and 16-bit adapter cards, and one slot is restricted to use by an 8-bit adapter card. The AST computer is equipped with 1M-byte on-board memory as standard, and memory can be expanded to 4M bytes on the system board. In comparison, the PC AT was manufactured with the ability to contain a maximum of either 512K bytes or 640K bytes of memory on its system board.

The last significant difference between the PC AT and the AST Premium 386 SX/16 is in built-in ports. The PC AT obtains its functionality through the addition of adapter cards that add serial and parallel ports, video display, and other functions. Although the AST Premium 386 SX/16 also increases its functionality through the installation of adapter cards, two serial ports and one parallel port are built into the computer's system board. Each of these ports is accessed through connectors mounted at the rear of the computer's system unit, freeing the use of system expansion slots for other types of adapter cards.

AST Premium Tower

The AST Premium 486/33TE illustrated in Figure 1.9 is one member of the AST Premium Tower EISA Series. This series of computers incorporates the Extended Industry Standard Architecture (EISA), which can be viewed as a superset of the PC AT's ISA. EISA extends the computer's bus to 32 bits, while retaining compatibility with the 8-bit PC and PC XT bus and the 16-bit PC AT bus. Thus, you can use 8-bit, 16-bit, and 32-bit adapter cards in an EISA computer. Because the 80386 and 80486 microprocessors can transfer data in 32-bit increments, the 32-bit bus significantly increases operating capability compared with 16-bit bus computers, making EISA computers well suited for operating as local area network servers onto which hundreds of users may store and retrieve programs and data files.

Figure 1.9 refers to the computer as a "tower" system, because of the vertical shape of its system unit. The system unit of the AST Premium 486/33TE has 6 bays—4 externally accessible and 2 internal—as well as 10 expansion slots. Through the tower design you can normally obtain more data storage and adapter card functionality than through the use of a desktop system unit.

Compatible Computer Selection Considerations

To provide information necessary to evaluate the capabilities of different types of PC AT compatible computers, this discussion explores the major components included in

Figure 1.9   AST Premium 486/33TE Computer. This tower system features 10 EISA slots that support 8-bit, 16-bit, and 32-bit adapter cards. (*Courtesy of AST Research, Inc.*)

the system unit of this category of personal computers. Pay particular attention to how these components can differ from one computer to another and what their differences mean to your computer needs.

RAM

Modern PC AT compatible computers differ from the PC AT in several respects in their random access memory. First, most compatibles have a minimum of 1M byte of RAM on the system board and many compatibles can have their system board memory expanded to 4M bytes, whereas some compatibles can support 16M bytes. In comparison, the maximum amount of memory that can be installed on the system board of the PC AT is either 512 or 640K bytes.

A second significant difference between the PC AT and compatible computers with respect to memory involves the memory chips used to populate the system board. Early versions of the PC AT used 64K-bit chips, whereas later versions of that computer used a mixture of 64K-bit and 256K-bit chips. In comparison, almost all compatible computers are now manufactured using either 256K-bit or 1M-bit individual chips or use single in-line memory modules (SIMMs) that contain individual rows of 256K-bit or 1M-bit chips mounted as a row of nine chips that are snapped into one socket.

The use of SIMMs enables memory to be expanded easier than when individual memory chips are used. In addition, SIMMs eliminate the common occurrence of bent memory pins when users press individual chips into chip sockets without correctly aligning the pins above the sockets.

A third difference between PC AT RAM and RAM contained on the system board of many compatible computers involves the method by which the memory is accessed. The microprocessor accesses PC AT RAM by addressing a static location defined by a row and column number similar to matrix addressing. On many compatible computers introduced after the PC AT was discontinued, vendors incorporated interleaved and page-mode memory access techniques to better match the faster microprocessor operating speed to the slower memory operating speed.

Interleaved memory subdivides memory into two or four sections that process information alternately. The microprocessor can then send information to one section while another section is being recharged, resulting in an increase in RAM storage. In the page-mode technique, back-to-back memory accesses occur within blocks of memory known as *pages*. This back-to-back memory access occurs without the necessity of using wait states to slow down the microprocessor during memory access.

A fourth significant difference between the PC AT and compatible computers is the use of shadow RAM by many compatible computers. Shadow RAM is a technology that loads slower ROM instructions and/or video BIOS directly into fast static RAM upon power-up, permitting the computer to obtain an increased level of performance and an enhanced video display capability.

ROM

The instructions contained in the PC AT's ROM, including BIOS, POST, and Cassette BASIC, represent copyrighted material that vendors marketing compatible computers could not legally duplicate. Although some third-party personal computer manufacturers, such as AST Research and Compaq Computer Corporation, designed their own ROM routines, many manufacturers selected ROM routines developed by a few companies that independently designed a legal emulation of IBM's ROM routines. Among the most prominent vendors that market ROM routines are Phoenix Technologies Ltd. and Award Software. A large portion of advertisements for PC AT compatible computers include the terms "Phoenix BIOS" or "Award BIOS," indicating the source of the BIOS. In actuality, these advertisements only partially explain the contents of the ROM chips, because POST is an integral part of BIOS.

Cassette BASIC contained in the PC AT's ROM represents a nucleus of BASIC language instructions that are supplemented by two programs included on the IBM PC-DOS diskette—disk BASIC and advanced BASIC. Instead of attempting to develop or purchase an independently developed kernel of BASIC statements in ROM, compatible computer manufacturers provide purchasers with a diskette-based version of this language. Developed by Microsoft Corporation and labeled GW-BASIC, this language is included on the MS-DOS diskette provided with most PC AT compatible computers.

Microprocessor

As an alternative to using the Intel 80286 microprocessor that was featured in the PC AT, a compatible computer microprocessor may be the Intel 80386, 80386SX, or 80486.

80286

The original PC AT used a 6-MHz 80286 microprocessor. Later versions of that computer incorporated an 8-MHz version of 80286. Although sales of 80286-based systems were surpassed by 80386, 80386SX, and 80486 based systems during 1991, new offerings of 80286 microprocessors have extended the processing capability of that microprocessor. Intel introduced 10-MHz and 12-MHz 80286 processors, whereas other semiconductor firms that manufacture the 80286 under license boosted their offerings with 16-MHz, 20-MHz, and 25-MHz versions. Each of these microprocessors provides an excellent level of performance for the most demanding DOS applications, and the low price of the 80286 in comparison to the cost of 32-bit microprocessors results in an extremely high price for the increased performance level. Only in the area of compute-bound applications typically involving mathematical modeling, graphics to support Microsoft Windows, and intensive input/output operations associated with LAN servers does the 80286 lack the power that many users will desire. In those environments, you should consider 80386- and 80486-based computers.

80386

In 1985, Intel released the 80386, which is a 32-bit microprocessor. The 80386 contains approximately 275,000 transistors, which is more than double the 130,000 transistors contained on the 80286.

The 80386 is a true 32-bit microprocessor, using a 32-bit bus to address memory. This significantly enhances the microprocessor's ability to retrieve and store data to RAM. However, most 80386 computers only contain one 32-bit expansion slot, which is designed primarily for the use of a memory adapter. The other expansion slots on most 80386-based computers consist of 16-bit and 8-bit slots, restricting the performance of the microprocessor when transferring data to diskette or fixed disk or to and from serial and parallel ports.

Currently available clock speeds of 80386 microprocessors include 16-, 20-, 25-, and 33-MHz rates. To take advantage of the higher processing capabilities of the 80386, many manufacturers of 80386-based computers include a *RAM cache* on their system board. The cache acts as a bridge between the microprocessor and slower RAM. The typical cache contains between 32K bytes and 256K bytes of fast static RAM (SRAM) chips. A cache controller on the system board is used to predict the data that the microprocessor may require next and reads that data into the cache before the microprocessor requests the data. Thus, the cache can significantly speed up memory access operations. If the cache incorrectly predicts the data, the microprocessor performs a direct read operation from RAM, which requires more time than a retrieval from cache SRAM.

When memory-intensive applications are performed on an 80386 operating at 33 MHz, its higher clock rate and 32-bit memory access capability will permit software to execute three to four times faster than on a 20-MHz or 25-MHz 80286. If you plan to use your computer for word processing and conventional spreadsheet operations, the difference between an 80286 and an 80386 computer may not be perceivable. Similarly, the difference between a 33-MHz 80386 and Intel's newest microprocessor, the more powerful 25-MHz 80486, may not be noticeable for most applications.

80386SX

The 80386SX can be considered a hybrid 80386 microprocessor. Although the 80386SX has all of the processing capability of the 32-bit 80386, the former microprocessor was designed to use the 16-bit data bus of an 80286. This bus reduction significantly reduced the cost of the microprocessor, so the cost of an 80386SX-based computer is usually several hundred dollars less than computers that use an 80386 microprocessor.

Currently 16-MHz and 20-MHz versions of the 80386SX are available. Although the 80386SX does not provide the level of power associated with the 80386 and 80486 microprocessors, it can be used in computers functioning as a workstation that perform graphic-intensive operations or as a server on a LAN.

The key difference between a 16-MHz 80286 and a 16- or 20-MHz 80386SX is the ability of the latter to support a true 32-bit operating system. However, at the time this book was prepared, IBM's new operating system known as OS/2 was only available as a 16-bit version that operates on 80286, 80386, 80386SX, and 80486 microprocessors. Thus, there is no version of OS/2 designed to take advantage of the ability of 386 and 486 microprocessors to execute 32-bit instructions. However, many application programs can run in 32-bit mode, including Paradox, Turbo CAD, and Windows 3.0.

80486

The 80486 is Intel's latest member of the 8088 series of microprocessors. Although similar to the 80386 in its use of a 32-bit bus, the 80486 incorporates a number of functions onto one chip that formerly required separate chips. The level of chip integration on the 80486 is best noted by the fact that that microprocessor incorporates approximately 1.2M transistors on one chip. In comparison, the 80386 contains approximately 275,000 transistors.

Unlike earlier microprocessors, the 80486 includes an on-chip numeric processor (eliminating the need for a separate 80487 chip) and an internal cache. The built-in numeric processor performs floating-point mathematical operations that required the use of a separate coprocessor with other microprocessors. The internal cache enables the 80486 to read many instructions and data at high speed without having to use the external bus.

Another significant difference between the 80486 and other microprocessors is the ability of the 486 to perform *pipelined execution*. In pipelined execution the 80486 subdivides the execution of each instruction into multiple stages. At any given time the 486 can have multiple instructions in different stages of execution, which further increases its processing capability. These features of the 80486 enable a 33-MHz 486 to provide a level of raw processing power of approximately 10 times that of the 8-MHz 80286 used in the PC AT.

Similar to 80386-based personal computers, most 80486-based machines normally have either one or two 32-bit expansion slots that are primarily designed· for use by memory adapter cards. Although 486-based computers offer a significant level of performance over earlier microprocessors, their power is not practical for the typical personal computer user. Areas where 80486-based systems excel include intensive mathematical operations where you might otherwise require the power of a mainframe, as a file server in a local area network supporting more than 50 LAN users, or as a sophisticated workstation.

Bus

PC AT compatible computers are manufactured with two different types of buses—the Industry Standard Architecture (ISA) 16-bit design that was used by IBM in the PC AT and the Enhanced Industry Standard Architecture (EISA) 32-bit bus.

The development of the EISA bus resulted from the design of microprocessors operating at higher clock rates. Many computer manufacturers found that the PC AT bus was too slow to keep up with memory access requirements of the 80286 microprocessor operating in excess of 8 MHz and that the bus design might not operate correctly with adapter boards at clock rates at and above 10 MHz. To overcome these problems, computer designers introduced *wait states*, which can be viewed as a delay induced for memory and bus access operations. Thus, one wait state resulted in the microprocessor using every second cycle to access memory and its bus, although instructions were performed at its clock rate. Another design addition was cache memory, which with a controller that attempts to predict the next memory access location reads data into fast SRAM. Although these design techniques considerably improved the performance of 80286 and 80386SX systems, the 16-bit ISA data bus would not enable the 32-bit operations at which the 80386 and 80486 excel.

IBM's answer to the problems of the 16-bit PC AT bus was its Micro Channel architecture introduced with its PS/2 family of computers. Unfortunately, the Micro Channel design was completely different from the ISA design, so Micro Channel slots were incompatible with adapter cards designed to support the ISA. This meant that the investment of individuals and companies that had previously acquired millions of ISA adapter cards was useless if the users wished to install those cards in the more powerful Micro Channel-based PS/2s.

To enable both companies and individuals to retain their ISA-based adapter cards while achieving better performance through the use of a 32-bit bus, a group of nine personal computer manufacturers developed the EISA. Most EISA personal computers only contain one or two 8-bit expansion slots, with the others being primarily 16-bit slots, although each computer will normally have one or two 32-bit slots. The 32-bit expansion slots are normally reserved for use by memory adapter cards, because their use significantly enhances the performance of memory operations when RAM is expanded beyond the capacity of the system board. The EISA provides downward compatibility with ISA adapters, so you can use 8-bit and 16-bit adapter cards in an EISA expansion slot.

Expansion Slots

Desktop PC AT compatible computers are normally manufactured with between 4 and 8 expansion slots; however, tower systems may include 10 or 12 slots. In addition to the number of slots on a system you consider purchasing, you should ascertain their type and availability. The *type of slot* references its support of 8-bit, 16-bit, or 32-bit adapter cards; *slot availability* references whether the computer is manufactured with the use of a slot reserved for a specific type of adapter.

Device Housing Areas

Both the number and accessibility of the computer's device housing areas as well as the number of bays in each area are important considerations for the use of on-line storage devices. Almost all desktop PC AT compatible computers have two device housing areas. Normally, one is accessible from the front of the computer, which enables you to fill its bays with removable storage devices, such as diskette drives and tape backup units. The second device housing area is normally hidden from view from the front of the computer, requiring you to remove the system unit cover to gain access to the bays. Due to this design constraint, you can only mount fixed disks in the bays in that device housing area.

Some PC AT compatible computers contain dual device housing areas that are both accessible from the front of the computer. This design provides you with more flexibility;

you can install on-line storage devices in the bays in either device housing area regardless of whether they use removable media.

Disk Controller

Because the fixed disk can be viewed as an extension of the computer's memory, the ability of the microprocessor to rapidly write data onto and retrieve data from on-line storage devices is an important performance consideration. The disk controller connects the microprocessor to diskette and fixed disk drives. The disk controller directs the mechanical operation of disk drives, converting storage and retrieval requests into positional information so read/write heads can access an appropriate disk location. In addition, the controller converts bytes into a serial bit stream and vice versa and contains a data separator that extracts digital data from the continuous analog signal detected by the disk drive's read/write head during data retrieval operations.

The three most common types of controllers used with PC AT systems are the Shugart ST-506, the Small Computer System Interface (SCSI), and the Enhanced Small Device Interface (ESDI). The ST-506 controller is used with most 80286 systems. For better performance required of 80386- and 80486-based computers, the manufacturers install either SCSI or ESDI controllers.

The SCSI controller uses the SCSI. This interface was developed to permit multiple tasks to be run across peripherals linked in a daisy chain by cabling. In comparison, the ESDI controller uses the ESDI, which was designed to provide a maximum diskette data throughput. This controller can only access two diskette drives at one time; an SCSI controller can normally support up to eight daisy chained devices.

Diskette Drives

IBM's marketing of PC AT components made drive selection fairly easy: Only two types of diskette drives and two types of fixed disks were originally offered for use in that computer. Today, PC AT compatible computer vendors allow purchasers a wide latitude in selecting the types of diskette and fixed disk drives for inclusion in a PC AT compatible. You can obtain 360K-byte and 1.2M-byte 5¼-inch floppy diskette drives or 720K-byte and 1.44M-byte 3½-inch rigid diskette drives, as well as tape backup units and fixed disks ranging in capacity from 10M bytes to 300M bytes. Refer to Chapter 3 for additional information about the operation and data storage capability of diskette and fixed disk drives.

To help you select appropriate components for a PC AT compatible computer, Table 1.5 lists the features for seven major types of components you may wish to consider. You can use this table to compare and contrast the features of two computers against your requirements or add additional columns to evaluate additional computers.

Third-Party Equipment

Although the PC AT and compatible personal computers are tremendously capable systems, no efficient method of backup is provided for the hard disk unless you add a tape backup unit. Otherwise, to back up the contents of a single 20M-byte disk requires 17 high-capacity 1.2M-byte diskettes. Although this is not an unreasonable number of floppy diskettes, if compatibility with the PC or PCXT is desired by installation of a 360K-byte diskette drive, backup would then require 55 diskettes. If two fixed disks are installed, one disk could be used as a backup for the other; this, however, would

Table 1.5
PC AT Compatible
Computer Selection
Guide

Feature	Your Requirement	Vendor A	Vendor B
RAM			
Installed on system board ___M bytes	_____	_____	_____
Chip size ___K bytes or ___M bytes	_____	_____	_____
RAM packaging: SIMM or chip	_____	_____	_____
Maximum on system board ___M bytes	_____	_____	_____
RAM type: static, interleaved, page-mode	_____	_____	_____
RAM cache	_____	_____	_____
ROM			
BIOS version and developer	_____	_____	_____
ROM shadowing into RAM	_____	_____	_____
Video shadowing into RAM	_____	_____	_____
Microprocessor			
Model	_____	_____	_____
Clock speed ___ MHz	_____	_____	_____
Expansion slots			
Type: ISA or EISA	_____	_____	_____
Number of 32-bit slots	_____	_____	_____
Number of 16-bit slots	_____	_____	_____
Number of 8-bit slots	_____	_____	_____
Device housing areas			
Number and accessibility	_____	_____	_____
Bays per housing area	_____	_____	_____
Disk controller type On-line storage			
Diskette drives	_____	_____	_____
Type: 3½ or 5¼-inch	_____	_____	_____
Storage capacity	_____	_____	_____
Tape backup unit	_____	_____	_____
Storage capacity ___M bytes	_____	_____	_____
Fixed disk	_____	_____	_____
Storage capacity ___M bytes	_____	_____	_____

be costly and limit you to one diskette drive, because only three devices can be supported by the diskette drive and fixed adapter card.

IBM continued a policy of open architecture for third-party vendors, and one of the first products third-party suppliers furnished for use in the AT was a controller board and cartridge tape drive to provide a mechanism for fixed disk backup. Some third-party vendors manufacture a stand-alone tape subsystem that is self-contained and connected to an adapter inserted into the AT's system unit; other vendors offer a tape unit that is designed for insertion into the system unit itself.

Tape Backup Units

Today, most tape backup units use industry standard quarter-inch tapes that look similar to audio cassettes. Other tape backup units are constructed to use 5¼-inch cartridges or ½-inch cartridge tapes. Figure 1.10 illustrates the Mountain Computer 5¼-inch disk cartridge system installed in the lower portion of the device housing area of an IBM PC AT. Each 5¼-inch disk cartridge can store 20M bytes of data, making the backup

Figure 1.10   Mountain Computer Micro Bernoulli. The Mountain Computer Micro Bernoulli internal tape backup unit can store 20M bytes of data on a removable disk cartridge. (*Courtesy of Mountain Computer.*)

process of a fixed disk faster as well as requiring less storage space for backup media compared to that for diskettes.

Figure 1.11 illustrates an external tape backup unit combined with a fixed disk installed in one device housing area. The system illustrated in Figure 1.11 is designed to be placed on top of the computer's system unit, next to the monitor, thereby requiring no additional desk space.

Method of Operation

In addition to internal and external systems, tape backup units can be classified according to their method of operation and interface. The two prevalent methods of operation are *start/stop* and *streamer*. In a start/stop method of operation, the tape moves only one record at a time during transfers from a fixed disk. Although its search-and-record capability makes a start/stop tape backup unit preferable for applications such as selective backup, the extra precision for its tape movement makes it the more expensive backup device.

The streamer type of tape backup unit is, as its name implies, designed for continuous recording. Streamer backup units are typically used to record the entire contents of a disk drive in a single session.

Typically, streamer tape backup units employ a microprocessor to control their servo mechanism. Although they have faster throughput and cost less than start/stop systems, they cannot perform selective retrievals.

Figure 1.11   Mountain Computer Series 7000 Combo System. The Mountain Computer Series 7000 Combo System consists of a fixed disk and tape backup unit in one external housing. Designed to be placed on top of the system unit of a PC XT or AT next to the monitor, the unit requires no additional desk space. (*Courtesy of Mountain Computer.*)

Interface Considerations

The interface required to operate a tape backup unit varies considerably among vendor products. Many tape backup units require a separate controller and require a system expansion slot to be available for its installation. Some tape backup units can be cabled to the rear connector of the disk controller, permitting one external tape backup unit to serve several personal computers. Although tape backup units connected to a disk controller have a lower data transfer rate than obtainable through the use of a separate controller, the portability afforded by the use of this interface and its ability to enable one unit to serve many computers usually outweigh the few extra minutes a full backup procedure may require.

Multifunction Boards

Although the PC AT and many compatible computers have eight expansion slots in their system units, only seven are actually available, because most models are shipped with a diskette and fixed disk controller installed in one expansion slot. After adding a display adapter, a serial/parallel adapter, and perhaps a few memory cards, you may rapidly run out of expansion slots. To alleviate this situation, many third-party vendors have introduced multifunction boards that contain several functions on one card and only require the use of a single expansion slot.

The first multifunction board developed for the PC AT was the AST Research Advantage. This multifunction board can expand the AT's memory to 3M-bytes as well as provide up to two serial ports, a parallel port, and an optional game port. Each Advantage board can be populated with 64K-byte or 256K-byte memory chips and can round out the AT's system board memory to 640K bytes and then continue memory expansion 1M byte at a time, permitting up to 3M bytes of memory to be obtained through the use of a single expansion slot.

More recent versions of the AST Advantage support the use of 1M-bit memory chips and have a significantly increased storage capacity over earlier versions of that adapter board. Because one of the key features of most multifunction boards is memory, it is important to distinguish between the three types of memory adapter cards support.

Extended and Expanded Memory

Until now, this chapter has basically discussed only conventional memory—physical memory within the contiguous 1M-byte address space that can be directly addressed by an 8088 microprocessor, or by an 80286, 80386, or 80486 microprocessor operating in its real mode (that is, when it is emulating an 8088).

Extended memory is the contiguous address space from 1M byte to 16M bytes on an 80286-based machine and up to 4 gigabits on an 80386 or 80486; however, the latter two are normally limited by design constraints to 16M bytes. The 8088 microprocessor, which has only 20 address lines, cannot directly address memory above 1M byte, nor can it operate in protected mode and run an operating system such as OS/2. When they operate in real mode as an 8088, the 80286, 80386, and 80486 are limited to memory use of 640K bytes, because the various versions of PC-DOS through 4.0 don't support more than 640K bytes of memory.

Expanded memory is defined by the Lotus-Intel-Microsoft (LIM) 4.0 specification (described in a moment) as any 64K-byte segment of memory above the 1M-byte boundary that is always addressed within the 1M-byte boundary but paged from "outside" the boundary. An 8088, or an 80286, 80386, or 80486 running in real mode, can access segments of expanded memory by means of paging, or bank switching. *Bank switching* is the process of electronically repositioning expanded memory into the microprocessor's address range. The expanded memory is divided into 16K-byte blocks called *pages*, and these are swapped into or out of an area of main storage called the *page frame*. This page frame effectively becomes a window that can look into various blocks of expanded memory, as shown in Figure 1.12.

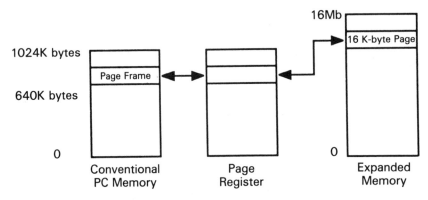

Figure 1.12 Expanded Memory Operation. When expanded memory is used, a page frame in conventional memory serves as a sliding window for using expanded memory. A location in memory, the page register, maintains the status of the associated page frame.

To use expanded memory, programs must be designed to operate with a switching scheme, taking into consideration such factors as the location of the page frame and page register as well as the size of the page. Fortunately, two specifications that are basically compatible with each other have attracted the widespread support of software developers.

The first specification to gain wide support was jointly introduced by Lotus Development Corporation, Intel Corporation, and Microsoft Corporation. Known as LIM EMS, this expanded memory specification uses up to four 16K-byte windows between memory locations 768 K and 896 K for bank switching to obtain a 64K-byte window to expanded memory. This window is the page frame. The LIM EMS supports up to 8M bytes of addressable memory and requires a device driver to act as an interface between an applications program and expanded memory.

Unfortunately, programs sold prior to the introduction of the LIM EMS, or programs not developed to use this standard, cannot take advantage of expanded memory. To do so you must obtain a new release of the program that supports the expanded memory specification or a multitasking shell program under which the application program can operate.

A second extended memory specification was introduced with backing from AST Research, Quadram Corporation, and Ashton-Tate. Known as the AQA Enhanced Extended Memory Specification (AQA EEMS), this specification can be considered as a superset of the original LIM specification. The EEMS specification initially uses 4-page frames that are the same as the LIM specification, which makes the two compatible. Where the EEMS specification differs from LIM is in its support of up to 64-page frames, although in actuality you can use only a subset at one time because of the physical constraints of conventional memory. LIM EMS Version 4.0 incorporates the older LIM EMS and EEMS specifications into its standard and supersedes both. Today there is only one expanded memory standard—LIM EMS.

Selecting Memory

Before you can use expanded memory, you must install 640K bytes of conventional memory in your computer. Some expanded memory cards permit memory on the card to be partitioned between conventional and expanded. Thus, say you have 512K bytes of memory installed on your system board. You would select 128K bytes on a card with partitioning capability in order to make up your conventional memory to the full 640K bytes, a function known as *backfill*. If the expanded memory card cannot be partitioned, you'll have to add a 128K-byte memory card before you can use expanded memory.

Representative Hardware

Above Board

Under the Above Board trademark Intel markets a variety of adapter boards for use in the PC AT and compatible computers, including the Above Board PS/AT and the Above Board/AT.

The Above Board PS/AT is a multifunction board, because it includes a parallel port and serial port as well as a clock/calendar on the card and is bundled with several programs. This adapter can be populated with 64K-bit or 256K-bit chips. The 64K-bit chips provide a maximum of 384K bytes of memory, which can be used as either conventional or expanded memory. The 256K-bit chips increase the capacity of the board to 1.5M bytes, of which up to 384K bytes can be used as conventional memory and the remainder (or all the memory on the board) as expanded memory.

The Above Board/AT is similar to the Above Board PS/AT in its ability to use either 64K-bit or 256K-bit memory chips. You can install as many as 2048K bytes of memory on the Above Board/AT, assigning up to 640K bytes as conventional memory and the remainder as expanded memory. A configuration switch on the board specifies the type of memory chips used to populate the card's sockets, the assignment of conventional and expanded memory, and the port address of the board.

Another interesting Intel Above Board product is that vendor's Above Board Plus 8 I/O adapter card. This board is manufactured with 2M bytes of memory and contains sockets that accept an additional 6M bytes of RAM. A piggyback board that holds another 6M bytes of RAM can be snapped onto this Above Board Plus 8 I/O, resulting in a total of 14M bytes of RAM available in one expansion slot. In addition to the RAM, this board includes one serial and one parallel port.

Memory on the Above Board Plus 8 I/O can be configured via software as conventional, expanded, and extended. Expanded memory conforms to the previously discussed LIM specification, so you can use this board to fill out the 640K of conventional RAM if your computer has less memory or to set the remaining memory on the board as expanded memory. If you are using the board in an 80286- or 80386-based computer, you can set all or a portion of the board's memory as extended to enable it to be used with OS/2.

Figure 1.13   STB Systems, Inc., Rapid MEG. This memory adapter uses SIMMs.

Another interesting and potentially valuable feature of the Above Board 8 I/O card is its ability to be used with PCs, XTs, and ATs. Although the card contains two connectors similar to other cards designed for use in the PC AT, a chip on the board controls its use of an 8-bit or 16-bit bus for memory transfer. Thus, you can use the Above Board Plus 8 I/O in an 8-bit bus IBM PC or PC XT and by the replacement of a chip on the board use it in a 16-bit bus PC AT.

STB Systems Rapid MEG

Another memory adapter marketed for use with PC AT and compatible computers is the STB Systems Rapid MEG, which is illustrated in Figure 1.13. This adapter was manufactured to accept 256K-byte or 1M-byte SIMM modules, which are inserted into sockets in the left portion of the card. Memory on the adapter is configured via menu-driven software that enables you to set up and reconfigure the adapter after it is installed without having to physically access the card. Once installed, memory can be configured in different combinations, including expanded, extended, and/or backfill for raising conventional memory of a computer to 640K bytes.

Software Installation

New versions of Intel Above Board add-in memory cards, as well as smaller third-party products, are software-installable. Marketed by Intel Corporation as the Above Board 286, Above Board PS/286, and Above Board Plus 8 I/O, these cards are packaged with an installation program you can use to initialize or modify the memory configuration. This feature eliminates the use of configuration switches, so you don't have to open the system unit of a PC to change a previously set configuration.

2 // System Setup

Although differences between the PC AT and compatible computers with respect to their design and use of components can be significant, the setup of most computers is similar. Thus, the focus of this chapter is the assembly of the major components of a PC AT into an operating computer system. The chapter discusses many of the differences between the IBM PC AT and compatible computers that will help you understand how your computer may differ from an IBM PC AT. Although the information presented in this chapter should not be viewed as a substitute for reading the specific hardware manual that should accompany your compatible computer, many times that manual is not available. Thus, the information presented in this chapter may be the only guide to the setup of your computer system, even though it was not written specifically for a particular brand of PC AT compatible computer.

For most systems, assembling the components of your PC AT in a work area four to six feet from a dual power receptacle will provide adequate access to power. If many options that are independently powered (such as a modem or a printer) are to be added to the system, additional power outlets will be needed. A power strip can be connected to your household receptacle to obtain several additional outlets, or you can use an extension cord. A standard six-plug power strip is recommended, because most include some degree of circuit breaker protection against overloads and have a built-in reset button, making it a safer, neater alternative to dangling extension cords.

AC Power Protector

Although devices that protect a personal computer from spikes, surges, noise, and brownouts are not necessary for the operation of the computer, they are one of the first accessories you should consider.

AC power protector products include surge suppressors, isolation transformers, and voltage regulators. Some devices perform just one of these functions; others may perform two or all three of the functions.

A *surge suppressor* rejects high-amplitude spikes and, depending on the manufacturer, may reject radio frequency interference (RFI) noise. An *isolation transformer* provides a higher degree of spike filtration than a surge suppressor and also rejects RFI noise. The most sophisticated AC power protector is a *voltage regulator*. This device includes a transformer that maintains a constant output voltage over a wide range of input voltages; it works fast enough to eliminate sudden as well as gradual surges and sags; and it suppresses short spikes as well as RFI that is carried by the house wiring. The independent windings isolate the load equipment from the house wiring and provide a high degree of protection against electrical shock in the event of a catastrophic malfunction in the load equipment's own power supplies.

Figure 2.1 illustrates the SSB Design Pure Power Plus, which is a combined multiple outlet, surge suppressor, and isolation transformer. The SSB Design Pure Power Plus provides six 115-VAC electrical outlets at the rear of the device; power activity is controlled by individual switches on the front of the unit. Although several manufacturers make similar devices, the current indicator at the front of the unit is probably unique and provides you with a visual indication of how much current your equipment is using. The voltage indicator tells you the condition of the line voltage, which can be especially valuable during the summer months when electric utilities sometimes reduce voltages during periods of peak consumer demand.

In addition to protecting against spikes and surges, the SSB Design Pure Power Plus includes EMI and RFI filtration. Because noise in the form of electromagnetic interference (EMI) or RFI can result in memory errors, this feature may be valuable for personal computers located in an industrial area.

Power-on Self-Test

To immediately ascertain the status of your system unit and keyboard prior to installing any optional equipment, you conduct the power-on self-test (POST). To perform this

Figure 2.1 The SSB Design Pure Power Plus. This unit is a combined surge suppressor and EMI/RFI filter. With six outlets at the rear of the unit, this device can be used to distribute up to 15 amps of power to a personal computer and five peripheral devices. (*Courtesy of SSB Design.*)

test, you should connect your keyboard to the circular receptacle in the rear of the system unit, as illustrated in Figure 2.2. Next, check the 115V–230V selector switch located above the two power receptacles on the rear of the system unit to ensure that it is in the correct position. For the United States and Canada, this switch should be set at 115V. As indicated in Figure 2.2, a screwdriver can be used to move the voltage selector switch to its correct position.

If your system unit is in the locked position, insert the tubular key into the lock on the front of the system unit. Turning the key counterclockwise unlocks the system unit. If you are using your system unit for the first time, check each diskette drive for the presence of a shipping insert and remove it from each drive prior to use.

If you are using the IBM monochrome display, its power cord can be connected to the lower left power receptacle on the rear of the system unit, permitting the system unit power switch to provide power to both the system unit and the monitor, as illustrated in Figure 2.2. Unfortunately, not all compatible computers supply this capability. The three-prong receptacle at the right is for attaching one end of the system unit's power cord; the other end of the cord should be connected to a wall outlet, electrical isolator, power protector, or power strip. Before you do this, make sure that the power switch on the system unit is in the off position. When you are ready, turn the power switch on the system unit to the upright, on position. Three things will happen. First, the keyboard status lights will blink on and off. Next, a memory test will occur and the amount of memory installed in your system unit followed by the letters "OK" should be displayed in the upper left corner of your screen. After the POST is completed, you should hear one short beep, indicating that your system unit has completed its self-test.

The time required to perform the POST depends on the amount of memory installed in the system unit and can range from 15 to 90 seconds. If you did not hear one short

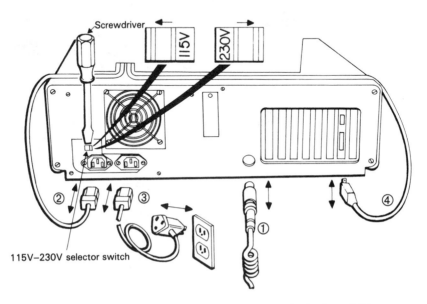

Figure 2.2   Preparing to Perform the POST. Connect the keyboard (1), power cords (2, 3), and video cable (4) to the system and set the voltage selector switch.

beep, there is a high probability that your system unit contains a defect, and you may wish to contact the dealer from whom you purchased it or try to run the diagnostic diskette contained in the IBM *Guide to Operations Manual* or a similar manual furnished with a compatible computer.

If you purchased you system from a dealer who did not install optional equipment you will be required to disassemble the system unit. If your dealer assembled your system, you may still have to run a setup program if the dealer did not, because this program is required to set the date, time, and installed options. Once the setup software is run, this information is stored in the CMOS RAM previously described in Chapter 1.

Setup

When you install your system for the first time, install certain options in your system unit, or replace the computer's battery, you will have to set the date, time, and installed options. This setup is accomplished by the use of the Diagnostic diskette, which configures your system to reflect the equipment installed. To use this diskette, you should first power-off all external devices, such as printers and monitors, as well as your system unit. After you insert the Diagnostic diskette into drive A (the top or left diskette drive) and close the drive lever, turn on all externally attached devices and then turn on the power. Once the POST is performed, a menu of options will appear on your screen, from which you can select the SETUP option. To successfully run this program, you must know what options were installed in your system unit. If your dealer did not furnish you with a list of installed options, you can ascertain what is installed by removing the cover on the system unit. This process is described here, because you must remove the cover to add memory, adapter cards, or additional storage devices as well.

Figure 2.3 illustrates the Setup menu for a PC AT compatible computer using Award Software's BIOS. This menu is used to define and modify the system configuration and is maintained in CMOS through means of a battery contained inside the computer's system unit.

The Setup menu illustrated in Figure 2.3 enables you to set the system date and time as well as to define the components installed in your computer and the functions the computer will perform when certain predefined conditions occur. Award BIOS supports four types of diskette drives, enabling you to define 360K-byte and 1.2M-byte 5¼-inch and 720K-byte and 1.4M-byte 3½-inch drives to be defined. Beside the "DISK 1" and "DISK 2" entries in Figure 2.3 you identify the types of fixed disks that your system has installed. If you have a high-performance disk controller, such as an ESDI or SCSI controller that has its own BIOS, you would only enter a number where "None" is located and ignore the other column entry positions. Otherwise, this Setup menu requires you to select specific, detailed information about each disk that is normally contained on a plate mounted on the top or side of each drive.

The Setup menu illustrated in Figure 2.3 supports two types of memory configurations—base and extended. In this particular example, the computer configuration is set up to indicate the installation of a total of 16M bytes.

The last four entries in the Setup menu enable you to define the functions the computer will perform when certain predefined conditions occur. The ERROR HALT entry enables you to store a setting for whether the computer should stop if an error is detected during power-up. The CACHE CONTROLLER entry enables you to enable or disable the operation of memory cache, because some programs and adapter cards

```
                        AWARD Software CMOS Setup
      DATE (MM/DD/YY)   1/1/80          TIME (HH:MM:SS) 0:00:00

      DISKETTE 1        None
      DISKETTE 2        None


                              CYLS.  HEADS  SECTORS   PRECOMP  LANDZONE

      DISK 1  **** MB    None
      DISK 2  **** MB    None


      VIDEO             EGA/VGA


      BASE MEMORY       640
      EXTENDED MEMORY   15232


      ERROR HALT        HALT ON ALL ERRORS
      CACHE CONTROLLER  ENABLE
      SHADOW RAM        ENABLE
      SECURITY FEATURES LOCKS DISABLED


                   MOVES BETWEEN ITEMS,         SELECTS VALUES
         F10 RECORDS CHANGES, F1 EXITS, F2 FOR COLOR TOGGLE
```

Figure 2.3   Award BIOS CMOS Setup Menu.

do not work when this feature is enabled. The SHADOW RAM entry can also be set to ENABLE or DISABLE. Although enabling SHADOW RAM results in BIOS being read into fast RAM from ROM and increases the level of system performance, on occasion programs and adapter cards may not be able to work with fast ROM. Although disabling cache RAM or SHADOW RAM will slow down the performance of the computer, it may enable programs and adapter cards that might not otherwise be usable to be run on your computer.

The last feature listed in Figure 2.3 enables you to set a password. If this feature is enabled, users will have to enter a password to complete each power-on system boot or to enter the Setup menu.

Adding System Unit Options

Prior to disassembling the system unit, you should disconnect the keyboard and set it aside. Next, you should ensure that the system unit power switch is off and then disconnect the power cord and all cables from the back of the unit. As a safety precaution, also disconnect the power cord plug from the wall outlet, power strip, surge protector, or voltage regulator.

Turning the system unit to allow easy access to the rear, you can use a flat-blade screwdriver to remove the five cover mounting screws as illustrated in the top part of Figure 2.4. After the screws are removed, set them aside in a convenient place, because they will be needed to fasten the cover when the unit is reassembled. Next, gently lift the system unit and turn it so the front panel with the IBM label is facing you and lower it onto your work area. Then, slide the system unit cover away from the rear and toward you until it slides off the base. This process is illustrated in the bottom part of Figure 2.4. Set the cover aside.

Inside the system unit there should be at least one expansion card in the eight system expansion slots, because each AT is shipped with a diskette and fixed disk adapter installed in slot 8. In addition, the high-capacity diskette drive comes installed as drive A. Now, turn to the foldout at the back of the *IBM PC AT Installation and Setup* manual to record the equipment installed in your system unit (if you haven't previously done so), as well as to denote any additional equipment you will install. This information is required to successfully run the setup program on the Diagnostic diskette, which configures your system for use.

If you have a PC AT compatible computer, the location of the diskette and fixed disk adapter as well as the type of diskette drive installed as drive A may differ. Most compatible computers have their disk controller card installed in the expansion slot closest to the first device housing area, similar to the manner in which the diskette and fixed disk adapter is installed in the PC AT illustrated in Figure 2.4. If the compatible computer has a different number of expansion slots than the PC AT, the location where its disk controller card is installed will differ. However, the compatible's controller card location will more than likely be the expansion slot closest to the device housing area, because this will facilitate cabling the controller card to on-line storage devices. In some

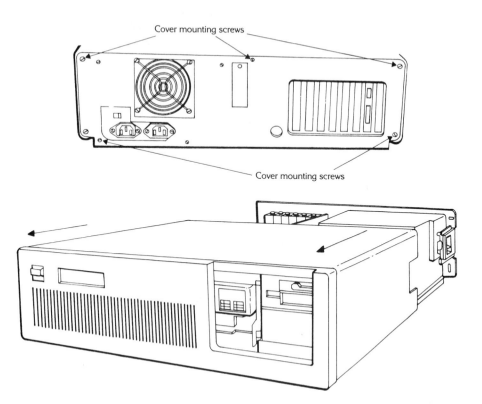

Figure 2.4 Removing the System Unit Cover. First remove the five cover mounting screws and then slide the cover forward.

instances the floppy controller will be built into the motherboard and will be located to facilitate cabling to the diskette drive.

Although most PC AT compatible computers have a 1.2M-byte 5¼-inch high-capacity drive installed as drive A, many computer vendors provide the option of selecting a high-capacity 1.44M-byte 3½-inch diskette drive for installation in that position. Thus, your computer may have a 3½-inch diskette drive with a storage capacity of 1.44M bytes installed as drive A in comparison to the 1.2M-byte 5¼-inch floppy diskette drive used by the IBM PC AT.

At the rear of the system unit to the right of expansion slot 8 is the battery, which should be connected to the system board connector if this has not been done by your dealer. To connect the battery requires you to locate the battery cable connector attached to the battery and to press it into the system board connector as shown in Figure 2.5.

On-Board Memory Expansion

PC AT Memory Expansion

For early versions of the PC AT, the minimum on-board RAM is 256K bytes, because this is the amount of memory installed in the basic model of the AT. In the lower left portion of the system unit you will find either two or four rows of nine memory modules. If only two rows are installed, you have a 256K system; four rows means the maximum 512K bytes of on-board RAM is installed if your system uses piggybacked 128K-byte chips. Later versions of the PC AT were manufactured to accept both 64K-byte and 256K-byte memory chips. If you have a later version of the PC AT, it uses 256K-byte

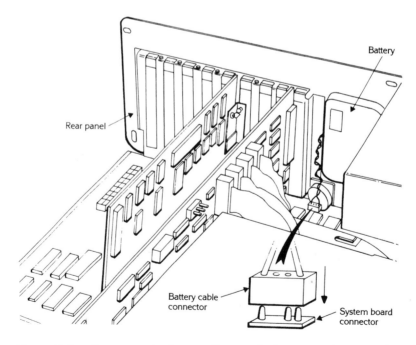

Figure 2.5 Connecting the Battery. Connect the battery to the system board by pressing the battery cable connector into the system board connector.

chips in memory banks 0 and 1 and 64K-byte chips in banks 2 and 3, resulting in a maximum of 640K bytes of RAM that can be installed on the system board.

If you have an older basic model PC AT, to install the 256K RAM memory kit to bring on-board memory up to 512K bytes will require the removal of any adapters installed in expansion slots 1 through 6. First, however, you should ground yourself by touching a metal part of the system unit or another device to prevent static damage from occurring.

If you have adapters installed in slots 1 through 6, they can be removed by first turning the screws that hold the adapters in place in a counterclockwise direction, as illustrated in Figure 2.6. After the screws are removed from each adapter, they should be placed in a convenient location; you will require them to refasten each adapter to its system expansion slot when you reinstall the adapter. Once the screw is removed, the adapter can be removed from the expansion slot by grasping it at the top and lifting it upward. Make a note as to which slot it was removed from and place the adapter in a safe place.

Once the adapters are removed, you are ready to insert your memory modules. Each module has a notch that must be aligned with the notch of the connector on the system board, as illustrated in Figure 2.7. Nine memory modules are required for each 128K-byte addition, because each memory byte on the AT includes a parity bit for memory error-status checking. In Figure 2.7 note the location of the factory-installed memory kit of 256K bytes, which is standard on all ATs manufactured prior to 1986. Once you have added your 256K-byte memory kit, your on-board memory will be 512K bytes.

The pins on the modules are easily bent and must be aligned with the connector before you press them into place. The left part of Figure 2.7 shows a memory module

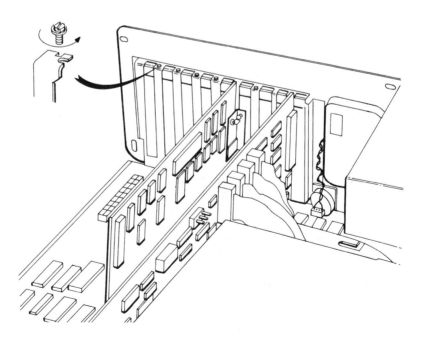

Figure 2.6 Removing Adapter Cards. Use a flat-blade screwdriver to unfasten and remove the screws that hold the adapters in place.

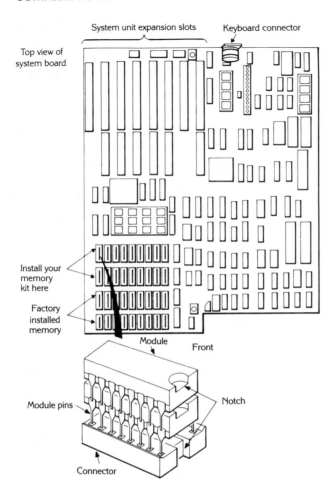

Figure 2.7 Installing Memory. Align the notch in each memory module with the notch on the system board. Note: only memory chips for the IBM PC AT are piggybacked, as shown in this diagram.

being inserted into a connector on the system board. Note that if you fail to properly align the module when you insert it into the connector, you can remove the module with a device known as a module puller or "dip puller." This tweezer type device can be purchased at most electronics stores. Place the module puller over each end of the module and gently tilt it back and forth to remove the module from the connector. If any pins are bent, you can use a pair of regular tweezers to carefully straighten them prior to reinserting the module in the connector. You can also use a small flat-blade screwdriver to remove a module by inserting it under the module and gently lifting it up.

Once the memory modules are installed, you should install any adapters you previously removed by holding the adapter by the top of the card and pressing it firmly into its expansion slot. When it is in its expansion slot, fasten it to the system unit by installing the adapter mounting screw you previously removed.

Compatible Computer Memory Expansion

Most IBM PC AT compatible computers manufactured since 1988 contain at least 1M byte of memory on the system board. Computers with 1M byte of memory that cannot have additional RAM installed on their system board used a mixture of 64K-byte and 256K-byte chips to populate four rows or banks of sockets, similar to the method by which the system board of the IBM PC AT is populated. Most compatible computers that have the ability to expand system board RAM beyond 1M byte do so through the use of SIMMs, which can be installed into sockets mounted directly on the system board or into a memory card whose RAM functions as system board random access memory.

Figure 2.8 illustrates the interior of a typical 80386- or 80486-based PC AT compatible computer that uses an adapter card to install system memory. For true 32-bit computers using the 80386 or 80486 microprocessor, a commonly used design is to populate system board memory through the use of a 32-bit memory card. This design

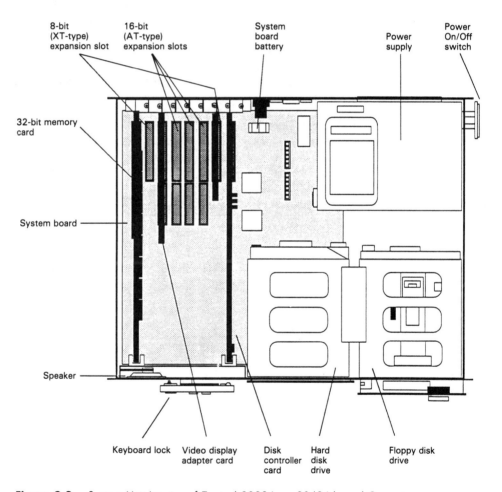

Figure 2.8   System Unit Interior of Typical 80386- or 80486-based Computer.

enables you to upgrade system board memory by adding memory to the memory card. Normally this design uses SIMMs to populate memory, enabling you to install a row of nine chips by simply snapping a SIMM Module into a socket on the card.

Display Adapters

Two of the more common display adapters originally used with the AT are the IBM monochrome display and printer adapter and the IBM color/graphics monitor adapter. Each of these display adapters should be installed in expansion slot 1 or 7. The rationale for using expansion slot 1 or 7 is because the color/graphics card has a skirt that restricts its installation to an 8-bit expansion slot.

If you are installing an EGA or VGA adapter, you must consider whether it is an 8-bit or 16-bit card prior to determining the system expansion slot to use for its installation. If the video adapter is manufactured as an 8-bit card and if it does not have a skirt, you can install it in any system expansion slot. However, if you install it in a 16-bit slot and an 8-bit slot was available, you are eliminating the potential use of a 16-bit expansion slot with a 16-bit adapter card for faster data transfers. If your video display adapter is manufactured as a 16-bit card, you must normally install it in a 16-bit expansion slot. Many 16-bit video cards are designed to be used in 8-bit slots. However, doing so eliminates the benefits you would obtain from the use of a 16-bit interface.

Because your PC AT comes with support brackets installed for all expansion slots except slot 1, you may first have to remove an expansion slot cover to insert your display adapter into slot 7. This is accomplished by removing the screw that holds the expansion slot cover in place by turning it counterclockwise, as illustrated in Figure 2.9.

After the expansion slot cover is removed, you should save it so that if you remove the adapter from that slot at a later date, you can re-cover the gap. Otherwise, the cover will not be needed. After the cover is removed, grasp the adapter by the top of the card and press it firmly into the expansion slot, ensuring that the adapter falls into the support bracket. Then install the screw you previously removed to fasten the adapter.

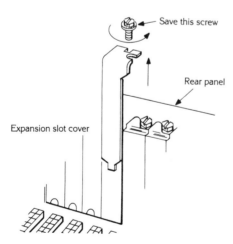

Figure 2.9   Expansion slot covers can be removed by removing the screw that holds the slot cover in place.

Once your display adapter or adapters are installed, you should set the display switch on the system board. The setting of this switch will govern the display adapter that will be used when you power on the system unit. If the monochrome display and printer adapter is to be the primary display, the switch should be pushed to the rear of the system unit, as indicated in Figure 2.10. If the color/graphics is to be the primary display, set the switch in the opposite direction.

If you install a more recent type of video adapter, such as the EGA or VGA card, you will probably not have to concern yourself with setting the display switch. In fact, most PC AT compatible computers marketed with an EGA or VGA card as a standard video display do not contain a video switch. Default video settings are either software selectable or set through the use of a DIP switch mounted on the rear of the card whose elements you can easily set or reset from the rear of the computer.

Other Adapters

A wide variety of IBM and third-party vendor adapters can be installed inside the system unit of the AT and compatible computers. Take care to ascertain which expansion slots each card must be inserted into and any configuration rules that govern the successful use of the adapter. As an example, consider the IBM 128K-byte memory expansion option adapter card. This card must be installed only in a slot between 2 and 6 and requires the system board to be at its maximum memory capacity of 512K bytes prior to its installation.

On certain adapters, such as the 512K-byte memory expansion cards, you must set a series of DIP switches for the option to work. Figure 2.11 illustrates the location of the two banks of DIP switches contained on the IBM 512K-byte memory expansion

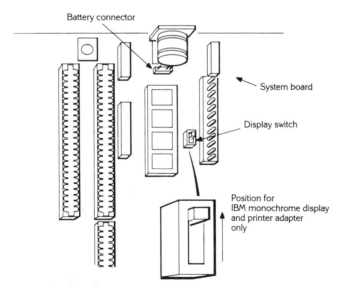

Figure 2.10   Setting the Display Switch. Push the display switch toward the rear of the system unit if the monochrome display and printer adapter is to be your primary display. If the color/graphics adapter is to be your primary display, push the switch in the opposite direction.

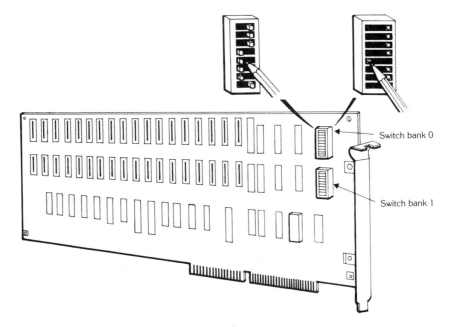

Switch bank 0

Switch bank 1

Figure 2.11 DIP Switch Locations. To install the IBM 512K-byte memory expansion adapter, you set two banks of DIP switches.

adapters. Figure 2.12 indicates the switch settings for each adapter you can install. A ball-point pen or similar object can be used to set the correct position of each switch.

After IBM discontinued manufacturing memory adapter cards for the PC AT, other vendors designed significantly improved cards for use in the PC AT and compatible computers. Many of these cards can be configured through software and allow memory on the card to be partitioned into conventional backfill memory to raise system memory to 640K bytes; remaining RAM on the card can be configured as extended or expanded memory.

Diskette Drives

If you have a PC AT, you can install a second high-capacity diskette drive or a double-sided diskette drive in the lower portion of the storage housing area in the system unit. To install either diskette drive, you must first remove the cover plate by unscrewing the two cover plate screws that fasten it to the system unit, as shown in Figure 2.13. Then, remove the four mounting screws and three mounting clips, of which the upper two screws fasten the standard high-capacity diskette drive to the system unit. In this way you can slide the previously installed diskette drive a few inches forward, enabling you to cable the drive to be installed in the lower part of the storage housing area. Next, locate the terminating resistor on the drive to be installed and remove it by inserting a small flat-blade screwdriver under the resistor and lifting it off. On some diskette drives this terminating resistor may be colored black; on other drives it may be colored blue. Thus, it is preferable for you to refer to the installation instructions furnished with the diskette drive to ensure that the terminating resistor is correctly removed.

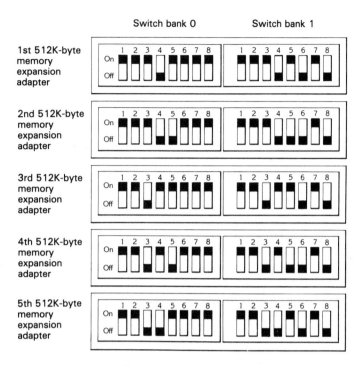

Figure 2.12 Specific Switch Settings for Memory Expansion Cards. Use the DIP switch setting for the correct 512K-byte memory expansion adapter.

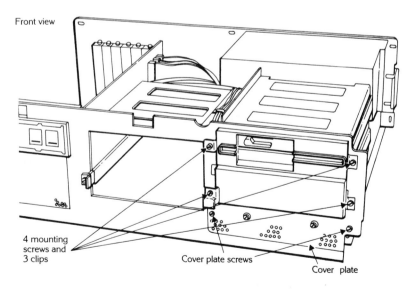

Figure 2.13 Preparing to Install a Second Diskette Drive. To install a second diskette drive, first remove the cover plate from the system unit base.

Once the terminating resistor is removed, slide the drive into the center slot of the system unit until it is even with the upper diskette drive that was previously moved forward several inches. Next, locate the signal cable that connects the hard disk and diskette drive adapter to the high-capacity fixed disk. As Figure 2.14 illustrates, one of the four connectors will be labeled B and must be connected to the second diskette drive. When you have identified the appropriate drive connector, you should align its locating key with the locating slot on the diskette drive, which is an edged surface area on the upper right-hand portion of the drive. Once they are aligned, press the connector firmly into place, as shown in Figure 2.15.

After the signal cable is attached, a power connector must be attached to operate the diskette drive. The power cable has a four-hole connector labeled P12 and is connected to four wires that run back to the power supply. The P12 connector should be inserted into the four-prong connector located on the upper right corner of the diskette drive. Because the high-capacity diskette drive that is standard equipment has the same connector, you can look at that connector as a reference.

Before you fasten the drives to the system unit, you must connect a ground wire to the new diskette. The ground wire connected to the standard high-capacity diskette drive can be used as a reference for this installation. This ground wire is fastened to and runs along the system unit to the left of drive A. Once the following wire attachments and connectors are made, both diskette drives should be slid into the system unit and fastened to the system unit's shell with four clips and mounting screws, as illustrated in Figure 2.16.

After the diskettes are fastened to the system unit, you can then install the cover plate that was removed to provide access for the second diskette. Actually, the cover plate contains a diskette face plate and a cover plate. Because you must have access to the newly installed diskette drive, you should remove the two screws that hold the diskette face plate to the cover plate for the lower drive, thereby permitting you to remove the face plate. Figure 2.17 shows this process. Then you can screw the cover plate to the system unit directly under the second diskette drive. Because diskette drives

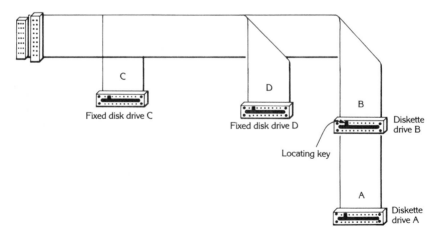

Figure 2.14   The Connector for Drive B. The connector on the signal cable labeled B must be used to connect the second diskette drive to the diskette and fixed disk adapter.

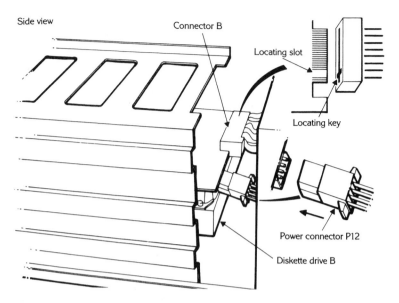

Side view   Connector B

Locating slot

Locating key

Power connector P12

Diskette drive B

Figure 2.15 Inserting the Drive Connector. The signal cable connector labeled B and the P12 power connector must be attached to the second diskette drive.

are normally shipped with an insert to protect the read/write heads, you should remove the shipping insert from the drive prior to using drive B.

Although the primary focus was on the installation of 5¼-inch diskettes, as previously noted both IBM and compatible PC AT computer manufacturers support the use of 3½-inch diskette drives. Unless your computer was specifically manufactured with device housing areas designed for 3½-inch drives, you have to use special mounting brackets to install 3½-inch storage devices into bays designed to hold 5¼-inch devices. Refer to mounting bracket instructions that are included with 3½-inch storage devices designed for installation in 5¼-inch bays for specific information concerning the installation of this category of on-line storage devices.

Fixed Disk Drive

Up to two fixed disk drives can be installed in the system unit of the PC AT and many compatible computers.

When you install a fixed disk drive, it is very important to handle it with the utmost care, because dropping, shaking, or rough handling could damage the drive and void the warranty. You should carefully read the installation instructions furnished with the fixed disk before you install it. Because of the sensitivity of this device to shock and vibration, it is recommended that the novice seek professional assistance for the installation of the drive.

Cabling the System

Once you have added the appropriate options to your system unit or you have removed its cover to ascertain the options for use in the setup program, it is time to replace the

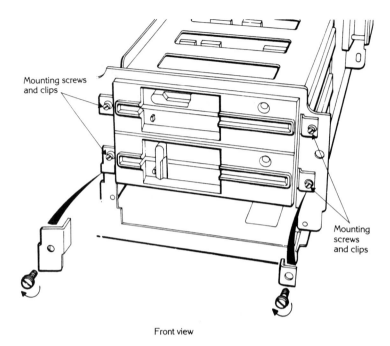

Mounting screws
and clips

Mounting
screws
and clips

Front view

Figure 2.16   Inserting the Connected Floppy Drives in the System Unit. After the connectors are properly connected and wire attachments are completed, slide both diskette drives into the system unit and fasten them to the shell with four clips and mounting screws.

system unit cover and cable the major system components together. After the cover is replaced, the entire system unit should be gently lifted up and turned so that the back of the unit faces you. At this time, the five mounting screws that were previously removed should be inserted and tightened by turning them clockwise with a flat-blade screwdriver. At this time, the system unit is ready to be cabled to your peripheral devices, powered on, and reconfigured if necessary by the use of the setup program.

Device Connection

The connection between the system unit and your display will be based on the type of display unit you are using. For example, if you are using the IBM monochrome display, it will be connected to the system unit via the 9-pin shell connector on the combined monochrome display and parallel printer adapter card that was installed in the system unit. If you are using the IBM composite color monitor or a television, either display can be connected to the color/graphics monitor adapter card mounted in the system unit. A composite monitor can be cabled to either the phono jack or the 9-pin shell connector on the color/graphics monitor adapter card.

The attachment of a printer to the PC AT will vary, based on the type of printer used. If you use a parallel printer, you can connect it to the 25-pin printer connector on the monochrome display and parallel printer adapter card, similar parallel printer connectors mounted on some EGA and VGA cards, or the parallel connector on the serial/parallel adapter card.

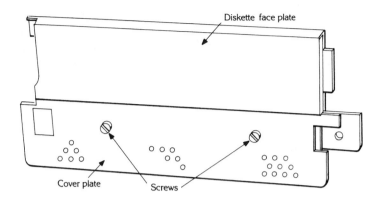

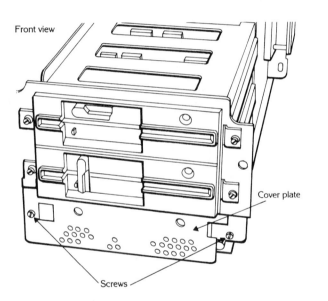

Figure 2.17 Reinstalling the Cover Plate Without the Diskette Face Plate. After the diskettes have been fastened to the system unit, remove the diskette face plate from the cover plate and fasten the cover plate to the system unit.

If you wish to use a serial printer, you must interconnect that type of device to the system unit via the serial connector on the IBM serial/parallel adapter. As previously discussed in Chapter 1, you will require a cable to connect this 9-pin connector to a standard 25-pin connector commonly used to connect serial devices to computers. This adapter card generates the serial bit stream required to operate a serial printer. Other devices that require a serial bit stream include a modem or coupler and a graphic tablet. Such devices are also connected to the system unit through a cable connection to the serial connector on the IBM serial/parallel adapter card.

After the PC AT is cabled and powered on, the POST will be initialized. A cursor will appear on the screen and a beep will indicate the successful operation of all components, after which a message asking you to enter the date or displaying the message IBM Personal Computer will appear on your display. If one or more actions of this three-sequence operation fail to materialize, a problem may exist with your system. To assist you in resolving operational or system failures, you should refer to the *IBM Guide to Operations* for the appropriate instructions concerning the use of the IBM diagnostic programs if you have a PC AT or an equivalent set of instructions for compatible computers.

Moving the System

If your computer has a fixed disk, you should execute the IBM diagnostic program and select option 3, Preparing System for Moving. This program "parks" the read/write heads of the fixed disk at a predefined location to prevent the loss of data when you move the system.

3 / Storage Media and Keyboard Operation

The purpose of this chapter is twofold. First, you will become acquainted with the different types of storage media used with the PC AT and compatible computers. Then you will get a broad view of the operation and uses of specific keyboard keys and key combinations that initiate predefined functions. Doing so will provide an overview of the more common methods for inputting and storing data.

In examining removable storage media, the chapter first explores the characteristics of 5¼-inch diskettes that were standard equipment in the original IBM PC AT. This is followed by an examination of the characteristics of more recent 3½-inch rigid case diskettes.

When introduced, the IBM PC AT used 5¼-inch diskettes and fixed disks for storing information. The 5¼-inch diskette is sold with a protective jacket, which shields the uncovered index hole and exposed recording surface during storage. Because every AT has at least one diskette drive, and diskettes provide a mechanism to exchange information with other personal computer users, this chapter first examines diskette storage.

5¼-inch Diskettes

The top section of Figure 3.1 illustrates the various parts of the 5¼-inch diskette with respect to its permanent protective jacket. The lower part provides a detailed view of the contents of the diskette.

The diskette is inserted into the diskette drive so that the end with the dual notches enters first, with the label side of the diskette facing upward. When the diskette is being read or information is being recorded on it, the diskette spins inside its jacket. The read/write head of the diskette drive will come into contact through the head aperture, which is a slot in the protective jacket through which reading or recording of information occurs.

Tracks, Bytes, and Sectors

Information in the form of data or programs is written onto and read from the diskette along concentric circles called *tracks*, as illustrated in Figure 3.2. There are 40 tracks on a conventional 5¼-inch diskette that are numbered from 0 to 39. A high-capacity 5¼-inch diskette contains 80 tracks, numbered from 0 to 79. Depending on the type of diskette drive used to format the diskette and the switches you include in the FORMAT command specification, each track can be subdivided into 8, 9, or 15 *sectors*, and each sector can store 512 8-bit bytes of information, where a *byte* represents 8 bits or one character of data. Each time the computer reads information from or writes information

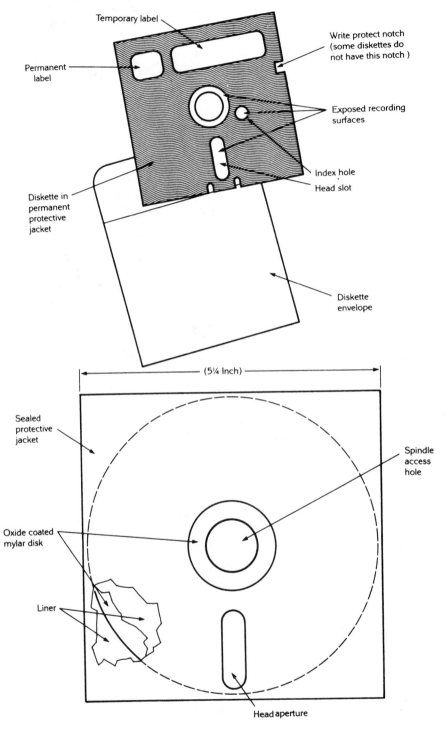

Figure 3.1   The Parts of a 5¼-inch Disk.

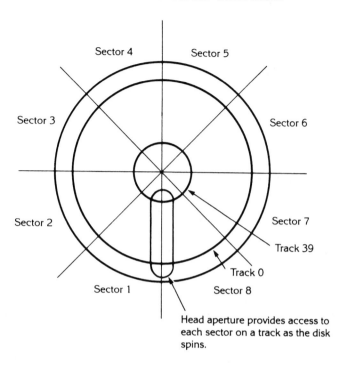

Sector 4 Sector 5

Sector 3 Sector 6

Sector 2 Sector 7

Track 39

Track 0

Sector 1 Sector 8

Head aperture provides access to
each sector on a track as the disk
spins.

Figure 3.2   5¼-inch Diskette Format.

onto a diskette, a minimum of one sector's worth of information is read or written.
The FORMAT command prepares a diskette to receive information, checks the diskette
for bad spots, and builds a directory to hold information about the files that will eventually be written onto it. This command, as well as other operating system commands,
will be covered in Chapter 4.

5¼-inch Diskettes and Drive Compatibility

Both double-sided and high-capacity 5¼-inch diskette drives can be installed in the PC
AT. The double-sided drive can read and write to single-sided and double-sided diskettes
but cannot read or write to high-capacity diskettes. Although the high-capacity diskette
drive can read data contained on single- and double-sided diskettes, if you write on
any of these two diskette types using a high-capacity diskette drive you may not be
able to read the diskette in a standard double-sided drive. Thus, it is recommended that
high-capacity diskettes be used in the high-capacity diskette drive if you wish to write
information onto a diskette using that drive. Table 3.1 summarizes the diskette and
drive compatibility between double-sided and high-capacity 5¼-inch drives.

3½-inch Diskettes

When IBM's first portable computer, the PC Convertible, was introduced in 1986, it
also represented the first personal computer product from that manufacturer to use

Table 3.1
5¼-inch Diskette and
Drive Compatibility
Reading/Writing

Double-sided Drive	High-capacity Drive
Single-sided diskette	Single-sided diskette*
Double-sided diskette	Double-sided diskette*
	High-capacity diskette

*If you write on any of these diskette types using a high-capacity drive, you may not be able to read the diskette in a single- or double-sided drive.

3½-inch diskette drives. Shortly after the PC Convertible went on sale IBM began to market 3½-inch diskette drives for use with the PC AT.

Initial 3½-inch diskette drives were known as *standard drives*. Diskettes in those drives were formatted with 80 tracks per side, using 9 sectors per track with each sector containing 512 bytes of information. Thus, 2 times 80 tracks per side times 9 sectors per track times 512 bytes per sector yielded 737,280 bytes, or 720K bytes of data storage capacity.

In 1987 IBM introduced the PS/2 family of computers. The PS/2 family supports two types of 3½-inch diskette drives—the previously mentioned standard drive and a high-capacity drive. The high-capacity drive enables you to format 3½-inch diskettes using either 9 or 18 sectors per track. When 18 sectors per track are used, the storage capacity of the diskette becomes 2 sides times 80 tracks per side times 18 sectors per side times 512 bytes per sector, yielding 1,474,560 bytes or 1.44M bytes of storage capacity.

The introduction of the 3½-inch high-capacity drive for PS/2 computers was rapidly followed by many vendors offering this drive for use with the PC AT. Shortly thereafter many PC AT compatible computer manufacturers began to offer this drive as well as the 3½-inch standard drive to customers.

Figure 3.3 illustrates the components of a 3½-inch diskette whose magnetic material used for recording information is encased in a shell of hard plastic to provide protection against damage. Access to the magnetic material is obtained via a sliding metal cover that is retracted only when the diskette is placed inside a diskette drive. The write-protector located at the bottom of the diskette provides you with the ability to prevent data from being recorded onto a disk. When the sliding protector is positioned so that the square hole in the disk is open, the diskette is write protected. When the sliding protector is positioned to close the hole as you look down from the top of a disk, information can be written onto the diskette. Some diskettes, such as the IBM Reference disk shipped with each PS/2 and some operating system diskettes, do not have this switch and are permanently write protected.

Diskette Operation

You insert a 3½-inch diskette into the diskette drive with the shutter on the upper shell facing toward the computer. As the diskette is inserted, its shutter retracts, providing the read/write heads of the diskette drive with access to the magnetic media.

Diskette Storage Capacity

The theoretical storage capacity of a diskette depends on the number of formatted sectors per track; the actual storage on the diskette is based on the manner in which data is written onto the diskette. Table 3.2 indicates the theoretical storage capacity

HARDWARE OVERVIEW

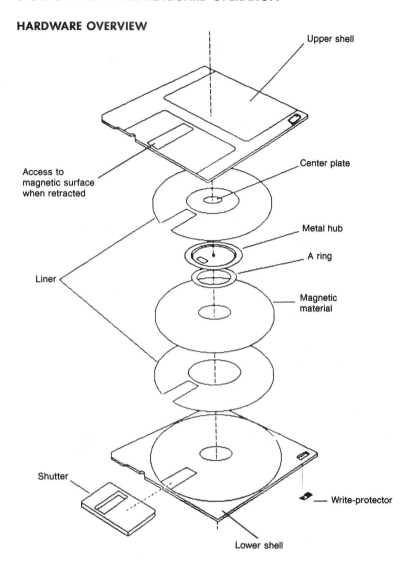

Figure 3.3 Components of a 3½-inch Diskette.

of single- and double-sided 5¼-inch and double-sided standard and high capacity 3½-inch diskettes. Note that only a 5¼-inch high-capacity diskette drive is capable of writing 15 sectors per track and should only do so when a high-capacity diskette is installed in that drive.

As an example of how the actual quantity of data stored on a diskette can be less than the theoretical storage capacity, consider a single-sided diskette. Although 40 tracks times 8 sectors times 512 bytes per sector results in 163,840 potential characters of storage, a lesser number normally results in actual usage of the diskette. First, the disk operating system uses portions of track 0 of each diskette for status information concerning the files on that diskette. Second, if you were to save a one-character

	Number of Sectors/Track	Number of Tracks	Storage Capacity in Bytes
Number of Sides			
5¼-inch Diskettes			
1	8	40	163,840
1	9	40	184,320
2	8	40	327,680
2	9	40	368,640
2	15	80	1,228,800
3½-inch Diskettes			
2	9	80	737,280
2	18	80	1,474,560

Table 3.2
5¼- and 3½-inch Diskette Storage Capacity

program, one sector of 512 bytes would be required, which would waste the remaining 511 bytes of storage. Similarly, a program containing 513 characters would require two sectors for storage and also result in 511 wasted 8-bit byte locations on that diskette.

The Formatting Process

Before you can use a blank disk, you must format it; that is, you must command the computer to write dummy data to all tracks in such a way that it can later identify precisely which part of the disk is currently under the read/write heads. During this formatting process, the computer divides the recording space into tracks numbered from 0 at the outer edge to either 39 or 79 at the inner edge, for a total of 40 or 80 tracks. For double-sided disks, there are two such tracks, one on each side of the disk. These upper and lower tracks are numbered identically, but are differentiated by the number of the head that reads or writes them (0 for the upper, 1 for the lower head).

To divide each track into sectors, the computer writes a synchronization pattern consisting of the track number, head number, and sector number, followed by the appropriate number of bytes of a special character (usually that with a value of E5 hexadecimal) that denotes an empty data area. After the last data byte, the computer writes two checksum bytes that will allow the detection of reading errors. The computer repeats this sequence of sector ID, data bytes, and checksum bytes as many times as there will be sectors on the track.

Care and Handling of Diskettes

Information on the diskette can be located quickly by the disk operating system reading track 0 to obtain the track and sector number that defines the location where a particular program or data file resides. If the head aperture opening on the diskette should become dirty, it may not only prevent access to a particular program but could also prevent access to all the information on the diskette if track 0 became unreadable. Therefore, you should be extremely careful when handling and storing diskettes. If possible, always consider the following safety rules with respect to diskette handling and storage.

- Never touch the exposed recording surfaces of the diskette formed by the head aperture and index hole.

- Due to the fragile nature of 5¼-inch diskettes, always try to store them in an upright position in their envelope to ensure that they do not bend or sag.
- Never place heavy objects on top of your diskettes.
- As soon as you remove your 5¼-inch diskette from the drive, place it in its envelope to prevent the accumulation of dust from occurring on its head slot.
- Store your diskettes in appropriate storage boxes away from sunlight and other heat sources as well as such magnetic field sources as telephones, electronic calculators, and other electronic equipment.
- If you label the information on a 5¼-inch diskette, do so only with a felt-tip pen to avoid damaging the diskette. Write on the labels, whenever possible, before you put them on the diskette.

Write Protection

The write protect notch on 5¼-inch diskettes (Figure 3.1, top) and write-protector slide on 3½-inch (Figure 3.3, lower right) diskettes provides the mechanism to safeguard information recorded on your diskette from accidental erasure. In order to use this feature, you must place a tab over the notch on 5¼-inch diskettes or move the write-protector slide to expose a square hole on a 3½-inch diskette so that data already recorded on the diskette cannot be erased or recorded over. Many purchased programs such as the IBM disk operating system come without this notch or protector slide, so that you don't have to take any action to protect the information stored on these diskettes; the protection is built in. Be aware, however, that some purchased programs do have the write protect notch or protector slide, and you will have to take action to protect data. If your requirements for protection change at a later date, you can always peel the tab off the notch or reposition the protector slide to permit new data to be recorded onto the diskette.

Fixed Disks

Fixed disk technology predates the personal computer by several decades. In 1953, legend has it that IBM's project to develop a fixed—nonremovable—disk (designated as product 3030) was dubbed "Winchester," after the .303 rifle. That name later became synonymous with the terms *fixed disk* and *hard disk*.

The fixed disks that can be used with the PC AT and compatible computers vary in capacity from 20M bytes to more than 300M bytes of storage.

Operation

The fixed disk operates in a very similar way to a floppy diskette drive. Inside a hermetically sealed housing are one or more platters with a read/write head for each surface. The read/write head is an electromagnet capable of detecting and producing a switchable magnetic field to read and write bit streams. The read/write heads are positioned by an arm from track to track, without the heads actually touching the disk surface as they float on an air cushion several millionths of an inch in height. Data is typically stored on each track in groups of 512 bytes—a sector. Many disks are formatted for 17 sectors per track, so that each track stores 8.5K bytes.

Tracks on a fixed disk are numbered from 0 near the circumference in ascending order toward the center of the platter, the actual number of tracks depending on the storage capacity of the disk. Figure 3.4 illustrates a schematic diagram of the track layout on a fixed disk.

To increase the capacity of a fixed disk, data bits can be recorded closer together, additional platters of data storage can be added to the device, or a combination of both techniques can be employed. When multiple platters are used in a fixed disk, multiple read/write heads are used to read and record data onto the corresponding track of each surface at the same time. The assembly of vertically corresponding tracks of each surface, the *cylinder*, is illustrated in Figure 3.4.

During a read or write operation, the head is first moved to the appropriate track. The time required to position the head is known as the disk's *seek time*; this time varies depending on the number of tracks across that the head must be moved in order to reach the desired track. For a single track movement, a seek time of a few milliseconds may be required, whereas a movement from the outermost to the innermost track end of the disk could require 100 milliseconds or more. The average time to position the read/write head across one-third of the disk to a random sector is known as the *average access time* and is usually published by fixed disk drive manufacturers. Other times

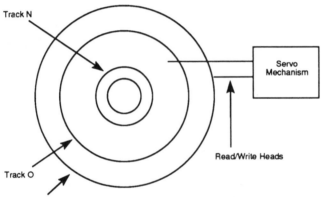

(A) Top View

Track N

Servo Mechanism

Read/Write Heads

Track O

Increasing tracks on a platter or increasing platters increases storage capacity.

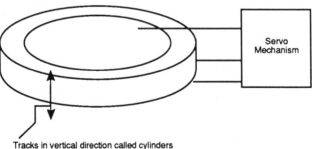

(B) Side View
Multiple Platters

Servo Mechanism

Tracks in vertical direction called cylinders

Figure 3.4   Fixed Disk Layout and Platter Operation.

published by some manufacturers include track-to-track seek and random reads based on defined seek widths. Once the read/write head is positioned on the appropriate track, another delay occurs until data can be read from or written onto the disk. This time is known as the *rotation* or *latency time* and is the delay until the platter rotates to position the first of the sectors to be accessed under the read/write head. For a disk spinning at 3600 revolutions per minute (rpm), the average rotation time is 8 milliseconds.

Interleave Factor

The fixed disk normally rotates at 3600 rpm (or some rate between 2400 and 3600 rpm). As the disk rotates, the first sector to be read or recorded onto passes under the head, and the data transfer begins. The gap between sectors is small, so the next sector is reached very quickly—too quickly, in fact, for most disk controllers, because they usually require some time to get ready for the transfer to or from the next sector. If the controller is not ready when the second sector passes under the head, the controller must wait for an entire revolution of the disk for the appropriate sector to be correctly positioned. To eliminate this waste of time, many disks are formatted to separate logically consecutive sectors by one or more physical sectors. This separation, called *interleaving*, provides the controller with additional time to read or record data onto consecutive logical sectors without requiring additional disk rotations.

Figure 3.5 shows two single platter disks, one formatted without sector interleaving, and the second formatted with an interleave factor of three—meaning that logically

No Interleaving

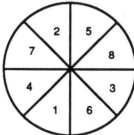

Interleave Factor of Three

Figure 3.5 Sector Interleaving.

consecutive sectors are separated by two physical sectors. Normally, the interleave factor can be considered as an important parameter in comparing the performance of two fixed disk drives. As an example of the differences between interleave factors, consider two disks, one with an interleave factor of two and another with an interleave factor of four. To retrieve all of the data on a track requires two disk revolutions when the interleave factor is two, but four disk revolutions if the interleave factor is four. Thus, a fixed disk with a low interleave factor is normally more efficient in storing and retrieving data than a disk with a higher interleave factor. Because the controller governs the interleave factor, you want to use the lowest interleave factor that the controller supports. If you have a 12-MHz or faster PC, you should always buy a drive and controller that do not require any interleave (1:1 interleave ratio), because those computers are fast enough to support that interleave factor.

Drive Motors

A fixed disk drive may use either a stepper motor or a voice coil motor to position the read/write heads. A stepper motor moves the heads a fixed distance and relies on the mechanical accuracy of the motor to position the heads to the correct location. Because the motor cannot adjust for media expansion or contraction, there are constraints on how closely tracks of information may be spaced in order to be recorded and retrieved correctly. These constraints limit the storage capacity of a stepper motor system.

In a fixed disk that uses a voice coil, the motor controls the read/write head movement electronically, based on reference data stored on the disk surface. The capability to alter the reference data enables a greater number of tracks to be formatted onto a disk. In addition, many voice coil drives are so designed that when primary power is lost or turned off, the remaining power stored in the power supply's capacitors is applied to the voice coil in such a way as to retract the heads quickly to a parking position outside the data storage area of the platter.

Stepper motor drives are normally two to three times slower than voice coil drives. In addition, stepper motor drives usually have less storage capacity than voice coil drives. However, stepper motor drives are also less expensive. If you do not require a large-capacity drive with fast access time, such as might be necessary for a personal computer functioning as a local area network server, a stepper motor drive will normally suffice. If large-capacity storage and quick access are of primary concern, consider purchasing a voice coil motor drive.

Cluster

Although it is a logical rather than a physical parameter and is controlled by software, the concept of the cluster is important to understanding the efficiency of fixed disk operations. The *cluster* is the smallest addressable unit of storage space in DOS. This unit of storage corresponds to an entry in the DOS File Allocation Table (FAT), which can be considered as a map of available space on a storage medium.

Under DOS 2.X, the FAT is 12 bits in length, permitting 4096 (2^{12}) unique numbers. If each number denoted a 512-byte sector, the maximum capacity of the disk would be 4096 times 512, or 2,097,152 bytes. To increase the available storage, DOS 2.X assigns each FAT number to a cluster of 8 logically consecutive sectors. There's a trade-off, of course. The total storage on the disk is now 4096 times 4096, or 16,777,216 bytes, but the smallest amount of storage that you can allocate to a file is 4096 bytes. Thus, saving a file that contains only one character results in wasting 4095 bytes of disk storage. You can, of course, read or write a single 512-byte sector, because each sector is physically identified on the disk, and the operating system can translate a logical sector number within a file to a physical track and sector number that the disk controller hardware can use.

Under DOS 3.X the FAT was changed so it could be either 12 or 16 bits in length. When 16 bits are used, the number of clusters supported increases to 65,535, permitting a cluster size of 4 sectors, or 2048 bytes, to be used. Thus, fixed disks formatted under DOS 3.X and later versions of the operating system store data more efficiently than do fixed disks formatted under DOS 2.X.

Landing Zone

To prevent data from being damaged due to vibrations or a bump to the computer system, many manufacturers incorporate a *landing zone* into their drives. The landing zone is a fixed location that does not contain data, onto which the read/write heads are positioned whenever power to the system turns off or is lost. Although the use of a landing zone alleviates potential damage to data due to vibrations or small bumps, before you move the computer you should use the IBM Diagnostic diskette and select the Preparing to Move option. If you have a PC AT or an equivalent program supplied with a compatible computer, this option "parks" the heads into a fixed position and is a much better protection mechanism than a reliance on the automatic landing zone.

Keyboard Use

The first keyboard marketed by IBM for use with the PC AT contains 84 keys and is divided into three sections, as illustrated in Figure 3.6. The left-hand section is composed of 10 function keys; the typewriter key area is in the middle section. A numeric keypad is in the third section on the right-hand side of the keyboard. In the upper right corner are three status lights that display the status of the Capitals (Caps) Lock, Numeric (Num) Lock, and the Scroll Lock keys.

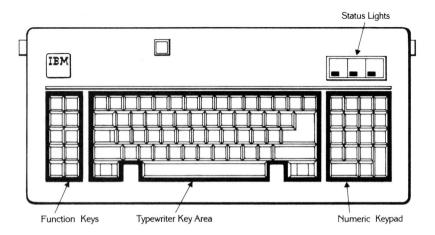

Figure 3.6 Original PC AT Keyboard Unit.

A few years after the PC AT was developed, IBM introduced its Enhanced Keyboard, which contains 101 keys. This keyboard later became a standard offering with that firm's PS/2 series of computers, and similar versions are now included with most compatible computer products.

The IBM Enhanced Keyboard is illustrated in Figure 3.7. In addition to having three status lights and a separate function key area, typewriter area, and numeric keypad, this keyboard also contains dual Shift keys with one on each side of the typewriter area, an Enter key on the keypad, and a special key area located between the typewriter area and the numeric keypad. This special key area contains five rows of keys. The top row contains three keys—Print Screen, Scroll Lock, and Pause. The Print Screen key causes all data on the screen to be printed and replaces the use of the Shift and Print Screen keys (the latter labeled PrtSc) on the original keyboard. The Scroll Lock key was relocated from its position above the numeric keypad on the original keyboard; the Pause key suspends program execution and replaces the multikey Ctrl+Num Lock combination used to perform that operation on the 84-key keyboard.

The second and third rows in the special key area contain the Insert, Home, Pg Up, Del, End, and Pg Dn keys. These keys are also included as alternate functions on the numeric keypad of both keyboards; however, when you use these cursor large-movement keys on the keypad you cannot simultaneously use the keypad to enter numeric data. Thus, the Enhanced Keyboard permits you to simultaneously use the separate bank of cursor large-movement keys in conjunction with the numeric keys in their calculator mode on the numeric keypad.

The last two rows in the special key area contain two rows of additional cursor movement keys for smaller moves. The first row has one key that moves the cursor up

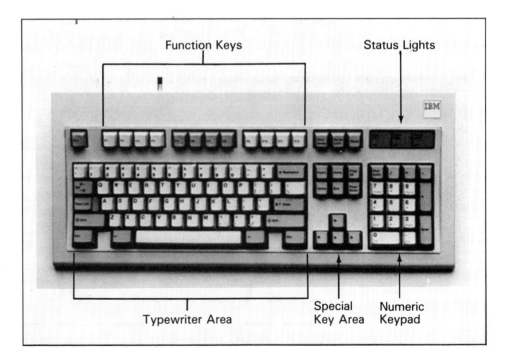

Figure 3.7   IBM Enhanced Keyboard.

one line. The last row has three cursor positioning keys, which respectively move the cursor to the left, down, or right one character position.

Function Keys

Examine the keyboards illustrated in Figure 3.6 and 3.7. On the left-hand side of the original PC AT keyboard are two columns of keys labeled F1 through F10. The top row of the Enhanced Keyboard above the typewriter key area is one row of 12 keys labeled F1 through F12. All of these keys are known as *program function keys* and can be used to make the PC AT perform predefined commands. If unaltered by programming, the first 10 function keys have been assigned for use with your IBM BASIC program to generate the predefined commands listed in Table 3.3.

Programming Assistance Keys

Surrounding the normal typewriter keys in the middle section of the keyboard is a series of keys that can be used for assistance in writing, updating, and executing programs. These keys are listed in Table 3.4, along with a description of their operation. Examples of the effective use of most of these keys will be covered shortly; however, read the description of the result of each key command operation to become familiar with the usage of each key.

Note that on the original PC AT keyboard several of the program assistance keys—including the Tab, Shift, Backspace, and Enter keys—were not labeled. On the Enhanced Keyboard each of these keys is labeled.

Numeric Keypad

When you press the Num Lock key, the numeric keypad is activated. This causes the cursor movement keys to switch to number keys and the shift keys to work in reverse. This keypad is arranged like a calculator and permits the easy entry of large quantities of numeric data.

With the Num Lock key activated, keys 1 through 9 on the numeric key pad produce the digits 1 through 9; the Delete key produces a decimal point, and the Insert key results in a zero.

Table 3.3
Function Key
Commands

Key	Command	Description
F1	LIST	Displays the lines of the program on the monitor display or television
F2	RUN	Causes the program to begin execution from the first line of the program
F3	LOAD	Reads designated program from auxiliary storage and stores it in main memory
F4	SAVE	Stores your program on the diskette or fixed disk
F5	CONT	Restarts a program after it has been interrupted by a Stop or Ctrl-Break
F6	LPT1	Refers to line printer and transfers data from the screen to the printer
F7	TRON	Means trace on and causes the line numbers of the program to be displayed as each program line is executed
F8	TROFF	Means trace off and cancels command F7
F9	KEY	Changes the function of other function keys
F10	SCREEN	Returns the program to character mode from graphics mode and turns off color

Table 3.4
Programming
Assistance Keys

Key	Meaning	Description
	Tab	Performs a tab function similar to a typewriter; tabs are set every eight characters
	Control	Always used with a second or third key to perform a function or command
	Shift	Changes lowercase letters to uppercase (capitals) or capitals to lowercase letters
	Alternate	Used with alphabetic keys to generate BASIC key words from abbreviated data entry
	Backspace	Moves the cursor to the left and removes one character for each key stroke
	Enter	Indicates the logical end of a line of input by moving the cursor from the last character on one line to the first character of the next line
	Space	Moves the cursor one position to the right
	Capitals Lock	A toggle key that causes letters to be typed in uppercase (capitals); pressing the key again causes a return to lowercase

Cursor Control and Editing

When the Num Lock key is not activated, the numeric keypad keys take on alternate meanings and function as a cursor control and screen editing mechanism. The alternate meanings of the numeric key pad keys are indicated in Table 3.5. As previously noted for the Enhanced Keyboard, many of the alternate meanings of keys on the numeric keypad are contained as separate keys in the special key area on that keyboard. Thus, you can maintain the use of the numeric keypad and obtain the ability to insert, delete, and perform other cursor positioning functions when you use an Enhanced Keyboard.

In addition to the previously discussed keys on the numeric key pad, there are several additional keys that can be used to perform special functions.

The Escape (Esc) key will perform functions defined in your operating system or by the application program used when depressed. Normally, this key is used to remove the line that the cursor is on for corrections, but does not delete the line from memory.

When the Scroll Lock key is pressed, the Scroll Lock light will be illuminated on your keyboard. When you press this key once, the cursor up and cursor down keys will move text up or down one line and lock the cursor to the line it is on. This key can also be used in conjunction with the Ctrl key to stop a job, as indicated in Table 3.6. Once the Scroll Lock light is on, it can be turned off by pressing the Scroll Lock key again, which will also turn off the Scroll Lock mode of operation.

The System (Sys) key, like the Esc key, has its functions defined by the operating system or through the application program you are using.

On the original PC AT keyboard the Print Screen (PrtSc) key will display an asterisk (*) when pressed; however, if you press and hold a Shift key and then press this key,

Table 3.5
Alternate Numeric
Key Pad Functions

Key	Description
7 Home	Home repositions the cursor to the first character of the top line of the screen
8 ↑	Moves the cursor up one line for each keystroke
4 ←	Moves the cursor to the left one character position for each keystroke
6 →	Moves the cursor to the right one character position for each keystroke
2 ↓	Moves the cursor down one line for each keystroke
1 End	End positions the cursor at the last character on the current line
Del	Deletes the character where the cursor is positioned
0 Ins	Insert sets the keyboard to the insert mode of operation; other keys entered to the right of the cursor and all data to the right will move to the right; terminate the insert mode by pressing the Insert key again or press the Enter key if all modifications have been completed on the line

Table 3.6
Multikey Program
and Screen Control

Key	Function	Description
Ctrl+Scroll Lock/Break	Break	Terminates execution of a program and identifies the line where it stops
Ctrl+Num Lock or Pause (Enhanced Keyboard)	Pause	Suspends program execution; press any key to continue program execution
Ctrl+→|	Tab	Moves the cursor to the next word on the current line
Ctrl+|←	Reverse Tab	Moves the cursor to the previous word on the current line
Ctrl+Home	Clear Screen	Moves all information from the screen and moves the cursor to the first character position on the first line
Ctrl+Alt+Delete	System Reset	Causes a reload from the diskette or fixed disk
Shift+PrtSc or Print Screen (Enhanced Keyboard)	Print Screen	Prints all data on the screen

the data that is displayed on your screen will be printed. On the Enhanced Keyboard, pressing the key labeled Print Screen performs the multikey Shift+PrtSc function, causing all data on the screen to be printed.

Multikey Operational Combinations

Using a key combination (pressing two or three keys simultaneously) you can perform a series of unique program control and screen control functions. These functions are listed in Table 3.6. Additional multikey operational combinations are applicable only to the use of IBM's disk operating system and are described in Chapter 4.

4 // The Disk Operating System

The disk operating system (DOS) can be viewed as a collection of programs that permits a computer system to supervise its own operations, automatically or under operator control, calling in program routines, languages, and data as required for a continuous throughput of a series of jobs. It is the central nervous system of the computer. Normally, an operating system consists of a nucleus of three elements—control programs, processing programs, and data management programs. The control programs provide for an automatic or enhanced operator control of the resources of the computer and permit an orderly and efficient flow of jobs through the computer system.

The processing programs are invoked as required by the control programs and consist of language processors such as compilers or interpreters that compile or interpret source programs as well as service programs that perform linkage between programs.

The operating system uses data management programs to control the organization and access of data for the application programs you will develop or purchase. As an entity, the programs that make up the operating system provide significant advantages not only in operating efficiency but also as an aid to programmers. The operating system provides easy access and usage of the higher-level languages, diagnostic aids, and libraries of programs you may wish to use.

DOS is a collection of programs on diskettes designed to facilitate running programs, create and manage files, and simplify functions using such devices as the line printer and diskette drives.

Versions of DOS

IBM announced the PC AT, together with PC-DOS Version 3.0, in 1984. Later releases of PC-DOS sold for use on the PC AT included PC-DOS Versions 3.1 and 3.2. After IBM discontinued the manufacture of the PC AT, PC-DOS Versions 3.3, 4.0, and 5.0 were introduced, all of which operate on the PC AT and compatible personal computers.

Versions of DOS marketed by IBM are formally known as PC-DOS, an acronym for Personal Computer Disk Operating System. PC-DOS is compatible with Microsoft's DOS, which is better known as MS-DOS. Microsoft markets MS-DOS for use on IBM PC compatible personal computers manufactured by more than 100 vendors. The major difference between the two versions of the operating system is in utility programs that access on-line storage devices written to perform input/output (I/O) directly with the hardware. These utilities often are varied to correspond to the differences between IBM personal computers and individual compatible systems. Thus, in some situations, one or more utility programs on an MS-DOS diskette may not work or may operate incorrectly if you use them on an IBM PC AT. Similarly, a PC-DOS utility program may not work or may operate incorrectly when executed on a compatible computer.

Despite these minor differences, the operation and use of MS-DOS and PC-DOS are applicable to both the IBM PC AT and compatible computers, using the operating system sold for use on your particular computer. Thus, this book will use the term DOS to refer to both MS-DOS and PC-DOS.

When the PS/2 family was introduced with DOS Version 3.3, Microsoft provided a similar DOS to PC AT compatible computer manufacturers. In mid-1988, DOS 4.0 was introduced, which contained many new and enhanced commands, as well as a shell menu system that facilitates its use. Because over 20 million copies of DOS 3.3 were sold for use with the PC AT and compatible computers and this version of the operating system was marketed concurrently with DOS 4.0, both versions are covered in this book. Due to the large degree of commonality between DOS 3.3 and DOS 4.0 and the recently introduced DOS 5.0, this chapter first examines specific operating system topics using DOS 3.3. Then you will learn of relevant enhancements available in DOS 4.0 and DOS 5.0. If a specific topic is the same for all three versions of the operating system, this discussion does not specify a particular version of DOS.

Device Designators

Prior to using DOS, you should become familiar with the *designator* or *specifier* used for each storage device installed in or attached to your computer. This familiarity is required because the manner in which you start DOS depends on the storage devices installed in or attached to your computer.

If your computer has only one diskette drive, it will be referenced as physical drive specifier A. If your computer has two diskette drives, the drive installed in the left side or top of the system unit is referenced as drive A. The drive installed in the right or lower portion of the system unit is referenced as drive B.

If you have only one physical diskette drive, DOS treats that drive as logical diskette drives A and B. Doing so enables you to copy the contents of all or a portion of one diskette onto another, with DOS prompting you to change or "swap" diskettes.

If your computer has one diskette drive and one fixed disk, the diskette drive functions the same as if you had only one diskette drive. That is, the floppy drive is referred to by DOS as both drive A and drive B. The fixed disk is referred to as drive C.

Although most computers have three or fewer drives, on occasion systems contain a second fixed disk. This disk drive is referenced as drive D.

Installing DOS 3.3

Your DOS 3.3 diskette contains a file named SELECT. This file can specify the keyboard layout you wish to use, the country code that will govern the format in which the date and time are displayed, and the currency symbol and decimal separator used by your computer. Using the SELECT file during the DOS 3.3 installation process, you automatically create a second copy of the operating system by responding to a few prompts issued by the command. The use of this command is applicable to all computer configurations, regardless of the number of diskette drives or fixed disks your system contains.

If your computer does not have a hard disk, installation requires at least one blank diskette, which becomes your "DOS Start-Up/Operating Diskette." If your computer has a fixed disk, the SELECT command transfers the contents of your original DOS 3.3 diskette to your fixed disk. Once this occurs, you can start DOS from your fixed disk and eliminate the requirement to use the original or a backup copy of the DOS 3.3 diskette.

Diskette-Based Systems

Before you initiate the SELECT command on your DOS 3.3 diskette you should determine the country and keyboard codes to be used with that command. These codes will be entered as command parameters; their permissible values are listed in Table 4.1.

After inserting your original DOS 3.3 Start-Up/Operating Diskette in drive A, you can either press **Ctrl+Alt+Delete** to start DOS if your system was previously powered-on, or you can simply turn on power to your computer. For either situation, you can ignore the date and time prompts by pressing the Enter key when DOS asks you to enter a new date and time. After DOS displays a copyright notice, the prompt A> displays. The character A signifies that DOS will use the diskette in drive A to process any file reference commands that are entered without a specified device name. This prompt is also known as the *default diskette prompt* or *default drive,* because DOS assumes that all file references without a drive specifier are to the drive indicated by the prompt.

Once A> appears on your display, you are ready to use the SELECT command, whose format is

SELECT *xxx yy*

where *xxx* is the country code and *yy* is the keyboard code with which you want to configure DOS to work. Assuming you wish to use the United States country and

	Country	Country Code	Keyboard Code
Table 4.1 DOS Country and Keyboard Codes	Arabic speaking	785	
	Australia	061	US
	Belgium	032	BE
	Canada (Eng.)	001	US
	Canada (Fr.)	002	CF
	Denmark	045	DK
	Finland	358	SU
	France	033	FR
	Germany	049	GR
	Hebrew speaking	972	
	Italy	039	IT
	Latin America	003	LA
	Netherlands	031	NL
	Norway	047	NO
	Portugal	351	PO
	Spain	034	SP
	Sweden	046	SV
	Switzerland (Fr.)	041	SF
	Switzerland (Ger.)	041	SG
	United Kingdom	044	UK
	United States	001	US

keyboard codes, from Table 4.1 you select 001 as the country code and US as the keyboard code. Then, you enter the SELECT command as follows:

SELECT 001 US

Figure 4.1 illustrates the screen display you should see as you start DOS 3.3 and enter the SELECT command. Note the warning message displayed after the SELECT command is entered. This message is given because the SELECT command invokes the DOS FORMAT command, which prepares a diskette or fixed disk for data recording. During this preparation, the FORMAT program writes marks on concentric circles that are used as indicators to position data as it is recorded to disk. These marks in effect erase any previously recorded data, so you are warned of this erasure in advance.

Because the SELECT command automatically initiates the FORMAT command, you do not have to understand how to use the FORMAT command and its options at this time. Later this chapter reviews its use. FORMAT is extremely important, because it is the first step in preparing or initializing blank diskettes as you make duplicate copies of application programs or store or copy data files.

Assuming you wish to continue the SELECT command process, DOS displays the character Y, so you simply press the **Enter** key to resume the operations initiated by the SELECT command. When this occurs you see the message:

```
Insert new diskette for drive B:
and strike ENTER when ready
```

If you only have one diskette drive, that physical drive will be used as logical drives A and B. Thus, the prompt Insert new diskette for drive B: in actuality tells you to remove the original DOS diskette from drive A and insert the new blank diskette in that drive.

If your computer has two diskette drives, insert the new diskette in physical drive B, the drive installed either in the right portion of the system unit or below the A drive.

Once you press the Enter key, DOS begins to format the target diskette, with the head and cylinder numbers continuously updated as the format operation progresses. After formatting is completed, the following message is displayed:

```
Format Complete
System transferred
```

The first line in the message indicates that the formatting process was completed and the disk is initialized for data recording. The second line refers to the fact that the SELECT command initiated the operation of the FORMAT command with a pa-

```
Current date is Thu  5-09-1991
Enter new date (mm-dd-yy):
Current time is 12:52:29.15
Enter new time:


The IBM Personal Computer DOS
Version 3.30 (C)Copyright International Business Machines Corp 1981, 1987
               (C)Copyright Microsoft Corp 1981, 1986

A>SELECT 001 US

SELECT is used to install DOS the first
time.  SELECT erases everything on the
specified target and then installs DOS.
Do you want to continue (Y/N)?  Y
```

Figure 4.1 Using the SELECT Command.

rameter that caused three system files to be transferred to the newly formatted diskette. By containing system files, the new diskette becomes "self-booting." This means that the diskette will contain files in predefined locations that are automatically loaded by a section of code in the computer's ROM when you turn on or reboot your computer. Once loaded, these files provide an interface between the user entering data from the keyboard and the operation of application programs. Later, this chapter examines the structure of the FORMAT command and how you can set its parameters to transfer system files to a newly formatted diskette.

After the format operation is completed and the system files are transferred, DOS displays three lines of statistics. The first line shows the total number of bytes of disk space; the second line indicates the number of bytes used by the system files. The third line displays the number of bytes available on the disk, which is the difference between the total disk space and the number of bytes used by the system files.

After displaying these statistics you see the following message:

```
Format another (Y/N)?
```

When you enter the letter **N** (uppercase or lowercase), subsequent action depends on whether your computer has one or two diskette drives. If your system has one diskette drive, DOS prompts you when to insert the original DOS diskette and the diskette for drive B. DOS displays Reading source file(s) when the original DOS diskette is inserted in drive A. After you insert your newly formatted diskette in physical drive A in response to the Insert diskette for drive B: prompt, the names of the files appear on your screen as they are copied. If your computer has two diskette drives, DOS automatically copies the files from the original DOS diskette onto the diskette installed in physical drive B without prompting you to Insert a diskette for drive B:. For either hardware configuration, the SELECT procedure is completed when the A> prompt is redisplayed. At this time, you should store your original DOS diskette in a safe place and use the recently created copy for everyday use.

Fixed Disk-Based Systems

If your computer system includes a fixed disk drive, you will probably want to install DOS 3.3 on that drive (drive C in most cases). By doing so you can subsequently load DOS from drive C, so you will not have to insert a diskette in drive A each time you wish to use your computer.

Prior to installing DOS 3.3 on your computer's fixed disk, you must prepare the disk to record data. To do so, use the DOS FDISK program. Insert the original DOS 3.3 Start-Up/Operating System diskette in drive A and power-up your computer. Then, after the prompt A> is displayed, type **FDISK** and press **Enter**. The FDISK main menu is displayed, which is similar to the illustration shown in Figure 4.2. If your computer system has two fixed disks, the menu includes a fifth choice, which enables you to select the next fixed disk drive after you have prepared the first drive.

FDISK can create a *DOS partition,* which is an area on your fixed disk reserved for DOS to use. It stores your operating system files, as well as application programs designed to work under this operating system. Many computer users require only one partition on their fixed disk; however, other users may require two or more partitions if they wish to install several operating systems. Examples of other operating systems include a Microsoft implementation of AT&T's UNIX system, called XENIX, and CP/M-86, the latter an updated version of Digital Research's Control Program for Microcomputers (CP/M) operating system.

```
IBM Personal Computer
Fixed Disk Setup Program Version 3.30
(C)Copyright IBM Corp. 1983,1987

FDISK Options

Current Fixed Disk Drive: 1

Choose one of the following:

        1. Create DOS Partition
        2. Change Active Partition
        3. Delete DOS Partition
        4. Display Partition Information




Enter choice: [1]




Press ESC to return to DOS
```

Figure 4.2   FDISK Main Menu.

```
Create DOS Partition

Current Fixed Disk Drive: 1

        1. Create primary DOS Partition
        2. Create extended DOS Partition

Enter choice: [1]

Press ESC to return to FDISK Options
```

Figure 4.3   Creating a DOS Partition.

To create a partition for DOS 3.3, you accept the default choice of item 1 enclosed in brackets by pressing **Enter**. This action displays the screen illustrated in Figure 4.3.

As indicated by the options displayed in Figure 4.3, DOS has two DOS partition types. The first is called a *primary DOS partition* and is the only one required to use DOS on a fixed disk. Under DOS 3.3 the maximum size of this partition was 32M bytes. However, several vendors of data storage devices offer extensions to DOS that break the 32M-byte barrier. In addition, under DOS 4.0 and DOS 5.0 the 32M-byte partition limit was removed, with a partition size equal to the maximum disk space possible. If you do not have one of the third-party software extensions or use DOS 4.0 or DOS 5.0, you can use FDISK to create up to three *extended DOS partitions*. These partitions can be any size and can be subdivided into multiple areas known as *logical drives*, with each logical drive limited in size to 32M bytes. Thus, if your fixed disk exceeds 32M bytes of storage capacity, under DOS 3.3 you would probably want to create an extended DOS partition and subdivide that partition into logical drives. Thereafter, when you load DOS 3.3, each logical drive is assigned a drive letter identifier you use to access the storage contained in the logical drive area.

To create a primary DOS partition, you select the default choice of 1 illustrated in Figure 4.3. This selection displays a new screen, illustrated in Figure 4.4. Normally, you want the primary DOS partition to be as large as possible if you do not intend to use another operating system. Thus, you would select the default choice of Y contained in brackets in Figure 4.4 by pressing **Enter**.

After the DOS partition operation is completed, the following message displays:

```
System will now restart

Insert DOS diskette in drive A:
Press any key when ready...
```

After you insert your DOS diskette in drive A and press a key, the "current" date and time are displayed, with DOS prompting you to enter a new date and time as previously illustrated in the top portion of Figure 4.1. Here the initial "current" date is a reference date and time when the original DOS Version 1.0 was produced and that you will obviously want to update to the true current date and time. Next, the copyright notice displays, after which the A> prompt appears. At this point you must use the SELECT command. This command sets your keyboard and country codes, formats your fixed disk, and transfers the files from the DOS diskette onto your fixed disk.

At the A> prompt you should enter the SELECT command using the following format:

```
SELECT C: XXX YY
```

Here C: is the drive specifier parameter that tells the command that it should operate on drive C. *XXX* is the country code, whereas *YY* is the keyboard code, with both codes selected from Table 4.1.

Once you enter the SELECT command, the same warning message as shown previously at the bottom of Figure 4.1 displays. If you continue the SELECT command process by pressing **Enter**, due to the severity of inadvertently formatting the fixed disk DOS displays

```
WARNING, ALL DATA ON NON-REMOVABLE DISK
DRIVE C: WILL BE LOST!
PROCEED WITH FORMAT (Y/N)?
```

To proceed with the formatting operation, enter **Y**. During the format operation DOS updates the head and cylinder number each time they change to identify the progress of the format. DOS displays a message when formatting is complete and displays the message System transferred to denote that the three system files have transferred from the diskette onto the fixed disk. Next, DOS prompts you to enter a volume label:

```
Volume label (11 characters, ENTER for none)?
```

```
Create Primary DOS Partition

Current Fixed Disk Drive: 1

Do you wish to use the maximum size
for a DOS partition and make the DOS
partition active (Y/N).........? [Y]

Press ESC to return to FDISK Options
```

Figure 4.4 Creating a Primary DOS Partition.

The volume label is normally used as an identifier for diskettes; however, it can also be used for fixed disks. Programs can be written to check the volume label to ensure that a correct diskette is used or that the program is executed on a computer whose fixed disk was assigned a specific volume label. As indicated by the displayed message, you can either enter a volume label or simply press **Enter** to omit the label. After either action, disk space statistics display on your screen, followed by the message

```
Reading source file(s)...
```

As the remaining files on the DOS diskette are copied to your fixed disk, their names display on your screen. When all files have been copied, the A> prompt displays. At this point you have successfully installed DOS on your fixed disk and can remove the DOS diskette from drive A and store it in a safe place.

Installing DOS 4.0

Under DOS 4.0 the SELECT program was significantly enhanced. This program operates as a full-screen utility that is automatically invoked when you power-on or press the Ctrl+Alt+Del keys to perform a system reset with the DOS 4.0 Install diskette in drive A. Prior to installing DOS 4.0 you should ensure that you have at least one available blank diskette if your computer has a 5¼-inch or 3½-inch high-capacity diskette drive or two blank diskettes if your computer has standard-capacity 720K-byte 3½-inch diskette drives.

Once you power-on your computer or perform a system reset with the Install diskette in drive A, the computer manufacturer's logo and the program name DOS SELECT that is initiated will be displayed. This will be followed by a copyright notice and instructions to press the Enter key to continue or the Esc key to cancel the program. As the SELECT program operates, it displays the action that occurs and provides you with the ability to display help information by pressing the F1 key. SELECT also prompts you when to insert diskettes.

Diskette-Based Systems

If your computer does not have a fixed disk drive, you will require two or four blank diskettes, depending on the storage capacity of the diskette drives installed in your computer. Figure 4.5 indicates the diskette requirements for the SELECT program. For example, if your computer uses 720K-byte diskettes, on one diskette the SELECT program places the DOS command files and utility programs. On the second diskette the SELECT program copies the DOS SHELL program and additional DOS utility programs. Thus, label the first diskette "Start-up" and the second, "Shell." Once the appropriate information is copied to the two diskettes, you can start DOS using either diskette. If you use the Start-up diskette, DOS 4.0 will be brought up in a command-based interface; whereas, if you use the Shell diskette, DOS 4.0 is initiated using the DOS Shell.

The DOS Shell is a graphics-based interface, and it presents a user-friendly display of available selections and incorporates an on-line help facility. Later sections of this chapter examine the operation and use of the DOS 4.0 Shell. Because the actual installation of DOS 4.0 is very similar for diskette and fixed disk operations, its use is described on a fixed disk system with notations about relevant differences between the fixed disk and diskette installation.

```
                        Welcome

        Welcome to DOS 4.00 and the SELECT program.  SELECT
        will install DOS 4.00 on your fixed disk or diskette.
        If you install DOS 4.00 on a diskette, the number of
        blank diskettes you need depends on the type and
        capacity of your diskette drive:

          Drive Type (Capacity)        Number of Diskettes

          5.25-Inch Drive (360KB)      four 5.25 (360KB)
          5.25-Inch Drive (1.2MB)      four 5.25 (360KB)
          3.5-Inch Drive (720KB)       two  3.5  (1MB)
          3.5-Inch Drive (1.44MB)      one  3.5  (2MB)

        If you install DOS 4.00 onto a fixed disk, you need
        one blank diskette:

          5.25-Inch Drive              one  5.25 (360KB)
          3.5-Inch Drive               one  3.5  (1 or 2MB)

          Press Enter (↵) to continue or Esc to Cancel


    Enter     Esc=Cancel
```

Figure 4.5   SELECT Program Diskette Requirements.

Fixed Disk-Based Systems

After the logo screen is displayed, the SELECT program displays a screen of information denoting the number of blank diskettes you should have based on the storage capacity of the diskette drives installed in your computer. In this display screen the term *720KB* refers to 3½-inch diskettes that have a formatted storage capacity of 720K bytes, whereas the term *1.44MB* refers to diskettes that have a 1.44M-byte formatted storage capacity. This screen is illustrated in Figure 4.5. As mentioned earlier, if your computer only has diskettes with a 720K-byte storage capacity, you will need two 3½-inch 1M-byte diskettes, whereas systems with one or more 1.44M-byte storage capacity diskette drives only require one blank 2M-byte diskette. Finally, as indicated in Figure 4.5, if your computer has a fixed disk you will only require one blank diskette.

After the information concerning the number of required blank diskettes is displayed, you specify a division between DOS functionality and program workspace. A new screen containing three entries displays; it is illustrated in Figure 4.6.

The second entry in Figure 4.6 is highlighted as the default value, which is selected if you press Enter. Essentially, this screen helps you to specify the amount of memory-resident DOS functions. Because DOS supports a maximum of 640K bytes of user memory unless you invoke the DOS 4.0 support of expanded memory that requires programs specifically written for this feature, maximizing DOS functionality reduces your program workspace to a minimum value. Unless you intend to execute very large spreadsheet programs, selecting option 2 is acceptable for most users and should be selected if your computer's RAM is 512K bytes. If you expect to perform operations on large spreadsheets, select option 1 only if you are using a computer other than an IBM PC AT that has 256K bytes of RAM. For all PC ATs and most compatible computers with more than 512K bytes of RAM select option 3. This option maximizes DOS functionality while permitting sufficient memory to execute programs.

Once you select the program workspace, the next DOS 4.0 SELECT screen sets the country and keyboard parameters. Unlike DOS 3.3, which requires you to enter codes,

```
                    Specify Function and Workspace

       SELECT sets up your computer to run DOS and your programs
       most efficiently based on the option you choose.

       Note:  You can review the results of your choice later
       in this program.

       Choose an option:


            1. Minimum DOS function; maximum program workspace

            2. Balance DOS function with program workspace

            3. Maximum DOS function; minimum program workspace




       ─────────────────────────────────────────────────────────

       Enter     Esc=Cancel     F1=Help
```

Figure 4.6   SELECT Function and Workspace Menu.

```
                          Country Selection


       Choose a country:

            United States              (001)   Norway                    (047)
            Canada (French Speaking)   (002)   Germany                   (049)
            Latin America              (003)   Australia                 (061)
            Netherlands                (031)   Japan                     (081)
            Belgium                    (032)   Korea                     (082)
            France                     (033)   Peoples Republic of China (086)
            Spain                      (034)   Taiwan                    (088)
            Italy                      (039)   Portugal                  (351)
            Switzerland                (041)   Finland                   (358)
            United Kingdom             (044)   Arabic Speaking           (785)
            Denmark                    (045)   Hebrew Speaking           (972)
            Sweden                     (046)




       ─────────────────────────────────────────────────────────

       Enter     Esc=Cancel     F1=Help
```

Figure 4.7   DOS 4.0 Country Selection.

under DOS 4.0 the U.S. country and keyboard codes are predefined and accepted if you simply press Enter. For a different country and keyboard, the DOS 4.0 SELECT program displays the available countries and their codes, as illustrated in Figure 4.7. Initially, a highlighted bar displays over the United States entry on the screen. You can use the Up and Down Arrows to reposition the highlight bar to the required country and press the Enter key to make your selection. In comparison, under DOS 3.3 you must first look up the appropriate country code and then enter its numeric value.

Once you complete the country and keyboard selections, the Select Installation Drive menu is displayed. This menu provides the capability to specify the drive on which DOS will be installed. If you have a fixed disk, one option shows the drive designator C, whereas a diskette-based system shows drive A for this option.

After you specify the drive on which to install DOS, the next menu contains options to specify a location in a hierarchical directory structure to which DOS files will be copied. Essentially, DOS supports a directory structure similar to an inverted tree, with the root directory denoted by the backslash character (\) at the top of the structure. Paths to subdirectories begin with a backslash, followed by the name or names of the subdirectories in the route to a specific subdirectory, with a backslash preceding each name.

Figure 4.8 shows the Specify DOS Location menu. This menu actually provides several other functions as well. First, as specified by the name of the menu, you can accept the default displayed location \DOS, which defines a subdirectory under the root directory on drive C that will be named DOS as the location where files will be copied from the Install diskette. For most computer users, this is acceptable; however, to locate DOS files elsewhere you can enter a string of up to 63 characters between the brackets shown in Figure 4.8. This is the maximum path length supported by DOS. If you enter a DOS location, the SELECT program creates a subdirectory to match your entry if a previously created directory does not exist.

As indicated in Figure 4.8, you can use the Specify DOS Location menu to have all DOS files on a fixed disk updated. This feature enables you to update DOS 3.3 to DOS 4.0. If you select option 2, you can have all nonsystem files copied to a specified directory whose name you enter in brackets.

Once DOS files are copied to the default or a specified subdirectory, the SELECT program displays several menus requesting information concerning the number and type of printers you have and the computer port(s) to which they are connected. From anywhere on these menus you can press the F1 key to obtain on-line assistance; a

```
                         Specify DOS Location


         You can accept the DOS directory name shown or type a new
         directory name.


         DOS Directory . . . .C:\[DOS                                        ]



         To select option 1 below, press Enter.  To change your
         option, press the tab key, highlight your choice and then
         press Enter.

            1. Update all DOS files on fixed disk

            2. Copy non-system files to directory specified



   _____

     Enter    Esc=Cancel    F1=Help
```

Figure 4.8   DOS 4.0 Specify DOS Location Menu.

sample help window appears in Figure 4.9. Note in the figure that a help message is superimposed over the Printer Selection menu as a result of pressing the F1 key.

Once appropriate printer information is entered, SELECT can accept the previously entered data and continue with the installation, or it can review, change, or add installation choices. Assuming you accept the previously entered data, SELECT makes a copy of the Install diskette and prompts you when to remove that diskette and to insert your backup diskette. After the copy of the Install diskette is made, SELECT copies the contents of that diskette and the Operating diskette to the fixed disk if you previously installed DOS 3.3 on the fixed disk. If this is the first time you are using the fixed disk, SELECT displays a menu that you use to partition the disk. Under DOS 4.0 partitions can exceed 32M bytes, so you can either let SELECT define the partition size—which sets it to the maximum storage capacity of the disk—or you can define the partition size.

After the partition size is defined, you are instructed to perform a system reset operation. Press the **Ctrl+Alt+Del** keys. At this time SELECT formats your fixed disk. During formatting, SELECT displays the percentage of the disk that is formatted in the upper left corner of the screen. Once formatting is complete, SELECT copies the files from the Install diskette to the subdirectory \DOS or another previously specified subdirectory. Then you are instructed to insert the Operating diskette, whose contents are now copied to the fixed disk. After the two copying operations are completed, SELECT prompts you to remove all diskettes and perform another system reset. This indicates that the DOS 4.0 installation process is completed, and a system reset brings up the DOS 4.0 Shell.

Installing DOS 5.0

The introduction of DOS 5.0 in mid-1991 represents a considerable advance in both the ease of installation and the capability of the operating system. While we will focus our attention on the installation process in this section, later in this book we will examine the features of DOS 5.0.

DOS 5.0 is distributed on both multiple 5¼-inch 360K-byte and 3½-inch 720K-byte diskettes. By placing diskette number 1 into your drive and entering the command A:SETUP, the installation process becomes almost a matter of inserting and removing

```
                            Printer Type Help

Printer.........    Use the Up or Down arrow keys to select the name of
                   your printer, then press Enter.  If the printer
                   attached to your system is not listed, select "Other"
                   to identify the type of printer you are using.  When
Choose a printer:  more than one printer is attached, this list
                   reappears for each printer. If you do not know the
                   name or type of printer you have, check the printer
  IBM 5152 Graph
  IBM 4201 Propr   Esc=Cancel     F1=Help        F9=Keys
  IBM 4201 Propr
  IBM 4202 Proprinter XL
  IBM 4207 Proprinter X24
  IBM 4208 Proprinter XL24
  IBM 4201 Proprinter (Serial)
  IBM 4201 Proprinter II (Serial)
  IBM 4202 Proprinter XL (Serial)
  IBM 4207 Proprinter X24 (Serial)
```

Figure 4.9   Help Message Window Displayed in Front of the Printer Selection Menu.

diskettes. Although the installation of DOS 5.0 is relatively easy, a word of caution is in order. You should have available a blank diskette, because when you install this new operating system in place of a previous version of DOS you can store your original DOS files onto that diskette.

Figure 4.10 illustrates the initial screen display resulting from the use of SETUP under DOS 5.0. By pressing the Enter key you will obtain a series of screen displays that will ask you if you are using a network or if you want your hard disk backed up. By responding affirmatively to these prompts you will be prompted to perform a few additional steps prior to proceeding with the actual installation of DOS 5.0.

During the setup process the program will determine your hardware and software (if applicable) configuration. In addition, it will provide you with an option to use the DOS Shell automatically upon startup if you so desire. Here the DOS Shell is similar to the DOS 4.0 Shell in that its graphical interface makes managing files and using the operating system easier.

As DOS 5.0 is being installed you will be prompted at appropriate times to insert other disks into your A drive. To facilitate informing you of the status of the installation process DOS 5.0 displays a long rectangular horizontal box and both labels the "percent complete" and fills the box with a solid bar in proportion to the percentage of the installation process that has been completed. Once the Setup process is complete you will be prompted to remove any floppy diskettes from your drives and then press Enter to start DOS 5.0. The resulting display will be similar to the illustration in Figure 4.11 if you selected the run DOS Shell on startup option.

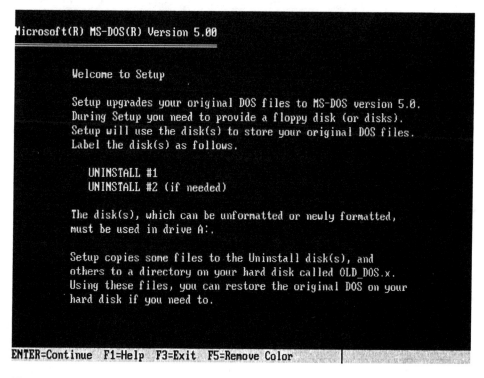

Figure 4.10 DOS 5.0 Setup Screen

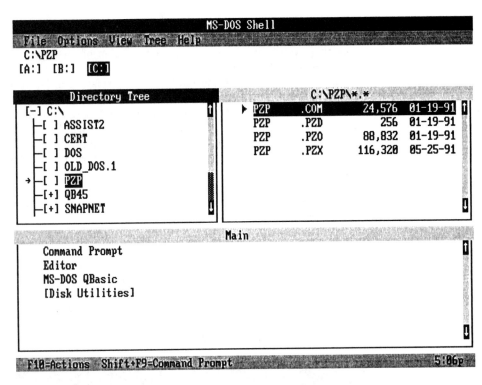

Figure 4.11   MS-DOS 5.0 Shell

DOS 4.0 Shell

The initial DOS 4.0 Shell menu, whose title is Start Programs, has an arrow in the upper left corner of the screen; it is the *mouse pointer*. The DOS 4.0 Shell supports both keyboard entries and the use of a mouse, whereas DOS 3.3 is limited to keyboard entries.

The three items listed under the date in the left portion of the Start Programs display—Program, Group, and Exit—are referred to as items on the *action bar*. By pressing the F10 key, you can use the action bar. Pressing this key highlights the Program entry on the action bar. This highlighting feature is the *selection cursor,* and it can be moved to other items in the action bar by pressing the Left and Right Arrow keys.

As an alternative to moving the selection cursor over an appropriate item, you can press the character key that appears underlined in the selection. As an example, you can type the character **G** to select Group or the character **X** to select Exit. Once you press the Enter key, a pull-down menu listing the options for the item in the action bar is displayed. As this chapter examines the operation and usage of DOS commands, it also investigates the use of the DOS Shell when appropriate. For now, look at the four entries in the vertical column in the left of the screen. These entries, starting with Command Prompt, are located in the Shell's group area. When the DOS Shell is initially displayed, the Command Prompt entry is highlighted. Using the Up and Down Arrow keys you can reposition the selection cursor to other items in the group area. Pressing

Enter when the Command Prompt item is highlighted switches DOS 4.0 to its command prompt mode of operation, similar to DOS 3.3. Figure 4.12 shows the message you see after you switch to this mode. Note that you can use command prompt mode anytime in the DOS Shell by pressing the key combination **Shift+F9**. You can type **EXIT** to return to the DOS Shell.

Also note that the default prompt used by DOS 4.0 is C:\DOS>, instead of C> for a fixed disk system using DOS 3.3. This change is caused by the INSTALL program, which creates a file called AUTOEXEC.BAT whose DOS PROMPT command alters the prompt. The AUTOEXEC.BAT file is automatically executed whenever you power-up your computer or perform a system reset operation, causing the PROMPT command in the file to be changed from the DOS 3.3 default. If you are more comfortable with the previous prompt display, remove the PROMPT command from the AUTOEXEC.BAT file. Further information concerning the use of batch files to include the AUTO-EXEC.BAT file appears in Chapter 6.

DOS 5.0 Shell

The DOS 5.0 Shell represents a considerable evolution in the shell from that available under DOS 4.0. As indicated in Figure 4.13, your screen is divided into several different areas. At the top of your screen is a Menu bar that is directly below the title bar labeled "MS-DOS Shell." This bar lists the names of available menus. To select a specific menu you would press the F10 key, which highlights File. Next, you can use the down cursor key to drop the menu or the right or left cursor key to move the highlight bar onto another menu. Figure 4.13 illustrates the pulldown of the File menu in the DOS 5.0 shell. The drive icons ([A:] [B:] [C:]) enable you to select a specific drive, whose directory is displayed in the Directory Tree window. To the right of that window is the file list area, which displays the files in the directory highlighted in the Directory Tree. Under the heading Main, which takes up approximately one-third of the screen, is the program-list area. By default the Main group is displayed in the program-list area. The Main group includes two programs that you can start directly from the MS-DOS Shell that represent a considerable improvement over prior versions of DOS—a full-screen editor and QBasic, an easy-to-use interpreter you can use to write Basic programs. Also included in the Main group is the entry Command Prompt. By selecting this entry you leave the MS-DOS Shell and go to the MS-DOS command line. To return to the shell you type **DOSSHELL** and press **Enter.**

Bringing Up DOS from Drive A

Now that you have either made a duplicate DOS diskette or installed DOS on your fixed disk, you are ready to start the operating system for everyday use.

```
When ready to return to the DOS Shell, type EXIT then press enter.


IBM DOS Version 4.00
        (C)Copyright International Business Machines Corp 1981, 1988
        (C)Copyright Microsoft Corp 1981-1986

C:\DOS>
```

Figure 4.12   Initialized DOS 4.0 Command Mode.

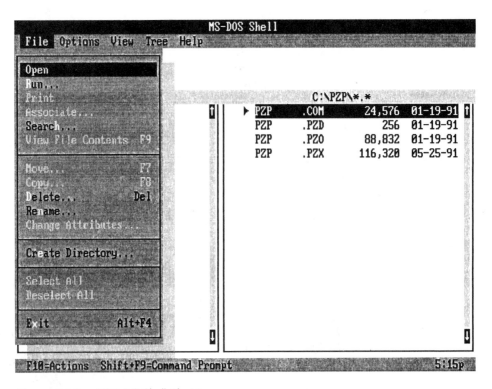

Figure 4.13   DOS 5.0 Shell File Menu.

There are two methods that you can use to start DOS. If power to the system unit is off, you can insert your DOS diskette in drive A. Then, after power is turned on, the internal power-on self-test (POST) is performed, and DOS is automatically loaded into the computer's memory. If your system was previously powered-up, you can perform a system reset operation (by pressing **Ctrl+Alt+Del**) to load DOS. When this operation is initiated, the computer clears its memory and restarts itself without performing a POST.

When either of the two previously discussed methods of starting DOS are performed, the computer's Basic Input/Output System (BIOS) in read-only memory (ROM) causes any disk in drive A to be searched. If the disk contains DOS system files, the computer's BIOS loads three files into memory. The first two files are named IBMBIO.COM and IBMDOS.COM if you are using PC-DOS. These files are *hidden files*, because they are not listed if you list a directory of the disk where the programs reside. The first file provides a standard interface to the hardware and supplements the BIOS contained in the computer's ROM. The second file is responsible for interpreting commands issued by application programs and converting those commands into a form recognizable by BIOS. The third file is called COMMAND.COM, which is a command processor that accepts and processes DOS commands you enter from the keyboard or from a *batch file*. A batch file contains a frequently used sequence of DOS commands.

After the three core DOS files are loaded, the current date is displayed if you are using DOS 3.3, and you are prompted to enter a new date or accept the displayed date. If you are using DOS 4.0, the DOS Shell is loaded and the date and time are displayed at the top left and right corners of the screen. If you are using DOS 5.0 and select the graphic Shell the shell will be automatically displayed on startup with the time displayed in the lower right corner of your screen. For DOS 3.3 and DOS 5.0, the current date is displayed, followed by the prompt shown here:

```
Current date is Fri 5-9-1989
Enter new date:
```

You can enter any month, day, and year as long as they fall within the following ranges:

month (m) is 1 or 2 digits from 1 to 12
day (d) is 1 or 2 digits from 1 to 31
year (y) is 2 digits from 80 to 99 or 4 digits from 1980 to 2099

The delimiters between the month, day, and year can be either a slash (/) or hyphen (-). If you enter an invalid date or delimiter, DOS repeats the message, as in

```
Enter new date: 12-23/89
Enter new date: 12-23-89
```

until the format is correct.

After an acceptable date is entered, DOS displays a message similar to

```
Current time is 0:01:21.85
Enter new time:
```

Note that under DOS the time is displayed in the following format:

hours:minutes:seconds.hundredths of a second

whereas only hours and minutes are displayed when the DOS 4.0 Shell is used. You can enter any time, as long as it falls within the following ranges:

hours is 1 or 2 digits between 0 and 23
minutes is 1 or 2 digits between 0 and 59
seconds is 1 or 2 digits between 0 and 59
hundredths of a second is 1 or 2 digits between 0 and 99

When you enter the time, be sure to enter a colon (:) after each time element (except hundredths of a second)—a slash (/) or a hyphen (-) will not work.

Time must be entered in a military format, with 1 p.m. expressed as 13 hours, 2 p.m. expressed as 14 hours, and so on. Due to this, be sure to convert the appropriate hour of the day to its correct military format. Also note that you can press the Enter key without entering a time to accept the displayed time, or you can enter just the hour or however much of the remaining levels of time information you wish.

Once you enter the date and time or respond to their prompts by pressing Enter, a copyright notice appears. Then the prompt A> displays, indicating that the diskette in drive A will be examined automatically to process any file reference commands that you enter without a specified device name. The complete DOS 3.3 initialization procedure for a diskette-based system is illustrated in Figure 4.14.

If you initialize DOS 4.0, the DOS Shell display is similar to that in Figure 4.11, with the icon for drive A highlighted instead of the icon for drive C. Then, if you press the Shift+F9 keys or select the Command Prompt option, you switch to the operating system's command mode of operation, with a display similar to that shown in Figure 4.10. The only difference for diskette initialization is that the prompt under DOS 4.0

```
Current date is Wed  5-08-1991
Enter new date (mm-dd-yy):
Current time is 11:00:38.08
Enter new time:


The IBM Personal Computer DOS
Version 3.30 (C)Copyright International Business Machines Corp 1981, 1987
            (C)Copyright Microsoft Corp 1981. 1986

A>
```

Figure 4.14   DOS 3.3 Initialization on Diskette-Based System.

is A:\> instead of C:\DOS> when the operating system is initialized from the fixed disk.

Bringing Up DOS from Drive C

If your computer has a fixed disk, you will normally initialize DOS from that device. By doing so you forgo placing a DOS diskette in drive A when you power-up your computer or perform a system reset operation.

If you previously installed DOS on drive C, that drive will be automatically searched for DOS when you power-up your computer or perform a system reset operation. The DOS initialization display for a system with a fixed disk is similar to that illustrated in Figure 4.14 when using DOS 3.3, except that the default prompt becomes C>, indicating that the fixed disk is the default drive. As previously explained, if you initialize DOS 4.0 or 5.0 from a fixed disk and select its command mode of operation, the prompt C:\DOS> is displayed.

Changing the Default Drive

You can change the DOS default drive designation prompt by entering a new drive designation letter followed by a colon. The following examples illustrate the resulting prompts when you change the default drive under DOS 3.3, DOS 4.0, and DOS 5.0.

DOS 3.3	DOS 4.0/5.0
C>	C:\DOS>
C>**A:**	C:\DOS>**A:**
A>	A:\>

Here, the original prompt in the first row is changed when you enter **A:** (shown in the second row), becoming a drive A prompt in the third row.

The key difference between the drive designation prompt for DOS 3.3 and 4.0 is that under DOS 4.0 the current directory is also displayed. Thus, C:\DOS> indicates that drive C is the default drive and the subdirectory DOS located under the root directory is the current directory. Similarly, A:\ indicates that drive A is the default drive and the root directory (\) is the current directory.

As a result of entering A followed by a colon, the default drive was changed to drive A. Now, A will be the drive DOS will search for any commands or file names you enter. Note that for computers that have only one diskette drive, changing the drive designation from A to B or from B to A has no effect on the physical drive that will be searched for commands or file names. This is because the one physical diskette drive will function as two logical drives in tandem with each drive designation change.

Editing Keys

To help you enter and modify commands, DOS assigns predefined editing functions to the first five function keys (F1 through F5), the Insert (Ins), Delete (Del), and escape (Esc) keys. In addition, the Backspace key can also be used for editing, eliminating one character to the left of the cursor each time that key is pressed.

Table 4.2 summarizes DOS editing keys and the functions associated with the use of each key. Note that no cursor control keys are listed in Table 4.2. This is because the normal cursor control keys are disabled when the computer is in the DOS command mode. Thus, you cannot move the cursor to a specific character location in a command to make corrections, unfortunately resulting in a rather primitive editing facility. However, you can use the Left and Right Arrow keys to delete and redisplay one character at a time from the command line. The Left Arrow key functions like the previously described Backspace key, and the Right Arrow key functions the same as the F1 key.

As data is entered from the keyboard it is placed into a temporary storage area known as an *input buffer*. Data remains in this buffer until you press Enter, after which the keystroke is processed. Due to this, you actually modify or repeat the contents of the input buffer when you edit a command line.

To illustrate how you can save keystrokes by using DOS editing keys, assume that in response to the DOS prompt C> or C:\DOS> you typed the following command line without pressing the Enter key.

DIR A:STAT.BAS

In the preceding command line the actual command invoked is the DOS directory command whose name is DIR. Here the DIR command operates on the contents of drive A, indicated by the letter A followed by a colon (:), and the file, whose name is STAT with the extension .BAS. Entering this command displays information concerning the file, including its size and date of creation. Everything to the right of the command (DIR) is the file specification. The actual construction of file specifications will be covered later in this chapter.

After you type the previously mentioned command line, use the Backspace key to erase that line from the display. Although the data is erased from the screen, the line is still in the input buffer.

Table 4.2
DOS Editing Keys

Editing Key	Function Performed
Delete	Deletes one character in the input buffer without moving the cursor.
Insert	Inserts characters.
Esc	Cancels the line currently displayed while the contents of the input buffer remain unchanged.
F1	Redisplays one character of previous command line from the input buffer.
F2	Redisplays all characters of previous command line up to a specific character.
F3	Redisplays all remaining characters of previous command line from the input buffer.
F4	Skips over all characters of previous command line in the input buffer until a specified character is encountered. This is the opposite of F2.
F5	Accepts the edited line for further editing, placing the currently displayed line in the input buffer.

Each time you press the F1 key, one character from the buffer is copied to the screen. Thus, pressing the F1 key twice results in the following screen display:

```
DI
```

The F2 key performs a function that is similar to the multiple use of the F1 key. That is, pressing the F2 key followed by a single character that functions as a delimiter results in the display of all characters from the input buffer up to but not including the first occurrence of the delimiter. As an example of the use of F2, press that key and type an S. The screen appears as follows:

```
DIR A:S
```

You can use the F3 key to copy all of the remaining characters from the input buffer onto the screen. Once the Enter key is pressed, only the characters on the screen are sent to the computer for processing. To illustrate the usefulness of the F3 key, suppose you wanted to check for the status of the file STAT.BAT on the diskette in drive A. By pressing F3, you would generate the display of the contents of the input buffer as follows:

```
DIR A:STAT.BAS
```

Now, you could use the Backspace key to erase the *S* character. Then you could type **T**, then press **Enter** to invoke the required operation. This would now provide a directory listing of the file STAT.BAT on drive A by changing one letter instead of typing a new command line. As you work with DOS editing keys you will find the F3 key to be most useful. This key can generate a previously entered command line. That line can be duplicated as much as you want, or you can modify the previously entered command before you send the command line to the computer for processing.

Like the F2 key, to use the F4 key you insert a delimiter. Here the delimiter informs DOS to skip all characters up to the first occurrence of the delimiter character when DOS displays the remainder of the contents of the input buffer. Note that if the specified character is not present in the input buffer, no characters are skipped.

To illustrate the use of the F4 key, assume your input buffer appears on your screen as follows:

```
DIR A:STAT.BAS
```

To list a directory of all files on the B drive whose extension is .BAS, either you could enter the appropriate command from scratch or you could take advantage of the commonality of one or more portions of the current input buffer using DOS editing keys. Here the command to list all files on drive B with the extension .BAS is

DIR B:*.BAS

The asterisk is a wildcard character whose use is covered later in this chapter. If you press the F3 key, the contents of the input buffer are displayed, which were previously entered as

```
DIR A:STAT.BAS
```

By pressing the **Backspace** key 10 times or holding the key down, you remove all characters up to and including the drive designator A. Now you can type the three characters **B:***. Next, press the **F4** key followed by a period, which causes all characters up to but not including the period to be skipped. Then, pressing the **F3** key causes the remainder of the input buffer to be copied to the screen:

```
DIR B:*.BAS
```

Insert/Delete

The Insert (Ins) and Delete (Del) keys, despite operating as their names imply, actually work on the contents of the input buffer when you are at the DOS command level. Thus, their usefulness for command line editing is minimal.

As an example of the use of the Insert and Delete keys, assume you want to check the status of the file FRED.BAS on drive B. The content of the input buffer is the line

```
DIR B:*.BAS
```

You first press **Backspace** five times or hold that key down until the period is removed from the display. Next, press the **Delete** key to erase the asterisk from the input buffer. Then press **Insert** to switch DOS to insert mode. Now you type the word **FRED**, causing each character to be inserted into the input buffer while all characters to the right of and including the period are shifted to the right. When you finish inserting the filename FRED, you press **Insert** a second time to leave the insert mode. Then you press the **F3** key, causing the remainder of the command line to be displayed, as in

```
DIR B:FRED.BAS
```

Now you can either press the **Enter** key to make this revision replace the data in the input buffer as well as send it to the computer for processing, or you can press the **F5** key to cause the contents of the displayed line to replace the contents of the input buffer for further editing. However, this does not send the command line to the system for processing. To distinguish this, DOS displays the @ character at the end of the line when the F5 key is pressed, after which the cursor is moved to the first position of the next line.

Control Functions

When you load DOS you can initiate five predefined control functions, based on the use of multikey combinations. These combinations and their operations under DOS are summarized in Table 4.3.

To perform the system reset, you simultaneously press **Ctrl+Alt+Delete**. This process reinitializes DOS, which is useful if your system freezes due to a bug in an application program or some other abnormality occurs.

If you are using DOS 3.3, the Shift+PrtSc key combination prints the text contents of the display. If you have an Enhanced Keyboard you can simply press the key labeled Print Screen to print the text contents of the display. If graphics are displayed, you can print them as well with Shift+PrtSc if a special DOS file named GRAPHICS was previously loaded and your computer is using the CGA display mode. Under DOS 4.0, the GRAPHICS program can print the contents of a screen that contains text and/or graphics in the CGA, EGA, and VGA video display modes.

Table 4.3
DOS Multikey
Functions

Key Combination	Function Performed	Description
Ctrl+Alt+Delete	System Reset	Reloads DOS from the diskette or fixed disk.
Shift+PrtSc	Print Screen	Prints all data on the screen.
Ctrl+PrtSc	Echo to Printer	Logs all input and output to the printer.
Ctrl+Num Lock	Suspend System Operation	Freezes the operation of the computer until a key is pressed.
Ctrl+Break	Break	Cancels current operation and returns to DOS prompt level.

The Ctrl+PrtSc key combination can be viewed as a logging facility. When this key combination is first pressed, it prints whatever you type and all system responses. This echoing of data to the printer continues until you press this pair of keys again. This multikey combination is normally used to obtain a hardcopy historical log of operational procedures, error messages, command use, and system responses. Then the log can be examined to determine the possible cause of unexpected events, used as a reference for creating or debugging batch files, or stored for future reference.

Because in its normal video mode your computer screen can only display 25 lines of data, many times the listing of a disk's directory or a long file causes data to scroll rapidly off the screen. To freeze the screen after a certain number of lines, press **Ctrl+Num Lock**. This key combination suspends the operation of your computer, freezing the display and enabling you to pause to think about your operation before you execute it. If you have an Enhanced Keyboard, you can press the **Pause** key to freeze the screen. To resume operations, just press any key. To stop a previously suspended command, you can press **Ctrl+Break**. In fact, Ctrl+Break can be used to terminate the entry of a command line and return you to the DOS prompt level, as illustrated by the following example:

```
C>DIR B:FRE

C>
```

When you press Ctrl+Break after typing FRE, no directory listing is generated.

Command Syntax (Format)

A common method to describe the parameters that can be included in each DOS command is presented in this section. This format notation is used in the remainder of this book to identify the basic format of DOS commands as well as to denote the parameters that can be contained in a command-line entry. Common format notations used for DOS commands include

- Keywords. Capital letters are used to identify DOS commands. Although keywords are shown here in capital letters, in actuality, you can enter DOS commands using any combination of uppercase and lowercase characters.
- Command Parameters. Items shown in lowercase italic letters are command parameters. You supply these items when you enter the command.
- Optional Parameters. Items enclosed in square brackets ([ ]) are optional. You may or may not include them in a command.
- Repeating Items. Items that may be repeated as many times as you want (up to the 255-character limit of command lines) are indicated by ellipses (. . .).
- Choose an Item. Items contained in braces ({ }) indicate you should select one item from the group.

Note that with the exception of square brackets, braces, and ellipses, all punctuation characters, such as commas, equal signs, and slashes, must be included as indicated in the command format.

Command Parameters

Drive Letter

The drive letter (*d*) followed by a colon is used to specify the drive that contains the command in the form of a file or the drive(s) the command will operate on.

If the drive letter precedes the command, DOS searches the indicated drive for a file containing the command to be acted on. For example, assume the default drive is A and you wish to execute the FORMAT command that resides on drive C. You would then enter the following command at the A> prompt:

C:FORMAT

Under DOS 4.0 and 5.0 the actual location of the FORMAT command is under the subdirectory \DOS on drive C if you accepted the default location when the SELECT program was executed. Although you could enter the command to include its path as C:\DOS\FORMAT, you can omit the path and simply enter the command as **C:FORMAT**. The reason why you can enter the command without the path \DOS is that the SELECT program creates a batch file named AUTOEXEC.BAT that contains the DOS command PATH C:\DOS. The AUTOEXEC.BAT file is automatically executed each time you power-up your computer or perform a system reset. The PATH command placed in that file by the SELECT program causes DOS to search the subdirectory \DOS for programs and files not found in the current directory. Specific information concerning the PATH command and the use of batch files is part of Chapter 6.

If a drive letter does not follow the FORMAT command, that command will assume that a diskette in the default drive (A) is to be formatted. Thus, if you want to format a diskette in drive B using the FORMAT command resident on drive C, you enter the following:

A>C:FORMAT B:

Recall that under DOS 4.0 and 5.0, the prompt A:\> is displayed, whereas under DOS 3.3 the prompt is A>.

When you power-up your computer, the initial default drive depends on your system's hardware configuration. If you do not have a fixed disk, when DOS is initialized the prompt A> or A:\> indicates that A is the default drive. If your computer system has a fixed disk on which DOS is installed, the prompt C> or C:\DOS> is displayed if you power-up your computer without a diskette in drive A. As indicated earlier in this chapter, you can change the default drive by entering a new designation letter followed by a colon.

Path

A path (*path*) is used in a tree-structured directory to specify the route to a file. The path follows the drive letter and precedes the filename.

Similar to the drive letter, the path to a file can be specified twice in most command lines. If the path follows the drive letter but precedes the command name, it indicates the route to the file on the drive that contains the command. If the path follows the command and drive letter, it identifies the route to the file the command will operate on. A preliminary discussion of tree-structured directories and the use of paths occurs later in this chapter. Also refer to Chapter 1 for a detailed explanation of tree-structured directories.

Filenames and Extensions

A filename consists of one to eight characters that can be used as a primary description of the information in the file. The file extension is an optional one to three additional characters separated from the filename by a period; it further defines the information contents of the file. Figure 4.15 illustrates the relationship of the filename and file extension.

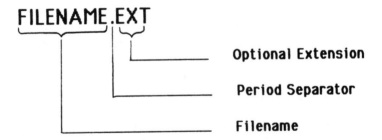

Figure 4.15   Filename and File Extension Relationship.

Table 4.4
Invalid Filename and
Extension Characters
in DOS 3.3, 4.0,
and 5.0

Symbol	Name	Symbol	Name
"	Quotation	:	Colon
/	Slash	;	Semicolon
\	Backslash	<	Less than
[	Left bracket	>	Greater than
]	Right bracket	.	Period
¦	Broken vertical bar	,	Comma
=	Equal		Space

Table 4.5
DOS Reserved
Names

Reserved Name	Device
CLOCK$	System clock device driver (DOS 4.0)
CON	Console keyboard/screen
AUX or COM1	First serial communications port
COM2	Second serial communications port
COM3	Third serial communications port
COM4	Fourth serial communications port
LPT1 or PRN	First parallel printer port
LPT2	Second parallel printer port
LPT3	Third parallel printer port
NUL	Nonexistent device for use in application program testing

Both uppercase and lowercase characters can be used in filenames and extensions; DOS does not distinguish between the two. Depending on the version of DOS used, certain characters may not be usable in filenames and extensions. Table 4.4 lists the invalid characters under PC-DOS Version 3.3, 4.0, and 5.0; they represent the majority of characters that cannot be used in filenames and extensions for all versions of DOS.

In assigning filenames and extensions, you should avoid certain reserved names that are used by the operating system to reference specific components in the computer. Table 4.5 lists the DOS reserved names that cannot be used as filenames and the computer component or device they reference.

Table 4.6 gives a list of extensions that have special meanings to DOS. Use these extensions *only* when you are creating one of the indicated file types or manipulating a previously created file with a DOS command. Otherwise, substantial confusion about the type of file can result, or the file may not operate correctly.

Table 4.6
Special Extensions

Extension	Meaning
BAK	Backup file
BAT	DOS batch file
CHK	Assigned to files recovered by CHKDSK
COM	Program file directly executable by DOS
EXE	Program file directly executable by DOS
MAP	Default extension for list file created by DOS linker program
OVL	Extension used by DOS for overlay files
REC	Extension used by DOS for recovered files
SYS	Extension used by DOS for files containing system configuration and device drivers
$$$	Extension used by DOS for temporary files

File-Naming Conventions

A key to maximizing the use of file reference commands is to establish and use consistent naming conventions. Although any group of legal characters can be used in developing filenames and extensions, naming conventions generate standards that both serve to boost productivity and to eliminate vagueness that can result in other users spending minutes or hours searching for a particular file.

The development of specific naming conventions depends on your preferences or your organization's requirements. As an example, a file containing accounts payable information for 1990 might be named ACTPAY90.DAT, with the extension DAT used to indicate that the file is a data file.

Naming conventions for filenames can be easily developed to fit a particular application. In comparison, a large number of file extensions have been predefined and are accepted as de facto standards in addition to those extensions in Table 4.6. Table 4.7 lists, in alphabetical order, de facto file extension standards.

Device Names

You can use names assigned to specific physical devices in DOS to direct the results of commands to those devices. Consider the names assigned to devices to be reserved names. As such, they cannot be used as diskette or fixed disk filenames, because the operating system assumes that they are assigned to specific physical devices.

Table 4.5 lists the names assigned by DOS to physical devices. If the console is used as an input device, the F6 (Ctrl+Z) key followed by Enter or Ctrl+Break can be used to terminate use of the console. Either action generates an end-of-file mark or character indication to DOS, which then terminates the operation. Concerning the NUL reserved name, the physical device assigned to this name is a dummy or nonexistent device that is used for test purposes. If you use this reserved name for testing as an input device, an immediate end-of-file character is generated. If this reserved name is used for testing as an output device, the write operations are simulated; however, no data is actually transferred. The NUL device can be very valuable in testing operations of batch files (collections of DOS commands). As an example, using the NUL reserved name instead of a printer name, you can test the logical structure of the operation of the commands in the file without having to print data. Batch files are covered in detail in Chapter 6.

Note that the colons that follow reserved names are optional. In addition, DOS ignores any drive parameter or filename extension erroneously entered with a reserved name.

Paths

The introduction of large storage capacity in the form of fixed disks with the PC XT was accompanied by a major revision to DOS: Version 2.0. Although several major and

Table 4.7
De facto File
Extension Usage

Extension	File Type
ASM	Assembly language program in source code
BAK	Backup file
BAS	BASIC program
BAT	Batch file containing DOS commands
BIN	Binary file
CHK	File recovered by CHKDSK
COB	COBOL language program in source code
COM	Command or program directly executable by DOS
DAT	Data file
DOC	Document file usually created by word processor
EXE	Executable relocatable program
FOR	FORTRAN program in source code
LIB	Library file
MAC	Macro for assembly language program
MAP	Link program listing
OBJ	Machine language (object) version of compiled program
OVL	Application program overlay file
OVR	Compiler program overlay file
PAS	Pascal language program in source code
PIC	Screen (picture) display image
REC	Recovered file
SYS	System configuration file
TMP	Temporary file
TXT	Text file
$$$	Temporary file

minor revisions to DOS have occurred since Version 2.0, the hierarchical file structure of that version remains the means for effectively working with a large number of files.

Under the hierarchical file structure of DOS Versions 2.0 and later, a root directory is automatically created on each diskette and fixed disk when the media is formatted. The root directory of a specific disk drive is indicated by a drive designator followed by a backslash. For example, A:\ is the root directory of a diskette in drive A, whereas C:\ is the root directory of the fixed disk assigned to drive C.

Recall that a mixture of files and other directories can be placed under the root directory, with the other directories commonly called *subdirectories,* because they are nested under the root directory. Figure 4.16 illustrates an example of a directory structure that, although appropriate for a fixed disk, could also be used on a diskette.

In examining Figure 4.16, note that two subdirectories have been established directly under the root directory—DOS and WP. Under the DOS subdirectory you might locate a majority of DOS utility programs to facilitate their use when required, which is what the SELECT program does under DOS 4.0. Under the WP subdirectory, a word processing program named EW.COM and word processing files are stored. Assuming that two operators use the word processor, it might be appropriate to separate their data files. To accomplish this, separate subdirectories could be established, with each person storing data files in his or her subdirectory. This is illustrated by the GIL and BEV subdirectories in Figure 4.16.

The use of a path to specify the route through the hierarchical file structure provides the mechanism for locating files and subdirectories. This in turn results in the requirement to add a pathname to the file specification.

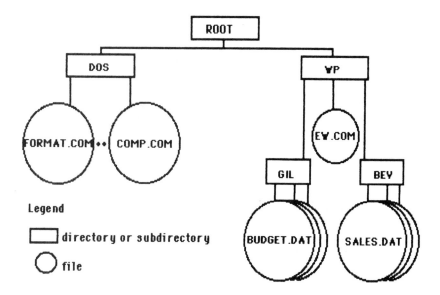

Figure 4.16 Sample Hierarchical Directory Structure.

In essence, the path is the route through directory names to create or access a file or subdirectory. The path consists of one or more directory names, each preceded by a backslash (\). If the path begins with a backslash, DOS starts its search from the root directory; otherwise, the search commences at the current directory. When a file-name is included in the path it must be separated from the last subdirectory name by a backslash.

In the hierarchy in Figure 4.16, the path to the file BUDGET.DAT from the route directory can be entered as

\WP\GIL\BUDGET.DAT

If the file is located on the fixed disk (drive C) and the default drive is drive A, the complete file specification required to access BUDGET.DAT becomes

C:\WP\GIL\BUDGET.DAT

Figure 4.17 illustrates the complete file specification broken down by its components.

In the preceding example, the drive identifier is optional if drive C is the default drive. Similarly, the path is optional if the user previously entered a DOS command to establish the subdirectory GIL as the current directory. Chapter 5 reviews DOS commands used for creating and navigating directories.

The format of a complete file specification follows; the items enclosed in brackets are optional.

[d:][pathname][filename[.ext]]

Global File (Wildcard) Symbols

The question mark (?) and asterisk (*) are two special symbols you can use in filenames and extensions to mean "any character." Due to the comparable usage of these symbols to a special type of card in a card game, they are also commonly known as *wildcards*.

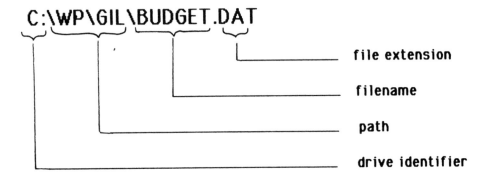

Figure 4.17 File Specification Components.

Table 4.8
Global Character
Usage Examples

Global Character Example	Meaning
.	All filenames
*.XYZ	All filenames with the extension .XYZ
XYZ.*	Any file named XYZ regardless of its extension
SAMPLE*.*	Any file whose name begins with SAMPLE, regardless of its extension
???PAY87.*	Any file with PAY87 in positions 4 through 8 of the filename, regardless of its extension

The ? character matches any single character in a filename or extension. This means that any one character can be in the position of the ?. For example, entering the directory (DIR) command

DIR ACTPAY??.???

causes any file in the directory that has ACTPAY in positions one through six of the filename to be displayed, regardless of its extension.

The * matches all characters from the asterisk's position to the end of the filename or extension. Thus, you can enter **DIR ACT*.*** to display all files in the directory that have ACT in positions one through three of their filenames, regardless of their extensions. Table 4.8 lists five examples of the use of global characters and their meaning.

DOS Commands

To use DOS effectively, you should have a firm understanding of the operation and usage of the commands included in the system. Although there are over 60 DOS commands you can use, focus initially on the small subset of those commands in this chapter. This subset of DOS commands are those most frequently used to perform a core of day-to-day computer operations. Knowledge of the operation and usage of these commands will enable you to perform such basic functions as setting and resetting the computer's date and time, formatting a disk, copying files from one storage medium to another, and obtaining a directory listing of files on a storage medium.

After reviewing the operation of these commands, this chapter examines the uses of the DOS Shell features of DOS 4.0 and 5.0.

Internal Versus External Commands

Table 4.9 lists 25 commonly used DOS commands whose structure, operation, and usage will be covered in the remainder of this chapter. As indicated by the Type column in Table 4.9, DOS commands can be categorized as internal or external. The coding to process internal commands is contained in the command interpreter file, COMMAND.COM, which is read into memory when the operating system is initialized. Thereafter, when you enter the name of an internal command the command interpreter file—which is now memory resident—executes the appropriate coding to process the command. Thus, internal commands are also referred to as *memory-resident* commands.

The coding for the processing of external commands is contained in program files that are fixed disk- or diskette-resident, depending on where your operating system resides. When you enter an external command, COMMAND.COM recognizes that the coding resides in a file and uses the default drive and current subdirectory or a specified drive and path included with the command entry to locate the file. Once located, the contents of the file are loaded into memory and executed.

External command files can be easily recognized in a directory listing, because their filename extension is BAT, COM, or EXE. One example of a frequently used external command is the FORMAT command. The coding that processes and executes this command resides on the FORMAT.COM file on your DOS diskette. When you enter the FORMAT command, DOS searches the default drive or a specified drive for that file, loads the file once it is located, and then executes its contents. When you enter an external command you can omit its filename extension, because it is optional. The following examples illustrate the use of the FORMAT command to initialize diskette and fixed disk media for data recording. Each of the following examples shows the default drive using the prompt displayed by DOS 3.3. If you are using DOS 4.0 or DOS 5.0, the prompt displayed when drive A is the default drive is A:\>, whereas the prompt displayed when drive C is the default drive is C:\DOS>.

FORMAT Command	*Result*
A>**C:FORMAT**	Formats diskette in drive A, which is the default drive, using the FORMAT.COM file located on drive C.
A>**FORMAT B:**	Formats the diskette in drive B using the FORMAT.COM file located on drive A.
C>**FORMAT A:**	Formats the diskette in drive A using the FORMAT.COM file located on drive C.
C>**FORMAT**	Formats the fixed disk using the FORMAT.COM file located on drive C.

These four examples of the FORMAT command limited the use of command parameters to a drive specifier. Later, this chapter examines the optional parameters you can include in this command line.

The fourth example illustrates how easy it is to inadvertently format your fixed disk. In that example, no drive specifier was included in the command line, causing the command to be executed on the default drive—the fixed disk.

Due to the potential effect of destroying tens to hundreds of millions of bytes of data by an inadvertent format of the fixed disk, DOS displays a warning message when you attempt to format a fixed disk that was previously formatted. Earlier versions of

Table 4.9
Commonly Used
DOS Commands

Command	Type	Activity Performed
ASSIGN	E	Routes disk I/O requests from one drive to another.
ATTRIB	E	Sets and resets the attribute byte and archive bit of a file or displays the status of the attribute byte and archive bit.
BREAK	I	Instructs DOS to check for a control break whenever a program requests DOS to perform an I/O operation.
CHKDSK	E	Checks the disk and displays a status report about its contents and your computer's memory.
CLS	I	Clears the display screen.
COMP	E	Compares the contents of two files.
COPY	I	Copies a specified file or set of files to the same or another disk.
DATE	I	Displays or stores a date in your computer.
DEL	I	Deletes a specified file or set of files (same as ERASE).
DIR	I	Displays the files stored on a disk that match your specifications.
DISKCOMP	E	Compares the contents of one diskette to another.
DISKCOPY	E	Copies the contents of one diskette onto another.
ERASE	I	Deletes a specified file or set of files (same as DEL).
FORMAT	E	Prepares a diskette or disk for use and optionally copies the operating system files to it.
GRAFTABL	E	Loads a table into memory that defines ASCII characters 128 through 255.
GRAPHICS	E	Permits the contents of the color graphics video display mode to be printed.
LABEL	E	Creates, changes, or deletes a volume label on a disk.
PROMPT	I	Sets a new DOS prompt.
RENAME	I	Changes the name of a file or set of files.
SYS	E	Transfers the operating system files.
TIME	I	Displays or stores the time in your computer.
TYPE	I	Displays the contents of a file on the screen.
VER	I	Displays the version of DOS you are using.
VERIFY	I	Verifies the data written onto a disk was correctly recorded.
VOL	I	Displays the disk volume label of a specified disk.

DOS did not include a warning message, and many persons inadvertently reformatted their fixed disk.

DATE (Internal) Command

The DATE command displays the current date known to your computer system and if you wish, changes that date. The format of this command is

$$\text{DATE} \left\{ \begin{array}{l} mm\text{-} dd\text{-} yy \\ dd\text{-} mm\text{-} yy \\ yy\text{-} mm\text{-} dd \end{array} \right\}$$

If you enter the command **DATE** by itself, DOS displays the current date and prompts you to enter a new date:

```
A>DATE

Current date is Fri 5-9-1989

Enter new date (mm-dd-yy):
```

Once the current date is displayed, you can enter a new date or press the Enter key to leave the current date unchanged. The actual format in which the current date is displayed, as well as the format you will use to enter a new date, depends on the country code used when you installed DOS. In North America, the month-day-year format (*mm-dd-yy*) is commonly used, with the other two DATE formats used primarily in European countries.

When you enter the DATE command with parameters or respond to the Enter new date prompt, the following constraints must be adhered to or DOS generates an Invalid date message.

The following date style applies to DATE:

m must be 1 or 2 digits from 1 to 12
d must be 1 or 2 digits from 1 to 31
y must be 2 digits from 80 to 99 or 4 digits from 1980 to 1999. For DOS 3.0 and higher the upper limit is 79 or 2079.

You can separate the parts of the date using a hyphen (-), slash (/), or period (.). The following examples illustrate the use of this command:

A>**DATE**
Current date is Thu 6-16-1988
Enter new date (mm-dd-yy):

A>**DATE 6-16-89**

A>**DATE**
Current date is Fri 6-16-1989
Enter new date (mm-dd-yy): **6-16-88**

A>**DATE**

Current date is Thu 6-16-1988
Enter new date (mm-dd-yy):

If a calendar is not available, the DATE command provides an equivalent mechanism to determine the day of the week for a particular date. As an example of this, say you enter the DATE command with the parameters 5-15-98. DOS informs you that that date is a Friday. This information displays when you enter the DATE command a second time, as indicated here:

C>**DATE 5-15-98**

C>**DATE**

Current date is Fri 5-15-1998
Enter new date (mm-dd-yy):

If you use the DATE command as a calendar, be sure to enter the current date in response to the Enter new date prompt. This action is required to reset your computer's date and is important to remember, because the system date is recorded in the directory whenever you create or modify a file.

TIME (Internal) Command

The TIME command displays or changes the time known to your computer system. The format of this command is

TIME [*hh*[:*mm*[:*ss*[.*xx*]]]]

where *hh* is 1 or 2 digits from 0 to 23 that represents hours, *mm* is 1 or 2 digits from 0 to 59 that represents minutes, *ss* is 1 or 2 digits from 0 to 59 that represents seconds, and *xx* is 1 or 2 digits from 0 to 99 that represents hundredths of a second.

Because the format or syntax of the TIME command may appear confusing, take a moment to review it. Because entries in brackets are optional, the TIME command can be entered without any parameters. You can also enter the command with just an hour; with an hour and minute; with an hour, minute, and second; or with an hour, minute, second, and hundredth of a second.

The hour parameter is expressed in military time, with 1 p.m. entered as 13, 2 p.m. as 14, and so on. Whereas a colon is used to separate hours from minutes and minutes from seconds, a period must be used to separate seconds from hundredths of a second.

If you enter the command without any parameters, you see the display of the current time and a prompt message to enter the new time:

A>TIME
```
Current time is 9:59:02.91
Enter new time:
```

To leave the time as currently displayed, press the **Enter** key without entering any values. If you only enter one parameter, such as a new hour, the remaining parameters are initialized to zero. This is partially illustrated by the following example:

A>TIME
```
Current time is 9:57:37.06

Enter new time: 11
```
A>TIME
```
Current time is 11:00:02.65
Enter new time:
```

In the preceding example, an 11 was entered for the new time. When the TIME command was entered a second time, the minute field was zero, but 2 and 65 hundredths of a second transpired between entering the new time and displaying the current time.

DOS 4.0 Shell Date and Time Setting

Using the DOS 4.0 Shell to set the date and time, as with many other Shell functions, you need not remember command formats. Unfortunately, this feature is not available under DOS 5.0, requiring you to use the command line entries DATE and TIME. This is because the DOS Shell simplifies the execution of many commands by displaying pop-up boxes that illustrate the format of the data to be entered. In addition, a help facility can be invoked by pressing the F1 key. It provides further information concerning the activity you are performing.

When the Start Programs screen in the Shell is initially displayed, the Command Prompt item in the Main Group is highlighted. Using the Down Arrow key, you can move the selection cursor over the DOS Utilities entry. Pressing the Enter key selects this item in the group area, resulting in the DOS Utilities screen display. This screen is illustrated in Figure 4.18. From this screen you can select from six DOS utilities, including one to set the date and time.

When the DOS Utilities screen is displayed, the selection cursor is positioned over the Set Date and Time entry. Pressing Enter to select this entry results in the display of a set of pop-up boxes, the first of which is illustrated in Figure 4.19. When each

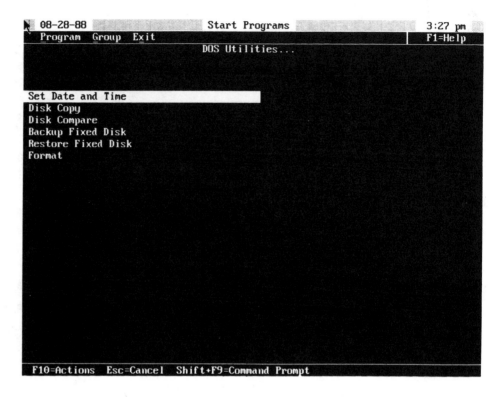

Figure 4.18   DOS 4.0 Utilities Screen.

pop-up box is displayed, a cursor is positioned at the first data entry position. As indicated by the row at the bottom of the pop-up box, you can press the Enter key to have DOS accept the data you entered, press the Esc key to cancel the operation, or press the F1 key for help. Pressing F1 displays a pop-up box.

Once you enter the date, a second pop-up box for entering the time is displayed. Unlike the command prompt mode of DOS where the time can be set to hundredths of a second, under the DOS Shell the time is set to the nearest minute. Thus, you may have to wait up to 59 seconds to enter a precise time when you use the DOS Shell.

After you complete the date and time pop-up box items, you can return to the Start Programs Main Group screen if you select an appropriate entry from the Exit item in the action bar. To make the selection, press **F10** to select the action bar, which highlights the Program item. Next you can either type **X**, which is underlined in the Exit item, or you can press the Right Arrow key to reposition the selection cursor over Exit and press the **Enter** key. This displays an Exit pull-down box. This pull-down box contains two entries—Exit Shell and Resume Start Programs—with the selection cursor positioned over the top item, Exit Shell. Note the first characters in the choices; under lined characters show which letters you can type. Alternatively, you can move the selection cursor over the Resume Start Programs entry and press the Enter key to return to the Start Programs screen.

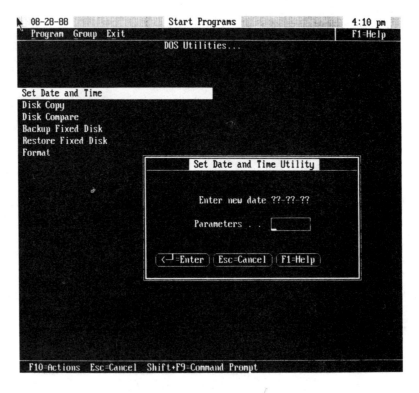

Figure 4.19   Setting the Date and Time Under DOS 4.0.

FORMAT (External) Command

As discussed earlier, the FORMAT command initializes a disk for recording data. During the disk initialization process, the FORMAT command analyzes the media for defective tracks and creates a directory and File Allocation Table (FAT). The directory is an area on the disk reserved to hold information about a file, subdirectory, or a volume label. The FAT is an area on the disk that serves as a pointer to the location where individual files reside on the disk.

Because formatting destroys all previously recorded data on the diskette or fixed disk, ensure that the medium to be formatted is correct. This is especially true for the fixed disk, whose inadvertent formatting can destroy tens to hundreds of millions of bytes of data.

The syntax of the FORMAT command under DOS 3.3 is

```
[d:][path]FORMAT
d:[/S][/1][/8][/V][/B][/4][/N:xx][/T:yy]
```

Under DOS 4.0, the optional parameter /V was changed to /V:label, and a new optional parameter, /F:size, was added to the syntax of the command.

Under DOS 5.0 the optional parameters /q, /u, /f:size, and /b were added to the FORMAT command. The /q parameter deletes the file allocation table and the root directory of a previously formatted disk and should be used only when you know a previously formatted disk is in good condition. The /u parameter specifies an unconditional format that destroys all existing data on a disk. The use of this parameter prevents you from unformatting a disk, a capability unique to DOS 5.0. The /f:size parameter, which enables you to specify the capacity of the floppy disk you wish to format, was extended under DOS 5.0. Under DOS 5.0 support was added for 2.88Mbyte 3½-inch diskettes. The last additional parameter added under DOS 5.0, /b, reserves space for the system files. In previous versions of DOS you had to reserve space prior to using the SYS command to copy the system files to the disk. This command parameter was added to DOS 5.0 to provide compatability with earlier versions of DOS.

The optional drive identifier and path preceding the command keyword are only required if the file FORMAT.COM is at a location other than the default drive or if it's located in a directory other than the current directory. Thus, the first command line (for DOS 3.3) and the second command line (for DOS 4.0 and DOS 5.0)

```
A>C:FORMAT B:
```

```
A:\>C:FORMAT B:
```

each tell DOS to retrieve the file FORMAT.COM from the current directory of drive C to format a diskette in drive B. Following the drive letter of the device to be formatted, you can enter a subset of eight (DOS 3.3), nine (DOS 4.0) or twelve (DOS 5.0) optional parameters. The actual parameters you can specify depend on the medium you will format (diskette or fixed disk), the type of diskette drive installed, and previously entered command-line parameters, because some parameters are mutually exclusive of one another.

When you specify the /S option, you copy the three operating system files— IBMBIO.COM, IBMDOS.COM, and COMMAND.COM in PC-DOS—to the formatted disk at the conclusion of the formatting operation. In MS-DOS the same files are named IO.SYS, MSDOS.SYS, and COMMAND.COM. Figure 4.20 illustrates the use of the /S option in the FORMAT command. In this example, DOS resides on a diskette in drive A and the format operation is performed on a diskette in drive B.

If you are using DOS 4.0 or DOS 5.0 and have a fixed disk, the INSTALL program you used to set up your system created an AUTOEXEC.BAT file with a PATH statement that contains the route to the subdirectory DOS on drive C. This means that DOS

```
A:\>FORMAT B:/S
Insert new diskette for drive B:
and press ENTER when ready...

Format complete
System transferred

Volume label (11 characters, ENTER for none)? FINANCE

    1457664 bytes total disk space
     107520 bytes used by system
    1350144 bytes available on disk

        512 bytes in each allocation unit
       2637 allocation units available on disk

Volume Serial Number is 2476-11FA

Format another (Y/N)?
```

Figure 4.20   Using the FORMAT /S Option.

automatically searches the C:\DOS disk/directory location for the file FORMAT.COM if it does not reside on the diskette in drive A. Once the format operation is invoked, under DOS 4.0 and 5.0 a percent of disk formatted message displays as the disk is being formatted and is erased from the screen when the operation is complete.

The message System transferred indicates that three system files were copied to the newly formatted disk.

Using the /S parameter in the FORMAT command makes the disk self-booting. This means you can place the resulting disk in drive A and use it to bring up your computer. The system files transferred to that disk prompt you to enter the date and time and display the copyright notice prior to displaying the prompt A> or A:\> under DOS 3.3 and DOS 4.0 and 5.0, respectively. After you format a diskette using the /S parameter, you can copy application programs to that diskette, so your application diskette becomes self-booting. This can be very handy for use on a computer that has only one diskette drive for distributing the application to users with that hardware configuration. This is because a self-booting diskette eliminates the necessity to first load DOS and then to remove the DOS diskette to use an application diskette.

Another difference between DOS 3.3 and DOS 4.0 and DOS 5.0 concerns volume label prompting. Under DOS 3.3, unless you enter the /V parameter you are not prompted to enter a volume label. Under DOS 4.0 and DOS 5.0, you are automatically prompted to enter a volume label unless you use the /V:label option in the command line to specify a label. Doing so results in DOS accepting the label and bypassing the display of a prompt asking you to enter a label.

The volume label uniquely identifies each disk and can be checked using the DIR command. Both the /S and /V parameters can be included in a FORMAT command, resulting in the transfer of system files to the disk, as well as the placement of a volume label on the media.

In general, as you assign volume labels to diskettes, be as explicit as possible about the contents of the media. Otherwise, simply assigning a volume label, such as FINANCE, to several diskettes can necessitate a substantial effort later to locate a diskette containing July 1989 financial data files.

The remaining format parameters are related to the different types of diskettes supported by the original IBM PC series, including the PC AT and the PS/2 family of personal computers. The /1 parameter formats a $5\frac{1}{4}$-inch diskette for single-sided use. The original IBM PC was introduced with single-sided disks in 1981. The /1 parameter enables you to format a diskette in a $5\frac{1}{4}$-inch drive attached to your computer, so that data from your $5\frac{1}{4}$-inch or $3\frac{1}{2}$-inch diskettes or fixed disk can be copied to $5\frac{1}{4}$-inch media that is compatible with computers using single-sided diskette drives.

The /8 parameter formats a diskette for recording data 8 sectors per track. This was the original recording method used by DOS Versions 1.0 and 1.1. In DOS Version 2.0, the FORMAT command defaulted to 9 sectors per track for conventional $5\frac{1}{4}$-inch drives and 15 sectors per track on high-capacity $5\frac{1}{4}$ diskettes installed in a 1.2M-byte high-capacity diskette drive.

The /B parameter formats a $5\frac{1}{4}$-inch diskette for 8 sectors per track as well as reserve space for two hidden system files, IBMBIO.COM and IBMDOS.COM. This parameter should be used with the FORMAT command to create a diskette on which any version of DOS can be placed by using that version's SYS command.

The /4 parameter formats a conventional double-sided $5\frac{1}{4}$-inch diskette in a 1.2M-byte high-capacity drive.

The /N:xx parameter specifies the number of sectors per track to format, with xx used to represent the number of sectors. The /T:yy parameter specifies the number of tracks to format. Both parameters are used in the FORMAT statement when you want to format a diskette to a capacity less than the maximum supported by the diskette drive. As an example of the use of these parameters, assume your computer has a high-capacity 3½-inch diskette drive and you wish to share data files with a friend who has a computer with standard 3½-inch diskette drives. The diskette drive used in your computer has a storage capacity of 1.44M bytes, whereas the drives used in your friend's computer have a storage capacity of 720K bytes. If you use the FORMAT command without any parameters, your computer formats a diskette with a capacity to store 1.44M bytes of data. This diskette cannot be used in your friend's computer, because the diskette drives in that computer are limited to a storage capacity of 720K bytes. To ensure compatibility with the diskette drives in your friend's computer, you enter the parameters /N:9/T:80 in the FORMAT command to format diskettes in a disk drive on your computer for use on your friend's computer.

The /F:size parameter was added to the FORMAT statement when DOS 4.0 was released. This parameter was included to provide a mechanism for computer users to easily specify a format for a medium with a storage capacity less than the maximum capacity of a diskette drive. When the /F:size parameter is used in the FORMAT statement, you can specify the storage capacity as a decimal number by itself or by adding several types of suffixes to the number to denote kilobyte or megabyte storage capacity.

Table 4.10 lists the permissible /F:size values based on diskette type. Note that you can only specify a lesser capacity disk format in a higher-capacity drive and the specifications must be media type compatible. That is, you cannot specify a 360K-byte disk format associated with a 5¼-inch diskette in a 3½-inch diskette drive, nor could you specify a 720K-byte disk format associated with a 3½-inch diskette if you are using a high-capacity 1.2M-byte 5¼-inch disk drive.

The data in Table 4.11 indicates the FORMAT parameters permitted based on the type of disk to be formatted.

DOS 4.0 Shell FORMAT Process

Similar to setting the date and time, you can initiate the formatting process under the DOS 4.0 Shell by selecting the DOS Utilities option from the Start Programs Main Group screen. Once this is accomplished, the DOS Utilities screen illustrated in Figure 4.18 is displayed. Move the cursor selection bar with the **Up** or **Down Arrow** key until it is positioned over Format. Then press **Enter** to display a pop-up box labeled Format Utility on the DOS Utilities screen, as illustrated in Figure 4.21. When this pop-up

Table 4.10
/F:size Values Based
on Diskette Type

Disk Type	Permissible Values					
160K bytes	160,	160K,	160K bytes			
180K bytes	180,	180K,	180K bytes			
320K bytes	320,	320K,	320K bytes			
360K bytes	360,	360K,	360K bytes			
720K bytes	720,	720K,	720K bytes			
1.2M bytes	1200,	1200K,	1200K bytes,	1.2,	1.2M,	1.2M bytes
1.44M bytes	1440,	1440K,	1440K bytes,	1.44,	1.44M,	1.44M bytes
2.88M bytes	2880,	2880K,	2880K bytes,	2.88	2.88M	2.88M bytes

Table 4.11
Format Parameter
Usage

Disk Type	Parameters Allowed
160K byte/180K byte	/S, /V, /1, /8, /B, /4, /F:size
320K byte, 360K byte	/S, /V, /1, /8, /B, /4, /F:size
720K byte, 1.44M byte	/S, /V, /N, /T, /F:size
1.2M byte	/S, /V, /N, /T, /F:size
2.8M byte	/S, /V, /N, /T, /F:size
Fixed disk	/S, /V

box is displayed, drive A is the default drive parameter in the Parameters box, with the cursor positioned under the letter a. You can accept that drive, enter a different drive, and enter any applicable FORMAT parameters at this time. Assuming you entered appropriate FORMAT parameters, pressing Enter invokes the FORMAT program, prompting you to insert a new diskette for drive A and to press the Enter key when you are ready.

After the format operation is completed, you are prompted to enter a volume label unless you entered the parameter /V:label in the Parameter box. Similar to the FORMAT operation previously illustrated in Figure 4.20, information concerning disk space and the volume serial number are displayed, followed by the prompt Format another (Y/N)?. Assuming you enter N, pressing any key in response to a Press any key prompt causes the DOS Utilities screen in the DOS Shell to be redisplayed.

Although the DOS Shell facilitates elementary formatting, you must remember the availability and syntax of optional parameters to make full use of this command. In fact, the Help pop-up box displayed in response to pressing the F1 key refers you to the IBM *Using DOS* book for information concerning the optional parameters you can use.

DOS 5.0 Shell FORMAT Process

To format a disk under DOS 5.0 you can select the Disk Utilities group in the program list shown in Figure 4.11. Then select Format, which will display a dialog box similar to the one illustrated in Figure 4.21.

CLS (Clear Screen) (Internal) Command

If you are working at the command prompt level and have entered a few of the examples covered in this chapter, your display screen may be cluttered with information. The CLS (clear screen) command erases previously displayed data with the exception of the DOS prompt, which is redisplayed. The format of this command is simply the command name:

    CLS

One popular use of the CLS command is to clear the screen of previous activity before you print a copy of some screen operation. Thus, enter **CLS**, followed by the actions you want to print, then press **Print Screen** or **Shift+PrtSc** if you do not have an Enhanced Keyboard to generate a hardcopy of desired activity that is not cluttered with other information. There is no equivalent command under the DOS Shell, because operations are based on the selection of items and filling boxes in pop-up screens that are automatically cleared after selection.

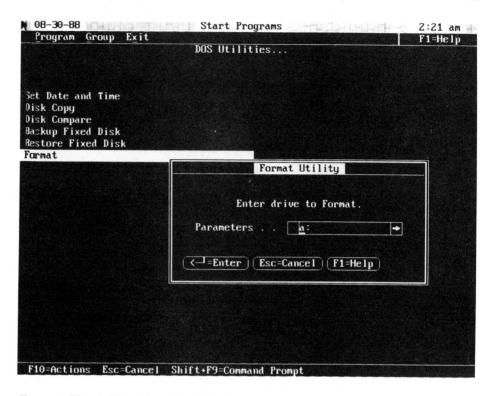

Figure 4.21 DOS 4.0 FORMAT Utility Pop-up Box.

BREAK (Internal) Command

Before you examine a series of commands that can be used to perform multiple operations, an examination of how to terminate DOS command mode operations is warranted. Normally, you can press the **Ctrl+Break** or **Ctrl+C** multikey combination to terminate a DOS command. Even under the DOS Shell, you can press this key combination to terminate the operation of an activity, such as formatting a diskette.

DOS normally checks for the Ctrl+Break multikey sequence when data is entered from the keyboard, displayed on the monitor, or printed. To increase the ability to break out of a program that produces few or no standard device operations—such as a computational intensive program—you can use the BREAK command. The format of this command is

$$\text{BREAK} \left[\left\{ \begin{array}{l} \text{ON} \\ \text{OFF} \end{array} \right\} \right]$$

When you enter **BREAK** without a parameter, the current state of the command (ON or OFF) is displayed. When BREAK is set to ON, DOS continuously checks for Ctrl+Break. Otherwise, when BREAK is set to OFF (its default value), DOS only checks for Ctrl+Break during standard input/output operations. The following example illustrates checking the state of the BREAK command under DOS 3.3 and setting its default value of OFF to ON. Under DOS 4.0 and DOS 5.0, the only change is in the DOS prompt, which is initially set to C:\> if your system has a fixed disk.

```
C>BREAK
BREAK is off
C>BREAK ON
C>BREAK
BREAK is on
C>
```

DIR (Directory) (Internal) Command

The DIR (Directory) command helps you determine the file and subdirectory contents of a storage medium. Using this command, you can obtain information about all directory entries or the entries for a single file or group of specified files. The format of this command is

```
DIR [d:][path][filename[.ext]][/P][/W]
```

The optional drive specifier (*d:*) indicates the drive for which a directory listing should be taken. If the drive identifier is omitted, the directory listing will be taken for the default drive's current directory. Thus,

A>**DIR** (DOS 3.3)

A:\>**DIR** (DOS 4.0 and DOS 5.0)

generates a directory listing of the contents of a diskette in drive A. Modifying the command line to

A>**DIR B:** (DOS 3.3)

A:\>**DIR B:** (DOS 4.0 and DOS 5.0)

lists the directories and filenames of a diskette in drive B.

The path option obtains a directory listing of a hierarchical or tree-structured storage medium. By incorporating a path to the DIR command, you can obtain a directory listing of specific subdirectories or a file or group of files located in a specific subdirectory. Examples of the use of path parameters in DIR commands, as well as a detailed examination of subdirectory related commands, are given in Chapter 5.

To illustrate the use of the DIR command and its optional parameters, examples here apply the command against a common diskette. In the example illustrated in Figure 4.22, a directory listing of a diskette in drive B was taken by entering the command DIR B:. In this example, *xxxxxxx*, which represents the number of bytes available for data storage, depends both on the size of currently stored data files and the storage capacity of the disk.

In the directory listing illustrated in Figure 4.22, the backslash (\) after the message Directory of B: indicates it is a directory of the root or top of a hierarchical directory structure. Unless you specify a path, the DIR command lists the contents of the current directory that, in this example, is the root directory.

You can obtain information about a specific file or a group of files by entering a filename and the ? and * global (wildcard) characters in the filename and filename extension. Table 4.12 lists three examples of the use of global characters and filenames in a DIR statement and the operational result of each command-line entry.

The example illustrated in Figure 4.23 shows the use of the asterisk wildcard character on the diskette in drive B. As indicated in Figure 4.21, this diskette contains four

```
A>DIR B:

Volume in drive B is DATACOM
Directory of B:\

COMMAND     COM     25307    3-17-87    12:00p
BLAST       EXE    158772    4-13-87     7:59a
INDEX       EXE     13596    4-13-87     7:56a
INSTALL     EXE     28252    4-13-87     7:56a
            4 File(s)        XXXXXX bytes free
```

Figure 4.22   Directory Listing of Diskette in Drive B.

Table 4.12
DIR Command
Examples

DIR Command	Operational Result
DIR A:*.*	Produces a directory listing of all files located on the diskette in drive A.
DIR B:*.EXE	Produces a directory listing of all files on the diskette in drive B whose extensions are EXE.
DIR PAY*.*	Produces a directory listing of all files located on the diskette in the default drive whose filenames start with PAY, regardless of the files' extensions.

```
A>DIR B:*.COM

Volume in drive B is DATACOM
Directory of B:\

COMMAND     COM     25307    3-17-87    12:00p
            1 File(s)        XXXXXX bytes free
```

Figure 4.23   Using a Global Character in a DIR Command.

files. Note that because the diskette only contains one file whose extension is COM, only one file is included in the new directory listing shown in Figure 4.23.

The /P parameter automatically pauses the display when the screen is filled. This parameter is valuable when the directory you wish to list is extensive and entries would otherwise rapidly scroll off the screen. When you use /P, the following prompt is displayed:

```
Strike a key when ready...
```

At this time, you can press any key to continue with the directory listing.

The /W parameter obtains a "wide" display of the directory. When you use this parameter in a DIR command, each row in the directory list contains up to five filenames. The example illustrated in Figure 4.24 shows the use of the /W parameter. Note that although the /W parameter displays up to five filenames on a line, the resulting directory listing excludes information concerning the size of the file and the day and date it was created or last modified.

DOS 4.0 Shell File System Directory Operations

The DOS Shell File System performs a variety of file and directory operations, including display of different types of directory listings. Because you were just introduced to the

A>DIR B:/W

Volume in drive B is DATACOM
Directory of B:\

COMMAND   COM   BLAST   EXE   INDEX   EXE   INSTALL   EXE
        4 File(s)   XXXXXX bytes free

Figure 4.24   Using the /W Parameter in the FORMAT Command.

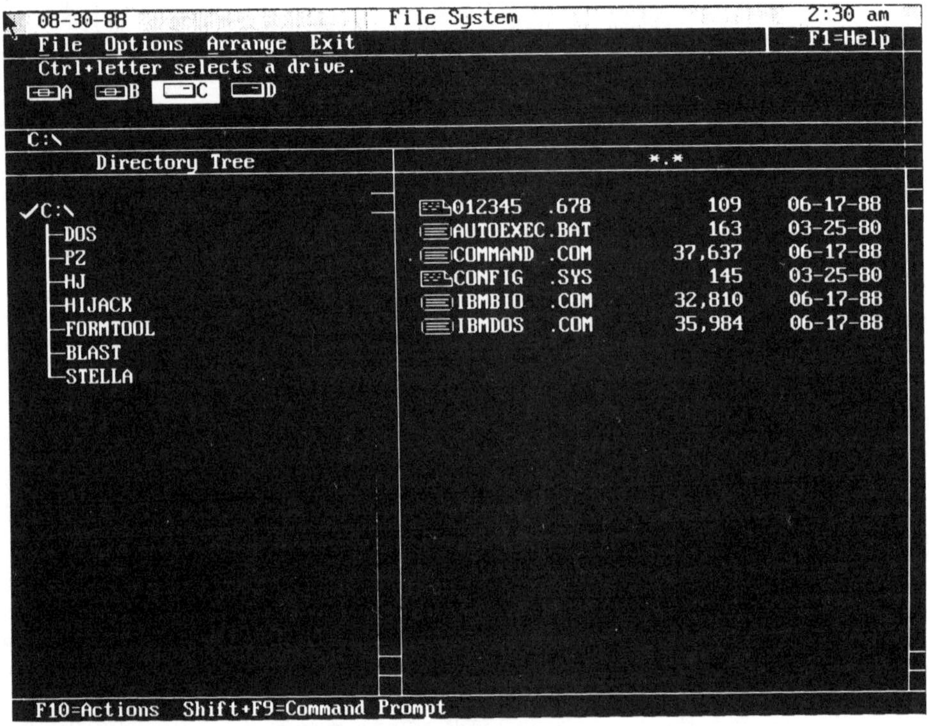

```
 08-30-88                    File System                    2:30 am
 File  Options  Arrange  Exit                             F1=Help
 Ctrl+letter selects a drive.
  ▭A   ▭B  ▭C   ▭D

 C:\
        Directory Tree                          *.*

 ✓C:\                        ▣012345  .678        109    06-17-88
   ├DOS                      ▤AUTOEXEC.BAT        163    03-25-80
   ├P2                       ▤COMMAND .COM     37,637    06-17-88
   ├HJ                       ▣CONFIG  .SYS        145    03-25-80
   ├HIJACK                   ▤IBMBIO  .COM     32,810    06-17-88
   ├FORMTOOL                 ▤IBMDOS  .COM     35,984    06-17-88
   ├BLAST
   └STELLA




 F10=Actions   Shift+F9=Command Prompt
```

Figure 4.25   DOS 4.0 File System Screen.

use of the DIR command, you can compare the use of the DOS Shell File System to perform equivalent operations.

The File System can be selected from the Start Programs Main Group by moving the selection cursor over File System and pressing **Enter**. Figure 4.25 illustrates the File System screen.

After you select the File System, a directory listing of the default drive and directory is automatically performed, with the results displayed. In examining Figure 4.25, note in the upper left that the icon for drive C is highlighted; this means that drive C is the default drive. You can select another drive by pressing **Ctrl** and the drive designator letter. The row with the entry C:\ under the drive identifier row displays the current path. In this example, it denotes the current location at the root directory on drive C.

The Directory Tree window along the left third of the screen displays the directory structure under the root directory of drive C. The right window displays the filenames that correspond to the selected directory. In this example, the check mark to the left of C:\ under Directory Tree indicates that the filenames in the root directory are to be displayed. The symbol *.* to the right of Directory Tree identifies the type of files to be displayed. When you invoke the File System, the default of *.* is used, which represents the global characters for all files and all extensions. Thus, the right window in Figure 4.25 displays all files in the root directory regardless of their extension. If you use the Up or Down Arrow key to select another directory, the filenames in this window automatically change. This is illustrated in Figure 4.26, where the subdirectory FORMTOOL was selected in the Directory Tree window, displaying all files in that directory regardless of their extension.

Press the **F10** key to move the selection cursor to the action bar. From there you can select any item in the action bar by entering the letter underlined in an item or using the **Left** or **Right Arrow** key to position the selection cursor over the item. After an action bar item is selected, you can press the **Down Arrow** key to display the pull-down menu associated with the item. Once a pull-down menu is displayed, you can use the Left or Right Arrow key to access pull-down menus associated with the other items in the action bar.

The File pull-down menu options perform such file-related operations as renaming, copying, and viewing files, as well as the ability to create a directory. A later section

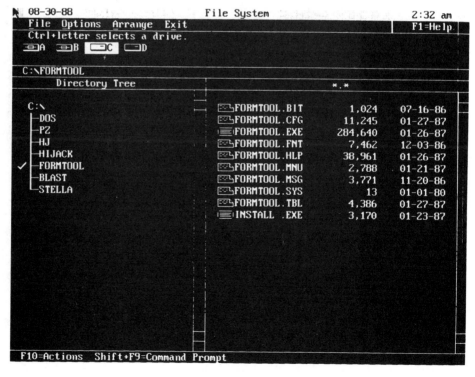

Figure 4.26   Changed Directory Under DOS 4.0 File System.

of the chapter examines the use of portions of this pull-down menu; here the equivalent command prompt operations are described.

Select the Options item in the action bar and press **Down Arrow** to display the Options pull-down menu shown in the upper left of Figure 4.27. Selecting the Display options item generates a Display Options pop-up box over the other File System windows on your screen, as illustrated in Figure 4.28. This pop-up box is the key to obtaining information about a specific file; set of files with a common name, common extension, portion of a common name or extension; or all files in the directory. In addition, this pop-up box offers the capability to sort files in a directory five different ways. As indicated in Figure 4.28, initially the cursor is positioned at the first entry position, the Name box. If you accept the default entry of *.*, all files in the currently checked subdirectory are displayed. Note that the button to the left of Name in the Sort by: column is highlighted. This is the default method of sorting directory entries. You can press the **Tab** key to move the selection cursor to highlight the Name entry in this column. Then use **Down Arrow** to select a different sorting method, including sorting by Extension, Date, Size, or Disk order.

Although the DOS 4.0 Shell File System facilitates the display of files better than do command mode operations that have no sorting capability, to effectively use this Display Options box you must be familiar with the use of global (wildcard) filename characters. Thus, entering *.COM in the Name box in Figure 4.28 displays all files whose extension is .COM that are located in the root directory of drive C. Similarly,

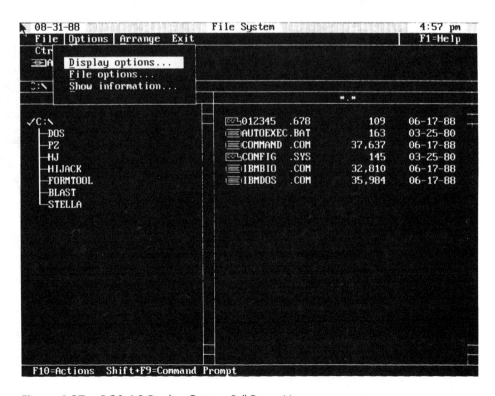

Figure 4.27   DOS 4.0 Display Options Pull-Down Menu.

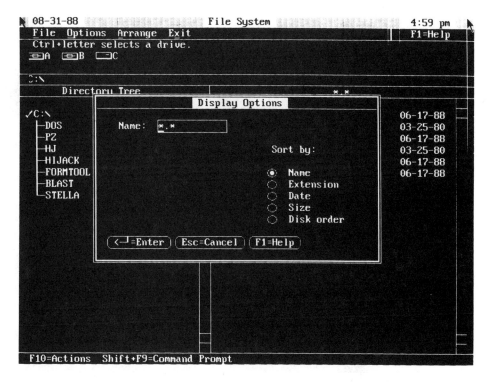

Figure 4.28   DOS 4.0 Display Options Pop-Up Box.

entering C*.* displays all files whose names start with the letter C and are located in the root directory of drive C.

Select File Options in the Options pull-down menu to verify certain file related activities, as well as to display files in more than one directory at the same time. Figure 4.29 illustrates the File Options pop-up box. The default for the Confirm on delete and Confirm on replace entries in the File Options pop-up box is checked (selected) here, meaning that a confirmation prompt is displayed before a file is deleted or moved or copied with a replace operation. The Select across directories entry enables you to select files in different directories. You can toggle the selection or deselection of any box item by pressing the **Up** or **Down Arrow** key to move the selection cursor over the item. Then, press the **Spacebar** to select or deselect the action; a check mark to the left of any item indicates it is selected.

The last item in the Options pull-down, Show information, displays information concerning a previously selected file or group of files or summarizes information concerning the current directory and the current drive. Summarized directory information includes the current directory name, total storage of files in the directory, and total number of files in the directory. Drive summary information includes the disk name, storage capacity denoted as Size, available storage capacity, labeled Avail, and the total number of files and directories on the disk. Thus, Show information can be viewed as an enhanced DIR command that provides information at the file, directory, and drive level.

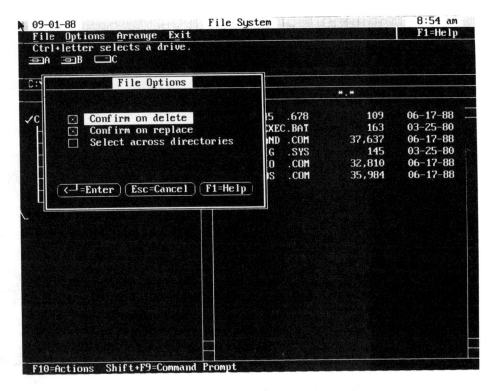

Figure 4.29   DOS 4.0 File Options.

The Arrange item on the action bar provides a pull-down menu containing three entries, as illustrated in Figure 4.30. The first entry, Single file list, is the default method by which the DOS Shell File System displays the Directory Tree and associated filenames. That is, a single file list is used for display purposes.

Selecting Multiple file list entry essentially splits your screen horizontally into two wide windows with two "panes" each, as Figure 4.31 shows. Initially, the same Directory Tree and associated filenames are displayed in each list. Because the area for the top list is slightly smaller than the area used for the display of the second list and each area is less than a single list area, a short directory structure and small number of files may not be completely visible in either window. When this occurs, press **Tab** to move the selection cursor to the first entry in the Directory Tree or filename pane in either window. Then, you can use the **Up** and **Down Arrow** keys to scroll through the contents of either pane.

One of the key benefits of the Multiple file list option is the capability it provides for viewing the contents of two separate directories at the same time. To display two directories, first use the **Tab** key to position the selection cursor at the top item in the Directory Tree area of either list. Then, position the selection cursor using **Up** or **Down Arrow** so the selection cursor highlights the directory whose contents you wish to view. Finally, press **Enter** to display the contents of the directory in the right pane. Figure 4.32 represents the display of the contents of two directories at the same time. To recap, this display resulted from selecting the Multiple file list option in the

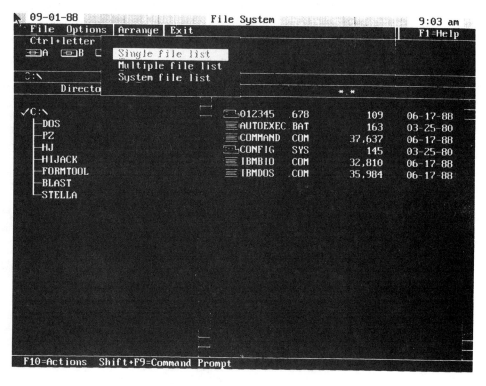

Figure 4.30   DOS 4.0 Arrange Pull-Down Menu.

Arrange pull-down menu and checking the FORMTOOL directory in the bottom window's Directory Tree.

Note that you can use any one of the three file list actions in the Arrange menu to select a program to execute. Once you have located the desired file, you can select it by moving the selection cursor until it highlights the filename. Then, pressing the **Spacebar** selects the file. At this time, you can press the **F10** key to select the File item in the action bar. Pressing **Down arrow** displays the File pull-down menu, the first selection item of which is Open (start). Then an Open File pop-up box is displayed, which appears in Figure 4.33. This pop-up box provides options to execute a program and to enter any optional parameters that may be associated with its execution.

As indicated in this section, the DOS Shell File System provides a similar, but enhanced, capability over DIR command prompt operations. Although with the File System you can view the contents of two directories at one time, sort directories five ways, and perform other enhanced operations, to use it effectively you should be familiar with wildcard characters.

DOS 5.0 Shell File Operations

DOS 5.0 Shell file operations are similar to DOS 4.0 in that you select the File menu to initiate file operations as previously shown in Figure 4.13. From the File menu you initially obtain 14 selectable options, ranging from Open at the top of the File pull-down menu to Exit at the bottom of the File menu. As indicated in Figure 4.13, you

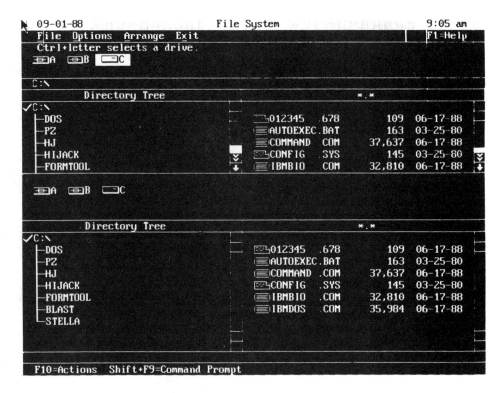

Figure 4.31   Initial Split Window.

can perform several types of file manipulations directly from the File menu, including opening text files, executing files with the Run option, and printing files. With the exception of Exit, selecting an entry will result in the display of a dialog box that facilitates the use of the selected command.

The Associate entry in the File menu enables you to associate one or more files you regularly use with a specific program. Then, when you open an associated file the program associated with those files will commence execution and load those files. For example, you can associate a budget file with Lotus 1–2–3. Then, by opening the budget file DOS 5.0 will automatically execute 1–2–3 and load the budget file.

The Search command in the DOS 5.0 Shell is a welcome addition for those of us with large capacity drives. Through the use of this command you can search a specific directory or an entire disk for a specific file or a group of files through the use of global file specifiers. If you compare the DOS 5.0 File menu shown in Figure 4.13 with the DOS 4.0 File menu shown in Figure 4.34 you will note the addition of the Run and the previously described Search command. The Run command now provides you with another mechanism to execute programs. As we continue our examination of Shell commands we will discuss the similarities and differences between DOS 4.0 and DOS 5.0 when applicable.

COPY (Internal) Command

The COPY command duplicates one or more files on the same or a different diskette or directory/drive. If you copy files to the same diskette, you must assign the copy a

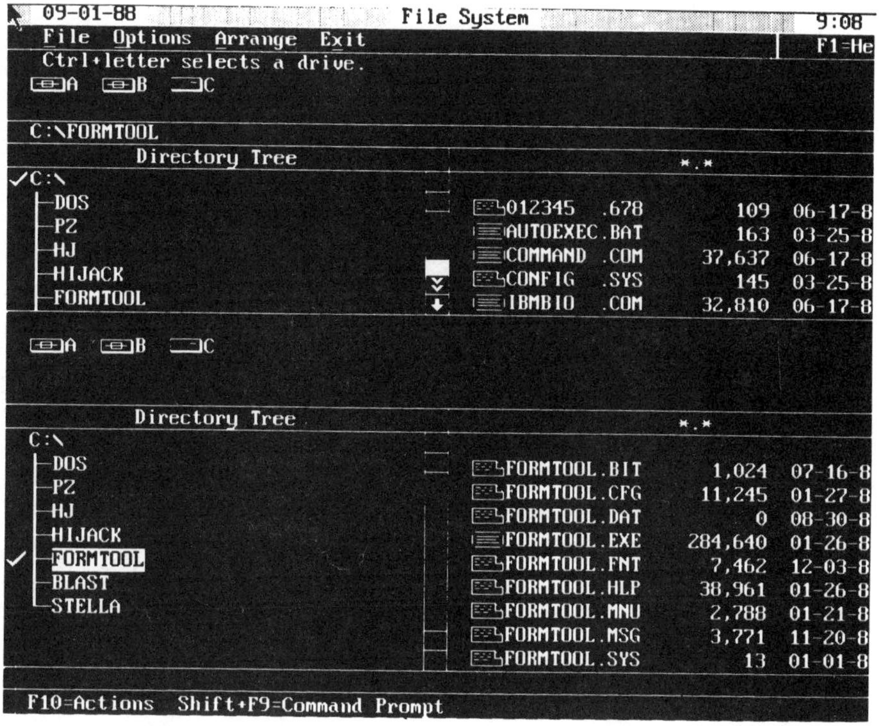

Figure 4.32   Split Window Showing Two Directories.

different name from the original, unless you have created multiple directories to store them. If you copy files to a different subdirectory on the same fixed disk or diskette or to a different fixed disk or diskette, you can use the same name for both the original and the copied file.

The general format of the COPY command is

```
COPY[/A][/B][d:][path][filename[.ext]][/A][/B]
[d:][path][filename[.ext]][/A][/B][/V]
```

Although at first glance the general format of the command appears formidable, a short discussion of the /A and /B parameters should help you revise the format into a more manageable syntax for a majority of your file-copying operations. The /A and /B parameters control the amount of data to be processed by the COPY command. When used with a source file, the /A parameter causes the file to be treated as an ASCII (text) file. This means that all data in the file up to but not including a Ctrl+Z (end-of-file) character is copied.

If you use the /B parameter with a source file, the entire file is copied. If the /A parameter is used with the target file specification, a Ctrl+Z character is added as the last character of the file, whereas the use of the /B parameter does not add an end-of-file character (Ctrl+Z) to the file.

Normally, you can accept the default value of /A when *concatenation* (the process of joining files) is being performed during a COPY operation or the default value of /B when concatenation is not being performed. In certain situations, a communications

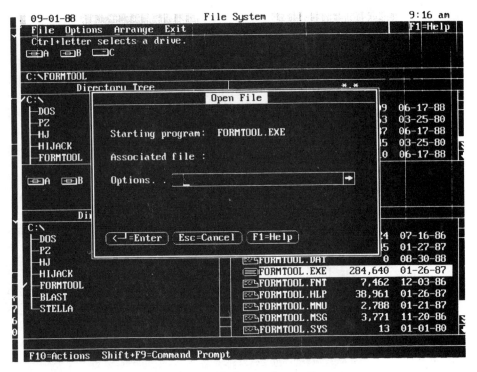

Figure 4.33   Using the Open File Pop-Up Box to Start a Program.

program may add a Ctrl+Z to a file being downloaded to a computer. If this occurs, the COPY command only copies a portion of that file, up to but not including the inadvertent end-of-file character. If you want to duplicate this type of file, use the /A parameter in the COPY command, with the source file specification.

Because a very large majority of COPY command operations can use the default value of the /A and /B parameters, the format of that command becomes more manageable, being rewritten as

COPY[*d:*][*path*][*filename*[*.ext*]][*d:*][*path*][*filename*[*.ext*]][/V]

The /V parameter causes DOS to verify that information copied is recorded properly. Because the verification process requires DOS to read the copied data to compare it with the original copy on a sector-by-sector basis, the /V switch causes the COPY command to operate slowly.

You can include both the ? and * wildcard (global) characters in the filename and extension parameters of both the source and target files. When you use either global character in the source file specification, the names of the files are displayed as the files are copied. This is illustrated in Figure 4.35.

The top of the figure shows a wide directory listing of a diskette in drive B. Note that there are four files on that disk. Next, the COPY command is entered to copy all files whose extension is SU from the diskette in drive A to the diskette in drive B. Once this COPY command is entered, DOS displays the name and location of each file as it is copied. After all files matching the source filename with its global character are copied, DOS summarizes the COPY operation by displaying the message

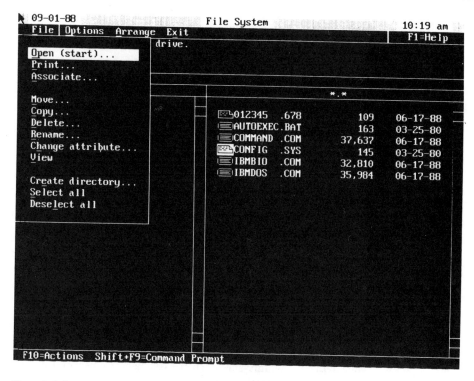

Figure 4.34   DOS 4.0 File Pull-Down Menu.

```
A>DIR B:/W

 Volume in drive B is INVOICEJLY8
 Directory of  B:\

COMMAND  COM    BLAST    EXE    INDEX    EXE    INSTALL  EXE
        4 File(s)     80896 bytes free

A>COPY A:*.SU B:
A:DEMOLINE.SU
A:DEFAULT.SU
A:TYMNET.SU
        3 File(s) copied

A>DIR B:/W

 Volume in drive B is INVOICEJLY8
 Directory of  B:\

COMMAND  COM    BLAST    EXE    INDEX    EXE    INSTALL  EXE    DEMOLINE SU
DEFAULT  SU     TYMNET   SU
        7 File(s)     77824 bytes free

A>
```

Figure 4.35   Using a Global Character in a COPY Command.

```
3 File(s) copied
```

DOS always gives a numeric value that denotes the number of files that it copies onto the target medium.

In the lower third of Figure 4.35, another wide directory listing of the contents of drive B appears. Note that seven files are now on the diskette in drive B, as a result of the COPY operation.

Physical Versus Logical Drives

The COPY command performed in Figure 4.35 was conducted on a computer with two diskette drives. If your computer has only one diskette drive and you attempt to copy a file from one diskette to another, DOS treats the single physical drive as two logical drives. In such circumstances, DOS prompts you when to change diskettes, as illustrated by the following example.

```
A>COPY PAY.JLY B:PAY89.JLY

Insert diskette for drive B: and strike
any key when ready

      1 File(s) copied
```

Table 4.13 lists five examples of the use of the COPY command and their operational result. Recall that under DOS 4.0 and DOS 5.0 the prompt A> is A:\> and the C> prompt is C:\DOS>, unless you use the DOS PROMPT command to change the prompts. The operational result of each command intentionally excludes mentioning that data is copied to the default subdirectory, because the use of the COPY command with a hierarchical directory structure is covered in detail in Chapter 5. That chapter examines how you can organize your fixed disk or diskette into subdirectories and place groups of related programs and data files in specific subdirectories.

Using Reserved Names

By using reserved device names in the COPY command, you can direct files to the printer, use the computer as a typewriter, and perform other interesting, unconventional operations. Several examples of the use of reserved device names within a COPY command are

```
A>COPY PAY.DAT LPT1:

C>COPY CON: RUN.BAT

C>COPY PAY.BAS CON:
```

	COPY Command	Operational Result
Table 4.13 COPY Command Examples	**A>COPY B:*.* C:**	Copies all files on the diskette in drive B to drive C.
	A>COPY PAY.BAS C:	Copies the file PAY.BAS from the default drive (drive A) to drive C.
	C>COPY A:*.BAS B:	Copies all files on the diskette in drive A whose extensions are BAS to the diskette in drive B.
	C>COPY A:*.BAS	Copies all files on the diskette in drive A whose extensions are BAS to the default drive (drive C).
	A>COPY PAY.BAS C:PAY89.BAS	Copies the file PAY.BAS from the default drive (drive A) to drive C and renames the file PAY89.BAS.

The first example routes the file PAY.DAT on the diskette in drive A to the printer attached to the LPT1 port.

In the second example, the console (CON) is used as the source device, and the file RUN.BAT is used as the target device. After you enter this COPY command, DOS routes keyboard input (from CON) to the file RUN.BAT, which DOS creates on drive C. This example illustrates one method by which you create batch files. To terminate keyboard input, you can either press the **F6** key or the **Ctrl+Z** multikey combination to generate an end-of-file character.

In the third example, the contents of the file PAY.BAS are routed to the console (CON) and are displayed on the screen.

A word of caution is in order when you copy files to the console or printer. Only files stored in an ASCII format are meaningful when printed or displayed with the COPY command. This is because the COPY command does not interpret and act on control codes embedded by word processors and other application software in a file. Thus, using the COPY command to print or display a file created with a word processing program that contains control codes for italics, underlines, and other attributes, or a BASIC program stored in a tokenized format, produces unexpected results in a display or printout. Printing or displaying the contents of such a file usually results in displaying or printing special characters that are not meaningful. This situation is illustrated by the use of the COPY command to print the contents of a small BASIC program whose output is shown in Figure 4.36.

DOS Shell COPY Operations

The File System of the DOS Shell can copy files. First, select the file you wish to copy. Similar to all file selection operations, you can use the **Tab** key to move the selection cursor to the filename area. Then use **Up** and **Down Arrow** keys to move the selection cursor onto the filename you wish to copy. Then press the **Spacebar**, which highlights the icon to the left of the filename.

Once the file or files you want copied are highlighted, you must select the Copy option from the File pull-down menu.

To display the File pull-down menu, press **Tab** to move the selection cursor to the File item in the action bar. Then press **Down Arrow** to display the File pull-down menu, illustrated in Figure 4.34. If you are using DOS 5.0 you would perform a similar operation, resulting in the display of a dialog box resembling the one illustrated in Figure 4.37.

After you have selected a file or set of files and accessed the File pull-down menu, you can move the selection cursor to the Copy option. Then press **Enter** to display the Copy File pop-up menu, shown in Figure 4.37. Note that the From box automatically contains the name of the selected file, whereas the To box displays the current drive and current directory, denoted as C:\ in this example, with the cursor positioned under the letter C. At this time, you can accept the current drive and current directory as the destination to which to copy the file, or you can enter a new location. Then you can enter the same filename or a different filename, depending on whether you changed the file's location and your naming requirements. You cannot have two files with the

πê Aτ§δæ A·ê CτAθ∞|ë   πê̂ Aτ̂§δ̂æ A·ê   CτAθ∞|ë

Figure 4.36   Printing a Non-ASCII File.

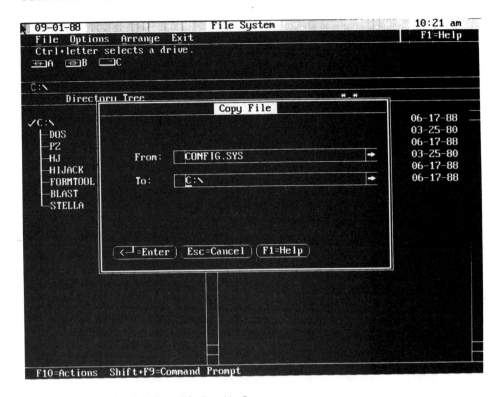

Figure 4.37   DOS 4.0 Copy File Pop-Up Box.

same name in the same directory; thus, if for example you want another copy of CONFIG.SYS in the root directory of drive C, you might name the copy CONFIG.OLD.

COMP (Compare Files) (External) Command

The COMP (compare files) command compares the contents of two files. This command should not be confused with the DISKCOMP command, which compares the contents of two entire diskettes.

The format of the COMP command is

```
[d:][path]COMP
[d:][path][filename[.ext]][d:][path][filename[.ext]]
```

This command originally came with PC-DOS only. Under MS-DOS you would use the FC (files compare) command. Under DOS 5.0 comp is supported by both PC-DOS and MS-DOS.

Similar to other external commands, the device identifier (d:) and path preceding the command name identify the location where the COMP command file resides.

The first set of parameters ([d:][path][filename[.ext]]) after COMP specifies the first file or set of filenames you want to compare with wildcard characters used to define a set of files. The second set of parameters defines the file or set of files the first file or first set of files will be compared against.

You can compare files on the same drive or different drives, in the same directory, or in different directories. If you omit the filenames or the second set of parameters when you enter the command, you will be prompted to enter them.

After a successful comparison, COMP displays the message

```
Files compare OK
```

When all comparisons between files are complete, COMP displays the message

```
Compare more files (Y/N)?
```

At this point, if you enter **Y** you are prompted to enter two new filenames. You can type **N** to terminate the COMP command.

If the files being compared do not match, an error message is displayed. This error message indicates the location in hexadecimal notation where a mismatch occurred, as well as the contents of the bytes in each file where the mismatch occurred. After 10 unequal comparisons, COMP assumes that further comparison is of no use and displays the following message:

```
10 Mismatches - ending compare
```

Table 4.14 contains three examples of the use of the COMP command and the operational result of each command line entry.

DISKCOPY (Copy Diskette) (External) Command

The DISKCOPY (copy diskette) command duplicates an entire diskette or just the first side of a diskette. This command also examines the target diskette to determine whether it was previously formatted, and, if not, the command formats the target diskette with the same number of sides and sectors per track as the source diskette. The format of the DISKCOPY command is

```
[d:][path]DISKCOPY [d:[d:]][/1]
```

The first drive specifier after the command name identifies the source drive, whereas the second drive identifier indicates the target drive. If you specify the /1 parameter, DISKCOPY copies only the first side of the diskette, even if you use a double-sided diskette.

If you have only one diskette drive on your computer, DOS prompts you when to insert the target and source diskettes at the appropriate times. If you use the command without entering drive specifiers, a single-drive copy operation will be performed using the default drive. Similarly, if you specify the same drive for source and target diskettes a one-drive copy operation will be performed. Table 4.15 illustrates three examples of the use and operational results of the DISKCOPY command. Note that this command

Table 4.14
COMP Command
Examples

COMP Command	Operational Result
A>**COMP PAY B:PAY.DAT**	Uses the COMP command file on the default drive (drive A) to compare the contents of the file PAY on drive A to the contents of the file PAY.DAT on drive B.
A>**C:COMP A:PAY B:PAY.DAT**	Uses the COMP command file on drive C to compare the contents of the file PAY on drive A to the contents of the file PAY.DAT on drive C.
C>**COMP A:*.DAT C:**	Uses the COMP command file on drive C to compare the contents of all files on drive A whose extensions are DAT to files on drive C that have that extension.

DISKCOPY Command	Operational Result
C>**DISKCOPY A: B:**	Uses the DISKCOPY command file on drive C to copy the contents of the diskette in drive A to the diskette in drive B.
B>**C:DISKCOPY B: A:**	Uses the DISKCOPY command file on drive C to copy the contents of the diskette in drive B to the diskette in drive A.
A>**DISKCOPY**	Uses the DISKCOPY command file on drive A to perform a one-drive copy operation. DOS prompts you when to insert the source and target diskettes in that drive.

Table 4.15
DISKCOPY
Command Examples

can only be used to copy similar capacity diskettes. Thus, you can use this command to copy a 720K-byte double-sided 3½-inch diskette to another 720K-byte diskette or a 1.44M-byte double-sided 3½-inch diskette to another 1.44M-byte double-sided 3½-inch diskette. Similarly, you could copy the contents of a 360K-byte double-sided 5¼-inch diskette to another 360K-byte diskette and a 1.2M-byte 5¼-inch double-sided diskette to another 1.2M-byte double-sided diskette. However, you could not copy a 720K-byte 3½-inch diskette to a 1.44M-byte diskette, a 1.44M byte 3½-inch diskette to a 720K-byte diskette, a 360K-byte 5¼-inch diskette to a 1.2M-byte diskette, or a 1.2M-byte diskette to a 360K-byte diskette.

DOS Shell Disk Copy Operations

You can perform a disk copy operation with the DOS Shell by selecting DOS Utilities from the Start Programs Main Group. This displays the DOS Utilities screen (see Figure 4.18). Move the selection cursor to Disk Copy and press **Enter** to display the Diskcopy Utility pop-up box on the DOS Utilities screen.

Figure 4.38 illustrates the Diskcopy Utility pop-up box. Note that the default entries in the Drives box are a: and b:, with the cursor positioned under a:. You can accept either or both drive designators for the source and destination drives, or you can enter a different source or destination drive designator.

If you are using DOS 5.0 Shell you can select the DISKCOPY command from the Disk Utilities entry. Doing so results in the display of a dialog box similar to the one illustrated in Figure 4.38.

DISKCOMP (Compare Diskette) (External) Command

The DISKCOMP (compare diskette) command compares the contents of similar capacity diskettes. Normally, this command is used to verify the operation of a previously performed DISKCOPY command. The format of the DISKCOMP command is

[d:][path]DISKCOMP[d:[d:]][/1][/8]

Like all external commands, the optional drive identifier (d:) and path preceding the command name indicate where the DISKCOMP command file resides. If you do not specify a location, the default drive and current directory are used to locate the command file.

If the optional /1 parameter is included, DISKCOMP compares only the first side of the diskettes in the specified drives, even if the diskettes are double-sided. The /8 parameter instructs the command to compare diskettes on an 8-sectors-per-track basis, even if the first diskette contains 9 or 15 sectors per track.

Similar to the DISKCOPY command, you can enter the DISKCOMP command without drive parameters or with the same drive parameters to perform a one-drive comparison. When this occurs, you are prompted when to swap diskettes.

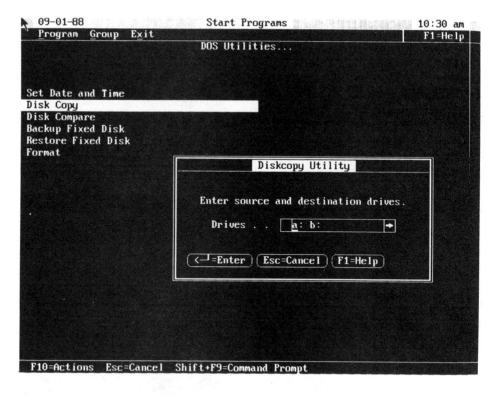

Figure 4.38 DOS 4.0 DISKCOPY Utility Pop-Up Box.

Table 4.16
DISKCOMP
Command Examples

DISKCOMP Command	Operational Result
C>**DISKCOMP A: B:**	Uses the DISKCOMP command file on drive C to compare the contents of the diskette in drive A to the contents of the diskette in drive B.
B>**C:DISKCOMP B: A:**	Uses the DISKCOMP command file on drive C to compare the contents of the diskette in drive B to the contents of the diskette in drive A.
A>**DISKCOMP**	Uses the DISKCOMP command file on the diskette in drive A to perform a one-drive diskette comparison operation. DOS will prompt you when to switch the source and target diskettes in that drive.

When the DISKCOMP command is executed, all tracks on the source and target diskettes are compared on a track-by-track basis. If the tracks are not equal, a message indicating the track number of unequal tracks and the side where the mismatch occurred is displayed. Once the comparison is completed, the following message is displayed:

```
Compare more diskettes (Y/N)?
```

Entering **N** terminates the command operation. If you enter **Y**, another comparison is performed on the same drives after you answer the prompts to insert the appropriate diskettes. Table 4.16 lists three examples of the use and operational results of the DISKCOMP command.

DOS Shell Disk Compare

Similar to the DOS Shell Disk Copy action, the Disk Compare option is selected from the DOS Utilities screen. This is only applicable to DOS 4.0, as this command is not included in the DOS 5.0 Shell. Once you move the selection cursor over Disk Compare and press **Enter**, the DISKCOMP Utility pop-up box displays, as illustrated in Figure 4.39. Drives a: and b: are displayed as the default drives in the Parameters box. You can change one or both drive designators, or you can enter an optional parameter. Unfortunately, pressing the F1 key for Help refers you to documentation concerning parameters used with this command. Thus, for this command—as well as other DOS commands performed under the DOS Shell—you should become familiar with the command-line parameters unless you are willing to accept the command's default values.

DELETE and ERASE (Internal) Commands

The DEL (delete) and ERASE commands are identical—they both have the same format and perform the same operation. Either command can be used to delete a specified file or group of files, the latter occurring when one or more global (wildcard) characters are used in the command line.

The difference between the two commands is the command name, with DEL used for delete and ERASE used for erase. The common format of these two commands is

$$\begin{Bmatrix} \text{DEL} \\ \text{ERASE} \end{Bmatrix} [d:][path]\, filename[.ext]$$

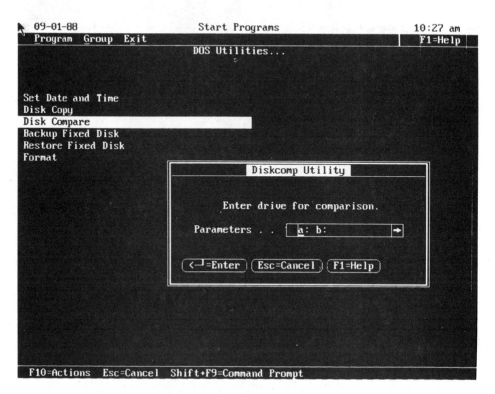

Figure 4.39   DOS 4.0 DISKCOMP Utility Pop-Up Box.

Both DEL and ERASE can erase all files except hidden files, such as IBMBIO.COM and IBMDOS.COM, or files that have been write protected by the DOS ATTRIB command. Figure 4.40 illustrates the use of the ERASE command using the asterisk wildcard to erase all files with the extension SU from the diskette in drive B. At the top of Figure 4.40 is a wide directory listing, which indicates that there are seven files on the diskette in drive B, including three files whose extensions are SU. In the middle of Figure 4.40, the ERASE command was used with an asterisk in the filename position. This command tells DOS to erase all files whose extension is SU on the diskette in drive B. At the bottom of Figure 4.40, another wide directory listing of the diskette in drive B appears. Note that the three files with the extension SU are no longer on the diskette.

In actuality, the use of DEL or ERASE does *not* physically remove the files from the diskette. When you use either command, an appropriate bit in the disk's File Allocation Table (FAT) is reset to inform DOS that previously used storage for that file can now be used to store other data. This is why many commercially available utility programs can recover previously erased files. If you should inadvertently erase a file, do not save any additional information on the disk before you use a data recovery program. This is because saving a file on a disk where a file was previously inadvertently erased may overwrite all or a portion of the sectors of the erased file with the new file. When this occurs, the previously erased file or a portion of that file is permanently lost.

Table 4.17 contains three examples of the use of the ERASE command. Each of these examples is applicable to the DEL command, because DEL has the same format and operational result as ERASE.

```
A>DIR B:/W

 Volume in drive B is INVOICEJLY8
 Directory of  B:\

COMMAND  COM    BLAST    EXE    INDEX    EXE    INSTALL  EXE    DEMOLINE SU
DEFAULT  SU     TYMNET   SU
         7 File(s)       77824 bytes free

A>ERASE B:*.SU

A>DIR B:/W

 Volume in drive B is INVOICEJLY8
 Directory of  B:\

COMMAND  COM    BLAST    EXE    INDEX    EXE    INSTALL  EXE
         4 File(s)       80896 bytes free
```

Figure 4.40   Using the ERASE Command.

Table 4.17
ERASE Command
Examples

ERASE Command	Operational Result
A>**ERASE B:*.***	Deletes all files in the current directory on the diskette in drive B.
A>**ERASE PAY.***	Deletes all files named PAY in the current directory on the default drive (drive A) regardless of their extension.
B>**ERASE C:*.BAS**	Erases all files whose extension is BAS that are located in the current directory on drive C.

If you use a filename that does not exist in an ERASE or DEL command, DOS returns the message

```
File not found
```

This message is applicable if you enter a specific filename and extension in an ERASE or DEL command that does not exist or if you use one or more global characters in the command and DOS fails to find a file that matches the entered specification.

DOS Shell Delete Operations

Similar to all file-related operations in the DOS Shell, you must first select a file or set of files. When operating with the DOS Shell, you can use the `Delete` option of the File pull-down menu (illustrated in Figure 4.34) to display the Delete File pop-up box. It is shown in Figure 4.41.

If you examine the bottom of Figure 4.41 carefully, you will note the icons for the files T.BAT and TEXT.BAT are highlighted; these files have been selected for deletion. This is why the `Delete` box displays the names of both files.

If you accept the default setting for `Confirm on delete` in the File Options pop-up box (see Figure 4.29), you are prompted for each file you want to delete. Figure 4.42 shows the options that enable you to skip the current file or delete it.

If you are using the DOS 5.0 Shell, you can select Delete directly from the File menu. Doing so results in the display of a dialog box similar to the DOS 4.0 Delete File dialog box illustrated in Figure 4.42.

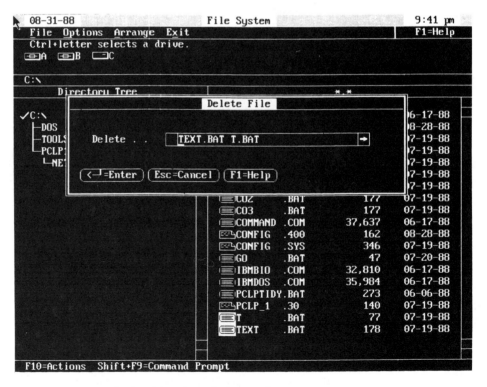

Figure 4.41   Initial DOS 4.0 Delete File Pop-Up Box.

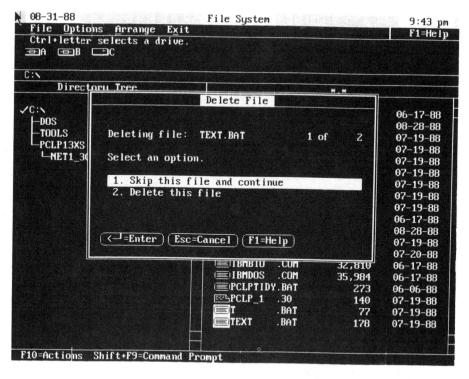

Figure 4.42   Using the DOS 4.0 Delete File Pop-Up Box.

DOS 5.0 UNDELETE Command

A significant addition to DOS 5.0 is the UNDELETE command that can be selected from the Disk Utilities option in the shell or entered as a command. The UNDELETE command is used to restore files previously deleted with the DELETE command. The format of the command is:

    UNDELETE [[d:][path]filename[.ext]] [/list/all][/dos]

The /list parameter is used to simply list deleted files that are available to be recovered. The /all parameter recovers all deleted files without prompting for confirmation prior to undeleting each file. The /dos parameter recovers files deleted by DOS, prompting confirmation prior to undeleting each file. When the command is entered without any parameters, it undeletes the specified file.

The addition of UNDELETE removes one of the key reasons many persons previously used to justify the purchase of a utility program and may by itself justify an upgrade to DOS 5.0.

RENAME (Internal) Command

The RENAME command changes the name of a file or group of files, as well as their extensions. The format of this command is

$$\begin{Bmatrix} \text{RENAME} \\ \text{REN} \end{Bmatrix} [d:][path]filename[.ext] filename[.ext]$$

As indicated in the format of the command, you can use either the full RENAME keyword or its abbreviation REN in a command line. The optional drive identifier (*d*:) and path following the command keyword indicate the location of the file or group of files whose name and/or extension are to be changed. The first filename and extension denote the present name and extension of a file or group of files, with the latter represented by the use of one or more wildcard characters. The second filename and extension in the command line denote the new name and/or extension of the file or group of files.

Figure 4.43 illustrates the use of the RENAME command to change the file named TYMNET.SU to TELENET.SU. At the top of that illustration, a wide directory listing of the contents of drive B appears. The middle of the figure shows that the RENAME command has been entered to change the filename of the TYMNET file shown in the directory. At the bottom of Figure 4.43, a second wide directory listing verifies that the name of the file has been changed.

Table 4.18 contains three examples of the use of the RENAME command and the operational result for each command. If you attempt to RENAME a file with a name that already exists in the current directory or if the file does not exist, DOS displays the following message:

```
Duplicate file name or file not found
```

```
C>DIR B:/W

 Volume in drive B is INVOICEJLY8
 Directory of  B:\

COMMAND  COM     BLAST    EXE     INDEX     EXE     INSTALL  EXE     DEMOLINE SU
DEFAULT  SU      TYMNET   SU
        7 File(s)       77824 bytes free

C>RENAME B:TYMNET.SU TELENET.SU

C>DIR B:/W

 Volume in drive B is INVOICEJLY8
 Directory of  B:\

COMMAND  COM     BLAST    EXE     INDEX     EXE     INSTALL  EXE     DEMOLINE SU
DEFAULT  SU      TELENET  SU
        7 File(s)       77824 bytes free

C>
```

Figure 4.43   Using the RENAME Command.

Table 4.18
RENAME Command
Examples

RENAME Command	Operational Result
A>**RENAME *.SU *.DAT**	Changes the name of all files on the diskette in the default drive (drive A) whose extension is SU to the extension DAT.
C>**RENAME B:PAY.JUN JUNE.PAY**	Changes the name of the file PAY.JUN on the diskette in drive B to JUNE.PAY.
C>**RENAME PAY.JUN JUNE.PAY**	Changes the name of the file PAY.JUN on the default disk (drive C) to JUNE.PAY.

DOS Shell RENAME Operations

Similar to all DOS Shell file operations, you must select a file prior to invoking the RENAME operation. Once you select a file or set of files, you can either press **F10** to move the selection cursor over File or press **Tab** one or more times, depending on the current location of the selection cursor. Then, press **Down Arrow** to display the File pull-down menu, which is the same as the menu illustrated in Figure 4.34.

Once you select Rename, the Rename File pop-up box will be superimposed on your screen. Figure 4.44 illustrates the Rename File pop-up box that contains the current filename, which was the filename previously selected. Note that if you select more than one filename, each filename is displayed and the box number increments from 1 of N to 2 of N, and so on, as you enter each new filename. Each time you enter a new filename and press **Enter**, the current file is renamed to the new filename.

If you are using the DOS 5.0 Shell, you can select the rename command from the File menu. This action will result in the display of a dialog box similar to the one illustrated in Figure 4.44.

TYPE (Internal) Command

The TYPE command provides convenient displays of ASCII file contents. The format of this command is

```
TYPE [d:][path]filename[.ext]
```

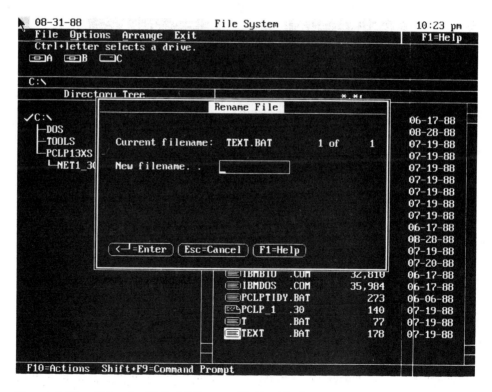

Figure 4.44 Using the DOS 4.0 Rename File Pop-Up Box.

Similar to other commands that operate on files, the optional drive specifier ($d:$) and path indicate the location of the file whose contents are to be displayed. If not included, the default drive and current directory on that drive are used to locate the specified file.

For lengthy files that would normally scroll off the screen, you probably prefer to obtain a hardcopy of their contents. To do so, press the **Ctrl+PrtSc** or **Ctrl+S** multikey combination prior to entering the TYPE command. This causes all I/O to be automatically logged to the printer. Another method to direct the output of the TYPE command to the printer is output redirection. The concept of output redirection is covered in Chapter 8.

Table 4.19 illustrates the use of three examples of the TYPE command. The legibility of the file being displayed depends on the method used to store the contents of the file on disk. If the file was created by an application program, such as a word processing file, it should be stored in ASCII format to use the TYPE command effectively. Otherwise, embedded control codes used to define such characteristics as italics, bold print, and so on, are displayed, using their ASCII value. This normally creates a "jumbled" display, because control code characters represent interesting graphics for display purposes that have no relation to their use within an application program. Similarly, BASIC programs stored in a tokenized format and object program files also appear unreadable, because they contain nonalphanumeric characters.

DOS Shell VIEW Command

A more sophisticated version of the TYPE command is included in the DOS Shell in the View function. The View function is contained in the File pull-down menu, illustrated in Figure 4.34.

As for all file reference operations, you must first select a file. Then, you can select the View function from the File pull-down menu, and a File View screen displays. It is similar to that illustrated in Figure 4.45.

Figure 4.45 shows the contents of the AUTOEXEC.BAT file that was previously selected. As indicated in the instructions displayed, you can press the **Pg Up** and **Pg Dn** keys to scroll through the contents of a file. This feature is not available with the TYPE command, and the capability significantly improves your ability to view the contents of large files. Another improvement incorporated in the View function is the ability to toggle the display of the contents of a file from Hex (hexadecimal) to ASCII by pressing the F9 key, a feature valuable for debugging programs.

Similar to the DOS 4.0 Shell, the DOS 5.0 Shell also includes a View function. This function, like the DOS 4.0 function, is selected from the File menu and results in the display of a dialog box similar to the one illustrated in Figure 4.45.

Table 4.19 TYPE Command Examples	**TYPE Command**	**Operational Result**
	A>**TYPE READ.ME**	Displays the contents of the file READ.ME residing on the default (drive A) diskette drive.
	C>**TYPE B:UPDATE.DOC**	Displays the contents of the file UPDATE.DOC residing on the diskette in drive B.
	B>**TYPE A:INFO**	Displays the contents of the file INFO residing on the diskette in drive A.

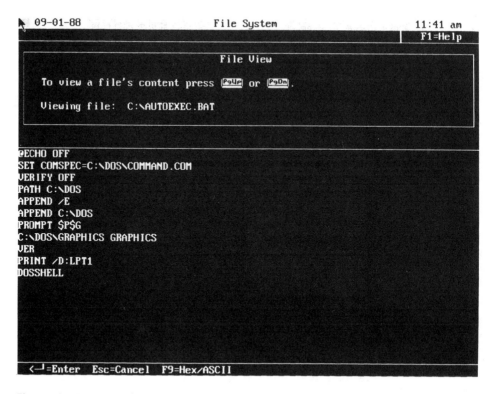

Figure 4.45 Using the DOS 4.0 View Facility.

LABEL (External) Command

The LABEL command creates, changes, or deletes a previously created volume label. The volume label can consist of 1 to 11 characters and serves as an identifier for a diskette or for a fixed disk. The format of the LABEL command is

[d:][path]LABEL [d:][volume label]

The optional device identifier (d:) and path preceding the command name identify the location where the LABEL command file resides. If you do not specify a location, the default drive and current directory are used to locate the command file. The optional drive identifier following the command name identifies the drive on which the volume label will be created, changed, or deleted. If no drive is specified, the default drive will be used. The last optional parameter—the *volume label*—can be up to 11 characters in length. If this parameter is omitted, you are prompted with the following two messages:

Volume in drive X is xxxxxxxxxxx

Volume label (11 characters, ENTER for none)?

If you press the **Enter** key without typing a volume label, the following prompt message is displayed:

Delete current volume label (Y/N)?

If you type **Y** and press **Enter**, any previously assigned volume label is deleted.

Figure 4.46 illustrates the use of the LABEL command. At the top of that illustration a wide directory listing of the diskette in drive B was taken. Note that the volume label of the diskette is INVOICE.JLY8. In the middle of Figure 4.46, the LABEL command was used to change the volume label of the diskette in drive B to DATACOM. A second wide directory listing at the bottom of Figure 4.46 verifies the result of the previous use of the LABEL command.

Table 4.20 contains three examples of the use of the LABEL command and the operational result of each command line entry.

VOL (Volume) (Internal) Command

The VOL (volume) command displays the disk volume of a specified drive. The format of this command is

```
VOL [d:]
```

If you do not specify a drive, the volume label on the default drive is displayed. The following example illustrates the use of this command:

```
C>VOL B:

Volume in drive B is DATACOM

C>
```

Table 4.21 illustrates three examples of the use of the VOL command.

```
C>DIR B:/W

 Volume in drive B is INVOICEJLY8
 Directory of  B:\

COMMAND  COM    BLAST    EXE    INDEX    EXE    INSTALL  EXE    DEMOLINE SU
DEFAULT  SU    TELENET  SU
        7 File(s)      77824 bytes free

C>LABEL B:DATACOM

C>DIR B:/W

 Volume in drive B is DATACOM
 Directory of  B:\

COMMAND  COM    BLAST    EXE    INDEX    EXE    INSTALL  EXE    DEMOLINE SU
DEFAULT  SU    TELENET  SU
        7 File(s)      77824 bytes free
```

Figure 4.46   Using the LABEL Command.

Table 4.20
LABEL Command
Examples

LABEL Command	Operational Results
A>**C:LABEL PAY**	Uses the LABEL command file in the current directory of drive C to assign the volume label PAY to the diskette in the default drive (drive A).
A>**LABEL B:PAY**	Uses the LABEL command file in the current directory of the default drive (drive A) to assign the volume label PAY to the diskette in drive B.
C>**LABEL A:**	Uses the LABEL command file in the current directory of drive C to change the volume label of the diskette in drive A. Once the command line is entered the DOS prompt Delete current volume label (Y/N)? is displayed.

	VOL Command	Operational Result
Table 4.21 VOL Command Examples	A>**VOL**	Displays the disk volume label of the default drive (drive A).
	A>**VOL C:**	Displays the disk volume label of the first fixed disk (drive C).
	C>**VOL B:**	Displays the disk volume label of the diskette in drive B.

VERIFY (Internal) Command

The VERIFY command ensures that data written to a disk has been correctly recorded. Unlike the /V switch in the COPY command that is in effect during the duration of that command, the VERIFY command remains in effect until you change its status by entering another VERIFY command or turn off power to your computer. The format of the VERIFY command is

$$\text{VERIFY } \left[\begin{Bmatrix} \text{ON} \\ \text{OFF} \end{Bmatrix} \right]$$

If you enter the VERIFY command without a parameter, the present state of the command is displayed. When you enter VERIFY ON, all data written to a disk is reread to verify that it was recorded without error. Due to the extra time required to read the data after it is written, VERIFY ON slows your computer's processing speed as it writes data to disk. The last command line option, VERIFY OFF, terminates any previous VERIFY ON command operation. The default value of VERIFY is OFF when DOS is initialized.

VER (Version) (Internal) Command

The VER (version) command, as its name implies, displays the DOS version number you are currently using. The format of this command is

VER

The following example illustrates the use of this command:

A>**VER**

IBM Personal Computer DOS Version 3.30

A>

Utility Commands

The remainder of this chapter examines the operation and use of eight DOS commands that perform utility functions. Although these commands are not as commonly used as the commands previously covered in this chapter, each performs a valuable function you may find helpful.

ASSIGN (Drive) (External) Command

The ASSIGN command routes disk I/O requests for one or more drives to other drives. The format of this command is

[d:][path]ASSIGN [x[=]y[. . .]]

Like all external commands, the optional drive specifier and path preceding the command identify the location of the command file. The x parameter in the command specifies the drive to which current disk I/O requests are routed. The *y* is replaced by the drive letter you want disk I/O requests routed to. If you do not specify *x* and *y* parameters, the command resets all drive parameters, resulting in the resumption of normal drive assignments. As noted in your DOS manual, you should never use an ASSIGN statement with the BACKUP, RESTORE, LABEL, JOIN, SUBSET, or PRINT commands.

Your usual use of the ASSIGN command is with programs that restrict file storage to certain drives. It is used prior to loading an application program that was written to perform I/O operations to a specific drive that you wish to change. Although a large majority of software now enables you to specify any disk for data storage, prior to the introduction of the PC XT many application programs restricted I/O operations to diskette drives A and B. Thus, if you are using a program with this limitation, the ASSIGN command enables you to store data files on your fixed disk.

In the example illustrated in Figure 4.47, the ASSIGN command assigns diskette drive B I/O references to the fixed disk, drive C. Next, the user obtains a wide directory listing of all files with the extension BAT on drive B. By examining the result of the use of the DIR command, it is obvious that physical drive C has been used, because no diskette currently marketed could have over 21 million bytes of available storage capacity.

CHKDSK (Check Disk) (External) Command

The CHKDSK (check disk) command helps you to analyze the directories, files, and the File Allocation Table (FAT) on a disk or diskette. The result of the execution of this command is a display of information concerning the available and used disk space of the designated drive and the computer's total and free memory status. The format of this command is

```
[d:][path]CHKDSK [d:][path][filename[.ext]][/F][/V]
```

The optional parameters preceding CHKDSK specify the drive and path to the directory that contains the CHKDSK command file. The /F parameter causes CHKDSK to fix any errors the program encounters in the disk's directory or FAT. The /V parameter generates a display of all files and their paths on the default or specified drive.

When you use the CHKDSK command, if you specify a filename the command displays the number of noncontiguous areas occupied by the file. If this number becomes very large due to the frequent use and modification of the contents of the file, you may want to consider "unfragmenting" the file. To do this, use the COPY command to copy the file to a newly formatted disk. Thereafter, disk file I/O times should be significantly

```
C>ASSIGN B=C

C>DIR B:*.BAT/W

 Volume in drive B is DATACOM
 Directory of  B:\

PMTUTOR  BAT    AUTOEXEC BAT    GOMOUSE  BAT    BEEP     BAT    DESIGN   BAT
COMPRESS BAT    TESTCOM  BAT
        7 File(s)   21729280 bytes free

C>
```

Figure 4.47   Using the ASSIGN Command.

faster, because DOS will be initially working with a file whose contents are stored in a contiguous location on the disk.

Figure 4.48 shows how to use the CHKDSK command under DOS 3.3 to check a diskette in drive B, as well as the number of noncontiguous blocks occupied by the file NEWINDEX.EXE located on the diskette in drive B.

Under DOS 4.0, the CHKDSK command and its parameters are used the same as under DOS 3.3. However, additional information concerning the data recorded on the disk is displayed. Figure 4.49 illustrates the use of the CHKDSK command under DOS 4.0. Note that when a fixed disk is checked, its volume serial number displays under this version of the operating system. In addition, for both fixed disks and diskettes, three lines of information concerning their *allocation units*—IBM's new name for clusters—are displayed.

As you examine Figure 4.49, note that there are 2048 bytes in each allocation unit, which means that data is recorded and retrieved in clusters of 2048 characters. Because there are a total of 10337 allocation units on the disk and each allocation unit contains 2048 bytes, multiplying the number of bytes in each allocation unit by the total number

```
C>CHKDSK B:NEWINDEX.EXE
Volume DATACOM       created Jun 21, 1988 8:13a

    362496 bytes total disk space
     53248 bytes in 3 hidden files
    244736 bytes in 7 user files
     64512 bytes available on disk

    655360 bytes total memory
    573792 bytes free

B:\NEWINDEX.EXE
    Contains 2 non-contiguous blocks.

C>
```

Figure 4.48   Using the CHKDSK Command.

```
C:\DOS>chkdsk

Volume DOS400       created 03-25-1980 1:45a
Volume Serial Number is 2E61-08E9

  21170176 bytes total disk space
     71680 bytes in 3 hidden files
     16384 bytes in 7 directories
   3639296 bytes in 182 user files
      6144 bytes in bad sectors
  17436672 bytes available on disk

      2048 bytes in each allocation unit
     10337 total allocation units on disk
      8514 available allocation units on disk

    655360 total bytes memory
    543920 bytes free

C:\DOS>
```

Figure 4.49   CHKDSK Display Under DOS 4.0.

of allocation units on the disk yields the total disk space—21170176 bytes in the example illustrated in Figure 4.49.

Table 4.22 contains three examples of the use and operational results of the CHKDSK command.

ATTRIB (Attribute) (Internal) Command

The ATTRIB (attribute) command displays or modifies file attributes for a single file, selected files in a directory, or all files in a subdirectory. The two attributes that can be set or displayed are the files read only attribute and its archive bit. The format of this command is

$$[d:][path]\text{ATTRIB } \left[\begin{Bmatrix} +R \\ -R \end{Bmatrix}\right] \left[\begin{Bmatrix} +A \\ -A \end{Bmatrix}\right] [d:][path][filename[.ext]][/S]$$

The optional +R and -R parameters are used to set and remove the read-only attribute of the specified file. Similarly, the +A and -A parameters are used to set and turn off the archive bit of the specified file. When either of these parameters is included in the ATTRIB command, you must include a file specification in the command line. This specification can include one or more wildcard characters in the filename and file extension fields.

The setting of the read-only attribute of a file is a valuable mechanism to prevent other users of your computer from modifying selected files. Figure 4.50 illustrates the use of the ATTRIB command. In the top portion of the figure, the +R parameter is included in the command to set the read-only attribute of the file BLAST.EXE located on drive B. In the middle of Figure 4.50, the user entered the ERASE command in an attempt to delete the file whose read-only attribute was previously set. Note the DOS message Access denied to the attempt to erase the file. This action occurred because the file's read attribute was previously set to read-only. This setting is confirmed by the use of the ATTRIB command without the R or A parameters in the lower portion

Table 4.22
CHKDSK Command
Examples

CHKDSK Command	Operational Result
A>C:CHKDSK B:	Uses the CHKDSK command file on the current directory in drive C to analyze the diskette in drive B.
A>CHKDSK	Uses the CHKDSK command file on drive A to analyze the diskette in that drive. The message Bad command or file name is displayed if the CHKDSK command file is not on the diskette in drive A.
C>CHKDSK A:PAY.DAT	Uses the CHKDSK command file on the current directory in drive C to analyze the diskette in drive A and the noncontiguous storage used by the PAY.DAT file on that diskette.

```
A>ATTRIB +R B:BLAST.EXE

A>ERASE B:BLAST.EXE
Access denied

A>ATTRIB B:BLAST.EXE
    A    R   B:\BLAST.EXE

A>
```

Figure 4.50 Using the ATTRIB Command.

of Figure 4.50. Here the line displayed after the ATTRIB command was entered denotes that the archive bit and the read-only attribute of the file are set.

If you include the optional /S parameter in the ATTRIB command, all files in the specified directory and any files in subdirectories under that directory are processed. Table 4.23 lists three examples of the use of the ATTRIB command and their operational results.

DOS Shell File Attribute Operations

Under the DOS Shell, you can view four types of file attributes—a for archive, h for hidden, s for system, and r for read-only. You can view the attributes associated with one or more files by first selecting the file. Then you can select the Show information item from the Options menu, which displays the files' attributes.

Although you can display four types of attributes, you can only change three types—hidden, read-only, or archive. To change a file attribute, first select the file by moving the selection cursor to the filename area. Then, use **Up** and **Down Arrow** keys to move the selection cursor over the first file whose attribute you want to change. Pressing the **Spacebar** selects the file, highlighting the icon to the left of the filename. After you have completed your file selection, press either **F10** or **Tab** to position the selection cursor over File in the action bar. Then, press **Down Arrow** to display the File pull-down menu, previously illustrated in Figure 4.34. After you move the selection cursor to Change attribute and press **Enter**, the Change Attribute pop-up box appears, as illustrated in Figure 4.51. As indicated by the entries in this pop-up box, you can change the attributes of files one at a time or you can change the attributes of all selected files at one time. Select the first option when you want to give different attributes to each of the selected files.

Once you select the method by which file attributes will be changed (one at a time or all at once), a new pop-up box is displayed that contains three entries—Hidden, Read Only, and Archive. You can change one or more attributes associated with a specific file or one or more attributes of all files by highlighting an item and pressing the **Spacebar**. This displays a mark to the left of the attribute name. You can change more than one attribute by moving the selection cursor to other attribute items and pressing the **Spacebar**. Finally, to effect the attribute changes, press the **Enter** key. If Hidden is selected, the DIR command will not display information about the file. However, the filename will still appear under the DOS Shell list. Both Read Only and Archive choices function in the same manner as when the ATTRIB command is used.

Although Figure 4.51 illustrated the changing of file attributes under the DOS 4.0 Shell, DOS 5.0 provides a similar capability. Once you select Change Attributes from the DOS 5.0 File menu your dialog box will be similar to the one illustrated in Figure 4.51.

	ATTRIB Command	Operational Result
Table 4.23 ATTRIB Command Examples	A>C:ATTRIB +R B:PAY.DAT	Uses the ATTRIB command file on drive C to set the read-only attribute of the file PAY.DAT on drive B.
	A>ATTRIB C:PAY.DAT	Uses the ATTRIB command file on the default drive (drive A) to display the attribute settings of the file PAY.DAT on drive C.
	C>ATTRIB +R -A PAY.DAT	Uses the ATTRIB command file on the default drive (drive C) to set the read attribute and reset the archive bit of the file PAY.DAT located on drive C.

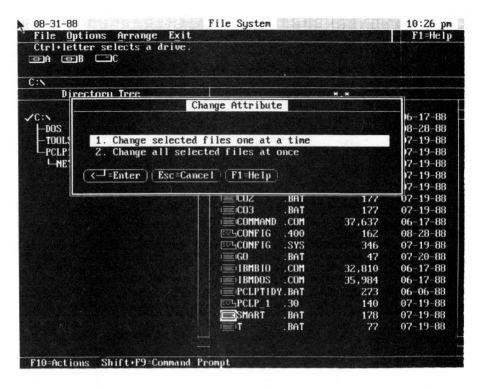

Figure 4.51   DOS 4.0 Change Attribute Pop-Up Box.

GRAPHICS (External) Command

Under DOS 3.3, the GRAPHICS command provides a printed copy of a graphics display when your computer is placed in a color/graphics monitor adapter (CGA) video mode (and if your printer can accommodate graphics). Under DOS 4.0, screen printing of text and/or graphics was extended to support Enhanced Graphics Adapter (EGA) and Video Graphics Array (VGA) hardware. Through this command, a screen containing graphics *picture elements (pixels),* including any text formed by pixels, is printed on the specified graphics-compatible printer when you press the **Print Screen** key if you have an Enhanced Keyboard or **Shift+PrtSc** if you have a keyboard manufactured earlier. The format of this command is

[*d:*][*path*]GRAPHICS [*printer type*][/R][/B][/LCD]

The two optional parameters that precede the command identify the location of the command file. Under DOS 3.3, the printer type option enables you to select one of six devices if you are using IBM's version of the operating system:

COLOR1   IBM PC Color Printer with black ribbon

COLOR4   IBM PC Color Printer with red, green, blue, black ribbon

COLOR8   IBM PC Color Printer with cyan, magenta, yellow, black ribbon

COMPACT   IBM PC Compact Printer

GRAPHICS IBM Personal Graphics Printer and IBM ProPrinter

THERMAL   IBM PC Convertible Printer

Under IBM's DOS 4.0, the printer type GRAPHICSWIDE was added and the number of printers supported by the GRAPHICS printer type was considerably expanded. GRAPHICS printers that are now supported include the IBM 5152 Graphics Printer Model 2, the ProPrinter, ProPrinter II, ProPrinter XL with 8.5-inch wide paper, ProPrinter X24 and XL24 with 8.5-inch wide paper, the Pageprinter and the IBM Quietwriter II and Quietwriter III. Under the GRAPHICSWIDE printer type, the IBM Quietwriter II, ProPrinter XL, and ProPrinter XL24 with 13.5-inch wide paper are now supported. The GRAPHICS and WIDEGRAPHICS printer parameters provide compatibility with a large number of non-IBM printers. This is because the IBM Personal Graphics Printer sold with the original IBM PC was manufactured by Epson Corporation, and its printer control codes are used in many other vendor devices, including the IBM ProPrinter series. If you do not specify a printer type in the command, the default is the GRAPHICS printer due to the popularity of such devices with compatible printer control codes.

Under DOS 5.0 a variety of Hewlett-Packard printers were added. New printers now supported are listed below.

HPDEFAULT	Any Hewlett-Packard PCL printer
DESKJET	A Hewlett-Packard Deskjet printer
LASERJET	A Hewlett-Packard LaserJet printer
LASERJETII	A Hewlett-Packard LaserJet II printer
PAINTJET	A Hewlett-Packard PaintJet printer
QUIETJET	A Hewlett-Packard QuietJet printer
QUIETJET PLUS	A Hewlett-Packard QuietJet Plus printer
RUGGARDWRITER	A Hewlett-Packard RuggardWriter printer
RUGGARDWRITERWIDE	A Hewlett-Packard RuggardWriterwide printer
THINKJET	A Hewlett-Packard ThinkJet printer

The /R parameter causes black to be printed as black and white as white. If you do not specify a setting, black is printed as white and white as black.

The /B parameter is required to print the background color and is only applicable to printer types COLOR4 and COLOR8. If this parameter is not specified, the background color is not printed.

When you invoke the GRAPHICS command, the resident size of DOS in memory is increased by the size of the program required to dump the pixels to the specified printer. Note that all text on the screen, as well as the graphics picture elements, is printed on the printer when you invoke this command.

GRAFTABL (Load Graphics Table) (External) Command

The GRAFTABL (load graphics table) command loads a table of data into your computer's memory that defines ASCII characters 128 through 255. Once GRAFTABL is invoked, ASCII characters 128 through 255 can be displayed when you use the color/ graphics adapter video mode. The format of this command is

[d:][path]GRAFTABL [country page code][/STATUS]

where the country page code numbers for available countries are

Country Page Code Number	Country
437	United States (default value)
860	Portugal
863	Canada (French)
865	Norway and Denmark

Entering an appropriate country page code number in the command line causes DOS to load a table of data into your computer's memory. This table defines the display characteristics of ASCII characters 128 through 255. You can subsequently display these characters when your computer uses the color graphics adapter video mode. If you use the /STATUS parameter, the command displays the number of the currently selected country page code.

Table 4.24 illustrates three examples of the use of the GRAFTABL command. Note that this command can be used multiple times to change the current table of data in memory to represent a different country.

SYS (System) (External) Command

Under PC-DOS the SYS (system) command transfers the operating system files IBMBIO.COM and IBMDOS.COM to a disk with an empty directory or a disk that was previously formatted by the FORMAT command that included the /S or /B parameters in the command line. Either parameter provides space for the system files to be transferred to occupy the first two entries on the target diskette, permitting that diskette to be used as a start-up or boot diskette. This command is normally used to transfer a copy of DOS onto application program diskettes that are designed to use DOS but that cannot be legally sold with the previously mentioned IBM files. Once you transfer the system files to the application diskette, you can thereafter use the application diskette without first bringing up DOS. This command is especially useful if you have a one-diskette drive system. Otherwise, you have to do the "floppy shuffle," where after bringing up DOS you remove the DOS diskette so you have an available drive for the application diskette.

The format of the SYS command is

```
[d:][path]SYS d:
```

The drive identifier (d:) after the command keyword identifies the disk drive that the operating system files will be transferred to. The following example shows the use of this command to transfer the operating system files from a diskette in drive A to a diskette in drive B.

```
A>SYS B:
System transferred
```

	GRAFTABL Command	Operational Result
Table 4.24 GRAFTABL Command Examples	A>C:GRAFTABL 860	Uses the GRAFTABL command file in the current directory on drive C to load the table of graphics characters for the Portuguese code page.
	A>C:GRAFTABL /STATUS	Uses the GRAFTABL command file in the current directory on drive C to display the number of the selected country code page.
	C>GRAFTABL 437	Uses the GRAFTABL command file in the current directory on the default drive (drive C) to load the table of graphics characters for the US code page.

If you attempt to transfer the system files to a diskette whose directory is not completely empty or to a diskette that was not formatted using a /S or /B parameter in the command line, the location where the system files must be located will be unavailable for use on the target diskette. To indicate this situation, DOS displays the following error message:

```
No room for system or destination disk
```

Table 4.25 lists two examples of the use of the SYS command and the operational result of each command line entry.

MEM (External) Command

The MEM command is new in DOS 4.0. This command can display the amount of used and unused memory, as well as programs currently in your computer's memory. The format of this command is

$$[d:][path]\text{MEM} \left[\left\{ \begin{array}{l} \text{/PROGRAM} \\ \text{/DEBUG} \end{array} \right\} \right]$$

When used without any parameters, MEM produces a display containing a summary of used and unused memory, as illustrated in Figure 4.52. The command will display extended memory only if memory above 1M byte is installed and if an expanded memory driver was loaded. The /PROGRAM option causes all programs currently memory resident to be displayed as well as a summary of used and unused memory. If the /DEBUG option is included in the command line, a complete summary of information, including system device drivers, install device drivers, all programs currently in memory, and all used and unused memory, will be displayed. Refer to Chapter 7 for additional information concerning device drivers.

Table 4.26 illustrates two examples of the use of the MEM command and the operational result of each command line entry.

PROMPT (Set System Prompt) (Internal) Command

This command sets a new DOS prompt or resets the prompt to its default value. The format of this command is

Table 4.25
SYS Command
Examples

SYS Command	Operational Result
A>C:SYS B:	Uses the SYS command file on the current directory of drive C to transfer the system files to the diskette in drive B.
A>SYS B:	Uses the SYS command file on the current directory of the default drive (drive A) to transfer the system files to the diskette in drive B.

```
C:\DOS>mem

    655360 bytes total memory
    654336 bytes available
    543920 largest executable program size

    393216 bytes total extended memory
    393216 bytes available extended memory

C:\DOS>
```

Figure 4.52   Using the DOS 4.0 MEM command.

MEM Command	Operational Result
C:\DOS>**MEM**	Uses the MEM command file located in the DOS directory of drive C to display the amount of used and unused memory.
C:\DOS>**MEM /PROGRAM**	Uses the MEM command file located in the DOS directory of drive C to display all programs in memory as well as a summary of used and unused memory.

Metastring	Meaning
$	$ character
t	The time
d	The date
p	The current directory of the default drive
v	The DOS version number
n	The default drive letter
g	> character
l	< character
b	¦ character
q	= character
h	A backspace; the previous character is erased
e	The Escape character
-	The CRLF (carriage-return line-feed) sequence; causes the cursor to go to the beginning of a new line on the display

```
PROMPT [prompt-text]
```

where *prompt-text* can contain metastrings in the form of $C and text that define the new system prompt. If you omit the optional *prompt-text*, the current prompt is reset to the normal DOS prompt. Table 4.27 lists the metastrings that you can include in the PROMPT command and summarizes their meanings.

To illustrate the use of the PROMPT command, enter the command **PROMPT $T $B NG** after the normal DOS prompt. As shown here, the metastring $T results in the display of the time, whereas the metastring $B generates the piping character (¦), and the metastring NG generates the default drive letter followed by the greater than sign.

```
C>PROMPT $T $B $N$G
16:27:35.81 ¦ C>
```

You can return to the normal DOS prompt by entering the command **PROMPT** with no characters. If you wish, you can include text in the PROMPT command, as indicated by the following example:

```
A>PROMPT COMMAND?$Q
COMMAND?=
```

The primary purpose for the inclusion of the PROMPT command in DOS was to provide a mechanism to structure a customized prompt to fit your organizational requirements. A secondary purpose of this command is to generate control codes through the use of the Escape character that can be included in batch files to perform predefined operations. Chapter 7 contains several examples of the use of the PROMPT command in batch files.

The AUTOEXEC.BAT file created by the DOS 4.0 INSTALL program also illustrates the use of the PROMPT command and explains why the DOS 4.0 prompt is initially different from the DOS 3.3 prompt. In examining Figure 4.45, in which the AUTO-EXEC.BAT file was displayed by the use of the DOS Shell function, note the line PROMPT PG. The inclusion of this PROMPT command in the AUTOEXEC.BAT file causes the current directory of the default drive ($P) followed by the > character ($G) to display as the system prompt. Thus, by removing or modifying this command you can automatically have your computer display a different system prompt whenever you perform a power-up or system reset operation.

5 / Fixed Disk Organization

This chapter focuses on the use and operation of DOS commands that enable you to use a fixed disk effectively. First, the chapter reviews the concept behind hierarchical directory structures. Next, you will examine several types of hierarchical directory structures so you can make an informed decision about which structure best satisfies your organizational requirements. Using the preceding information as a base, you can then explore DOS directory-related commands to construct a predefined directory structure. Once this is accomplished, the text explains the use of paths in DOS commands to load applications onto and operate them from a fixed disk. Although this chapter describes the DOS command prompt mode of operation, when applicable it also informs you when you can use the DOS Shell to perform equivalent operations.

Hierarchical Directory Structures

Until DOS Version 2.0, the IBM PC was limited to supporting a single directory on diskette storage. The IBM PC XT included a 10M-byte fixed disk, which increased the storage capacity available to personal computer users more than thirtyfold. Whereas this additional storage capacity was welcomed by personal computer users, without a hierarchical directory structure it would have presented several problems that users had not heretofore encountered with the limited storage capacity of diskettes.

First, access to files on a fixed disk could become exceedingly slow, because the operating system might have to search a directory that could contain hundreds to thousands of files.

Second, from an organizational perspective, storing all program and data files under a common directory would tax the mental capability of most computer users. As an example, a user storing several hundred files on a fixed disk would have a difficult time remembering which shared data files various users had created, or even which data files were generated, say, by a word processor, and which by a spreadsheet or database manager.

To alleviate these problems, the introduction of the IBM PC XT was accompanied by DOS Version 2.0, which included support for hierarchical directory structure operations. This feature, which remains part and parcel of the latest computer systems, enables you to establish an almost infinite number of subdirectory structures that can be customized to meet both individual and organizational data storage requirements on fixed disks.

The top of the directory in a hierarchical directory structure is the *root directory*. This name is derived from the fact that a hierarchical directory structure is similar to an inverted tree. Like the root system of a tree in which nutrients flow from the root to branches, access to subdirectories flows through the root directory.

Entries in a hierarchical structure can consist of DOS files or other directories. For subordinate levels of directories, the entry is more accurately known as a *subdirectory*. Figure 5.1 illustrates the nesting capabilities of a hierarchical directory structure, showing how you can organize your storage media to place files in predefined directories.

Two subdirectories, SD1 and SD2, are illustrated in the figure. Subdirectory SD1 is located directly under the root directory, whereas subdirectory SD2 is nested under SD1. You can access a file or subdirectory by establishing a path through the directory structure to the desired file or subdirectories. Here the path is the route that informs DOS of the specific location on a storage media where files and subdirectories are located. Once you access a hierarchical directory structure, you can move up and down the structure by specifying an appropriate path name.

Directory Structures to Consider

Under DOS's hierarchical directory structure, when you use the FORMAT command DOS automatically creates a root directory on each diskette and fixed disk. The root directory for a specific device is indicated by the drive designator followed by a backslash. As an example,

    C:\

indicates a current position at the top of the tree structure or the root directory of the fixed disk, whereas

    A:\

indicates the root directory of a diskette in drive A.

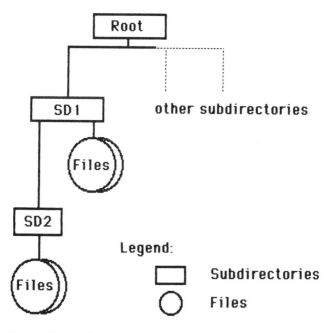

Figure 5.1 Nesting Subdirectories.

Although you can use a hierarchical directory structure on diskettes, in most situations you will probably maintain one directory structure and locate files under a common root directory for this storage medium. This is because you will probably prefer to organize your data and program files by diskette, placing a word processing program and its data files on one diskette, a spreadsheet program and its data files on a second diskette, and so on. When you use a fixed disk, its large storage capacity is best organized by structuring its storage. This structuring can take almost an infinite number of shapes because of the flexibility DOS provides in naming and nesting subdirectories. Two of the more general hierarchical directory structures you may wish to consider are illustrated in Figure 5.2.

The top portion of Figure 5.2 represents an application-oriented directory structure. In this type of directory structure, application programs and their data files are organized under specific subdirectories. Thus, a word processing program and data files created by that program might be placed under a subdirectory named WP, a telecommunications program and its data files under a subdirectory named TELCOM, and so on.

In the lower portion of Figure 5.2, a personnel-oriented directory structure shows a structure common in multiuser systems and networks. This type of directory structure

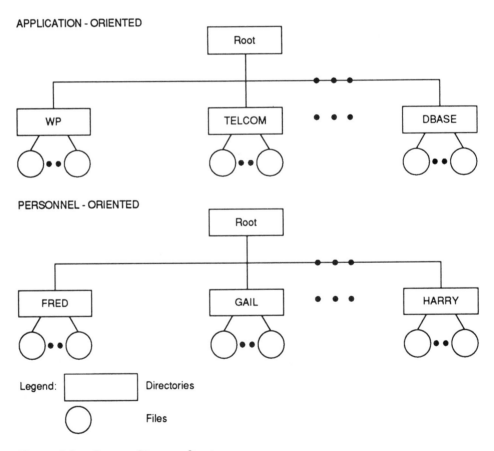

Figure 5.2   Common Directory Structures.

is recommended when several persons share one personal computer or one large-capacity fixed disk. Because the directory structure shown in the lower portion of Figure 5.2 could result in each person maintaining separate copies of application programs, this structure can waste a considerable amount of fixed disk storage. To minimize the potential waste, a combination of application- and personnel-oriented directories should be considered. Figure 5.3 illustrates an example of this combined directory structure.

In the directory structure illustrated in Figure 5.3, the application program files are placed under specific subdirectories. Other subdirectories with the names or abbreviations of individuals who use specific application programs are created under appropriate application directories. This structure permits individuals to place their data files under specific subdirectories assigned to their use while they can access common application programs placed at specific locations in the directory structure.

Directory and Path Names

Subdirectory names follow the same conventions as standard DOS filenames. That is, they can be up to eight characters in length and can optionally contain a three-character extension, with a period to separate the directory name from its extension. Thus, although the subdirectory names previously illustrated in Figures 5.1 through 5.3 are perfectly valid, you could add extensions to them to better reflect the contents of a

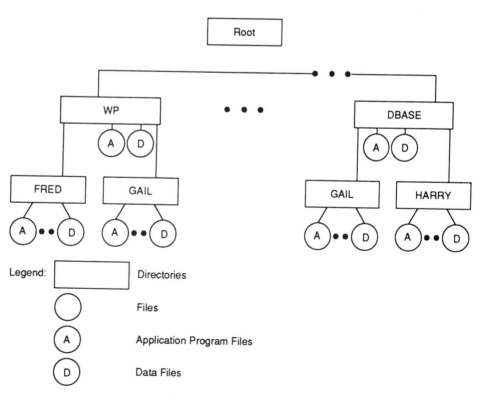

Figure 5.3   Combined Application/Personnel Directory Structure.

particular subdirectory. In most cases, eight characters are sufficient to define the contents or purpose of a subdirectory, so examples in this chapter use directory names of eight or fewer characters.

Path names are the route the operating system establishes through a hierarchical directory structure to locate a specific file or subdirectory. Path names start at the root and consist of strings of directory names separated from one another by the backslash character. Thus, to access a file named PAY.DAT under the subdirectory FRED in Figure 5.3, your route or path name would become

\WP\FRED\PAY.DAT

Here, the backslash preceding the WP subdirectory indicates that the route commences at the root directory. If the directory structure illustrated in Figure 5.3 resides on drive C, the complete file specification that defines the location of the file PAY.DAT becomes

C:\WP\FRED\PAY.DAT

Because each subdirectory has a unique path address, you can assign the same name to files located in different subdirectories. As an example, GAIL could also create a file named PAY.DAT. If GAIL did so, the complete file specification for that file would be

C:\WP\GAIL\PAY.DAT

With one PAY.DAT file located under Gail's subdirectory and a similarly named file located under Fred's subdirectory, the operating system considers each as a separate entity. Otherwise, if you attempt to create a file under a subdirectory for which another file with the same name exists, DOS displays an error message. Although the subdirectory structure illustrated in Figure 5.3 appears balanced, in actuality you can nest several levels of subdirectories under one directory and none under another directory or mix a level of nesting under different directories. The only restriction you have to consider is the maximum path length permitted by DOS, which is 63 characters.

Locating DOS

Until now, this chapter has deferred discussion of where the operating system files should be located in a hierarchical directory structure. Although there are essentially an almost infinite number of ways you can structure your disk, most persons prefer to keep their operating system files in one of two popular locations—under the root directory or in a separate subdirectory named DOS. The latter location is where the DOS 4.0 INSTALL program and the DOS 5.0 SETUP program will place the operating system files unless you enter a different subdirectory location.

The advantages associated with locating DOS system files directly under the root are twofold. First, the root directory is the default current directory at which DOS positions you at power-up or if a system reset is performed. Thus, without having to change directories you can immediately enter command keywords. In addition, you do not have to prefix a command with a path to the command file. Second, no matter where you are located in the hierarchical directory structure, you can simply prefix a command filename with one backslash to inform the operating system that the file is located in the root directory.

The second popular location for DOS files is a separate directory under the root directory that most persons appropriately name DOS. If you use this organization concept, ensure that the file COMMAND.COM, the DOS command interpreter, remains in the root directory. Otherwise, on power-up or a system reset you are placed at the root directory, and DOS will not be able to automatically load COMMAND.COM to interpret subsequent commands entered from the keyboard.

Two other files that must be placed in the root directory are IBMBIO.COM and IBMDOS.COM, because both of these files must be loaded at power-up or system reset to successfully operate your computer. Each of these is a hidden file that is automatically placed in the root directory by the operating system. If you want to place COMMAND.COM in the DOS directory, you should place the statement PATH C:\DOS in an AUTOEXEC.BAT file in the root directory. Doing so means that AUTOEXEC.BAT is executed each time your computer is powered-up or a system reset operation is performed, causing the operating system to automatically search the directory named DOS under the root directory for commands or batch files that are not found by a search of the current directory. Then, if you switch to a directory other than DOS and enter the command FORMAT, as an example, the operating system first searches the current directory for the file FORMAT.COM. If it does not find that file in the current directory the operating system then searches the DOS directory for that file. Additional information concerning the use of the PATH command occurs later in this chapter.

A separate directory for DOS command files is primarily created by users who structure their directories. In placing DOS command files in a subdirectory named DOS under the root directory, you must remember to prefix external command keywords with the path \DOS\, with the second backslash followed by the command keyword whenever you are located outside of the DOS subdirectory. As an alternative to prefixing commands with the path \DOS\, you can include the statement PATH C:\DOS in the AUTOEXEC.BAT file, or you can enter this PATH command from the keyboard. Either method causes DOS to search the directory \DOS on drive C after it searches the current directory for commands or batch files.

Directory-Related Commands

DOS includes several commands that can be used to perform such functions as the creation and deletion of subdirectories, as well as to move from one directory to another. To review the operation and use of these commands, follow this section's example of creating a predefined directory structure on a fixed disk and copying several files from different diskettes to different subdirectories on the fixed disk.

Suppose you will be using your PC AT or compatible computer to perform word processing, form design, graphing, database functions, and communications operations, as well as various types of budgeting and financial analysis calculations with a spreadsheet program. In addition, assume the operating system files will be located in a subdirectory named DOS under the root directory. To store your application programs on a fixed disk using separate directories for each category of software, a fixed disk organization that could satisfy your requirement would be similar to that illustrated in Figure 5.4. To understand the creation of nested subdirectories, assume that two persons would share the use of the form design program. For the two persons, FRED and GAIL, the desired hierarchical directory structure includes subdirectories labeled with their names under the FORMTOOL directory.

Now that the desired directory structure is in place, examine the use of DOS commands to implement this structure. Table 5.1 lists nine commonly used DOS directory-related command prompt commands covered in the remainder of this chapter. The Type column in that table indicates whether the command is internal (I) or external (E). As

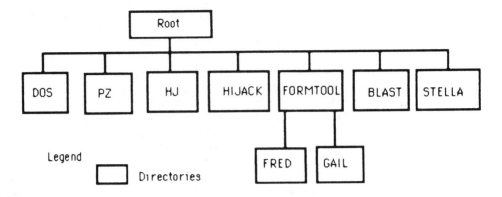

Figure 5.4 Desired Hierarchical Directory Structure.

Table 5.1
Commonly Used DOS
Directory-Related
Commands

Command	Type	Activity Performed
APPEND	I/E	Locates files outside of the current directory with extensions other than COM, EXE, or BAT.
CD or CHDIR	I	Displays or changes the current directory.
JOIN	E	Connects a drive to a directory on another drive, resulting in a single directory structure from two separate directories.
MD or MKDIR	I	Creates a subdirectory.
PATH	I	Establishes one or more routes to different subdirectories DOS will search if a command or batch file is not found in the current directory.
RD or RMDIR	I	Removes a subdirectory from a disk.
SUBST	E	Assigns a drive identifier to another drive or to a path on a drive.
TREE	E	Displays the directory paths on a drive and optionally lists the files in each directory.
XCOPY	E	Selectively copies groups of files that can include lower-level subdirectories.

previously explained in Chapter 4, internal commands are memory resident when DOS is initialized, whereas the code to perform external commands is stored in command files that must be loaded into memory.

In reviewing the operation and use of directory-related commands, assume that your fixed disk was just formatted by the DOS 4.0 INSTALL program and the operating system files were transferred to the subdirectory DOS that is automatically created by that program. Using the directory command (DIR), your directory listing would be similar to that illustrated in Figure 5.5. Note that the DOS 4.0 INSTALL program automatically places the COMMAND.COM file, as well as the AUTOEXEC.BAT file, under the root directory.

MKDIR (Make Directory) (Internal) Command

The MKDIR (make directory) command creates a new directory. The format of this command is

$$\begin{Bmatrix} MD \\ MKDIR \end{Bmatrix} \ [d:]path$$

```
Volume in drive C is DOS400
Volume Serial Number is 2E61-08E9
Directory of C:\

COMMAND  COM    37637  06-17-88  12:00p
AUTOEXEC BAT      163  03-25-80   1:45a
DOS         <DIR>       03-25-80   1:45a
        9 File(s)    XXXXXXXX bytes free
```

Figure 5.5 Initial Directory Structure.

As do several other directory-related commands, this command has an abbreviation. Thus, you can enter either MD or MKDIR for the command name. As an internal command, it does not have to be prefixed with the drive designator and path to a command file, because the command is memory resident when DOS is loaded. With this knowledge, you can use the MKDIR command to create the remainder of the hierarchical directory structure illustrated in Figure 5.4.

To create the six remaining subdirectories that are directly under the root directory, you can simply type MKDIR or MD followed by the appropriate subdirectory name six times. No path is required in the command line, because the current directory is the root directory and the use of the MKDIR command without a path creates a subdirectory under the current directory.

Figure 5.6 illustrates the commands entered at the C:> prompt to create the six directories and the use of the DIR command to verify their presence.

In the top portion of Figure 5.6, the entry of MD and MKDIR was purposely varied to illustrate how both keywords can be used to create subdirectories. Note that when the DIR command displays a directory listing, each subdirectory entry is followed by the word DIR to identify the entry as a subdirectory. Otherwise, the entry would be a file and simply show any file extension in this location in the directory listing. At the bottom of the directory listing note the message 9 File(s). Although this message may appear confusing because there are seven subdirectories, DOS treats each subdirectory as a file to include naming conventions for the subdirectory name and its optional extension.

Now that four subdirectories exist under the root directory, complete your hierarchical directory structure by creating the subdirectories FRED and GAIL under the FORM-TOOL subdirectory. In creating these subdirectories, experiment with two different methods using the MKDIR command. The first method involves issuing additional MKDIR commands while you are at the root directory level. To do so, you include the full path names of the desired subdirectories; otherwise, DOS creates the subdirectories under the root directory at the same level as the previously created subdirectories.

To create the subdirectory FRED you could issue either of the following commands using the command keyword MKDIR or the keyword MD.

MKDIR\FORMTOOL\FRED

MKDIR FORMTOOL\FRED

Similarly, to create the subdirectory GAIL under the FORMTOOL directory, you could enter either of the following commands using the keyword MKDIR or the keyword MD.

MKDIR\FORMTOOL\GAIL

```
C:\>MD PZ

C:\>MKDIR HJ

C:\>MD HIJACK

C:\>MKDIR FORMTOOL

C:\>MD BLAST

C:\>MKDIR STELLA

C:\>DIR

    Volume in drive C is DOS400
    Volume Serial Number is 2E61-08E9
    Directory of C:\

COMMAND  COM    37637  06-17-88  12:00p
AUTOEXEC BAT      163  03-25-80   1:45a
DOS          <DIR>     03-25-80   1:45a
PZ           <DIR>     08-29-88   9:32p
HJ           <DIR>     08-29-88   9:33p
HIJACK       <DIR>     08-29-88   9:34p
FORMTOOL     <DIR>     08-29-88   9:36p
BLAST        <DIR>     08-29-88   9:43p
STELLA       <DIR>     08-29-88   9:52p
        9 File(s)   XXXXXXXX bytes free
```

Figure 5.6   Creating Directories Under the Root Directory.

MKDIR FORMTOOL\GAIL

Assuming that you enter two appropriate make directory commands to create the subdirectories FRED and GAIL and use the DIR command to verify that they were created, what is displayed? If you entered the DIR command, the resulting directory would be very similar to that shown in the lower portion of Figure 5.6. In fact, the only difference would be in the number of bytes free, with the directory listing taken after the FRED and GAIL subdirectories were created showing 24 fewer bytes free. An examination of the directory listing shows that the subdirectories FRED and GAIL are conspicuous by their absence from the listing, yet 24 bytes were used. So, an obvious question is, where are the two subdirectories you just created?

If you examine the directory listing in Figure 5.6, which is essentially equivalent to the listing you would see after creating the subdirectories FRED and GAIL, you will note that you are presently located at the root (\) as you perform the directory listing operation. Therefore, the directory command performed as it was designed to operate, only listing those subdirectories and files, if any, located *directly* under the root directory.

To obtain a listing of the subdirectories under the FORMTOOL directory, you must either change directories (which is the next major topic) or indicate to DOS that you want to list the directory of FORMTOOL by specifying the path from the root directory to that subdirectory as shown in Figure 5.7.

Note that the directory command used in Figure 5.7 includes the path \FORMTOOL, informing DOS to list a directory of the contents of the FORMTOOL subdirectory. The

```
C:\>DIR \FORMTOOL

    Volume in drive C is DOS400
    Volume Serial Number is 2E61-08E9
    Directory of C:\FORMTOOL

.               <DIR>       08-29-88   9:36p
. .             <DIR>       08-29-88   9:36p
FRED            <DIR>       09-03-88  10:36a
GAIL            <DIR>       09-03-88  10:36a
        4 File(s)     XXXXXXXX bytes free

C:\>
```

Figure 5.7   Listing the Contents of the FORMTOOL Subdirectory.

```
C:\>DIR \FORMTOOL\FRED

    Volume in drive C is DOS400
    Volume Serial Number is 2E61-08E9
    Directory of C:\FORMTOOL\FRED

.               <DIR>       09-03-88  10:36a
. .             <DIR>       09-03-88  10:36a
        2 File(s)     XXXXXXXX bytes free

C:\>
```

Figure 5.8   Examining the FRED Subdirectory.

directory listing shows four DIR entries, a dot (.), double dot (..), FRED, and GAIL. The single dot designates the current or working directory and is the directory where the system is currently located. The double dot designates the directory immediately above the current directory, also known as the *parent directory*. Both dot entries, as well as subdirectories, are treated as files; hence the entry 4 File(s) in the last line of the display results from the use of the DIR command.

To solve the mystery of the use of 24 bytes of storage when the subdirectories FRED and GAIL were created, now list the FRED subdirectory. This is illustrated in Figure 5.8. Note that the FRED directory contains two files—dot and double dot. Thus, the creation of a directory entry uses 12 bytes of storage for the two files associated with the directory and their creation date.

DOS Shell Create Directory Operations

When you operate within the DOS Shell, directory-related operations are performed in a manner similar to the file related operations covered in Chapter 4. That is, you must first select a directory or directory location, then select the directory-related operation after you access the File pull-down menu from the File System screen.

The Create Directory operation under the DOS Shell requires you to select the higher-level directory under which you wish to create a new directory. Thus, if your disk was just formatted you would only have the root directory denoted by the backslash (\) symbol under the Directory Tree to select.

Figure 5.9 illustrates the Create Directory pop-up box displayed under DOS 4.0 after you select the Create directory option from the File pull-down menu. This menu was previously illustrated in Figure 4.34. Note the check mark to the left of the BLAST directory in the Directory Tree, which indicates that this directory was previously selected. Also note that COMM has been entered in the New directory name box. Once you enter a new directory name and press the **Enter** key, the new directory is created under the selected directory. Figure 5.10 illustrates the result of the previous Create Directory operation. Note that COMM is now a subdirectory under BLAST and that BLAST is still the selected subdirectory. If you are using DOS 5.0, you would also select Create Directory from the File menu, resulting in the display of a dialog box similar to the one illustrated in Figure 5.9.

Before you examine an alternate method that can be used to create the subdirectories under FORMTOOL, take a moment to review the operation and utilization of the CHDIR command.

CHDIR (Change Directory) (Internal) Command

The CHDIR (change directory) command alters the current or working directory level. The format of this command is

$$\begin{Bmatrix} \text{CD} \\ \text{CHDIR} \end{Bmatrix} [d:]path$$

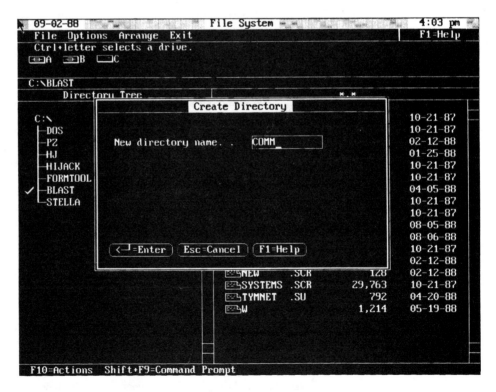

Figure 5.9   DOS 4.0 Create Directory Pop-Up Box.

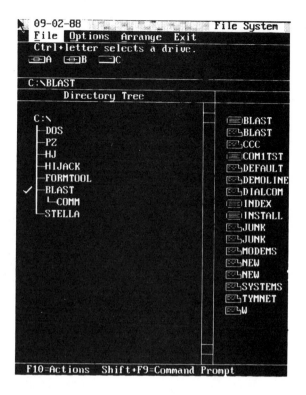

Figure 5.10   Results of the Create Directory Operation.

Similar to the Make Directory command, you can use one of two keywords in the Change Directory command line—CD or CHDIR. Using the Change Directory command, you can easily reposition your location to any existing subdirectory, as long as you remember the hierarchical directory structure you created. If you forget your directory structure, you can use the TREE command to obtain a report. This command is covered later in this chapter.

To move down the hierarchical directory structure to FORMTOOL from the root directory, you would enter the command

CHDIR\FORMTOOL

Once you have moved the current directory to FORMTOOL, you can issue the DIR command without specifying the path \FORMTOOL and obtain the same result as if you had specified the path when you were located in the root directory. Figure 5.11 shows the alternate method of obtaining a directory listing of a subdirectory without specifying a path in the DIR command.

Again note in Figure 5.11 that the use of the DIR command provides a listing limited to the contents of the current directory. Thus, any files and subdirectories that exist on other directories on the disk are not displayed. After a while this concept will become more obvious, because by noting the message Directory of... you will be reminded by DOS that the directory listing is of the subdirectory FORMTOOL.

C:\>CD\FORMTOOL

C:\FORMTOOL>DIR

    Volume in drive C is DOS400
    Volume Serial Number is 2E61-08E9
    Directory of C:\FORMTOOL

```
.             <DIR>      08-29-88   9:36p
. .           <DIR>      08-29-88   9:36p
FRED          <DIR>      09-03-88  10:36a
GAIL          <DIR>      09-03-88  10:36a
      4 File(s)    XXXXXXXX bytes free
```

C:\FORMTOOL>

Figure 5.11   Obtaining a Directory Listing of a Subdirectory Without Using a Path in the DIR Command.

If you did not previously create the subdirectories FRED and GAIL, you can do so without specifying a path in the MKDIR command, because you previously used the CD command to change the current directory to FORMTOOL. Thus, entering the commands

    A>**MKDIR FRED**

    A>**MKDIR GAIL**

would create the desired subdirectories under FORMTOOL, without requiring you to specify a path.

To move back to the root directory, simply enter the command

    CHDIR

Here the backslash as the last character informs DOS to make the root directory the current directory. As an alternative, you can use the double dot (..) designator in a CHDIR command as follows:

    CHDIR..

Because the double dot designates the directory immediately above the current directory and you were located at FORMTOOL, using CHDIR.. moves you back to the root directory level.

Now that you have created the subdirectory structure previously illustrated in Figure 5.4, review the hierarchical level of each directory. Table 5.2 summarizes the relationship between directories, including the path from the root directory and its hierarchical level.

With the DOS Shell you can simply place the selection cursor over the desired directory in the Directory Tree and press the **Enter** key to view the contents of the directory. When you do so, DOS automatically changes directories, which is the reason why there is no "Change Directory" option in the File pull-down menu.

File Operations

When using a hierarchical directory structure, you must include the drive identifier and path to a file unless the file is located on the default drive in the current directory. In

Directory	Path	Hierarchical Level
Root	\	root
DOS	\DOS	level 1
PZ	\PZ	level 1
HJ	\HJ	level 1
HIJACK	\HIJACK	level 1
FORMTOOL	\FORMTOOL	level 1
FRED	\FORMTOOL\FRED	level 2
GAIL	\FORMTOOL\GAIL	level 2
BLAST	\BLAST	level 1
STELLA	\STELLA	level 1

```
C:\>DIR \FORMTOOL\FRED

      Volume in drive C is DOS400
      Volume Serial Number is 2E61-08E9
      Directory of C:\FORMTOOL\FRED

.              <DIR>       09-03-88  10:36a
. .            <DIR>       09-03-88  10:36a
PAY      DAT      54  09-03-88  11:36a
         3 File(s)     XXXXXXXX bytes free

C:\>
```

Figure 5.12   Verifying the COPY Operation.

such situations, the optional drive identifier and path name are not required, because the default drive and current directory provide DOS with the correct location.

Directory Structure Example

To understand the use of drive identifiers and path names in a hierarchical directory structure, assume you want to load a file named PAY.DAT on a diskette in drive A onto the subdirectory named FRED on drive C. You could use the full DOS command, including all drive identifiers:

COPY A:PAY.DAT C:\FORMTOOL\FRED

If you previously changed the current directory on drive C to FRED by entering CD\FORMTOOL\FRED, you could enter a simpler COPY command as follows:

COPY A:PAY.DAT C:

To verify that the file PAY.DAT was transferred to the subdirectory FRED, you could use the DIR command:

DIR \FORMTOOL\FRED

or, if you changed the current directory to FRED, you could simply enter the command **DIR.**

Figure 5.12 illustrates the use of the "long" DIR command, whose path begins at the root directory to obtain a directory listing of the FRED subdirectory.

In the event FRED is fired and a new employee named ALVIN is assigned to use the form creation program, you can investigate additional directory related operations required to rename a directory. Unfortunately, there is no DOS command under the DOS command prompt mode of operation that renames directories, forcing you to remove the directory named FRED. To do this, you use the Remove Directory command, whose operation and utilization will be covered after you examine how to rename a directory under the DOS Shell.

DOS Shell Rename Directory Operation

Unlike the DOS command prompt mode of operation, which does not provide an easy method to rename a directory, both the DOS 4.0 and the DOS 5.0 Shell rename directories simply. The key to renaming a directory is the Rename option in the File pull-down menu on the File System screen.

Similar to file-related operations, you must first select the directory to rename. Use the **Tab** key and the **Up** and **Down Arrow** keys to position the selection cursor on the directory to be renamed. Then, press the **Spacebar** to select the directory; a check mark is positioned to the left of the selected directory. Now you can press the **F10** key or the **Tab** key to position the selection bar on the File item on the action bar. Then, pressing **Down Arrow** displays the File pull-down menu.

Once you select the Rename option, the Rename Directory pop-up box displays over the File System screen, as illustrated in Figure 5.13, if you are using DOS 4.0. If you

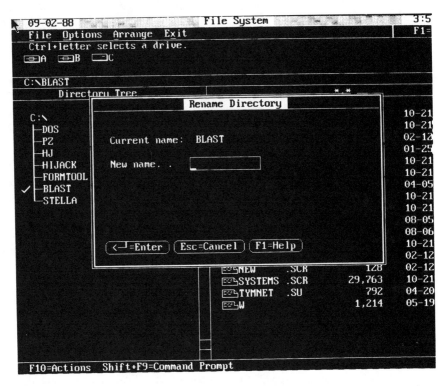

Figure 5.13   DOS 4.0 Rename Directory Pop-Up Box.

are using DOS 5.0, the three buttons at the bottom of the screen are relabeled OK, CANCEL, and HELP. Note that the pop-up displays the name of the selected or current directory and positions the cursor at the first position in the New name box. After you enter the new directory name and press the Enter key, you see the result of the rename operation, with the new directory name replacing the current name in the Directory Tree area.

RMDIR (Remove Directory) (Internal) Command

The RMDIR (remove directory) command removes a previously created subdirectory. Similar to the directory-related commands described earlier, you can invoke this command using either of two keywords—RMDIR or RD. The format of this command is

$$\begin{Bmatrix} RD \\ RMDIR \end{Bmatrix} [d:]path$$

To successfully use this command, first you must remove all files (except for the dot [.] and double dot [..] entries, which as you recall represent directory levels) from the directory. Then, you must ensure that the current directory is positioned *above* the directory you are removing.

Assuming that the PAY.DAT file under the FRED directory can be used by ALVIN, try creating a subdirectory using the name ALVIN and copying that file to it. Then you can use the DOS ERASE command to remove the file prior to eliminating the subdirectory named FRED.

Assuming the current directory is the root directory, you could use the MD command to create the subdirectory ALVIN under the FORMTOOL directory, as shown here:

C>MD\FORMTOOL\ALVIN

Now, to copy the file PAY.DAT from the subdirectory FRED to the subdirectory ALVIN enter the command

COPY \FORMTOOL\FRED\PAY.DAT \FORMTOOL\ALVIN

Now that the data file has been copied, use the RMDIR command to attempt to remove the subdirectory FRED. After you enter **RMDIR FRED** or **RD FRED**, note the resulting error message. The error occurs because the file PAY.DAT has not been removed from the subdirectory you are trying to eliminate.

C>RMDIR \FORMTOOL\FRED

```
Invalid path, not directory,
or directory not empty
```

Now use the DOS ERASE command to remove the file PAY.DAT, as indicated next.

ERASE \FORMTOOL\FRED\PAY.DAT

Note that if you do not specify a path name, the ERASE command searches the root directory that is the current directory for the file PAY.DAT, which, in this case, is not your intention.

Now that the only file in the FRED subdirectory has been removed, you can remove the FRED subdirectory:

RMDIR\FORMTOOL\FRED

DOS Shell Delete Directory Operation

Similar to the command prompt mode of operation, the DOS Shell requires you to remove all files from a directory prior to deleting the directory.

To delete a directory, you first select it from the Directory Tree area in the File System screen. Assuming that you previously deleted all files in that directory, you can successfully select the Delete option from the File pull-down menu. Once this action is accomplished, the Delete Directory pop-up box is displayed. This pop-up box, illustrated in Figure 5.14, displays the current directory that will be deleted and two options you can select. As the figure indicates, the default option is Do not delete this directory, forcing you to move the selection cursor to option 2 prior to pressing **Enter**. If you forgot to remove one or more files on the directory to be deleted, the message Access denied is displayed. As previously mentioned in the discussion of the Shell Rename option, under DOS 5.0 the buttons at the bottom of the dialog box have slightly changed.

If you are operating in the DOS command prompt mode, after establishing and deleting directories, as well as copying and erasing files, you might become confused concerning the directory structure you have. Fortunately, DOS includes the TREE command that you can use to generate a report of the structure of a disk.

TREE (External) Command

The TREE command displays a report of the directory structure of a diskette or hard disk. This report can be limited to the directory paths or can include a listing of all files stored on the disk. The format of this command is

    [d:][path] TREE [d:][/F]

Similar to all DOS external commands, the drive identifier and path preceding the command name identify the location of the command file. The drive identifier following the command keyword can specify the drive whose directory paths you want displayed. If not included in the command line, the default drive is used. Finally, the /F option causes all files in each directory to be listed.

Because an extensive directory structure rapidly scrolls off the screen, there are several methods you can consider to better view the directory. First, you can press **Ctrl+PrtSc** to obtain a hardcopy listing of the directory as it is being displayed. If you just wanted to view the directory structure, you could use the Pause Screen function. As another option, you can perform a *piping operation* to the DOS MORE filter to display the results of the TREE command one screen at a time. The use of pipes and filters, as well as additional DOS commands (including the MORE command) is covered in Chapter 7.

Assuming you want a report of the directory structure of the disk you have been manipulating in this chapter, you can enter the following command line:

    C:\>**TREE**

The report generated by the TREE command is illustrated in Figure 5.15. Note that the display of the execution of the TREE command from the DOS command prompt mode of operation produces the same display that you will see in the Directory Tree of the File System screen under the DOS Shell. This is why there is no TREE function included in the DOS Shell.

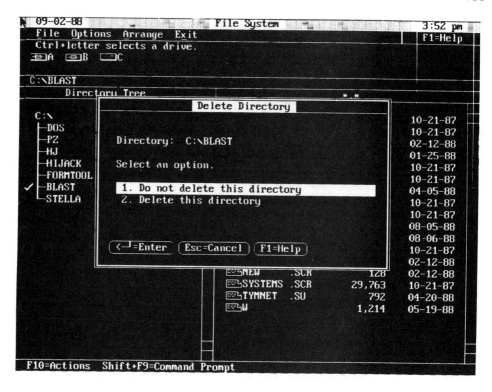

Figure 5.14   DOS 4.0 Delete Directory Pop-Up Box.

```
C:\>TREE
Directory PATH listing for Volume DOS400
Volume Serial Number is 2E61-08E9
C:.
├───DOS
├───PZ
├───HJ
├───HIJACK
├───FORMTOOL
│       ├───ALVIN
│       └───GAIL
├───BLAST
└───STELLA

C:\>
```

Figure 5.15   TREE Command Report.

Under DOS 5.0, a Tree menu was added to the shell. The selection of the Tree menu provides options to Expand One Level of the displayed tree, Expand Branch, Expand All, and Collapse Branch.

File Location Commands

To simplify the process of accessing files in a hierarchical directory structure, two file location commands are included in DOS—PATH and APPEND. PATH only finds files that can be executed, such as files with the extension COM, EXE, and BAT. APPEND can be considered to be the inverse of PATH, because the command locates files outside the current directory that have extensions other than those PATH looks for.

Because the PATH command was incorporated into earlier versions of DOS prior to IBM's adding the APPEND command, it is appropriate to review the operation and use of each command in the order they first appeared in DOS.

PATH (Set Search Directory) (Internal) Command

The PATH command responds to the names of one or more directory names you enter by telling DOS to search them for executable files after it examines the current directory. The format of this command is

$$\text{PATH} \begin{Bmatrix} ; \\ [[d:]path[[;[d:]path]]] \end{Bmatrix}$$

If you enter the command PATH without any parameters, the current PATH search settings are displayed. Entering PATH with a semicolon resets the search path to null, the initial DOS 3.3 default. If you are using DOS 4.0, the INSTALL program places the command PATH C:\DOS in the AUTOEXEC.BAT file that INSTALL creates in the root directory.

To examine the use of the PATH command, assume you are using DOS 3.3 and wish to automatically access operating system command files located in a subdirectory named DOS under the root directory on drive C. To inform the operating system to search that drive and subdirectory for executable files not found in the current directory, you enter the command

    C>**PATH C:\DOS**

Thereafter, each time you enter the name of an external DOS command on a command line, DOS automatically searches the DOS subdirectory if the command file is not found in the current directory. To verify the PATH setting, you can enter the command without parameters as shown here:

    C>**PATH**

    PATH=C:\DOS

You can include a list of drives and path names separated by semicolons as long as the total number of characters in the command does not exceed 128. Thus, if you wanted DOS to search the subdirectory FRED located under the FORMTOOL directory, which, in turn, is located under the root directory on drive C, you could modify the command as follows:

    C>**PATH C:\DOS;C:\FORMTOOL\FRED**

APPEND (Internal/External) Command

As previously mentioned, the APPEND command can be considered as performing an operation similarly but inversely to the PATH command. That is, the APPEND command enables DOS to search for files outside of the current directory whose extensions are other than COM, EXE, and BAT. Thus, using this command you can store applications once on a fixed disk and use them without changing to the directory in which they are located.

The first time you use the APPEND command, it functions as an external command and will be loaded from a file into memory. The format for this command when used as an external file is

$$[d:][path]\text{APPEND} \begin{Bmatrix} d:path[;[d:][path...]] \\ \text{APPEND}[/X][/E] \end{Bmatrix}$$

As with all external commands, the drive specifier and path preceding the keyword APPEND are used to specify the location where the command file resides. If the command is used without its optional /X and /E parameters, you can specify the paths to subdirectories DOS should search to access nonexecutable files stored outside the current directory. This will probably be the most popular format of the APPEND command, because it enables you to access overlay files and additional software such as help files that PATH does not provide access to. Very few programs are made up of a single executable program, so you will probably use the PATH command followed by an APPEND command with similar syntax to obtain full access to modern application programs.

Thus, to complement the previously discussed PATH command, you could enter the APPEND command as follows:

C>**APPEND C:\DOS;C:\FORMTOOL\FRED**

This APPEND command would cause DOS to automatically search the subdirectories DOS and FRED for nonexecutable files not found in the current directory.

The /X optional parameter causes paths specified by a previous APPEND command to be searched on the occurrence of certain function calls. If you specify the /E parameter, the current APPEND path is stored in the DOS environment and can be changed by the SET command. The DOS environment and several additional commands are discussed in Chapter 7.

Once APPEND has been loaded it functions as an internal command for the duration of the current work session. At this time its format becomes

$$\text{APPEND} \begin{Bmatrix} d:path[;[d:]path...] \\ [;] \end{Bmatrix}$$

When you use the APPEND command with a semicolon, any previous APPEND list of paths is reset to null, which is its default value when DOS is initialized.

The only action under the DOS Shell that performs a similar function to the APPEND command is Associate. This action, which is invoked from the File pull-down menu on the File System screen, enables you to associate filename extensions with a program. Then, whenever you select a file with the previously specified extension and also select the Open (start) action, the program associated with the selected file is invoked. This feature enables you to keep data files in separate directories from program files but select a data file to start the associated program.

Utility Commands

This section examines the operation and use of three DOS directory-related utility commands—XCOPY, JOIN, and SUBST. XCOPY is similar to, but much more powerful than, the DOS COPY command. XCOPY helps you to selectively copy groups of files that can include lower-level subdirectories. JOIN enables you to form a single directory structure from two separate directories, whereas SUBST enables you to assign a drive identifier to another drive or to a path on a drive.

XCOPY (External) Command

The XCOPY command selectively copies groups of files, including lower-level subdirectories. The format of this command is

$$[d:][path]\text{XCOPY} \left\{ \begin{array}{l} [d:][path] filename[.ext] \\ [d:]path[filename[.ext]] \\ d:[path][filename[.ext]] \end{array} \right\} \ [d:][path][filename[.ext]]\text{parameters}$$

where the optional parameters are

/A to copy only files whose archive bit was set to one without changing the bit setting.

/D to copy only files whose date is the same or later than the date specified by entering the date format in one of the following formats:

/D:*mm-dd-yy*

/D:*dd-mm-yy*

/D:*yy-mm-dd*

where the date format entered is based on the country code you specified when the SELECT or COUNTRY command was used.

/E to create subdirectories on the target drive, even if they are empty after all copying is completed. If /E is not specified, empty subdirectories are not created.

/M to copy only those files whose archive bit is set to one, then turn off the archive bit of the source file.

/P to copy on a file-by-file basis, prompting you prior to copying each file.

/S to copy all files on the source disk regardless of subdirectory position to be copied. This optional parameter does not create an empty subdirectory on the target disk unless the /E parameter is also specified in the command. If the /S parameter is not included, only files with the specified or current directory are copied.

/V to verify that data copied to the target disk is recorded properly.

/W to display the message

    Press any key to begin copying file(s)

This parameter provides you with the opportunity to insert different diskettes before the XCOPY command executes.

To illustrate the use of the XCOPY command, assume the diskette in drive A and your fixed disk in drive C have the tree structures illustrated at the top of Figure 5.16.

By entering the XCOPY command as shown here, the resulting target directory structure illustrated at the bottom of Figure 5.16 is created.

XCOPY A:\ C:\FORMTOOL/S

In this XCOPY command, A:\ informs DOS that the root directory of drive A is the starting point for the command. The identifier and path C:\FORMTOOL specifies the target drive and path XCOPY will copy files to. The /S parameter tells DOS to copy all files below the starting source directory.

If you prefer to copy specific files, you can add filenames to the preceding example. Assuming you only want to copy files with the extension ASC, you can enter the following command line.

XCOPY A:*.ASC C:\FORMTOOL/S

If you want to copy all files with the extension ASC but rename the extension of each file to DAT, you can enter the following command line:

XCOPY A:*.ASC C:\FORMTOOL*.DAT/S

JOIN (External) Command

The JOIN command can connect a drive to a directory on another drive, forming a single directory structure. Through this command, you can let application programs that are diskette resident take advantage of the storage capacity of fixed and virtual disks. The format of this command is

$$[d:][path]\text{JOIN} \begin{Bmatrix} [d: & d:\backslash\text{directory}] \\ [d: & /\text{D}] \end{Bmatrix}$$

As for all external commands, the drive identifier and path preceding the command identify the location where the JOIN command file resides. If you enter the command without any parameters, the currently joined drives and directories, if any, are displayed.

Initial Tree Structure

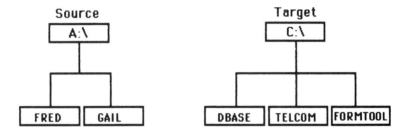

Command Line   C>XCOPY A:\C:\CALC /S

Resulting Target Drive Tree Structure

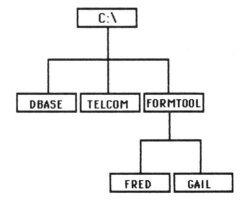

Figure 5.16   Using the XCOPY Command.

The drive identifier immediately after JOIN denotes the drive to be connected or disconnected to or from a directory on another drive. If the drive identifier is followed by a second drive identifier and directory path, the first drive is joined to the second drive under the specified directory. Note that the specified directory must contain no files other than dot (.) and double dot (..) if the directory has been created already. If it does not exist, DOS creates the specified directory. The resulting operation of the JOIN command is illustrated in Figure 5.17. If the parameter /D follows the first drive identifier, the specified drive is disconnected from any previously JOINed directory.

Figure 5.18 illustrates the operation and verification of a JOIN command. Note that the contents of the diskette in drive A are joined to drive C as a directory named DISKETTE. Then, the DIR command verifies the operation of the JOIN command.

Note that the JOIN command should not be used with drives affected by a SUBST or ASSIGN command. Nor should you use BACKUP, RESTORE, FORMAT, DISKCOPY, or DISKCOMP with a drive affected by JOIN.

SUBST (Substitute) (External) Command

The SUBST (Substitute) command assigns a drive to a path on another drive. The primary use for this command is to permit application programs that do not recognize paths to do so by making a subdirectory masquerade as a disk drive. That is, SUBST enables you to assign a drive identifier to an existing disk drive and subdirectory,

Initial Drive C Directory Structure

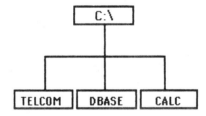

Using the JOIN command

C>JOIN A: C:\DISKETTE

Resulting Joined Drive C Directory Structure

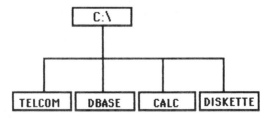

Figure 5.17 Using the JOIN Command.

C:\>JOIN A: C:\DISKETTE

C:\>DIR

    Volume in drive C is DOS400
    Volume Serial Number is 2E61-08E9
    Directory of C:\

```
COMMAND  COM     37637  06-17-88  12:00p
AUTOEXEC BAT       163  03-25-80   1:45a
DISKETTE       <DIR>    09-03-88   1:27p
DOS            <DIR>    03-25-80   1:45a
PZ             <DIR>    08-29-88   9:32p
HJ             <DIR>    08-29-88   9:33p
HIJACK         <DIR>    08-29-88   9:34p
FORMTOOL       <DIR>    08-29-88   9:36p
BLAST          <DIR>    08-29-88   9:43p
STELLA         <DIR>    08-29-88   9:52p
        10 File(s)    XXXXXXXX bytes free
```

C:\>

Figure 5.18   Verifying the Use of the JOIN Command.

permitting data routed to the assigned disk drive and subdirectory in actuality to flow to the assigned drive.

The format of the SUBST command is

$$[d:][path] \text{SUBST} \begin{Bmatrix} [d: \quad d:path] \\ [d: \quad /D] \end{Bmatrix}$$

The first drive identifier after SUBST denotes the drive to be substituted for or have its association deleted from another drive or path. This drive identifier can be a physical or a logical drive. If the drive identifier is higher than E, which is the highest DOS normally permits, you must include a LASTDRIVE assignment in your CONFIG.SYS file.

The second drive identifier and path following the SUBST keyword references the drive and subdirectory you want to operate as if it were an independent disk drive. If you follow the first drive identifier with the parameter /D, any previously set substitution is deleted, whereas simply specifying the keyword without any parameters displays the currently assigned substitutions.

As an example of the use of the SUBST command, assume drive C has the directory such that the path C:\FORMTOOL\GAIL exists on that drive. Issuing the command

    SUBST E: C:\FORMTOOL\GAIL

provides you with two ways to access the subdirectory GAIL on drive C as a result of the substitution. You can still use the physical drive and path name, or you could use the disk drive identifier E. Once the substitution is accomplished disk drive E, in effect, becomes an abbreviated method of referencing the path \FORMTOOL\GAIL on drive C.

6 / **Batch File Operations**

Batch files both automate operations and significantly boost the productivity of DOS and its users. With batch files you can customize DOS for other computer users, simplify complex systems, and perform other operations to facilitate the use of a personal computer.

A batch file consists of a series of DOS commands that are executed when a single command referencing the name of the file is entered. Because you normally test the operation of a batch file prior to using it on a permanent basis or providing it to others, its use eliminates many common causes of DOS operational problems. Such problems can include users typing complex DOS commands incorrectly, performing unintentional DOS operations, or lacking the ability or training necessary to perform DOS related operations.

This chapter first examines ways to create and use batch files. Then, using this information as a base, it examines the operation of specific batch commands and shows how to create several batch files to boost the productivity of your personal computer. In concluding, this chapter explores a special type of batch file designed to hold commands used to configure your computer system. This examination includes the operation and utilization of configuration commands that can be placed in this special batch file.

Creating and Using Batch Files

A batch file consists of ASCII text that represents one or more DOS commands. Each command occupies a separate line in the file. To identify the file as a batch file, its extension must be BAT. However, to execute the batch file you can enter the name of the file without its extension on the DOS command line. When you do so, DOS searches the current directory for a COM, EXE, or BAT file with a name that matches the name you entered. You should therefore avoid assigning a name to a batch file that duplicates the name of a DOS command.

Because a batch file is restricted to ASCII text, it must be created by a process that generates that type of data. One of the most common methods of creating batch files is to use the DOS COPY command to copy data from the console to your file. As an illustration of the use of the COPY command, consider the following example, which creates the batch file named WP.BAT.

```
C>COPY CON: WP.BAT
  CD \WP
  WRITE
  CD \
  ^Z
```

In this example you must enter a Ctrl+Z multikey combination, pressing the Ctrl and Z keys and Enter to terminate the COPY operation. Once you do so, the data entered from the console is written onto the file WP.BAT. Then, by simply entering the command WP, three separate command line entries will be executed.

The first line entry in the WP.BAT file changes the directory to WP. The next line entry, WRITE, is assumed to be a command entry that results in the execution of a word processing program with that name. Finally, the third line entry changes the current directory to the root directory after you exit the program. Although this example is simple, it illustrates how you can create a program that, while transparent to the user, navigates through a hierarchical directory structure to execute a program and then returns to the root directory once the use of that program is terminated. Thus, batch files can be extremely useful in simplifying operations for users not well versed in the use of the operating system.

Although the DOS Shell enables you to easily navigate through a directory structure, you must use batch files to predefine a sequence of operations. Thus, under the DOS Shell you can create one or more batch files to further simplify computer operations. Then you can simply move the section cursor over a batch file's name and press the **Spacebar** to select it, after which invoking the Open (start) action from the File pull-down will initiate the predefined sequence of operations.

Instead of using the COPY command to create batch files, you can create them with the EDIT or EDLIN text editor that is included with DOS, or you can use most word processors. If you use a word processor, make sure that the resulting data is written onto disk as an ASCII file and not as the word processor's normal binary file or as an encoded text file. Otherwise, DOS will not be able to correctly interpret the information contained in the file.

Replaceable Parameters

One of the most helpful features incorporated in a batch file is the ability to use replaceable parameters. DOS enables up to 10 replaceable parameters to be used at a time within a batch file. These parameters are replaced by data supplied by the computer operator in the DOS command line when the batch file is executed.

The replaceable parameters that can be specified must be labeled %0 through %9, with %0 always replaced by a drive specifier, if required, and the filename of the batch file. As an example of replaceable parameters, consider the following batch file.

```
A>COPY CON: WRITE.BAT
CD \WRITE
COPY %1.DAT %1.BAK
WRITE %1
```

Suppose the previously created batch file was executed by entering the DOS command line

WRITE JANEMEMO

Here JANEMEMO is substituted for the replaceable parameter %1. Thus, after the directory is changed to WRITE, the batch program substitutes JANEMEMO for %1, resulting in the file JANEMEMO.DAT being copied to the "backup" file JANE-MEMO.BAK. Then, the batch program automatically executes a word processing program named WRITE, using the file JANEMEMO.DAT as input.

If you change the COPY command in the previously illustrated batch file to **COPY %1.DAT %2.BAK,** two filenames would be required to be entered in the DOS command line. In this instance, entering WRITE JANEMEMO JANEBKUP would result in the sequential substitution of JANEMEMO for %1 and JANEBKUP for %2.

Batch Commands

When DOS 1.0 was introduced, it included only two commands designed specifically for use in batch files—REM and PAUSE. DOS 2.0 added five additional batch commands—ECHO, FOR, GOTO, IF, and SHIFT, as well as the undocumented ability to include comments by prefixing line entries with a period (.). This undocumented capability is also known as the *dot command*.

When DOS version 3.0 was released, the batch commands remained essentially unchanged. However, the undocumented dot command was eliminated. The only major change to batch commands occurred with the introduction of DOS version 3.3, which added the CALL command. This batch command enables you to program one batch file and to execute another batch file (that is, it acts like a subroutine call in conventional programming). Then, when execution of the CALLed batch file is complete, control is passed back to the original batch file (just as a subroutine returns control to a main program).

Table 6.1 indicates the batch commands that are supported by different versions of DOS. You can use this table to determine whether you should obtain a more recent version of the operating system for the creation of batch files on your computer system.

REM Command

The REM command is an abbreviation for REMark. It documents your batch files by including comments at appropriate locations. The format of this command, which is only used in batch files, is

```
REM [remark]
```

As an example of the use of this command, try modifying your previously created WP.BAT file. The following example illustrates how you might identify each line in the batch file that performs an operation.

```
REM Change to WP directory
CD \WP
REM Execute word processing program
```

Table 6.1
DOS Batch
Command Support

Batch Command	DOS Support			
	1.X	**2.X**	**3.0**	**3.3/4.0/5.0**
REM	yes	yes	yes	yes
ECHO	no	yes	yes	yes
PAUSE	yes	yes	yes	yes
FOR	no	yes	yes	yes
GOTO	no	yes	yes	yes
IF	no	yes	yes	yes
SHIFT	no	yes	yes	yes
CALL	no	no	no	yes

```
WRITE
REM Return to root directory
CD \
```

For clarity, many persons prefer to group REM commands together. Thus, as an alternative the file might be created using REM commands as follows:

```
REM Change to WP directory
REM Execute word processing program
REM Return to root directory
CD \WP
WRITE
CD \
```

The DOS commands used in the sample three-line batch file are essentially self-explanatory and for many persons probably do not require documentation. However, you'll be saved hours of future effort if you have to modify a previously created batch file and the documentation is explicit in explaining the operation of complex statements in the file.

ECHO Command

This command can be used to enable or disable the display of DOS commands as they are executed from within a batch file. The format of this command is

$$\text{ECHO} \left[\left\{ \begin{matrix} \text{ON} \\ \text{OFF} \end{matrix} \right\} \right] \text{[message]}$$

When ECHO is entered with no parameters, the command causes the current ECHO state to be displayed as indicated here.

A>**ECHO**
Echo is ON

ECHO ON is the default state when your system is powered-up or a system reset is performed. By issuing an ECHO OFF command, you instruct DOS to inhibit the display of the DOS prompt and commands on the screen as they are executed from within a batch file. Similarly, an ECHO ON command displays the DOS prompt and commands on the screen as they are executed from within a batch file. If you include a message in the ECHO command, it is displayed regardless of the ECHO state. As an alternative to ECHO OFF, you can prefix any command with an @ symbol to inhibit its display. Unfortunately, this does not prevent DOS from displaying messages generated by the execution of commands, such as x File(s) copied. To suppress these messages, you should direct the output to the NUL device by adding >**NUL** after any DOS command that normally generates a message on the display.

PAUSE Command

The PAUSE command can be used to temporarily suspend the execution of a batch file. The format of this command is

PAUSE [*remark*]

When the PAUSE command is executed, it first displays any remark included in the command line. Then, the command temporarily suspends the execution of the batch file it is included in and displays the message Strike a key when ready... on a new line. Once a key is pressed, the batch file resumes execution at the next line following the line containing the PAUSE command. The following short batch program illustrates how the PAUSE command can be used to provide information to the operator of the personal computer. Note that FORMAT is a dangerous command to play with unless you absolutely know what you are doing.

```
COPY CON: FORMAT.BAT
ECHO OFF
PAUSE press a key to initiate formatting
XFORMAT A:
```

Assuming you previously renamed the DOS FORMAT file as XFORMAT and named your batch file FORMAT, the result of entering your new FORMAT command is

C>FORMAT
```
Insert new diskette for drive A:
and strike ENTER when ready
```

Note that the preceding batch file changed the use of the DOS FORMAT command to restrict its usage to diskettes in drive A. Later this chapter examines in detail several methods you can use to prevent formatting the hard disk inadvertently.

FOR Command

The FOR command enables the iterative execution of a specified DOS command. The format of this command is

```
FOR %%variable IN(file set)DO command
```

When the FOR command is executed, a single-letter *variable* included in the *command* is set sequentially to each member of the *file set*. After the *variable* is set to a member of the *file set*, the command following the DO specification is executed. This process repeats until all file set members are processed. As an example of the use of FOR, assume you want to obtain a listing of all the batch files and data files under the subdirectory DBASE. To accomplish this, you could create a batch file like this:

```
COPY CON: LSTDBASE.BAT
CD \DBASE
FOR %%X IN(*.BAT *.DAT)DO TYPE %%X>LPT1:
CD \
^Z
```

Once the batch file named LSTDBASE is created, entering its filename causes the directory to be changed to DBASE. Then, the FOR command assigns the variable X to the file *.BAT, which is actually a potential set of files, because the asterisk global character is included in the file specification. Next, the TYPE command is executed for all files whose extension is BAT, after which the variable X is assigned to the file set *.DAT and the process of printing the contents of all files whose extension is DAT occurs. As indicated in this example, global filename characters can be included in the FOR command to increase the power and utility of this batch command.

GOTO Command

The GOTO command performs branching operations. This command, as you will soon see, can be used with any combination of commands or conditional operators.

The format of the GOTO command is

```
GOTO [:]label
```

The *label* is required here because it indicates a destination point in the batch file to which branching should occur.

The *label* is a string of up to eight characters, which must be prefixed by a colon (:) when the label is used as a branch entry point. When used in this manner, the label is contained on a separate line in the batch file. The following example illustrates the use of the GOTO command, as well as the inclusion of a label in a batch file.

```
:START
PAUSE Insert the disk to be copied in drive A
COPY A:*.* C:\LOTUS\JOHN
GOTO START
```

In the preceding example a continuous loop through the batch file occurs, so you must press Ctrl+Break to terminate the batch job and return to the DOS prompt level of operation. When you examine the IF command you will use that command to construct a conditional branching example. This example more fully demonstrates the capability of the GOTO command that occurs when its use is combined with another batch command.

IF Command

The IF command is one of the most useful batch commands, because it enables you to incorporate conditional branching into a batch file. The format of this command is

```
IF [NOT] condition command
```

where the *condition* parameters are

```
ERRORLEVEL number
String1 == String2
EXIST filespec
```

When the IF command is executed, the specified *condition* in the *command* is evaluated. If the condition is True, the command specified after the condition is executed. If the condition is False, the command specified after the condition is ignored and control is passed to the next line in the batch file.

The ERRORLEVEL number refers to the value of an optional exit code that a previously executed program may have set. When a program completes its execution correctly, it returns to DOS with an unset error flag. If the program terminates incorrectly, its error flag is set, causing DOS to examine a specific location to determine what the error code means.

Four DOS commands that return error codes if they terminate with an error that can be checked are FORMAT, REPLACE, BACKUP, and RESTORE. As an example of the use of error codes, assume you are creating a batch program file to automate BACKUP operations. In using an ERRORLEVEL X conditional operator in the IF command, the command will be executed if the returned error code is X or higher. Thus, the following simple batch file demonstrates the use of the ERRORLEVEL operator in the batch IF command:

```
BACKUP
IF ERRORLEVEL 1 ECHO!Backup Aborted!
```

The condition String1==String2 in an IF command is true when both strings are identical. Unlike normal string comparisons, string values used in an IF command cannot include data redirection characters or such command line delimiters as a comma, equal sign, colon, or semicolon. As an example of the use of a string comparison condition in IF commands, consider the batch file in Listing 6.1, which includes the COPY command in line 1 that creates the batch file.

Listing 6.1 LISTDISK.BAT

```
COPY CON: LISTDISK.BAT
IF %1==LEFT GOTO DRIVEA
IF %1==RIGHT GOTO DRIVEB
ECHO YOU OBVIOUSLY DON'T KNOW WHAT TO DO
GOTO END
:DRIVEA
DIR A:>LPT1:
GOTO END
:DRIVEB
DIR B:>LPT1:
:END
```

This batch file enables you to simply enter the name of the file followed by the word LEFT or RIGHT to obtain a directory listing of an appropriately located drive. When this batch file is executed, the first entry in the command line following LISTDISK is assigned to the replaceable parameter %1. Thus, if the command line entry is

A>LISTDRIVE LEFT

the replaceable parameter %1 would be assigned the value LEFT. Because the first IF command is true, a branch to the label DRIVEA occurs in the program. The line after that label contains the DOS command DIR A:, causing the directory of that drive to be printed, after which a branch to the end of the batch file occurs. Similarly, if you enter the command

LISTDISK RIGHT

the directory of the diskette in drive B is printed. Although this is a trivial example, it illustrates the capability of using string comparisons in an IF command.

The last condition that you can test in an IF command is the existence or nonexistence of a file specification. By using the conditions EXIST or NOT EXIST, you can test for the existence of a file in the default directory of a specified drive. The following portion of a batch file illustrates how you can test for the presence of a required file on a diskette in a specific drive and display an appropriate message if it is not found.

```
:START
PAUSE Insert disk labeled XYZ in drive A
IF EXIST A:JAN91.WKS GOTO DOIT
PAUSE Wrong disk inserted into drive A
GOTO START
:DOIT
REM Program continues
```

SHIFT Command

The SHIFT command enables you to use more than 10 replaceable parameters in a batch file. When included in a batch file, this command changes the order in which the parameters %0 through %9 are replaced. That is, each SHIFT command causes every parameter to be shifted to the left. Because this may sound confusing, clarify the use of this command by creating a batch file that uses the SHIFT command. The contents of the file, named SHOSHIFT.BAT, appear in Listing 6.2.

Listing 6.2 SHOSHIFT.BAT

```
ECHO OFF
ECHO %0 %1 %2 %3 %4 %5 %6 %7 %8 %9
SHIFT
ECHO %0 %1 %2 %3 %4 %5 %6 %7 %8 %9
SHIFT
ECHO %0 %1 %2 %3 %4 %5 %6 %7 %8 %9
```

Next, assume you entered the following command line:

SHOSHIFT A B C D E F G H I J K

which displays:

```
A>ECHO OFF
A B C D E F G H I
B C D E F G H I J
C D E F G H I J K
```

As indicated in this example, you can use the SHIFT command to extend the number of replaceable parameters that can be used in a batch file. Although 10 replaceable parameters are usually sufficient for most applications, for creating complex batch processes the SHIFT command can be extremely useful.

CALL Command

Added with the introduction of DOS 3.3, this batch command enables a second batch file to execute without requiring the first one to terminate. The format of this command is

```
CALL [d:][path]filename
```

The following portion of a batch file named RUN.BAT illustrates the use of the CALL command.

```
IF %1 == LOTUS CALL C:LOTUS
IF %1 == DBASE CALL D:DBASE
REM Program continues
```

By entering the DOS command line **RUN LOTUS**, the file LOTUS on drive C is called. Similarly, entering the DOS command line **CALL DBASE** invokes the batch file named DBASE located on drive D.

Common Uses of Batch Files

This section describes and lists the commands in popular batch files to give you a start. Once you master use of these files, you may want to create more on your own.

The AUTOEXEC.BAT File

The AUTOEXEC.BAT file is a special batch file you can use to automatically execute DOS commands. This special file is searched for by DOS each time your computer is powered-up or a system reset is performed. If this file is located in the root directory of the drive from which DOS is initialized, it is automatically executed.

The primary use of an AUTOEXEC.BAT file is to execute a series of DOS commands that are always initially required for the operation of your computer system. One example of the usefulness of AUTOEXEC.BAT is to display a menu system to facilitate the use of the computer by personnel who are not educated in the DOS commands. Later this chapter presents several menu systems that can be generated through the use of an AUTOEXEC.BAT file. Even if you are using DOS 4.0 or 5.0, you may wish to develop a customized menu system to facilitate the operations of your organization.

Boosting Productivity

Batch files can perform a variety of tasks related to files and subdirectories and can make the interface between the user and the computer much simpler. As an example, instead of issuing separate commands to first change the DOS current directory and then invoke a program such as Lotus 1-2-3, you might simply create a batch file to run 1-2-3. Then, issuing one batch filename would automatically change the directory and execute the desired program.

This section describes the use of batch programs for operations that are normally performed on files and subdirectories. Some of the major topics covered include the development of several format protection schemes, a method to enhance diskette copying operations on systems that have only one diskette drive, and methods to create your own help files, as well as several menu systems to simplify fixed disk usage.

Because you assign the names to your batch files, it is important that your batch files do not duplicate names of DOS commands. It is also crucial not to create two batch files with the same name to perform different functions.

Format Protection Schemes

Because the formatting of a disk destroys any previously recorded data, a mechanism for preventing inadvertent formatting is highly desirable. This section explains two format protection schemes that can be used to satisfy different operational requirements.

If you have a fixed disk system, the FORMAT.EXE file from the DOS distribution diskette was probably copied to the root directory or to a subdirectory named UTILITY or DOS. If another person using the computer is at the C> prompt level and enters the command FORMAT, the resulting action depends on the version of DOS used. Although versions of DOS from 3.0 onward provide a warning, earlier versions of DOS simply initiate the format operation, destroying any data previously recorded on the hard disk. Even when a warning message is displayed, if it is late at night or if you or another user are distracted while performing this operation, it is quite possible that entering the wrong response to a warning message can destroy months or years of effort.

To prevent the inadvertent formatting of the fixed disk you can first rename the FORMAT.EXE file to a less obtrusive name. Because the format process prepares a disk for use, you could rename it as indicated here:

RENAME FORMAT.EXE PREPARE.EXE

Next, you could create a one-line batch file to restrict formatting to drive A. To create this batch file, use the name FORMAT for the file as indicated here:

```
COPY CON: FORMAT.BAT
PREPARE A: %1 %2 %3 %4 %5 %6
```

In this example, entering the command FORMAT invokes the execution of a batch file with that name. This file causes the FORMAT.EXE program that was previously renamed PREPARE.EXE to be executed. Up to six replaceable parameters are passed to the renamed formatting program. This means you can pass six of the eight parameters that can be specified in the FORMAT command. In addition, the drive specifier A: is always passed to the formatting program, restricting the use of the program to formatting diskettes in drive A.

The following illustrates the execution of the previously created batch file and the resulting execution of the renamed FORMAT command:

C>**format**

C>**PREPARE A:**

```
Insert new diskette for drive A:
and strike ENTER when ready
```

Because the previously created one-line batch file executes the command PREPARE, it is displayed on the user's screen. If you feel this may cause confusion, you could prefix the PREPARE command with an ECHO OFF command. The modification of the previously created batch file and its execution is

C>**copy con: format.bat**

```
echo off
prepare a:%1 %2 %3 %4 %5 %6
^Z
     1 File(s) copied
```

C>format

```
C>echo off
Insert new diskette for drive A:
and strike ENTER when ready
```

Considering Device Names

Because many users are familiar with device names, they would probably enter the command FORMAT A: to format a diskette in drive A. If this entry occurs as you use the previously created batch file, the error message Invalid parameter is displayed and the batch program terminates. This happens because the drive specifier A: was previously included in the batch file. To permit additional flexibility in using the FORMAT command, you can rename FORMAT.EXE as PREPARE.EXE and create the batch file listed in Listing 6.3 to execute the renamed FORMAT program.

Listing 6.3 Considering Device Names

```
ECHO OFF
IF %1==A: GOTO OK
IF %1==a: GOTO OK
IF %1==B: GOTO OK
IF %1==b: GOTO OK
ECHO This program only formats diskettes in drive A or B
GOTO END
:OK
```

```
PREPARE %1 %2 %3 %4 %5 %6
:END
```

This second example is more flexible for many users, because it enables formatting to occur on diskettes in drive A or drive B. In this example, lines two through five test the replaceable parameter for the value A, a, B, or b and result in a branch to the label OK if a match occurs. If no match occurs, the message This program only formats diskettes in drive A or B is displayed and a branch to the label END occurs.

Enhancing Single-Drive Copying Operations

Although many computers containing one floppy diskette drive are fine machines, they are not easily used for diskette copying operations. When you need to use the DISKCOPY A: B: command or its near equivalent, COPY A:*.* B:, DOS uses your one physical drive as two logical devices. Due to this, you will be treated to what is known as the "floppy shuffle" as you are alternately prompted to insert source and target diskettes as each file is copied. If you have to duplicate a large number of files on the diskette, you can conceivably spend 20 minutes or more performing the floppy shuffle.

To alleviate the floppy shuffle, you will see how to create a batch file that automatically uses a portion of the capacity of your fixed disk as a second diskette drive. This batch file creates a temporary directory named TEMPCOPY under the root directory and copies all files from the diskette to be copied to that directory. Next, your batch file prompts the user to place a formatted disk in drive A, copies the contents of the TEMPCOPY directory to the diskette in drive A, erase the contents of the temporary directory, and then remove the directory. Listing 6.4 shows the creation of this batch file using the DOS EDLIN text editor program.

Listing 6.4 FASTCOPY.BAT

```
 1: ECHO OFF
 2: ECHO Place Diskette to be copied in Drive A
 3: PAUSE
 4: MD C:\TEMPCOPY
 5: COPY A:*.* C:\TEMPCOPY
 6: ECHO Place target Diskette in Drive A
 7: PAUSE
 8: COPY C:\TEMPCOPY *.*A:
 9: ECHO Enter Y in response to next prompt
10: ERASE C:\TEMPCOPY\*.*
11: RD C:\TEMPCOPY
```

In the batch file listed, line 1 turns the echoing of executed commands off, and line 2 prompts the user to place the diskette to be copied in drive A. The PAUSE command in line 3 displays the prompt Strike a key when ready.... Once a key is pressed, line 4 creates the directory named TEMPCOPY under the root directory.

Copying the contents of the diskette in drive A to the subdirectory TEMPCOPY results from the execution of the COPY command in line 5. Next, the ECHO command in line 6 prompts the computer user to place the diskette in drive A onto which the files will be copied. The PAUSE statement in line 7 again displays the prompt Strike a key when ready... on the screen.

After the files are copied to the diskette, it is assumed that they are of no use on the fixed disk and should be removed. Because the use of the ERASE command with the global asterisk characters for filename and extension generates the DOS message

Are you sure (Y/N)?, line 9 was included in the batch file to prompt the user how to respond to that message. Then, the execution of line 10 erases all files in the directory TEMPCOPY on drive C once the user enters the letter Y in response to the previously described DOS message. Finally, line 11 removes the directory TEMPCOPY from the fixed disk.

The following interactive example illustrates how to execute the FASTCOPY.BAT batch file. In this example, a diskette containing six files was to be copied. Using FASTCOPY instead of the DOS COPY command reduces the number of diskette insertions on a one drive system from 12 to 2, which illustrates the major advantage in using this batch file.

```
C>FASTCOPY

C>ECHO OFF
Place DISKETTE to be copied in Drive A...
Strike a key when ready...
A:AVG.PIC
A:PERF.WKS
A:WK1.PIC
A:WK2.PIC
A:WK3.PIC
A:WK4.PIC
      6 File(s) copied
Place Target Diskette in Drive A...
Strike a key when ready...
C:\TEMPCOPY\AVG.PIC
C:\TEMPCOPY\PERF.WKS
C:\TEMPCOPY\WK1.PIC
C:\TEMPCOPY\WK2.PIC
C:\TEMPCOPY\WK3.PIC
C:\TEMPCOPY\WK4.PIC
      6 File(s) copied
Enter Y in response to next prompt
Are you sure (Y/N)?Y

C>
```

Creating DOS Command HELP Files

If you or your users operate a computer and are not well versed in the use of DOS commands, on-line assistance can be a most helpful feature to provide. In this section you create a batch file named HELP.BAT that enables users to enter the command HELP followed by a DOS command to obtain on-line assistance concerning the use of the specific command.

Although the DOS Shell contains a context-sensitive help facility invoked by pressing the F1 key, this facility has many limitations. As an example, for most DOS commands the help facility will refer you to the DOS manual for information concerning the parameters available for use with a command. By creating your own help files, you may be able to substantially improve the use of your computer, as you will see by developing a comprehensive ERASE help file that provides the computer user with substantially more information concerning the use of the ERASE command than can be obtained using the DOS Shell help facility.

Listing 6.5 shows the creation of the HELP.BAT file.

Listing 6.5 HELP.BAT

```
COPY CON: HELP.BAT
ECHO OFF
IF EXIST %1.HLP GOTO LOCATE
IF "%1==" GOTO HELP
ECHO HELP NOT AVAILABLE FOR %1
GOTO END
:LOCATE
TYPE %1.HLP
GOTO END
:HELP
TYPE HELP.HLP
:END
^Z
```

After turning ECHO off, the IF command checks for the existence of a file whose name is the first replaceable parameter used when you run the program and whose extension is HLP. If the file exists, a branch to the label LOCATE occurs, after which the TYPE command displays the file whose name was entered in the command line when the batch file was initiated and whose extension is HLP.

If the name of the DOS command assigned to the replaceable parameter %1 does not exist with the extension HLP in the current directory, the second IF command will be executed. This IF command is included in the batch file to avoid the need to type HELP HELP in order to display a master HELP file that explains how to obtain help for selected DOS commands. Instead, entering HELP by itself results in the replaceable parameter %1 being assigned a null value of "". Because this value results in a match in the string comparison, a branch to the label HELP occurs. Then, the next line in the batch file displays the HELP.HLP file on the screen. If you plan to have more than one screenful of help on a topic, incorporate the MORE command so that the text doesn't scroll off the screen before it's read.

If you create separate ASCII files that explain the use of such DOS commands as COPY, DIR, FORMAT, and ERASE, you only have to enter the command

HELP *command*

where **command** is a DOS command for which there is an ASCII file explaining the use of the command. Then, the contents of that file are displayed to give on-line assistance.

Listing 6.6 shows how to create the file ERASE.HLP, using the EDLIN text editor contained on the DOS diskette. The file contains text that explains the use of the ERASE command. The following display shows exactly what you'll see on the screen if you enter HELP ERASE to obtain information on the use of the DOS ERASE command.

Listing 6.6 ERASE.HLP

```
1:*The ERASE command is used to erase a file from disk.
2:*
3:*The format of ERASE is
4:*                                      ERASE [d:][path]filename[.ext]
5:*      where:
6:*              [d:]           - disk drive where file is located
7:*              [path]         - directory path to the file
```

```
 8:*                      filename    - name of the file to erase
 9:*                      [.ext]      - filename extension (if present)
10:*
11:*  Examples:
12:*                      ERASE B:\123\GRAPH1.PIC
13:*
14:*                      ERASE SAMPLE.HLP
```

A>**help erase**

A>echo off
The ERASE command is used to erase a file from disk.

The format of ERASE is
                      ERASE [d:][path]filename[.ext]
where:

                      [d:]   - disk drive where file is located
                      [path]   - directory path to the file
                      filename   - name of the file to erase
                      [.ext]   - filename extension (if present)
         Examples:
                      ERASE B:\123\GRAPH1.PIC

                      ERASE SAMPLE.HLP

Expansion to Application Programs

You can also create other ASCII text files with the extension HLP to provide on-line assistance relating to application programs. As an example, assume you have two application programs named BEST and WORST for which you would like to provide users with on-line assistance. You simply create text files with EDLIN named BEST.HLP and WORST.HLP, in the same way in which you created the ERASE.HLP file in Listing 6.6. Then, entering the command HELP BEST (or HELP WORST) causes the HELP.BAT file displaying the contents of BEST.HLP (or WORST.HLP) on the screen.

Master Menus for Fixed Disk Systems

The use of fixed disk systems became much more prevalent after the introduction of the PC AT because of the decreasing cost and increased availability of fixed disk storage devices. Many users today place multiple applications on their fixed disks, resulting in a requirement for an easy way to navigate between applications. You can design a simple batch menu system to assist with this task, or you can create a more complex system that accomplishes a similar function in a more elegant manner. This discussion examines several methods of creating master menus, beginning with a simple method that helps you navigate among directories.

Suppose you have a computer with a large fixed disk and wish to use 1-2-3, dBASE IV, and WordPerfect. A simple menu scheme enables users to choose among each of these applications by simply selecting a letter or number from the menu. An example of this menu is

```
                                        GILBERT'S MAIN MENU
==================================================================
                                        A - LOTUS 123
                                        B - DBASE IV

                                        C - WORDPERFECT

                                        X - Exit MENU System to DOS
```

Enter your selection -

Once this menu is displayed, you (or any other user) can simply type the letter of your choice and press the **Enter** key to use a selected application. To practice this technique, create files named A.BAT, B.BAT, and C.BAT to begin each of the applications and a batch file called X.BAT to provide a means to exit the MENU system and return to the DOS prompt. A file called MENU.BAT will be used to display the menu on the screen and give the user a choice. The MENU.BAT file is shown in Listing 6.7.

Listing 6.7 MENU.BAT

```
1:*echo off
2: cls
3: type menu.txt
4: prompt Enter your selection -
```

Line 1 of MENU.BAT turns off the echo of commands to the screen so you do not see what commands are issued. Line 2 clears the screen, and line 3 places the menu on the screen by typing a file called MENU.TXT. This file is

```
 1:*                                    GILBERT'S MAIN MENU
 2: ================================================================
 3:
 4:                                     A - LOTUS 123
 5:
 6:                                     B - DBASE IV
 7:
 8:                                     C - WORDPERFECT
 9:
10:
11:
12:                                     X - Exit MENU System to DOS
```

Line 4 of the MENU.BAT file changes the DOS prompt from the standard of default disk drive and greater than symbol to the words Enter your selection -. When the menu is placed on the screen, the user is asked to select one of the choices on the menu, as shown:

```
                                        GILBERT'S MAIN MENU
==================================================================
                                        A - LOTUS 123
                                        B - DBASE IV
                                        C - WORDPERFECT

                                        X - Exit MENU System to DOS
```

Enter your selection -

The X.BAT file exits from the menu and returns control to the DOS system. In reality, however, control is still at the DOS level but the prompt has been changed. All the X.BAT file in Listing 6.8 has to do is return the prompt to its standard symbol, the default disk drive and the greater than symbol (>).

Listing 6.8 X.BAT

```
1:*echo off
2: cls
3: prompt $n$g
```

Line 1 simply turns the echo of commands to the screen off. Line 2 clears the screen, and line 3 changes the DOS prompt back to its standard symbol, the default disk drive followed by the greater than symbol.

The A.BAT file invokes 1-2-3. This batch file is illustrated in Listing 6.9.

Listing 6.9 A.BAT

```
1:*echo off
2: cls
3: cd \123
4: lotus
5: cd \
6: menu
```

Line 1 turns the echo of commands to the screen off, and line 2 clears the screen. Then, line 3 uses the DOS Change Directory (CD) command to change the current directory to the subdirectory containing the 1-2-3 software. In this example, it is assumed that 1-2-3 resides in the directory named 123. Next, line 4 executes the 1-2-3 software. When the user exits 1-2-3, DOS executes the next command in the batch file, called LOTUS, resulting in line 5 changing the current directory back to the highest level or root directory. Finally, line 6 issues the MENU command, which executes the MENU.BAT file and places the master menu back onto the screen.

The B.BAT file invokes the dBASE IV program. This batch file appears in Listing 6.10. Notice that it is structured exactly the same as the A.BAT file, except that line 3 changes the current directory to the DBASE subdirectory and line 4 executes the dBASE software. Lines 5 and 6 are used to return to the master menu.

Listing 6.10 B.BAT

```
1:*echo off
2: cls
3: cd \dbase
4: dbase
5: cd \
6: menu
```

The last file required to create the simple menu is the C.BAT file. This file is used to invoke WordPerfect word processing software and is illustrated in Listing 6.11. Note that it is the same as the A.BAT and B.BAT files, except that line 3 changes the current directory to the WORDPERFECT subdirectory while line 4 executes the WordPerfect software.

Listing 6.11 C.BAT

```
1:*echo off
2: cls
```

```
3: cd \wp
4: wp
5: cd \
6: menu
```

Using BASIC

A different method of developing a menu system uses the BASIC interpreter that comes with DOS. You start the interpreter by issuing the command BASIC, or BASICA for the advanced BASIC, or GWBASIC for the BASIC provided with many versions of MS-DOS developed for clones.

Listing 6.12 shows an example of a BASIC program for controlling software selections on Jane's PC. This program has three options from which to select: word processing, spreadsheet, or database applications. The BASIC SHELL command is used to execute a batch program corresponding to the selection made from the menu. When you terminate the word processor, spreadsheet, or database function, control is returned to the BASIC program and the menu is again displayed on the screen. Although we will review the operation of many BASIC statements in this chapter, you should refer to Chapters 8 through 11 for specific information concerning the use of the BASIC programming language.

Listing 6.12 BASIC Language Program for Controlling Software Selection

```
10 REM *******************************************************************
20 REM *
30 REM * Main Menu for JANE's PC
40 REM *
50 REM *******************************************************************
60 CLS
70 PRINT "                          JANE's PC MAIN MENU"
80 PRINT "--------------------------------------------------------------------"
90 PRINT
100 PRINT
110 PRINT "           1 - WORDPROCESSING"
120 PRINT
130 PRINT "           2 - SPREADSHEET"
140 PRINT
150 PRINT "           3 - DATABASE"
160 PRINT
170 PRINT
180 PRINT
190 PRINT
200 INPUT "Enter the NUMBER of your choice... ";N
210 IF N=1 THEN SHELL "C:\BATUTIL\WP.BAT"
220 IF N=2 THEN SHELL "C:\BATUTIL\SS.BAT"
230 IF N=3 THEN SHELL "C:\BATUTIL\DB.BAT"
240 GOTO 60
250 END
```

Lines 10 through 50 are simply remarks within the program using the BASIC REM statement. These lines provide anyone who looks at the program with information the author of the program feels is important. In this example, it's simply a remark that this is the main menu for Jane's PC. Other information could be added, such as the name of the program and the date it was created, as well as the name of the program developer.

Line 60 is the BASIC CLS statement that simply clears the screen on the PC similarly to the DOS CLS command. Lines 70 through 190 use the PRINT command to place the menu on the PC screen. Line 200 uses the INPUT command to obtain a menu selection from the user. The INPUT command first asks the user to enter a number of his or her choice from the menu and waits for the user to enter a number into the variable N. Line 210 checks whether the number entered is a 1 and if so executes the SHELL command to run a batch file named WP.BAT under the BATUTIL subdirectory on the C drive. Lines 220 and 230 work in a manner similar to line 210. That is, they check whether the number entered is a 2 or 3 and execute batch files named SS.BAT and DB.BAT, respectively, on encountering the predefined number. If the user enters anything other than a 1, 2, or 3, the GOTO command at line 240 is executed. This GOTO causes the program to start over at line 60, which first clears the screen and then places the menu back onto the screen. Line 250 is an END command that indicates the end of the program.

Although the DOS ECHO command performs the same general function as the BASIC print statement, BASIC provides greater flexibility for performing the required tasks. As an example, BASIC programming statements enable you to compare keyboard input against predefined values and to then perform branching operations based on the value of the input. In comparison, batch file processing only permits data input in the form of replaceable parameters that are entered when the batch file is executed. Thus, you can easily construct a BASIC program to accept keyboard input to perform different operations, whereas attempting to do the same with batch files can be either extremely difficult or impossible.

A second advantage in the use of BASIC for creating menus is the ease of screen control in that language. With the BASIC COLOR statement you can easily set foreground, background, and border colors, as well as perform highlight and blinking operations. Whereas these operations can also be performed from within batch files, many readers familiar with BASIC will prefer to perform those operations from within that language. Thus, the use of the SHELL command is the key to obtaining the ability of increased menu programming flexibility from within BASIC.

The BASIC SHELL Command

The SHELL command runs a command or batch file from within a BASIC program and is the key to how the menu works properly. In essence, the BASIC program is simply put to "sleep" while the batch file or DOS command is executed. When the batch file is finished with its work or the DOS command is completed, the DOS command EXIT is used to return to the BASIC program, "wake" it up, and allow it to continue operating at the point where it was last running.

Figure 6.1 shows what the BASIC program looks like on the screen when it is executed.

Suppose the program is saved on your hard disk under the name MENU.BAS. To run the program, simply enter the command

BASIC MENU

This causes the BASIC interpreter to start and automatically loads and executes the program MENU.BAS. Of course, the BASIC interpreter must be in your current directory or pointed to by the DOS PATH command, whereas the program MENU.BAS

```
                        JANE's PC MAIN MENU
-----------------------------------------------------------------

              1 - WORDPROCESSING

              2 - SPREADSHEET

              3 - DATABASE



Enter the NUMBER of your choice... ?
```

Figure 6.1   Resulting BASIC Program Display.

must also be in your current directory or in a directory pointed to by the DOS PATH command.

Instead of entering the command yourself, you can set up a system to automatically start this menu by creating an AUTOEXEC.BAT file as shown:

```
1: echo off
2: path = \DOS
3: BASIC MENU
```

This file turns off the echo of commands to the screen in line 1. In line 2, the DOS PATH command sets up search paths to the subdirectory \DOS, which is where the BASIC interpreter is assumed to reside. Then, line 3 executes the BASIC interpreter and the MENU.BAS program.

Listing 6.13 illustrates the contents of the WP.BAT file.

Listing 6.13 WP.BAT File

```
1:*echo off
2: cd \mm
3: mm
4: exit
```

Line 1 turns off echoes of commands to the screen. Line 2 uses the DOS CD command to set the \MM subdirectory as the current directory, and line 3 executes the word processor program. Line 4 is the DOS EXIT command, which is executed when the word processor is finished.

This EXIT command returns control to the BASIC program that called the batch file and is necessary because the SHELL command was used within the program. Similarly, the SS.BAT and DB.BAT files are shown in Listings 6.14 and 6.15. These files operate exactly like the WP.BAT file but use different subdirectories and call a spreadsheet and database, respectively. That is, the SS file changes the directory to 123, whereas the DB file changes the directory to DBASE. Then, each file issues the appropriate command to initiate the program in each subdirectory.

Listing 6.14 SS.BAT File

```
1:*echo off
2: cd \123
```

```
3: lotus
4: exit
```

Listing 6.15 DB.BAT File

```
1:*echo off
2: cd \dbase
3: dbase
4: exit
```

Increasing Menu Functionality

To add additional functionality to the BASIC menu, increase the documentation with REM statements and add an error routine to catch simple errors. Listing 6.16 shows an updated BASIC program that retains the name MENU.BAS.

Listing 6.16 Revised BASIC Program

```
10 REM ***********************************************************
20 REM *
30 REM * Program name:    MENU.BAS
40 REM * Author:          Tom Domore
50 REM * Last update:     December 12, 1990
60 REM *
70 REM * This program is the main menu for JANE's PC
80 REM *
90 REM ***********************************************************
100 CLS
110 PRINT "                      JANE's PC MAIN MENU"
120 PRINT "--------------------------------------------------------------------"
130 PRINT
140 PRINT
150 PRINT "              1 - WORDPROCESSING"
160 PRINT
170 PRINT "              2 - SPREADSHEET"
180 PRINT
190 PRINT "              3 - DATABASE"
200 PRINT
210 PRINT
220 PRINT
230 PRINT "              0 - EXIT...Return to DOS"
240 PRINT
250 PRINT
260 INPUT "Enter the NUMBER of your choice... ";N
270 IF N=0 THEN CLS :SYSTEM
280 IF N=1 THEN SHELL "C:\BATUTIL\WP.BAT"  :GOTO 100
290 IF N=2 THEN SHELL "C:\BATUTIL\SS.BAT"  :GOTO 100
300 IF N=3 THEN SHELL "C:\BATUTIL\DB.BAT"  :GOTO 100
310 PRINT
320 PRINT "*** ERROR ***  -->  You must enter a NUMBER between 0 and 3..."
330 PRINT
340 INPUT "Press <ENTER> or <RETURN> key to try again...";X$
350 GOTO 100
360 END
```

Lines 10 through 90 are all remarks, but this time the program has added information that may be beneficial in a business environment. The program name is MENU.BAS, the author is Tom Domore, and the date the program was last changed was December 12, 1990. This information could be used by someone who later was given the task of changing the menu on all PCs in the company to add additional menu options for such applications as communications or graphics.

Line 100 still clears the screen, and lines 110 through 250 use the PRINT command to put the menu on the screen. Notice that the option 0 - EXIT...Return to DOS was added to the menu. You may have a user who wishes to work at the DOS level and is knowledgeable about PCs. This option offers an easy and "clean" way to safely exit the BASIC MENU program. Line 260 uses the INPUT command to request the user to select from the menu and places the value selected into the variable N. Line 270 is used to check for the selection of 0, indicating that the user wishes to exit to DOS. If the choice is 0, the screen is cleared with the CLS command, and the SYSTEM command returns control to the DOS system. SYSTEM is actually a BASIC command that closes the BASIC program, stops the BASIC interpreter, and turns control back over to the disk operating system.

Lines 280 through 300 each checks for a selection from the menu and, based on the number selected, executes a batch file using the SHELL command. When the batch file is completed, the next command after the SHELL command is executed and, in this case, it is the GOTO 100 command. This returns the program to the clear screen routine and places the menu back on the screen so the user can make another selection. This simple modification to the program now accepts any selection that is not a number 0 through 3 to fall through the program to line 310. Lines 310 through 340 print an error message on the screen telling the user to enter a number between 0 and 3. The INPUT command at line 340 simply allows the program to pause long enough for the user to read the error message before line 350 is executed. Line 350 returns control to line 100, which clears the screen and places the menu back on the screen. An example of the execution of this program is shown in Figure 6.2.

There is still one problem with this program as it is written. What if someone enters a letter or special character and not a number as planned for? In this situation, BASIC

```
                        JANE's PC MAIN MENU
    ------------------------------------------------------------------


              1 - WORDPROCESSING

              2 - SPREADSHEET

              3 - DATABASE



              0 - EXIT...Return to DOS

    Enter the NUMBER of your choice... ? 7

    *** ERROR ***   --)  You must enter a NUMBER between 0 and 3...

    Press <ENTER> or <RETURN> key to try again...?
```

Figure 6.2 Execution of Revised BASIC Program.

is looking for a numeric value (or number) for the variable N in line 260, and any character other than a numeric value triggers a BASIC error that displays a question mark and prompts the user to Redo from start, meaning to enter the number again. This message is not very meaningful to someone who is not familiar with computers and the BASIC programming language, raising the potential of a degree of user confusion if it is displayed. Figure 6.3 illustrates the program's response to a user entering **QUIT** instead of 0 for EXIT. Note that the ?Redo from start message generated by the BASIC interpreter is followed by the program displaying the Enter the NUMBER of your choice...? message a second time. To the novice user, is this a request to start all over or should the user simply enter a number?

To eliminate the potential confusion, you should eliminate the possibility of the error message being generated. Change line 260 of the program to accept any character, whether numeric or alphabetic, using a string variable N$ in the statement. Then, if a string variable is used, lines 270 through 300 of the program must be modified to check for the numbers 0 through 3 in the form of string values. The changes to lines 260 through 300 of the program previously listed in Listing 6.15 are

```
260 INPUT "Enter the NUMBER of your choice...";N$
270 IF N$="0" THEN CLS :SYSTEM
280 IF N$="1" THEN SHELL "C:\BATUTIL\WP.BAT" :GOTO 100
290 IF N$="2" THEN SHELL "C:\BATUTIL\SS.BAT" :GOTO 100
300 IF N$="3" THEN SHELL "C:\BATUTIL\DB.BAT" :GOTO 100
```

As a result of the modification of the program to accept keyboard input as strings, let us again execute the program and enter invalid data. Figure 6.4 illustrates the execution of the BASIC program designed to accept string data. Note that the improper keyboard entry of QUIT does not result in the generation of the BASIC ?Redo from start error message. Because N$ does not equal the string 1, 2, or 3, the error message at line 320 in the program is executed. Then, once the user presses the **Enter** key the program branches to line 100, clears the screen, and redisplays the menu.

Strictly BATCH

Now try creating a menu of strictly batch files and placing this menu and all associated batch files in a subdirectory called \BATUTIL. Once this is accomplished, you can

```
                          JANE's PC MAIN MENU
-------------------------------------------------------------------------


        1 - WORDPROCESSING

        2 - SPREADSHEET

        3 - DATABASE



        0 - EXIT...Return to DOS

Enter the NUMBER of your choice... ? QUIT
?Redo from start
Enter the NUMBER of your choice... ?
```

Figure 6.3   BASIC Language-Generated Error Message.

```
                        JANE's PC MAIN MENU
-------------------------------------------------------------------

              1 - WORDPROCESSING

              2 - SPREADSHEET

              3 - DATABASE


              0 - EXIT...Return to DOS

Enter the NUMBER of your choice... ? QUIT

*** ERROR ***  --)  You must enter a NUMBER between 0 and 3...

Press <ENTER> or <RETURN> key to try again...?
```

Figure 6.4   Execution of BASIC Program That Accepts String Data.

execute this menu with the change directory (CD) command to the \BATUTIL sub-directory and entering the command MAINMENU to run the MAINMENU.BAT file. You can also create a batch file called MENU.BAT that simply runs the MAIN-MENU.BAT file by including the one line command MAINMENU in that file. Another method to get the menu to appear automatically on the screen is to create an AUTO-EXEC.BAT file in the root directory that automatically changes to the \BATUTIL directory and executes the MAINMENU.BAT file. An example of an AUTOEXEC.BAT file that performs the previously described operations whenever the computer is powered up or a system reset is performed is shown in Listing 6.17.

Listing 6.17 AUTOEXEC.BAT File

```
1: echo off
2: cls
3: path = \DOS;\BATUTIL
4: cd \batutil
5: MAINMENU
```

This AUTOEXEC.BAT file turns off the echo of commands to the screen in line 1. Line 2 clears the screen and line 3 sets the DOS search paths for commands and files to first look at the \DOS subdirectory and then look at the \BATUTIL subdirectory. Line 4 changes the current directory to the \BATUTIL subdirectory, and line 5 executes the MENU.BAT file to place the menu on the screen.

Listing 6.18 shows the contents of the MAINMENU.BAT file.

Listing 6.18 MAINMENU.BAT File

```
1:*echo off
2: cls
3: type mainmenu.txt
4: prompt Enter your selection please. . . .
```

Lines 1 and 2 turn echo of commands off and clear the screen, respectively. Line 3 types out a file called MAINMENU.TXT that contains the text that forms the menu. Line 4 changes the DOS prompt from the standard A> (C> on a hard disk) to the words Enter your selection please.... Now, whenever the menu is displayed the user will see the Enter your selection... prompt instead of the C> prompt. Using the DOS PROMPT command to change the prompt has made the menu much more meaningful and easy for a novice to use. An experienced user will quickly recognize that the computer is still at DOS level and only the prompt has been changed. Any DOS command can still be given at this prompt.

Listing 6.19 shows the contents of the MAINMENU.TXT file, which in this example contains a menu for Tom. Notice that six options with numbers are available for use and an option for U for Utilities or 0 to exit to DOS can be chosen. Each of the options 1 through 6 is similar to the previous example of batch menus where the entry of a numeric results in batch files called 1.BAT, 2.BAT, 3.BAT, and so on, being invoked.

Listing 6.19 Text File MAINMENU.TXT

```
 1:*
 2:                          MAIN MENU FOR TOM
 3: =====================================================================
 4:
 5:
 6:     1 - SPREADSHEET                    U - Utilities
 7:
 8:     2 - WORD PROCESSING
 9:
10:     3 - DATABASE
11:
12:     4 - PROFS
13:
14:     5 - HARVARD GRAPHICS
15:
16:     6 - PAGEMAKER                      0 - Return to DOS
17:
18:
```

Listing 6.20 shows the 1.BAT file.

Listing 6.20 1.BAT File

```
1:*echo off
2: cls
3: cd \123
4: lotus
5: cls
6: cd \batutil
7: type mainmenu.txt
```

Here, lines 5, 6, and 7 are used to clear the screen and return to the main menu after the selected spreadsheet software is exited. Similarly, files 2.BAT through 6.BAT can be constructed, the only differences among them being in the location where the change of directory occurs (line 3) and in the command used to invoke the application program (line 4). But what about this option 0, which supposedly enables you to return to DOS? Listing 6.21 shows the O.BAT file.

Listing 6.21 O.BAT File

```
1:*echo off
2: cls
```

```
3: echo... Returning to DOS....
4: cd \
5: prompt $n$g
```

Lines 1 and 2 simply turn echo of the following commands to the screen off and clear the screen. Line 3 tells the user that the system is returning to DOS control, and line 4 changes the current directory to the root directory. Line 5 again uses the DOS PROMPT command to change the prompt back to the current disk drive and the greater than symbol (C> in this case). Remember that you changed the prompt in MAIN-MENU.BAT and this simply changes the prompt back to its original value.

Listing 6.22 shows the U.BAT file, which brings up a Utility menu. Lines 1 and 2 simply turn off the echo of commands and clear the screen, and line 3 places the UTIL.TXT file, which contains the Utility menu, on the screen. The prompt has not been changed since MAINMENU.BAT, and you are still asked to Enter your selection please...

Listing 6.22 U.BAT File

```
1:*echo off
2: cls
3: type util.txt
```

Listing 6.23 shows the contents of the UTIL.TXT file used to create a utility menu. Note that each of the utilities in this menu uses letters for its execution. This is because these batch files are M.BAT, D.BAT, S.BAT, and so on. These are not explained here, but using the concepts provided in this book you could easily generate your own utility batch files for this menu. Then, to return to the MAINMENU.BAT file you would create a two-line R.BAT file whose contents would be ECHO OFF followed by MAINMENU on the second line.

Listing 6.23 UTIL.TXT File

```
 1:*
 2:                              UTILITY MENU
 3: ================================================================
 4:
 5:
 6:    M - Move files
 7:
 8:    D - Display file
 9:
10:    S - Sort Directory
11:
12:    P - Printer Control
13:
14:    L - Label generation
15:
16:    F - File locater                  R - Return to MAIN MENU
17:
18:
```

The Configuration File

The configuration file is a special type of batch file designed to hold commands to configure your computer system. This batch file must be given the name CONFIG.SYS and can be created in the same manner as other batch files. That is, the CONFIG.SYS file can be created by the use of EDIT or EDLIN, a word processor capable of creating ASCII files, or by using the DOS COPY command as shown here.

COPY CON: CONFIG.SYS

Similar to terminating input to any batch file when you are copying data from the console, you must press the F6 key or simultaneously press Ctrl+Z to terminate keyboard input to the CONFIG.SYS file.

Once you create a CONFIG.SYS file its execution will receive priority over all other files with the exception of the three system files—IBMBIO, IBMDOS, and COM-MAND.COM—when you are using PC-DOS and equivalent files when you are using MS-DOS. This priority of execution includes any AUTOEXEC.BAT file that may reside on your disk, because the commands contained in the CONFIG.SYS file can govern the operation of commands in the AUTOEXEC.BAT file. Figure 6.5 illustrates the relationship between the execution of the CONFIG.SYS file and an AUTOEXEC.BAT file with respect to the tasks performed by DOS during its initialization process. As indicated in this figure, each time you power-up your computer or perform a system reset, DOS searches the root directory of the drive it was initiated from for the file CONFIG.SYS. Then, if found, the file is executed.

Use of CONFIG.SYS

Commands that can be placed in the CONFIG.SYS file can be used to specify a country date and time format, specify the maximum number of drives that can be open at one time, specify a file or files that contain device drivers, and set other configuration-related parameters, such as whether DOS should check for Ctrl+Break. When shipped in the United States, DOS 3.3 normally contains a one-statement configuration file as illustrated.

C>TYPE CONFIG.SYS

```
COUNTRY=001
```

Here, the statement COUNTRY=001 specifies the time and date format for the United States. This can be easily altered by changing the country code to another three-digit code supported by DOS.

As under DOS 4.0, if you used the INSTALL program to place DOS on a fixed disk, your configuration file will appear similar to

```
BREAK=ON
BUFFERS=20
FILES=8
LASTDRIVE=E
SHELL=C:\DOS\COMMAND.COM /P /E:256
DEVICE=C: \DOS\ANSI.SYS
INSTALL=C:\DOS\FASTOPEN.EXE C:=(50,25)
```

The BREAK=ON statement results in DOS checking for the Ctrl+Break key sequence whenever the statement is entered. Otherwise, DOS only checks for it when I/O operations are performed. The BUFFERS=20 statement causes DOS to allocate 20 disk buffers in memory when it starts, whereas the FILES=8 statement permits up to 8 files to be open at the same time.

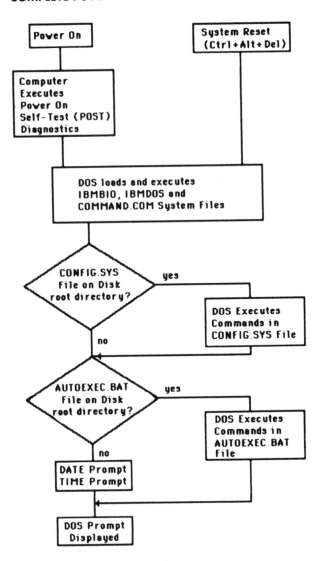

Figure 6.5   DOS Initialization Process.

The LASTDRIVE=E sets the maximum number of drives you may access to five, including virtual disks created in memory. By changing this statement you can increase the maximum number of drives you can access to 16.

The SHELL=C:\DOS\COMMAND.COM statement loads and starts the DOS command processor, COMMAND.COM, located in the DOS subdirectory on drive C. The /P parameter installs COMMAND.COM as a permanent command processor, whereas the /E:256 optional parameter specifies an environment size of 256 bytes. This is the location where DOS keeps track of the path or paths to search for commands not found in the current directory, the path DOS should use to reload the command processor when necessary, and other key information. You can display the current environment setting by entering the DOS SET command without parameters.

The DEVICE=C:\DOS\ANSI.SYS statement causes the ANSI.SYS file located in the DOS directory on drive C to be installed. The ANSI.SYS file contains an enhanced standard input and standard output device driver that replaces IBM's standard I/O support. ANSI is an acronym for the American National Standards Institute, and the use of ANSI.SYS provides a standard method of support for programming that performs such functions as reassigning the keyboard key, manipulating the cursor, and displaying color attributes.

The last statement in the CONFIG.SYS file normally created by the DOS 4.0 IN-STALL program causes the FASTOPEN.EXE file to be installed when DOS is initialized. This program enables your computer to retrieve recently opened files faster than in earlier versions of DOS by storing file information in memory. The statement contained in the CONFIG.SYS file allocates 50 directory or file entry buffers in memory and 25 continuous space buffers for the files on drive C.

Configuration Commands

This section examines the operation and utilization of seven commonly used configuration file commands. Each of these commands can be included by itself or with any other configuration commands in a CONFIG.SYS file.

BREAK Command

The BREAK command enables or disables DOS checking for Ctrl+Break. If this command is not included in the CONFIG.SYS file, a default value of BREAK=OFF is assumed. The format of this command is

$$\text{BREAK=} \left[\left\{ \begin{matrix} \text{ON} \\ \text{OFF} \end{matrix} \right\} \right]$$

With BREAK=OFF, DOS checks for Ctrl+Break only during keyboard, printer, and asynchronous communications operations.

BUFFERS Command

The BUFFERS command tells your computer how much RAM to reserve for data buffers. DOS allocates up to 99 buffers, which are temporary storage areas of 512 bytes used as intermediate storage when data is accessed from disk. When requested to retrieve disk data, DOS sequentially examines the contents of each buffer until it finds the requested data. If it is not found, DOS performs a disk read, causing sectors on a track to be read into disk buffer storage and a search of the buffer contents to be repeated.

As a good rule of thumb, you should have at least one buffer for every open file. In actuality, the computation of an optimum number of buffers is almost impossible, because different application programs specify different BUFFER requirements. Normally, you should set the BUFFER=XX command in your CONFIG.SYS file to the maximum value required by the application program you use most frequently. If you do not include a BUFFERS command in your CONFIG.SYS file, DOS uses a default of 15.

The format of the BUFFERS configuration command under DOS 3.3 is

BUFFERS=m

where *m* is a number between 1 and 99. Although it is difficult to set an optimum number of BUFFERS, for most applications a value set equal to the highest requirement of your set of application programs will suffice. Under DOS 4.0, BUFFERS can be set to 1 through 10,000, if expanded memory is available. In addition, BUFFERS now supports *look-ahead buffers,* which is the term used to represent the number of sectors your computer can read in advance of processing any input operation. Under DOS 4.0 the format of the BUFFERS command is

BUFFERS=*m*, *n*

where *n* is the number of look-ahead buffers that can be set from 1 through 8.

Under DOS 5.0, the BUFFERS command has the same format as under DOS 4.0. However, the parameters *m* and *n* and their possible values are now a mixture of DOS 3.3 and DOS 4.0. That is, *m* specifies the number of disk buffers and must be in the range 1–99, while *n* specifies the number of buffers in a secondary buffer cache and must be in the range of 1–8.

Under DOS 5.0 the secondary cache is used to store the contents of files currently being used by programs. When a program requests a portion of a file stored on disk, DOS provides the program with the requested information and then stores the next portion of the file in a secondary buffer cache, if the cache is available.

COUNTRY Command

As previously mentioned, the COUNTRY configuration command sets the date and time format of your computer. In addition, this command automatically sets the currency symbol and decimal separator for a country based on the three-digit country code specified in the command.

The format of the COUNTRY configuration command under DOS 3.3 is

COUNTRY=*XXX*

where *XXX* is a three-digit international country code for the telephone system of the country. Table 6.2 lists the country codes currently supported by DOS.

Under DOS 4.0 the COUNTRY configuration command was expanded to support the code page of the desired country. The *code page* is a table that translates numeric information stored in your computer into the letters, symbols, and characters used in a particular language. The code page can be specified in COUNTRY configuration command by following the three-digit international country code by a comma and then entering the code page in the statement.

Table 6.2
DOS 3.3 Supported
Country Codes

Country	Country Code	Country	Country Code
Australia	061	Middle East	785
Belgium	032	Netherlands	031
Canadian-French	002	Norway	047
Denmark	045	Portugal	351
Finland	358	Spain	034
France	033	Sweden	046
Germany	049	Switzerland	041
Italy	039	United Kingdom	044
Israel	972	United States	001

Table 6.3 lists the country codes and code pages supported by DOS 4.0. Refer to the DOS 4.0 and DOS 5.0 manuals for specific information on how you can switch among several pairs of code pages.

DEVICE Command

With the DEVICE configuration command you can specify the name of a file containing a device driver. Before the DEVICE statement became available, you normally had to separately load a COM program to support special hardware to include mice and scanners, as well as virtual disks and other nonstandard devices. With the support of a DEVICE statement, you can now tell the system which files to load and where they are located. This capability enables device drivers to be automatically invoked to coordinate the activities of DOS and nonstandard hardware. The format of this command is

```
DEVICE=[d:][path]filename[.ext]
```

Device drivers included on the DOS 3.3 diskette are ANSI.SYS, DRIVER.SYS, and VDISK.SYS. ANSI.SYS, as previously discussed, is an enhanced standard input and output device driver. DRIVER.SYS is a block device driver that permits disks to be referenced to a logical letter, and VDISK.SYS is a virtual disk device driver. Of the three device drivers supplied on DOS 3.3, VDISK.SYS is probably most popular, because it enables you to reserve a portion of RAM to be used as if it were a disk drive. Because a RAM disk provides far faster file access or data transfer than an electromechanical

Table 6.3
DOS 4.0 Supported Country Codes and Code Pages

Country	Country Code	Code Pages Supported
Arabic-speaking	785	864,[1] 850
Australia	061	437, 850
Belgium	032	850, 437
Canada (French-speaking)	002	863, 850
Denmark	045	850, 865
Finland	358	850, 437
France	033	437, 850
Germany	049	437, 850
Hebrew-speaking	972	862,[1] 850
Italy	039	437, 850
Japan	081	932,[1] 437
Korea	082	934,[2] 437
Latin America	003	437, 850
Netherlands	031	437, 850
Norway	047	850, 865
Portugal	351	850, 860
Simplified Chinese	086	936,[2] 437
Spain	034	437, 850
Sweden	046	437, 850
Switzerland	041	850, 437
Traditional Chinese	088	938,[2] 437
United Kingdom	044	437, 850
United States	001	437, 850

Notes:
[1] This code page is supported only with a country supplement.
[2] This code page is supported only with the Asian version of DOS 4.0 on Asian hardware.

diskette or fixed disk, its use can be highly advantageous for programs that require numerous I/O operations.

Under DOS 4.0 the device drivers DISPLAY.SYS, DRIVER.SYS, and PRINTER.SYS were added. DISPLAY.SYS enables you to use code page switching on EGA displays and on the IBM PC Convertible LCD display. DRIVER.SYS allows DOS to assign a logical drive letter to any internal or external diskette drives you might add to your system. The third device driver added to DOS 4.0, PRINTER.SYS, enables you to use code page switching on some IBM ProPrinters and the IBM Quietwriter III printer.

DOS 5.0 has added several additional device drivers, including EGA.SYS, EMM386.EXE, HIMEM.SYS, RAMDRIVE.SYS, SETVER.EXE, and SMARTDRV.SYS. EGA.SYS is used to save and restore an EGA screen with the DOS 5.0 Task Swapper on a computer using an EGA monitor. EMM386.EXE uses extended memory to simulate expanded memory for programs that can use expanded memory. RAMDRIVE.SYS is the DOS 5.0 version of VDISK; SETVER.EXE is used to load the DOS version table into memory. This table lists the names of programs and the number of the DOS version with which each program is designed to execute.

Once the SETVER.EXE device drive is initiated, you can use the SETVER command (which is new to DOS 5.0) to display or modify the version table.

The last new device driver, SMARTDVR.SYS, is used to create a disk cache in extended or expanded memory. To illustrate the use of a device driver, take a moment to examine the use of VDISK.SYS.

To set up a virtual disk, you insert the DEVICE statement in your configuration file with the following format:

```
DEVICE=[d:][path]VDISK.SYS[size][sector][entries]
```

The optional drive letter and path denote the location where the VDISK.SYS file resides; size specifies the virtual disk size in K bytes, with 64K bytes used as a default value; sector is the sector size in bytes, with allowable sizes 128, 256, and 512, with a default value of 128; entries specifies the number of directory entries (files) that the virtual disk can contain. The range of the entries parameter is 2 to 512, with its default value being 64.

As an example of the use of the DEVICE configuration command, assume you want to set up a virtual disk of 360K bytes of RAM with a sector size of 512 bytes that can contain up to 64 files. To set this up, you enter the following statement in your configuration, assuming that the VDISK.SYS file resides in the root directory of the drive containing DOS. If the VDISK.SYS file is located on a different disk or directory, you must prefix its name with a drive designator and path to denote its location.

```
DEVICE=VDISK.SYS 360 512 64
```

Assuming you wish to set the time and date format to be used by DOS to that used for the United States and automatically create a virtual disk, you can use the COPY command to create a two-line CONFIG.SYS file. Its contents are

```
C>COPY CON: CONFIG.SYS
COUNTRY=001
DEVICE1=VDISK.SYS 360 512 64
^Z

        1 File(s) copied
C>
```

Note that similar to a batch file, the entry of data to the CONFIG.SYS file is terminated by pressing either the F6 key or the Ctrl+Z multikey combination.

Now that you created or modified an existing CONFIG.SYS file, you must reboot your system to execute the commands contained in that file. Thus, when you power up your computer the next time or if you perform a system reset operation, the following message will be displayed, indicating that 360K bytes of memory were allocated to a virtual disk that was provided the drive designator D.

```
VDISK Version X.0 virtual disk D:
      Buffer size:          360 KB
      Sector size:          512
Directory entries:    64

Current date is Sun 11-11-1988
Enter new date (mm-dd-yy):
```

Note that the virtual disk drive designator is based on the first unused disk on your system. Thus, if you already have two diskette drives called A and B, the virtual disk is designated C. Similarly, if you have drives A, B, and C, the virtual disk is designated D. DOS automatically supports up to five drives, through drive designator E. If you require the use of more than five drives, use the LASTDRIVE configuration command in the CONFIG.SYS file.

FILES Command

The FILES configuration command specifies the maximum number of files that an application program can have open at one time. The format of this command is

```
FILES=XXX
```

where *XXX* can have a value between 5 and 255. If the command is not included in a CONFIG.SYS file, a default value of 8 is used by DOS.

When DOS is initiated, it automatically opens five files—standard input, standard output, standard error, standard printer, and standard auxiliary device for each process. Thus, a default value of 8 is normally sufficient for most application programs. However, if your application program should return an error message indicating an insufficient number of files, you can use the FILES= configuration command to increase the maximum number of open files supported by DOS. To avoid an error message and having to change your configuration file, you should set FILES= to the maximum number of open files required by the application programs you use.

LASTDRIVE Command

The LASTDRIVE configuration command increases the maximum number of disk drives DOS will support. With this command you can add support for logical drives whose numbers exceed the number of physical drives installed in your system.

DOS permits the use of five disk drive names, A through E, in its default mode of operation. In order to have DOS recognize as valid a disk drive letter beyond E, include the LASTDRIVE command in your CONFIG.SYS file. The format of this command is

```
LASTDRIVE=letter
```

where the *letter* represents the last valid disk drive you want to be able to use on your system. Any letter up to Z is permitted, permitting DOS to support up to 26 "disks" on your computer.

SHELL Command

The SHELL configuration command specifies any executable program to be loaded as a top-level shell processor. The top-level shell is a resulting user interface between the two system files, IBMBIO and IBMDOS, and an executing application. Normally this interface is COMMAND.COM, which is the DOS default shell.

The format of the SHELL command is

```
SHELL=[d:][path]COMMAND[.COM][d:][path][/C][/P][/D][E:n][/F]
```

The device identifier and path indicate where the initial copy of COMMAND.COM is located. The second drive and path are optional and are used to specify where COMMAND.COM should look when it needs to reload itself. If this location is not specified, COMMAND.COM reloads itself from the location where the initial copy of the program resides. This reloading is necessary because COMMAND.COM was designed to split itself into a resident and a transient partition to provide more memory for the execution of application programs. This enables large programs to overwrite the transient portion of COMMAND.COM, which is located in high memory. Then, after the program is terminated, the resident portion of COMMAND.COM attempts to reload the transient portion from its old location or another location specified in the SHELL statement. This also explains why, as an example, you may see the message Insert disk with COMMAND.COM in drive X displayed after an application program is terminated.

The /C (Command) parameter is used to cause a newly loaded COMMAND.COM to perform a specified internal command or to load and execute the program following the letter. The /P parameter tells COMMAND.COM it should make itself permanent. In addition, it also tells COMMAND.COM to locate, load, and execute your computer's AUTOEXEC.BAT file. The /D parameter, when used with the /P parameter, disables the automatic execution of the AUTOEXEC.BAT file when COMMAND.COM becomes permanent.

The /E parameter specifies the size in bytes to allocate to the environment. You can specify a range of numbers (n) from 160 to 32,768 (32K) bytes, with the default being 160 bytes.

The /F option causes the error handling code in COMMAND.COM to automatically fail any error. Thus, even though the familiar Abort, Retry, Ignore message will still be displayed, you do not have to enter any response to continue operations. This option should be used if you are operating your computer via remote communications. Then, if you accidentally caused a critical error, you could continue operations without having to go to your computer to enter a keyboard reply to a critical error.

7 // Advanced DOS

This chapter describes many of the advanced features of the disk operating system. Features covered in this chapter include I/O redirection, which encompasses the use of pipes and filters; file backup and restoration; and the DOS environment.

I/O Redirection

To understand the principle behind I/O redirection, a short review of standard computer I/O operations is warranted. This information provides a basis for understanding the principles of I/O redirection.

In the normal or default state of operation of your computer, the operating system expects to receive input from the keyboard while output is directed to the video display. These two devices—keyboard and video display—are also known as DOS's standard I/O devices. Unless specified otherwise, DOS commands result in standard I/O operations. Thus, a directory listing normally is displayed on your screen, whereas the command DIR that results in the display is normally input from your keyboard. Although standard I/O is the default method by which I/O is serviced and will suffice for most applications, on occasion you will want to redirect I/O operations. To accomplish this, you can use the greater than (>) and less than (<) characters in a DOS command line.

Input Redirection

To specify input redirection, use the less than symbol (<) between a command and a reserved name or file specification. Thus, the format for input redirection is

$$\text{DOS } \textit{COMMAND} < \begin{Bmatrix} \textit{reserved name} \\ \textit{file specification} \end{Bmatrix}$$

where the braces indicate that a choice of one of the enclosed items is to be made.

One of the more common uses of input redirection is to change the execution requirements of programs. As an example of this, consider a program named PAYROLL whose execution normally requires the computer user to sit at the terminal and type a series of keyboard entries when the program executes. Using input redirection, you can first use the EDIT or EDLIN text editor included on the DOS diskette or a word processor to create an ASCII file containing the keyboard entries required to execute the program. Assuming that the name of the file containing the keyboard entries is JAN88.DAT, the command

PAYROLL<JAN88.DAT

causes the PAYROLL program to execute with input to the program occurring from the file named JAN88.DAT.

One of the major advantages of input redirection is its automation of program execution. A secondary advantage that may be just as important with respect to productivity is the ability to store program input data in files. Then, if there are minor changes to the input data between successive program executions, a word processor or text editor can expedite making the required changes.

Output Redirection

Output redirection is similar to input redirection in that both can be used with reserved names or file specifications. The format of output redirection is

$$\text{DOS } \textit{COMMAND} \left\{ \begin{matrix} > \\ >> \end{matrix} \right\} \left\{ \begin{matrix} \textit{reserved name} \\ \textit{file specification} \end{matrix} \right\}$$

When output is redirected to a file, DOS first checks whether the file exists. If it does, DOS overwrites the existing file with the output *unless* two greater than symbols (>>) are included in the output redirection. In this case, DOS appends the requested output to the end of a previously created file. If the file does not exist, DOS creates and automatically saves the requested file.

To understand the benefits of output redirection, consider the following DOS command line:

DIR>LPT1:

When this command line is executed, DOS routes the directory listing to the first parallel printer port, providing a mechanism to automatically obtain a hard copy of the directory.

Returning to the PAYROLL program discussed under input redirection, suppose the output of the program directed to the screen contains successful or error messages for five modules. In addition, assume that the messages scroll off the screen as the next module executes. Because the creation and use of an input file to respond to the program's prompts might still require the computer operator to read each screen, the operation is not really automated. In this instance, you might consider combining input and output redirection, as shown in this command:

PAYROLL<JAN88.DAT>SCREEN.PIC

In this example the payroll program receives input from the file JAN88.DAT and sends screen output to the file SCREEN.PIC. Later, the operator can use the DOS TYPE command to examine the screen information previously generated by the program.

Pipes and Filters

Piping enables you to chain DOS commands and programs with the automatic redirection of standard I/O, permitting the screen output of one command to be used as the keyboard input to another command or program.

The special symbol ($\vdots$) denotes a pipe and serves as a delimiter between the output of one command and the input to the second command. The second command, which accepts data from a standard input device, modifies the data and then outputs the results to a standard output device, is commonly known as a *filter*. Currently, DOS includes three filter commands—SORT, MORE, and FIND.

SORT (External) Command

The SORT command reads data from a specified input device, sorts the data, and then writes it to the standard or a specified output device. The format of this command is:

```
[d:][path]SORT[/R][/+n]
```

Here the optional /R switch causes the sort to be performed in reverse order, whereas the /+n switch causes the sort to start with column n. If the second option is not specified, the sort or reverse sort starts in column 1.

The format of the piping of standard I/O is

$$
\text{DOS } \textit{COMMAND} \mid \text{DOS } \textit{COMMAND} \left\{ \begin{matrix} > \\ >> \\ < \end{matrix} \right\} \left[\begin{matrix} \textit{reserved name} \\ \textit{file specification} \end{matrix} \right]
$$

As an example of piping using the SORT command, consider the following command line entry.

```
DIR C: ¦ SORT>LPT1:
```

In this example the video output that normally results from the directory (DIR) command is first piped into the SORT command, which sorts the directory and then directs the output of the sorted directory to the first parallel printer port.

MORE (External) Command

The MORE command is a filter that displays one screen of 24 lines of data and the message -More-, then pauses. By pressing any key you can display the next screenful of data. The format of this command is

```
[d:][path]MORE
```

As an example of the use of the MORE filter, consider the following command line entry:

SORT/R<MEMO.DAT ¦ MORE

The preceding command line causes the file MEMO.DAT to be sorted in reverse order and then displayed one screen at a time. Note that the SORT command sorts data according to the ASCII values of the characters it encounters. This means that when you use MORE with a data file, the file must be in ASCII format. In addition, because uppercase letters have a lower ASCII value than lowercase letters, the results of a sort operation can be unexpected. For example, PREPARATION will appear before Parameter. For this reason, good sort utilities (which the DOS SORT command is *not*) internally convert the sort keys to a single case before comparing them, so that the sorted output is in proper alphabetical order. SORT is also slower than a sick tortoise—don't try to sort more than 50 items with it unless your patience is infinite!

FIND (External) Command

The third filter in DOS is the FIND command. This command can be used to search an ASCII file for the occurrence or nonoccurrence of a string included in the command. The format of the command is

```
FIND[/V][/C][/N]"string"[file specification]
```

The /V switch causes FIND to display all lines that do *not* contain the specified string. The /C switch causes FIND to count the number of lines that contain the specified string, whereas the /N option causes the command to include the line number for each displayed line.

The FIND command provides a valuable mechanism for constructing a sequence of commands to perform database-related operations. To better understand the utility of this command, assume you have an ASCII file named PHONE.DAT whose record format is illustrated in Figure 7.1.

Suppose the file was created and is maintained with the aid of a word processing program at a central office within an organization. Other persons in the organization might be interested in obtaining a telephone directory of persons in their department. To do this, they would use the FIND filter to locate all records in the file that contain the string associated with their department code. If the department code of interest is A106, all the records containing that string could be printed using the following command line.

```
FIND "A106" PHONE.DAT>LPT1:
```

If for some reason you desired a directory listing based on the department code for the entire organization, you could use the SORT command with the FIND command in one line to print it. Because the department code commences in column 37 of each record, you must signify this in the SORT command using the /+n option, with n assigned the value 37. Thus, you could use the FIND and SORT commands, piping the output of FIND to SORT and directing the output of the SORT command to the printer, as shown here:

FIND "A106" PHONE.DAT | SORT/+137>LPT1:

Pipe and Filter Applications

To better understand the use of pipes and filters you can experiment with batch files that sort directories in several different ways, including devising a menu system to provide the user with several types of directory listings. These examples are followed by the creation of a batch file that can be used to rapidly locate files on a hierarchical directory structure.

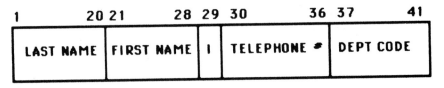

Figure 7.1   Telephone Record Format.

Sorting a Directory

The first application for batch files demonstrates how you can create batch files that use the filename, filename extension, file size, and menus to sort filenames within a directory.

Using the Filename

You can use the SORT command to sort the filenames in the directory of your choice, but you must pass information about the filenames to the command. This can be accomplished by passing the DIR command to the SORT command using the piping feature built into DOS. The following command sorts all files on the B drive in order by filename.

DIR B: ¦ SORT

Assuming the initial directory is as shown in Figure 7.2, after the directory is sorted using the command DIR B: ¦ SORT, it would appear in alphabetical order, as indicated in Figure 7.3.

Because the default output from this command is to the screen display, you can see the sorted directory of drive B on the display. If you want to save this sorted directory, you could simply send the output of the SORT command to a file using the piping facilities of DOS:

DIR B: ¦ SORT >B:SORTDIR.TXT

This command would place the sorted directory listing of drive B into a file called SORTDIR.TXT. You could then display this file at any time with the TYPE command and get a sorted listing of all files on drive B. As an alternative, you could include the line TYPE B:SORT ¦ DIR.TXT in a batch file to display the results of the sort automatically.

To print the sorted directory, you could again use the SORT command with the piping facilities to send the output to the standard printer device PRN:

DIR B: ¦ SORT >PRN

```
A>dir b:

 Volume in drive B has no label
 Directory of  B:\

NOTEUSERS DIC       14   1-04-80   1:03p
JUNK             216    8-23-87   3:48p
TEMP      BAT      37  11-05-87   9:15p
FILE3     TXT     222  10-25-87   4:09p
GOODSTUF  DOC     263  10-25-87   4:21p
SAMPLE    XYZ      14   1-04-80   1:03p
         6 File(s)   723968 bytes free

A>
```

Figure 7.2   Initial Directory Listing.

```
A>dir b: ¦ sort



        6 Files(s)   723968 bytes free
Directory of B:\
Volume in drive B has no label
FILE3    TXT    222  10-25-87   4:09p
GOODSTUF DOC    263  10-25-87   4:21p
JUNK            216   8-23-87   3:48p
NOTEUSRS DIC     14   1-04-80   1:03p
SAMPLE   XYZ     14   1-04-80   1:03p
TEMP     BAT     37  11-05-87   9:15p


A>
```

Figure 7.3   *Directory Sorted by Filename.*

This SORT command sends a sorted listing of the directory of drive B to the current standard printer, creating a screen dump of the alphabetically listed directory contents.

Using the Filename Extension

Suppose you want to sort the directory by filename extension to group all files of a type together. The SORT command can specify the starting column to sort on. Because the filename extension begins in column 9, the command to sort by filename extension would be:

```
DIR B: ¦ SORT /+9
```

Figure 7.4 shows a sample result of this command. Note that the period separating filename from extension does *not* appear in a directory entry.

Once again, it is simple to send this output to a file or to the printer using the DOS piping facilities:

```
DIR B: ¦ SORT /+9 >B:SORTDIR.TXT
or
DIR B: ¦ SORT /+9 >PRN
```

Here, the first command line directs the sorted output to the file SORTDIR.TXT on drive B; the second command line directs the sorted output to the printer. If a subdirectory is to be sorted, the command would be:

```
DIR B: \SUBDIR1 ¦ SORT /+9
or
DIR B: \SUBDIR1 ¦ SORT /+9 >B:SORTDIR.TXT
or
DIR B: \SUBDIR1 ¦ SORT /+9 >PRN
```

Using the File Size

To sort the directory by file size, the commands shown for sorting by filename extensions would be repeated, except for the column passed to the SORT command. To sort on the file size, you would inform the SORT command to begin in column 14:

```
DIR B: ¦ SORT /+14
```

```
A>dir b: | sort /+9


JUNK            216    8-23-87    3:48p
TEMP    BAT      37    11-05-87   9:15p
NOTEUSRS DIC    14     1-04-80    1:03p
GOODSTUF DOC   263    10-25-87    4:21p
FILE3   TXT    222    10-25-87    4:09p
SAMPLE  XYZ     14     1-04-80    1:03p
        6 File(s)    723968 bytes free
Volume in drive B has no label
Directory of  B:\


A>
```

Figure 7.4 Directory Sorted by Filename Extension.

```
A>dir b: | sort /+14


NOTEUSRS DIC    14     1-04-80    1:03p
SAMPLE  XYZ     14     1-04-80    1:03p
TEMP    BAT     37    11-05-87    9:15p
JUNK           216     8-23-87    3:48p
FILE3   TXT    222    10-25-87    4:09p
GOODSTUF DOC   263    10-25-87    4:21p
Directory of  B:\
        6 File(s)    723968 bytes free
Volume in drive B has no label


A>
```

Figure 7.5 Directory Sorted by File Size.

This will result in a sorted directory listing of drive B on the screen, as shown in Figure 7.5.

You could similarly send the output to a file or the printer with the following commands:

```
DIR B: | SORT /+14 >B:SORTDIR.TXT
or
DIR B: | SORT /+14 >PRN
```

A Batch File for Different Directories and Outputs

You just saw how to sort directories in several different ways and how to send the output of the sorting to the screen, printer, or file. Now examine a batch file in which the user tells the SORT command which directory to sort and where the output should go (the screen or the printer). The batch file called SDIR.BAT can be created using the EDIT or EDLIN facility or the COPY command. The contents of the file SDIR.BAT are

```
ECHO OFF
CLS
DIR %1 ¦ SORT %2
```

Notice that the %1 and %2 parameters are values that the user passes to the SDIR.BAT batch file. To execute the file, type SDIR followed by the directory you wish to sort followed by the place you want the output sent. Some examples are

```
SDIR B:\SUBDIR1 >PRN

SDIR B: >CON

SDIR B:\SUBDIR2 >B:\SUBDIR2\DIRSORT.TXT
```

The first example sorts the SUBDIR1 subdirectory on drive B and sends the output to the printer. The second example sorts all files on drive B and sends the output to the screen. The third example sorts the SUBDIR2 subdirectory of drive B and stores the output in a file called DIRSORT.TXT in the SUBDIR2 subdirectory. You could create a batch command similar to the preceding examples to sort by file size, as follows:

```
ECHO OFF
CLS
DIR %1 ¦ SORT /+14>%2
```

In this example after ECHO is turned off for batch file commands and the screen is cleared, a directory specified by using the first replaceable parameter is listed. Next, the directory is sorted by file size, and output is directed to the device specified by the second replaceable parameter.

A command to sort by filename extension would look like this:

```
ECHO OFF
CLS
DIR %1 ¦ SORT /+9>%2
```

A Sorting Menu System

You can easily develop a menu system that sorts in different ways when users select choices on a menu. Suppose you wanted a menu to look like Figure 7.6.

By using the menu illustrated in Figure 7.6, you could sort a directory by filename, size, or filename extension and have the output sent to the screen or the printer, or you could obtain a wide listing of your directory. For example, by simply typing a 1 followed by the name of the directory you wish to sort you would obtain a sorted listing on the screen. A batch file can display a menu on the screen and ask the user to select an option. Listing 7.1 illustrates the creation of a batch file using the EDLIN text editor.

Listing 7.1 Batch File to Display Menu

```
Batch File to Display Menu

1:*echo off
```

```
2: cls
3: type sdir.txt
4: prompt ENTER NUMBER FOLLOWED BY DIRECTORY $q$g
```

The first line in the file turns off the echo of commands to the screen, so users do not see the commands being executed. Line 2 clears the display. Line 3 is used to put the menu on the screen. In this example, the menu was placed in a file called SDIR.TXT (Listing 7.2) and the TYPE command in DOS is used in line 3 of Listing 7.1 to display it on the screen. Line 4 changes the standard DOS prompt from A: to words that tell the user what to do next (for example, enter the number of your choice from the menu and follow the number with the directory you wish to have sorted).

Listing 7.2 Directory Mapping Functions

```
 1:*
 2:
 3:        DIRECTORY MAPPING FUNCTIONS
 4:        =============================
 5:
 6:        1 - Sort Directory by Filename to screen
 7:        2 - Sort Directory by Filename to Printer
 8:        3 - Sort Directory by Size to Screen
 9:        4 - Sort Directory by Size to Printer
10:        5 - Sort Directory by Filename Extension to Screen
11:        6 - Sort Directory by Filename Extension to Printer
12:        7 - Display Wide Directory Listing
13:        0 - END - Return to DOS
```

A batch file named 1.BAT will be created next to perform the sorting; it will look like Listing 7.3.

Listing 7.3 1.BAT File to Perform Sorting by Filename to Screen

```
1:*echo off
2: cls
3: dir %1 ¦ sort ¦ more
4: pause
5: cls
6: type sdir.txt
```

```
DIRECTORY MAPPING FUNCTIONS
=============================


1 - Sort Directory by Filename to Screen
2 - Sort Directory by Filename to Printer
3 - Sort Directory by Size to Screen
4 - Sort Directory by Size to Printer
5 - Sort Directory by Filename Extension to Screen
6 - Sort Directory by Filename Extension to Printer
7 - Display Wide Directory Listing
0 - END - Return to DOS
```

Figure 7.6 Desired Menu System.

The first line in the 1.BAT file turns off the echo of the commands to the screen so that the user doesn't see what commands are issued by the batch file. The second line clears the screen, and the third line actually sorts the specified directory. Notice that line 3 looks very similar to the sorting batch files developed earlier but also contains a MORE command. When a large directory is being sorted and more than 24 files are to be listed, the list will scroll off the top of the screen as the successive lines are displayed. MORE is the DOS command that stops the screen from scrolling when it is full and tells the user that -MORE- information is to be displayed after looking at this screen. To display the next full screen and continue scrolling, simply press any key.

The fourth line contains a PAUSE command. This batch command causes a temporary halt to the processing of batch commands until the user is ready to continue. When the PAUSE command is executed, it tells the user to Strike any key when ready . . . on the screen. The PAUSE is needed at this point in the batch file because you want to look at the sorted directory display just produced. Line 5 is a clear screen command; if the PAUSE command were not placed just prior to the CLS command you would not have time to look at your sorted directory before the screen was cleared. The sixth and final command in the 1.BAT file again displays the menu of choices to the user.

The peculiar name of this batch file—1—was selected to correspond to an option on the main menu. That is, if the user responds to the main menu by selecting option 1, the batch file with that name executes.

Similarly, you can create additional batch files with numeric names to correspond to the other options on the main menu. The file named 2.BAT sorts a directory and sends the results to the printer. The 2.BAT file is shown in Listing 7.4. Notice that there is no need to include a clear screen command (CLS) at the beginning of this procedure because the output is going directly to the printer. There is also no need to PAUSE after the sort is printed because the user is not using the screen to look at the sorted directory listing. The command on line 2 performs the sort of the directory specified by the user and sends the output to the printer. Line 3 clears the screen and line four redisplays the menu for another selection.

Listing 7.4 2.BAT File to Perform Sorting by Filename to Printer

```
1:*echo off
2: dir %1 ¦ sort >prn
3: cls
4: type sdir.txt
```

Program Listings 7.5 through 7.8 show the contents of files 3.BAT through 6.BAT, respectively. These files are very similar to files 1.BAT and 2.BAT, except for the directory that is sorted. Listing 7.9 shows the contents of the file 7.BAT, where line 2 results in the specified directory being displayed on the screen in a wide format.

Listing 7.5 3.BAT File to Sort Directory by Size to Screen

```
1:*echo off
2: cls
3: dir %1 ¦ sort /+14 ¦more
4: pause
5: cls
6: type sdir.txt
```

Listing 7.6 4.BAT File to Sort Directory by Size to Printer

```
1:*echo off
2: dir %1 ¦ sort /+14 >prn
3: cls
4: type sdir.txt
```

Listing 7.7 5.BAT File to Sort Directory by Filename Extension to Screen

```
1:*echo off
2: cls
3: dir %1 ¦ sort /+9 ¦more
4: pause
5: cls
6: type sdir.txt
```

Listing 7.8 6.BAT File to Sort Directory by Filename Extension to Printer

```
1:*echo off
2: dir %1 ¦ sort /+9 >prn
3: cls
4: type sdir.txt
```

Listing 7.9 7.BAT File to Display Wide Directory Listing

```
1:*echo off
2: dir %1 /w
3: pause
4: cls
5: type sdir.txt
```

Listing 7.10 shows the contents of file 0.BAT, which probably requires a little explanation. Because choice 0 on your menu is End--Return to DOS you want to remove your menu from the screen and put the standard DOS prompt back when this option is selected. Line 2 in the file performs the clear screen operation, whereas line 3 resets the DOS prompt back to the default drive letter (A in this case, but C if you have a hard disk drive), followed by a greater than symbol (>). At this point you have exited your sorted directory menu system and returned control to DOS.

Listing 7.10 File 0.BAT

```
1:*echo off
2: cls
3: prompt $n$g
```

The File Locator

Since the introduction of hierarchical directory structures with DOS Version 2.0, finding files that are not in the current directory has become more complex and time-consuming. Fairly expensive commercial file-finding software is available, but there is a less costly solution. Using a batch file that takes advantage of the results of executing the CHKDSK command, you can develop a mechanism to locate files easily in a complex hierarchical directory structure.

To understand the concept of CHKDSK, you can create a sample directory structure and place a few files under each subdirectory. Figure 7.7 illustrates the directory structure. For simplicity, the six files are labeled using a single alphabetic character.

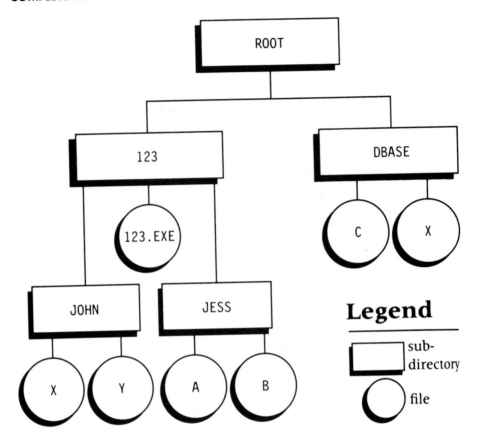

Figure 7.7   Sample Directory Structure.

If you enter the DOS command **CHKDSK d:/V**, all directories and files on the specified drive will be displayed as well as any encountered errors and a summary of disk space and memory usage. The following illustrates the resulting action from the use of the CHKDSK command on the sample directory.

```
A>chkdsk  /v
Directory A:
Directory A:\123
Directory A:\123\JOHN
        A:\123\JOHN\X
        A:\123\JOHN\Y
Directory A:\123\JESS
        A:\123\JESS\A
        A:\123\JESS\B
        A:\123\123.EXE
Directory A:\DBASE
        A:\DBASE\C
        A:\DBASE\X

    730112 bytes total disk space
```

```
   4096 bytes in 4 directories
   7168 bytes in 7 user files
 718848 bytes available on disk

 524992 bytes total memory
 477520 bytes free
```

When CHKDSK executes, it displays a list of all directories and files contained on the disk. By first directing the output of the CHKDSK command to a temporary file, you can process that file with the FIND command. Listing 7.11 illustrates the creation of the batch file named LOCATE.BAT, which is constructed to provide a mechanism to rapidly locate any file on a disk.

Listing 7.11 Creating a File Locator Program

```
copy con: LOCATE.BAT
echo off
if "%1" == "" goto :error
echo FILE LOCATOR COMMENCING...PLEASE WAIT...
chkdsk /V >temp.$$$
find "%1" temp.$$$
erase temp.$$$
echo END OF SEARCH...
goto :end
:error
echo FILENAME MUST BE ENTERED AFTER LOCATE...TRY AGAIN...
:end
^Z
        1 File(s) copied

A>
```

In Listing 7.11 the DOS COPY command copies the input from the keyboard (CON) to the file named LOCATE.BAT. The first line turns the echo of commands from the batch file off. The second line checks whether the user entered a filename to search for. If no filename is entered (the %1 parameter is null) the batch file LOCATE transfers to an error routine (:error) that tells the user to enter the required filename. The third line echoes a message to the user that the LOCATE program is starting to run. The fourth line actually executes the CHKDSK command and sends the output to a file called TEMP.$$$. Line 5 uses the DOS FIND command to find the filename entered by the user in the TEMP.$$$ file. This FIND command will show the user every line in the TEMP.$$$ file that contains the filename being searched for. The sixth line erases the TEMP.$$$ file, which is no longer needed. The seventh line tells the user that the search for the filename is completed. Line 8 bypasses the error message display previously described and goes to the end of the program.

The use of the LOCATE.BAT file is illustrated in the following:

```
A>locate X

A>echo off
FILE LOCATOR COMMENCING...PLEASE WAIT...

---------- temp.$$$
       A:\123\JOHN\X
       A:\123\123.EXE
       A:\DBASE\X
END OF SEARCH...

A>
```

Note that entering the command LOCATE X located two files named X—one under the subdirectory JOHN and another in the subdirectory DBASE. Also notice that the filename 123.EXE was also shown as being found by the LOCATE command. This is because it contains the X character in its name and was picked up by the FIND command in line five of the LOCATE.BAT file.

Expanding the Locate Capability

You can expand the previously created batch file to locate either directories or files by name. To do so, first define a command format that will be used as follows, with the items in braces indicating a choice of one of the two.

$$\text{LOCATE} \begin{Bmatrix} \text{DIR} \\ \text{FILE} \end{Bmatrix} \text{NAME}$$

The preceding command format requires two replaceable parameters—one for DIR or FILE, the other for the name of the directory or file to locate. Listing 7.12 illustrates the revised LOCATE.BAT file.

Listing 7.12 Revised LOCATE.BAT File

```
 1:*echo off
 2: if "%2" == "" goto :error
 3: if "%1" == "DIR" goto :dir
 4: if "%1" == "FILE" goto :file
 5: echo "DIR" OR "FILE" MUST BE ENTERED AFTER LOCATE...TRY AGAIN
 6: goto :end
 7: :dir
 8: chkdsk /v ¦FIND "Directory" >temp.$$$
 9: find "%2" temp.$$$
10: erase temp.$$$
11: goto :end
12: :file
13: chkdsk /v >temp.$$$
14: find "%2" temp.$$$
15: erase temp.$$$
16: goto :end
17: :error
18: echo "NAME OF DIR" OR "FILENAME" TO LOCATE MISSING...TRY AGAIN
19: end
```

Line 1 of this revised file is similar to the previously created file, because it uses the ECHO command to turn off the echo of batch commands to the screen. Line 2 checks whether the user entered a filename or directory name to search for. If no name was entered, an error message is issued and the LOCATE command is ended. Lines 3 and 4 check to see if the correct syntax of the LOCATE command was used and the word DIR or FILE was entered immediately after entering LOCATE. If DIR was entered, control passes to the part of the file that processes the directory searching following the label :dir. If FILE was entered, control passes to the part of the file that processes filename searching following the label :file.

Lines 5 and 6 tell the user that the DIR or FILE keywords must be entered after LOCATE and the program is ended by a branch to the label :end. Line 8 uses the CHKDSK and FIND commands to find all directories on the disk and place them in a file called TEMP.$$$. Line 9 searches the TEMP.$$$ file for the directory name the user is looking for and displays it on the screen. Lines 10 and 11 clean up previous work by deleting the TEMP.$$$ file and ending the program. Lines 13 through 15 are the same as in the previous LOCATE.BAT file (with the exception that the parameter is %2 here) and are used to find the filename you are looking for.

Here are several examples of executing the revised LOCATE.BAT file:

A> **locate**

```
A>echo off
"NAME OF DIR" OR "FILENAME" TO LOCATE MISSING...TRY AGAIN
```

A>**locate DIR**

```
A>echo off
"NAME OF DIR" OR "FILENAME" TO LOCATE MISSING...TRY AGAIN
```

A>**locate 123**

```
A>echo off
"DIR" OR "FILE" MUST BE ENTERED AFTER LOCATE...TRY AGAIN
```

A>**locate FILE**

```
A>echo off
"NAME OF DIR" OR "FILENAME" TO LOCATE MISSING...TRY AGAIN
```

A>**locate DIR 123**

```
A>echo off

---------- temp.$$$
Directory A:\123
Directory A:\123\JOHN
Directory A:\123\JESS
```

A>**locate FILE X**

```
A>echo off

---------- temp.$$$
    A:\123\JOHN\X
    A:\123\123.EXE
    A:\DBASE\X

A>
```

File Backup and Restoration

Three of the most important, but frequently forgotten, DOS commands for fixed disk operations are BACKUP, XCOPY, and RESTORE. Although each of these commands can be used to back up files from one diskette to another, their primary use is in providing computer users with a mechanism to back up the contents of a fixed disk to diskette storage and to restore files from diskette storage to a fixed disk. By performing backup operations on a regularly scheduled basis, you can minimize the effect of a hard disk head crash that could conceivably wipe out tens to hundreds of millions of bytes of storage, as well as countless hours of prior effort.

BACKUP (External) Command

The BACKUP command duplicates one or more files from one type of disk to another, as long as the drive specifiers in the command are not duplicated. The format of this external DOS command is

```
[d:][path]BACKUP
d:[path][filename[.ext]]d:[/S][/M][/A][/D:mm-dd-yy]
[/T:hh:mm:ss][/F][/L[:[d:][path][filename[.ext]]]]
```

The drive specifier following the command keyword denotes the source drive, which contains one or more files to be backed up. The path, filename, and extension are used to identify the location of the files to be backed up, whereas the optional parameters further define the characteristics and attributes to be used during the backup process. Table 7.1 lists the operational result of each of the BACKUP command parameters.

By including one or more optional parameters in the command line, you can precisely control the files to be backed up based on their directory location and date and/or time of creation. In addition, when you use diskette storage for backup under DOS 3.3, it is advisable to include the /F parameter in the command line. Otherwise, if you run out of formatted diskettes you will have to use a different computer to format additional disks. To do so on your computer, you must terminate the BACKUP operation and restart the operation when you have the correct number of formatted diskettes.

Under DOS 4.0 the target diskette is automatically formatted if it was not already formatted by the FORMAT command. Due to this, the /F parameter has been eliminated from the BACKUP command under DOS 4.0 and 5.0.

Even though using the DOS Shell simplifies the BACKUP and RESTORE operations, you should be familiar with the optional parameters of these commands as well as other DOS commands. Figure 7.8 illustrates the Backup Utility pop-up box that is displayed when you select the Backup Fixed Disk action from the DOS Utilities screen. Note that the default parameter setting is

```
c:\*.* a: /s
```

Here c:*.* denotes all files in the root directory of drive C, whereas a: indicates those files should be backed up onto a diskette in drive A. Finally, the /S parameter causes the backup of subdirectory files in addition to the files in the root directory, in effect causing the entire contents of drive C to be backed up.

Because a complete backup of a fixed disk can take a significant amount of time, you will probably prefer to use other parameters after the first backup operation is performed. Thus, becoming familiar with the use of command parameters can significantly increase your efficiency in using your computer.

Table 7.1
BACKUP Command
Parameters

Parameter	Operational Result
/S	Backs up subdirectory files in addition to the files in the specified or current directory.
/M	Backs up files modified since the last BACKUP operation.
/A	Appends files to files already present on the backup disk.
/D	Backs up files modified on or after the specified date.
/T	Backs up files modified on or after the specified time on the specified date.
/F	Formats the target diskette if it is not.
/L	Creates a log file. If a filename is not specified, a default of BACKUP.LOG will be created in the root directory of the source drive.

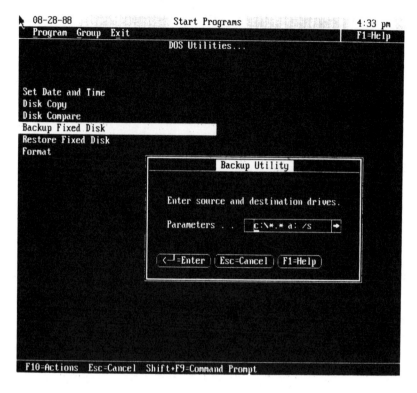

Figure 7.8 Backup Utility Pop-Up Box.

The number of diskettes required for backup operations depends on your backup requirements and your diskette storage capability. If your personal computer has a 20M-byte fixed disk that is half full, to back up the 10M bytes of data requires twenty-eight 360K-byte or nine 1.2M-byte 5¼-inch diskettes or fourteen 720K-byte or seven 1.44M-byte 3½-inch diskettes. Because it is very difficult to estimate the amount of data that changed from the time of a previous backup operation, a good rule of thumb is to always have a blank box of diskettes available, as well as to use the /F parameter in the BACKUP command line if you are using DOS 3.3.

Note that BACKUP is not the same as COPY and should not be used to duplicate files. This is because the COPY command creates an exact duplicate of a file or group of files, whereas the BACKUP command chains files together and inserts control information that precludes its use unless restored to its original format by the use of the RESTORE command.

When you use the BACKUP command with a diskette drive as the target drive, you are prompted to insert a new diskette after the currently inserted diskette is filled. You should always label each diskette to include recording its date and diskette number, because the RESTORE operation requires backup diskettes to be inserted in the order they were created. In addition to prompting you to insert an appropriate diskette, BACKUP issues a warning that any files previously stored in the root directory of the disk used for backup will be erased. This warning arises from the BACKUP technique of creating two files in the root directory on a target diskette—BACKUP.XXX and

CONTROL.XXX. The BACKUP.XXX file contains all the files chained together, whereas the CONTROL.XXX file contains such control information as path names and filenames. The following illustrates the use of the BACKUP command to back up all files on drive C in the HIJACK subdirectory onto a diskette in drive A. Note that once the command is in operation, the name of each file backed up is displayed as it is transferred to the backup media.

C>**BACKUP \HIJACK A:**

Insert backup diskette 01 in drive A:

Warning! Files in the target drive
A:\ root directory will be erased
Strike any key when ready

∗∗∗ Backing up files to drive A: ∗∗∗
Diskette Number: 01

\HIJACK\UPDATE
\HIJACK\HIJACK.EXE
\HIJACK\CONVERT.EXE
\HIJACK\CAPTURE.EXE
\HIJACK\EGA.EXE
\HIJACK\TOSHIBA.EXE
\HIJACK\ATT.EXE

To help you better understand the BACKUP command, Table 7.2 illustrates three command line entries and their operational results. As indicated by the first example in Table 7.2, you can use global characters in the BACKUP command to specify file sets.

RESTORE (External) Command

The RESTORE command can be considered to be the complement of the BACKUP command, because it reinstates on the fixed disk one or more files that were previously backed up onto another medium. The format of this command is

[d:][path]RESTORE d:[d:][path]filename[.ext][/S][/P][/B:mm-dd-yy]
[/A:mm-dd-yy][/M][/N]:[/L:time][/E:time]

The first drive identifier following the command keyword denotes the drive that contains one or more files previously produced by the use of the BACKUP command. The option drive identifier, as well as the following path, filename, and extension, specify

Table 7.2 BACKUP Command Examples	BACKUP Command	Operational Result
	C>BACKUP *.* A:/S	Uses the BACKUP command file on the default drive (drive C) in the current directory to back up all files on that drive to the diskette in drive A.
	C>BACKUP *.DAT A:/D:9-11-91	Uses the BACKUP command file on the default drive (drive C) in the current directory to back up all files in the current directory with the extension DAT on drive C modified on or after 9-11-91 to drive A.
	A>C:BACKUP C:\ A:/F	Uses the BACKUP command file on drive C in the current directory to back up all files from the root directory on drive C to drive A. If a diskette inserted in drive A is not formatted, BACKUP formats it prior to backing up any files.

the location where you want the files restored and what files are to be restored. Similar to the BACKUP command, you can use global characters in the filename and extension fields to specify a file set.

The optional parameters following the filename extension govern the conditions under which file restoration will occur. Table 7.3 lists the operational result of each of the RESTORE command parameters.

If you want to restore the files previously backed up in the sample backup procedure, enter the command

C>**RESTORE A: C:\HIJACK**

The preceding command restores all files in the directory HIJACK on drive A to the fixed disk, drive C. When you use the RESTORE command, remember that the first drive identifier indicates the source, the second drive identifier and path indicate the target, and the following file specification indicates what files from the source you want restored. Thus, the RESTORE command requires you to enter parameters in the sequence source, target, source. The following illustrates the use of the RESTORE command to recover the files in the directory HIJACK on drive A that were previously backed up. Table 7.4 illustrates the operational result from three RESTORE command line entries.

C>**RESTORE A: C:\HIJACK**

```
Insert backup diskette 01 in drive A:
Strike any key when ready

*** Files were backed up 06/30/1988 ***

*** Restoring files from drive A: ***
Diskette: 01
```

Table 7.3
RESTORE Command
Parameters

Parameter	Operational Result
/S	Restores all files in the specified directory and subdirectories under the specified directory.
/P	Causes RESTORE to prompt you prior to restoring files that have changed since the last backup or that are marked read only.
/B:*mm-dd-yy*	Restores all files modified on or before the specified date.
/A:*mm-dd-yy*	Restores all files modified on or after the specified date.
/M	Restores all files modified or deleted since they were backed up.
/N	Restores files that no longer exist on the target drive.
/L:*time*	Restores only those files modified at or after the specified time.
/E:*time*	Restores only those files modified at or earlier than the specified time.

Table 7.4
RESTORE Command
Examples

RESTORE Command	Operational Result
C>RESTORE A: \HIJACK*.PIX	Uses the RESTORE command file on the default drive (drive C) in the current directory to restore files whose extension is PIX in the subdirectory HIJACK on drive A to drive C.
C>RESTORE A: C:*.* /S	Uses the RESTORE command file on the default drive (drive C) to restore all files on the backup diskette(s) to drive C.
A>C:RESTORE A: C:*.* /S/N	Uses the RESTORE command file on drive C in the current directory to restore all files on the backup diskette(s) that no longer exist on drive C.

```
\HIJACK\UPDATE
\HIJACK\HIJACK.EXE
\HIJACK\CONVERT.EXE
\HIJACK\CAPTURE.EXE
\HIJACK\EGA.EXE
\HIJACK\TOSHIBA.EXE
\HIJACK\ATT.EXE
\HIJACK\HERC.EXE
\HIJACK\MONO.EXE
```

XCOPY (External) Command

Unlike the BACKUP command, which creates files you must RESTORE prior to usage, you can use files created by the XCOPY command without executing an intermediate command. XCOPY can be used in a backup procedure by specifying the /M optional parameter in the command line. This option turns off the archive bit of the source file, which informs both subsequent XCOPY and BACKUP commands that the file was not created or modified since the last use of either command. Because of this, you can intermix the use of XCOPY and BACKUP to satisfy your specific requirements. Refer to Chapter 5 for specific examples covering the use of the XCOPY command.

8 / BASIC Overview

Three versions of BASIC are bundled with the IBM PC AT. The version or versions operable on your system will depend on how much disk storage your system has and whether you have a copy of the DOS diskette in drive A or have placed DOS on your fixed disk. In comparison, most compatible computers include Microsoft Corporation's GW-BASIC on the PC-DOS diskette sold with their computer. The main difference between the versions of BASIC furnished with the IBM PC AT and compatible computers concerns the use of read-only memory (ROM) for storing a nucleus of BASIC.

When IBM developed the PC AT it stored Cassette BASIC in ROM and furnished two additional versions of BASIC on the DOS diskette, each of which uses the ROM Cassette BASIC routines. In comparison, GW-BASIC is entirely disk resident and is equivalent to IBM's more sophisticated BASIC called Advanced BASIC.

Cassette BASIC

Cassette BASIC can be considered as a nucleus BASIC, because it is available on every IBM PC AT. This BASIC is contained in 32K bytes of ROM located in the system board inside the system unit.

If your PC AT has only one diskette drive, you should remove any diskette in the drive. Then, when you switch power on, Cassette BASIC will be "brought up" or initialized.

When Cassette BASIC is initialized, your screen will display a copyright notice and the words Version C followed by the release number and the number of free bytes of memory available for use. In Cassette BASIC, the only data and program storage device that is available is a cassette tape recorder. Because the PC AT does not contain a cassette port, you cannot store information using this version of BASIC. Thus, IBM PC AT users should not use Cassette BASIC, because each AT comes with a minimum of one high-capacity diskette drive installed, which enables the use of two upwardly compatible versions of Cassette BASIC—Disk BASIC and Advanced BASIC.

Disk BASIC

Disk BASIC was originally supplied as a program file on the IBM DOS diskette and must be loaded into memory in order for you to use it. Note that with the release of DOS 3.3 Disk BASIC was essentially eliminated from the DOS diskette. Although you can still enter the Disk BASIC command **BASIC**, that command now results in the initialization of Advanced BASIC. Thus, the remainder of the information presented in this section is only applicable to IBM PC AT users that operate their computers under an old version of DOS. If you have DOS 3.3 or a later version of the operating system, skip to the section Advanced BASIC.

The method employed to load Disk BASIC will depend on where your DOS files reside.

If you have only diskette drives on your AT, you must bring up DOS from drive A prior to loading BASIC. If power to your AT was off, you can insert a diskette with DOS on it in drive A and turn power on. Once you power up the computer, the self-test diagnostics will be executed and then the initial portion of DOS will be read from drive A. During the DOS initialization process, you will be requested to enter the date and time. Because the AT has a battery-operated clock/calendar, in most situations you will simply press the Enter key if the date and time are correct. If not, you can enter a new date or time, using the same format in which the date and time are displayed. The DOS day and time prompts as well as the IBM DOS initialization message and the command required to load Disk BASIC are illustrated below. The DOS initialization message is displayed after the date and time are entered and consists of a copyright notice and information concerning the version of DOS being used.

```
Current date is Tue 08-13-1991
Enter new date (mm-dd-yy):
Current time is 19:51:40.74
Enter new time:

The IBM Personal Computer DOS
Version 3.00 (C)Copyright IBM Corp 1981, 1982, 1983, 1984

A>BASIC
```

After the initialization message is displayed, one line will be skipped and the prompt message A> will be generated. Here, the character A says you are working with diskette drive A, and the > character says you are at the DOS system level of operation. By typing the word BASIC and pressing the Enter key, you will inform DOS that you wish Disk BASIC to be loaded from the diskette in drive A. The result of entering the BASIC command is illustrated in Figure 8.1. The words Version D in the Disk BASIC initialization display inform you that you are in Disk BASIC, and the number following the character D tells you the revision level of the software you are operating with. Normally, a digit is used for major revisions, and a fractional change in the revision number indicates a minor revision. The number of free bytes of memory available for use by Disk BASIC will also be displayed. The 25th line will have the initial values of the soft keys displayed. The prompt Ok is issued by BASIC and indicates it is ready for operation.

Disk BASIC is a superset of Cassette BASIC in that it can execute all Cassette BASIC statements as well as several additional BASIC statements. Key differences between disk and Cassette BASIC are Disk BASIC's ability to support I/O to the diskette and fixed disk in addition to a cassette, communications support, an internal clock to keep track of the date and time, and the ability to support up to two printers attached to the system unit in place of the one printer Cassette BASIC supports.

Note that when Disk BASIC is initialized, the values of the soft keys are displayed on line 25. The number preceding each soft key indicates the function key you must press to generate the literal assigned to the key. Later in this chapter you will learn

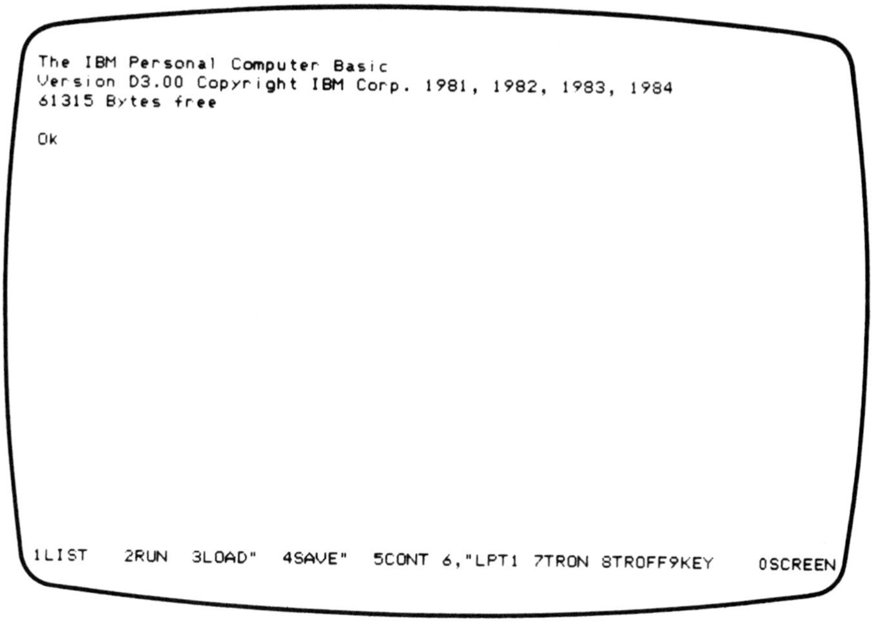

```
The IBM Personal Computer Basic
Version D3.00 Copyright IBM Corp. 1981, 1982, 1983, 1984
61315 Bytes free

Ok
```

```
1LIST   2RUN  3LOAD"  4SAVE"  5CONT 6,"LPT1 7TRON 8TROFF9KEY      0SCREEN
```

Figure 8.1 Disk BASIC Initialization Display.

how to use the function keys as a labor-saving device to perform predefined functions, such as listing the contents of a program by pressing the F1 key and the Enter key instead of typing the word LIST into your system.

If your IBM PC AT is powered up and you previously transferred DOS to the root directory of your fixed disk, you can load Disk BASIC from that device. If you are at the root directory level of drive C, you can simply enter the command **BASIC** to initialize Disk BASIC. Otherwise, if you were in a different directory and the BASIC program was in the root directory, you would enter the command CD\ to change to the root directory prior to entering the command BASIC.

If your system was powered off but DOS was on the root directory of drive C and no diskette was in drive A, as you powered up your system the root directory of drive C would be searched for DOS. This would result in the familiar request to enter the date and time, as well as the display of the DOS copyright notice. Once the prompt C> is displayed, you can bring up Disk BASIC by entering the command BASIC as illustrated here:

```
Current date is Tue 08-14-1990
Enter new date (mm-dd-yy):
Current time is 22:08:36.44
Enter new time:

The IBM Personal Computer DOS
Version 3.00 (C)Copyright IBM Corp 1981, 1982, 1983, 1984
```

C>**BASIC**

Once the command BASIC is entered, Disk BASIC will be initialized and your display screen will appear as previously illustrated in Figure 8.1.

If DOS was on the root directory of drive C and drive A was the default drive, you could enter the command **C:BASIC** to initialize Disk BASIC. Again, the Disk BASIC initialization message illustrated in Figure 8.1 would appear and the Ok prompt would signify that Disk BASIC was awaiting your action.

Advanced BASIC

The most extensive form of BASIC available on the IBM PC AT DOS diskette—Advanced BASIC—can be viewed as a superset of both disk and Cassette BASIC.

Because the original PC was manufactured with only 16K of random access memory (RAM), IBM offered three versions of BASIC, each version requiring a larger amount of memory to operate. Cassette BASIC requires a minimum of 16K, Disk BASIC requires 48K, and Advanced BASIC requires 64K bytes of RAM. Because every IBM PC AT has a minimum of 256K of memory, you will normally use Advanced BASIC, because it operates on every AT and is upwardly compatible with Disk and Cassette BASIC.

Like Disk BASIC, Advanced BASIC is supplied as a program on the IBM DOS diskette, which must be loaded into memory to use. Advanced BASIC can be loaded like Disk BASIC, except that you enter the command **BASICA** in response to the DOS prompt character instead of **BASIC**. The following three examples illustrate three command entries that can be used to bring up or initialize Advanced BASIC.

A>**BASICA**	DOS on drive A, default drive is A
A>**C:BASICA**	DOS on drive C, default drive is A
C>**BASICA**	DOS on drive C, default drive is C

The last two examples assume that DOS is in the root directory of drive C. As previously noted, if you are using DOS 3.3 or a later version, a request for Disk BASIC results in the initialization of Advanced BASIC. Thus, IBM PC AT users with DOS 3.3 or above can substitute **BASIC** for **BASICA** in the previous examples.

If you are using DOS 5.0, interpretive BASIC was renamed QBASIC. The QBASIC program is very similar to QuickBASIC, in that it includes a full-screen text editor and online help. However, unlike QuickBASIC, which is a compiler, QBASIC is an interpreter whose operation and capability are similar to BASICA. When you use QBASIC under DOS 5.0, its operation will resemble the screens covered under QuickBASIC. However, some of the capabilities of QuickBASIC were removed in QBASIC. For example, the Run menu only enables Start, Restart, and Continue operations, whereas Quick BASIC provides four additional operations from the Run menu. Because all QuickBASIC menus with the exception of Calls are supported by QBASIC, you can use the discussion of QuickBASIC menus while working with QBASIC to help you understand the use of each QBASIC menu.

Once Advanced BASIC is loaded, the words Version A followed by a number indicating the revision level of the software will be displayed, along with the number of bytes of memory available for use. Figure 8.2 illustrates the screen display initialization message once Advanced BASIC is loaded. Like Disk BASIC, Advanced BASIC can be initialized in many ways, depending on where DOS is located and whether your AT is powered on.

The preceding examples for the initialization of Disk BASIC are applicable to Advanced BASIC; simply replace the command **BASIC** with the command **BASICA**.

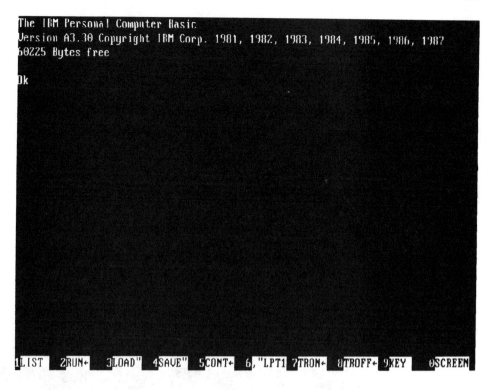

The IBM Personal Computer Basic
Version A3.30 Copyright IBM Corp. 1981, 1982, 1983, 1984, 1985, 1986, 1987
60225 Bytes free

Ok

```
1LIST  2RUN←  3LOAD"  4SAVE"  5CONT←  6,"LPT1  7TRON←  8TROFF←  9KEY  0SCREEN
```

Figure 8.2   Advanced BASIC Initialization Display.

GW-BASIC

Although called GW-BASIC, this version of BASIC that is supplied with many versions of PC-DOS is contained on an EXE file named BASIC.EXE. Thus, to initiate GW-BASIC you can simply enter the command **BASIC** at the DOS prompt. Figure 8.3 illustrates the resulting screen display when GW-BASIC is initialized. In comparing the initialization of Advanced BASIC and GW-BASIC, you will note that both versions of the BASIC language assign the same meanings to the first ten function keys. In fact, due to the similarity of each version of BASIC, we will normally refer to both of them collectively as *interpretive BASIC* or simply *BASIC* in the remainder of this book.

Returning to DOS

To return from BASIC to DOS, you must have a DOS diskette in drive A or a copy of DOS on your fixed disk. Once the BASIC prompt, Ok, appears on your display you can type the command **SYSTEM** and press Enter. This command exits BASIC and returns to DOS, causing the DOS prompt (A> or C>) to appear, which indicates that DOS is ready for you to give it a command. The following example shows the screen as you return to DOS from BASIC:

```
The IBM Personal Computer Basic
Version A3.30 Copyright IBM Corp. 1981, 1982, 1983, 1984, 1985, 1986, 1987
60225 Bytes free

Ok
```
SYSTEM

```
C>
```

Note that if the soft keys for BASIC were displayed, on entering the SYSTEM command those keys would disappear from view.

Interpreters Versus Compilers

Both IBM's Advanced BASIC and Microsoft's GW-BASIC are interpreter-based versions of the BASIC language. This means that both programs translate your BASIC statements into executable code one statement at a time, every time you run the program.

A second type of BASIC language translator is a *compiler*. When a BASIC compiler is used, this program translates all statements into executable code prior to executing the converted program—a one-time process.

Contrasting a BASIC interpreter to a BASIC compiler, you can make two general observations. First, the use of a compiler provides executable code that normally operates faster than the step-by-step translation performed by an interpreter. Second, because

Figure 8.3   GW-BASIC Initialization Display.

a compiler checks all statements for syntax prior to program execution, the compiler enhances your ability to rapidly detect programming errors.

In addition to the two general observations, a brief examination of Microsoft Corporation's QuickBASIC will reveal several additional advantages associated with the use of more modern compiled versions of the BASIC language over an interpretive BASIC.

Microsoft QuickBASIC

Figure 8.4 illustrates a QuickBASIC screen in which the File pull-down menu is displayed. QuickBASIC is a menu-based compiler that incorporates pull-down menus. This compiler includes a help facility that explains features in dialog boxes. In addition, as you move a highlight bar over each entry in a menu the 25th line on the display provides information concerning the selection of the highlighted entry. For example, the highlighted entry New Program results in the display Removes currently loaded program from memory. QuickBASIC supports a mouse, so you can rapidly scroll through program listings by placing the cursor on the upper or lower arrows on the right side of Figure 8.4 and pressing the mouse selection button. This provides you with more flexibility than does interpretive BASIC, which requires you to list statements by line numbers, and which, when statements are scrolled off the screen, requires you to enter another command referencing the line numbers so you can view the scrolled statements again.

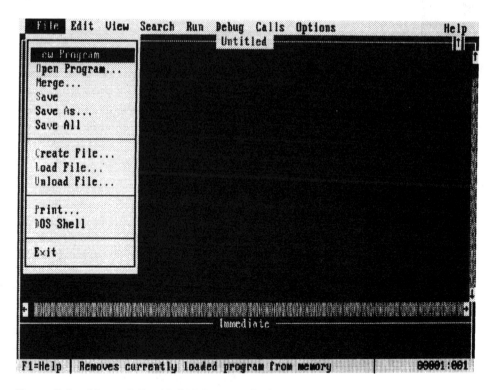

Figure 8.4 Microsoft QuickBASIC Screen with File Menu Pulled Down.

Although QuickBASIC is superior in many instances to interpretive BASIC, you must purchase it separately; it is not included on an MS-DOS or PC-DOS diskette. Most of the statements and commands supported by QuickBASIC are equivalent to those supported by Advanced BASIC and GW-BASIC. Thus, this discussion will focus on the use of the BASIC language, noting differences between interpretive and compiled BASIC when appropriate, with Microsoft Corporation's QuickBASIC used for noting the capabilities and limitations of a compiled BASIC.

Interpretive BASIC Modes of Operation

Once any version of interpretive BASIC becomes operational, the prompt Ok will be displayed on your monitor. This prompt message means that BASIC is ready for you to tell it what to do. This state is also known as the *BASIC command level*, because BASIC is awaiting your command. At this point, interpretive BASIC can be used in either of two modes of operation—direct or indirect.

The *direct mode* is used to tell interpretive BASIC to immediately perform your request after you terminate an input line by pressing the Enter key. BASIC automatically differentiates between direct and indirect modes by examining the input line for the presence or absence of a line number. If no line number is at the beginning of the input line, BASIC will immediately execute the statement or command entered. If a line number is encountered, BASIC will treat the line input as part of the program to be stored in memory. This is the *indirect mode*, and you can execute the resulting program by entering the RUN command or by pressing the F2 key.

Direct Mode

The direct mode provides you with the capability of a calculator to solve computations that do not require the use of a complete BASIC program. In addition, direct mode operations can be employed to debug a program by interspacing program execution and direct mode computations. Direct mode computations occur immediately after the Enter key is pressed, so this mode is also referred to as the *immediate program mode*.

The top part of Figure 8.5 illustrates the entry and execution of several direct program mode operations. In each example, the PRINT statement is a BASIC language statement that causes the display of the resulting operation to appear on the screen. In the first direct mode operation, the numerical quantity 317.5 is added to the quantity 4.106. Here, the plus sign (+) is the BASIC operator employed to conduct addition. After the line is entered, the results of the computation are displayed on the next line. In the following five examples, numerical data is operated on using the subtraction (−), multiplication (*), division (/), and exponentiation (^) BASIC operators. The apostrophe (') to the left of the comment on each line concerning the type of operation performed serves as an indicator to BASIC that all of the following characters on the line should be treated as comments. This comment indicator character (') can be used in both direct and indirect modes. The last direct mode example illustrates how BASIC can operate on data strings. In this example, concatenation or the combining of two strings into one is shown. The wide range of BASIC operators available for use in both direct and indirect modes will be covered in detail later in this chapter.

DIRECT

```
Ok
PRINT 317.5+4.106          ADDITION
 321.606
Ok
PRINT 350-105              SUBTRACTION
 245
Ok
PRINT 27.5*10              MULTIPLICATION
 275
Ok
PRINT 14.515/3.14159       DIVISION
 4.620272
Ok
PRINT 2^5                  EXPONENTIATION
 32
Ok
PRINT 2^5-12+1.7*5/3       COMBINED
 22.83334
Ok
PRINT "PUF*"+"NTOOT"       CONCATENATION
PUFFNTOOT
Ok
```

INDIRECT

```
Ok
1 PRINT 50/2
RUN
 25
Ok
2 PRINT 2^4
RUN
 25
 16
Ok
```

Figure 8.5 Direct and Indirect Program Modes in Interpretive BASIC.

Indirect Mode

The indirect mode of operation is the more powerful of the two available BASIC modes. This is because many statements can be entered as part of a program and executed with one command. The first example in the lower portion of Figure 8.5 shows a one-line program entered into memory. With the program in memory, you can enter the RUN command to execute the program, or you can simply press F2. The example in the lower portion of Figure 8.5 shows what happens after a second line is added to the program and the two-line program in memory is then executed by entering the RUN command. Note that the program prints two lines of output, one for each program line that contained a PRINT statement.

QuickBASIC Modes of Operation

If you are using Microsoft's QuickBASIC, note the two windows labeled Untitled and Immediate in Figure 8.4. The window labeled Untitled is used to develop programs that you can execute by either pressing the Shift+F5 key combination or by selecting Start from the Run menu. Figure 8.6 illustrates the QuickBASIC pull-down Run menu. Once you select Start or press Shift+F5, the program located in the upper window is executed. When this occurs, a new screen referred to as the *output screen* that contains the results of the program's execution is displayed. This screen also displays the message Press any key to continue on the last line. Once a key is pressed, the original QuickBASIC screen is displayed. Thus, you can see that the top window of QuickBASIC provides an indirect mode of operation, and the lower window, Immediate, corresponds to the direct mode of interpretive BASIC.

You can move down one window by pressing the F6 key or by clicking the mouse pointer anywhere in the lower window. To move to the upper window from the lower window, press the key combination Shift+F6 or move the mouse pointer anywhere in the upper window and click. Two additional window manipulation operations that warrant attention are window expansion and restoration. By pressing Ctrl+F10 you can expand the current window to cover the entire screen. Once this is accomplished, pressing F6 or Shift+F6 makes the next or previous window, respectively, active in the full-screen mode. By pressing Ctrl+F10 a second time, you can restore the screens to their default proportions.

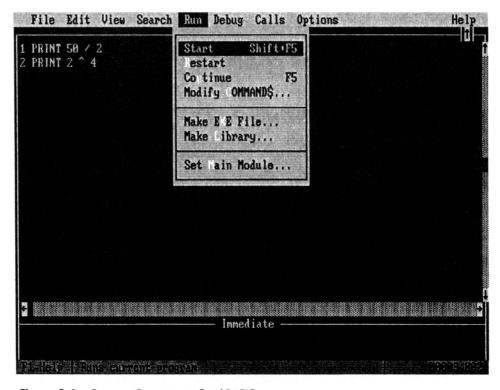

Figure 8.6   Program Execution in QuickBASIC.

Lines, Statements, and Elementary Commands

Although you may not recognize the fact at this time, you have already entered and executed your first BASIC program in both interpretive and compiled versions of that language. In interpretive BASIC, every BASIC program consists of one or more line numbers. In turn, each line number contains one or more BASIC statements, such as the PRINT statements shown in Figure 8.5.

Interpretive BASIC

In most flavors of the language, a BASIC program line begins with a line number and is terminated by pressing the Enter key. Valid line numbers range between 0 and 65,529 and may contain a maximum of 255 characters, including the Enter character. When this logical line exceeds 80 characters in length, it will "wrap" itself onto the next physical line as you continue to enter data, as shown here:

```
Ok
NEW
Ok
10PRINT"DUE TO THE POSITIONS REQUIRED ON A LINE FOR A LINE NUMBER AND THE PRINT
STATEMENT AN 80-CHARACTER MESSAGE WOULD REQUIRE MORE THAN ONE PHYSICAL LINE"
RUN
DUE TO THE POSITIONS REQUIRED ON A LINE FOR A LINE NUMBER AND THE PRINT STATEMEN
T AN 80-CHARACTER MESSAGE WOULD REQUIRE MORE THAN ONE PHYSICAL LINE
Ok
```

If the logical line exceeds 255 characters in length, the extra characters will be truncated when you press Enter. Although the extra characters will appear on your display, they will not be processed by BASIC.

To determine what the contents of memory are at a particular point in time when you are using an interpretive BASIC, you can use the LIST command. In its elementary form, this command will cause the program currently in memory to be listed on the display. Later, when you read about this command in detail, you will see how you can list single lines or segments of a program. Returning to the two-line indirect program illustrated in the lower part of Figure 8.5, suppose that program is currently in memory. The effect of the LIST command results in the complete two-line program being displayed as shown:

```
Ok
LIST
1 PRINT 50/2
2 PRINT 2^4
Ok
```

Now suppose you wish to modify the program currently residing in memory. If you wish to add one or more new lines to the program, you can do so by entering a valid line number followed by at least one nonblank character and then press Enter. Each line so entered will be added to the BASIC program in memory. If a line already exists with the same line number as the line entered, then the old line number will be erased and replaced by the newly entered one. If line numbers are entered out of sequence,

BASIC will internally sort the program lines into sequence, as shown here. In the following, the user added line 0 into memory after the listing of the file displayed its contents, showing it combined two lines, numbered 1 and 2. After entering line 0, the user again listed the program, and BASIC displayed the program in numerical line number sequence.

```
Ok
LIST
1 PRINT 50/2
2 PRINT 2^4
Ok
0 PRINT "ANSWERS FOLLOW"
LIST
0 PRINT "ANSWERS FOLLOW"
1 PRINT 50/2
2 PRINT 2^4
Ok
```

QuickBASIC

In comparison to an interpreter, which requires line numbers for each statement, a compiler treats this method of statement reference as an option. This difference results from the fact that when using a compiler that has a full-screen edit capability every statement in the program is immediately available for editing, enabling you to use cursor control keys or the mouse to scroll through the program as a single entity even though only a small portion of the program may be displayed. If you are using QuickBASIC, the position of the cursor is displayed in the lower right corner of your screen. For example, Figure 8.6 indicates that the cursor is at line 3, column 2, when the Run menu was pulled down.

Another significant difference between QuickBASIC and interpretive BASIC concerns the method used to edit statements. As previously explained, in interpretive BASIC you can remove a statement by entering the line number of the statement followed by pressing Enter. In QuickBASIC, line numbers are actually considered as a special type of label, requiring a different method for editing. QuickBASIC Edit menu options are illustrated in Figure 8.7.

The Edit menu in QuickBASIC provides a significant advantage for program editing compared with interpretive BASIC. For example, you can select the Undo option (for which there is no interpretive BASIC equivalent) to reverse the most recent edit and restore the current line to its condition before the last change. Other Edit menu options include Cut, Copy, Paste, and Clear, each of which operates on a block of text that is defined by pressing the mouse button down and dragging the mouse pointer to the end of the block you wish to manipulate.

The Cut option removes the selected text; however, it is placed in a special storage area called the clipboard. The clipboard functions as a temporary storage area, allowing you to move a block from the clipboard to a position defined by the location of the cursor when you select the Paste option from the Edit menu. Thus, Paste copies a block of text from the clipboard to a defined location in an active window.

If you wish to duplicate a portion of your program you can use the Copy option. This command copies a block of text into the clipboard without changing the original block. Then you can use the Paste option to duplicate the block at other locations in the active window. The last Edit option, Clear, deletes a selected block of text from

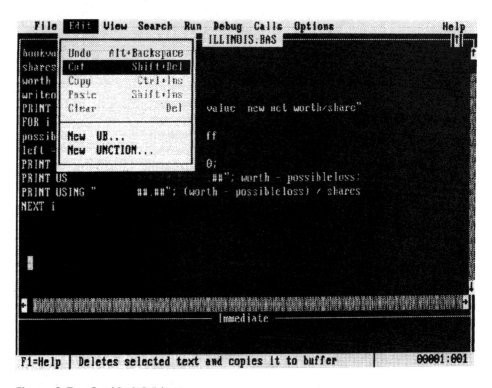

Figure 8.7 QuickBASIC Edit Menu.

the active window without copying it to the clipboard, in effect providing you with a mechanism to rapidly delete portions of a program.

Line Format in Interpretive BASIC

When an interpreter is used, each BASIC program line entered will follow this format:

nnnnn BASIC statement[:BASIC statement. . .]['comment]

The characters *nnnnn* indicate the line number, which can be from one to five digits, ranging in magnitude from 0 to 65,529. The line number is, in essence, the address of a program statement or series of statements. The latter occurs when multiple statements are contained on one line. Normally, program execution is in sequential line number order, beginning with the first statement in the program and continuing until the physical end of the program is reached. An example of this is the following:

```
START ————————→ 10 ⌉
                 ⌊ 20 ⌐
                 ↳ 30 ⌉
                 ⌊ 40 ⌐
                 ↳ 50 → END
```

BASIC contains many statements that you can use to alter the sequence in which operations are performed, so you can develop programs that execute lines or groups of lines nonsequentially:

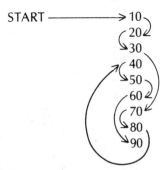

Because line numbers are the address of one or more statements contained on a program line, they are a necessary mechanism in most implementations of the language to identify changes in the sequence of the execution of statements within a program.

The line number is followed by one or more BASIC statements where the brackets in the format indicate optional items that can be contained within the format. To have multiple BASIC statements on a line, you simply separate each statement from the preceding statement by a colon(:). Although multiple statements on a line sometimes reduce the clarity of a program for debugging purposes or the visual comprehension of a program's actions, the program uses less memory for storage and execution. This fact is illustrated by the simple three-line program shown next. Lines 1 and 2 print the results of two computations; line 3 prints the number of bytes in memory not being used by BASIC. This is accomplished by the use of the FRE function. The FRE function uses what is known as a *dummy argument* and returns the number of available or free bytes of memory not used by BASIC. In this example, 60,854 bytes are shown to be available;

```
Ok
LIST
1 PRINT 50/2
2 PRINT 2^4
3 PRINT FRE(0)
Ok
RUN
 25
 16
 60854
Ok
```

Now, modify line 1 to incorporate the BASIC statement contained in line 2 and delete line 2 from memory. LIST and RUN this program as shown below.

```
Ok
LIST
1 PRINT 50/2 :PRINT 2^4
3 PRINT FRE(0)
Ok
RUN
```

```
25
16
60857
Ok
```

Note that available memory has increased by 3 bytes from the previous program, in which the first two BASIC statements were on individual lines. By combining line 2 with line 1, you eliminate one line number as well as the carriage return and line feed characters associated with that line.

If you have previously programmed other computers, you may be aware that some implementations of the BASIC language allow statements with no separations between keywords as well as between keywords and operators. With each version of interpretive BASIC, separators in the form of a space are required or a syntax error will occur when you run your program. An example of a syntax error due to the improper separation between the BASIC keyword PRINT and the operand is

```
Ok
LIST
1 PRINT50/2
3 PRINT FRE(0)
Ok
RUN
Syntax error in 1
Ok
1 PRINT50/2
```

When a syntax error is discovered while a program is running, BASIC will automatically display the line that caused the error so you can correct it. In the previous example, line 1 is displayed and the cursor is positioned under the digit 1. You can move the cursor right to the 5 in 50 and press the Insert key to put you in the insert mode. Doing so will change the cursor from a line to a square. You can then press the Spacebar to insert the required space between the keyword PRINT and the operand. By pressing the Enter key, you will store the corrected line back into memory and can now return the program:

```
Ok
LIST
1 PRINT50/2
3 PRINT FRE(0)
Ok
RUN
Syntax error in 1
Ok
1 PRINT 50/2
RUN
 25
 60864
Ok
```

In the preceding example, the second statement on the first line was purposely omitted. Note that available memory increased by 10 bytes, from 60,854 to 60,864. This shows that you can easily determine the amount of memory required for one or more BASIC statements. This can be a valuable tool if you have limited memory in your system unit or if you are developing a very large program and have to examine various ways to economize on the use of memory.

One useful feature of BASIC is the ability to document what a particular statement or group of statements is designed to perform. This can be accomplished by adding comments to the end of a line by using the single quotation mark (') to separate the comment from the rest of the line. Thus, if you were computing and printing the circumference of a circle whose radius is 24 feet, you might add the appropriate comment to the BASIC statement as shown:

```
Ok
LIST
10 PRINT 3.14159*24^2 'CIRCUMFERENCE IN FEET
Ok
RUN
 1809.556
Ok
```

Note that when the one-line program is executed, the comment is ignored. This part of the line is referred to as being *nonexecutable*. Later, when BASIC is covered in detail, you will see that there is a REM statement (for remark) that enables you to add nonexecutable comments to a program.

Comments can be valuable for interpreting what is occurring in a program. Although comments are nonexecutable, they require memory for storage that would otherwise be available for program execution.

Line Numbers and Labels in QuickBasic

If you are using QuickBASIC, line numbers are optional and are primarily employed to control branching within a QuickBASIC program. A second branching reference in QuickBASIC is the *label*, which is a string of alphanumeric characters followed by a colon that marks, precedes, or denotes a specific location in a program. For example, you might have the label COMPUTE prefix a statement:

COMPUTE: X=410*5

Here, the label COMPUTE identifies the location of the statement X=410*5 in the program.

You could also insert the label preceding the statement:

COMPUTE:
X=410*5

To branch to the label, you would add the label to a GOTO statement. In doing so the colon becomes optional, enabling you to enter **GOTO COMPUTE** or **GOTO COMPUTE:** to branch to the label COMPUTE.

In QuickBASIC a line number can be considered as a special type of label that, when it is used to reference a location, does not have to include a terminating colon. Thus, changing the label COMPUTE to 1000 enables you to prefix the statement **X=410*5** in the previous example as **1000** or **1000:**.

Most of the BASIC language examples presented in this book use interpretive BASIC or assign line numbers to each statement when using QuickBASIC. The rationale for this method of presentation is that the use of line numbers helps you find statements being described in different programming examples.

BASIC Character Set

The BASIC character set consists of alphabetic characters, numeric characters, and special characters that have specific meanings in BASIC. The character set that BASIC recognizes is a subset of the 256 characters that can be printed or displayed by using BASIC. Although you can use the additional characters for printing or display purposes, they have no particular meaning to BASIC.

The alphabetic characters in BASIC are the 26 uppercase and 26 lowercase letters of the alphabet. Although BASIC keywords can be entered in any combination of upper- and lowercase alphabetic characters, BASIC automatically converts keywords to uppercase characters after they are entered. In this book, all BASIC keywords are shown as uppercase characters, although you could enter them in upper- and lowercase.

Similar to the conventional alphabet, the numeric characters recognized by BASIC are the 10 digits, 0 through 9. Table 8.1 contains a listing of the special characters that have a specific meaning in BASIC.

Reserved Words

When you program in BASIC, certain words are interpreted as a request to perform predefined operations. As an example, the word PRINT tells BASIC to display data on

Table 8.1
Special Characters
Recognized by BASIC

Character	Meaning
	Blank
=	Equal sign or assignment symbol
+	Plus sign or concatenation symbol
—	Minus sign
*	Asterisk or multiplication symbol
/	Slash or division symbol
\	Backslash or integer division symbol
^	Up Arrow, circumflex, or exponentiation symbol
(	Left parenthesis
)	Right parenthesis
%	Percent
#	Number (or pound) sign
$	Dollar sign
!	Exclamation point
&	Ampersand
,	Comma
.	Period or decimal point
'	Single quotation mark (apostrophe)
;	Semicolon
:	Colon
?	Question mark
<	Less than symbol
>	Greater than symbol
"	Double quotation mark
_	Underline

the screen. Such *reserved words* include all BASIC commands, statements, function names, and operator names.

If you are using variable names to represent values that are used in a BASIC program, you may not use any reserved word as a variable name. Otherwise, BASIC would attempt to perform the predefined operation associated with the reserved word and, most likely, some type of syntax error would result. Thus, instead of using the reserved word PRINT in an assignment statement, you could change PRINT to APRINT to avoid obtaining an error, as indicated in the following interpretive BASIC example:

```
Ok
10 PRINT=4.5←incorrect (reserved word)
RUN
Syntax error in 10
Ok
10 PRINT=4.5
10 APRINT=4.5←changing reserved word
RUN
Ok
```

In the top portion of the preceding example, you were trying to assign the value 4.5 to the variable named PRINT. PRINT is a reserved word that operates on a given syntax that differs from the equality sign in which you are attempting to associate the value 4.5 with the variable name. The result of this attempted operation will be a syntax error. By changing PRINT to APRINT, the word is no longer reserved for a predefined operation, and you can now associate a value with the variable name.

If you are using QuickBASIC, syntax errors are denoted by the appearance of a dialog box, as illustrated in Figure 8.8. This dialog box contains two selection items that are command buttons. You can select OK, which enables you to continue entering your program, and Help, which when selected displays the Help: Syntax Error dialog box that contains hints that may explain the cause of the syntax error. You can select a dialog box entry by moving the mouse pointer to the entry and clicking the mouse button. As an alternative, you can use the Tab key to move the cursor from one command button to another and press the Enter key to select the command button on which the cursor is positioned.

When you wish to use a reserved word, you should ensure that it is appropriately delimited. This will permit BASIC to recognize the word. You delimit reserved words by using spaces or other special characters that may be permissible according to the syntax of the command, statement, function name, or operator name. A list of all the reserved words in BASIC is contained in Table 8.2.

Constants and Variables

Numerical quantities are referred to in BASIC as numbers or constants. There are five ways to indicate numeric constants: integer, fixed point, floating point, hexadecimal, and octal. When you are using QuickBASIC, a sixth method is added through its support of long integers. In addition, BASIC permits a second type of constant, which is called a *string constant*. Here, a string constant is a sequence of up to 255 characters that

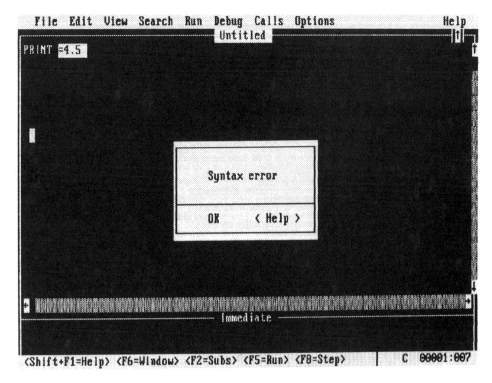

Figure 8.8   QuickBASIC Syntax Error Dialog Box.

is enclosed in double quotation marks if you are using an interpretive BASIC; a string length of up to 32,767 characters is allowed in QuickBASIC.

Numeric Constants

Numeric constants are positive or negative numbers that may be preceded by a plus or minus sign. If the sign does not appear, the number is considered positive. Numeric constants cannot contain commas and can be expressed in one of five ways, as indicated in Table 8.3.

Examples of valid integer numeric constants include the following:

```
   0
   1
 +10
 -4
 -0
```

Note that the positive sign is optional, because the number is taken to be positive if the sign is not included. Because two 8-bit bytes of storage are used for storing integer variables, their range of values must lie between $-32,768$ and $+32,767$.

Examples of valid fixed point numeric constants include the following:

$$5$$
$$-14.75$$
$$14.75$$
$$+14.75$$
$$0$$
$$146$$

Floating-point numbers are similar to scientific notation except that the base 10 is replaced by the letter E for single-precision or D for double-precision data representation. A floating-point constant consists of an optionally signed integer or a fixed point

Table 8.2
BASIC Reserved Words

ABS	DIM	KEY	OR	SLEEP[1]
AND	DO[1]	KILL	OUT	SOUND
ASC	DRAW	LBOUND[1]	PAINT	SPACE$
ATN	EDIT	LCASE[1]	PALETTE[1]	SPC(
AUTO	ELSE	LEFT$	PCOPY[1]	SQR
BEEP	END	LEN	PEEK	STATIC[1]
BLOAD	ENVIRON	LET	PEN	STEP
BSAVE	ENVIRON$	LINE	PLAY	STICK
CALL	EOF	LIST[2]	PMAP	STOP
CDBL	EQV	LLIST[2]	POINT	STR$
CHAIN	ERASE	LOAD[2]	POKE	STRING
CHDIR	ERDEV	LOC	POS	STRINGS$
CHR$	ERDEV$	LOCATE	PRESET	SUB[1]
CINT	ERL	LOCK[1]	PRINT	SWAP
CIRCLE	ERR	LOF	PRINT#	SYSTEM
CLEAR	ERROR	LOG	PSET	TAB(
CLNG[1]	EXIT[1]	LOOP[1]	PUT	TAN
CLOSE	EXP	LPOS	RANDOMIZE	THEN
CLS	FIELD	LPRINT	READ	TIME$
COLOR	FILEATTR[1]	LSET	REDIM[1]	TIMER
COM	FILES	LTRIM$[1]	REM	TO
COMMAND$[1]	FIX	MERGE	RENUM[2]	TROFF
COMMON	FNxxxxxxxx	MID$	RESET	TRON
CONST[1]	FOR	MKDIR	RESTORE	TYPE[1]
CONT	FRE	MKD$	RESUME	UCASE$[1]
COS	FREEFILE[1]	MKI$	RETURN	UEVENT[1]
CSNG	FUNCTION[1]	MKL$[1]	RIGHT$	UNBOUND[1]
CSRLIN	GET	MKS$	RMDIR	UNLOCK[1]
CVD	GOSUB	MKSMBF$[1]	RND	USING
CVI	GOTO	MKDMBF$[1]	RSET	USR
CVL[1]	HEX$	MOD	RTRIM$[1]	VAL
CVS	IF	MOTOR[2]	RUN	VALPTR$
CVSMBF[1]	IMP	NAME	SADD[1]	VALPTR
CVDMBF[1]	INKEY$	NEW[2]	SAVE[2]	VIEW[1]
DATA	INP	NEXT	SCREEN	WAIT
DATE$	INPUT	NOISE[2]	SEEK[1]	WEND
DECLARE[1]	INPUT#	NOT	SELECT[1]	WHILE
DEF	INPUT$	OCT$	SETMEM[1]	WIDTH
DEFDBL	INSTR	OFF	SGN	WINDOW
DEFINT	INT	ON	SHARED[1]	WRITE
DEFSNG	INTER$	OPEN	SHELL	WRITE#
DEFSTR	IOCTL	OPTION	SIN	XOR
DELETE	IOCTL$			

[1] Only applicable to QuickBASIC.
[2] Not applicable to QuickBASIC.

Table 8.3
Types of
Numeric Constants

Types of Numeric Constants	Ways to Indicate Numeric Constants
Integer	Whole numbers between −32,768 and +32,767; integer constants do not contain a decimal point
Long integer	Whole numbers between −2,147,483,648 and +2,147,483,647 (only applicable to QuickBASIC)
Fixed point	Positive or negative real numbers that can contain a decimal point
Floating point	Positive or negative numbers represented in exponential form
Hexadecimal	Hexadecimal numbers with up to 4 digits in interpretive BASIC and up to 10 digits in QuickBASIC can be expressed by using the prefix &H
Octal	Octal numbers with up to 6 digits in interpretive BASIC and 10 digits in QuickBASIC can be expressed by using the prefix &O or the prefix &

number known as the *mantissa*, which is followed by the character E and an optionally signed integer known as the *exponent*. The two formats for numbers represented in floating-point notation are as follows:

    number E +/− *ee*
    number D +/− *ee*

where number is an integer, a whole number with a decimal fraction, or just a decimal fraction—the number portion of the notation contains its significant digits and is called the mantissa, and if an integer is employed that contains no decimal point, the decimal point is considered to be to the right of the mantissa; E stands for single-precision exponential notation; D signifies double-precision exponential notation; +/− is an optional plus sign or a minus sign; and *ee* is a one- or two-digit exponent. The exponent specifies the magnitude of the number, which is the number of places to the right (positive exponent) or left (negative exponent) that the decimal point must be moved to obtain its true decimal point location. The maximum exponent value in all versions of BASIC is 38 for single-precision numbers. In QuickBASIC, a maximum exponent value of 308 is obtainable for double-precision numbers, whereas in interpretive BASIC double-precision numbers are limited to the same exponent value as single-precision numbers, with double precision only increasing the number of digits that can be displayed and stored.

Some examples of floating-point constants include

    −4.76E+3
    .1E−4
    5E+10

In the first example, −4.76 is the mantissa and +3 is the exponent. This number could be read as −4.76 times 10 to the third power and could be written as −.00476 in regular fixed-point notation. The second example is equivalent to expressing the number as .00001 in fixed-point notation; the third number is equivalent to 50000000000. Double-precision floating-point constants permit numbers to be stored with 17 digits of precision and printed with up to 16 digits of accuracy. In comparison, with single precision, up to 7 digits can be stored and printed, although only 6 digits will be accurate.

When you are using an interpretive BASIC, any number from 10E−38 to 10E+38 can be represented as a floating-point constant; however, greater mantissa accuracy is obtained when a double-precision floating-point constant is used, because the mantissa can be expanded from 7 to 17 digits. Unlike interpretive BASIC, QuickBASIC double precision increases both the number of digits in which a number is represented and the exponent value of the number. In QuickBASIC, double precision extends the exponent range to -324 to $+308$, whereas numbers can be stored with 17 digits of precision with up to 16 digits of accuracy. Various examples of numeric constant precision will be covered later in this chapter.

Hexadecimal numbers with up to four digits in interpretive BASIC and eight digits in QuickBASIC can be expressed by using the prefix &H. Hexadecimal digits are the numbers 0 through 9 and the letters A through F, which represent the decimal digits 10 through 15. Thus, decimal 255 can be represented in a hexadecimal as &HFF. Other examples of hexadecimal numbers include the following:

&H1234
&HAB7
&H5F

Octal numbers with up to 6 digits in interpretive BASIC and up to 10 digits in QuickBASIC can be expressed in BASIC by using the prefix &O or just & before the number. Octal digits include the numbers 0 through 7. Some examples of octal numbers include the following:

&O1717
&O147676
&77

String Constants

A string constant is a sequence of characters bounded by quotation marks. The sequence of characters can include most characters from the ASCII character set to include blanks, letters, numbers, and special characters such as $, +, -, /, and so on. The string cannot include quotation marks because this terminates the string, nor can it include certain characters that have special meanings such as the backspace character. The maximum number of characters that can be included in a string in interpretive BASIC is 255, which is the maximum size of one logical line of information. In QuickBASIC a string can be up to 32,767 characters long. We will typically use strings to represent such nonnumeric information as names and addresses as well as to label numeric output data and to print messages. Some examples of string constants include the following:

"TRY AGAIN"
"THE ANSWER IS"
"$2,500,000"

Numeric Constant Precision

Numeric constants can be stored internally in memory as integer, single precision, or double precision, whereas QuickBASIC adds the support for long integers. When constants are entered in integer, hexadecimal, or octal format, two bytes of memory are used and the numbers are interpreted as integers, which are whole numbers without a decimal point. In QuickBASIC, a long integer doubles the number of bytes of memory over a standard integer, resulting in four bytes of memory used to store data.

A single-precision constant is any numeric constant that is not an integer constant and is written with seven or fewer digits, uses the character E in exponential form, or has a trailing exclamation point (!). By using the exclamation point, you can declare a numeric constant to be single precision.

When expressed in double precision, numeric constants will be stored with up to 17 digits of precision and are printed with up to 16 digits. A double-precision constant is any numeric constant that contains eight or more digits or the character D when expressed in exponential format or contains a trailing number sign (#). By using the number sign, you can declare a numeric constant to be double precision. Examples of single- and double-precision numeric constants are listed in Table 8.4.

Roundoff

As mentioned earlier in this section, BASIC stores up to 7 digits in single precision and up to 17 digits in double precision. If you have more than 7 digits in single precision or 17 digits in double precision, your computer will round off the excess digits. This is illustrated by the following example.

```
k
10 A=12345678:PRINT A
RUN
1.234568E+07
Ok
```

Scalar Variables

Variables are names that are used to represent numbers or strings in a BASIC program. Similar to constants, there are two types of variables—numeric and string.

Within each type of variable are two classes—scalar variables and array variables. A *scalar variable* has only one value associated with it at any particular point in time; an *array variable* can have one or more values associated with it at any time. An example of the latter would be an array containing five elements, in which each element is initialized to a unique value different from the value of each of the other elements. The following discussion focuses on scalar variables, and array variables will be examined as a separate topic later in this chapter.

A *numeric variable* always has a value that is a number. If you use a numeric variable prior to assigning a value to it, BASIC will assume its value is zero without generating an error message. Therefore, it is important to ensure that your variables are assigned values prior to their use.

One method to assign the value of an expression to a variable is through the use of the LET statement. The following examples illustrate the assignment of values to numeric variables:

Table 8.4
Examples of
Numeric Constants

Single Precision	Double Precision
27.44	27.44143207
27.44!	27.44143207#
1.76E+12	1.76304159D+12

```
Ok
10 LET A=347.16
20 LET PIE=3.14159
30 RATIO =PIE/A
40 PRINT A,PIE,RATIO
RUN
 347.16        3.14159        9.049401E-03
Ok
```

In line 10, the variable A is assigned the value 347.16. In line 20, the variable PIE is assigned the value 3.14159. In line 30, an optional form of the assignment statement excluding the word LET is shown. Here, the variable RATIO is assigned the value of PIE divided by A. In line 40, the values of the three variables are printed through the use of the PRINT statement.

A string variable can range anywhere from 0 to 255 characters in length in interpretive BASIC and up to 32,767 characters in length in QuickBASIC. String variables are initially assumed to have a null value and a length of zero before you assign values to them. String variables can have a constant value, in which case they are string constants, or you can set the value of the string based on the result of some computation or the value of data input from the keyboard or from a data file. In this case, the string will be variable.

Some examples of the assignment of values to string variables are shown here. Note that the name of each string variable terminates with a dollar sign, which indicates to BASIC that it is a string variable. Variable naming conventions are described shortly.

```
Ok
10 NAME$="JOHN DOE"
20 ADDRESS$="6750 PROGRAMMERS ROW"
30 CITY$="COMPUTERVILLE"
40 PRINT NAME$,ADDRESS$,CITY$
RUN
JOHN DOE        6750 PROGRAMMERS ROW        COMPUTERVILLE
Ok
```

The type of variable used, string or numeric, must match the type of data assigned to it or a Type mismatch error will occur. Thus, string variables must be assigned string values and numeric variables must be assigned numeric values.

In the following example, a Type mismatch in line 10 occurred, since assigning a numeric value to a string variable was attempted.

```
Ok
LIST
10 NAME$=3.14159
20 PRINT NAME$
Ok
RUN
Type mismatch in 10
Ok
```

You could either change NAME$ to NAME or 3.14159 to "3.14159" to remove the mismatch. In the first case, NAME would be a numeric variable name. In the second case, we would be converting the number to a string.

Variable Names

BASIC variable names can be any length up to 255 characters; however, BASIC differentiates only the first 40 characters.

Numeric variable names can consist of letters, numbers, and the decimal point. The first character in a variable name must be a letter and a special character that identifies the type of variable permitted as the last character of the variable name. If the last character in the variable name is the dollar sign ($), the variable is considered to be a string variable. The format for variable names is:

```
Numeric variable name = LC. . .CT
```

where *L* is a letter; *C* is letters, numbers, or decimal point, of which up to 39 characters are significant, and a maximum of 254 characters permitted; and *T* represents the type—% for integer, & for long integer (QuickBASIC only), ! for single precision, # for double precision, and $ for string variable. If the type is not specified, single precision is assumed by BASIC.

Although a variable name cannot be a reserved word, it may contain embedded reserved words as long as it is not a reserved word with one of the type declaration characters such as %, !, &, #, or $ appended to the end of the word. Thus,

```
10 FRE = 50
```

is illegal, because FRE is a reserved word. If you change the preceding statement to

```
10 FREE = 50
```

the statement is legal, because FRE is only part of the variable name. Table 8.5 lists some examples of legal and illegal BASIC variable names. Can you ascertain why the illegal examples are invalid? In addition, can you differentiate between numeric and string variables and understand the type of numeric variable listed? If not, you may want to read this section a second time.

Table 8.5
Examples of
Variable Names

Names	Type/Reason
Valid	
A$	String
ADDRESS$	String
AMOUNT	Numeric
AMOUNT%	Numeric integer
AMOUNT&	Numeric long integer[1]
SSN$	String
SSN#	Numeric double precision
TAX!	Numeric single precision
TAX5	Numeric
TAX.SALES#	Numeric double precision
Invalid	
ADDRESS > STREET	Only letters, numbers, and decimal point permitted
AMOUNT!#	Only one type declarator permitted
CLEAR	Reserved word
$TAX	First character must be a letter

[1] Only applicable to QuickBASIC.

Variable Storage and Operation Considerations

Numeric variable names can be declared as integer, long integer, single-precision, or double-precision values by appending, respectively, the characters %, !, &, #, or $ to the variable name. Although you may obtain less accuracy by performing computations with integer and single-precision variables, there are several storage and program operational considerations that may favor declaring a variable to be a particular precision.

Table 8.6 lists the storage requirements for numeric variables of different precision. Variables of a higher precision require more storage than lower-precision variables. Thus, it may become important to sacrifice precision if memory space is insufficient for your program's operation. If you try to add a line to a program when there is no more room in memory, you will receive an `Out of memory` error message, and the line will not be added to the program. If this should occur, you may want to consider changing the precision of some variables to obtain additional storage, or you could subdivide your program into two or more logical programs that could be "chained" together.

Another reason to change the precision of variables is because you require program speed optimization. Whenever possible, you should use integer counters in loops, because only 2 bytes are acted on when integers are used. This can be extremely important if you are writing a communications program where you must perform a repetitive computation and then quickly sample the communications buffer to process the next group of received data. Here, if you cannot sample the buffer quickly enough you could lose data as incoming characters could overlay data previously sent to the AT.

In addition to declaring the precision of a numeric variable or defining a string variable with a trailing declaration character, interpretive BASIC has four type declaration statements that perform similar operations. These declaration statements can be used to declare variables as integer (DEFINT), single precision (DEFSNG), double precision (DEFDBL), or string (DEFSTR). If you are using QuickBASIC, you can use the previously mentioned type declaration statements as well as DEFLNG to define long integers. If such statements are used, they should be placed at the beginning of your program and must be executed prior to using any variables that they declare. A few examples of the use of type declaration are illustrated by the following programs:

```
Ok
LIST
10 DEFINT I,J,K
20 DEFSNG X,Y,G
30 I=26/5
40 X=2/3
50 X#=2/3
60 PRINT "I=",I
70 PRINT "X=",X
```

Table 8.6
Numeric Variable
Storage Requirements

Variable Type	Storage Requirement
Integer	2 bytes
Long integer[1]	4 bytes
Single precision	4 bytes
Double precision	8 bytes

[1] Only applicable to QuickBASIC.

```
80 PRINT "X#=",X#
Ok
RUN
I=              5
X=              .6666667
X#=             .6666666865348816
Ok
```

In this example, the DEFINT statement in line 10 declares that the variable names beginning with the letters I, J, and K will be integer. The DEFSNG statement declares variable names beginning with X, Y, and G to be single precision. In line 30, the division of 26 by 5 is rounded to an integer and will be printed with the value 5 as a result of the PRINT statement in line 60. In line 50, a type declaration character is used to denote that the variable X is a double-precision variable even though it was defined as a single-precision variable by the DEFSNG statement.

When a type declaration character—such as %, !, &, #, or $—occurs in a program, it takes precedence over a DEF type statement in the typing of a variable. Thus, when 2 is divided by 3 and converted to double precision in interpretive BASIC, the result is .6666666865348816. The reason that this value is not accurately expressed as .6666666666666667 is that the computation was performed in single precision and then rounded upward when the results of the operation were converted to double precision. Note that in line 40 the assignment of the computation of 2 divided by 3 is printed in line 70 as .6666667, because all operators are in single precision. In the following example, line 50 was changed so that the numerator is in double precision prior to its being divided. As shown, this results in an accurate 16-digit fraction.

```
Ok
LIST
10 DEFINT I,J,K
20 DEFSNG X,Y,G
30 I=26/5
40 X=2/3
50 X#=2#/3
60 PRINT "I=",I
70 PRINT "X=",X
80 PRINT "X#=",X#
Ok
RUN
I=              5
X=              .6666667
X#=             .6666666666666667
Ok
```

Array Variables

When you are writing a computer program, it is often convenient to refer to an entire collection of items at one time. Such a collection is normally referred to as an *array*. In BASIC, an array can be considered as a group or table of values that is referenced by the same name. Each individual value in the array is known as an *element*. The elements in the array can be either numerical quantities or string values; however, all of the elements in a given array must be of the same type, either all numerical quantities or all string values.

In mathematical notation, you might write A_0, A_1, A_2 . . . A_N to denote the N elements of a one-dimensional array named A. Because there are no subscripts in BASIC, you are forced to find an alternate method to denote the elements of an array. This alternate method is obtained by using parentheses to define the elements of an array. In BASIC, you will use the left and right parentheses after the name of an array as delimiters in which the specific element of the array you wish to examine or operate on will be defined. Thus, the preceding mathematical notation of N elements of the array A would be referenced as A(0), A(1), A(2) . . . A(N) in BASIC, and the fifth element of the array A would be referenced as A(4) if your base element were zero.

To better visualize the usefulness of arrays, consider the following problem. Suppose you know the daily sales of a store during a 31-day period and wish to perform a statistical analysis on those sales. Without arrays, you would have to assign a unique variable name to each of the daily sales figures. Just to obtain the sum of the sales might require a laborious statement such as the following:

```
10 LET TOTAL=SALES1+SALES2+ . . . SALES 31
```

Using the array variable named SALES, you could give the entire monthly table of sales one name and identify daily sales activity by their position within the table. You could view the array named SALES as the following table, filled in with some arbitrary daily sales values:

SALES ARRAY

127.14	215.13	419.87	. . .	310.54
SALES(1)	SALES(2)	SALES(3)	. . .	SALES(31)

If you wished to sum the value of sales within the month, you could build a counter in BASIC that would add the value of each element in the SALES array to a counter as shown here:

```
Ok
10 TOTAL=0
20 FOR I=1 to 31
30 TOTAL=TOTAL+SALES(I)
40 NEXT I.
```

In the preceding example, line 10 initializes the value of the TOTAL counter to zero. The FOR and NEXT statements form a boundary in which all statements in between are executed as the I counter loops in value from its initial of 1 to a final value of 31. Thus, each time the loop occurs, line 30 is executed, and the value of TOTAL is incremented by the value of SALES(I). When I is 1, the value of the first element of SALES, SALES(I), which is 127.14, is added to TOTAL, and so on. Note that in this example your array base is one (1). In BASIC, your array base is always zero, but you can reset it with the OPTION BASE statement. Suppose you had a requirement to add 365 daily sales figures. You would then change the end loop parameters in line 10 from 31 to 365. As you can see, arrays can provide a convenient mechanism for manipulating data.

In addition to one-dimensional arrays, BASIC permits you to have two-dimensional arrays. In fact, you can have up to 255 dimensions in an array in interpretive BASIC with a maximum of 32,767 elements per dimension, although doing so could rapidly use up large segments of program memory. In QuickBASIC you can have up to eight dimensions in an array, with up to 32,767 elements per dimension. A two-dimensional array can be thought of as being composed of horizontal and vertical columns. The first of two subscripts then refers to the row number and the second subscript refers to the column number. An array of three rows and three columns would be expressed in mathematical notation as

$$A_{0,1} \; A_{0,2} \; A_{0,3}$$
$$A_{1,1} \; A_{1,2} \; A_{1,3}$$
$$A_{2,1} \; A_{2,2} \; A_{2,3}$$

In BASIC, the element of the second row, second column, would be expressed as A(1,2). As shown, each array element will be named or referenced by the name subscripted through the use of a pair of parentheses with a number or sequence of numbers separated by commas. A three-dimensional array could be used to define a particular object and a point on that object might be expressed as A(5,20,15).

Numeric variable array names are similar to numeric variable names; however, no type declaration character is permitted. Thus, all numeric variable array names will consist of single-precision values. In addition, numeric variable array names are followed by a pair of left and right parentheses that define the specific size of or element of the array.

When you operate with arrays, you must first inform the computer how much memory to set aside for the array. This process is known as *defining* or *dimensioning* the array. You can do this through the use of the BASIC DIM statement, which is used to specify the maximum values for array variable subscripts and allocate storage accordingly. Because 0 is the lowest position of an element in an array unless changed by the BASIC OPTION BASE statement that declares the default lower bound for array subscripts, you can dimension a 10-element array named TAXRATE as follows:

```
100 DIM TAXRATE(9)
```

Once TAXRATE is dimensioned, you can initialize the various elements of the array to 10 specific tax rates and perform tax computations using the index of the array to retrieve a specific tax rate.

String variable arrays are named similarly to numeric variable arrays, with the only exception being that a trailing dollar sign is appended to the name. This signifies to the BASIC interpreter that the values of the elements of the array are strings. Thus, to dimension space for 100 names and addresses, you could use the following DIM statement:

```
10 DIM NAME$(99), ADDRESS$(99)
```

BASIC has an automatic dimensioning feature that you can use to your advantage if the number of elements in an array does not exceed 11. If you use an array element prior to defining the array, BASIC will automatically assume that it is to be dimensioned with a maximum subscript of 10, permitting you to have up to 11 elements in an array without dimensioning it.

In programming, you should observe caution in the mechanism you employ to dimension variables. Although the maximum dimension for an array is 255 in interpretive BASIC and 32,767 in QuickBASIC, a four-dimension array of 10 by 10 by 10 by 10 would require 10,000 locations to be set aside. If the array were numeric and thus consisted of single-precision values, four bytes would be required to store each value, resulting in a total of 40,000 bytes of memory being reserved for the array.

Operators and Numeric Expressions

In BASIC you must use special symbols, called *operators*, to indicate the operation you wish to perform. BASIC operators can be divided into four categories: arithmetic, relational, logical, and functional. The operators are used to connect numbers, numeric variables, or string variables, thus forming formulas or expressions. Thus, a formula can be composed of a single number or a single numeric variable as well as some combination of numbers, numeric variables, and operators. A numeric variable must be assigned some numerical quantity prior to its appearing in a formula, or it will be used in the formula with a 0 (zero) value.

The failure to assign values to numeric variables may cause expressions to be evaluated incorrectly, resulting in an erroneous computation that, if embedded in a lengthy program, may be hidden from casual observation. In some cases, the failure to assign values to numeric variables can result in the unintentional generation of an error message by the program in addition to obtaining a nondesired value. Both situations are illustrated by the following interpretive BASIC program:

```
Ok
10 LET X=A*42.5
20 PRINT "X=",X
30 LET V=23.5/A
40 PRINT "V=",V
RUN
X=              0
Division by zero
V=              1.701412E+38
Ok
```

In line 10, the multiplication operator (*) is used to multiply the value of the variable A by 42.5. Because A has not been assigned a value in the program prior to its use in line 10, it is used in the formula computation with a 0 value. This results in X being assigned the value 0, which may not be what you really wanted to occur. In line 30, the slash (/) character is used as a division operator to divide 23.5 by the value of A and assign that value to V. A has not been assigned a value, so division by zero is attempted. This results in a Division by zero error message, because machine infinity with the sign of the numerator is supplied as the result of the division. Note that the value assigned to the variable V is the largest value that interpretive BASIC can compute.

If you are using QuickBASIC a Division by zero dialog box will be displayed when the compiler attempts to convert line 30 into machine code. This dialog box terminates the attempted execution of the program, highlighting the statement causing the division by zero. Then you can correct the program.

Arithmetic Operators

Table 8.7 lists the BASIC arithmetic operators according to their hierarchy of operations. The hierarchy of operations is important, because together with the order of execution, it defines how a formula is evaluated. BASIC formulas are evaluated equivalently to mathematical expressions, in that operations are conducted from left to right with a

	Operator Symbol in BASIC	Operation	Hierarchy	Sample Expression Using Operator
Table 8.7 Arithmetic Operators	^	Exponentiation	1	A^B
	—	Negation	2	—A
	*,/	Multiplication, floating point division	3	A*B A/B
	\	Integer division	4	A\B
	MOD	Modulo arithmetic	5	A MOD B
	+,—	Addition, subtraction	6	A+B A—B

given hierarchical group. As an example, consider the following formula expressed using BASIC operators:

```
A+B/C+D^2
```

Proceeding from left to right, the value of the variable A is added to the value of the variable B divided by the value of variable C. Next, the previously computed value is added to D squared. Suppose the mathematical formula you wished to evaluate was $A+B/C + D^2$. Then, the initial formula you expressed using the preceding BASIC operators would be incorrect. You can alter the way operations are conducted in BASIC through the insertion of pairs of parentheses into formulas. When parentheses are inserted into formulas, the operations within the parentheses are performed as separate entities. If several pairs of parentheses are nested within a formula, the operators within the innermost pairs of parentheses are performed first, followed by the operations within the second innermost pair, and so on. Within each pair of parentheses, the hierarchy of operations as shown in Table 8.7 will apply unless it is altered by other pairs of parentheses that are embedded inside the outer pair. To properly express the required mathematical formula in BASIC, you could use parentheses to modify the initial BASIC expression as follows:

```
(A+B)/C + D^2
```

Now, the value of variable A will be added to the value of variable B and the sum will then be divided by the value of variable C.

Table 8.8 illustrates the conversion of 10 mathematical expressions to their BASIC language equivalents.

Although most of the operators listed in Table 8.7 should be familiar to you, two of them may appear unfamiliar due to their limited use in day-to-day computations. These are the integer division and modulo arithmetic operators.

Integer Division

An integer division operation is denoted by the backslash (\) character. When integer division is specified, the operands are first rounded to integers if they are not integer values, and then integer division is performed. The operators must lie in the valid range of numbers between —32,768 and 32,767 or between —2,147,483,648 and 2,147,483,647 when long integers are used in QuickBASIC. After division is performed, the quotient is truncated to an integer. Several examples of the results obtained from the use of integer division are illustrated by the following program:

```
Ok
10 LET A=10\4
20 LET B=11\4
30 LET C=12\4
40 LET D=13\4
50 PRINT A,B,C,D
60 LET E=40.25\5
70 LET F=36.49\6
80 LET G=36.51\6
90 PRINT E,F,G
RUN
 2           2           3           3
 8           6           6
Ok
```

Note that in integer division no rounding occurs. Only the "whole" or integer portion of the division is assigned to the appropriate variable and the remainder is discarded.

Modulo Arithmetic

In BASIC, modulo arithmetic is denoted by the operator symbol MOD. Integer division results in a quotient truncated to an integer, whereas the remainder is discarded. Modulo arithmetic, on the other hand, gives the integer value that is the remainder of an integer division. The following program shows several results of modulo arithmetic operations:

```
Ok
LIST
10 A=14 MOD 3
20 B=16.8 MOD 4
30 C=25.49 MOD 5
40 D=25.51 MOD 5
50 PRINT A,B,C,D
```

Table 8.8
BASIC Equivalents of Mathematical Expressions

Mathematical Expression	BASIC Language Equivalent
$A+\dfrac{B}{C}$	`A+B/C`
$\dfrac{A}{B+C}$	`A/(B+C)`

$\dfrac{A \cdot B}{C \cdot D}$	`(A*B)/(C*D)`
	 or
	 `A*B/(C*D)`
	 or
	 `(A/C)*(B/D)`

$A-(B-C)$	`A-(B-C) or A-B+C`
$A_x{}^5+D^E$	`A(X)^5+D^E`
$A \cdot X^3+B \cdot X^2+C$	`A*X^3+B*X^2+C`
$-X$	`-X`
$A_1+A_2{}^2+A_3{}^3$	`A(1)+A(2)^2+A(3)^3`
$\dfrac{(A+B) \cdot (A-C)}{D+E}$	`((A+B)*(A-C))/(D+E)`
$3.14159 \cdot R^2$	`3.14159*R^2`

```
Ok
RUN
 2            1            0            1
Ok
```

If the results of some of the computations appear to be off by 1 from what you may have hand calculated, you probably forgot that BASIC rounds when converting numbers to integers. Thus, 25.49 is rounded to 25, whereas 25.51 is rounded to 26. Then, 25 MOD 5 is 0, because 25/5 has a remainder of zero. Likewise, 26/5 is 5 with a remainder of 1.

Mixed Precision within Statements

When variables or constants of mixed precision occur within a statement, BASIC will perform variable assignment values or computations based on a series of predefined rules.

If a numeric value in one precision is assigned to a numeric variable typed to a different precision, the number will be stored with the precision of the target variable, as illustrated by the following example:

```
Ok
LIST
10 A%=100/3  :PRINT A%          'INTEGER
20 B!=100/3  :PRINT B!          'SINGLE PRECISION
30 C#=100/3  :PRINT C#          'DOUBLE PRECISION
Ok
RUN
 33
 33.33333
 33.33333206176758
Ok
```

The preceding examples converted a lower-precision number to a higher-precision number. Note that the resulting higher-precision number can only be as accurate as the lower-precision number. If you wish to increase the precision, you must use arithmetic operations instead of an assignment statement. This is because in an assignment statement, if you would assign a single-precision value to a double-precision variable, only the first six digits of the double-precision variable will be accurate, because only six digits of accuracy are supplied by a single-precision value. If you use arithmetic operations in a statement, all of the operands in the arithmetic operation will be converted to the most precise operand. This is illustrated by the following example:

```
Ok
LIST
10 A%=100!/3  :PRINT A%         'INTEGER
20 B!=100!/3  :PRINT B!         'SINGLE PRECISION
30 C#=100#/3  :PRINT C#         'DOUBLE PRECISION
Ok
RUN
 33
 33.33333
 33.33333333333333
Ok
```

Note that by typing the value 100 in line 30 as double precision, the resulting division became accurate to 16 places.

In the preceding examples, lower-precision values were assigned to higher-precision variables. What happens if you wish to assign a higher-precision value to a lower-precision variable? The answer to this question is provided by the following program:

```
Ok
10 A%=33.33333! :PRINT A%
20 B!=33.33333333333333# :PRINT B!
RUN
 33
 33.33333
Ok
```

In the preceding examples, the result of the assignment of a higher-precision value to a lower-precision value causes the assigned number to be rounded.

Relational Operators

In order to carry out what are known as *conditional branching operations* in BASIC, a mechanism is required to express conditions of equality and inequality. This mechanism is provided by the use of relational operators. When relational operators are used to compare two values expressed as numerics or strings, you must ensure that similar type operands are used on both sides of the relational operator sign. That is, you cannot mix numeric and string constants or variables. Doing so would violate the grammatical construction of the language and result in a syntax error. Table 8.9 lists the relational operators available in BASIC.

Relational operators can be used to control program execution flow by initiating branching based on certain conditions. In addition, they can be employed to cause a BASIC statement or sequences of BASIC statements to be executed when certain conditions occur.

The results of relational comparisons are bistable. They are either "true" (-1) or "false" (0). The result of the relational comparison is normally used to determine where a program statement will branch to or what sequence of program statements will be executed.

A detailed description of the use of relational operators will be deferred until later in this book, but some elementary examples are in order. In the short program segment that follows, a numeric value is read from the keyboard through the use of the BASIC INPUT statement and assigned to the variable X. Next, three conditional tests are conducted to see if the value entered is equal to, less than, or greater than 5. If the

Table 8.9	Operator Symbol	Relation Tested
Relational Operators	=	Equality
	<> or ><	Inequality[1]
	<	Less than
	>	Greater than
	<= or =<	Less than or equal to
	>= or =>	Greater than or equal to

[1]QuickBASIC automatically converts an inequality entered as >< to <>.

result of a comparison operation is "true," the appropriate branch to the indicated line number in the program occurs. If the results of the comparison are "false," the next program line number is executed.

```
Ok
LIST
10 INPUT;X
20 IF X=5 THEN 500
30 IF X<5 THEN 1000
40 IF X>5 THEN 1500
500 PRINT " EQUAL":STOP
1000 PRINT " LESS THAN":STOP
1500 PRINT " GREATER THAN":STOP
Ok
RUN
? 5 EQUAL
Break in 500
Ok
```

When the program was executed with the RUN command, the value 5 was entered. This resulted in a branch to line 500 in the program where the string EQUAL was printed. The STOP statement on that line caused the message Break in 500 to be generated, and the program terminated its execution. In the following example, the value of X is used as a decision variable regarding the value of the variable P in the program. If X is equal to 2, then P will be set equal to 7; otherwise, P will be assigned the value 3.

```
Ok
LIST
10 INPUT;X
20 PRINT
110 IF X=2 THEN P=7:ELSE P=3
120 PRINT "FOR X= ";X;"P= ";P
Ok
RUN
? 1
FOR X= 1 P= 3
Ok
RUN
? 2
FOR X= 2 P= 7
Ok
RUN
? 3
FOR X= 3 P= 3
Ok
```

When arithmetic and relational operators are combined in one expression, the arithmetic operations are performed prior to the relational test. As an example, consider the following BASIC statement:

```
10 IF (A+B) ^2<=C THEN 50
```

First, the values of A and B are added and the combined value is then squared. The result of the arithmetic operations is then compared to the value of C. If the square of A plus B is less than or equal to C, the branch to program line 50 occurs. Thus, if the expression is true (−1), the branch occurs. If the expression is false (0), then the next sequential program statement is executed. For the expression to be false, the value of A plus B squared must be greater than C in this example.

When strings are compared, the comparison is based on the ASCII value of the characters in the string. The ASCII codes of the character set used by the AT and compatible computers are listed in Appendix A. If you turn to Appendix A, you will note that the first 32 characters in order of their ASCII value are control characters that are used for video display or communications. These characters are followed by a series of punctuation characters, including the space character, exclamation point, quotation symbol, and so on. Next, the 10 decimal digits occur, followed by a few additional punctuation characters and all the uppercase letters of the alphabet. After a few more punctuation characters, the 26 lowercase alphabetic characters are encountered, followed by a series of special characters to include graphics, language, and mathematical symbols.

For string comparisons consisting of digits and alphabetic characters, you can think of the comparison being conducted in alphabetical order. This is because the ASCII value of the digits appears first, followed by the uppercase alphabet, which is then followed by the lowercase alphabet. Thus, numbers are "less than" letters and uppercase alphabetic letters are "less than" lowercase alphabetic letters.

When two strings are compared, the computer actually takes one character at a time from each string and compares their ASCII values. If the ASCII values are the same, the computer will continue comparing, examining the next character in each string. If all the characters in each string are in the same order, the strings are equal. If the ASCII values of the strings differ, the string with the lower ASCII value is less than the string with the higher value. If two strings of different lengths are compared, if the end of the shorter string is reached during the comparison, the shorter string is considered to be smaller. Both leading and trailing blanks are significant, because each such blank has the ASCII value of 32 for string comparison purposes. Table 8.10 lists several true and false string comparisons. If you cannot easily determine why these comparisons are true or false, you may wish to review the preceding material concerning relational operators.

In addition to individual string comparisons, strings can be joined together and pairs of strings can be compared. The joining together of strings is called *concatenation*, and several examples of string concatenation are shown below.

```
"SALES" + "REPORT"    becomes "SALESREPORT"
"STATE" + "ZIP"       becomes "STATEZIP"
N$ + Z$               becomes the value of N$ followed by the value
                         of Z$
```

In the preceding examples, the plus sign (+) is used as the concatenation operator.

Table 8.10	**True Comparisons**	**False Comparisons**
String Comparisons	"1AX" < "2AA"	"4UIPROGRAM" < "1HECKOFAJOB"
	"TEST" > "ZETA"	"PAYROLL.1" < "PAYROLL"
	"four" > "FOUR"	"GILBERT" > "GILBERT HELD"
	"TIMEOUT" > "TIME"	

By concatenating strings, you can perform many important sorting functions expediently. As an example, you could concatenate state and zip code strings to sort addresses by zip code within a state.

Boolean Operators

Boolean operators provide BASIC programs with the ability to make logical decisions on numeric data under program control. Hence, Boolean operators are often referred to as logical operators. There are six Boolean operators: NOT, AND, OR, XOR, IMP, and EQV.

Each of the Boolean operators takes a combination of true/false values and returns a true or false result. The operand of a Boolean operator is considered to be true if it is not equal to zero or false if it is equal to zero. This is similar to the -1 and 0 results obtained from relational operators. The result of a Boolean operation is a number that is considered to be true if it is not equal to zero or false if it is equal to zero. The number is computed by performing the Boolean operation on the operand or operands bit by bit. To obtain a firm understanding of Boolean operators, examine each of the operators in detail through the use of what is known as truth tables as well as looking at some examples of its use in BASIC statements. Each of these Boolean operators will be discussed in order of its precedence of operation. That is, the NOT operator will have its operands evaluated prior to the operands of an AND operator, if those two Boolean operators appear in one expression.

NOT

The NOT operator is also known as the *logical complement operator*. The truth table showing the results of this Boolean operator is

A	NOT A
T	F
F	T

An example of the NOT operator used in a BASIC statement is

```
10 IF NOT A THEN 500
```

In this example, the program will branch to line 500 if A is not true. This is because NOT A is true only if A is false, because NOT A would be false only if A is true.

AND

Also known as a *conjunction operator*, the AND operator can be employed to join two operands together as shown in the following truth table:

A	B	A AND B
T	T	T
T	F	F
F	T	F
F	F	F

In examining this truth table, the conjunction of the two operands has the value true only if both operands are true. It has the value false if either or both operands are false. The AND operator is a valuable mechanism for testing for ranges of values, as shown by the following BASIC statement:

```
10 IF AGE>=20 AND AGE<=40 THEN 500
```

In the preceding statement, the program will always branch to line 500 if a person's age is found to be between 20 and 40.

OR

The OR or *disjunction operator* performs an inclusive operation on two operands as shown in the following truth table.

A	B	A OR B
T	T	T
T	F	T
F	T	T
F	F	F

The result of the OR operation has the value true if either or both operands are true. The result of the operation has the value false only if both operands are false. Suppose age requirements were immaterial if a person's height were under 5 feet. Maybe you have a secret mission for short people! You could modify the BASIC statement used to explain the AND operator as follows:

```
10 IF AGE>=20 AND AGE<=40 OR HEIGHT <5 THEN 500
```

You would now always branch to line 500 if a person's age were between 20 and 40 or if their height were less than 5 feet.

XOR

The results of the XOR (exclusive OR) operation on two operands are illustrated by the following truth table:

A	B	A XOR B
T	T	F
T	F	T
F	T	T
F	F	F

If both operands are true or if both operands are false, the result has the value false. If either operand differs in value from the other, the result has the value true. The following program statement illustrates the use of the XOR operator in BASIC:

```
10 IF HEIGHT <5 AND AGE XOR TESTAGE THEN 500
```

For the branch to line 500 to occur, HEIGHT has to be less then 5 AND AGE must be different from TESTAGE.

IMP

The IMP or *implication operator* has the value false only if the value of the first operand is true and the value of the second operand is false. Otherwise, the value of the implication operation is true. This is shown by the following truth table:

A	B	A IMP B
T	T	T
T	F	F

F	T	T
F	F	T

EQV

The results of the EQV or *equivalence operator* are true if both operands are true or both operands are false. Otherwise, the value of the equivalence operation is false. This is shown by the following truth table:

A	B	A EQV B
T	T	T
T	F	F
F	T	F
F	F	T

Binary Manipulation

The Boolean operators provide the means to perform binary manipulation of data. Boolean operands are converted to integers in the range −32,768 to 32,767 and two 8-bit bytes are used to store the resulting binary number. This is illustrated with the decimal value of each binary position indicated as well as the sign bit of the two-byte integer in the following:

S	16384	8192	4096	2048	1024	512	256	128	64	32	16	8	4	2	1

A sign bit of 0 indicates the number is positive. Negative numbers are expressed in what is known as *twos complement form*. First, the complement of the binary number is obtained and then a binary 1 is added to obtain its twos complement. As an example of twos complement notation, consider the decimal number 15. It would be stored as

0	0	0	0	0	0	0	0	0	0	0	0	1	1	1	1

Its ones complement would be

1	1	1	1	1	1	1	1	1	1	1	1	0	0	0	0

To obtain its twos complement, a binary 1 is added to the ones complement, resulting in the storing of minus decimal 15 in twos complement notation as in

1	1	1	1	1	1	1	1	1	1	1	1	0	0	0	1

If the Boolean operands fall outside the range −32,768 to +32,767, an Overflow error will occur. When a Boolean operation occurs, the operation is performed on a sequence or sequences of 16 bits. Each bit position in the result is determined by the corresponding bits in the operand or two operands, according to the previously defined truth tables. For binary manipulation, a 1 bit is considered to be "true," and a 0 bit is considered to be "false." To see how Boolean operators manipulate binary information, examine the following sample program statements:

```
10 LET A=15 AND B
```

Suppose when line 10 is executed the value of B is decimal 10. Because 15 = binary 1111 and 10 = binary 1010, 15 AND 10 will be 1010 in binary, which is 10 decimal. Now consider the following program statement:

```
10 IF A AND B=12 THEN 1000
```

In this example, only if the result of the conjunction operation is binary 1100 will the branch to line 1000 occur. By using Boolean operators, you obtain the ability to "mask" bit positions. This provides you with the ability to test the status of the contents of memory locations, machine I/O ports, and unique portions of memory bytes. If you wanted to perform a certain operation only if bit position 2 were set, you could "mask" all the other bits by ANDing by 2. The following statement would then cause a branch to line 1000 only if bit 2 in the variable named A were set:

```
10 IF A AND 2=2 THEN 1000
```

Precedence of Operators in Expressions

Although the precedence of operators within a given category has been discussed, what happens if you have a program statement that requires the execution of different types of operators? The different categories of numeric operations have their own order of precedence. In an expression, all function calls will be evaluated first. Although a detailed discussion of function calls will be deferred for the time being, you can view them being used in an expression similar to a variable; however, their use results in a predefined operation being performed. As an example, the SQR(X) function returns the square root of X.

After function calls are performed, arithmetic operations will be conducted. These operations are followed in sequence by relational operations while Boolean operators are conducted last. Table 8.11 summarizes the operator precedence for arithmetic, relational, and Boolean operations.

Loading and Running Programs

If a program is stored on the fixed disk or diskette, you can easily load and execute it by using the LOAD command in interpretive BASIC, whose format is

```
LOAD"filespec[,R]
```

The file specification, or *filespec* for short, describes the physical file in the form of the device where it resides, the path to the file, and the filename. The device name tells BASIC where to look for a file, the path tells BASIC which directory contains the file, and the filename informs BASIC which file you are looking for on a particular device in a particular directory.

The file specification is a string expression of the form

```
[device][path]filename[.ext]
```

Note that the *device*, *path*, and *ext* are optional. If the device is omitted, the default drive is assumed. Omitting the path causes the current directory to be used as the directory to be searched for loading the indicated file when a LOAD command is entered.

Table 8.11
Operator Precedence

Operator	Operation
Arithmetic	
^	Exponentiation
−	Negation
*,/	Multiplication, floating point division
\	Integer division
MOD	Modulo arithmetic
+,−	Addition, subtraction
Relational	
=	Equality
<> or ><	Inequality[1]
<	Less than
>	Greater than
<= or =<	Less than or equal to
>= or =>	Greater than or equal to
Boolean	
NOT	Complement
AND	Conjunction
OR	Disjunction
XOR	Exclusive or
IMP	Implication
EQV	Equivalence

[1] The inequality symbol, ><, is automatically converted to <> by QuickBASIC.

When you are using QuickBASIC, pull down the File menu to load programs into memory. Figure 8.4 shows the QuickBASIC File menu, which you pull down by either pressing the ALT+F key combination or clicking the mouse pointer on the File label. Selecting the Open Program option displays the Open Program dialog box, which is illustrated in Figure 8.9.

As you examine the File menu illustrated in Figure 8.4, note the distinction between the Open Program and Load File options. Open Program is used to clear memory and load an existing program from disk. In comparison, Load File does not clear memory prior to loading a file.

The Open Program dialog box illustrated in Figure 8.9 initially displays all files with the extension BAS in the current directory. This is because the default value assigned to the File Name text box is *.BAS, which results in all files with the extension BAS being displayed in the Files list box. Here the File Name text box is the rectangular box to the right of the File Name label, whereas the Files list box is the rectangular box under the Files label. Above the Files list box note C:\QB45, which indicates that the current directory is QB45 under the root directory on drive C. You can change the directory and drive by moving the cursor to a directory or drive indicator in the Dirs/Drives list box and then click the mouse button on an entry or move the highlight bar over an entry and press Enter. Once you have located the specific program you want to load you simply double-click the mouse when a highlight bar is positioned on the program name and QuickBASIC then loads the program, changing the title bar at the top center of the window to reflect the name of the program just loaded. If you do not have a mouse, you can use the tab and arrow keys to position a highlight bar over the program you wish to load and then press Enter to inform QuickBASIC to load the

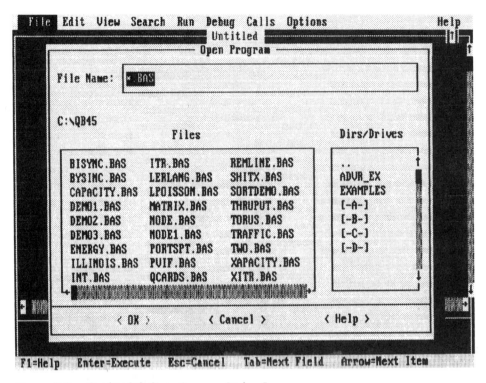

Figure 8.9   QuickBASIC Open Program Dialog Box.

program. Once you have loaded a program, you can select the Start option from the Run menu or press the Shift+F5 key combination to execute the program.

Device Names

The device name consists of one to four characters and is terminated by a colon(:). Table 8.12 contains a list of currently available device names and their association with a physical device. Once the device name is specified, you must provide BASIC with the path and the filename you are looking for on a particular device, because storage devices can contain more than one directory and the same filenames may exist in different directories.

Path

A *path* is a list of directory names separated by backslashes (\). If you have a directory named FINANCE under the root directory on drive C, the device and path specifiers in the LOAD command for interpretive BASIC that load a file named INCOME in that directory can be

A>**LOAD"C:\FINANCE\INCOME"**   if default drive is A
c>**LOAD"\FINANCE\INCOME"**   if default drive is C

When naming files, a series of file naming conventions must be adhered to.

Table 8.12
Device Names

Name	Physical Device Addressed
KYBD	Keyboard (input only)
SCRN	Display (output only)
LPT1	First printer (output only)
LPT2	Second printer (output only)
LPT3	Third printer (output only)
COM1	First asynchronous communications adapter
COM2	Second asynchronous communications adapter
CAS1	Cassette tape player (input and output)[1]
A	First diskette drive (input and output)
B	Second diskette drive (input and output)
C	First fixed disk (input and output)
D	Second fixed disk (input and output)

[1] Although this device is supported by early versions of DOS, there is no cassette port on the AT and compatible computers.

Filename Conventions

For both disk and diskette files, hereafter referred to as *disk files*, the filename may consist of two parts separated by a period (.). The part to the left of the period is the name of the file; the part to the right of the period is the file extension. Thus, disk files are of the form *name.extension*.

The name of the disk file must be eight or fewer characters in length. If you have more than eight characters in the name of the file, BASIC will insert a period after eight characters and use up to the first three extra characters as the extension. Thus, a disk filename specified as PAYROLLDATA would be stored as PAYROLLD.ATA. Only the characters A through Z, digits 0 through 9, and the ( ), { }, @, $, %, ^, &, !, –, –, ", /, and ~ characters can be used for a filename or extension. If you use a filename longer than eight characters and have specified an extension, an error message will be displayed. Normally, you will use the extension to define the type of the file for reference purposes as illustrated here:

PAYROLL.BAS
EMPLOYEE.DAT
STAT105.FTN

In this example, PAYROLL could be a program file written in BASIC, and you will use the abbreviation BAS in the file extension to indicate this. The EMPLOYEE file might contain data to be used by the PAYROLL program, and you indicate that it is a data file by adding DAT as its extension. The STAT105 could be a statistical program for course number 105 you are taking, and if you wrote the program in FORTRAN, you could so indicate by adding FTN as its file extension. DOS reserves certain predefined functions for files with these extensions: COM (command), BAK (backup), and BAT (batch). Unless you specifically intend to use a file with one of those three extensions for a specific system function, you should normally attempt to use some other extension in your file extension naming process.

R Option

If the R option is specified in the LOAD command for interpretive BASIC, the program will commence execution immediately after it is loaded. Program execution will then begin at the first program statement in the file.

Keyboard Program Entry

When you are using interpretive BASIC, prior to typing a program into your computer you may want to enter the NEW command into the system. The NEW command is used to delete the program residing in memory from the system and to clear all variables. If you just powered up the system, there would be no current program in memory, and you could load a program from disk or enter a program from the keyboard without having to use the NEW command. If you previously entered a program, loading a new program will clear memory automatically unless you use the MERGE command. This command could result in a mixture of two programs in storage. This is illustrated by the following example. Assume line numbers 5, 15, and 25 represent a three-line program in memory. If you merge another three-line program from disk that consists of line numbers 10, 20, and 30, what do you wind up with in memory? As shown here, you would wind up with a six-line program that is a mixture of the old program previously entered into the system and the new program.

```
Old program   New program    Resulting program
     5 ─────────── 10 ───────────────→ 5
    15 ─────────── 20 ───────────────→ 10
    25 ─────────── 30 ───────────────→ 15
                                     → 20
                                     → 25
                                     → 30
```

If you do not require the old program to be merged with the new program, you can eliminate it from memory by using the NEW command, as in

```
Ok
NEW
Ok
```

The effect of the NEW command can be shown by the following example:

```
Ok
10 REM TRIAL PROGRAM
20 PRINT "HI THERE"
NEW
LIST
Ok
```

In this example, your short two-line program is erased from memory when you enter **NEW**. This is verified by the use of the LIST command, which does not list the previously entered program because it has been erased from memory.

If you are using QuickBASIC, selecting the New Program option from the File menu (Figure 8.4) performs an operation equivalent to the interpretive BASIC NEW command. That is, it clears memory before enabling you to create a new program.

Program Execution

If you did not use the R option when loading your interpretive BASIC program, you can either press the F2 key or enter the keyword RUN to execute your program. Pressing the F2 key generates the keyword RUN followed by a return, causing any BASIC program in memory to be executed. Similarly, if you entered a program from the keyboard after BASIC was initialized, pressing the F2 key or entering the keyword RUN will cause your program to execute.

If you are using QuickBASIC, you can either select the Start option on the Run menu or press the Shift+F5 key combination to execute the program in memory.

9 // Basic Operations in BASIC

This chapter focuses on a variety of processing, branching, and I/O statements. These statements can be viewed as forming the nucleus of the BASIC language common to all versions of BASIC that can operate on your computer. Prior to examining one or more examples of each statement, the format that must be followed to obtain the correct construction of the statement will be defined. In this and succeeding chapters, the following notations will be used for BASIC format specifications:

format: Common to all versions of BASIC
format$_Q$: Applicable to QBASIC and QuickBASIC

Each of the formats presented for BASIC commands, statements, and functions will be constructed based on the following syntax construction rules:

- Words in capital letters are keywords and must be entered as shown. Keywords may be entered in any combination of upper- and lowercase characters; however, BASIC will convert keywords to uppercase.
- Items shown in lowercase are to be supplied by you when creating a command, statement, or function.
- Items in brackets ([ ]) are optional and may or may not be included in the format based on a particular circumstance.
- Braces ({ }) indicate that a choice of one of the enclosed items is to be made. Braces do not appear in the actual statements.
- Ellipses (. . .) are used to indicate an item that may be repeated as many times as you wish.
- All punctuation characters with the exception of square brackets must be included as shown in the format.

In developing format conventions, several generic terms and abbreviations have been employed to develop a standard scheme for presenting each BASIC language statement. The terms and abbreviations that will be used throughout this book are listed in Table 9.1.

Processing Statements

REM Statement

The REM statement is an abbreviation for REMark. This statement permits the insertion of explanatory remarks into a program. The format of this statement is illustrated below:

Table 9.1
Generic Terms
and Abbreviations

Term	Meaning
A	Option added to a *filespec* to denote an ASCII file.
address	Memory location.
arg	Argument.
arrayname	String or numeric array name.
aspect	Ratio of X-radius to the Y-radius.
background	Background color of screen.
boundary	Edge of screen or of a figure to be filled with color.
col	Screen column number between 1 and 40 or 1 and 80, depending on screen width.
color	Numeric value that indicates color selection.
constant	Actual value BASIC uses during program execution; can be string or numeric.
constant$	String constant.
dummy	Dummy argument.
dummy$	Dummy string argument.
errorcode	Number associated with an error message.
expr	Expression.
expr1, *expr2*	Expressions that are evaluated.
expr$	Any valid string constant, variable, or expression.
exprlist	List of expressions.
exprnm	Any numeric constant, variable, or expression.
exprnm%	Any integer numeric constant, variable, or expression.
exprnm&	Any long integer numeric constant, variable, or expression.
exprnm#	Any double-precision numeric constant, variable, or expression.
exprnm!	Any single-precision numeric constant, variable, or expression.
filenum	File number assigned to a file that was opened.
filespec	File specification of a program to be loaded or a data file.
foreground	Foreground color of screen.
length	Numeric expression with a value between 1 and 65,535 that specifies a range.
letter	Any letter in BASIC character set, A through Z.
*line*ᵢ	The *i*th line number of a BASIC program.
memadr	Memory address.
n	References the communications adapter (0 through 4) when referring to communications statements or a microprocessor hardware port.
newnum	New BASIC program line number.
numvar	Numeric variable name.
offset	Numeric expression with a value between 1 and 65,535 that specifies a starting point.
oldnum	Previous or old BASIC program line number.
P	Option added to *filespec* to denote encoded binary files
palette	Color mix selection.
promptmsg	Prompt message displayed on screen.
R	Option added to *filespec* to denote execution from first line in program after program loading.
range	Group of line numbers affected by a command.
recnum	Record number.
remark	Nonexecutable comment.
row	Screen row number between 1 and 25.
statement(s)	One or more BASIC language statements.

Table 9.1
(continued)
Generic Terms
and Abbreviations

Term	Meaning
sub	Subscript.
var	Numeric or string variable.
varnm	Numeric variable.
var$	String variable.
xctr	x-axis center point of drawing.
yctr	y-axis center point of drawing.
&	Current line number, when used as expression suffix, identifies a long integer.
&H	Hexadecimal number prefix.
&O	Octal number prefix.
;	Continue printing or display on same line.
.	Current line.

$$\text{format: } \left\{ \begin{matrix} \text{REM} \\ , \end{matrix} \right\} \text{-remark}$$

The REM statement provides you with a mechanism to internally document a program by adding information concerning calculations, variable assignments, and the like to a program. While the REM statement is nonexecutable, it is output exactly as entered when the program is listed and provides you with a mechanism to "internally document" a program.

In addition to the REM statement, you can also use a single quotation mark followed by your comments. This allows you to add comments to a line containing a BASIC statement or to put comments on a separate line. If you have a program line containing multiple statements, any REM statement on that line must be the last statement on the line. Some examples of the use of REM statements and remarks preceded by a single quotation mark are shown here:

```
100 REM Initialization Section
110 REM Variable Naming Assignments
120 REM SALES(X) Array containing daily sales receipts
 .
 .
 .
500 'Lines 500 through 600 compute regression analysis
 .
 .
1000 X=X+1 'increment counter
 .
 .
1500 Flag=1 : REM Reset flag
```

The addition of comments to a program can be extremely helpful if you desire to modify the program at a later date; however, a word of caution is in order. Comments take up space in memory and will slow program execution time. For these reasons, it is advisable to use comments selectively and supplement "internal documentation" with external documentation in the form of notes concerning the intricacies of your program.

Although REM statements are nonexecutable, like all interpretive BASIC statements they are preceded by a line number. If you are using QBASIC or QuickBASIC you can also prefix a REM statement with a line number or label. This means that you can have a branch to a REM statement within a program. When a branch to a REM statement occurs, program execution will continue with the first executable statement that follows the REM statement. Thus, REM statements can be used both to document looping activities and to provide entry and exit points to loops.

Assignment Statements

In BASIC, there are several methods to assign a numerical or a string value to a variable. One of the most popular methods employed is through the use of the assignment statement whose format is shown below:

format: [LET] *var = expr*

In some versions of BASIC, this statement is known as the LET statement because of the understood keyword. In all versions of interpretive BASIC and QuickBASIC, the word LET is optional. Here, the equal sign is sufficient when you assign an expression, numeric, or a string value to a variable. The following example uses the assignment statement:

```
10 LET X=1
20 LET NAME$ = "GIL"
30 A=B+C+D
40 PRODUCT=A*B*C*D
```

In line 10, the numeric variable X is assigned the value 1. Because the keyword LET is optional, this statement could have been written as:

```
10 X=1
```

In line 20, the string variable NAME$ is assigned the string value "GIL". In line 30, the sum of the values associated with the variables B, C, and D is assigned to the variable named A. If, at the point of assignment, the variables in a statement are undefined, BASIC will assign a value of zero to such variables. While forgetting to assign values to variables prior to their use can cause incorrect results, it can also cause an overflow error if the unassigned variable is used as a divisor in an equation. In such instances, this will cause a Division by zero error message to occur.

From the preceding examples, note that the variable to the left of the equal sign and the term to the right must be of the same type, numeric or string. If you attempt to assign a numeric value to a string variable or a string value to a numeric variable, you will obtain a Type mismatch error as shown below.

```
Ok
100 REM BET WE GET AN ERROR
110 NAME$=105
RUN
Type mismatch in 110
Ok
```

Although there are many assignment terms that look like algebraic equations, there are certain assignment terms that make little sense if you view them as an algebraic equation. One example of this is

```
100 LET X=X+1
```

The assignment term X=X+1 does not correspond to an algebraic equation, since the equation X=X+1 has no meaning from an algebraic equation standpoint. When written in BASIC, you are increasing the value of the numeric variable X by one unit. Here, the assignment term becomes logical when you interpret it to mean you wish to add 1 to the value represented by the variable X and then assign this new value to X. This new value of X will then replace the old value. Later, you will see that this type of assignment statement is frequently used as a counter in BASIC.

Although some BASICs allow multiple assignments of the form,

```
100 A=B=C=0
```

such assignments are not permitted in any version of BASIC covered in this book. Instead, you must use several assignment statements, although you can include multiple assignment statements on a single line as long as each statement is separated from the preceding statement by a colon (:). An example of this is

```
100 A=0:B=0:C=0
```

READ and DATA Statements

Many BASIC programs require that a large number of variables be initialized or changed to certain values within a program. Although you can use many assignment statements to accomplish this, it may be cumbersome to do so. Instead, you may use one or more pairs of READ and DATA statements. When used in BASIC, a READ statement must always be used in conjunction with one or more DATA statements. DATA statements contain the values of constants that READ statements will assign to the variables in the READ statement. READ statement variables may be numeric or string; however, the values read from the DATA statement must correspond to the types of constants in the DATA statements. That is, a string variable in a READ statement must correspond with a string constant in a DATA statement, and a numeric variable in a READ statement must correspond to a numeric constant in a DATA statement. The formats of the READ and DATA statements are

```
format: READ var[,var . . .]
format: DATA constant[,constant . . .]
```

An example of the use of a pair of READ, DATA statements is shown below:

```
100 READ A,B,C,X$,E
110 DATA 5,10,15,"GIL",20
```

In the preceding example, the statement in line 100 specifies that you should read the values for five variables from one or more DATA statements. The first three variables are numeric and must be expressed as numeric constants in the associated DATA statement or statements. The fourth variable is a string variable and the value in the associated DATA statement must be a string. The fifth variable in the READ statement is a numeric variable, and the value of the associated DATA statement must be a numeric constant. In the above example, the execution of line 100 results in the assignment of the value 5 to A, 10 to B, 15 to C, "GIL" to X$, and 20 to E. A single READ statement can access the constant values from a number of DATA statements, so you could rewrite the preceding example in a number of ways to include using two DATA statements:

```
100 READ A,B,C,X$,E
110 DATA 5,10,15
120 DATA "GIL",20
```

Although two DATA statements are shown following the READ statement, they can be placed anywhere within a program. All DATA statements are nonexecutable and merely reserve space in memory for the values of the constants associated with each DATA statement. Then, each variable in a READ statement will have a sequential value taken from memory and assigned to the variable. We can visualize the effect of the DATA statement as generating a pool of values in sequential order. As more DATA statements occur in a program, the values associated with each statement are appended to the end of the pool in the sequence of occurrence. Thus the two DATA statements from the previous example can be visualized as creating the following data pool.

```
100 DATA 5,10,15
110 DATA "GIL",20
```
→ | 5 | 10 | 15 | "GIL" | 20 |

When a READ statement is encountered in a program, you can visualize that it causes a pointer to move from one value to the next value for each variable in the statement. In effect, a value is obtained from the data pool and assigned to a variable in the READ statement, and the pointer will then move to the right one position, ready to assign the next value in the data pool to the next variable in the READ statement.

If there are more variables in the READ statement or statements than there are constants in one or more DATA statements, when the pointer is shifted to the right and encounters no data, the error message Out of DATA will occur and the program will terminate. This is shown by the following example, which attempts to read three elements from a data pool that only contains two data items.

```
50 READ A,B,C
75 DATA 1,2
RUN
Out of DATA in 50
Ok
```

You can have multiple READ statements within a program. When this occurs, the second and subsequent READ statements will continue to take values from the data pool in sequence, with each value assigned to the variable in each READ statement in its order of occurrence. This is shown by the following example:

```
100 DATA 1,3,5,9,"MIGHTY","FINE"
500 READ A,B,C
750 READ D,XRAY$
1000 READ OHMY$,X$
1500 DATA "SUNSET","STRIP"
```

The three DATA statements generate the values assigned to the data pool as follows:

| 1 | 3 | 5 | 9 | "MIGHTY" | "FINE" | "SUNSET" | "STRIP" |

With the pointer at the beginning of the data pool, the READ statement in line 500 can be thought of as causing the following pointer actions to occur:

| 1 | 3 | 5 | 9 | "MIGHTY" | "FINE" | "SUNSET" | "STRIP" |

When A was READ, the pointer moved to the first value and assigned the contents of the first position in the data pool to that variable. Thus, A was given the value 1. Next, B was assigned the value 3, and C was assigned the value 5. Note that the pointer is now at the position where the value 5 was held in the pool. Upon encountering the READ statement in line 750, the pointer would again move to the right one position for each variable in the READ statement. Here, the variable D would be assigned the value 9 and the string variable XRAY$ would be assigned the string value MIGHTY. The movement of the pointer in response to the second read statement is shown here:

| 1 | 3 | 5 | 9 | "MIGHTY" | "FINE" | "SUNSET" | "STRIP" |

There are two variable names contained as part of the READ statement in line 1000, so the execution of this statement will cause the pointer to move two positions to the right through the data pool. As the pointer moves over the string "FINE", this string will be assigned to the string variable OHMY$, while the string "SUNSET" will be assigned to the string variable X$. Note that in this short program example, the number of data constants in the data pool exceeds the number of string variables in READ statements. This is perfectly valid, because sometimes you may branch around one or more READ statements and forgo assigning constants to variables based on certain program conditions. In such cases, the extra data will be ignored. The opposite of this situation, however, is not permitted. That is, you cannot read more variables in READ statements than there are constants in data statements, unless you reread the constants. The mechanism to reread constants is obtained through the RESTORE statement, which will be covered shortly.

Two final notes on READ and DATA statements. You can obtain an idea of the rationale for using these statements instead of multiple assignment statements by comparing the previous example using READ and DATA statements to a program segment performing the same variable assignments using assignment statements as shown here:

```
100 A=1
110 B=3
120 C=5
130 D=9
140 XRAY$="MIGHTY"
150 OHMY$="FINE"
160 X$="SUNSET"
```

From this example, it is apparent that READ and DATA statements are labor-saving devices for the assignment of constant values to variables.

Although the preceding examples showed quotation marks around string constants contained in DATA statements, there are occasions where you can safely do without such string specifiers. If a string does not have commas, semicolons, or significant leading or trailing blanks, you can place that string in a DATA statement without surrounding quotation marks. This is illustrated by the following example:

```
10 PRINT "LAST NAME","FIRST NAME","SSN"
20 READ LAST$,FIRST$,SSN$
30 DATA Held,Gilbert,000000000
40 PRINT LAST$,FIRST$,SSN$
```
RUN
```
LAST NAME       FIRST NAME      SSN
Held            Gilbert         000000000
Ok
```

RESTORE Statement

There are many programming situations in which you would like to read the data more than once. To do this requires a mechanism to move the position of the pointer in the data pool back to its initial position at the beginning of first data element. This repositioning of the data pool pointer is accomplished by the RESTORE statement whose format is

$$\text{format: RESTORE } \left[\left\{ \begin{array}{l} [\textit{line}] \\ [\textit{label}]^1 \end{array} \right\} \right]$$

When a RESTORE statement is executed, the first variable in the next READ statement in the program will be assigned the value of the first item in the first DATA statement in the program. If a line number is specified in the RESTORE statement, the first variable in the next READ statement will be assigned the value of the first item in the DATA statement specified by the line number of the RESTORE statement. If you are using QBASIC or QuickBASIC, you can specify both line numbers and labels in a RESTORE statement to reference specific DATA statements. As indicated, specifying a line number or label within a RESTORE statement permits us to selectively move the data pool pointer through the data pool. This is shown by the following example:

```
Ok
```
LIST
```
10 READ A,B,C,D
20 DATA 1,3,5,9,11,13
30 PRINT A,B,C,D
40 DATA 15,17,19,21
50 RESTORE
60 READ X,Y,Z
70 PRINT X,Y,Z
80 RESTORE 40
90 READ X,Y,Z
100 PRINT X,Y,Z
```
RUN
```
1       3       5       9
1       3       5
15      17      19
Ok
```

---

[1] Only applicable to QBASIC and QuickBASIC.

In this example, the data pool contains 10 constants, formed by the data in lines 20 and 40. The READ statement in line 10 results in the assignment of 1 to A, 3 to B, 5 to C, and 9 to D. The PRINT statement in line 30 outputs the values of the four variables. Here, the commas (,) between variables are print control mechanisms that permit data to be placed in fixed positions on a line when used as a separator in the PRINT statement. The use of print separators will be covered in detail later in this chapter when the PRINT statement is examined.

The RESTORE statement in line 50 moves the pointer back to the beginning of the data pool, because no line number was specified. The execution of line 60 will cause the values of 1, 3, and 5 to be assigned to the variables X, Y, and Z. The result of the PRINT statement in line 70 confirms the assignment of these values. In line 80, the line number appended to the RESTORE statement causes the pointer in the data pool to be repositioned to the first element in the referenced DATA statement. Now, the READ statement in line 90 will result in the assignment of the values 15, 17, and 19 to the variables X, Y, and Z. This is confirmed by the execution of the PRINT statement in line 100.

The preceding example showed how the RESTORE statement enables you to assign the same or a different sequence of values to different variables. Although specifying a line number in a RESTORE statement permits you to move the data pool pointer, its movement is controlled by the number of constants contained in a particular DATA statement. If you wish to selectively move the pointer to the right, you can do so by introducing dummy variables into your READ statements. In such cases, the dummy variable will be assigned a value; however, because you will not use the variable in the program, its assignment is immaterial. To see the use of dummy variables, assume that a pointer was positioned in a data pool as shown in the following:

```
  1 | 3 | 5 | 9 | 11 | 13 | 15 | 17 | 19 | 21
```

If you wanted to assign the values 15 to X, 17 to Y, and 19 to Z, you would have to first skip over the number 13. If all the data elements were contained in one DATA statement, you would have no such mechanism. You would have a similar problem if you had several DATA statements but the number 15 in the data pool was not at the beginning of a DATA statement that you could reference the line number of in a RESTORE statement. The solution to such problems is the use of one or more dummy variables in a READ statement. One example of the use of a dummy variable follows:

```
100 READ DUM,X,Y,Z
```

In line 100, the variable DUM will be assigned the value 13 as a mechanism to move the pointer so variables X, Y, and Z can be assigned the required values of 15, 17, and 19. Although DUM is assigned the value 13, because you have no intention of using it within the program with that value, it is known as a dummy variable. Although the variable name DUM was used for this dummy variable, you could use any valid name as long as you insulate it from use within the program.

INPUT Statement

Until now, the only methods that have been covered to assign values to variables were internally within a program. What happens if you wish to control the value of variables during program execution? One method might be to include every possible variable value in numerous assignment or READ and DATA statements and branch to the appropriate point in the program based on certain predefined criteria. Obviously, this would be extremely difficult, if not impossible. Far easier and more effective would be allowing input from the keyboard during program execution. This is accomplished by the use of the INPUT statement whose format is

format: INPUT[;]["*prompt msg*"]$\left\{ \begin{matrix} ; \\ , \end{matrix} \right\}$*var*[,*var . . .*]

When an INPUT statement is encountered, program execution is temporarily suspended and a question mark is displayed. The question mark is a BASIC program-level prompt character that serves as an indicator to the computer operator that the program is awaiting data input. If you include a "*prompt message*" in the statement, the string contained in quotation marks will be printed prior to the question mark if the prompt message is followed by a semicolon, as shown by the following example:

```
Ok
100 INPUT "Enter the radius of the circle";R
RUN
Enter the radius of the circle?
```

The question mark will be suppressed if you use a comma in place of the semicolon after the prompt message. This is shown in the following, which replaces the semicolon in the previous example with a comma and reexecutes the one-line program:

```
100 INPUT "Enter the radius of the circle",R
RUN
Enter the radius of the circle
```

When you respond to an INPUT statement, you must enter the same number of data items as there are variables in the variable list of the INPUT statement. Data items must be separated from one another by commas and the type of data—string or numeric—must agree with the type specified by the variable name in the variable list. An example of the use of an INPUT statement for multiple assignment of values to variables is

```
100 INPUT "ENTER WIDGETS SOLD AND COMMISSION RATE";SOLD,RATE
110 LET COM=500*SOLD*RATE/100
120 PRINT "COMMISSION=",COM
RUN
ENTER WIDGETS SOLD AND COMMISSION RATE? 100,5
COMMISSION=    2500
Ok
```

If you make a mistake and respond to an INPUT statement with too many or too few data items or with the wrong type of data, such as entering a string value for a numeric variable, the error message ?Redo from start will be displayed. At this point, you must reenter all values.

When you enter strings in response to an INPUT statement, the use of quotation marks is optional, as illustrated by the following example:

```
Ok
100 INPUT "Enter your name,rank and serial number,",N$,R$,S
110 PRINT N$,R$,S
```
RUN
```
Enter your name,rank and serial numberMarval,CPT,007
Marval        CPT              7
Ok
```

Notice in the preceding example that there was no space between the printout of the prompt message contained in the INPUT statement and the first character entered in response to the prompt. To make the response to such prompt messages more legible, you can insert a blank character after the last character of the prompt message. This is shown in the following example, in which a blank is appended to the end of the word number in line 100. Note that the response is now positioned to the right one character, separating the prompt message from the response.

```
100 INPUT "Enter your name,rank and serial number ",N$,R$,S
110 PRINT N$,R$,S
Ok
```
RUN
```
Enter your name,rank and serial number Wonder,Boy,0
 Wonder         Boy              0
Ok
```

If you are familiar with other versions of BASIC or are developing programs on your computer for use on other computers, you may wish to retain quotation marks to delimit strings. This will make your program easier to convert to a different computer if the requirement should arise.

The second format of the INPUT statement is only relevant for disk and Advanced BASIC. Here, the use of the optional semicolon immediately following the keyword INPUT is designed to suppress the generation of a carriage return and line feed sequence once you press the enter key. The use of the semicolon is intended to have the cursor remain on the same line as the user's response and will be a valuable tool for permitting multiple input responses on a single line.

INKEY$ Variable

You can use a secondary method to enter data from the keyboard during program execution with the INKEY$ variable. The use of this variable permits the program to read data on a character-by-character basis and is similar to the GET statement found in other versions of BASIC. The format of the INKEY$ variable is

format: *var*$=INKEY$

When a BASIC statement containing an INKEY$ variable is executed, a single character string will be input to the program from the keyboard. No characters will be displayed on the screen unless the program was written to echo input characters onto the display through the use of a PRINT statement. A null string will be returned if a key is not pressed when the INKEY$ variable is executed. You can force a program to wait for a certain character or group of characters by repeatedly looping back to the statement containing the INKEY$ variable, as illustrated by the execution of the following program segment:

```
Ok
100 PRINT "Enter C to continue"
110 A$=INKEY$
120 IF A$="C" GOTO 140
130 GOTO 110
140 REM program continues
```
RUN
```
Enter C to continue
Ok
```

After the `Enter C to continue` message is displayed, the INKEY$ variable in line 110 will return a character string from the keyboard whose value will be assigned to the string variable A$. In line 120, the value of A$ will be compared to the character C by the use of the BASIC IF statement. If A$ equals C, the program will branch to line 140. If A$ does not equal C, then line 130 will be executed, which will cause the program to branch back to line 110. This will cause the keyboard to be scanned again, and this looping will continue until C is pressed.

Note that because you are testing for an uppercase C, entering a lowercase c or any character other than the uppercase C will cause the program to cycle between lines 110 and 130. If you wish to test for either uppercase or lowercase, you would change line 120 as follows:

```
120 IF A$="C" OR A$="c" GOTO 140
```

You can also force a program to wait for the input of one or more characters by the use of multiple statements on a single line. In the following example, line 110 performs the exact functions of lines 110 through 130 in the previous example:

```
110 A$=INKEY$:IF A$="C" GOTO 140:ELSE GOTO 110
```

INKEY$ returns a string, so if you wish to input a digit and compare it to one or more digits in the program, you must convert the input string to a numerical value or compare the input string to a string consisting of one or more digits in the program. You can obtain the numerical value of a string by using the VAL function, whose use is illustrated by the following program segment:

```
100 PRINT "Remove single part paper, insert multipart paper"
110 PRINT "Enter 1 when ready to resume"
120 X$=INKEY$
130 X=VAL(X$)
140 IF X=1 GOTO 160
150 GOTO 120
160 REM program continues
```
RUN
```
Remove single part paper, insert multipart paper
Enter 1 when ready to resume
Ok
```

In the preceding example, the VAL function will return the numerical value of the specified string. A word of caution is in order, because VAL(X$) will return 0 (zero) if X$ is not numeric. Thus, if you were testing for 0, pressing any nonnumeric key would cause you to continue, which may not be what you intended to do. An easier method when testing for numeric characters is to perform the test against the numeric value employed as a string as shown by line 130 in the following example:

```
100 PRINT "Remove single part paper, insert multipart paper"
110 PRINT "Enter 1 when ready to resume"
120 X$=INKEY$
130 IF X$="1" GOTO 150
140 GOTO 120
150 REM program continues
```

When the INKEY$ variable is used, a zero-, one-, or two-character string can be returned. If a null (zero-length string) is returned, this indicates that no character was pressed at the keyboard when it was scanned. You can continuously cycle in a loop awaiting the entry of a character by the use of the following or a similar statement:

```
100 X$=INKEY$:IF X$="" GOTO 100
```

Note that the double quotation marks follow one another in line 100 so that the program will continuously cycle back to line 100 if no character has been entered.

In the preceding example, the first statement in line 100, X$=INKEY$, causes a character to be read from the keyboard and assigned to the variable X$. The second statement on that line, IF X$="" GOTO 100, causes the program to branch back to line 100 if no key has been pressed. If a key is pressed, X$ will not equal a null string of length zero, and the next sequential statement in the program will be executed.

If a one-character string is entered when the INKEY$ variable is encountered in a program, the string will contain the actual character that was pressed at the keyboard. This will be the primary result of the use of the INKEY$ variable. In certain instances, however, a two-character string will result from the use of the INKEY$ variable. This two-character string is generated to differentiate certain characters from the characters in the ASCII character set. Because your computer can only have 256 distinct characters by using the different combinations of an 8-bit byte, adding a prefix character permits an extension of the character set. When this occurs, a null character (ASCII code 000) is returned as the first character of a two-character string. The second character in the string will then have a different meaning from its normal ASCII representation.

A list of extended two-character codes and their meanings is contained in Appendix B. For an example of comparing these codes with standard ASCII codes, consider the character in Appendix A that has an ASCII value of 71. In the normal ASCII character set, the character G has the ASCII value of 71. In Appendix B, a two-character string with the first character being an ASCII 000 (null character) and the second character being an ASCII 71 is considered to be the cursor "Home" control character.

Because the first character in an extended code is ASCII 000, a logical question at this point is how you can differentiate a 00071 from a 71. To differentiate between the two characters numerically is impossible: 00071 is the same as 71. Because one character is actually a two-character string, you must differentiate between the two characters based on their string length. You can use the LEN function for this purpose, because it can be employed to obtain the number of characters in a string. The format of this function is

format: LEN(var$)

format$_Q$: LEN(*var*)

Note from these formats that the QuickBASIC LEN function operates on both strings and variables. When the program is operating on a string, the LEN function returns the number of characters similar to an interpretive BASIC LEN function. When the code is operating on a variable, the LEN function returns the number of bytes required by a variable.

If you wish to test the character or characters entered when an INKEY$ variable is executed, you can use programming logic similar to that of the following program:

LIST
```
100 X$=INKEY$:IF X$=""THEN 100
110 IF LEN(X$)=2 THEN 140
120 PRINT "One character code",X$
130 GOTO 100
140 PRINT "Two character code",X$
150 GOTO 100
```
RUN
```
One character code    1
One character code    a
Two character code     G
Two character code     H
Two character code     I
```

Enter this program in your computer, then press the F2 key in interpretive BASIC or the Shift+F5 key combination in QBASIC and QuickBASIC to run the program. As you press different keys, look in Appendixes A and B and note which keys are returned as one-character strings and which are returned as two-character strings. Note that no characters are displayed on the screen when you press a key. This means that the INKEY$ variable is appropriate for controlling the movement of a game's hero or vehicle when predetermined characters will be entered to change direction. You can use INKEY$ for controlling the screen display that you wish to print out when you do not wish to clutter the screen with the characters entered. Note that all two-character code strings are printed shifted one position to the right. This is because the first part of the string is a nonprintable null. To exit this endless loop program, press Ctrl+Break.

Another case in which the INKEY$ variable is valuable is in a program that displays mathematical problems and awaits the operator's responses. Here, you might construct a loop to read one digit at a time from the terminal. You could test each character obtained from the use of the INKEY$ variable for the ASCII value 13. When a 13 is encountered, it would indicate that a carriage return was entered. When the ASCII value of 13 is found, you would exit from the loop. You might wish to echo each character entered onto the display, so you could use a PRINT statement to perform this function. In the following example, the ASC function is used to return the ASCII code for the first character of the string indicated within the function. The format of this function is

format: ASC(*expr$*)

The result of the ASC function is a numerical value that is the ASCII code of the first character of the string specified in the parentheses. The following example uses the ASC function to test for the entry of a carriage return character:

```
Ok
10 B$=""
20 PRINT "15 X 24 ="
30 A$=INKEY$:IF A$="" THEN 30 'wait for character
40 PRINT A$;
50 IF ASC(A$)= 13 THEN 80      'echo to screen
60 B$=B$+A$                    'concatenate
70 GOTO 30
80 REM program continues
```

In this example, all numeric responses are concatenated into the string B$ until a carriage return is entered. Then the program branches to line 80. Later you could use the VAL function to obtain the numeric value of B$ to test it to the correct answer.

Because you wish to retain control of certain operational functions, there are four characters or character combinations that will not be passed through to the program by the use of the INKEY$ variable. These multikey combinations and their meanings are

Key combination	Meaning
Ctrl+Break	Stop program execution
Pause or Ctrl+NumLock	Put system into a pause state
Alt+Ctrl+Del	System reset
Print Screen or Shift+PrtSc	Print the screen

PRINT Statement

Just as there are a number of statements that can be used to input data values into a program, a variety of methods exists to transmit numerical or string output data from the computer. Two of the most commonly used statements are in PRINT and LPRINT statements. The LPRINT statement will be covered later.

The PRINT statement provides you with the mechanism to display data on your screen. The LPRINT statement works much like the PRINT statement, except that LPRINT sends data to the attached printer instead of the display.

The PRINT statement consists of a line number, the keyword PRINT, and an optional list of expressions that can consist of numbers, formulas, or strings. The two formats of this statement are:

$$
\text{format:} \left\{ \begin{array}{l} \text{PRINT}[exprlist] \left\{ \begin{array}{l} [,] \\ [;] \end{array} \right\} \\[2em] ?[exprlist] \left\{ \begin{array}{l} [,] \\ [;] \end{array} \right\} \end{array} \right\}
$$

Although both formats are applicable to interpretive BASIC and QuickBASIC, when you use the latter product the ? is automatically converted to the word PRINT when you press Enter to terminate a line. Thus, by pressing ? you can enter the keyword PRINT with one keystroke.

By themselves, the keyword PRINT or the question mark character will cause a blank line to be displayed. This is equivalent to generating a carriage return and line feed character. Thus, you can use the PRINT statement to control horizontal spacing when you desire to display a heading and skip one or more lines prior to printing the body of a report.

Concerning vertical spacing within a PRINT statement, the position of each printed item will be determined by the punctuation character employed to separate the items in the list of expressions. Successive items in the list of expressions must be separated by either a comma (,) or a semicolon (;).

Interpretive BASIC, QBASIC, and QuickBASIC are all similar to most BASICs in that a print line is divided into print zones that contain 14-character-wide zones, as illustrated in Figure 9.1. When a comma is used as a separator between items in the list of expressions, the next value in the list will be printed at the beginning of the next zone.

If more than 5 items are in the list of expressions and you are using commas as separators, items 6 through 10 will be printed on a second line, with their positions on that line corresponding to the positions of the zones shown in Figure 9.1. Similarly, items 11 through 15 would be printed on a third line, and so on. A printout that "wraps" around from line to line is shown by the following example. Note that BASIC always prints positive numbers preceded by a space if you wish to verify the zone positions in this example:

```
Ok
1 PRINT "123456789012345678901234567890123456789012345678901234567890"
2 PRINT 1,2,3,4,5,6,7,8,9,10,11,12,13,14,15
RUN
123456789012345678901234567890123456789012345678901234567890
 1             2             3             4             5
 6             7             8             9             10
 11            12            13            14            15
Ok
```

Expressions listed in a PRINT statement may be numeric or string; however, string constants must be enclosed in quotation marks or they will be considered to be variables. If they are unassigned a value, then they will be shown as having a zero value. When you use a semicolon as an item separator, the value of the next item will be printed immediately after the previous value. This enables you to display more data items on one line than using commas as separators. In the following example, 10 items are printed on 1 line by using semicolons as separators. You could also use 1 or more spaces between items, because BASIC will treat the spaces similarly to the use of semicolons. However, this feature is not common on many BASICs available on other machines.

	Zone 1		Zone 2		Zone 3		Zone 4		Zone 5	
First line	1	14	15	28	29	42	43	56	57	70	71	80

Figure 9.1 BASIC Print Zones. Each print zone contains 14 print positions. A logical line containing more than one physical line will have the second and subsequent print lines contain similar print zones.

```
Ok
10 PRINT 1;"TWO";3;"FOUR";5;"SIX";7;"EIGHT";9;"TEN"
```
RUN
```
 1 TWO 3 FOUR 5 SIX 7 EIGHT 9 TEN
Ok
```

Because using a comma enables you to place data items into predetermined positions, it provides an elementary mechanism for formatting data output. This is shown by the following program segment:

```
Ok
100 PRINT "COLUMN ONE","COLUMN TWO"
110 X=123.33
120 PRINT X,X/2
```
RUN
```
COLUMN ONE     COLUMN TWO
 123.33         61.665
Ok
```

A carriage return will be generated at the end of the print line when you terminate a PRINT statement without a comma or semicolon. Then, the next PRINT statement will cause a new line of information to be displayed. If you use a comma or semicolon at the end of the PRINT statement, the carriage return will be suppressed and the next PRINT statement will cause information to be displayed on the same line. This function is shown by modifying the previous example as shown here:

LIST
```
100 PRINT "COLUMN ONE","COLUMN TWO"
110 X=123.33
120 PRINT X,X/2,
130 PRINT X/3,X/4
```
RUN
```
COLUMN ONE     COLUMN TWO
 123.33         61.665           41.11     30.8325
Ok
```

Although either a comma or semicolon can be used at the end of a PRINT statement to signify that the next PRINT statement should display data on the same line, the semicolon will also serve to compress the next printed item out of its zone. This is shown by changing the terminator in line 120 to a semicolon in the following example.

LIST
```
100 PRINT "COLUMN ONE","COLUMN TWO"
110 X=123.33
120 PRINT X,X/2;
130 PRINT X/3,X/4
```
RUN
```
COLUMN ONE     COLUMN TWO
 123.33         61.665           41.11     30.8325
Ok
```

Many types of displays and monitors can be attached to the AT and compatible computers, so a WIDTH statement can be used to set the number of characters that will appear on one line of the display.

WIDTH Statement

When used to set the output line width, the format of the WIDTH statement is

format: `WIDTH size`

Here, the `size` is the number of characters you wish to set the output line width to. As an alternate format, you can include the device name in the WIDTH statement as shown here:

format: `WIDTH device, size`

Valid devices are SCRN:, LPT1:, LPT2:, LPT3:, COM1:, or COM2:. To set the width of the display, you could use

WIDTH *size*

or

WIDTH "SCRN:", *size*

A screen of 40 or 80 columns is always permitted; however, WIDTH 40 is not valid if you are using the IBM monochrome display. If your computer has an EGA or VGA monitor, the WIDTH statement will also control the number of lines on your screen, permitting 25 for EGA and 43 for VGA. If the line to be printed exceeds the length defined by a WIDTH statement, BASIC will cause the following data to be printed on the next physical line. This is demonstrated by the execution of the previous program where line 10 has been added that incudes a `WIDTH 40` statement:

```
Ok
LIST
10 WIDTH 40
100 PRINT "COLUMN ONE","COLUMN TWO"
110 X=123.33
120 PRINT X,X/2;
130 PRINT X/3,X/4
Ok
RUN
COLUMN ONE      COLUMN TWO
 123.33          61.665  41.11
 30.8325
Ok
```

When you print exactly 80 characters when the screen width is set to 80, an additional line feed will be generated by BASIC.

One of the primary uses of the WIDTH statement is to obtain the ability to print wide reports. For example, suppose your printer supports 136-character-per-line printing. To use this feature you would use the statement `WIDTH"LPT1:",136` in your program.

Numerical Treatment of Output

BASIC will always print positive numbers preceded by a space. This means that if you are using commas as listed separators, positive numbers will be printed in columns 2, 16, and so on. No matter what separator is used, BASIC will automatically append a space to the end of a number. This eliminates the possibility of two numbers being interpreted as one.

When the value of a variable is to be printed, its significance will depend on the type of the variable as explained in Chapter 8.

Prior to concluding this initial discussion of the PRINT statement, the review of two additional BASIC functions is warranted—the SPC function and the TAB function.

SPC Function

The SPC function can be used to space the cursor to the right a given number of spaces. Its format is

format: SPC (*exprnm*)

In addition to being used with the PRINT statement, the SPC function can be used with the LPRINT and PRINT# statements, to be discussed later.

When used with the PRINT statement, SPC will print the number of spaces specified by the numeric expression, in effect, moving the cursor *exprnm* positions to the right on the screen. Because a logical line in interpretive BASIC can be up to 256 character positions, the numeric expression must be in the range of 0 to 255. In QBASIC and QuickBASIC the expression's value can be up to 32,767, with the cursor moved by the expression value MOD80 if the screen is set to 80 positions. The use of this function in a PRINT statement is illustrated by the following program segment:

```
Ok
200 PRINT "DEBITS" SPC(30)"CREDITS"
RUN
DEBITS                        CREDITS
Ok
```

In the preceding example, the SPC function results in 30 spaces or column positions between the words DEBITS and CREDITS.

In the following example, note that if a floating point number is used, it will be rounded to an integer. Thus, X=14.51 results in 15 spaces, whereas Z=14.49 results in 14 spaces prior to printing the appropriate string.

```
Ok
LIST
10 X=14.51
20 PRINT SPC(X)"BASIC"
30 Y=15
40 PRINT SPC(Y)"OVERVIEW"
50 Z=14.49
60 PRINT SPC(Z)"OF SPC FUNCTION"
Ok
RUN
               BASIC
               OVERVIEW
              OF SPC FUNCTION
Ok
```

For interpretive BASIC, QBASIC, and QuickBASIC, if the specified value in the SPC function is greater than the width of the device, the value used will be *exprnm* MOD width.

TAB Function

Another function that can be used to control the cursor location on a line is the TAB function. This function is used in a PRINT statement, and its format is

format: TAB (*exprnm*)

Instead of spacing over the number of positions specified by the numeric expression, the TAB function causes the cursor to move to the right to the position specified by the numeric expression. When this function is used, *exprnm* must be between 1 and 255 in value in interpretive BASIC and between 1 and 32,767 in QBASIC and QuickBASIC. The leftmost position on the display is position 1, whereas the rightmost position is the defined WIDTH. Like the SPC function, the TAB function can only be used in PRINT, LPRINT, and PRINT# statements. The following program segment illustrates the use of the TAB function in several PRINT statements:

```
Ok
10 PRINT TAB(32)"INVENTORY REPORT"
20 PRINT
30 PRINT TAB(5)"PRODUCT" TAB(20)"UNITS ON HAND" TAB(40)"UNIT COST";
40 PRINT TAB(60)"PRODUCT COST:
RUN
                        INVENTORY REPORT

      PRODUCT          UNITS ON HAND      UNIT COST      PRODUCT COST
   Ok
```

In the preceding example, the TAB function in line 10 causes the string INVENTORY REPORT to be printed starting in column 32. Line 20 causes one blank line to be printed, and lines 30 and 40 cause four strings to be printed starting at columns 5, 20, 40, and 60, respectively. Note that the semicolon at the end of line 30 serves as a print continuation identifier to BASIC, informing the interpreter that the output of the next PRINT statement should follow on the same line.

LPRINT Statement

Although the PRINT statement causes data to be displayed on the screen, the LPRINT statement provides you with a mechanism to print information on the printer under program control. While you could output data to the screen and use the Print Screen key or the Shift+PrtSc keys to obtain a printed copy of the display, many times you will prefer to use the BASIC LPRINT statement to automatically generate printed information. The distinction between using the Print Screen key or the Shift+PrtSc keys and the LPRINT statement may not appear too meaningful when you are printing a few lines of data, but consider the case in which you have to output a report consisting of hundreds of lines of data. Obviously, you would prefer not to hit the Print Screen key or the Shift+PrtSc keys every time 24 lines of data are displayed. Thus, you will have a tendency to use the LPRINT statement to generate reports or substantial data output, whereas you may prefer to use the PRINT statement when you need the results of some computation and hard copy may not be necessary or can be easily obtained by the Print Screen key or the Shift+PrtSc keys. The format of the LPRINT statement is

format: LPRINT [*exprlist*] $\left\{ \begin{matrix} ; \\ , \end{matrix} \right\}$

In comparison to the PRINT statement, the only difference in formats is the prefix of L in the keyword. This L indicates that the expressions in the list will be printed. This statement functions similarly to the PRINT statement, including the use of the SPC and TAB functions within the statement. The key difference between statements is that the PRINT statement causes data to be displayed on the screen, whereas the LPRINT statement causes the output to be listed on the printer.

The LPRINT statement assumes a default value of an 80-character-width printer. This width can be changed if your printer is capable of recognizing special control characters to perform condensed printing, has switches for changing print width, or has a platen greater than 80 characters in width. You can also change the printer width through the use of the WIDTH statement. When BASIC is initialized, the value of the printer width is set to 80 characters. Some printers, like the IBM 80-cps graphics printer, are capable of printing up to 132 characters per line in a condensed print operating mode. Other printers have extended carriages and can normally print up to 132 characters per line in their normal print mode.

If your printer is capable of changing its settings by receiving special codes, you can change its operation under program control. Table 9.2 contains a list of special print functions and their control codes for the IBM 80-cps graphics printer.

The IBM Graphics printer was actually manufactured by Epson Corporation, so that the printer control codes came to be commonly but incorrectly referred to as "Epson control codes." Epson manufactures many types of printers whose control codes vary slightly among devices. In spite of control code differences among Epson printers, as well as between the IBM Graphics printer and other IBM printers, the control codes listed in Table 9.2 represent a core of functions supported by most printers.

Although many, if not all, of the functions listed in Table 9.2 can be obtained on printers manufactured by other vendors, the control codes may differ. Therefore, it is recommended that you consult your printer manual to ascertain the appropriate control codes to perform the printing functions available if you have a non-IBM printer attached to your system.

In addition to sending data to the printer, you can send "special" codes that the printer uses for such functions as printing narrow or wide letters, double printing, and printing the actual graphic characters shown on your screen. To perform these functions requires the use of one or more CHR$ functions in an LPRINT statement.

CHR$ Function

The CHR$ function converts an ASCII code to its character equivalent and can be used to send special characters to the screen or a printer. For the screen, you would use the CHR$ function in a PRINT statement; the printer output requires CHR$ to be used in an LPRINT statement. The format of this function is

format: X$=CHR$(*exprnm*)

Table 9.2
IBM 80-cps
Graphics Printer
Control Codes

Function	Code	ASCII Values
Bell	BEL	7
Cancel	CAN	24
Cancel ignore paper end	ESC 9	27 57
Cancel skip perforation	ESC O	27 79
Carriage return	CR	13
Compressed character	SI	15
Compressed character Off	DC 2	18
Double strike	ESC G	27 71
Double strike Off	ESC H	27 72
Double width (one line)	SO	14
Double width	ESC W1	27 87 1
Double width (SO only)	DC 4	20
Emphasized	ESC E	27 69
Emphasized Off	ESC F	27 70
Escape	ESC	27
Form feed	FF	140
Home head	ESC<	27 60
Horizontal tab	HT	9
Ignore paper end	ESC 8	27 56
Line feed	LF	10
Null	NUL	0
Select character set 1	ESC 7	27 55
Select character set 2	ESC 6	27 54
Set horizontal tab stops	ESC D	27 68
Set length of page	ESC C	27 67
Set lines per page	ESC C	27 67
Set skip perforation	ESC N	27 78
Set variable line feed 0.12 mm (1/216 in.)	ESC 3	27 51
Set variable line feed 0.35 mm (1/72 in.)	ESC A	27 65
Start variable line feed 0.35 mm (1/72 in.)	ESC 2	27 50
Subscript-superscript On	ESC S	27 83
Subscript-superscript Off	ESC T	27 84
Underline	ESC__	27 45
Unidirectional printing	ESC U	27 85
Variable line feed 0.12 mm (1/216 in.)	ESC J	27 74
3.18 mm (1/8 in.) line feed	ESC 0	27 48
2.47 mm (7/72 in.) line feed	ESC 1	27 49
480-bit-image graphics mode	ESC K	27 75
960-bit-image graphics mode	ESC L	27 76
960-bit-image graphics mode normal speed	ESC Y	27 89
1920-bit-image graphics mode	ESC Z	27 90

There are 256 characters in the ASCII character set, and the numeric expression can range in value from 0 to 255. You can use this function in an LPRINT statement to send special characters to the printer, or you can use it in a PRINT statement to display special characters. In either situation, the numeric expression represents the ASCII code of the character you wish to send to the screen or printer. The ASCII character set showing each of the 256 characters and their ASCII code values is contained in Appendix A.

Now that you know how to send special characters to the printer, you can actually operate some of the printer's functions under program control. Suppose you wish to produce the title of a report in double-width characters. According to Table 9.2, you must transmit an ASCII 14 to the printer to enable double-width printing. You can use the CHR$ function in an LPRINT statement as follows:

```
Ok
100 LPRINT CHR$(14)"REPORT TITLE"
```

This results in the following action on your printer:

REPORT   TITLE

If you wish to center the report title on the page in double width, you could use the TAB function, as shown by the following LPRINT statement:

```
200 LPRINT TAB ((40-12)/2) CHR$(14)"REPORT TITLE"
```

Because the printer is operating in double width, you only have 40 character positions per line. Thus, you will tab out to position 14 when the expression in the TAB function is evaluated. Although you could have simply put TAB(14) in the statement, you purposely put the expression in its place so you can see how you can compute where to center a string for output. The term *report title* contains 12 character positions to include the space between report and title, so subtract 12 from 40. Then divide the difference by 2 to obtain the position where the string will be centered.

The two-line program and its execution result on the printer follow. Note that the second line that was printed has the output centered on the page:

```
100 PRINT CHR$(14)"REPORT TITLE"
200 LPRINT TAB((40-12)/2) CHR$(14)"REPORT TITLE"
```

REPORT   TITLE
REPORT   TITLE

Double-width printing operates on a line-by-line basis on the IBM printer when an ASCII 14 is transmitted to that device. That is, once turned on by an ASCII 14 on one line, it will terminate at the end of that line. Unless you use an ASCII 14 in the next line to be printed, that line will be printed in single width. Thus, the double-width feature can be viewed as having an automatic shutoff feature. If you transmit an ESC W followed by a 1, this double-width mode is not canceled by a line feed and will remain in effect until it is canceled by an ESC W followed by a 0 (zero). On other printers, like the C.ITOH 8510, this feature will remain on until turned off by sending another special character to the printer to signify double-width inhibit. If you are using the 8510 printer, a "shift-in" character (ASCII 15) can be used to turn off the double-width feature on that printer. If you wish to print both double width and single width on the same line, you can turn double width off by using ASCII 20 in a CHR$ function. An example of normal and double-width printing on a single line is shown in the following example:

```
LIST
100 LPRINT "NORMAL" CHR$(14) TAB(10)"DOUBLE" CHR$(20)TAB(20)"NORMAL"
RUN
Ok
```

The result of this execution of this statement is

NORMAL   DOUBLE   NORMAL

What happens if your report is chock full of columns of data—so much data that you require more than 80 columns to be printed? In such a situation, you place the printer in the compressed-character print mode, which permits up to 132 characters to be printed on one line. To switch to the compressed-character print mode, send an ASCII 15 to the printer. Once sent, the printer will remain in the compressed-character print mode until an ASCII 18 is transmitted. Again, these control characters are listed in Table 9.2. The use of compressed-character printing is shown in the following:

THIS IS AN EXAMPLE OF COMPRESSED PRINTING

You can mix both double-width and compressed-mode printing on one line. When you do so, double-width printing includes 66 characters per line instead of 40 characters per line. In Table 9.3 a comparison of line printing capacity by mode is tabulated.

Now, take a look at the double-strike printing feature available on the IBM 80-cps graphics printer. From Table 9.2, you see that to enable this option requires you to issue an ESCAPE code plus an ASCII G. The ESCAPE code should not be confused with the Esc key. In DOS and when using interpretive BASIC, pressing the Esc key causes an entire logical line to be erased from the screen. An ESCAPE code is the ASCII value 27, which is normally used as part of a two-character sequence to perform some predefined function. Here, an ESCAPE character followed by an ASCII G will place the printer in a double-strike operational mode. When this occurs, everything on a program line will be printed twice. Because the paper is rolled up just $1/216$ of an inch before the second printing, this helps to fill in the spaces resulting from the dot matrix printhead and results in a bold and solid output that makes the print quality appear similar to typewriter quality. Once the printer is placed in the double-strike mode, it remains in that mode until an ESCAPE H character sequence is sent to the printer. This will return printing to the normal print mode of operation. On some printers, the double-strike mode is called "bold printing," and different character sequences are used

Table 9.3
Line Print Capacity

Mode	Characters per Inch
Normal width	80
Normal width/compressed	132
Double width	40
Double width/compressed	66

to enable and inhibit this feature. The following example illustrates one possible use of the double-strike print capability on the IBM graphics printer. You use the ESCAPE G and ESCAPE H character sequences to turn on and off bold printing:

```
100 LPRINT "Mr. George Deadbeat"
120 LPRINT "Anycity, USA"
130 LPRINT
140 LPRINT "Dear George:"
150 LPRINT
160 LPRINT "Reference our invoice dated July 16, 1776.  It has come to our"
170 LPRINT "attention that "; CHR$(27); CHR$(71); "PAYMENT IS LONG OVERDUE."
180 LPRINT CHR$(27); CHR$(72); "Hope your check is in the mail."
190 LPRINT
200 LPRINT "With much thanks."
```

```
Mr. George Deadbeat
Anycity, USA

Dear George:

Reference our invoice dated July 16, 1776.  It has come to our attention that
PAYMENT IS LONG OVERDUE.
Hope your check is in the mail.

With much thanks.
```

STRING$ Function

Now that you know how to place into operation many of your printer's features, examine one additional control mechanism. This control mechanism provides the ability to easily print a string containing characters that all have the same ASCII code when you use the STRING$ function. Its two formats are

format:
$$\begin{cases} var\$ = \text{STRING}\$(exprnm_1\ exprnm_2) \\ var\$ = \text{STRING}\$(exprnm, expr\$) \end{cases}$$

The STRING$ function returns a string of length $exprnm_1$ in which all characters will have the ASCII code specified by $exprnm_2$ or by the first character of $expr\$$. The use of this function in an LPRINT statement is

```
Ok
100 LPRINT TAB(30)"VERY LONG REPORT TITLE"
110 LPRINT TAB(30)STRING$(22,42)
RUN
                              VERY LONG REPORT TITLE
                              **********************
```

In this example, the function STRING$(22,42) results in 22 asterisks being printed (ASCII code 42 is the asterisk character), commencing at column 30.

Alternatively, you would have to type a string of 22 asterisks in line 110 or use a loop to control the printing of the asterisks if you did not use the STRING$ function. You can also use this function in a PRINT statement to display a string of similar characters or use it in a program to initialize a string to a particular character setting of a certain length.

When using the second format the STRING$ function enables you to easily duplicate the first character in a string. This is illustrated by

```
100 A$="WXYZ"
110 LPRINT STRING$(10,A$)
RUN
WWWWWWWWWW
```

WRITE Statement

The operational result of the execution of the WRITE statement is very similar to the PRINT statement. The difference between these two statements is that the WRITE statement inserts commas automatically between items to be displayed and delimits strings with quotation marks. The format of this statement is

format: WRITE[*exprlist*]

Like the PRINT statement, if the list of expressions is omitted, the WRITE statement generates a blank line. Although you will normally display data without commas between items and quotation marks surrounding strings, on occasion you may wish to use this statement to display examples of how data should be entered into a program. The following example illustrates one possible use of the WRITE statement for this purpose:

```
200 PRINT "USE THE FOLLOWING EXAMPLE FOR DATA ENTRY"
210 X=14:Y$="NEW YORK,NY":Z=31221
220 WRITE X,Y$,Z
RUN
USE THE FOLLOWING EXAMPLE FOR DATA ENTRY
14,"NEW YORK,NY",31221
Ok
```

Branching

Normally, the statements in a BASIC program are executed in sequential order. On occasion, you may wish to change the flow of program execution and jump to another part of the program. You can accomplish this change of program execution flow by using a number of branching statements. These statements alter the sequence of execution of the statements in a program. Several branching statements are discussed here, starting with what is commonly known as the unconditional branching statement.

GOTO Statement

The GOTO statement is known as an *unconditional branching statement*. The execution of GOTO always results in a branch out of the normal program sequence to a specified line number. The format of this statement is

format: GOTO *line*
format₍Q₎: GOTO *label*

Note that the keyword GOTO is one word and must be entered as such.

The execution of a GOTO statement causes the program to branch to the referenced line number. If the referenced line number contains a REM or a DATA statement, program execution will resume at the first executable statement after the REM or

DATA statement. If the line number references an executable statement, then the program will immediately branch to the referenced line and execute the referenced statement. The listing of a program segment illustrating the use of a GOTO statement and its execution with sample data follows. Note that as constructed, this program contains an infinite loop by repeatedly branching back to line number 100:

```
100 INPUT "ENTER A NUMBER ",N
110 S=N*N
120 PRINT "THE SQUARE OF ";N;" IS ";S
130 GOTO 100
OK
RUN
ENTER A NUMBER 5
THE SQUARE OF  5 IS 25
ENTER A NUMBER 7
THE SQUARE OF  7 IS 49
ENTER A NUMBER 99
THE SQUARE OF  99 IS 9801
ENTER A NUMBER
```

To terminate the execution of this program, you could enter the multikey combination Ctrl+Break. Later, you will examine a conditional branch that automatically terminates a program under predefined conditions.

In addition to using the GOTO statement within a program, when using interpretive BASIC you can also use GOTO in direct mode without a line number. In this manner, you can directly jump to a desired line within a program. This can be extremely useful for diagnostic purposes. An example of the use of the GOTO statement in this manner is

```
Ok
100 PRINT "DEMONSTRATION PROGRAM"
110 PRINT "TO SHOW THE USE OF A DIRECT MODE GOTO STATEMENT"
120 PRINT "LET'S SEE IF WE CAN SKIP THE FIRST TWO"
130 PRINT "LINES OF THIS PROGRAM"
GOTO 120
LET'S SEE IF WE CAN SKIP THE FIRST TWO
LINES OF THIS PROGRAM
Ok
```

In the preceding example, the direct mode GOTO 120 statement causes the program in memory to begin execution at line 120. This is equivalent to entering the BASIC command RUN 120.

If you are using QBASIC or QuickBASIC, you can use both line numbers and line labels as reference points for unconditional branches. For example, the prior program could be written as follows, where START represents a line label.

```
START:
INPUT "ENTER A NUMBER",N
S=N*N
PRINT "THE SQUARE OF ";N;" IS ";S
GOTO START
```

Computed GOTO Statement

The computed GOTO statement causes the branch to one of several specified line numbers, with the precise branch taken dependent on the value resulting from the evaluation of an expression contained in the statement. The format of the computed GOTO statement is

format: ON *exprnm* GOTO *line*[,*line*] . . .
format$_Q$: ON *exprnm* GOTO *label*[,*label*] . . .

The value of the numeric expression (*exprnm*) can be a constant, variable, or expression. This value will determine which line number in the list the program will branch to. If *exprnm* is not an integer, it will be rounded. The following program segment illustrates the use of this program statement:

```
Ok
100 PRINT "ENTER COMPUTATION DESIRED"
110 PRINT TAB(5)"(1) REGRESSION"
120 PRINT TAB(5)"(2) CORRELATION"
130 PRINT TAB(5)"(3) NONLINEAR REGRESSION"
140 INPUT "ENTER CHOICE (1, 2, OR 3) ",CHOICE
150 ON CHOICE GOTO 300,500,750
300 REM REGRESSION MODULE
500 REM CORRELATION MODULE
750 REM NONLINEAR REGRESSION MODULE
```

In the preceding example, the statements in lines 100 through 130 cause a heading and three program choices to be displayed. The display of program choice is normally called a menu, since the computer operator is provided with a number of items to select his or her action from. The INPUT statement in line 140 will first cause the prompt message ENTER CHOICE (1, 2, OR 3) to be displayed. Then the program will halt execution, awaiting a response from the keyboard. When a number is entered, it will be assigned to the variable named CHOICE. The computed GOTO statement in line 150 will cause a branch to one of the line numbers in the list depending on the value of the variable named CHOICE. If CHOICE is 1, the program will branch to line number 300. If CHOICE is 2, the program will branch to line number 500, while a value of 3 will cause the program to branch to line 750.

The menu displayed by the execution of this program segment is

RUN
```
ENTER COMPUTATION DESIRED
    (1) REGRESSION
    (2) CORRELATION
    (3) NONLINEAR REGRESSION
ENTER CHOICE (1, 2, OR 3)
```

Suppose the keyboard character entered does not correspond to one of the selection numbers in the menu. What will occur when the program gets to line 150 and the number of the variable differs from the number of lines in the list? If the number of the variable is zero or it is greater than the number of items in the list but less than 256, BASIC will continue program execution at the program line following the computed

GOTO statement. If the value of the variable is negative or greater than 255, an Illegal function call error will occur, terminating program execution.

You can trap potential errors prior to their occurrence by sampling data before it is used in a statement. In the following example, several lines of code have been added to the previous computed GOTO example. Lines 142 through 146 check the value entered in response to the INPUT statement. If the value entered is not 1, 2, or 3, an error message is displayed, and the program branches back to line 140 to accept the operator's next choice.

```
Ok
LIST
100 PRINT "ENTER COMPUTATION DESIRED"
110 PRINT TAB(5)"(1) REGRESSION"
120 PRINT TAB(5)"(2) CORRELATION"
130 PRINT TAB(5)"(3) NONLINEAR REGRESSION"
140 INPUT "ENTER CHOICE (1, 2, OR 3) ",CHOICE
142 IF CHOICE=1 OR CHOICE=2 OR CHOICE=3 THEN 150
144 PRINT "NUMBER MUST BE 1, 2, OR 3"
146 GOTO 140
150 ON CHOICE GOTO 300,500,750
300 REM REGRESSION MODULE
500 REM CORRELATION MODULE
750 REM NONLINEAR REGRESSION MODULE
Ok
```

The comparison in line 142 tests whether the value of the variable CHOICE is equal to 1 or 2 or 3. If the value of CHOICE is 1, 2, or 3, the program will branch to line 150. If the value of CHOICE does not equal 1, 2, or 3, the next program statement will be executed. Thus, line 144 would cause the message NUMBER MUST BE 1, 2, OR 3 to be displayed, and the program would then branch back to line 140 as a result of the GOTO statement in line 146. At line 140, the INPUT statement would again cause the prompt message ENTER CHOICE (1, 2, OR 3) to be displayed. Then, the program will halt, awaiting keyboard input of data. If you run the program and purposely enter an invalid choice, you can see the response generated by the addition of lines 142 through 146:

```
RUN
ENTER COMPUTATION DESIRED
    (1) REGRESSION
    (2) CORRELATION
    (3) NONLINEAR REGRESSION
ENTER CHOICE (1, 2, OR 3) 4
NUMBER MUST BE 1, 2, OR 3
ENTER CHOICE (1, 2, OR 3)
```

Using Labels

If you are using QBASIC or QuickBASIC, you can use labels in a computed GOTO statement to better define branch reference locations. You can select label names that reflect either the location of a label or the statement or group of statements that the label provides a branch entry point access for. In fact, when using QuickBASIC, you can mix line numbers and labels as entry point access locations, as illustrated by the following example:

```
START:
INPUT "ENTER YOUR AGE ", A
IF A > 3 GOTO 200
ON A GOTO YOUNG, MEDIUM, OLD
YOUNG:
PRINT "YOU'RE A BABY"
GOTO 100
MEDIUM:
PRINT "YOU'RE 2 YEARS OLD"
GOTO 100
OLD:   PRINT "AGE=3"
100 GOTO START
200 END
```

In the prior computed GOTO example, the label START: was used to denote the beginning of the program. After the INPUT statement is used to obtain a person's age, an IF statement was used to compare the value of the variable A to 3, resulting in the program branching to line number 200 if A exceeds 3. If not, the computed GOTO statement results in a branch to labels YOUNG, MEDIUM, or OLD if the value of A is 1, 2, or 3, respectively. Note that a mixture of line numbers and labels was used in the preceding example. If you are using interpretive BASIC, you would be restricted to using line numbers, because neither Advanced BASIC nor GW-BASIC support the use of labels.

Now that you have explored one use of what is commonly called the IF-THEN statement, take a deeper look at this statement.

IF-THEN-ELSE Statement

The IF-THEN statement in both interpretive BASIC and QuickBASIC differs from those on many other microcomputers using BASIC, since an optional ELSE clause can be contained as part of the statement. The format of this statement is

$$\text{format: IF } expr \begin{Bmatrix} \text{THEN } clause \\ \text{GOTO } line \end{Bmatrix} [[,]\text{ELSE } clause]$$

Any expression (expr) in the statement is evaluated. If the expression is determined to be true (not zero), the THEN or GOTO portion of the statement is executed. The clause following THEN can be either a line number that will serve as a reference for branching or one or more statements to be executed based on the evaluation of the expression. The GOTO portion of the statement is always followed by a line number. If the evaluation of the expression is determined to be false (zero), the THEN or GOTO portion of the statement is ignored, and program execution continues with the next executable program statement. Ignoring the optional ELSE portion of the statement for the time being, examine a few examples of the use of the IF-THEN statement by looking at the following program segment:

```
Ok
200 INPUT "ENTER AGE",AGE
210 IF AGE >30 THEN 500
220 IF AGE >10 AND AGE <30 GOTO 800
```

After the prompt message ENTER AGE is printed as a result of the INPUT statement, the program halts execution, awaiting data input. When you enter a numeric variable representing an age, that number is assigned to the variable labeled AGE. In line 210, the value assigned to AGE is compared to 30. If AGE is greater than 30, a branch to line number 500 occurs. Suppose the number 29 is entered in response to the ENTER AGE prompt. Because AGE is not greater than 30, no branch will be taken and the THEN portion of the statement will be ignored. With execution continuing at the next executable program statement, line 220 will be executed. In line 220, another comparison occurs. This time, you are comparing AGE to the range of values exceeding 10 and less than 30. Mathematically, this can be denoted as

$$10 < AGE < 30$$

Because AGE lies within this range, the branch to line 800 in the program will occur. Now, check how you can use a clause in an IF-THEN statement to change the value of a variable automatically within a program based on the results of the evaluation of an expression. Consider the following statement:

```
500 IF(A+B-C)^2<(D/E)^3 THEN P=4
```

When line 500 is executed, the values of the variables A and B will be added, and the value of the variable C will be subtracted from the previously computed sum. Next, the resulting quantity will be squared. This value will then be compared to the cube of the values of variables D divided by E. If the left-hand expression is determined to be less than the right-hand expression, the variable P will be assigned the value 4. If the left-hand expression is not less than the right-hand expression, the clause will be ignored.

Now, you can expand the IF-THEN statement to investigate how to use the ELSE portion of the statement. When included in an IF-THEN statement, the ELSE clause is executed when the results of the evaluation of the expression are false (zero). This is illustrated by modifying the previous example as follows:

```
500 IF(A+B-C)^2<(D/E)^3 THEN P=4 ELSE P=2
```

In this example, when the left-hand expression is less than the expression to the right of the less-than sign, P will be set to 4; otherwise, P will be set to a value of 2.

Look at several more examples of the IF-THEN-ELSE statement. First, consider the following statement:

```
100 IF DISPLAY THEN PRINT"ANSWER IS" ELSE LPRINT "ANSWER IS"
```

In the preceding example, the IF-THEN-ELSE statement provides a mechanism to print your output either on the display or on the printer. If the variable named DISPLAY has a nonzero value, output from that statement will be directed to the screen; otherwise, program output from this statement will go to the printer. Note that the IF-THEN-ELSE statement should be used as an entity. That is, the ELSE clause should not be contained on a line separate from the rest of the statement. As an example, consider the execution of the following program segment:

```
Ok
LIST
```

```
110 INPUT "ENTER VALUE ",A
120 IF A=4 THEN B=1 ELSE B=3
130 PRINT A,B
Ok
```
RUN
```
ENTER VALUE 1
 1              3
Ok
```
RUN
```
ENTER VALUE 4
 4              1
Ok
```

In the first execution of the program segment, the value 1 was entered. A did not equal 4, so B was set equal to 3. In the second execution of the program segment, the value 4 was entered. Line 120 sets B equal to 1 when A is 4, so the PRINT statement in line 130 verifies this assignment.

Now consider what happens if you separate the ELSE clause from the rest of the IF statement:

LIST
```
110 INPUT "ENTER VALUE ",A
120 IF A=4 THEN B=1
125 ELSE B=3
130 PRINT A,B
Ok
```
RUN
```
ENTER VALUE 1
 1              0
Ok
```
RUN
```
ENTER VALUE 4
 4              1
Ok
```

When the ELSE clause is separated from the IF-THEN statement, it is ignored by BASIC. Thus, entering the value 1 for A does not assign 3 to B, and because B is undefined, its value is 0. When you execute the program segment a second time with the value 4 assigned to A, B is assigned the value 1. Thus, you should be extremely careful to ensure the ELSE clause is contained in the IF-THEN statement when used.

Before you move on to a new group of statements, a discussion of data precision is warranted. As you have seen previously in this book, the internal representation of numerical values may not be exact in many situations, because single- and double-precision values are stored internally in floating-point binary representation. In addition, when you convert a lower-precision type to a higher-precision type, you retain the accuracy of the lower-precision type. This is demonstrated by the following program segment:

```
Ok
100 A=2/3:PRINT A
110 B#=A:PRINT B#
```

```
120 C#=2#/3:PRINT C#
```
RUN
```
 .6666667
 .6666666865348816
 .6666666666666667
Ok
```

Based on the preceding, you may wish to test the result of a single- or double-precision computation against the range within which the accuracy of the value may vary. A single-precision computation is accurate to ±.000001, so suppose you wished to compare a computed variable named X with the value 27.4. Consider X to be equal to 27.4 if X is 27.4−.000001 or 27.4+.000001. Thus, you wish to test the absolute value of X−27.4 to .000001. In BASIC, you can use the ABS function to obtain the absolute value of an expression. The format of this function is

format: ABS(*exprnm*)

where *exprnm* is the numeric expression you wish to obtain the absolute value of. You can then write your comparison as follows:

IF ABS(X−27)<.000001 THEN ...

Because .000001 is 1.0E−6 in exponential notation, the test comparison can be rewritten as follows:

IF ABS(X−27)<1.0E − 6 THEN ...

Block IF-THEN-ELSE statement

One of the problems associated with the previously described IF-THEN-ELSE statement involves its use to effect complicated alternative actions. In using a series of IF-THEN-ELSE statements to code a group of alternative actions, you may not only spend a considerable amount of time doing programming but also develop code that is very difficult to understand and modify. Recognizing this problem, Microsoft Corporation added a block IF-THEN-ELSE statement and a SELECT CASE statement to QBASIC and QuickBASIC. Each of these statements allows the appearance of the code you develop to be based on program logic, so you don't crowd many statements together. Thus, using either statement you can develop code to handle complex series of alternative actions while you improve the readability of the code.

The format of the block IF-THEN-ELSE statement in QuickBASIC is

```
format_Q: IF expr THEN
             [statement-block₁]
          [ELSEIF expr THEN
             [statement-block₂]]
          [ELSE
             [statement-blockₙ]]
          END IF
```

When you use the block IF-THEN-ELSE statement, each IF, ELSEIF, and ELSE clause is followed by a block of statements that can range in scope from a simple one-line variable assignment to a series of complex statements. The first statement in each block must start on a separate line after the IF, ELSEIF, or ELSE clause, because

QuickBASIC would consider the block IF-THEN-ELSE to be a single-line IF-THEN statement if the block begins on the same line as one of these three statements.

When you create a block IF-THEN-ELSE statement, QuickBASIC evaluates each of the expressions in the IF and ELSEIF clauses from top to bottom. If the expression is false, the statements in the statement-block are skipped. If the expression is true QuickBASIC then executes the statements in the statement-block and branches out of the block to the statement following the END IF clause. If none of the expressions in the IF or ELSEIF clauses is true and an ELSE clause is included, QuickBASIC executes the statements in the statement-block following that clause. Otherwise, the program jumps to the next statement after the END IF clause.

The following program segment example illustrates the use of a block IF-THEN-ELSE statement to assign premiums to male and female applicants. In this example, if the string variable SEX$ is not MALE or FEMALE, an error has occurred. Thus, the ELSE clause is followed by a PRINT statement denoting a data entry error and a branch back to the label START at the beginning of the program segment.

```
START:
INPUT "ENTER SEX OF APPLICANT ", SEX$
IF SEX$="FEMALE" THEN
        PREMIUM = 45.9
ELSEIF SEX$="MALE" THEN
        PREMIUM=51.67
ELSE
        PRINT "DATA ENTRY ERROR": GOTO START
        END IF
PRINT PREMIUM
```

To verify the execution of statement-blocks, try running the program. The following example shows an intentional misspelling of MALE as MAIL and then entry of the term correctly. Note that, when entered correctly, the statement-block PREMIUM=51.67 is executed as it is contained in the first true expression, a condition verified by the PRINT PREMIUM statement at the end of the program segment example.

```
ENTER SEX OF APPLICANT MAIL
DATA ENTRY ERROR
ENTER SEX OF APPLICANT MALE
 51.67
```

SELECT CASE Statement

The SELECT CASE statement is similar to the block IF-THEN-ELSE statement, in that it provides the ability to easily program a multiple-choice decision structure. However, unlike the block IF-THEN-ELSE statement that can be used to evaluate completely different expressions, the SELECT CASE statement is restricted to evaluating a single expression.

The format of the SELECT CASE statement is

```
formatₒ:  SELECT CASE expr
          CASE exprlist₁
            [statement-block₁]
          [CASE exprlist₂
            [statement-block₂]]
```

```
                    .
                    .
                    .
        [CASE ELSE
           [statement-blockₙ]]
        END SELECT
```

The SELECT CASE statement can be very powerful, because it supports a range of expressions and relational operator expressions. This is accomplished by the CASE statement syntax:

```
CASE expr TO expr
CASE IS relational-operator expr
```

When the first CASE statement syntax is used, the statements in the statement block are executed within the range of expression values. For example,

```
CASE 5 TO 10
```

would result in the statements in the statement-block associated with the CASE statement being executed when the expression is greater than or equal to 5 and less than or equal to 10. You can also include multiple ranges in a case statement, such as

```
CASE 1 TO 7, 9 TO 13, 17
```

When using the keyword TO in a CASE statement you must place the lesser value first. For example, CASE −10 TO −1 would result in a valid range from negative 1 to negative 10 being treated, because −10 is less than −1.

When the second CASE statement syntax is used, you can use any valid BASIC relational operators in an expression. Thus, CASE IS <10 would result in the statements in the statement-block associated with CASE being executed when the expression is less than 10. You can even encode multiple expressions or ranges of expressions for each CASE format. In addition, you can employ strings in relational operator expressions or ranges, in which case ASCII values of characters in the string are used for comparison purposes. As an example of multiple expressions, consider the following:

```
CASE 5 TO 10, 25 TO 50, OLD
```

In this example, if the value of the expression is equal to or greater than 5 and less than or equal to 10, equal to or greater than 25 and less than or equal to 50, or equal to OLD, the statements in the statement-block associated with the CASE are executed.

The following example illustrates the use of a simple SELECT CASE statement to check the value assigned to YEAR for three ranges, printing the century the year is in. If the value of YEAR does not fall into a predefined century, the optional CASE ELSE clause was included to print an error message.

```
INPUT YEAR
SELECT CASE YEAR
        CASE 1800 TO 1899
                PRINT "19TH CENTURY"
```

```
                    CASE 1900 TO 1999
                            PRINT "20TH CENTURY"
                    CASE 2000 TO 2099
                            PRINT "21ST CENTURY"
                CASE ELSE
                        PRINT "INVALID CENTURY"
        END SELECT
```

```
    ? 1872
    19TH CENTURY
    ? 2155
    INVALID CENTURY
```

The following example illustrates the use of string comparisons in a CASE clause. In this example a string expression (GRADE$) is evaluated in the SELECT CASE block of statements. If the string is within the range A to D the message PASSED is printed while a grade of F causes the message FAILED to be displayed. Any other grade causes the message INVALID GRADE to be printed.

```
    INPUT GRADE$
    SELECT CASE GRADE$
            CASE "A" TO "D"
                        PRINT "PASSED"
            CASE IS="F"
                        PRINT "FAILED"
            CASE ELSE
                        PRINT "INVALID GRADE"
    END SELECT
```

Screen Control

Numerous programming techniques can be used to control the display of information. As previously noted, you can use the INPUT and PRINT statements to display information. In this section, several statements and functions that can be used to clear the display, position the cursor to a specific location, read the contents of a specific display location, or obtain the current cursor column position will be examined. Discussion will be limited to the text mode of operation; in later chapters some of these statements will be reexamined to ascertain their use when you are using a graphics operating mode.

CLS Statement

You can clear the screen by including the CLS statement. The format of this statement is

format: CLS

format$_Q$: CLS $\left[\left\{ \begin{matrix} 0 \\ 2 \end{matrix} \right\} \right]$

When used in the direct mode without a line number in interpretive BASIC, this statement immediately clears the screen and returns the cursor to the home position in the upper left-hand corner of the screen. This provides you with a handy mechanism to immediately clear the display and reposition the cursor if you have previously filled the screen with data you no longer wish to reference. Note that the use of this statement does not clear the contents of memory of a previously entered program. To delete the program memory and clear all variables, enter the NEW command if you are using interpretive BASIC or select CLEAR from the file menu in QBASIC or QuickBASIC. Because the NEW command does not clear the screen, you might wish to follow it with the CLS statement entered in direct mode, or you can press the Ctrl+Home keys to clear the screen in interpretive BASIC.

You can also enter CLS in the Immediate window in QBASIC or QuickBASIC to clear the program output screen. To accomplish this, you must first switch to the Immediate window. Then you would enter **CLS** and press Enter. If you are using a viewpoint (which is described later in this chapter) you can use **CLS 2** to clear the contents of the viewport but retain the contents of the remainder of the display. To clear the entire screen, including the contents of the viewport, you would enter **CLS 0**, because CLS has no effect when a viewport is active.

Within a BASIC program, the execution of a CLS statement clears the screen under program control. Because screen clearing will occur automatically many times, you may wish to insert a status prompt to enable the program's user to acknowledge that he or she is ready to continue before your code clears the screen. This is particularly important if your program is displaying the results of some computation that cannot fit on one screen and you wish to clear the screen and continue the display of output. Without some control mechanism, the output would be displayed at the AT's operating speed and the execution of the CLS statement would then clear the display. This could conceivably make it difficult—if not impossible—for the user to determine the results of the computation. When used after the data input process is completed, no such prompt may be necessary. In this type of situation, you may wish to clear the screen prior to displaying the results of some computation based on previously entered data. The use of prompt messages prior to a CLS statement is illustrated by the following segment:

```
100 PRINT "ENTER C TO CONTINUE"
110 A$=INKEY$:IF A$<>"C"THEN 110
120 CLS
```

In this program segment, after the message ENTER C TO CONTINUE is displayed, the program constantly loops in line 110 until the appropriate character is entered. Once the character C is entered, line 120 is executed and the screen is cleared. This type of control mechanism is important if you wish to provide time for the user to print the contents of the display with the Print Screen key or the Shift+PrtSc keys prior to the program continuing with a new screen of information.

LOCATE Statement

You can position the cursor to a specific row and column on the screen through the use of the LOCATE statement. Before you examine the use of this statement, examine in some detail the screen positions resulting from text mode operation.

The format of the screen in text mode is illustrated in Figure 9.2. As illustrated, characters can be displayed on 25 lines across the screen. These lines are numbered 1

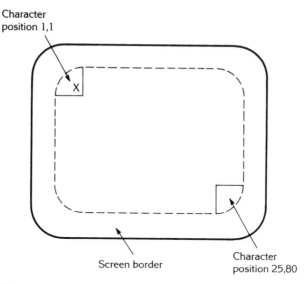

Figure 9.2 Text Mode Screen Format.

through 25, from top to bottom. The number of character positions per line will be 40 or 80, depending on the use of the BASIC WIDTH statement. The character positions on a line are numbered 1 to 40 or 1 to 80 from left to right. Although line 25 is used for the soft key display, you can use this line on the screen if you turn the soft key display off. This can be accomplished in direct mode or under program control by using one version of the KEY statement where the word OFF follows KEY, as shown here.

    100 KEY OFF   Turns off soft key in indirect program mode
    KEY OFF   Turns off soft key in direct mode method

Now that you have completed the initial examination of the text mode screen format, refocus on the LOCATE statement. In addition to positioning the cursor on the screen, optional parts of this statement enable you to turn the cursor on or off and to define its size. The format of this statement is

    format: LOCATE[*row*][,[*col*][,[*cursor*][,[*start*][,*stop*]]]]

where *row* is the screen line number and is a numeric expression in the range 1 and 25; *col* is the screen column number (this must be a numeric expression between 1 and 40 or 1 and 80, based on the screen width); *cursor* is a value that will define whether the cursor is visible (a value of 0 turns the cursor off, 1 turns the cursor on); *start* is the cursor starting scan line and must be a numeric expression between 0 and 31; and *stop* is the cursor stop scan line and must be a numeric expression between 0 and 31. Figure 9.3 shows the 8 bars that define the cursor when a color graphics adapter is used. These lines are numbered from 0 at the top of the character position to 7 at the bottom. Note that by defining the appropriate start and stop scan lines you can vary the size of the cursor. If a monochrome display adapter is used, the bottom scan line is 13, so you can use 14 bars to define the cursor.

If any format parameter is entered that is outside the specified range of values, an illegal function call error will result. Any parameter can be omitted, in which

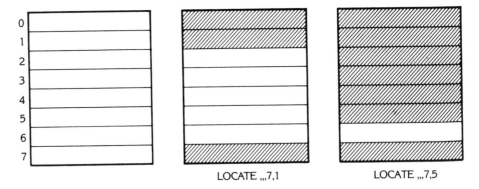

Figure 9.3 Bars That Form the Cursor Using Color/Graphics Video Adapter.

case the omitted parameter will assume the current value. Now take a look at some examples of the use of this statement to obtain a feel for its use within a program.

The default value of the cursor is off when a program runs. Suppose you wish to turn it on; you can do so with the following statement:

```
100 LOCATE,,1
```

Similarly, you can turn the cursor off by using a value of 0 for the cursor. Thus, the statement 100 LOCATE,,0 would turn the cursor off.

Note that by using two commas prior to turning the cursor on you have omitted the row and column positions from the specification. This means they will assume the current value and the cursor will become visible where the program first places it on the screen. Now, suppose you wish to print the message SPACEMAN on line 12, starting at column position 36. You can first position the cursor to that location, because subsequent I/O statements to the screen will place characters beginning at the specified location. Thus, you can satisfy your requirement through the use of the following two statements:

```
100 LOCATE 12,36
100 PRINT"SPACEMAN"
```

Line 100 causes the cursor to be positioned on row 12 at column 36. The PRINT statement on line 110 causes the string SPACEMAN to be displayed on line 12, starting at column 36. Suppose you wish to display a screen of questions and position the cursor to an appropriate location to receive the response to each question. This can be accomplished by multiple LOCATE statements, as indicated by the following program segment:

```
LIST
100 CLS
110 LOCATE 5,15,1
120 PRINT "PART NUMBER"
130 LOCATE 7,15
140 PRINT "QUANTITY ON HAND"
150 LOCATE 9,15
160 PRINT "UNIT COST"
170 LOCATE 5,40
180 INPUT "",PN
```

```
190 LOCATE 7,40
200 INPUT "",QTY
210 LOCATE 9,40
220 INPUT "",COST
```

In the preceding program segment, the LOCATE statement in line 110 positions the cursor at row 5, column 15, and turns it on. The PRINT statement in line 120 causes the string PART NUMBER to be displayed on line 5, commencing at column 15. The LOCATE and PRINT statements in lines 130 through 150 cause the strings QUANTITY ON HAND and UNIT COST to be displayed on lines 7 and 9, each left justified in column 15. Now that you finished displaying the items you wish values to be entered for, you can reposition the cursor to appropriate locations to receive data input. Assuming you wish data to be entered at column 40 on each line where the string was displayed, you can use the LOCATE statements in lines 170, 190, and 210 for that purpose. After you move the cursor to the appropriate position, the following INPUT statement will be used to assign the data to a variable. Note that the word INPUT is followed by a null character signified by double quotes. This null character was used to suppress the generation of a question mark by the INPUT statement. The execution of this program segment with sample data input follows. Note that you are able to align responses to questions on a line-by-line basis and space and position questions and responses through the use of the LOCATE statement.

PART NUMBER   **3433**

QUANTITY ON HAND   **122**

UNIT COST   **14.75**

You can use the start and stop parameters in the LOCATE statement format to vary the size of the cursor. This is accomplished by indicating the starting and ending scan lines. Scan lines are numbered from 0 at the top of the character position to 7 or 13, depending on whether you are using a color adapter or the monochrome adapter. By using the LOCATE statement with appropriate start and stop values, you can change the cursor from a dash to a square or into a rectangular shape. In addition, you can split the cursor into equal or nonequal segments, as illustrated in the right-hand portion of Figure 9.3. Once set, the cursor will retain that shape until it is altered by a subsequent LOCATE statement. The following examples illustrate the use of the LOCATE statement by changing the size of the cursor:

```
100 LOCATE ,,,0,13
```

Here, the position and cursor visibility remain unchanged. The cursor will cover the entire character cell on the display, starting at scan line 0 and ending on scan line 13.

```
100 LOCATE 1,1,1,0,6
```

Here, the cursor will move to the home position in the upper left-hand corner, the cursor will become visible and cover one-half of the character cell, starting at scan line 0 and ending at scan line 6.

When specifying scan lines, you can omit either or both values. If start is given and stop is omitted, stop will take on the value of start. If you specify a start value greater than stop, you will obtain a two-part cursor. In this event, the cursor will "wrap" itself from the bottom line back to the top.

BASIC contains a function for locating the current cursor column position and a variable that can be used to obtain the cursor's row location.

PART NUMBER	**3433**
QUANTITY ON HAND	**122**
UNIT COST	**14.75**

You can use the start and stop parameters in the LOCATE statement format to vary the size of the cursor. This is accomplished by indicating the starting and ending scan lines. Scan lines are numbered from 0 at the top of the character position to 7 or 13, depending on whether you are using a color adapter or the monochrome adapter. By using the LOCATE statement with appropriate start and stop values, you can change the cursor from a dash to a square or into a rectangular shape. In addition, you can split the cursor into equal or nonequal segments, as illustrated in the right-hand portion of Figure 9.3. Once set, the cursor will retain that shape until it is altered by a subsequent LOCATE statement. The following examples illustrate the use of the LOCATE statement by changing the size of the cursor:

```
100 LOCATE ,,,0,13
```

Here, the position and cursor visibility remain unchanged. The cursor will cover the entire character cell on the display, starting at scan line 0 and ending on scan line 13.

```
100 LOCATE 1,1,1,0,6
```

Here, the cursor will move to the home position in the upper left-hand corner, the cursor will become visible and cover one-half of the character cell, starting at scan line 0 and ending at scan line 6.

When specifying scan lines, you can omit either or both values. If start is given and stop is omitted, stop will take on the value of start. If you specify a start value greater than stop, you will obtain a two-part cursor. In this event, the cursor will "wrap" itself from the bottom line back to the top.

BASIC contains a function for locating the current cursor column position and a variable that can be used to obtain the cursor's row location.

POS Function

The POS function can be used to obtain the current column (horizontal) position of the cursor. The format of this function is

format: X=POS(*dummy*)

Here, a dummy argument is used in the function call. The returned value of the function call will be between 1 and 40 or 1 and 80, depending on the current WIDTH setting. The use of this function is demonstrated in the following program segment:

```
100 IF POS(X)>50 THEN 130
110 PRINT A$
120 GOTO 150
```

```
130 LOCATE 10,1
140 PRINT A$
150 REM Program continues
```

In this example, you assumed you would display variable length information. If so, you may wish to see where the cursor is located prior to continuing output to the screen. In line 100, you compared the cursor's column position to 50. If it is less than or equal to 50, the program will display the string contained in A$ and then branch to line 150. If the cursor's column position is greater than 50, the program will branch to line 130, where the cursor will be relocated to line 10, column 1, and the string A$ will be displayed starting at that position.

CSRLIN Variable

The CSRLIN variable can be used to obtain the vertical coordinate (row) of the cursor. The format of the use of this variable is

format: *varnm*=CSRLIN

If you are developing a program that has the number of output lines displayed based on user response, you could use the CSRLIN variable to test the row cursor position before the code generated a CLS statement that would clear the display and return the cursor to home position, 1,1. Another use of this variable is in conjunction with the POS function to obtain the current row and column positions of the cursor prior to generating a message at a location on the screen. Once the message is generated, you could restore your cursor to its previous location, as indicated by the following program segment:

```
Ok
100 KEY OFF        'Turn off soft keys
.

.

.
500 X=CSRLIN       'Get current line
510 Y=POS(0)       'Get current column
520 LOCATE 25,10
530 PRINT "WRONG ANSWER-ENTER C TO CONTINUE"
540 A$=INKEY$:IF A$<>"C"THEN 540
550 LOCATE 25,10   'Clear error message from screen
560 PRINT "                          "
570 LOCATE Y,X     'Restore cursor position
```

In this example, the statement in line 100 causes the "soft key" display associated with interpretive BASIC to be turned off. The statements in lines 500 and 510 assign the column and row positions of the cursor to the variables X and Y. In line 520, the cursor is repositioned to column 10 in line 530 and the message WRONG ANSWER-- ENTER C TO CONTINUE is displayed. The statements in line 540 cause the program to await the entry of the uppercase character C from the keyboard prior to resuming program execution Once C is entered, the error message is cleared from the screen and the cursor is relocated to its previous location by the statement in line 570. In line 570, the position of the cursor is restored to what were the current line and current column positions prior to generating and clearing the indicated error message.

VIEW PRINT Statement

One of the problems associated with developing programs in interpretive BASIC is that on reaching the bottom of the screen, additional output results in information at the top of the screen scrolling off and becoming lost. Thus, if you want to provide instructions for data entry while displaying a variety of information, you have to add instructions to keep track of the number of lines displayed and then refresh the screen with a new set of instructions each time the prior set of instructions scrolls off the screen. In addition to requiring an extensive amount of coding to perform, the scrolling of instructions will appear awkward. It appears that Microsoft Corporation recognized this problem, resulting in the inclusion of the VIEW PRINT statement in QuickBASIC.

The use of the VIEW PRINT statement enables you to restrict output to a horizontal portion of the display known as a *viewport*. The format of this statement is

format$_Q$: VIEW PRINT [*top line* TO *bottom line*]

Here the values for top line and bottom line define the rows where the viewport begins and ends. If the statement is entered without parameters, VIEW PRINT terminates the viewport. Thereafter, a previously defined viewport will have its contents scrolled off the screen as additional lines of information are displayed. To illustrate the use of the VIEW PRINT statement, consider the following example:

```
CLS
LOCATE 3, 5
PRINT "THE VIEWPORT IS CONTAINED IN ROWS 5 THRU 20"
LOCATE 4, 1
PRINT STRING$(72, "*")
LOCATE 21, 1
PRINT STRING$(72, "*")
LOCATE 22, 5
PRINT "YOU CAN ALSO FIX INSTRUCTIONS UNDER THE VIEWPORT"
VIEW PRINT 5 TO 20
FOR I=1 TO 30
PRINT "THIS IS LINE", I
NEXT I
```

In this example the screen is cleared (CLS) and the cursor is located at row 3, column 5. Next, the message THE VIEWPORT IS CONTAINED IN ROWS 5 THRU 20 will be displayed in row 3, beginning at column 5. The first STRING$ function is used to generate 72 asterisks that begin in column 1 of row 4; the second function also generates 72 asterisks, starting at column 1 in row 21. After displaying another message under the intended viewport, the VIEW PRINT statement creates a viewport from rows 5 through 20. Once this viewport is created, scrolling takes place only between the top and bottom lines of the viewport. This is illustrated by the use of the FOR-NEXT loop, which is used to print 30 lines. The viewport is 15 lines high, so on execution of this program, lines 16 through 30 will remain displayed in the viewport as lines 1 through 15 scroll off the screen, as verified by the following screen (note that the operation of the FOR-NEXT statement pair is described in detail later in this chapter):

```
THE VIEWPORT IS CONTAINED IN ROWS 5 THRU 20
*************************************************************************
THIS IS LINE 16
THIS IS LINE 17
```

```
THIS IS LINE 18
THIS IS LINE 19
THIS IS LINE 20
THIS IS LINE 21
THIS IS LINE 22
THIS IS LINE 23
THIS IS LINE 24
THIS IS LINE 25
THIS IS LINE 26
THIS IS LINE 27
THIS IS LINE 28
THIS IS LINE 29
THIS IS LINE 30
***********************************************************************
    YOU CAN ALSO FIX INSTRUCTIONS UNDER THE VIEWPORT

Press any key to continue
```

When using a viewport, you can use the screen positioning statements such as LOCATE. In addition, you can clear the contents of the viewport by entering **CLS 2**. If you wish to clear the entire screen, including the contents of the viewport, you would enter **CLS 0**.

Program Execution Control

You can terminate program execution and return to command level through the use of an END or a STOP statement. The format of each statement is

```
format: END
format: STOP
```

END Statement

The END statement may be placed anywhere in a program. Once executed, the program will terminate. Unlike many other versions of BASIC, the use of an END statement at the end of a program written in interpretive BASIC, QBASIC, or QuickBASIC is optional. In addition to terminating program execution and returning to command level, the END statement automatically closes any open files. The use of this statement is illustrated by the following program line:

```
100 IF X<Y THEN END ELSE 500
```

In the preceding example, if the value of X is less than Y the program will terminate. Because the only message displayed will be the Ok command-level prompt in interpretive BASIC, you might consider revising the previous example as follows:

```
100 IF X>=Y THEN 120
110 PRINT "X<Y CAUSED PROGRAM TERMINATION":END
120 REM Program continues
```

Now, when X is less than Y, the message X<Y CAUSED PROGRAM TERMINATION will be displayed prior to the command-level prompt Ok appearing on the screen.

STOP Statement

When a STOP statement is encountered, the program will terminate execution. If you are using interpretive BASIC the program will display the message Break in *nnnnn* and then generate the command-level prompt Ok.

Here, *nnnnn* is the line number where the STOP statement was executed. Unlike the END statement, this statement will not close any open files. The use of this statement is illustrated by the following program segment.

```
Ok
100 INPUT "ENTER LENGTH AND WIDTH ";L,W
110 A=L*W
120 IF A>0 THEN 140
130 STOP
140 PRINT "AREA= ";A
150 END
RUN
ENTER LENGTH and WIDTH ? -2,4
Break in 130
Ok
```

In the preceding example, the STOP statement was used to halt program execution when an apparent illogical computation had occurred.

If you are using QBASIC or QuickBASIC, the execution of a STOP statement changes your display from the output screen to the program screen and highlights the STOP statement that was executed. If you wish to view the output screen, you can press the F4 key to toggle back to that display.

CONT Command

You can resume program execution after a break when you are using interpretive BASIC by including the CONT command. Although BASIC commands will be discussed as an entity in the next chapter, it is worthwhile to point out the use of this command here. The format of this command is

format$_{D/A}$: CONT

This command can be used to resume program execution after a STOP or END statement has been executed, after Ctrl+Break has been pressed, or after an error has occurred. The CONT command causes program execution to continue at the point where the break occurred.

The use of this command to resume execution of the prior program whose execution was halted by a STOP statement follows:

```
Ok
100 INPUT "ENTER LENGTH AND WIDTH ";L,W
110 A=L*W
120 IF A>0 THEN 140
130 STOP
140 PRINT "AREA= ";A
150 END
RUN
```

```
ENTER LENGTH AND WIDTH ? -2,4
Break in 130
Ok
CONT
AREA= -8
Ok
```

Normally, you will use this command in conjunction with a STOP statement for program debugging purposes, as illustrated by the following example:

```
Ok
100 X=47.5
110 Y=32.5
120 Q=X*Y
130 PRINT "Q= ";Q
140 STOP
150 LET V=Q+250:PRINT V
```
RUN
```
Q = 1543.75
Break in 140
Ok
Q=1500
Ok
CONT
 1750
Ok
```

In this example, after program execution terminated as a result of the STOP statement, a direct mode statement (Q=1500) was used to change the value of a variable prior to resuming execution with the CONT command. Alternatively, you could use a direct mode GOTO statement, which would also cause program execution to resume at the referenced line number.

Note that the CONT command will be invalid if you edit the program during the break. In comparison, the use of a direct mode GOTO statement will always cause the program to resume execution at the referenced line number. As indicated by the format for this command, it is only applicable to interpretive BASIC.

Loop Control

A computer loop can be defined as a repeating sequence of program statements. Using the GOTO and IF-THEN statements, you can construct a program loop as illustrated by the following example, which results in a table of squares for the numbers 1 to 5.

```
Ok
```
LIST
```
5 PRINT"NUMBER","SQUARE"
10 I=1
20 IF I>5 THEN 60
30 PRINT I,I^2
40 I=I+1
50 GOTO 20
```

```
60 END
Ok
```
RUN

NUMBER	SQUARE
1	1
2	4
3	9
4	16
5	25

```
Ok
```

In this example, a loop control variable was initialized to 1 in line 10. In line 20, the value of the loop control variable was tested against the value you wanted in order to exit from the loop when reached. In this example, you wished to exit the loop and branch to line 60 when the value of I exceeded 5. In line 30, the PRINT statement will cause the value of I and its square to be displayed. This loop shows only the repeated use of a PRINT statement, but you could construct a loop to repeatedly obtain a set number of input data items or to perform a series of computations a desired number of times. In line 40, your loop control variable is incremented by 1 and line 50 causes the program to unconditionally branch back to line 20, where the program again tests the value of the loop control variable against 5. Once you cycle through the loop five times, you will have the value 6 and the statement in line 20 will cause the program to branch to line 60, terminating the loop.

Note that this method of constructing a loop requires you to set the initial value of the loop control parameter, test for the loop exit value, increment the loop control parameter, and have a branching mechanism to return you to the loop parameter comparison once the loop variable has been incremented. By the way, you can also have loops that decrement by initializing the loop parameter to the end value and testing for the lowest permissible loop value. This can be accomplished by decrementing the value of the loop variable each time you pass through the loop, as illustrated by the execution of the next program segment:

```
Ok
```
LIST
```
5 PRINT"NUMBER","SQUARE"
10 I=50
20 IF I<10 THEN 60
30 PRINT I,I^2
40 I=I-10
50 GOTO 20
60 END
Ok
```
RUN

NUMBER	SQUARE
50	2500
40	1600
30	900
20	400
10	100

```
Ok
```

FOR and NEXT Statements

Loops are used so routinely in programming that BASIC provides you with a built-in set of loop control statements known as the FOR and NEXT statements. The format of each statement is:

format: FOR varnm=exprnm$_1$ TO exprnm$_2$[STEP exprnm$_3$]
format: NEXT[varnm][,varnm] . . .

The NEXT statement specifies the boundary in which a series of instructions will be executed a given number of times. The beginning of the loop is specified by the FOR statement whose parameters will control the number of times the loop is executed. The initial value of the counter that controls the loop is specified by *exprnm$_1$*, whereas the value of *exprnm$_2$* specifies the final value of the counter. The program lines bounded by the FOR and NEXT statements will be executed until the NEXT statement is reached. At this time, BASIC will increment or decrement the counter by the amount specified by the STEP value (*exprnm$_3$*). If *exprnm$_3$* is positive, the counter will be incremented, whereas a negative value will result in the counter being decremented. If *exprnm$_3$* is not specified, an increment of 1 will be assumed. After the increment or decrement operation is performed, a comparison of the value of the counter against the final value *exprnm$_2$* will occur. If incrementing was specified and the value of the counter is less than or equal to the final value, BASIC will branch back to the statement following the FOR statement, and the process will be repeated. If the counter exceeds the final value, execution will continue with the statement that follows the NEXT statement.

If *exprnm$_3$* is negative and the counter is decremented, the test will be reversed. Here, the counter will be decremented each time through the loop and the process will be repeated until the counter is less than the final value *exprnm$_2$*. Some examples of the use of a single FOR-NEXT loop follow.

```
Ok
LIST
5 PRINT"NUMBER","SQUARE"
10 FOR I=I TO 5
20 PRINT I,I^2
30 NEXT I
Ok
RUN
NUMBER      SQUARE
  1           1
  2           4
  3           9
  4           16
  5           25
Ok
```

Note that the preceding example provides the same loop control mechanism as obtained through the use of IF-THEN and GOTO statements combined to generate a looping mechanism. You can generate a loop by decrementing the counter as illustrated by executing the following program segment.

```
Ok
LIST
```

```
5 PRINT"NUMBER","SQUARE"
10 FOR I=100 TO 50 STEP -10
20 PRINT I,I^2
30 NEXT I
Ok
```
RUN
```
NUMBER      SQUARE
 100        10000
  90         8100
  80         6400
  70         4900
  60         3600
  50         2500
Ok
```

You can specify a zero increment if you wish to perform some operation a number of times but do not know how many times are required. The use of a zero increment will cause an infinite loop to be created; however, you can construct your program to terminate the loop by setting the counter greater than the final value or by branching out of the loop when your goal is reached. An example of the use of zero increment in a FOR statement is illustrated by the following program segment:

```
Ok
```
LIST
```
100 K=1:X=0
110 FOR I=1 TO 2 STEP 0
120 K=K+1/K^2
130 X=X+1
140 IF K>=3 THEN 160
150 NEXT I
160 PRINT X;"ITERATIONS FOR K= ";K
```
RUN
```
 7 ITERATIONS FOR K= 3.011531
Ok
```

In this example, you wish to determine the number of iterations of the sequence $1 + 1/1^2 + 1/2^2 + 1/3^2 + \ldots 1/N^2$ that is required for the sum of the sequence to equal or exceed 3. Initialize K to 1 and a counter labeled X to 0 in line 100. The FOR statement has a zero STEP, which will keep you in the loop until K equals or exceeds 3. Once this occurs, the program will branch out of the loop due to the statement in line 140. Here, seven iterations were required until K exceeded 3.

If the initial value of the counter is greater than the final value when the STEP value is positive, the body of the loop will be skipped. This is indicated by the following program segment:

```
Ok
10 A=10:B=20
20 FOR X=B TO A STEP 5
30 PRINT X
40 NEXT X
```
RUN
```
Ok
```

If the STEP value is negative and the initial value of the counter is less than the final value, the body of the loop will also be skipped over.

The FOR and NEXT statements become invaluable as a mechanism for easily performing many computations. As an example, consider factorial numbers when $n! = n \cdot (n-1) \cdot (n-2) \ldots 2 \cdot 1$. The following program can be used to compute any factorial number between 1 and 33 when interpretive BASIC is used. The reason the upper limit is 33 is that factorials beyond this number exceed the largest number interpretive BASIC can operate on. If you are using QBASIC or QuickBASIC, the maximum factorial you can compute is 170 when you use double-precision variables. Doing so results in a value of 7.257415615308004D+306 for factorial 170.

```
Ok
LIST
10 INPUT "ENTER FACTORIAL DESIRED 0 TO EXIT ",F
20 IF F=0 THEN 90
30 X=1
40 FOR I=F TO 1 STEP-1
50 X=X*I
60 NEXT I
70 PRINT F;" FACTORIAL = ";X
80 GOTO 10
90 END
Ok
RUN
ENTER FACTORIAL DESIRED 0 TO EXIT 4
 4  FACTORIAL =  24
ENTER FACTORIAL DESIRED 0 TO EXIT 33
 33  FACTORIAL =  8.683316E+36
ENTER FACTORIAL DESIRED 0 TO EXIT 34
Overflow

 34  FACTORIAL =  1.701412E+38
ENTER FACTORIAL DESIRED 0 TO EXIT
```

Another valuable use of FOR and NEXT statements is to provide an easy mechanism for the manipulation of array elements. Suppose you have an array containing 50 data elements and you wish to obtain the average value of all elements. You can accomplish this task easily as shown by the following program segment.

```
100 FOR I=1 TO 50
110 X=X+A(I)
120 NEXT I
130 PRINT "AVERAGE= ";X/50
```

Here, the Ith element of array A will be added to the counter labeled X each time the FOR-NEXT loop is executed. When all 50 elements have been added to X, the loop will terminate, and the line following the NEXT statement, line 130, will be executed. The PRINT statement on this line will cause the string AVERAGE= to be displayed, and the value of X will be divided by 50 prior to being displayed on the screen.

Suppose you have a two-dimensional array. How could you use a FOR-NEXT loop to add the elements of that type of array? Because FOR-NEXT loops can be *nested*, you can use several such loops to perform the required loop control mechanism. In this instance of nested loops, one FOR-NEXT loop is placed inside another FOR-NEXT loop. An example of the use of nested FOR-NEXT loops follows:

```
100 FOR I=1 TO 10
110 FOR J=1 TO 5
120 X=X+A(I,J)
130 NEXT J
140 NEXT I
```

Here, the FOR J loop is known as the *inner loop* and the FOR I loop is known as the *outer loop*. When loops are nested, each loop must be assigned a unique variable name as its counter. The NEXT statement for the inner loop must appear prior to the occurrence of a NEXT statement for the outer loop, or an error will occur. To examine the use of nested FOR-NEXT statements, execute this short program segment:

LIST
```
100 FOR I=1 TO 6 STEP 2
110 FOR J=10 TO 30 STEP 10
120 PRINT I,J
130 NEXT J
140 NEXT I
```
RUN
```
1          10
1          20
1          30
3          10
3          20
3          30
5          10
5          20
5          30
Ok
```

In this example, the I counter is initialized to 1 in line 100. The J counter is initialized to 10 in line 110. The execution of the complete inner loop will occur for each loop cycle, so J will vary from 10 to 30 in increments of 10 when I is 1. Once the inner loop is completed, the program continues and initializes another outer loop cycle when the following NEXT statement is encountered. Thus, I is incremented by 2 to a value of 3 in the outer loop. This causes the inner loop to be repeated a second time, and the process will be repeated a third time with I having a value of 5 as J varies from 10 to 30. Note that in BASIC you can replace lines 130 and 140 with the common NEXT statement.

```
130 NEXT I,J
```

The error message FOR without NEXT will be generated if a FOR statement is encountered without a matching NEXT. This can result from a loop being initialized and a cycle being in progress when an END, STOP, or a RETURN statement is encountered in the program. The error message NEXT without FOR will occur if a NEXT statement is encountered prior to its corresponding FOR statement. A good technique for checking the validity of FOR-NEXT loops is to draw a line on the left-hand side of your program listing to connect each FOR statement with its corresponding NEXT statement. This will ensure a one-to-one correspondence. In addition, if the lines form concentric brackets that do not intersect, the FOR-NEXT statements are used in their appropriate order. If the lines drawn between statements cross, the FOR-NEXT statements will not operate and the variable assignments must be changed. The following examples illustrate the use of lines to connect FOR-NEXT statements:

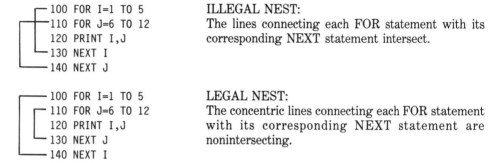

```
100 FOR I=1 TO 5          ILLEGAL NEST:
110 FOR J=6 TO 12         The lines connecting each FOR statement with its
120 PRINT I,J             corresponding NEXT statement intersect.
130 NEXT I
140 NEXT J
```

```
100 FOR I=1 TO 5          LEGAL NEST:
110 FOR J=6 TO 12         The concentric lines connecting each FOR statement
120 PRINT I,J             with its corresponding NEXT statement are
130 NEXT J                nonintersecting.
140 NEXT I
```

EXIT FOR Statement

Although you can use an IF statement referencing a line number or label in QuickBASIC to effect a branch out of a FOR-NEXT loop, QuickBASIC also provides what may be viewed as a more elegant method of exit through the use of the EXIT FOR statement. This statement is used in conjunction with an IF statement to exit a FOR-NEXT loop. Its format when used in conjunction with an IF statement is

format$_Q$: IF *expr* THEN EXIT FOR

You can include any number of EXIT FOR statements within a single FOR-NEXT loop and place those statements anywhere within the loop. However, if you have nested FOR-NEXT loops, the EXIT FOR statement is only applicable for the smallest enclosing FOR-NEXT loop in which it appears.

The following program segment illustrates the use of the EXIT FOR statement. This example computes the sum of the squares of the numbers from 1 to 10 but stops when the sum exceeds 25.

```
X = 0!
FOR A = 1 TO 10
IF X > 25 THEN EXIT FOR
X = X + A * A
NEXT A
PRINT A, X
```

Now examine the effect of the EXIT FOR statement when it is used with nested FOR-NEXT loops. In the following example, the EXIT FOR statement was placed within an inner FOR-NEXT loop, simply causing an exit to the NEXT statement associated with the loop to occur. The outer loop is still active, so control passes right back to the inner loop. Thus, the program segment runs to completion, as indicated by the printout of the execution results that follows the listing:

```
CLS
FOR I = 0 TO 6 STEP 2
FOR J = 1 TO 6 STEP 2
```

```
PRINT I, J
IF J > 4 THEN EXIT FOR
NEXT J
NEXT I
PRINT "END NESTED LOOP"
```

```
    0               1
    0               3
    0               5
    2               1
    2               3
    2               5
    4               1
    4               3
    4               5
    6               1
    6               3
    6               5
END NESTED LOOP
```

If the intention of the preceding example was to exit the nested FOR-NEXT loop when the value of J exceeds 5, the EXIT FOR statement cannot be used. EXIT FOR exits only the smallest enclosing loop, and the outer loop then passes control back to the inner loop. In place of the EXIT FOR statement, this code should include a conventional IF statement with a branch to a line number or label. Note that in the following example the IF statement causes a branch out of the nested FOR-NEXT loop once the value of J exceeds 4, regardless of the value of the index of the outer loop variable I:

```
CLS
FOR I = 0 TO 6 STEP 2
FOR J = 1 TO 6 STEP 2
PRINT I, J
IF J > 4 THEN GOTO 9
NEXT J
NEXT I
9 PRINT "END NESTED LOOP"
```

```
    0               1
    0               3
    0               5
END NESTED LOOP
```

SLEEP Statement

One common use of the FOR-NEXT loop in interpretive BASIC was to insert a pause into a program. This is accomplished by using an empty FOR-NEXT loop that simply counts the numbers within the range expressed in the loop. For example, the statement

```
FOR I= 1 TO 5000:NEXT I
```

would cause a program to pause for the length of time it took the computer to cycle through the loop incrementing I from 1 to 5000. Although the method of effecting a program pause is satisfactory when you do not require an exact interval of program suspension, it may not be sufficient when a precise time interval is required. This inexactness is caused by computers with different microprocessors or the same microprocessor operating at different clock rates, which can change the pause duration as they execute the FOR-NEXT loop. In addition, there is no elegant method of suspending a program in interpretive BASIC until a key is pressed other than writing a routine that uses the INKEY$ function with an IF statement. Recognizing this problem, Microsoft added the SLEEP statement to QBASIC and QuickBASIC, whose format is

format$_Q$: SLEEP [*seconds*]

When you enter the statement without an argument, SLEEP causes the program to suspend operation until a key is pressed or a predefined event occurs. If an argument is specified, the program pauses for the indicated number of seconds each time it is executed or until the user presses a key, whichever comes first. To illustrate the use of the QuickBASIC SLEEP statement, the previously illustrated FOR-NEXT program segment can be modified.

Suppose you want time for the user to consider the results displayed on the screen on a line-by-line basis. To accomplish this, you could insert a SLEEP statement either before or after the PRINT I,J statement. In the following example the SLEEP statement was inserted after the PRINT I,J statement. Therefore, when you execute the program segment, the value 0 1 is displayed and the execution of the program is then suspended until the user presses any key. Thereafter, each line of output is followed by the suspension of the program until the branch to line 9 occurs.

Following is the revised code:

```
CLS
FOR I = 0 TO 6 STEP 2
FOR J = 1 TO 6 STEP 2
PRINT I, J
SLEEP
IF J > 4 THEN GOTO 9
NEXT J
NEXT I
9 PRINT "END NESTED LOOP"
```

WHILE-WEND Statements

The WHILE and WEND statements provide another mechanism for executing a series of statements in a loop. Unlike the FOR and NEXT statements that directly control the number of times the statements within a loop will be executed, the WHILE and WEND statements cause the statements bounded by those two statements to be executed as long as a given condition is true. The format of these two statements is

format: WHILE *expr*
format: WEND

As long as the expression in the WHILE statement is true (not zero), the statements bounded by the WHILE and WEND statements will be executed. Each time the WEND statement is encountered, BASIC will pass control back to the WHILE statement and check the value of the expression in that statement. If the expression is still true, another pass through the loop will occur. If the expression is false, BASIC will cause the program to resume execution with the statement following the WEND statement. The following program segment illustrates the use of these two statements:

```
Ok
100 REM ACCEPT INPUT UNTIL COMPUTED VALUE EXCEEDS TOTAL
110 X=0:COUNT=0:TOTAL=132.65
120 TEST=1
130 WHILE TEST
140 INPUT "ENTER VALUE ",VALUE
150 X=X+VALUE/3.14159
160 COUNT=COUNT+1
170 IF X>TOTAL THEN TEST=0
180 WEND
190 PRINT "NUMBER OF ENTRIES= ";COUNT
RUN
ENTER VALUE 13.212
ENTER VALUE 32
ENTER VALUE 543
NUMBER OF ENTRIES=  3
Ok
```

In this example, two counters, X and COUNT, were initialized to 0 in line 110, and the value tested for, TOTAL, was initialized to 132.65. The expression used to control the WHILE-WEND loop execution, TEST, is initialized to 1 in line 120. In line 140, the INPUT statement will cause the prompt ENTER VALUE to be displayed, and the program will temporarily halt execution awaiting a numeric quantity to be entered. This quantity will be assigned to the variable VALUE. In line 150, the counter X will be incremented by the quantity VALUE divided by 3.14159. In line 160, the counter, COUNT, which is used to keep track of the number of items entered, is incremented by 1. When the value of X exceeds the predefined value contained in the variable TOTAL, TEST will be reset to 0 in line 170. This will cause the program to resume execution at the statement after the WEND statement, and the number of entries will then be printed as a result of the BASIC statement in line 190. As shown, three entries were required until the WHILE-WEND loop was exited.

Like FOR-NEXT loops, WHILE-WEND loops can be nested. Each WEND statement will match the most recent WHILE statement, as illustrated here:

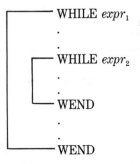

Error messages resulting from the improper usage of WHILE and WEND statements are similar to the error messages from the improper use of FOR and NEXT statements. An unmatched WHILE statement will cause a WHILE without WEND error message, and an unmatched WEND statement will result in a WEND without WHILE error message.

Subroutines

Many times in programming you recognize that a sequence of statements that performs one or more functions requires repeated usage. You can construct these statements as a subroutine and easily invoke their usage by branching to the statement where the subroutine starts. In addition, BASIC provides you with a mechanism to conveniently return program execution to the statement after the statement that invoked the subroutine or to any other program statement you may desire to resume program execution.

GOSUB Statement

The most common method to reference a subroutine is by means of the GOSUB statement, whose format is

format: GOSUB$\left\{\begin{array}{l} line \\ label^2 \end{array}\right\}$

The execution of the GOSUB statement causes the program to branch to the line number indicated in the statement or to a label if you are using QuickBASIC. Program execution will continue at the indicated line number or label until a RETURN statement is encountered.

RETURN Statement

The RETURN statement defines the physical end of the subroutine. The format of this statement is

format: RETURN$\left[\left\{\begin{array}{l} line \\ label^2 \end{array}\right\}\right]$

In all versions of BASIC, the RETURN statement will cause BASIC to branch back to the statement following the most recently executed GOSUB statement. The optional line number in the RETURN statement enables you to resume program execution at any line in the program, although the use of this feature must be carefully considered, because any other GOSUB, FOR, or WHILE statement that was active will remain active. If you are using QBASIC or QuickBASIC you can specify a label as the point where program execution will resume.

The subroutine itself does not require any special statement at its beginning. Thus, a subroutine can begin with a REM statement, a FOR statement, a CLS statement, and so on. The last statement, however, must be a RETURN statement. As an example of the use of subroutines, suppose you are developing a program that requires many screens of information to be displayed, each screen requesting the entry of several items of data. Furthermore, suppose that, after the last item of data is entered on each screen, you wish to provide a mechanism for the operator to either reenter the data elements in case one or more items were previously entered incorrectly or clear the display prior

---

[2] Applicable only to QuickBASIC.

to generating the next screen display and requesting the entry of new data elements. The main program with the appropriate subroutine branches might be constructed as follows:

```
100 REM Display first screen section
  .
  .

200 GOSUB 4000
210 IF X=1 THEN 100
  .

300 REM Display second screen section
  .
400 GOSUB 4000
410 IF X=1 THEN 300
  .

  .
4000 REM Beginning of subroutine
4010 X=0                          'Reset X
4020 LOCATE 25,10
4030 PRINT"ENTER C TO CONTINUE R TO REENTER DATA"
4040 A$=INKEY$:IF A$<>"C" OR A$<>"R" THEN 4040
4050 IF A$="R" THEN X=1
4060 CLS
4070 RETURN                       'End of subroutine
```

In this example, each GOSUB 4000 statement causes the program to transfer control to the subroutine that begins at line 4000. Here, the first statement in the subroutine is a nonexecutable REM statement. The second statement in the subroutine sets the variable labeled X to 0. This variable will be used for control purposes when you return to the main program. Line 4020 positions the cursor at row 25, column 10, where the message ENTER C TO CONTINUE R TO REENTER DATA will be printed, starting at row 25, column 10. Line 4040 uses the INKEY$ variable to read a character from the keyboard and causes a branch back to this line if neither the uppercase C nor R is entered. Line 4050 compares the value of A$ to the character R. If A$ equals R, then X will be reset to 1. If A$ does not equal R, the X will retain its initialized value of 0. The CLS statement in line 4060 causes the screen to be cleared, and the RETURN statement in line 4070 causes the program to transfer control to the statement following the most recent GOSUB statement.

Thus, if lines 100 through 200 of the program display the first screen and obtain the values for the appropriate data elements, if one enters the character R when the subroutine prompt message is displayed, the RETURN from the subroutine to line 210 will cause the program to branch back to line 100 and redisplay the screen. This is because the variable X was set to 1 in the subroutine. This RETURN feature permits all previous entries to be changed and provides an easy mechanism for reentering previously entered data elements within a program.

Before you examine what is commonly known as a computed subroutine statement, a word of caution concerning the usage of subroutines is in order. Subroutines can be physically located anywhere within a program, but good programming practice is to place them at the end of a program for ease of visual reference in program debugging. This can simplify program debugging considerably, because in BASIC a subroutine may be called from within another subroutine and the only limit to such nesting of subroutines is available memory.

If you place subroutines at the end of your program, their physical structure appears as illustrated in Figure 9.4.

When the last line in the main program is executed, what occurs next? If the last statement is not a STOP, END, or a GOTO statement that branches to a STOP or END statement, the first subroutine will be executed again. This is obviously not your intention, so you should place a STOP, END, or GOTO statement that will branch to a STOP or END statement at the end of the main program when you physically locate subroutines at the end of a program. This fact is illustrated by the execution of the following program segment:

```
Ok
LIST
100 REM Main program
110 INPUT "NAME ",N$
120 GOSUB 500
130 INPUT "ADDRESS ",A$
500 PRINT "I LIKE ";N$
510 RETURN
Ok
RUN
NAME GIL
I LIKE GIL
ADDRESS 4736 OXFORD ROAD
I LIKE GIL
RETURN without GOSUB in 510
Ok
```

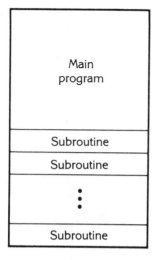

Figure 9.4   Recommended Program Structure. Subroutines are grouped together at the end of the program.

In this example, after line 130 is executed, the program falls back into the subroutine. This results in the unintentional printing of the I LIKE message in the subroutine a second time and causes the RETURN without GOSUB in 510 error message to be displayed. By placing a STOP or END statement in line 140 as shown next, this extra and unwanted fall into the subroutine is prevented:

```
100 REM Main program
110 INPUT "NAME ",N$
120 GOSUB 500
130 INPUT "ADDRESS ",A$
140 END
500 PRINT "I LIKE ";N$
510 RETURN
Ok
RUN
NAME GIL
I LIKE GIL
ADDRESS 4736 OXFORD ROAD
Ok
```

ON-GOSUB Statement

BASIC contains a computed GOSUB statement whose format and functional operation are very similar to the computed GOTO statement. The computed GOSUB statement provides you with the capability to branch to one of two or more subroutines based on the value of a numeric expression. The format of this statement is

format: ON *exprnm* GOSUB $\begin{Bmatrix} line[,line] & . & . & . \\ label[,label] & . & . & .^3 \end{Bmatrix}$

The value of the numeric expression, *exprnm*, will determine to which line number or label in the list the program will branch when the statement is executed. If the value of the expression is not an integer, it will be rounded. If the value of the numeric expression is zero or greater than the number of items in the list but less than or equal to 255, BASIC will ignore the statement and resume execution with the next executable statement following the ON-GOSUB statement. When the value of the numeric expression used for branch control is negative or greater than 256, an Illegal function call error will result, and program execution will be halted.

The use of this statement is most beneficial if you wish to divide your program into segments and control the branch to the appropriate segment by the user. This can be accomplished by providing an initial menu and associating a value with the response to branch to the desired program segment that was written as a subroutine. Once the subroutine is completed, the RETURN statement will provide you with a mechanism to branch back to the line following the computed ON-GOSUB statement where you can provide the program operator with another segment by branching back to the menu. This concept is demonstrated by the following program segment.

---

[3] Applicable only to QBASIC and QuickBASIC.

```
100 CLS
110 LOCATE 10,15
120 PRINT "PROGRAM SECTION SELECTION"
130 PRINT
140 PRINT TAB(15)"(1) CONVERTIBLE BOND ANALYSIS"
150 PRINT TAB(15)"(2) INTEREST RATE ANALYSIS"
160 PRINT TAB(15)"(3) HOME MORTGAGE ANALYSIS"
170 PRINT TAB(15)"(4) RETIREMENT FUNDING ANALYSIS"
180 PRINT TAB(15)"(5) EXIT PROGRAM"
190 PRINT
200 LOCATE 18,15
210 INPUT "ENTER SECTION DESIRED",X
220 ON X GOSUB 1000,2000,3000,4000,5000
230 GOTO 100
1000 REM Convertible bond analysis subroutine
 .
 .
 .
1990 RETURN
 .
 .
 .
5000 END
```

In this example, the section number desired is used as the mechanism to control which subroutine the program will branch to. Note that the entry of a number greater than 5 will cause line 230 to be executed, which redisplays the initial menu. In addition, each RETURN statement in the program will also cause line 230 to be executed, redisplaying the menu and allowing the operator to select another program section. If 5 is entered, a branch to line 5000 will occur. Here, an END statement is used to terminate the program. The initial menu displayed on the screen is

```
PROGRAM SECTION SELECTION

(1) CONVERTIBLE BOND ANALYSIS
(2) INTEREST RATE ANALYSIS
(3) HOME MORTGAGE ANALYSIS
(4) RETIREMENT FUNDING ANALYSIS
(5) EXIT PROGRAM

ENTER SECTION DESIRED
```

SUB Procedure and CALL Statement

By using subroutines you can simplify programming, subdividing programs into their logical components. However, the variables in subroutines come to be considered as global. That is, once used in a subroutine, the value of the variable is retained in the remainder of the program unless the user specifically alters the value. This is illustrated by the following program segment, which employs a GOSUB statement to branch to the subroutine labeled TEST. Note that the value of 37.5 assigned to the variable X in the subroutine is retained in the main program module, resulting in the PRINT X statement output of 37.5.

```
X = 5
GOSUB TEST
PRINT X
END
TEST:
X = 37.5
RETURN

37.5
```

Now consider modifying the previous program segment to use a SUB procedure in place of the GOSUB subroutine. First, however, examine the format of the SUB procedure, the differences between a procedure and a subroutine, and how you can use the QuickBASIC menu to create a procedure. In doing so you will create several small procedures to which you compare and contrast the subroutine previously created in this section.

The format of the SUB procedure is

```
formatₒ: SUB name [parameter-list][STATIC]
         .
         .
         [EXIT SUB]
         .
         .
         END SUB
```

As indicated in the format, the SUB statement defines the beginning of a subprogram; the END SUB statement defines the end of the subprogram. Within the subprogram you can have any number of optional EXIT SUB statements, which when executed cause control to return to the main program.

The name of the SUB procedure can be up to 40 characters long, and it represents both the title of the SUB procedure and the mechanism to reference the procedure through a CALL statement. The format of the CALL statement is

```
format: CALL name [argument-list]
```

where the *name* associated with the CALL statement references the subroutine that control will be passed to.

If you compare the format of the SUB statement to the CALL statement, you will note that the CALL statement has an optional *argument-list*, whereas the SUB statement format includes an optional *parameter-list*. The *argument-list* can contain constants, variables, or expressions whose values are substituted into corresponding variables in the parameter-list. An example of argument passing from a CALL statement to a parameter list in a SUB statement is

```
procedure call       CALL Example (AI, SEX$, SSN&)
                     .
                     .
                     .
procedure definition SUB example (Integer, SEX$, NMBR&)
```

In this example note that although the names in an argument-list and a parameter-list do not have to be the same, they must be the same type. In addition, the number of arguments in the argument-list must equal the number of parameters in the parameter-list.

Returning to the SUB statement format, the last part of that format is the optional keyword STATIC. When included in the SUB statement, STATIC causes local variables in the procedure to retain their values between calls to the procedure. If the keyword is omitted, the local variables in the procedure are initialized to zeros or null strings each time the procedure is called.

The key differences between a SUB procedure and a GOSUB-RETURN subroutine is the ability of the procedure to support local variables. In comparison, subroutines invoked through the use of GOSUB statements only support global variables. As previously illustrated from the GOSUB routine at the beginning of this section, a change in a variable inside the subroutine changes the value of the variable everywhere it appears in the program to include locations outside the subroutine. Thus, you have to be extremely careful when you create subroutines as well as when you have one subroutine call another subroutine to avoid conflicts between variable names resulting in unexpected value assignments.

Because the QBASIC and QuickBASIC menu systems facilitate the creation of SUB procedures, take a moment to examine their use. To create a SUB procedure, you can select New SUB from the Edit menu. Once this action occurs, both QBASIC and QuickBASIC display a dialog box labeled New SUB. Figure 9.5 illustrates the New SUB dialog box into which the name of the new SUB procedure is entered. It is accepted by clicking on the OK button or pressing Enter. Then QuickBASIC opens a new window

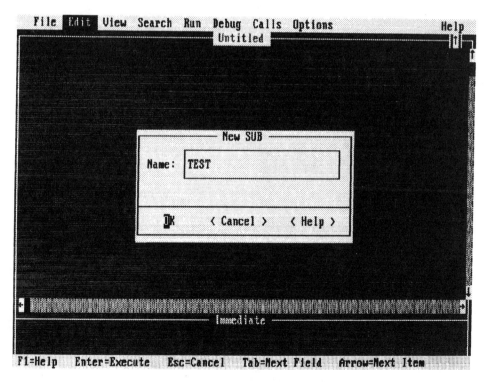

Figure 9.5 QuickBASIC New SUB Dialog Box.

into which the SUB and END SUB statements are generated, enabling you to focus on creating the procedure.

As an alternative to using the menu system, you can enter **SUB TEST**, and QuickBASIC automatically displays a new window containing your entry followed by a blank line and an END SUB statement, with the cursor positioned on the blank line to accept the procedure you will enter. The new window will retain the prior window's title, adding as a suffix a colon (:) followed by the name assigned to the procedure. Thus, entering SUB TEST would result in the suffix :TEST being displayed in the new window's title bar.

Once you complete the procedure you can use the SUBs option in the VIEW menu or press the **F2** key to return to the main program code, another procedure, or another program by displaying the QuickBASIC edit selection screen. For example, if the main program is named CCC and the procedure is named TEST, selecting SUBs from the VIEW menu or pressing the **F2** key would display the screen illustrated in Figure 9.6. By moving the highlight bar over CCC.BAS and pressing the Enter key or clicking the mouse button, you can display the program contained in CCC.BAS. Because both the SUB procedure and main program would be displayed in a "full screen" above the Immediate window, to better visualize the main program and the SUB procedure you could select the Split option. Split enables you to view both the main module and SUB procedure code at the same time in separate windows, as illustrated in Figure 9.7. If you again select the Split option from the View menu, the bottom window

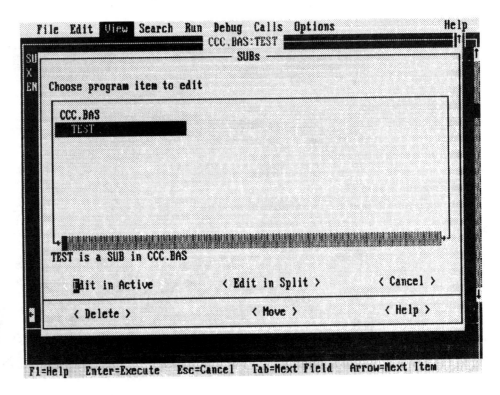

Figure 9.6   QuickBASIC Selection Display.

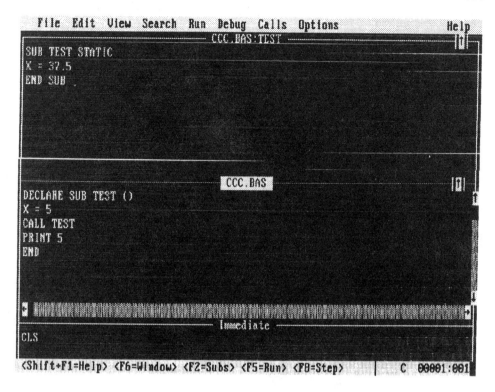

Figure 9.7 A Split Screen in QuickBASIC.

(CCC.BAS) will be closed and the top (CCC.BAS.TEST) will be expanded in size to cover the area formerly occupied by the bottom window.

Having reviewed the method by which a SUB procedure is created and the difference between a procedure and a subroutine, you are ready to focus on several examples of SUB procedures. In the following example, a value of 5 has been assigned to the variable X in the main program and then a procedure labeled TEST has been called, in which the variable X is assigned the value 37.5. Note that the statement following the CALL statement in the main program prints the value of X, which is 5. This illustrates that the values of variables in procedures are indeed local in comparison to subroutine variables, which are global.

```
X = 5
CALL TEST
PRINT X
END

SUB TEST STATIC
X = 37.5
END SUB

 5
```

Up to now you haven't saved the short program containing the SUB procedure. When you save a program, QuickBASIC automatically inserts a DECLARE statement into the main program. Thus, it is important to examine this statement before you investigate how to modify the previously created program.

DECLARE Statement

A DECLARE statement is used to state the references to QuickBASIC procedures and functions as well as to invoke argument checking. The format of this statement is

$$\text{format}_Q: \text{DECLARE} \left\{ \begin{array}{l} \text{SUB} \\ \text{FUNCTION} \end{array} \right\} \textit{name} \; [\textit{(parameter-list)}]$$

As indicated in the statement format, each DECLARE statement contains the keyword DECLARE followed by the words SUB or FUNCTION, the name of the procedure or function, and an optional set of parameters contained in parentheses. The purpose of the *parameter-list* is to invoke the type checking of arguments passed to the procedure to ensure they agree with the number and type of parameters in the DECLARE statement.

The following example illustrates both the use of the DECLARE statement and how to pass a value back from the SUB procedure to the main program through the use of an argument in the CALL statement and a variable in the SUB procedure *parameter-list*.

```
DECLARE SUB TEST (X)
X = 5
CALL TEST(X)
PRINT X
END

SUB TEST (X) STATIC
X = 37.5
END SUB

  37.5
```

In the preceding example, note that the value of X printed by the main program is now 37.5 instead of 5. This is because the variable labeled X was included in both the calling argument-list in the main program and the called parameter-list in the SUB procedure, so that the value of X was passed from the procedure back to the main program.

The next two examples illustrate the effect of local and global values through argument-parameter passing. In the first example that follows, the procedure labeled NEWTEST was added to the prior program, with a CALL statement used to access the new procedure from the previously created procedure labeled TEST. Note that the absence of a variable in the new CALL statement and new SUB TEST statement localizes the assignment of 99 to the variable X to the procedure labeled NEWTEST. Hence, the assignment of 37.5 to X in the procedure labeled TEST is applicable to the main program, because the result is passed between the procedure labeled TEST and the main program through the incorporation of a parameter and an argument in the CALL and SUB TEST statements.

```
DECLARE SUB TEST (X)
X = 5
```

```
CALL TEST(X)
PRINT X
END

SUB NEWTEST
X = 99
END SUB

SUB TEST (X) STATIC
X = 37.5
CALL NEWTEST
PRINT "NEWTEST X=", X
END SUB

NEWTEST X=      37.5
 37.5
```

In the next example, the program segment was modified to enable the passing of the value of X between both procedures. Note that the main program assigns the value 5 to the variable X and calls the procedure TEST. In that procedure X is assigned the value 37.5. However, after the assignment, the procedure NEWTEST is called in which the value of X is set to 99. Both the CALL NEWTEST and SUB NEWTEST statements now include the parameter X, so the value of X from the second procedure becomes global. This is illustrated by the PRINT statements in the calling procedure and the main program, both of which display 99 as the value for the variable X.

```
DECLARE SUB TEST (X)
X = 5
CALL TEST(X)
PRINT X
END

SUB NEWTEST (X)
X = 99
END SUB

SUB TEST (X) STATIC
X = 37.5
CALL NEWTEST(X)
PRINT "NEWTEST X=", X
END SUB

NEWTEST X=      99
 99
```

Error Handling

Several variables and error-handling statements are contained in BASIC. These statements and variables provide you with the capability to enable error trapping, obtain an error code and line number associated with an error, simulate the occurrence of an error, or define an error code that will be used for error trapping by your program.

ERR and ERL Variables

BASIC contains two predefined variables that will return the error code and line number in which an error was detected. The variable labeled ERR contains the error code for the last error encountered within a program, whereas the variable labeled ERL will contain the line number in the program where the error was detected. The format of these two variables is

format: *varnm*=ERL
format: *varnm*=ERR

You can use the ERL and ERR variables in IF-THEN statements to control program execution within an error-handling routine you may wish to include in a program. Because a logical question is how you should develop an error-handling routine, examine this aspect of BASIC and then see how you can use the ERR and ERL variables within such a routine.

ON ERROR GOTO Statement

The BASIC statement that enables trapping is the ON ERROR GOTO statement, whose format is

format: ON ERROR GOTO *line*

Once this statement is executed, error trapping will be enabled, and any detected error will cause the flow of program control to branch to the line number indicated in the statement. All errors, including syntax errors resulting from improper grammatical construction of statements within a program, will cause a branch to the indicated line. Normally you will insert the ON ERROR GOTO statement into your program after it has been completely tested with the exception of your error-handling routine. You should follow this procedure, because the ON ERROR GOTO statement can result in an infinite program loop if you have an error that is not trapped in your error-handling routine and use a RESUME statement at the end of the routine to return to the line where the error originated.

Your error-handling routine will typically check for recoverable errors such as a device timeout or a printer-out-of-paper error. In these situations, you can test for those error codes that signify these errors and display predefined messages to alert the operator to take appropriate action and then resume program execution after such action is completed.

RESUME Statement

To continue program execution after the completion of an error recovery procedure requires the use of the RESUME statement, whose format is:

format:
$$\begin{cases} \text{RESUME [0]} \\ \text{RESUME NEXT} \\ \text{RESUME } line \\ \text{RESUME } label^4 \end{cases}$$

---

[4] Applicable only to QBASIC and QuickBASIC.

Any of the preceding formats of the RESUME statement can be used with the exception of the last format, which is only applicable to QBASIC and QuickBASIC, with the precise format based on where you want program execution to resume after your error-recovery procedure is completed. The RESUME or RESUME 0 statement will cause program execution to resume at the statement that caused the error. A RESUME NEXT statement will cause program execution to be resumed at the statement following the one that caused the error. A RESUME LINE statement will cause program execution to resume at the specified line number. Similarly, a RESUME LABEL statement will cause program execution to resume at the specified label. Now that you have an overview of how to enable error trapping and resume program execution, you can develop the appropriate BASIC coding to perform a predefined error-handling routine.

Suppose you are developing a program that prints a report. Normally, if you are running a program and the printer runs out of paper, the computer will sense this fact, generate an Out of paper message on the display, and terminate program execution. This could result in untold hardship if your program was updating files at the same time it was printing the report. Here you might not be able to simply rerun the program, because it would update a portion of the files a second time, which is not what you would normally want to occur. You would either have to develop a mechanism to reenter the program at the point where the updating stopped or add an error-handling procedure to suspend execution while you add paper and then resume program execution once your printer is ready to continue printing the report.

Because this discussion concerns error control, examine how you can accomplish the latter. Appendix C lists all of the BASIC error messages and their associated error codes. Note that error code 27 results from the printer being Out of paper. This error condition will result if the printer is out of paper or if the printer is not powered up. The error-handling routine and the enabling of error trapping is indicated by the following program segment:

```
100 ON ERROR GOTO 5000
    .

    .
5000 REM Error handling routine
5010 IF ERR <> 27 THEN 5070
5020 CLS
5030 LOCATE 12,20
5040 PRINT "PRINTER NOT READY - CHECK PAPER AND POWER"
5050 PRINT TAB(20);"ENTER R WHEN READY TO RESUME"
5060 A$=INKEY$:IF A$<>"R"THEN 5060
5070 RESUME
```

In this example, line 100 enables error trapping and causes the program to branch to line 5000 if an error should occur. In line 5010, the program tests for error code 27. If error code 27 did not occur, the program will branch to line 5070 where the RESUME statement causes the program to RESUME execution at the line that enabled error trapping. If you wish to check for several errors, you might branch to line 5080, where you would add another comparison of the ERR variable with the next error code you wish to develop a procedure to process. If error code 27 occurred, the program will clear the screen and generate the messages PRINTER NOT READY--CHECK PAPER AND POWER and ENTER R WHEN READY TO RESUME. Once the character R is entered, the RESUME statement in line 5070 will cause the program to resume execution at the statement that caused the error. From the preceding, you can view error trapping as similar to constructing a subroutine, the key difference being that the program will branch from any line to the beginning of the error recovery routine on the detection of an error, whereas you have to specify each branch to a subroutine with a GOSUB statement. A RETURN statement causes the program to pass control to the statement following the last GOSUB, but an error recovery routine will use a RESUME statement to continue program execution after an error-recovery procedure has been performed.

Once you enable error trapping, it will remain on until disabled. You can disable error trapping by having the program execute an ON ERROR GOTO 0 statement. Once error trapping is disabled, subsequent errors will cause the appropriate error message to be printed and program execution will halt. Returning to the previous example, if you only wish to take corrective action on the occurrence of error code 27, you could change line 5070 in the program to

```
5070 ON ERROR GOTO 0
```

This statement will cause an error message to be printed, and the program will terminate execution if any error other than error code 27 should occur. It is good programming practice to include an ON ERROR GOTO 0 statement in your error-trapping routine to identify all errors for which no recovery procedure has been implemented. Otherwise, the use of a RESUME statement at the end of the error-handling routine could cause the program to loop continuously between the line causing the error and the recovery procedure, as indicated by the execution of the following program segment:

```
Ok
10 ON ERROR GOTO 5000
20 INPUT "ENTER WIDGETS SOLD ",W
30 C=365/W
.
.
5000 REM Error recovery routine
5010 IF ERR<>27 THEN 5070
5020 CLS
5030 LOCATE 12,20
5040 PRINT "PRINTER NOT READY - CHECK PAPER AND POWER"
5050 PRINT TAB(20)"ENTER R WHEN READY TO RESUME"
5060 A$=INKEY$:IF A$<>"R"THEN 5060
5070 RESUME
RUN
ENTER WIDGETS SOLD 0
Division by zero

^C
Break in 5010
Ok
```

In this example, the entry of a 0 value in response to the WIDGETS SOLD prompt message will cause a Division by zero error and the program will branch to the error-trapping routine starting in line 5000. The routine ends with a RESUME statement in line 5070, so the program will automatically go into a loop, executing lines 10, 5000, 5010, 5070, and back to 10. The poor terminal operator will think something productive is taking place; however, unknown to him or her the program is in a loop. Although it is obvious that line 30 will cause a `Division by zero` error, other errors may not be as obvious, and you should account for their possible occurrence by placing an `ON ERROR GOTO 0` statement at the end of your error-trapping routine. In the example, a Ctrl+Break key combination was used to terminate the infinite program loop.

Based on our discussion of error control, a logical question that should arise is how can you test the error-trapping routine you program? It is easy to remove the paper from the printer, but there are other error conditions you may wish to check for that are difficult to establish, especially in the area of device and file errors. Fortunately, BASIC has an ERROR statement by which you can simulate the occurrence of a BASIC error.

ERROR Statement

The format of the BASIC ERROR statement is

format: `ERROR varnm`

Here, the numeric variable, *varnm*, is an integer expression between 0 and 255. This variable is used to define an error code. If the defined error code is the same as an error code used by BASIC, this statement will simulate the occurrence of that error. If you previously developed an error-handling routine and enabled that routine by the use of an ON ERROR GOTO statement, the ERROR statement will cause the program to pass control to the error-handling routine. Thus, the ERROR statement provides you with a mechanism to test the programming logic of your error-handling routine.

Add the statement

```
15 ERROR 27
```

to the previous program segment. Now when you execute the program, error code 27 will be simulated. This results in the screen being cleared and the error trap message being displayed. Note that if you entered the ERROR statement in a line prior to the ON ERROR GOTO statement, your program would terminate when it was executed as the error trap would not be enabled when the error was simulated. This is illustrated by the next printout, where the statement previously entered in line 15 was erased and placed in line 5 of the program.

```
Ok
15
5 ERROR 27
```
RUN
```
Out of Paper in 5
Ok
```

If you are using QBASIC or QuickBASIC, a dialog box indicating the type of error will be displayed whenever a BASIC error occurs. Because you normally do not use line numbers in QBASIC or QuickBASIC, the error message displayed in the dialog box is `Out of paper` without a line number reference; however, the statement generating the error message will be highlighted, which enables you to quickly determine the location of the statement causing the error.

If no error-handling routine is in your program, the ERROR statement will cause the error message that corresponds to the number associated with the ERROR statement to be printed and the program will then halt execution. This is indicated by the following interpretive BASIC example:

```
Ok
10 X=27
20 ERROR X
RUN
Out of Paper in 20
Ok
```

If you are using QBASIC or QuickBASIC, the execution of the ERROR statement would display a dialog box with the label Out of paper. In addition, the statement that generated the error message in the dialog box would be highlighted, facilitating the location of the statement.

You can also use the ERROR statement to define your own error codes. Because the highest error number presently used by BASIC is 76, it is good practice to use values greater than that number. This user-defined error code can then be tested in your error-handling routine similarly to testing any other error. The use of user-defined error codes is illustrated by the following program segment.

```
100 ON ERROR GOTO 5000
110 INPUT"ENTER CITY ",C$
120 IF LEN(C$)>15 THEN ERROR 100
  .
  .
  .
5000 IF ERR=100 THEN PRINT"ONLY 15 CHARACTERS ALLOWED--REENTER DATA"
ELSE GOTO 5030
5020 RESUME 110
5030 REM program continues
RUN
ENTER CITY MAXWELLSMARTSVILLE
ONLY 15 CHARACTERS ALLOWED--REENTER DATA
ENTER CITY
```

In this example, error code 100 was associated with the occurrence of a string representing the name of a city that exceeds 15 characters in length. When the operator enters the name of a city that exceeds 15 characters, the program will automatically transfer control to the error-handling routine beginning at line 5000. At this line number, an error code of 100 is tested for by use of the ERR variable. If the error code is equal to 100, the message ONLY 15 CHARACTERS ALLOWED--REENTER DATA will be displayed.

Library and User-Defined Functions

Prior to concluding this initial examination of BASIC, a group of frequently used internal BASIC routines that form an integral part of the language will be presented. These routines are known as *functions*. They include the BASIC library functions, which are prewritten routines that can be accessed by invoking their names followed by the appropriate information you must supply to the function, or you can use the capability of BASIC to develop your own functions.

BASIC contains over 50 library functions: numeric, string-related, string, and I/O and miscellaneous. Some of the more commonly employed functions have already been covered, such as the TAB and SPC functions. In this section the use and operation of several commonly used BASIC functions are discussed. You access each of these functions, unless noted otherwise, by stating its name followed by whatever information must be supplied to the function, enclosing the information supplied in parentheses. The numeric quantity or string value passed to the function for use by its prewritten routine is known as its *argument*. Once you access the function and specify an argument, the desired operation will be conducted automatically.

Numeric Functions

Table 9.4 lists the BASIC numeric functions and their operations. One of the simplest ways to show the use of a function is by examining its use in a program. Suppose you wanted to obtain the square root of a number. Without the SQR function, you would have to develop your own routine to perform this function. To do this, you might first divide the number you wish the square root of by 2. You could then multiply that number by itself and test it against the original number. If it is greater than the original number, your derived number is too large. You can make it smaller by subtracting some small amount from it and repeat the process. When the derived number times itself is less than the original number, you number is too small, and you can now add a small increment to the number and again repeat the process.

Eventually, the derived number times itself will equal the number you wish to obtain the square root of or be very close to that number. Once you fall within a certain range, you can stop the repetitive process and consider the derived number to be the square root of the number you seek. Wow! All this just to obtain the square root of a number. By now you can begin to appreciate functions that automatically perform the desired operations for you once you specify the argument. Now take a look at how easy it is to use functions. Suppose you want the square roots of 2, 4, 6, and 8. The arguments to be passed to the SQR functions are 2, 4, 6, and 8. You can use a FOR-NEXT loop to control the passing of the arguments as follows:

Table 9.4
Numeric Functions

Function	Operational Result
ABS(*exprnm*)	Returns the absolute value
ATN(*exprnm*)	Returns the arctangent in radians
CDBL(*exprnm*)	Converts the expression to a double-precision number
CINT(*exprnm*)	Converts the expression to an integer by rounding
CLNG(*exprnm*)	Converts the expression to a long integer by rounding[1]
COS(*exprnm*)	Returns the cosine of an angle expressed in radians
CSNG(*exprnm*)	Converts the expression to a single-precision number
EXP(*exprnm*)	Returns the base of the natural logarithm (e) raised to the specified power
FIX(*exprnm*)	Truncates the specified expression to an integer
INT(*exprnm*)	Returns the largest integer that is less than or equal to *exprnm*
LOG(*exprnm*)	Returns the natural logarithm of the specified number
RND(*exprnm*)	Returns a random number
SGN(*exprnm*)	Returns +1 if *exprnm* is positive, −1 if negative, and 0 if its value is zero
SIN(*exprnm*)	Returns the sine of an angle expressed in radians
SQR(*exprnm*)	Returns the square root
TAN(*exprnm*)	Returns the tangent of an angle expressed in radians

[1] Applicable only to QBASIC and QuickBASIC.

```
Ok
LIST
10 PRINT "NUMBER","SQUARE ROOT"
20 FOR I=2 to 8 step 2
30 PRINT I,SQR(I)
40 NEXT I
Ok
RUN
NUMBER          SQUARE ROOT
  2               1.414214
  4               2
  6               2.44949
  8               2.828427
Ok
```

If you require the square root of a variable within a program, your program statement might be

```
100 X=SQR(Y)
```

Here, the variable X is set equal to the square root of the variable Y.

The ABS function returns the absolute value of a numeric expression. That is, the absolute value of a number is its value with its sign discarded; hence, the ABS function will first evaluate an expression and then discard its sign. The following example shows the use of this function operating on an expression:

```
10 X=3.14159
20 B=-12.5
30 PRINT ABS(X*B)
RUN
 39.26988
Ok
```

The INT function returns the largest integer part of a numeric expression used as the argument in the function call. In the following example, note that the integer of both 12.51 and 12.49 is 12. Because -3 is less than -2.49, the integer of -2.49 is -3.

```
10 X=12.51:PRINT INT(X)
20 Y=12.49:PRINT INT(Y)
30 Z=-2.49:PRINT INT(Z)
RUN
 12
 12
-3
Ok
```

Although the use of most of the functions listed in Table 9.4 should be apparent, some notes concerning the use of the trigonometric functions and a description of the exponential and logarithm functions may be in order for those not familiar with their use. Each trigonometric function, such as the SIN, COS, TAN, and ATN functions, is used to calculate the trigonometric value when the argument is expressed in radians. You can do this by multiplying degrees by pi/180, where pi = 3.141593. Each trigonometric function is calculated in single precision, so it is irrelevant to carry the value of pi to any further degree of precision. The following example shows how you can generate a table of values of the sine and cosine of an angle as the angle varies from 0 to 360° in increments of 45°:

LIST
```
100 PRINT "ANGLE","SINE(ANGLE)","COSINE(ANGLE)"
110 FOR I=0 TO 360 STEP 45
120 PRINT I, SIN(I*3.141593/180),COS(I*3.141593/180)
130 NEXT I
```
RUN

ANGLE	SINE(ANGLE)	COSINE(ANGLE)
0	0	1
45	.7071068	.7071068
90	1	-3.74507E-07
135	.7071066	-.7071068
180	-3.74507E-07	-1
225	-.7071068	-.7071065
270	-1	6.516827E-07
315	-.7071063	.7071075
360	6.516827E-07	1

Ok

Several items in the preceding example require some elaboration. Those familiar with trigonometry know that the sine function starts at a zero value at 0°, peaks at a value of 1 at 90°, and decreases to a value of zero at 180°. In the preceding example a value of $-3.74507E-07$ is given for 180°. This and other slight variances are due to the fact that pi was entered rounded to six significant positions. The small magnitude of the error, although insignificant, does not do justice to any type of tabular output you may desire. You can avoid this problem by using a formatted PRINT statement and specifying the precision of accuracy you desire. Thus, specifying values of, say, five significant positions would result in a zero value being printed.

The EXP function calculates the exponential function that can be expressed mathematically as e^x, where e represents the base of the natural (Naperian) logarithm whose value is approximately 2.718282. In interpretative BASIC, the power must be less than 88.02969, or an overflow will occur. If the power exceeds this value, an Overflow message will be displayed, and program execution will continue with positive machine infinity used as the result of the function call. If you are using QBASIC or QuickBASIC, when the power exceeds 88.02969, a dialog box containing the error message Overflow will be displayed, halting the execution of the program.

The LOG function calculates the natural logarithm of a numeric variable. If X represents the numeric variable, the use of the function represents the mathematical expression $\log_e X$, where e is the base of the natural system of logarithms previously discussed.

One of the most interesting numeric functions has been saved for the end of this short discussion—the RND function. This function enables you to easily generate random numbers. The use of this function returns a seven-digit decimal fraction greater than zero but less than one. The numeric variable in the argument is optional. If it is positive or omitted, the next RND function call will generate the next random number in the sequence of random numbers generated each time the program is executed. Because a fixed computational procedure is used by the RND function to generate random numbers, the numbers obtained from the RND function are not actually random. Thus, every time a program containing the RND function is executed, the same sequence of numbers will be generated. This is illustrated by running the following program two times.

```
Ok
10 FOR I=1 TO 5
20 PRINT RND;
30 NEXT I
RUN
 .6291626   .1948297   .6305799   .8625749   .736353
Ok
RUN
 .6291626   .1948297   .6305799   .8625749   .736353
Ok
```

Although the ability to regenerate a random number sequence may be very helpful for program-debugging purposes, many times it is desirable to generate a different sequence of random numbers each time a program is executed. This can be accomplished by reseeding the random number generator. The random number generator can be reseeded by using a negative numeric variable in the function call. This will generate a particular sequence of random numbers for the numeric variable used, so you can generate a different sequence each time the program is executed by using a different starting value each time the program runs. One way to accomplish this is to use the value of the system clock as the mechanism for entry into the random number generator. If you use the elapsed time in seconds and hundreds of seconds as your starting place in the random number generator, it becomes highly unlikely that anyone can turn on the system and execute the program twice at exactly the precise time in hundredths of seconds.

A second method to reseed the random number generator is through the use of the RANDOMIZE statement, whose format is

format: ⎰ RANDOMIZE [*exprnm*] ⎱
format_A: ⎱ RANDOMIZE TIMER   ⎰

By using the RANDOMIZE statement you can specify a different starting point for the random number generator. If the numeric expression is omitted, the program's execution will be suspended when the RANDOMIZE statement is executed, and the message

```
Random Number Seed(-32768 to 32767)?
```

will be displayed. On entering the value of the seed, program execution will resume. Because the RANDOMIZE statement reseeds the random number generator, this statement must precede the first reference to the RND function in a program. The use of this statement is illustrated by the execution of the following program segment:

```
Ok
10 RANDOMIZE
20 FOR I=1 TO 5
30 PRINT RND;
```

```
40 NEXT
```
RUN
```
Random number seed(−32768 to 32767)? 1
 .9527948  1.293463E-02  .7467608  .9900456  .3634014
Ok
```
RUN
```
Random number seed(−32768 to 32767)? 2
 .3591821  .1843976  6.049669E-02  .5644628  9.327507E-02
Ok
```
RUN
```
Random number seed(−32768 to 32767)? 1
 .9527948  1.293463E-02  .7467608  .9900456  .3634014
Ok
```

In this example, note that the use of the same seed (first and third program RUNs) results in the same sequence of random numbers. If you are familiar with tables of random numbers, you can view the seed as a page of random numbers and the numeric expression in the RND function as a particular random number on the page.

In Advanced BASIC and GW-BASIC, you can obtain a different starting point for the random number generator without being prompted to enter a new random number. This is accomplished by using the RANDOMIZE TIMER statement.

One of the tricks associated with using random numbers is to convert the decimal functions obtained from the use of the RND function into an appropriate range of numeric values you wish to associate with some activity to be simulated. As an example, suppose you desire to simulate the roll of a die. Since a die is six-sided with one to six dots on a side, you must use the RND function to generate a random number having a value between 1 and 6. The following statement can be used to obtain this range of values:

```
10 D=1+INT(6*RND)
```

As you analyze this statement, note that the RND function's maximum value is .9999999, whereas its minimum value would be .0000001. Thus, the minimum value assigned to the variable labeled D would be $1+INT(.0000001)$, which results in a value of 1, whereas the maximum value that could be assigned to that variable would be $1+INT(5.9999999)$, which results in a value of 6. Using the preceding information, you can use the following program segment to simulate 20 rolls of the die.

LIST
```
5 FOR I=1 TO 20
10 D=1+INT(6*RND):PRINT D;
15 NEXT I
Ok
```
RUN
```
 4 2 4 6 5 6 1 6 1 1 5 3 5 1 1 4 6 1 4 2
Ok
```

User-Defined Functions

BASIC provides the capability to avoid repeated programming steps to conduct the same computation. This is accomplished by the use of the DEF FN statement. This statement enables you to define your own functions. The format of this statement is

format: DEF FN *name*[(*arg*[,*arg*] . . .)] = *expr*
format_Q: DEF FN *name*[*arg*[,*arg*]. . .)]
.
.
.

    FN*name*=*expr*
.
.
.

    END DEF

If you are using QBASIC or QuickBASIC, note that a second type of DEF FN statement is available that enables you to develop a multiline function.

The function name can be any valid variable name. When preceded by the keyword FN, this name becomes the name of the function. The arguments in the function are variable name(s) that will be replaced with a value when the function is called in a program. The expression performs the operation of the function with the values assigned to the argument(s) when the function is called.

The function name may be numeric or string, and the expression defined must match the type of the name. That is, if the function name is a numeric variable, the expression associated with the function must perform operations on numeric variables. Similarly, your expression must operate on strings if your function name is a string variable. If the expression does not match the function type, a Type mismatch error will result.

In comparison to other BASICs that limit a program to 26 separate functions labeled A through Z, both interpretive BASICs, QBASIC, and QuickBASIC permit you to have virtually an unlimited number of functions, because any variable name can be used as the function name. Similar to the functions defined with other BASICs, each DEF FN statement is limited to a single line unless you use the second format supported by QuickBASIC.

The following program segments illustrate the use of the DEF FN statement:

```
10 DEF FNEQUATION(A,B,C)=A^3+3*B^2+2*C+27.5
20 LET X=FNEQUATION(1,2,3):PRINT X
30 LET Y=FNEQUATION(4,5,6):PRINT Y
```
RUN
```
 46.5
 178.5
Ok
```

In this example, line 10 defines the function FNEQUATION, which computes the expression $A^3 + 3 \cdot B^2 + 2 \cdot C + 27 \cdot 5$. The function is called in line 20 with argument values 1, 2, and 3 that will replace the variables named A, B, and C in the expression when it is evaluated. Similarly, line 30 calls the function for evaluation with 4, 5, and 6 used to replace the variables named A, B, and C. From this example, you see that the DEF FN statement only defines a function. To evaluate the function, you must refer to the function name elsewhere in the program by specifying the name of the function and providing the values of the arguments within a BASIC statement.

You can include one or more library functions within a DEF FN statement as illustrated by the next program segment:

```
10 DEF FNROOT(A,B,C)=SQR(A^3+B^2+C)
20 PRINT FNROOT(1,2,3)
```
RUN

```
  2.828427
Ok
```

You can also define string operations as indicated by the next program segment:

```
10 N$="NAME "
20 A$="ADDRESS"
30 DEF FNONE$(X$,Y$)=N$+A$
40 PRINT FNONE$(N$,A$)
```
RUN
```
NAME ADDRESS
Ok
```

From the preceding examples, you may have noticed that the DEF FN statement precedes the reference of the function within a program. This is because you must define the function prior to calling it. You can see this by reversing lines 30 and 40 in the previous example and then attempting to execute that program statement. Note in this example, the error message Undefined user function in 30 tells you that at the time of the function call the function was undefined. If you were using QBASIC or QuickBASIC, the attempted execution of the PRINT statement would result in the display of a dialog box containing the error message Function not defined.

```
Ok
```
LIST
```
10 N$="NAME "
20 A$="ADDRESS
30 PRINT FNONE$(N$,A$)
40 DEF FNONE$(X$,Y$)=N$+A$
Ok
```
RUN
```
Undefined user function in 30
Ok
```

When using user-defined functions, it is good programming practice to group together all DEF FN statements and place them in one area of the program prior to the first function call. This not only improves the legibility of the program, but can simplify program modifications and reduce any program debugging time that may be required.

To illustrate the multiline DEF FN statement that is applicable to QBASIC and QuickBASIC, refer to the following small program segment and its operational result:

```
DEF FNBOOLEAN (A, B)
PRINT "WHEN A= "; A; "AND B="; B; " THEN A AND B="; A AND B
PRINT "WHEN A ="; A; "AND B="; B; " THEN A OR B="; A OR B
END DEF
'MAIN PROGRAM
X = 10
Y = 3
K = FNBOOLEAN(X, Y)
Q = 23
R = 42
Z = FNBOOLEAN(Q, R)
```

```
WHEN A=  10 AND B= 3   THEN A AND B= 2
WHEN A = 10 AND B= 3   THEN A OR B= 11
WHEN A=  23 AND B= 42  THEN A AND B= 2
WHEN A = 23 AND B= 42  THEN A OR B= 63
```

In this example, the function named BOOLEAN was developed to compute and display the values resulting from the logical ANDing and ORing of two numbers. Note that the main program calls the function twice, the first time passing the values of the variables X and Y, the second time passing the values of the variables Q and R to the function. The multiline function then uses two PRINT statements to compute and display the logical AND and logical OR values for each numeric pair passed to the function.

In addition to a multiline DEF FN, QBASIC and QuickBASIC also support a FUNCTION procedure, described next.

FUNCTION Procedure

Similar to a subroutine, the values of variables within a function are global, which can lead to unexpected results unless you are careful in assigning variable names. This is illustrated in the following example, in which a function named EXAMPLE computes the sum of two numbers, assigning the result to the variable named C. Note that the main program assigns the value of 999 to C. However, once the function is invoked the value of C becomes 10, as indicated by the resulting output from the PRINT statement.

```
DEF FNEXAMPLE (A, B)
LET C = A + B
END DEF
'MAIN PROGRAM
C = 999
X = 7
Y = 3
K = FNEXAMPLE(X, Y)
PRINT "C=", C

C=              10
```

In comparison to the DEF FN statement treating variables as global, a FUNCTION procedure treats variables as local to the procedure unless you use a SHARED statement (described later in this section). The format of the FUNCTION procedure is similar to the SUB procedure, as indicated here:

```
format_Q: FUNCTION name [(parameter-list)][STATIC]
           [statement-block_1]
           .

           [EXIT FUNCTION]
           .

           [statement-block_n]
           .

           END FUNCTION
```

As indicated in this format, the FUNCTION keyword marks the beginning of a function procedure, and the procedure name can be up to 40 characters long. Similar to a SUB procedure, the *parameter-list* is a list of variables separated by commas that must correspond to the number and type of variables in an argument-list used to pass values to the function. The inclusion of the STATIC keyword results in the local variables within the function retaining their values between calls to the procedure. If the keyword STATIC is omitted, the local variables in the FUNCTION procedure are then initialized to zero or null strings.

Within a FUNCTION procedure you have any number of EXIT FUNCTION statements whose execution returns you to the line after the function call. Concerning the method used to call a FUNCTION procedure, unlike a SUB procedure that requires the use of a CALL statement, a FUNCTION procedure is called by using the FUNCTION procedure name within your program. Finally, the FUNCTION procedure is terminated by the END function statement.

The creation of a FUNCTION procedure is similar to that described for the SUB procedure. That is, you can enter the keyword FUNCTION followed by an optional parameter-list, and both QBASIC and QuickBASIC will display a new window with a title bar containing the FUNCTION name as a suffix to the program name, separated from the program name by a colon (:). When the new window is displayed, it will contain two line entries—the keyword FUNCTION followed by the function name and any specified parameters and the END function statement, with the latter separated from the former by a blank line on which the cursor is positioned to enable you to enter FUNCTION procedure statements. As an alternative, you can select the New Function option from the View menu, which displays a dialog box labeled New FUNCTION into which you can enter the name of the function.

The following example illustrates how variable values unless passed between an argument-list and a parameter-list or by the use of a SHARED statement are local to the FUNCTION procedure. In the following example, C is assigned the value 999 in the main program but computed as 10 in the FUNCTION EXAMPLE. After the function is invoked the main program uses a PRINT statement to display the value of C, which as noted is still 999. As noted, although C has a value of 10 in the FUNCTION EXAMPLE, that value is local to the function.

```
'MAIN PROGRAM
C = 999
X = 7
Y = 3
K = EXAMPLE(X, Y)
PRINT "C=", C
END

FUNCTION EXAMPLE (A, B)
LET C = A + B
END FUNCTION

C=                999
```

SHARED Statement

To provide access to variables without passing them as parameters, you can use the SHARED statement, whose format is

format$_Q$: SHARED var [AS type][,var[AS type]] . . .

The SHARED statement can be used in either a SUB or a FUNCTION procedure. The following example illustrates its use in the previously created FUNCTION, resulting in the value of variable C becoming global, which changes its value from 999 to 10 when printed in the main program.

```
'MAIN PROGRAM
C = 999
X = 7
Y = 3
K = EXAMPLE(X, Y)
PRINT "C=", C
END

FUNCTION EXAMPLE (A, B)
SHARED C
LET C = A + B
END FUNCTION

C=              10
```

Without the use of the SHARED C statement in the function, you would have to modify both the argument-list and the parameter-list to pass the value of C from the function back to the main program. To do this you would change the argument-list to X, Y, C. The parameter-list following the function name would be changed to A, B, C.

String and String-Related Functions

BASIC includes many string and string-related functions that provide the capability to easily manipulate data. These functions and the operations they perform are listed in Table 9.5.

Although some of these, including the ASC, VAL, CHR$, and STRING$ functions, have been discussed previously in the context of their use within certain statements, the use of each of these functions will be reviewed in more detail in this section. These functions provide the ability to perform special computer-related operations through the BASIC language, including communications processing, forms control, symbol generation, and so on.

You can examine the use of the functions listed in Table 9.5 by constructing several program segments that can demonstrate their operational results.

Suppose you wish to output a string on a character-by-character basis, one character on each line of the display. You may not know the length of the string, but you can employ the LEN function to determine its length and use the length in a FOR-NEXT statement to control its output. If you wish to obtain the characters in the string in sequence from left to right, you can use the MID$ function as shown in the following program segment:

```
100 INPUT"ENTER STRING ",X$
110 X=LEN(X$)
120 FOR I=1 TO X
130 PRINT MID$(X$,I,1)
140 NEXT I
RUN
ENTER STRING GIL
```

G
I
L
Ok

The LEN function in line 110 will return the number of characters in the string argument to include blanks and any unprintable characters such as control characters. The variable X is assigned the length of the string and is used in line 120 as the loop control mechanism, because you wish to print each character of the string on a character-by-character basis. The MID$ function in line 130 is used to obtain one character beginning at the Ith character in the string. Note that as I increases in value because the FOR-NEXT loop counter increments, each character in the string will be obtained in sequence. If you added a semicolon to the end of line 130, each character in the

Table 9.5
String and
String-Related
Functions

Function Format	Operational Result
String Functions	
CHR$(exprnm)	Converts an ASCII code to its character equivalent
LCASE$(expr$)	Returns a string expression with all letters converted to lowercase[1]
LEFT$(expr$,exprnm)	Returns the leftmost exprnm characters of expr$
LTRIM$(expr$)	Returns a string with leading spaces truncated (removed)
MID$(expr$,exprnm₁[,exprnm₂])	Returns exprnm₂ characters from expr$ beginning with character exprnm₁
RIGHT$(expr$,exprnm)	Returns the rightmost character specified by exprnm in string expr$
SPACE$(exprnm)	Returns a string consisting of exprnm spaces
STRING$(exprnm,expr$)	Returns a string of length exprnm in which all characters have the ASCII code of the first character in expr$
STRING$(exprnm₁,exprnm₂)	Returns a string of length exprnm₁ in which all characters have the ASCII code specified by exprnm₂
UCASE$(expr$)	Returns a string expression with all letters converted to uppercase[1]
String-Related Functions	
ASC(expr$)	Returns the ASCII code of the first character of a string
COMMAND$	Returns the command line used to invoke QuickBASIC[1]
CVD(expr$)	Converts an 8-byte string to a numeric variable
CVI(expr$)	Converts a 4-byte string to a numeric variable
CVL(expr$)	Converts a 4-byte string to a long integer[1]
CVS(expr$)	Converts a 2-byte string to a numeric variable
HEX$(exprnm)	Returns a string representing the hexadecimal value of a numeric expression
INSTR([exprnm,]string₁,string₂)	Searches for string₁ in string₂ starting at position exprnm
LEN(expr$)	Returns the length of the specified string
MKD$(exprnm#)	Converts the specified double-precision expression to a string
MKI$(exprnm%)	Converts the specified integer expression to a string
MKL$(exprnm&)	Converts the specified double precision expression to a string[1]
MKS$(exprnm!)	Converts the specified single-precision expression to a string
OCT$(exprnm)	Returns a string representing the octal value of a numeric expression
STR$(exprnm)	Returns the string value of the numeric expression
VAL(expr$)	Returns the numeric value of a string

[1] Applicable only to QBASIC and QuickBASIC.

string would be printed on the same line. Normally, a group of BASIC statements similar to the previous example but with a semicolon as the print line terminator will be used for communications processing. This will provide you with the ability to read a string of unknown length from the communications buffer and output that string to the display, to the line printer, or to another device.

In addition to being used as a function, you can use MID$ as a statement. When used in this manner, its format is:

format: MID$(expr$_1,exprnm_1[,exprnm_2])=expr$_2

When used as a statement, the characters in $expr\$_1$, beginning at position $exprnm_1$, are replaced by the characters in $expr\$_2$. The optional $exprnm_2$ can be used to specify the number of characters from $expr\$_2$ that will be used by the replacement. If $exprnm_2$ is omitted, all of $expr\$_2$ will be used in the replacement; however, the length of the original string, $expr\$_1$, will not change. The following program segment illustrates one possible use of the MID$ statement:

```
Ok

100 X$="CHICAGO,ILL. 22045"
110 MID$(X$,14)="33111"
120 PRINT X$
RUN
CHICAGO,ILL.  33111
Ok
```

The LEFT$ and RIGHT$ functions can be used to extract a portion of the specified string beginning at the left or right end of the string. The next program segment shows how these functions are used:

```
LIST
50 X$="JANFEBMARAPRMAYJUNJLYAUGSPTOCTNOVDEC"
60 PRINT RIGHT$(X$,3)
70 PRINT LEFT$(X$,3)
80 PRINT LEFT$(X$,88)
Ok
RUN
DEC
JAN
JANFEBMARAPRMAYJUNJLYAUGSPTOCTNOVDEC
Ok
```

The RIGHT$ function in line 60 causes the rightmost three characters of the specified string to be printed. The LEFT$ function in line 70 provides the leftmost three characters of the specified string. For both functions, if the number of characters requested exceeds the length of the string, the entire string will be returned by the function call. This is shown by the execution of line 80 in the program segment. If the second argument is specified as zero, a null string of length zero will be returned by the function call.

The CHR$ function provides you with the ability to convert an ASCII code to its character equivalent. The value of the argument used in the function call must be between 0 and 255, which represents the ASCII values of the character set used by the AT. You can use this function to send special characters to the communications buffer, printer, the screen, or another device. For example, if you wish to display the square root symbol on the screen, you could do so by including the following statement:

```
100 PRINT CHR$(251)
```

In this statement, 251 is the ASCII value that represents the square root symbol (see Appendix A). If you wish to alert the operator to special conditions or perhaps preface an error message with sound, you can do so by the use of CHR$(7). Here, the ASCII 7 represents the BEL character, which, when encountered in a PRINT statement, will beep the speaker in the system unit. An example of the use of this function to alert the operator to an error is illustrated by the next program segment.

```
100 INPUT"ENTER VALUE BETWEEN 1 AND 30 ",X
110 IF X>=1 AND X<=30 THEN 140
120 PRINT CHR$(7) "FOLLOW INSTRUCTIONS"
130 GOTO 100
140 REM Program continues
```

The STRING$ function can be used to obtain a string of specified length whose characters all have a specified ASCII code or are set to the first character of a specified string. This function is valuable for generating runs of similar characters that can be used for such purposes as report title or column heading highlighting. Several examples of the use of this function are illustrated by the following program segment:

```
100 PRINT TAB(30)"HEADING GOES HERE"
110 X$=STRING$(17,42)
120 PRINT TAB(30) X$
RUN
                              HEADING GOES HERE
                              *****************
Ok
```

In this example, the STRING$ function assigns a string of 17 asterisks (ASCII code 42) to the string variable X$. The following example shows two other methods to produce the same result. Note that each of these methods is slightly more complex than using the STRING$ function.

```
Ok
LIST
100 PRINT TAB(30)"HEADING GOES HERE"
110 LOCATE ,30
120 FOR I=1 TO 17
130 PRINT "*";
140 NEXT I
Ok
RUN
                              HEADING GOES HERE
                              *****************
```

```
LIST
100 PRINT TAB(30)"HEADING GOES HERE"
110 PRINT TAB(30)"****************"
Ok
```
RUN
```
                              HEADING GOES HERE
                              ****************
```
```
Ok
```

The use of the second format of the STRING$ function is illustrated by the next program segment. Here, a string of specified length will consist of the first character of the string used in the argument call.

```
100 XRAY$="DONALD"
110 Q$=STRING$(10,XRAY$)
120 PRINT Q$
```
RUN
```
DDDDDDDDDD
Ok
```

The last string function to be examined is the SPACE$ function. This function returns a string of spaces, the number of spaces returned based on the value of the argument in the function call. The use of this function is illustrated by the following program segment:

```
Ok
10 X$="GIL"
20 Y$=SPACE$(20)
30 Z$="HELD"
40 PRINT X$+Y$+Z$
```
RUN
```
GIL                 HELD
Ok
```

Note that, since a string can be up to 256 characters in length, the argument in the function call must be in the range of 0 to 255.

To illustrate the use of case conversion, which is only applicable to QuickBASIC, consider the following example. Note that the UCASE$ function converts the defined string to uppercase characters. This is followed by the use of the LTRIM$ function, which removes leading spaces from the string we are converting to uppercase. Thus, the second PRINT statement converts the string to uppercase and strips its leading spaces prior to printing the string.

```
A$ = "   arnold the wonder dog"
PRINT UCASE$(A$)
PRINT LTRIM$(UCASE$(A$))

   ARNOLD THE WONDER DOG
ARNOLD THE WONDER DOG
```

String-Related Functions

The ASC function is the inverse of the previously discussed CHR$ function, returning the ASCII code for the first character of the string specified in the function call. This is illustrated by the following example:

```
10 X$="*XYZ"
20 PRINT ASC(X$)
RUN
 42
Ok
```

In this example, 42 is the ASCII value of the asterisk character, as listed in Appendix A. If the string used in the function call is a null string, an Illegal function call will result. You can alleviate this potential error from occurring in a program by checking the length of a string with the LEN function and taking appropriate action if it is a null string.

Four functions are available in BASIC to convert string variables to numeric variables. The CVI function converts a 2-byte string to an integer while the CVS function results in the conversion of a 4-byte string to a single-precision number. The third string conversion function, CVD, results in the conversion of an 8-byte string to a double-precision number, whereas the CVL function—which is only supported by QuickBASIC—converts a 4-byte string into a long integer. The primary use of these functions is in random file operations. This is because numeric values that are read from such files are stored as strings and must be converted from strings into numbers.

BASIC also contains other functions that can be used to convert numeric number values to string values. The MKI$ function can be used to convert an integer to a 2-byte string, while the MKS$ function converts a single-precision number to a string. The third function in this category, MKD$, converts a double-precision number into an 8-byte string, whereas the MKL$ function—which is only supported by QBASIC and QuickBASIC—converts a double-precision number to a string. These functions will be typically used when you are programming random files, because numeric values placed in such files through the use of certain BASIC statements must be first converted into strings. Use of these statements will be covered with data file manipulation techniques later in this book.

The last two functions that will conclude this discussion of string and string-related functions are the STR$ and VAL functions. These functions in effect are the inverse of each other.

The STR$ function returns a string representation of the numeric expression appearing in the calling argument. The VAL function returns the numerical value of the string used in the calling argument.

To enter one or more data elements numerically and convert them to a string, use the STR$ function. This conversion of numeric values to string representation is illustrated by the following program segment:

```
100 INPUT"ZIP CODE ",ZIP
100 IF ZIP <99999 THEN 140
120 PRINT "ZIP CODE CANNOT EXCEED 5 DIGITS"
```

```
130 GOTO 100
140 ZIP$=STR$(ZIP)
150 X$=NAME$+ADDRESS$+CITY$+STATE$+ZIP$
```

In this example, the program reads the value of ZIP as a numeric variable to facilitate its comparison to a numeric quantity for error-checking purposes. In line 140, the numeric value of ZIP is converted to a string and assigned to the variable ZIP$. In line 150, ZIP$ is concatenated with strings representing the name, address, city, and state to form one record of information labeled X$.

I/O and Miscellaneous Functions

Eighteen I/O and miscellaneous functions have been grouped together to conclude this preliminary discussion concerning functions. The operational result from the use of these functions is indicated in Table 9.6.

Table 9.6
I/O and
Miscellaneous
Functions

Function	Operational Result
CSRLIN	Returns the current line position of the cursor
EOF(filenum)	Returns (–1) true if end of file reached, 0 if the end of file has not been reached
FRE(dummy)	Returns the number of bytes in memory not being used by BASIC
FREEFILE	Returns the next BASIC file number available for use[1]
INP(exprnm)	Returns the byte read from port n
LOC(filenum)	Returns the number of characters in the communications buffer waiting to be read, the number of records read or written to a sequential file since it was opened, or the record number of the last record read or written to a random file
LOF(filenum)	Returns the length of a file in multiples of 128 bytes or the amount of free space in the communications input buffer
LPOS(exprnm)	Returns the current position of the printhead
PEEK(memadr)	Returns an integer value between 0 and 255 that represents the byte read from the designated memory position
PEN(exprnm)	Returns the value of the light pen coordinates according to the supplied numeric argument
POINT(exprnm₁, exprnm₂)	Returns the color of the specified point on the screen for graphics operation
POS(exprnm)	Returns the current cursor column position
SCREEN(row,col[,exprnm])	In text mode returns the ASCII code for the character (if exprnm zero) at the specified location or the character's attribute (if exprnm nonzero)
SEEK(filenum)	Returns the current file position
STICK(exprnm)	Returns the X and Y coordinates of the two joysticks based on the value of exprnm
STRIG(exprnm) $\begin{Bmatrix} ON \\ OFF \end{Bmatrix}$	Enables and disables the trapping of the joystick buttons in advanced BASIC
USR[digit](exprnm)	Causes a branch to a machine language subroutine with the argument specified by exprnm
VARPTR(exprnm)	Returns the address in memory of the specified variable

[1] Applicable only to QuickBASIC.

The processing, branching, and I/O statements lie at the heart of BASIC programming. These commands and functions manipulate a set of data, handle various conditional circumstances, and manage the entry and outcome of data changed by the program. QBASIC and QuickBASIC enhance the power and flexibility of traditional implementations of the BASIC programming environment and extend its application to the users of today's 80286, 80386, and 80486 level of personal computers.

10 // BASIC Commands

In interpretive BASIC a command is commonly referred to as a *system command*, because it is recognized by BASIC as a request to perform a predefined operation on the entire program. Thus, commands are normally entered in direct mode without a line number; however, most commands in interpretive BASIC can be entered in either direct or indirect mode. In comparison, a BASIC language statement is an instruction within a BASIC program that will be interpreted by that BASIC language interpreter to perform an operation within the program. Thus, commands can be thought of as initiating operations at the system level, while statements initiate operations at the program language level.

Because QBASIC and QuickBASIC both contain a full-screen editor, interpretive BASIC commands used to generate line numbers and list portions of a program defined by a set of lines are not supported. Similarly, both QBASIC and QuickBASIC provide a menu system for loading and saving files as well as for executing programs in memory, so some other commands applicable to interpretive BASIC are not applicable to QBASIC and QuickBASIC. Both QBASIC and QuickBASIC may, however, contain menu-selected commands (options) that perform operations similar to interpretive BASIC commands entered as keywords. For brevity as well as in recognition of the commonality of QBASIC and QuickBASIC, these chapters refer to similar commands and statements applicable to both as QuickBASIC. Only when QBASIC differs from QuickBASIC will the text reference the appropriate language.

Command Overview

Table 10.1 lists each BASIC command, its format, and an operational description of its usage. A format indicated as format$_I$ means that the particular command is only applicable to interpretive BASIC; a format indicated as format$_{I/Q}$ means that the particular command is applicable to both interpretive BASIC and QuickBASIC. From reviewing the operational description of the commands in Table 10.1, you will note that many BASIC commands have DOS counterparts. Those commands and their DOS counterparts are listed in Table 10.2.

BASIC commands can be divided into six logical areas—directory reference commands, line reference commands, file reference commands, program reference commands, program tracing commands, and system reference commands—and will be covered here according to their logical area of use. In this chapter any reference to disk will refer to both the fixed disk and diskette storage; references to a diskette will be denoted as such.

Table 10.1
BASIC Commands

Command	Format	Description
AUTO	format_i: AUTO[.][number][,[increment]]	Generates line numbers automatically after the Enter key pressed.
BLOAD[1]	format_{I/O}: BLOAD filespec[,address]	Loads a memory image file into the computer's memory at the specified address.
BSAVE[1]	format_{I/O}: BSAVE filespec,offset,length	Saves portions of memory on the specified device starting at the specified address for the specified length.
CHDIR[1]	format_{I/O}: CHDIR path	Changes the current directory on the disk.
CLEAR	format_{I/O}: CLEAR[,[exp_1][,exp_2]][,int]]	Initializes numeric variables to zero and string variables to null; optionally sets the end of memory (exp_1) and the amount of stack space (exp_2) and the number of bytes to be set aside for video memory.
CONT	format_i: CONT	Causes program execution to resume after a break.
DELETE	format_i: DELETE[.][line_1][-line_2][;]	Erases the specified range of lines from the program.
EDIT	format_i: [.][line]	Displays a program line for editing.
FILES[1]	format_{I/O}: FILES[filespec]	Displays the names of all files or a specified file stored on a disk.
KILL[1]	format_{I/O}: KILL filespec	Deletes a file from the disk.
LIST	format_i: LIST[line_1[.][-line_2[.]]][,filespec]	Causes the program in memory or on the device specified by filespec to be listed on the display.
LLIST	format_i: LLIST[line_1[-[line_2]]]	Prints all or a specified part of the program currently in memory.
LOAD[1]	format_i: LOAD filespec[,R]	Loads a program from the device specified by filespec into memory and optionally (R) commences its execution.
MERGE[1]	format_i: MERGE filespec	Merges the specified ASCII program with the program currently in memory.
MKDIR[1]	format_{I/O}: MKDIR path	Creates a directory on the disk.
NAME[1]	format_{I/O}: NAME filespec AS filename	Renames the file specified by filespec to filename.
NEW	format_i: NEW	Deletes the program currently in memory.
RENUM	format_i: RENUM[new#][,[old#][,incr]]	Renumbers a program beginning with old line number; assigning new numbers starting at new one, with increments incr.
RESET	format_{I/O}: RESET	Closes all disk files and clears the system buffer.
RMDIR[2]	format_{I/O}: RMDIR path	Removes a directory from the specified disk.
RUN[2,3]	format_{I/O}: RUN { [line] / filespec[,R] }	Begins execution of the program currently in memory or loads and executes a program specified by filespec.

Table 10.1 continued next page

Table 10.1
(continued)
BASIC Commands

Command	Format	Description
SAVE[2]	format[1]: SAVE filespec $\left\{ \begin{array}{c} [A] \\ [P] \end{array} \right\}$	Saves a BASIC program in compressed binary format, ASCII (A) or protected encoded binary (P) format.
SYSTEM	format[I/Q]: SYSTEM	Causes an exit from BASIC and a return to DOS.
TRON	format[I/Q]: TRON	Enables program tracing.
TROFF	format[I/Q]: TROFF	Disables program tracing.

[1]Commands with DOS counterparts listed in Table 10.2.
[2]Commands that allow the specification of a path in the filespec.
[3]R option in RUN only applicable to interpretive BASIC.

Table 10.2
BASIC Commands
and Their DOS
Counterparts

BASIC Command	DOS Command
CHDIR	CHDIR
FILES	DIR
LIST[1]	TYPE
KILL	ERASE
MKDIR	MKDIR
NAME	RENAME
RMDIR	RMDIR

[1]Not applicable to QuickBASIC.

This review of BASIC commands first indicates the applicability of the command to interpretive BASIC and QuickBASIC. If the command is only applicable to interpretive BASIC but an equivalent menu-based command exists in QuickBASIC, following the interpretive BASIC command a note covers the operation of the equivalent QuickBASIC menu command.

Directory Reference Commands

CHDIR Command (Interpretive and QuickBASIC)

The CHDIR command functions like its DOS counterpart previously described in Chapter 5, providing you with a mechanism to move through a tree-structured directory. You can use this command in both direct and indirect modes as well as in the immediate and program modes in QuickBASIC; however, the path must be preceded by quotes. The following examples illustrate the use of this command. Note that you can optionally enclose a path with a pair of quotes.

Command Structure	Operational Result
CHDIR "\	Changes to the root directory from any directory
CHDIR "C:\SALES"	Makes SALES on drive C the current directory

CHDIR "A:\SALES\EAST"   Makes EAST under the directory SALES on the
diskette in drive A the current directory

MKDIR Command (Interpretive and QuickBASIC)

The MKDIR command also functions like its DOS counterpart previously described in Chapter 5, providing you with the capability to create a directory on a disk from BASIC. Like the CHDIR command, the path in the MKDIR command must be preceded by quotes.

To see how this command works, assume you are on the root directory of drive C and want to create a directory named SALES under the root directory on that drive. Thus, you would enter

MKDIR"\SALES

or

MKDIR"\SALES"

if you wish to enclose the path within a pair of quotes. If you were logged onto drive A, you would enter

MKDIR"C:\SALES

Note that you can specify a path in the MKDIR command, or you can use the CHDIR command in combination with the MKDIR command. Thus, you could enter

CHDIR"C:\SALES"
MKDIR"\EAST"

to create the directory named EAST under the directory named SALES on drive C or you could just enter the command

MKDIR"C:\SALES\EAST"

RMDIR Command (Interpretive and QuickBASIC)

The RMDIR command provides you with a mechanism to remove a directory from a specified disk or the default disk through BASIC. When you use this command, the directory must first be empty of all files and subdirectories before it can be removed, with the exception of the dot (.) and double dot (..) entries (like its DOS counterpart). In addition, you must be located in a different directory prior to removing the specified directory. To see how this command operates, assume you are in the directory EAST and wish to delete that directory. You could first enter the KILL command (to be covered later in this chapter) with global specifiers to delete all files in that directory. This would be accomplished by entering the following command:

KILL"C:*.*"

A word of caution is warranted concerning the use of the KILL command. Unlike the DOS DEL command that will generate the prompt message Are you sure? when you attempt to erase all files in a directory, the use of the KILL command with global specifiers results in the automatic deletion of all files in the current directory.

Next, you would change directories by using the CHDIR command. Here, you could change to the root directory, back up to the directory named SALES, or change to any other directory as long as it is not the directory to be deleted. Thus, you might enter

CHDIR"\SALES"

Now, because the directory named EAST is directly under the current directory, you would enter the following command to remove it from the disk:

RMDIR "\EAST"

Note that the three directory reference commands can be used in both direct and indirect modes in interpretive BASIC and in the program and immediate modes in QuickBASIC. When used in an indirect mode by including a line number with the command in an interpretive BASIC program or in a program in QuickBASIC, these commands provide a mechanism to manipulate program and data files in tree-structured directories under program control. Thus as an example, you could keep your sales analysis program in one directory and your monthly sales in a second directory. Then your program could be written to read the required data from the directory in which the sales data files are stored.

Line Reference Commands

AUTO Command (Interpretive)

The AUTO command can be a very valuable mechanism for speeding the entry of BASIC program statements into your computer when you are using an interpretive BASIC. This command automatically generates a line number each time you press the Enter key, permitting you to avoid manually entering program line numbers. Because line numbers will increment by some specified value, you should write your program prior to entering it with the AUTO command. This will permit you to correctly reference statements you wish to branch to and permit you to fully use the capability of the command.

The AUTO command creates line numbers beginning at the number you specify in the command, and each subsequent line number is incremented by the specified increment. When both values are omitted, the default values of 10,10 will be used. If the beginning line number is followed by a comma but the increment is not specified, the increment previously specified by a previous AUTO command will be used. If the beginning line number is omitted, but the increment is included, line numbering will commence with line 0.

Now take a look at some examples of the use of the AUTO command in interpretive BASIC prior to continuing this discussion of various options available with this command.

To generate a sequence of line numbers beginning at 10 and incrementing by 10, you can use the AUTO command as follows:

AUTO

or

AUTO 10,10

Suppose you wish to begin your program line numbering at 1000 and increment each line by 25. This can be accomplished by using the AUTO command with the parameters 1000 and 25, as shown here:

```
AUTO 1000,25
```

The execution of the preceding command will generate line numbers 1000, 1025, 1050, and so on. By now your curiosity should be aroused about how you exit from automatic line numbers. You can exit AUTO by pressing Ctrl+Break. When you exit the AUTO command, the line in which Ctrl+Break is entered will not be saved. Thus, once you have completed the entry of the program lines you wish to place in memory you should press the Enter key to terminate that line and generate one additional line number. Then you can use the Ctrl+Break keys to terminate the AUTO command without losing any information.

If after entering a program segment you wish to use the AUTO command again, you can omit the increment and the command will use the increment specified in the previous AUTO command. Thus,

```
AUTO 2000,
```

will generate line numbers 2000, 2025, 2050, and so on, because 25 was the increment used in the previous AUTO command.

If you already have a program in memory when you initiate the AUTO command, an asterisk (*) will be printed as a warning that any input will replace the current line in memory. By pressing Enter immediately after the asterisk is generated, the line in memory will not be replaced, and the AUTO command will generate the next line number. The following example illustrates the process:

```
10 READ X,Y,Z
20 DATA 1,3,5,9,11
30 PRINT X,Y,Z
AUTO 30,10
30*
40 READ Q,R
50 PRINT Q,R
60
Ok
RUN
  1      3      5
  9     11
Ok
```

There are two other features of the AUTO command that deserve mention. As indicated in Table 10.1, a period (.) may be used in place of the line number to specify the current line. Since the AUTO command permits you to make changes only to the current line, if you wish to change another line in an existing program or a line previously entered with this command, you must first exit AUTO by the Ctrl+Break keys. Then you can use normal editing procedures to change another line.

In comparing interpretive BASIC to QuickBASIC, the inclusion of a full-screen editing capability in which the contents of a program can be scrolled through a window eliminates the necessity of prefixing each QuickBASIC statement with a line number. This in turn eliminates the need for an AUTO command in QuickBASIC and explains why that version of BASIC does not support this command.

DELETE Command (Interpretive)

The DELETE command provides you with an easy mechanism to delete a range of program lines from a program in memory when using interpretive BASIC. In addition, you can use this command to delete a specific program line. The latter use is equivalent to entering a specific line number followed by pressing the Enter key, which also serves to delete the specified line from memory. The following examples illustrate the use of this command and alternate means to accomplish the same function.

Command Structure	Operational Result
DELETE 30	Deletes line 30
or	
30	
DELETE 20-50	Deletes lines 20 to 50
DELETE -80	Deletes all line numbers up to and including line 80
DELETE .-50	Deletes all line numbers from the current line up to and including line 50
DELETE 80-.	Deletes all line numbers from 80 up to and including current line

In the last two examples, a period was used to indicate the current line. If the DELETE command is invoked with a line number that does not exist, an Illegal function call error will result.

Cut Menu Command (QuickBASIC)

In QuickBASIC you can use the Cut command from the Edit menu to obtain an equivalent capability similar to the interpretive BASIC DELETE command. That is, you can highlight a single line or select a block of lines and use Cut command from the Edit menu or press the Shift+Del key combination to delete the selected text. Unlike interpretive BASIC, the QuickBASIC Cut command stores the removed data in the clipboard from which it can be pasted to another location in an active window if you so desire. In addition, the QuickBASIC Undo command provides you with the ability to reverse a prior Cut command. Unfortunately, in interpretive BASIC you can only undo a DELETE Command by rekeying the entries previously deleted.

EDIT Command (Interpretive)

When you are using an interpretive BASIC, the EDIT command enables you to display a line from a program in memory for editing. Once the line is displayed, you can use any of the editing keys on the keyboard to modify the line. This command is similar to the LIST command that will be covered next; however, note that the EDIT command only displays one line, whereas the LIST command displays one or a range of program lines.

As indicated in Table 10.1, a period can be used in the command to indicate that you wish to edit the current line. This is a handy mechanism to redisplay the last line entered for editing. The following examples indicate the use of this command.

Command Structure	**Operational Result**
EDIT 10	Displays line 10 for editing
EDIT .	Displays the current line for editing

If the line specified in the EDIT command does not exist, an Undefined line number error message will be displayed.

There is no equivalent command to EDIT in QuickBASIC, because that BASIC provides you with a full-screen edit capability that allows you to scroll your program through a window.

LIST Command (Interpretive)

The LIST command, which is only applicable to interpretive BASIC, allows you to list a portion of or an entire program in memory on the screen or onto a specified device. When the file specification indicated in the command format in Table 10.1 is omitted, the specified line or lines will be listed on the screen. You can explore the utility of this command by examining several versions of the use of this command.

Note that in interpretive BASIC pressing the F1 key automatically generates the word LIST on your screen. This permits you to generate the keyword of the command with one keystroke.

Command Structure	**Operational Result**
LIST	Lists the entire program in memory on the screen
LIST 10	Lists line 10 in memory on the screen
LIST 10-50	Lists line 10 through line 50 on the screen
LIST 10-	Lists line 10 through the last line in memory on the screen
LIST -50	Lists all lines from the beginning of the program through line 50 on the screen
LIST .-100	Lists all lines from the current line through line 100 on the screen
LIST 500-.	Lists all lines from line 500 through the current line on the screen
LIST 50,"LPT1:"	Lists line 50 on the printer
LIST 50-500,"LPT1:"	Lists lines 50 through 500 on the printer
LIST -500,"LPT1:"	Lists all lines from the beginning of the program in memory through line 500 on the printer
LIST 10-300,"A:JOB1.BAS"	Lists lines 10 through 300 from the program in memory to a file named JOB1 with the extension BAS on the diskette in the A drive

When you list all or a portion of a program in memory to a file on disk, the specified lines will be saved in ASCII format. Such files may then be used with the MERGE command whose use is also restricted to interpretive BASIC. The MERGE command can be used to merge lines from an ASCII program file into a program currently in memory. In comparison, a SAVE command will save a file in a compressed binary (tokenized) format unless an optional parameter is added to save the program in ASCII format. Because programs saved in ASCII can be read as data files, if you wish to transmit such files through the communications adapter you must normally save them in ASCII format.

Once you invoke a LIST command, it will continue until it reaches its specified range if the listing is directed to a specified device such as a printer. You may conceivably change your mind about listing a 3000 line program on the printer, so you can turn off the printer and obtain an Out of paper error message, which will terminate the execution of the LIST command. You can suspend or terminate a listing directed to the screen or to the printer by pressing Ctrl+NumLock and Ctrl+Break, respectively; however, data in the printer's buffer will continue to be printed until the buffer is emptied. You can also stop printing immediately by turning the printer off.

Similar to EDIT, the LIST command also has no direct equivalent in QuickBASIC. You can select the PRINT command in the QuickBASIC File menu to list selected text, the contents of the active window, the current module, or the contents of all loaded files on your printer, which provides a capability similar to using the interpretive BASIC LIST command with device address LPT1 in that command.

LLIST Command (Interpretive)

The LLIST command, whose use is restricted to interpretive BASIC, has the capability of listing all of or a specified range of lines of a program in memory on the printer with device address LPT1:.

The ways in which you can specify line numbers for the LLIST command are the same as previously indicated for the LIST command. Similar to using the LIST command with the filespec LPT1:, LLIST can be interrupted by a Ctrl+Break key sequence, or you can immediately stop the listing on the printer by turning it off. This will result in an Out of paper error message and return you to the BASIC command level. Examples of the use of this command are as follows:

Command Structure	Operational Result
LLIST	Prints the entire program
LLIST 30	Prints line 30
LLIST 10-50	Prints lines 10 through 50
LLIST 200-	Prints all lines from line 200 through the end of the program in memory
LLIST -200	Prints the first line through line 200
LLIST 10-.	Prints lines 10 through the current line
LLIST .-100	Prints the current line through line 100

The F1 key generates the keyword LIST, so you can reduce the LLIST keyword to a two-keystroke operation. This is accomplished by typing L followed by the F1 key.

Print Menu Command (QuickBASIC)

As previously noted for QuickBASIC, you can use the Print command from the File menu to print a portion of a program, the contents of the active window, the contents of the current module to include any procedures associated with the module, or the contents of all loaded files. To print a portion of a program, you select the text to be printed by highlighting that portion of the program you want to print. Then you select the Print command from the File menu, which displays the dialog box labeled Print. You would then select the Select Text entry in the Print dialog box and click on the OK button to have the selected text printed. Figure 10.1 illustrates the Print dialog box, which is superimposed upon five lines in a program named LERLANG.BAS that were selected for printing and which are highlighted on the display.

RENUM Command (Interpretive)

In interpretive BASIC, the RENUM command provides the ability to renumber the lines of a program currently in memory. When this command is used, all line references following GOTO, GOSUB, THEN, ELSE, ON-GOTO, ON-GOSUB, RESTORE, RE-SUME, and ERL test statements will be changed automatically to reflect the new line numbers. As illustrated by the format in Table 10.1, up to three line numbers can be specified in this command. The new number is the first line number to be used in the

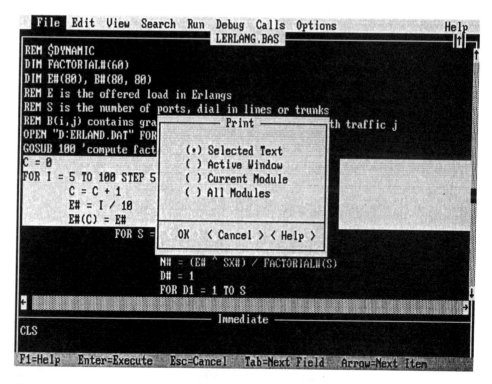

Figure 10.1 QuickBASIC Print Dialog Box.

renumbering process. If not specified, a default value of 10 will be used by the command. Old number specifies the line in the current program where the renumbering will begin. If not specified, line renumbering will begin at the first line of the program. The third line number that can be specified in the command defines the increment to be used in the renumbering process. If omitted, a default value of 10 will be used.

The RENUM command not only enables you to renumber lines in a program but also provides you with a mechanism to verify that all line number references reference an existing program line in an interpretive BASIC program. If you use the RENUM command and a statement references a nonexistent line number, the following error message will be displayed:

```
Undefined line number xxxxx in yyyyy
```

Although the incorrect line number reference (xxxxx) will not be changed by RENUM, line number *yyyyy*, which indicates the location where the undefined line number reference occurred in the program, may be changed from the original program. If your program has the sequence of line numbers 10,20,30 . . . and you use the RENUM command with default values, the new line numbers will match the old line numbers. Thus, you can use the RENUM command to check your program for nonexistent line number references. This is illustrated by the following example, which has an undefined line number reference that was added purposely.

```
Ok
10 INPUT"ENTER QUANTITY ",Q
20 IF Q>30 THEN 50
30 COM=Q*.07
40 GOTO 70
50 COM=Q*.09
60 PRINT "COMMISSION= ",COM
RENUM
Undefined line 70 in 40
Ok
```

QuickBASIC does not contain any command equivalent to RENUM. This is because this version of BASIC does not require each line to have a line number, eliminating a requirement to renumber lines.

Program Reference Commands

This section examines the use of four interpretive BASIC commands and their QuickBASIC equivalents. These commands can be grouped into the category of program reference commands.

CLEAR Command (Interpretive and QuickBASIC)

The CLEAR command has the capability of setting all numeric variables to zero and all string variables to null. Optionally, you can use this command to set the end of memory and the amount of stack space that is used by the computer for controlling FOR-NEXT loops and GOSUB references and the total number of bytes to be set aside for video memory. The last option is used to control the number of video pages available within video memory.

The BASIC stack can be thought of as a data structure like a stack of books. New items can be added to the top of the stack, which results in the position of all the previous books becoming one less in reference to the top of the stack. An item previously entered into a BASIC stack can only be removed when the items above it are removed. This type of stack can be considered as a push-down, pop-up stack where items are popped off the stack in the reverse of the order in which they were pushed on. It is this stack space that is a physical area of memory set aside for branching references that can be increased by the use of the CLEAR command.

An example of the use of the CLEAR command in direct mode follows:

```
Ok
A$="NEXT"
Ok
PRINT A$
NEXT
Ok
CLEAR
Ok
PRINT A$

Ok
```

In the indirect mode, you can use the CLEAR command to reset the pointer in your data pool in a way similar to the RESTORE statement:

```
Ok
100 READ X,Y,Z
110 DATA 1,2,3,4,5
120 PRINT X,Y,Z
130 A$="HOHOHO"
140 PRINT A$
150 CLEAR
160 READ A,B
170 PRINT A,B
RUN
 1           2           3
HOHOHO
 1           2
Ok
```

When the first optional parameter listed in Table 10.1 is added to the CLEAR command, you can set the maximum number of bytes that will be available in memory to store your program and data. Thus,

```
CLEAR ,32768
```

would permit a maximum of 32,768 bytes in memory to be used by this BASIC program and data. Normally, you would incorporate this optional parameter if you wished to reserve space in memory for one or more machine language programs that you would link to your BASIC program.

If you have a BASIC program with numerous nested GOSUBs or FOR-NEXT loops, you will probably have to increase the stack space size above the default value, which is the smaller of 512 bytes or one-eighth of available memory. You can increase the size of the BASIC stack space by using the second optional parameter in the CLEAR command as indicated here:

```
CLEAR ,,2000
```

This command would set the stack space to 2000 bytes.

CONT Command (Interpretive)

In interpretive BASIC, the CONT command has the ability to resume program execution after a Ctrl+Break key combination, when a STOP or END statement is executed in a program or after an error is encountered that causes a program to terminate. The following examples illustrate the use of this command.

```
LIST
10 INPUT"SALES ",S
20 XOM=.045*S
30 PRINT "COMMISSION= ";XOM:END
40 PRINT "NOW WE RESUME"
Ok
RUN
SALES 12
COMMISSION= .54
Ok
CONT
NOW WE RESUME
Ok
```

Note that the STOP statement in a program may not be the final termination if you use the CONT command:

```
10 X=47
20 Y=2
30 PRINT X+Y
40 STOP
50 PRINT X+Y
RUN
 49
Break in 40
Ok
Y=3
Ok
CONT
 50
Ok
```

In the second example, once execution is stopped you can change the value of any variables by using one or more direct mode statements and then resume execution by using the CONT command. Now, consider the following example where an error has been deliberately introduced into a program. The error will be corrected after the program terminates execution, and then the CONT command will be used to try to resume program execution.

```
10 INPUT "FACTORIAL ",F
20 N=1
30 FOR I=F TO 1
40 N=N*F
50 NEXT N
```
RUN
```
FACTORIAL 5
NEXT without FOR in 50
Ok
```
LIST 50
```
50 NEXT F
```
CONT
```
Can't continue
Ok
```

Note that the use of CONT is invalid, because the program was edited during the break.

Continue Menu Command (QuickBASIC)

Using QuickBASIC, you can achieve the ability to resume program execution by the selection of the Continue option from the Run menu or by pressing the F5 key. Thus, you can enter break points into a QuickBASIC program through the use of the STOP and END statements or by pressing the Ctrl+Break key combination and resume program execution by selecting the Continue option from the Run menu. Figure 10.2 illustrates the selection of the QuickBASIC Continue option from the Run menu. If you are using QBASIC the Run menu only provides you with the top three menu options shown in Figure 10.2.

NEW Command (Interpretive)

In interpretive BASIC, the NEW command can be used to delete the program currently in memory. This command should be used to free memory if you have previously entered a program and then wish to enter a new program. Otherwise, there will be the potential of one or more of the lines of the previous program becoming part of the newly entered program. Once this command is entered, any open files will be closed, and BASIC will return you to its command level signified by the prompt Ok. This is illustrated by the following example:

```
10 X=5
20 PRINT X
```
RUN
```
 5
Ok
```
NEW
```
Ok
```
RUN
```
Ok
```

New Program and Unload File Menu Commands

You can use the QuickBASIC New Program option in the File menu to obtain a capability similar to the NEW command in interpretive BASIC. In addition, in QuickBASIC you

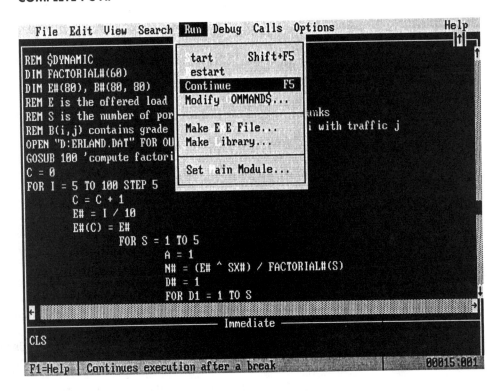

Figure 10.2 QuickBASIC Continue Option in the Run Menu. QBASIC only provides the top three commands in the Run Menu.

can obtain a more powerful capability than that afforded by the interpretive BASIC NEW command by selecting the `Unload File` option from the QuickBASIC File menu. However, this command is not available in QBASIC. This action results in the display of the Unload File dialog box illustrated in Figure 10.3, which enables you to delete an unwanted module from memory. Thus, if you previously loaded several modules into memory QuickBASIC provides you with the ability to selectively remove modules. In comparison, the interpretive BASIC NEW command and the `New Program` menu option in QBASIC and QuickBASIC clear all memory.

RUN Command (Interpretive and QuickBASIC)

The first format of the RUN command listed in Table 10.1 can be considered a program reference command. Although the second format does reference a program, it requires a file specification, so it will be covered under the file reference commands later in this chapter.

The RUN Command is used to initiate the execution of a program. In its first format,

`RUN[line]`

this command begins the execution of a program currently in memory. If the optional line parameter is specified, program execution will begin with the specified line number.

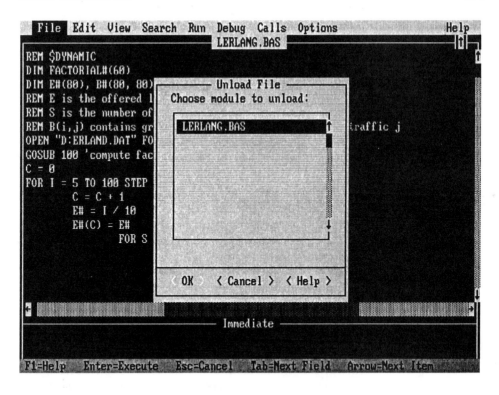

Figure 10.3 QuickBASIC Unload File Dialog Box.

The use of this command and its optional *line* parameter is shown in the following example:

```
Ok
100 PRINT "SEGMENT ONE"
500 PRINT "SEGMENT TWO"
750 PRINT "SEGMENT THREE"
RUN 500
SEGMENT TWO
SEGMENT THREE
Ok
RUN 750
SEGMENT THREE
Ok
RUN
SEGMENT ONE
SEGMENT TWO
SEGMENT THREE
Ok
```

Note that you can only use the F2 key using interpretive BASIC or you can select Start from the Run menu in QuickBASIC to execute a program in memory beginning at its first program line. This is because the F2 key generates the characters RUN followed automatically by an enter character while the START command in QuickBASIC causes program execution to commence at the first executable statement.

You can also use the RUN command to execute a program located on a different directory by including a path to the program in the command. Thus, you could enter the following command to execute the program named ANALYSIS under the SALES directory on drive A, assuming the SALES directory is under the root directory:

```
RUN "A:\SALES\ANALYSIS"
```

File Reference Commands

In this section, nine interpretive BASIC commands and their QuickBASIC equivalents with the common function of performing operations on defined file specifications will be reviewed. Although up to now commands have been discussed in alphabetical order in each section, discussion of the BLOAD and BSAVE commands will be deferred to the end of this section, because their usage is best explained by first covering the LOAD and SAVE commands.

Explaining Drive B

Although the original hardware configuration of most personal computers includes only one diskette drive, you can use any of the BASIC commands presented in this chapter to reference drive B. When a command referencing drive B is executed, DOS will prompt you to insert the diskette for drive B: and strike any key when ready. This prompt message, in effect, tells you to remove a diskette in your disk drive A if you do not want the command to operate on that diskette. Then, you can insert another diskette into drive A and press any key to have the BASIC command operate on the diskette placed into drive A. If you have a second diskette drive, issuing a BASIC command that references drive B will cause the command to take effect immediately without requiring you to remove and insert diskettes in drive A. Of course, if you have a fixed disk containing DOS, issuing a BASIC command without a drive specifier when C is the default drive will cause the command to take effect immediately on drive C.

FILES Command (Interpretive and QuickBASIC)

The FILES command is the counterpart of the DOS DIR command. This command has the capability to display the names of the files residing on the current directory of a disk. Unlike the DIR command, you cannot obtain information about the file size or the date the file was created. Similar to the DIR command, you can use the question mark (?) and asterisk (*) as global characters in your file specification. The question mark will serve as a replacement for any character in the file name or extension. When used as the first character in the file name or extension, the asterisk will cause a match of any name or extension on a diskette. If the file specification is omitted, all the files on the default or specified disk will be listed. The following examples illustrate the use and resulting operation of this command.

Command Structure	Operational Result
FILES	Displays all files on the current directory of the DOS default drive
FILES "B:*.BAS"	Displays all files with an extension of BAS on the current directory on drive B
FILES "STAT???.BAS"	Displays all files on the current directory of the DOS default drive that begin with STAT followed by three or less other characters and having the extension of BAS
FILES "C:\SALES"	Displays all files on drive C under the directory SALES

The use of this command in the direct mode is illustrated by the following example.

```
Ok
FILES
C:\SALES
                .   <DIR>           . .  <DIR> ANALYSIS.BAS
  45056 Bytes free
```

As a result of the preceding FILES command you can tell that drive C is the DOS default drive and that the current directory on that drive is SALES, which contains the file ANALYSIS.BAS.

KILL Command (Interpretive and QuickBASIC)

The KILL command is the counterpart of the DOS ERASE command, providing you with the capability to delete a file from a disk at the BASIC operating level. When invoked, you must specify the file extension, if one exists. The following examples illustrate the different structures of this command and their operational result. Again note that you can specify a path to the file in the file specification and that the trailing quotation mark is optional.

Command Structure	Operational Result
KILL "STAT.BAS"	Deletes file STAT with extension BAS from disk in default drive
KILL "A:STAT.BAS"	Deletes file STAT with extension BAS from diskette in drive A
KILL "C:\SALES\EAST"	Deletes file EAST from the SALES directory on the fixed disk

Like all diskette file specification references, if you omit the device name, you will default to the current drive. If the file does not exist or a referenced file is currently open, an appropriate error message is displayed.

The KILL command can be used in both direct and indirect modes in interpretive BASIC and in program and immediate modes in QuickBASIC. The following shows a direct mode use of this command in interpretive BASIC that could also be entered as an immediate command in QuickBASIC.

KILL "A:SPACE.BAS

You can write a BASIC program that will automatically delete a file from a diskette by using this command within the program. This is shown by the following program segment. Note that in this example the diskette was write protected and the program terminated after the appropriate error message was displayed:

```
LIST
100 REM AFTER A FILE MANIPULATION PROCESS YOU MAY
110 REM WISH TO DELETE A FILE THAT YOU NO LONGER REQUIRE
120 REM BY USING THE KILL COMMAND IN INDIRECT MODE
130 KILL "SPACE.BAS
135 PRINT
140 PRINT "PROGRAM CONTINUES"
Ok
RUN
Disk Write Protected in 130
Ok
```

If the diskette had not been write protected, the file SPACE.BAS would have been deleted from the diskette under program control if the file existed on the diskette in the default drive.

LOAD Command (Interpretive)

In interpretive BASIC, the LOAD command provides you with the capability to load a program from a specified device into memory. When the R option indicated in the command format in Table 10.1 is specified, the program will begin execution at the first statement after loading is completed.

When you load a file from the fixed disk or diskette, you must include a device specifier or the default drive is assumed. In addition, if you have a tree-structured directory, you must specify the path to the file or the file is assumed to be in the current directory.

Loading from disk can be conducted in either direct or indirect modes. The following examples indicate the command structure and operational results of the use of the LOAD command in the direct mode.

Command Structure	Operational Result
LOAD "STAT"	Loads the program file named STAT from the default drive
LOAD "C:\SALES\ANALYSIS"	Loads the program file named ANALYSIS in the SALES directory on drive C
LOAD "A:SALES.BAS"	Loads the program file named SALES with extension BAS from the diskette in drive A
LOAD "B:SALES.BAS,R	Loads and runs the program file named SALES with extension BAS on the diskette in drive B

To automatically load a program file from within a program, you can do so by the use of an indirect mode LOAD command. Several examples of the command structure and operational result of this mode follow:

Command Structure	Operational Result
`100 LOAD "A:SALES.BAS,R`	Loads and runs the program file named SALES with extension BAS from the diskette in drive A
`200 LOAD "C:\SALES\DATA"`	Loads but does not run the program file named DATA on the fixed disk under the directory named SALES

A word of caution is in order concerning the use of the R option. The indirect statement

`100 LOAD "SPACE`

will load the file SPACE from the disk into memory. However, the statement

`100 LOAD "SPACE,R`

will cause a `File not found in 100` error message, because you must use the appropriate file extension when the R option is used or BASIC will use R as the extension in its search for the file. This is shown by the following two indirect mode operations:

LIST
```
100 LOAD "A:SPACE,R"
```
RUN
```
File not found in 100
Ok
```

LIST
```
100 LOAD "SPACE.BAS,R
```
RUN
```
Ok
```

From the preceding examples, note that the only difference between the direct and indirect mode formats of the LOAD command is the inclusion of a program line number for the latter. When you are using a LOAD command in the indirect mode, a `File not found` error message will be displayed if the requested file does not exist on the disk in the specified drive or in the directory you are currently logged onto. Thus, if you are writing a program that uses program files on multiple diskettes, you should prompt the operator to insert the appropriate diskettes before the operator executes the LOAD command in the program. Otherwise, the wrong diskette will cause the `File not found` error message to be displayed and the program will terminate.

Note that under DOS you can assign labels to diskettes and under program control check to ensure that the correct diskette is inserted into the appropriate drive.

Open Program and Load File Menu Commands (QuickBASIC)

When you are using QuickBASIC you can use either the `Open Program` or the `Load File` option (not available in QBASIC) in the File menu to obtain a capability similar to the interpretive BASIC LOAD command. The `Open Program` option provides the ability to load an existing program, which then appears in a window with the filename indicated in the title bar. If you select the `Load File` option, you can load single program modules as one of three types of files supported by QuickBASIC—Module, Include, and Document. A Module file represents a discrete program component whose contents are checked by the QuickBASIC editor. An Include file is a text file whose statements will be compiled into your program, such as a file created using a text editor. A Document file represents a text file that is not checked by the QuickBASIC editor for syntax and formatting. Figure 10.4 illustrates the display of the dialog box resulting from the selection of the Load File option from the File menu. As previously indicated, this command is not applicable in QBASIC. In comparing this to Figure 8.9, you will note that the dialog box is very similar to the Open Program dialog box and simply adds the Load as options line above the OK, Cancel, and Help buttons.

MERGE Command (Interpretive)

In interpretive BASIC, the MERGE command provides the capability to merge the lines from an ASCII program file on disk with the program currently in memory. Whereas the LOAD command clears memory automatically, this command loads the specified ASCII file into memory without clearing existing memory. Any lines loaded from the specified file will replace the corresponding lines in memory, and any lines in memory that do not have a corresponding line number in the specified file will remain in memory. After the merge operation is completed, BASIC will return to the command level, and you will have one merged program representing the prior contents of memory and the specified file that was merged with those contents.

The MERGE command is very useful if you previously developed a comprehensive program as a series of modules saved as individual files and then wish to merge them

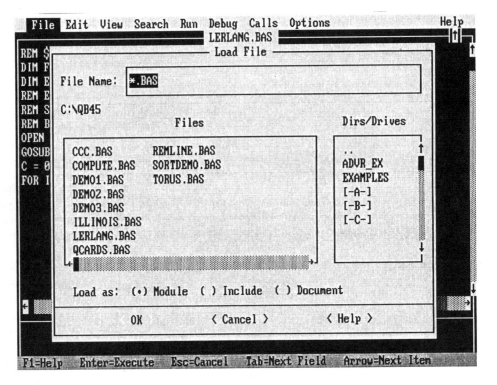

Figure 10.4   QuickBASIC Load File Dialog Box.

together into one program. If you did not use a distinct range of line numbers for each module, you should use the RENUM command to do so prior to merging the modules. Otherwise, when you merge each file, one or more line numbers in one module in effect could erase the line number of a previous program module. To use the RENUM command, you first have to load each module, renumber the lines in the module, and then save the module. Then, you could merge each module into memory to obtain one program.

The following examples illustrate the command structure and operational result from the use of the MERGE command. Note that you must specify a path to the file if it is not in the directory you are currently logged onto.

Command Structure	Operational Result
MERGE "A:STAT.BAS	Merges the ASCII program file named STAT with extension BAS on the diskette in drive A into the program in memory
MERGE "C:\SALES\DATA"	Merges the ASCII program file named DATA on the fixed disk under the SALES directory into the program in memory

A Bad file mode error will result if the program you attempted to merge was not saved in ASCII format using the A option parameter in the SAVE command. You can then save the program in memory and if the program you wish to merge is unprotected, you can LOAD it into memory and resave it using the A option parameter. Then, you can reload the original contents of memory and merge the newly formed ASCII file.

Merge Menu Command (QuickBASIC)

QuickBASIC provides a Merge option in the File menu, which is used to insert the contents of a text file into the currently loaded file based on the position of the cursor. Thus, you would first position your cursor at the location where you wish to insert a text file consisting of ASCII characters. After you select the Merge option from the File menu, QuickBASIC displays a dialog box labeled Merge, enabling you to select the file whose contents will be inserted into the previously loaded file at the location specified by the cursor's position. This command is only applicable to QuickBASIC and was not included in the File menu of QBASIC.

NAME Command (Interpretive and QuickBASIC)

The BASIC NAME command is the counterpart of the DOS RENAME command. This command provides the ability to change the name of a disk file.

Similar to most BASIC commands, the NAME command can be used in both direct and indirect modes in interpretive BASIC and in program and immediate modes in QuickBASIC. If the file to be renamed is not in the current directory a path to the file must be included in the file specification. The following example illustrates the command structure and operational result of this command.

Command Structure	Operational Result
NAME "A:STAT" AS "DATA"	Renames the file STAT on the diskette in drive A to DATA

If the file you wish to rename does not exist or the name you wish to change it to already exists on the diskette, an error will result. If the file you wish to rename is not on the current directory, you must include a path in the file specification. This is illustrated by the following use of the NAME command to change the name of the program file ANALYSIS.BAS located in the SALES directory on the DOS default drive to DATA.BAS:

```
Ok
NAME "\SALES\ANALYSIS.BAS" AS "\SALES\DATA.BAS"
Ok
```

In the indirect and program modes, the NAME command enables you to change the name of a disk file within a program. In developing a program that updates sequential files, this provides the ability to construct a continuous update cycle in a program. Refer to the flowchart in Figure 10.5. In the file update and report generation program process in Figure 10.5, the update program reads the data on the file named OLD. After updating the data, the program will output it to a file named NEW and print a report. Once the updating is complete, the NEW file will become the OLD file for the next update process. Performing the file manipulation required within your update program requires the following operations:

1. Save the file named NEW.
2. Delete the file named OLD.
3. Rename OLD as NEW.

The preceding operations can be performed in the indirect mode, as indicated by the following program segment:

```
500 SAVE "NEW
510 DELETE "OLD
520 NAME "NEW AS "OLD
```

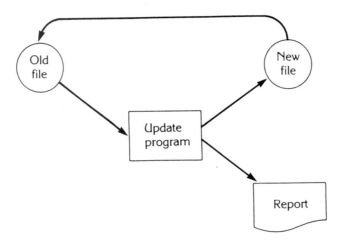

Figure 10.5   Cyclic File Update and Report Generator Program.

Before you write a program using file reference commands, read Chapter 12. This chapter covers the use of BASIC file statements that are necessary to read and write data items to and from sequential and random files.

RESET Command (Interpretive and QuickBASIC)

The RESET command closes all diskette files and clears any data in file buffer areas. It can be used in both direct and indirect modes in interpretive BASIC and in the program and immediate modes in QuickBASIC.

In indirect and programming modes, you can use it in a program to close all open files if you have previously opened the maximum number of files permitted and wish to manipulate data on other files. When file operations are covered in Chapter 12, you will see that this command is the same as a CLOSE statement, with no file number assigned to the statement. In direct mode, this command is invoked by entering the keyword RESET.

RUN Command

As previously discussed under Program Reference Commands in this chapter, the RUN command is both a program reference and a file reference command, depending on the format of the command. In this section, the second format indicated in Table 10.1 will be examined. This format requires a file specification, which is why it falls into the file reference command category. Note that if the program to be executed is on a different drive or directory from the default drive or directory, you must specify the drive and a path to the file.

The RUN command clears memory and loads and runs a file from disk. If the R option, which is only applicable to interpretive BASIC, is included, all open data files will remain open. Because you must specify the file, you cannot use the F2 key in interpretive BASIC, because that key generates the keyword RUN followed by an enter character and is effective only for executing a program currently in memory.

The following examples illustrate the command structure and operational results from the use of various RUN commands that reference files. Note that the default file extension BAS will be automatically supplied when such files are referenced:

Command Structure	Operational Result
RUN "ANALYSIS"	Loads and runs the file named ANALYSIS from the diskette in the default drive
RUN "ANALYSIS.BAS,R	Loads and runs the file named ANALYSIS from the diskette in the default drive; keeps all open files open
RUN "C:\SALES\EST"	Loads and runs the file named EST located under the directory SALES on drive C

Similar to the R option in the LOAD command when you are using interpretive BASIC, you must enter the complete extension of the file when you use the R option, or BASIC will confuse the R as part of the file extension and return the message File not found. You can also place the end quotation mark after the file specification to ensure that BASIC recognizes that the R option is not part of the file extension.

The ability to keep all open files open with the R option enables you to have one program automatically continue using a file accessed by a previous program.

Similar to most commands, the RUN command can be used in both direct and indirect modes in interpretive BASIC and program and immediate modes in QuickBASIC. To obtain a feel for the effectiveness of the Run command in the indirect program mode, assume you wish to construct a program that permits the operator to select one of five programs from a menu in a main program. After the menu is displayed and the program number requested is entered, your program segment might be

```
100 ON X GOTO 110,120,130,140,150
110 RUN "STAT1.BAS
120 RUN "STAT2.BAS
130 RUN "STAT3.BAS
140 RUN "STAT4.BAS
150 RUN "STAT5.BAS
```

Because the execution of the RUN command deletes the contents of memory before loading and running the specified file, you do not have to worry about a second RUN statement in a following line in the main program being executed after the command in the line number you branched to is executed. At the appropriate point in each of the five programs, you can automatically load and rerun the main program containing the menu by using a statement similar to the following in each STAT program:

```
500 RUN "MAIN.BAS
```

To see how you can employ a path in the RUN command, consider the following example. In this example, you list the program named FIRST located in the root directory. Then you use the CHDIR command in direct mode to change the current directory to SALES (CHDIR "C:\SALES") and load and list the program named ANALYSIS located in the SALES directory. After this is accomplished, you again use the CHDIR command in direct mode, this time to change the current directory to the root directory (CHDIR "\"). Now you can load and run the program file named FIRST located in the root directory. Notice that the program FIRST automatically executes the program named ANALYSIS, even though it is not in the same directory, because the appropriate path was specified in line 40 of the first program.

```
Ok
LIST
10 REM lets execute one program from another
20 PRINT "first program here"
30 PRINT "lets get next one"
40 RUN "C:\SALES\ANALYSIS"
Ok
CHDIR "C:\SALES"
Ok
LOAD "ANALYSIS"
Ok
LIST
10 PRINT "test"
Ok
CHDIR "\"
Ok
```

LOAD "FIRST"
```
Ok
```
RUN
```
first program here
lets get next one
test
Ok
```

SAVE Command (Interpretive)

In interpretive BASIC, the SAVE command provides the ability to save a BASIC program file on disk. If you are saving a file on disk and do not specify a file extension, BAS will be automatically added to the file directory as the file extension.

In the format of this command listed in Table 10.1, the A option results in saving the program in ASCII format. If you wish to read such files as data files for transmission to another computer or for other purposes, you should save them using this option. The P option saves the program in an encoded binary format that protects its contents from being listed or edited. This option should be used with care, since no way is provided to "unprotect" such files. Normally, you will want to use this option to create a copy of a program for someone when you do not desire to allow that person the ability to modify or list the program's contents. If no option is specified, the program will be saved in a compressed (tokenized) format. In this format, the ASCII code resulting from the Alt key combined with one of the alphabetic keys is used to replace certain BASIC keywords as indicated in Table 10.3. The indicated key combination replaces a keyword, so tokenized files take up less storage space on disk. If you wanted to read such files as data files, you would first have to write a program to detokenize them. Thus, it is simpler to save such files using the A option if you wish to use them as data files. If you wish to save the program in memory on a device other than the DOS default drive or in a different directory, you must include a drive specifier and/or a path in your file specification.

The following examples illustrate the command structure and operational result from the use of the SAVE command. Note that in interpretive BASIC you can use the F4 key to generate the keyword SAVE followed by a quote sign.

Table 10.3
BASIC Keyword Tokens

Alt Key Plus	Keyword	Alt Key Plus	Keyword
A	AUTO	N	NEXT
B	BSAVE	O	OPEN
C	COLOR	P	PRINT
D	DELETE	Q	(No word)
E	ELSE	R	RUN
F	FOR	S	SCREEN
G	GOTO	T	THEN
H	HEX$	U	USING
I	INPUT	V	VAL
J	(No word)	W	WIDTH
K	KEY	X	XOR
L	LOCATE	Y	(No word)
M	MOTOR	Z	(No word)

Command Structure	Operational Result
SAVE "A:STAT	Saves program under name STAT in tokenized format on diskette in drive A
SAVE "A:STAT,A	Saves program under name STAT in ASCII format on diskette in drive A
SAVE "A:STAT,P	Saves program under name STAT in protected format on diskette in drive A
SAVE "C:\SALES\EST"	Saves program under name EST in the directory named SALES on the fixed disk drive C

The SAVE command can be used in both direct and indirect program modes. In the indirect mode, you can use the SAVE command to automatically save a data file without operator intervention.

Save Menu Commands (QuickBASIC)

In QuickBASIC you can select among three Save options from the File menu to save information currently in memory. Selecting Save from the File menu displays a dialog box and copies the contents of the file currently displayed in the active view window to disk. If the file was not previously named, QuickBASIC prompts you to enter the file name and format that should be used for saving the file. As indicated in Figure 10.6 from the display of the Save dialog box, QuickBASIC supports two file formats— QuickBASIC, which is similar to interpretive BASIC token format; and text, in which data is stored in ASCII format.

The Save As option in the File menu saves a program under a different name than the filename from which you loaded the program. You should use this command after you modified a program and wish to keep copies of both the original program and the modified program.

The third QuickBASIC file-saving option, Save All (not available in QBASIC), provides the ability to save all changed module files when you are working with a multiple-module program. If the main module was just created and currently unnamed, QuickBASIC prompts you for the name and format of that module when you select the Save All option. This displays a dialog box labeled Save All, which (other than the label) is the same as the Save dialog box illustrated in Figure 10.6.

BSAVE Command (Interpretive and QuickBASIC)

The BSAVE command, along with the BLOAD command, provides the capability to load a memory image (binary) file into memory and to save a specified portion of the computer's binary memory on a specified device. After reviewing how a specified portion of memory can be saved with the BSAVE command, the BLOAD command will be examined.

As indicated in Table 10.1, you must include a file specification and offset and length parameters in the BSAVE command. In addition, if you wish to save the memory image onto a file located on a directory different from the current directory, you must include a path in your file specification. The offset parameter is a numerical expression that specifies where in the currently defined segment of memory saving will commence. The

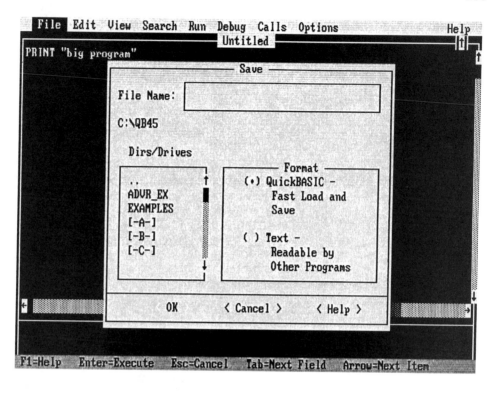

Figure 10.6 QuickBASIC Save Dialog Box.

length parameter specifies the number of bytes of storage from the offset position that will be saved. To understand how you use the offset parameter to specify where in a segment of memory saving commences requires you to examine the DEF SEG statement, because the offset parameter points into the segment of memory declared by the last use of the segment.

DEF SEG Statement

The design of the original IBM PC was based on the use of the Intel 8088 microprocessor, which uses a 16-bit address bus and an 8-bit data bus. If restricted to simply using its address bus, the PC would have been limited to addressing 2^{16} memory locations. Thus, PC designers developed a technique known as segmented addressing to reference memory. In this technique, two 16-bit numbers are used to reference memory. The first number is known as the *segment address* and is multiplied by 16, which is equivalent to adding 4 binary zeros to it, making it 20 bits long. The second 16-bit number is used as is and is known as the *relative portion* of the address. By adding both numbers, a 20-bit address is formed that can be used to reference any memory address up to 1024K bytes. Thus, the segment can be viewed as a base address, whereas the relative address provides an offset relative to that base address. Segment addressing is also used in Intel 80286, 80386, and 80486 computers operating DOS, which places the computer in a real mode that provides 8088 compatibility. Thus, both interpretive BASIC and QuickBASIC—which are real-mode languages—use the addressing scheme of the 8088 even when they operate on more modern microprocessors.

The DEF SEG statement defines the memory segment address portion of the address. The format of this statement is

format: DEF SEG=[*address*]

Here, the address is a numerical expression between 0 and 65535. If the address is omitted, the beginning of user work space in memory will be used as the default value. When an address is specified, its value should be based on a 16-byte boundary and should be one-sixteenth of the desired address. This is because the specified value is shifted 4 bit positions to the left, which is equivalent to multiplication by 16 to form the segment address for subsequent operations. As an example, suppose you wish to define your memory segment to be the address where the buffer for the color screen begins. This address in hexadecimal is B8000. Dividing by 16 results in B800. Thus, the DEF SEG statement that would set the memory segment to the beginning location of the color screen buffer would become

```
100 DEF SEG=&HB800
```

Digress for a moment from your consideration of the BSAVE and BLOAD commands to see how the DEF SEG segment can be employed. Suppose you wish to write a program to "dump" the contents of the screen to the printer. Knowing where the buffer that holds the contents of information displayed on the screen is located solves part of the programming problem. The PEEK function provides the ability to read a byte of information from a specified memory location.

PEEK Function

The format of this function is

format: *varnm*=PEEK(*exprnm*)

Each value returned will be an integer between 0 and 255, which will be the ASCII value of the location in memory PEEKed. The numeric expression used in the function call will be offset from a current segment if you used a DEF SEG statement in your program. Thus, you can write the following short subroutine to dump the contents of the screen to the printer.

```
100 DEF SEG=&HB800
110 FOR I=0 TO 3838 STEP 2
120 X=PEEK(I)
130 LPRINT CHR$(X);
140 NEXT I
150 DEF SEG
160 RETURN
```

If you are puzzled as to why the FOR-NEXT loop goes from 0 to 3838 in increments of 2, an explanation is in order. First, your display is assumed to be 25 lines of 80 characters, or a total of 2000 characters. Then, why do you vary I from 0 to 3838? This is because each 16-bit location that specifies a character on the display consists of two parts. The first 8 bits define the character (ASCII 0 to 255); the second 8 bits specify its attribute. Now you can see the rationale for incrementing the variable I by

2 to skip over the attribute, because you wish only to dump the contents of the screen to the printer.

The screen can be represented by character positions as indicated in Figure 10.7 in decimal notation, so why does your incremental value stop at 3838? This is because that is the last character position of the twenty-fourth line. Thus, this subroutine allows you to dump the entire screen with the exception of the twenty-fifth line, which you could then use as a program continuation or print request area. If you wish to dump the entire screen, changing the final value to 3998 would accomplish this task. The DEF SEG statement in line 150 resets your segment to the initial value. Otherwise, any additional PEEK statements in your program would reference memory using an offset of hexadecimal B800. If in doubt, try the preceding program. You may wish to vary the starting and ending parameters of the loop to dump a specified portion of the screen to the printer. If you wish to try the preceding screen dump for the screen buffer on the IBM monochrome display and parallel printer adapter, change line 100 in the program to read DEF SEG=&HB000, which is the address of that display.

Suppose you wish to save the screen image on the color screen buffer at a particular point in your program. The color screen buffer is 16K bytes in length, so your program segment to perform this function would appear as follows:

```
100 DEF SEG=&HB800
110 BSAVE "C:\GRAPH\PIX",0,&H4000
```

In this example, the DEF SEG statement sets the segment address to the start of the color screen buffer. Address B800 is used, because you must divide the actual address of B8000 by 16. In line 110, you use the BSAVE command with a zero (0) offset and length of Hex 4000 to specify that the entire 16K screen buffer is to be saved. The file named PIX will be created on the disk and will then contain the image of the screen.

In addition to saving memory images, the BSAVE command can be used to save machine language programs. One example of the command structure and operational result of the BSAVE command is listed in the example that follows.

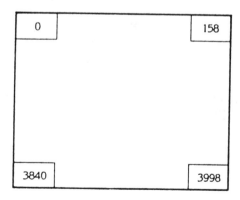

Figure 10.7   Character Positions on Display When WIDTH Is 80.

Command Structure	Operational Result
BSAVE "WAR,100,&H100	Saves 256 bytes from the buffer starting at offset position 100; memory image is saved on the diskette in the current drive on the file named WAR

The BSAVE command can be used in both direct and indirect modes. In the indirect program mode, this command is very useful to store graphic images after they have been developed on the screen. Then the BLOAD command can be used to load those images previously saved on a file into memory to automatically re-create the screen image. Thus, these commands provide the ability to save the results of many complex programs that generate one or more screen displays and simply reference those displays through a BLOAD command.

BLOAD Command (Interpretive and QuickBASIC)

The BLOAD command has the capability to load a memory image (binary) file into memory. The use of this command requires a file specification parameter; the offset parameter is optional. As indicated in the format listed in Table 10.1, the offset parameter is a numeric expression between 0 and 65,535 that specifies where in the segment declared by the last DEF SEG statement loading will occur. Thus, the offset parameter can be viewed as a pointer into the currently defined memory segment.

The BLOAD command can be used in both direct and indirect modes in interpretive BASIC and in program and immediate modes in QuickBASIC. Examples of the command structure and resulting operation from the use of the BLOAD command follow:

Command Structure	Operational Result
BLOAD "A:XRAY.MEM,0	Loads the memory image file named XRAY with extension MEM from the diskette in drive A; a zero offset will be used
BLOAD "C:\GRAPH\PIX.MEM",0	Loads the memory image file named PIX with extension MEM from the directory GRAPH on the fixed disk drive C into memory; a zero offset will be used

In the previous examples, it should be noted that the omission of an offset parameter informs BASIC to use the offset value used in the BSAVE command that previously saved the file. This will ensure that the file will be loaded into the same location from which it was saved. If you specify an offset parameter, you should include a DEF SEG statement prior to the BLOAD command. This will inform BASIC that you wish to load the memory image file at a location other than that from which it was saved.

Program Tracing Commands

Interpretive BASIC contains two program tracing commands, QuickBASIC supports the same commands as well as 11 additional menu based commands, whereas QBASIC supports six commands that represent a subset of QuickBASIC DEBUG commands that can be employed to assist you in ascertaining the flow of program execution.

TRON Command (Interpretive and QuickBASIC)

In interpretive BASIC, the TRON command enables a trace flag in the system that will cause each line number of the program to be displayed as it is executed. To distinguish the line number from any data output to the screen, the line numbers are enclosed in square brackets. The TRON command can be entered in direct or indirect mode. Function key F7 can be used to generate this command in direct mode in interpretive BASIC.

In QuickBASIC you can use the TRON command as a statement within a program or enter it directly in the Immediate window. Either action will result in the highlighting of each line in the program to occur as the program is executed, with program execution occurring on a line-by-line basis in slow motion. In addition, TRON causes the last 20 lines that were executed in a program to be recorded prior to the termination of the program, enabling you to use the Shift+F8 and Shift+F10 keys to scroll backward and forward through each of the last 20 lines of executable code. In addition to placing TRON into a program you can select the Trace On option from the Debug menu to perform the previously mentioned functions. This menu-based command will be discussed later in this chapter.

TROFF Command (Interpretive and QuickBASIC)

In interpretive BASIC, the TROFF command or the NEW command can be used to disable the tracing of program statements. You should use the former in the indirect mode, because the NEW command not only disables program tracing but also deletes the program currently in memory, which is probably not your intention when you wish to terminate tracing the execution of a program. In interpretive BASIC, the TROFF command can be generated by the F8 function key. The following examples illustrate the use of these commands in both direct and indirect modes.

In the direct mode in interpretive BASIC, you can press the F7 key to enable program tracing. In the following example after tracing was enabled, the F2 key was pressed to RUN the program in trace mode. After execution was completed, the F8 key was pressed to disable program tracing.

```
Ok
LIST
100 INPUT"ENTER VALUE ",R
110 FOR X=1 TO R
120 PRINT X^3,X
130 NEXT X
Ok
TRON
Ok
RUN
[100]ENTER VALUE 3
[110][120] 1    1
[130][120] 8    2
[130][120] 27        3
[130]
Ok
TROFF
Ok
```

Using the TRON and TROFF commands in indirect mode in interpretive BASIC provides the ability to selectively trace a portion or portions of a program. This capability is illustrated by the following program segment:

```
LIST
100 INPUT"ENTER VALUE ",R
110 FOR X=1 TO R
115 TRON
120 PRINT X^3,X
130 NEXT X
140 TROFF
150 FOR J=1 TO 5
160 PRINT J;
170 NEXT J
Ok
RUN
[100]ENTER VALUE 3
[110][115][120] 1        1
[130][115][120] 8        2
[130][115][120] 27       3
[130][140] 1 2 3 4 5
Ok
```

Note that in both examples, the tracing of program execution statements does not inform you as to what the values of variables are internally within the program. To obtain this information, which at times can be more valuable than obtaining the sequence of the execution of program statements, you can insert "dummy PRINT" statements into your program. These statements are called *dummy statements*, because once you diagnose what is wrong with your program, if anything, you will remove these statements from the program. Thus, these statements serve to provide you with information about what is happening to the variables internally and will not be used in the final version of your program. In the following example, line 115 has been added to a program as a dummy PRINT statement. As a result of the execution of this statement, the value assigned to the variable K will be displayed. Without this statement, you would not know the internal value assigned to this variable when the program is run:

```
LIST
100 INPUT"ENTER VALUE ",X
110 K=X^2+X^4
115 PRINT "K= ";K;" WHEN X= ";X
120 TRON
130 FOR I=2 TO X
140 PRINT I ,I*K
150 NEXT I
160 TROFF
Ok
RUN
ENTER VALUE 4
K= 272 WHEN X= 4
[130][140] 2 544
[150][140] 3 816
```

```
[150][140] 4 1088
[150][160]
Ok
```

If you are using QuickBASIC, the TROFF command can be entered as a statement within a program or in the Immediate window. If entered as a program statement, TROFF turns off line tracing when the statement is executed. In comparison, when entered in the Immediate window TROFF immediately turns off line tracing until another TRON statement is executed when you resume program execution.

Debug Menu

Although the capability of TRON and TROFF in QuickBASIC is limited in comparison to interpretive BASIC, you can use commands from the Debug menu in QuickBASIC to obtain a much better capability than is afforded by interpretive BASIC. Options on the Debug menu enable you to examine the values of variables in your program, suspend program execution when a predefined event occurs, and obtain other information that can assist you in the development and correction of a program. Figure 10.8 illustrates the Debug menu in QuickBASIC. In QBASIC the Debug menu contains six commands.

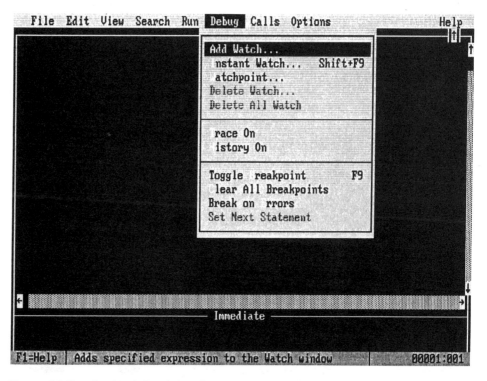

Figure 10.8 QuickBASIC Debug Pull-Down Menu. Only Trace On, Toggle Breakpoint, Clear All Breakpoints, and Set Next Statement as well as added Step and Procedure Step are applicable to QBASIC.

Common commands with QuickBASIC include Trace On, Toggle Breakpoint, Clear All Breakpoints, and Set Next Statement. New DEBUG statements added to QBASIC include Step and Procedure Step, which enable you to trace the execution of a program on a step-by-step or procedure basis.

Add Watch Menu Command (QuickBASIC only)

The Add Watch option provides you with the ability to continuously watch the value of a variable or the condition of an expression (–1 if true, 0 if false) as your program executes. Each of the variables assigned to be watched will be displayed in a Watch window that will appear at the top of your screen.

When you select the Add Watch option, an Add Watch dialog box displays. This box enables you to enter a variable or expression to be watched, which is then placed into the Watch window. Figure 10.9 illustrates the Add Watch dialog box superimposed on a program named LERLANG.BAS for which a Watch window was opened previously with the Add Watch option. If you examine the second and third lines in Figure 10.9, you will note the entries LERLANG.BAS I: and LERLANG.BAS E#:, each entry representing variables previously assigned to the Watch window through the use of the Add Watch dialog box. When your program executes, the values associated with variables and expressions entered into the Watch window are continuously updated as the program

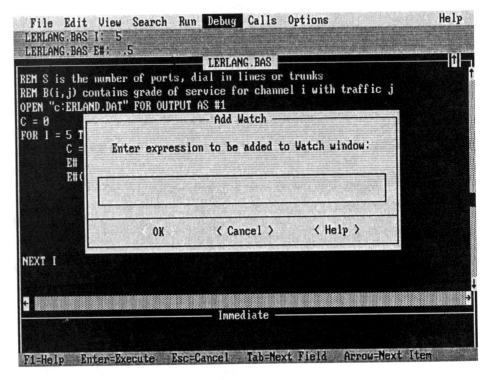

Figure 10.9 QuickBASIC Add Watch Dialog Box.

executes. When you interrupt the program's execution by pressing the Ctrl+Break multikey combination the current value of any variables and expressions assigned to the Watch window are displayed. Note that in Figure 10.9 the value of I was 5, whereas the value of E# was .5 when the program was interrupted.

Instant Watch Menu Command (QuickBASIC Only)

The Instant Watch option on the QuickBASIC Debug menu enables you to examine the current value of a variable or the condition of an expression and, if desired, add the variable or expression to the Watch window. To use the Instant Watch option you must suspend program execution, after which you can move the cursor onto the variable or expression whose value you wish to examine. Once this is accomplished, you can select Instant Watch from the Debug menu or press the Shift+F9 key combination. After either action, a dialog box displaying the selected variable or expression and its current value appears, as illustrated in Figure 10.10. In this illustration note that the value of the variable S was 10 when program execution was suspended. Also note that by clicking on the Add Watch button you can add the variable S to the Watch window.

Watchpoint Menu Command (QuickBASIC Only)

The Watchpoint option provides the ability to suspend program execution when a defined variable or expression obtaining a specified value or condition occurs. Selecting

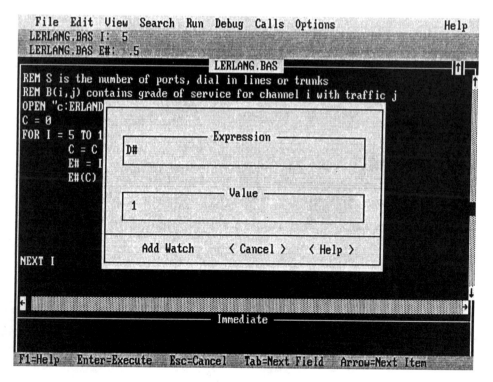

Figure 10.10 QuickBASIC Instant Watch Dialog Box.

the Watchpoint option from the Debug menu results in the display of a dialog box labeled Watchpoint. In this dialog box you enter the value of the variable or expression that, when reached, will cause the program to stop. After you enter a watchpoint, the variable or expression and its assigned break value and current condition will be displayed in the Watch window. For example, if you assigned D#=1 in the Watchpoint dialog box and its value was less than 1, the display would be D#=1:<FALSE> in the Watch window.

Delete Watch Menu Command (QuickBASIC Only)

The Delete Watch option provides the ability to remove variables and expressions previously assigned to the Watch window one at a time. Selecting this command from the Debug menu results in the display of a dialog box labeled Delete Watch, as illustrated in Figure 10.11. Moving the highlight bar over the variable or expression you wish to remove and clicking on the OK button or pressing the Enter key removes the variable or expression from the Watch window.

Delete All Watch Menu Command (QuickBASIC Only)

The Delete All Watch option is used to remove all variables and expressions from the QuickBASIC Watch window. Once this option is selected, the Watch window is automatically closed.

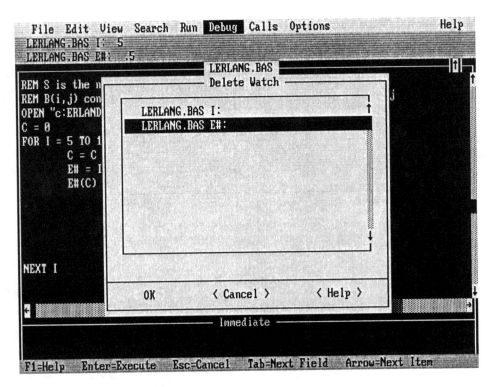

Figure 10.11   QuickBASIC Delete Watch Dialog Box.

Trace On Menu Command

As previously mentioned for the TRON command, you can also select Trace On from the Debug menu to perform the exact same function as TRON. In addition, the selection of the Trace On option functions as a toggle, alternating between TRON and TROFF operations. If a TRON operation is in effect, a dot precedes the option's entry in the Debug menu.

History On Menu Command (QuickBASIC Only)

The History On option also functions as a toggle, enabling and disabling the operation of your program at full speed and the recording of the last 20 lines of executed code prior to a program termination. Selecting the Trace On menu option automatically enables the History On option; however, the opposite is not true. That is, selecting History On without Trace On will result in your program operating at full speed with the results of the last 20 lines of executed code prior to program termination being saved. Then you can use the Shift+F8 and Shift+F10 key combinations to step backward and forward one line at a time to review the last 20 program actions.

Toggle Breakpoint Menu Command

You can select the Toggle Breakpoint option from the Debug menu or press the F9 key to effect a breakpoint. Either action will cause the line where the cursor resides to become a breakpoint, which will cause your program to pause when the breakpoint is reached. Then you can select the Continue option from the Run menu or press the F5 key to resume program execution.

The selection of a breakpoint causes the breakpoint line to be highlighted. Selecting the Toggle Breakpoint option a second time or again pressing the F9 key will clear the breakpoint where the program stopped. If you previously established several breakpoints in your program, you can move your cursor onto each breakpoint and press the F9 key or select the Toggle Breakpoint option to remove each breakpoint. As an alternative, you can select the Clear All Breakpoints option from the Debug menu to remove all breakpoints from your program.

Break On Errors Menu Command (QuickBASIC Only)

The Break On Errors option also functions as a toggle. When enabled, the option causes your program to halt at the first statement in the most recently executed error handling subroutine, providing you with the capability to identify the source of an error. When this command is enabled it also enables the History On option, enabling you to examine the last 20 statements executed prior to the error-handling subroutine.

Set Next Statement Menu Command

The last option in the Debug menu is Set Next Statement. You can use this option to change the sequence of the execution of your program to the statement that the cursor is on.

System Reference Command

The only system reference command in BASIC is SYSTEM. This command provides the capability to exit BASIC and return to DOS. Because this command causes a return to DOS, obviously it requires the use of DOS. The use of this command results in the closing of all open files prior to returning to DOS. As indicated in Table 10.1, no parameters are specified in the command and it is invoked by entering the keyword **SYSTEM**. The default drive prompt will be displayed in response to this command as shown:

SYSTEM

A>

When used in QuickBASIC, SYSTEM only works when placed in the Immediate window. Then it will generate the dialog box message One or more loaded files are not saved. Save them now? if one or more files are open when the command is set to be executed. In comparison, SYSTEM can be used from within a program or in immediate mode with interpretive BASIC.

11 / Advanced Concepts in BASIC

This chapter focuses on a variety of Advanced BASIC statements applicable to interpretive BASIC and QuickBASIC. Once again, because of the similarity of QBASIC and QuickBASIC, this chapter refers to both collectively as QuickBASIC. If a statement is applicable to all versions of BASIC, there is no specific version of BASIC notation following the statement heading. Topics that will be examined in this chapter include array processing, including table lookup programming, sorting procedures, the implementation of formatted displays and formatted printing, date and time processing, subroutine interrupts, and event trapping (which covers the use of function and cursor control keys in interrupts).

Array Processing

An *array* or *matrix* is a set of variables of the same type that is known and referenced by one name. The individual elements of an array are specified by the addition of a subscript to the array name. Thus, A(5) would be the fifth element of the numeric array A, whereas A$(15) would be the 15th element of the string array A$. Integer, single-precision and double-precision arrays are permitted in interpretive BASIC, and QuickBASIC adds support for long integer arrays. Integer arrays occupy 2 bytes per element; single- and double-precision arrays require 4 and 8 bytes of storage per element, respectively.

Many BASICs use 1 as the lowest position of an element in an array, but the default value in interpretive BASIC and QuickBASIC is 0 (zero). This lowest position can be changed by the OPTION BASE statement, which is examined later in this section.

Although most BASICs permit a maximum of two dimensions, interpretive BASIC permits up to 255 dimensions for an array; QuickBASIC supports 8 array dimensions. The maximum number of elements per dimension is 32,767 in both interpretive BASIC and QuickBASIC.

A one-dimensional array can be thought of as a single column of many rows. The elements are specified by a single subscript, indicating the row desired as shown in the left portion of Figure 11.1. A two-dimensional array consists of a specified number of rows and columns that can be visualized as organized into a table. This is illustrated in the right portion of Figure 11.1. In a two-dimensional array, each element is specified by a pair of subscripts separated by a comma. The first subscript indicates the row, and the second subscript indicates the column position within the table.

Unlike many other BASICs, both interpretive BASIC and QuickBASIC permit two-dimensional string arrays. In fact, up to 255 dimensions can be used for both string

ONE-DIMENSIONAL

Column

Row	
0	A(0)
1	A(1)
2	A(2)
3	A(3)
4	A(4)
5	A(5)

TWO-DIMENSIONAL

Column

Row	0	1	2
0	A(0,0)	A(0,1)	A(0,2)
1	A(1,1)	A(1,1)	A(1,2)
2	A(2,1)	A(2,1)	A(2,2)
3	A(3,1)	A(3,1)	A(3,2)
4	A(4,1)	A(4,1)	A(4,2)
5	A(5,1)	A(5,1)	A(5,2)

Figure 11.1　One- and two-dimensional arrays.

and numeric arrays in interpretive BASIC, whereas up to 8 dimensions are supported in QuickBASIC.

Arrays in a BASIC program are defined in one of two ways. If you use an array element prior to defining the array, it will be assumed to be dimensioned with a maximum subscript of 10, providing 11 elements. This implicit declaration is only valid for one-dimensional arrays having a maximum subscript of 10. Thus, if BASIC encounters the statement

```
200 X(4)=37
```

and the array X was not previously defined, BASIC will set X to a one-dimensional array of 11 elements and assign the value 37 to the fourth element of array X. The second way to define an array is through the use of a DIM statement.

DIM Statement

The DIM Statement provides the mechanism to reserve storage for arrays and to set the upper bounds on the number of elements permitted in each array. The format of this statement, common to both interpretive BASIC and QuickBASIC, is

```
format: DIM var(subscripts)[,var(subscripts)] . . .
```

Here, the variable names the array and the subscripts specify the amount of storage to be reserved and set the upper bounds on the number of elements in the array.

The DIM Statement can appear anywhere in a program, as long as it precedes the first reference to the array. As shown by the following example, the placement of a DIM statement after the reference to the array will result in a Subscript out of range message. Note that moving the DIM statement to a location before the reference to the array eliminates this error condition.

```
Ok
LIST
80 FOR I=1 TO 50
90 X(I)=0
95 NEXT I
100 DIM X(50)
Ok
RUN
Subscript out of range in 90
```

```
Ok
```

LIST
```
70 DIM X(50)
80 FOR I=1 TO 50
90 X(I)=0
95 NEXT I
Ok
```
RUN
```
Ok
```

The DIM statement is nonexecutable and, if you branch to that statement in a program, execution will resume at the next executable statement following the DIM statement. Several examples of the use of this statement follow:

```
100 DIM A(5),B(3,3)
110 REM A has 6 rows, 1 column
120 REM B has 4 rows, 4 columns
130 REM A has 6 elements - 0 to 5
140 REM B has 16 elements 0,0 to 3,3
```

LIST
```
10 X=0
20 PRINT "STOCK","PRICE","SHARES"
30 DIM STOCK$(2),PRICE(2),SHARES(2)
40 FOR I=0 TO 2
50 READ STOCK$(I),PRICE(I),SHARES(I)
60 X=X+PRICE(I)*SHARES(I)
70 PRINT STOCK$(I),PRICE(I),SHARES(I)
80 NEXT I
90 DATA AMERICAN ICE,4.50,110
100 DATA BASIC BARGINS,1.875,50
110 DATA OHVEY INC,.125,5000
120 PRINT "TOTAL VALUE =",X
Ok
```
RUN

STOCK	PRICE	SHARES
AMERICAN ICE	4.5	110
BASIC BARGINS	1.875	50
OHVEY INC	.125	5000
TOTAL VALUE=	1213.75	

```
Ok
```

In the second example, one of several methods that assign values to arrays was used. Here, a READ statement contained within a FOR-NEXT loop assigned the appropriate values to each element of the arrays STOCK$, PRICE, and SHARES. You could also use the assignment statement or use individual elements in an INPUT statement. Note that after the counter that stores the value of each stock (price times number of shares) is incremented in line 60, the PRINT statement in line 70 is used to print data from the arrays. This shows you that printing data from arrays is parallel to the mechanism used for filling arrays. You can print individual elements by using a PRINT statement or you can use that statement within a FOR-NEXT loop to print all or a portion of the elements within an array. This concept will be illustrated by several examples in which you will initialize each element of an array to a value and then print out individual elements and selected portions of elements on the display:

```
10 DIM Q(100)
20 FOR I=0 TO 100  'set value of each element
30 Q(I)=I*I         'to its square
40 NEXT I
50 PRINT "SQUARE OF TEN IS ";Q(10)
60 FOR I=18 TO 22
70 PRINT "SQUARE OF ";I;" IS ";Q(I)
80 NEXT I
RUN
SQUARE OF TEN IS 100
SQUARE OF  18  IS 324
SQUARE OF  19  IS 361
SQUARE OF  20  IS 400
SQUARE OF  21  IS 441
SQUARE OF  22  IS 484
Ok
```

To understand some of the potential problems that can occur in array processing, these program segments, designed to be nonoperable, will be created and executed:

```
LIST
50 DIM X(20)
60 Z=12
70 FOR I=Z TO Z+15
80 X(I)=I
85 PRINT X(I)
90 NEXT I
Ok
RUN
 12
 13
 14
 15
 16
 17
 18
 19
 20
Subscript out of range in 80
Ok
```

When using variables to define the elements of arrays you wish to operate on, you should be careful to use such variables correctly. In the previous example, the subscript became greater than that specified in the DIM statement and caused a Subscript out of range error to occur.

In the next example, the type of the arrays used in line 120 purposely does not match the type of the items in the DATA statements. Note that a syntax error occurred, even though it is really a type mismatch. The error was corrected by reversing the array items in line 120 to correspond to the appearance of the type of data in the DATA statements in lines 140 and 150. Line 140 could have been changed, but the items in line 150 would also need to be changed, so changing the sequence of the arrays in the READ statement is easier to correct this error:

```
LIST
100 DIM P$(20),Q(20)
110 FOR I=0 TO 1
120 READ P$(I),Q(I)
125 PRINT P$(I),Q(I)
130 NEXT I
140 DATA 1,WASHINGTON
150 DATA 2,ADAMS
Ok
RUN
Syntax error in 140
Ok

120 READ Q(I),P$(I)
RUN
WASHINGTON      1
ADAMS           2
Ok
```

The next example results in another Type mismatch error; however, this results in the display of the correct error message. Here, a numeric value was associated with an element in a string array, which generated the error:

```
100 DIM P$(20),Q(20)
110 LET P$(1)=87.50
RUN
Type mismatch in 110
Ok
```

Because numeric array elements are stored as single-precision variables, each element will occupy four memory locations. The following example illustrates how easy it is to run out of memory from the dimensioning of just a few large arrays:

```
Ok
LIST
5 PRINT FRE(X)
10 DIM A(2,2,2,2)    '81 elements
15 PRINT FRE(X)
20 DIM B(5.5)        '36 elements
25 PRINT FRE(X)
30 DIM X(49,49)      '2500 elements
35 PRINT FRE(X)
40 DIM Q(19,19,19)   '8000 elements
45 PRINT FRE(X)
50 DIM R(9,9,9,9)    '10000 elements
Ok
RUN
 60650
```

```
60311
60156
50145
18132
Out of memory in 50
Ok
```

As indicated, arrays can rapidly reduce the amount of memory available for program computations. If you require the use of several large arrays in a program, you may wish to use the ERASE statement to eliminate from the program those arrays whose operations are complete.

If you are using QuickBASIC, a second format of the DIM statement is supported:

format$_Q$: DIM[SHARED] *var*[(*subscripts*)][AS *type*]
                    [,*var*[*subscripts*][AS *type*]] . . .

The optional SHARED keyword results in arrays being shared between the module-level code and all procedures included in the module, such as SUB and FUNCTION procedures. The AS keyword provides the ability to define variable types within a DIM statement. For example,

```
DIM A(5) AS STRING
```

would allocate six storage locations for the string array labeled A.

Another interesting feature of the QuickBASIC DIM statement is its support of a TO clause for defining subscripts. For example,

```
DIM A(50 TO 100)
```

would allocate space for the array named A with subscripts 50 through 100. This feature can be quite valuable, because it provides a high degree of array declaration flexibility. As an example, suppose you needed an array bounded by the value of the variables X and Y at a certain point in your program. You could add the statement

```
DIM A(X TO Y)
```

to obtain an automatic dimension for subscripts A_X to A_Y as long as X and Y are integers.

ERASE Statement

The ERASE statement enables you to eliminate previously DIMensioned arrays from a program. In addition, you use it to redimension arrays within a program, because without the prior erasing of an array, you would obtain a Duplicate definition error. The format of this statement is indicated below.

format: ERASE *arrayname*[,*arrayname*] . . .

Suppose you had an array of 1001 elements in your program and only required the data contained in elements 0 through 200. If you wished to make available additional space for your program, you could first dimension a new array of 201 elements, transfer the values of the elements from the old array to the new and smaller array, and then erase the original array.

A program segment that illustrates this concept is listed below. Note that you merely have to list the array name in the ERASE statement.

```
100 DIM X(1000)
  .
  . .
  .
200 DIM Y(200)
210 FOR I=0 TO 200
220 Y(I)=X(I)
230 NEXT I
240 ERASE X
  .
  .
  .
```

Another use for the ERASE statement is in a program that uses INPUT statements to enter data into one or more elements of arrays. Also, at the end of the program, it provides the operator with the option of requesting another program cycle. Here, instead of constructing one or more loops to zero the array elements, you could ERASE the arrays and then branch back to the beginning of the program where your DIM statement could be located. This concept is illustrated by the following program segment.

```
10 DIM X(30),Y(40),Z(800)
  .
  .
  .
5000 PRINT "ANOTHER (C)YCLE OR (E)XIT"
5010 A$=INKEY$:IF A$="E"THEN 5050
5020 IF A$<>"C" THEN 5010
5030 ERASE X,Y,Z,
5040 GOTO 10
5050 END
```

OPTION BASE Statement

An OPTION BASE statement is provided so that interpretive BASIC and QuickBASIC can become compatible with other versions of BASIC that use a minimum value of 1 for array subscripts. The format of this statement is

format: OPTION BASE *value*

Here, the default base is 0 and can be specified as such by the statement, or you can use the OPTION BASE statement to change the minimum value of array subscripts to 1. This statement must precede any DIM or array reference statement within a program. You may have a natural tendency to operate with subscript elements starting at 1, but using the OPTION BASE statement accordingly could eliminate storage allocation for array elements you do not intend to use in your program.

```
10 OPTION BASE 1
20 DIM X(30),Y(30),Z(30)
```

Thus, this example would free 12 storage locations, because each element requires four memory locations. Without the OPTION BASE statement, one extra element requiring four memory locations of storage would have been reserved for each array.

Processing Examples

Now examine some additional examples of how you can use arrays in BASIC.

Multiple Report Headings

Suppose you wish to print a financial report that will be 12 pages in length, each page projecting a cash flow analysis for a different month of the year. If the title on each page remains the same and only the month changes, you could use the following program segment that calls a subroutine to print the appropriate heading on each page:

```
100 DIM M$(12)
110 FOR I=1 TO 12
120 READ M$ (I)
130 NEXT I
140 DATA JANUARY,FEBRUARY,MARCH,APRIL,MAY,JUNE
150 DATA JULY,AUGUST,SEPTEMBER,OCTOBER,NOVEMBER,DECEMBER
.
.
.
500 FOR I=1 TO 12
510 GOSUB 5000
. 'report computations
. 'and data output generator
1000 NEXT I
1010 END
.
.
.
5000 LPRINT TAB(30) "CASH FLOW FOR ";M$(I)
5010 RETURN
```

In this example, lines 100 through 150 set aside 12 locations in storage for the array M$ and then initialize each element of the array to the appropriate month. The FOR-NEXT loop bounding lines 500 to 1000 first calls a subroutine that prints the heading of the report for the appropriate month and then calculates and prints the computations to be displayed for that particular month. An END statement was placed in line 1010 to prevent an unintentional fall through the main program into the subroutine. Note that in this example, the subroutine merely prints the string CASH FLOW FOR followed by the month. A space was purposely left between the R in FOR and the double quote sign in line 5000 to separate the word FOR from the appropriate month that will be printed.

Data Entry Error Processing

Now, examine how you can use arrays to allow data to be entered from the terminal and correct data entry errors without rerunning the program.

Suppose you wish to construct a program to compute the mean, standard deviation, variance, and coefficient of variation on data elements obtained from a survey of the number of persons living in homes located in several geographical areas. Further suppose you have 20 people surveying different neighborhoods and you wish to construct one program that can be used to obtain the necessary computations for each geographical area. Because each geographical area most likely has a different number of households, you may wish to construct the program so that it will have an array dimensioned in size based on the number of households surveyed. This can be accomplished by the following two statements, which illustrate how you can automatically dimension arrays during program execution:

```
100 INPUT "NUMBER OF HOMES SURVEYED ",X
110 DIM H(X)
```

After you enter the number of homes surveyed, the program should then request the number of occupants of each home to be entered and read this information into the appropriate elements of the H array. This can be accomplished by the following program statements:

```
120 PRINT"ENTER NUMBER OF OCCUPANTS"
130 FOR I=1 TO X
140 PRINT"HOUSEHOLD #";I;"=";
150 LOCATE ,18
160 INPUT " ",H(I)
170 NEXT I
```

The FOR-NEXT loop results in the prompt Household # and the numbers 1 to the value of X being printed on the display. The LOCATE statement in line 150 repositions the cursor to column 18 on the current line, and the INPUT statement in line 160 will assign the data value entered to the appropriate element of the H array.

The space between the pair of double quotation marks in line 160 forces a space between the displayed equal sign resulting from the execution of line 140 and the terminal operator's data entry in response to the INPUT statement in line 160. The execution of lines 100 to 170 of the program segment developed up to this time is shown here:

```
RUN
NUMBER OF HOMES SURVEYED 3
ENTER NUMBER OF OCCUPANTS
HOUSEHOLD # 1 =  3
HOUSEHOLD # 2 =  2
HOUSEHOLD # 3 =  4
Ok
```

Once all values have been entered into the program, the following statements can be used to correct any data element previously entered incorrectly. These statements permit such changes to occur prior to the program's performing the required computations.

```
180 PRINT "ANY DATA ELEMENT ENTERED INCORRECTLY -Y/N "
190 A$=INKEY$:IF A$="N" THEN 250
200 IF A$<> "Y" THEN 190
210 INPUT "WHICH HOUSEHOLD DO YOU WISH TO CHANGE ",C
220 INPUT "ENTER NEW VALUE ",H(C)
230 PRINT "MORE CORRECTIONS -Y/N "
240 GOTO 190
250 REM start computations
```

If data was previously entered incorrectly, the operator will specify which household to change. The household number (C) will be used as a pointer to the element in the H array for entering the new value into the appropriate element of that array. Note that the operator can enter no corrections or correct as many previously entered data elements as needed as a result of the preceding code.

This facet of the program is shown by executing the statements in lines 100 to 250. In the following example, the operator first entered the values of 4, 8, 9, and 6 as the number of occupants in homes 1, 2, 3, and 4. Then, he indicated he wished to change household 3 to a new value of 4 and the program automatically changed the value of H(3) to 4.

```
RUN
NUMBER OF HOMES SURVEYED 4
ENTER NUMBER OF OCCUPANTS
HOUSEHOLD # 1 =   4
HOUSEHOLD # 2 =   8
HOUSEHOLD # 3 =   9
HOUSEHOLD # 4 =   6
ANY DATA ELEMENT ENTERED INCORRECTLY -Y/N
WHICH HOUSEHOLD DO YOU WISH TO CHANGE 3
ENTER NEW VALUE 4
MORE CORRECTIONS -Y/N
Ok
```

Digressing for a moment, review some elementary statistics. The arithmetic average or mean is defined as the sum of the values of the items divided by the number of items. Mathematically, this is noted as follows:

$$\overline{X} = \frac{\sum\limits_{i=1}^{n} X_i}{n}$$

where $\overline{X}$ is the arithmetic average or mean, X_i is the ith element of X, and n is the number of items.

The standard deviation is a measurement of the extent of variation or dispersion of a distribution. The more spread out the distribution, the larger the standard deviation. The more concentrated the distribution, the smaller the resulting standard deviation. Hence, the standard deviation is a more meaningful measure than the average and is expressed mathematically as

$$Sx = \sqrt{\frac{X^2 - \frac{(\Sigma X)^2}{n}}{n-1}} = \sqrt{\frac{\Sigma(X - \overline{X})^2}{n-1}}$$

The square of the standard deviation, S_x^2, is called the variance. The larger the variability among the items, the larger the standard deviation and consequently the larger the variance.

The coefficient of variation, CV(X), gives you a measure of relative variation, because

$$CV(X) = \frac{Sx}{X} \cdot 100$$

Returning to the program, the number of persons in each household can be summed by the following code.

```
260 S=0
270 FOR I=1 TO X
280 S=S+H(I)
290 NEXT I
```

In line 260, S is initialized to zero, because it will serve as a counter as you cycle through all elements of the H array, adding the value of each element to S in line 280. Although both interpretive BASIC and QuickBASIC automatically set all unused variables to zero, it is good programming practice to set counters to zero before you use them. Otherwise, you may forget that you previously used a variable elsewhere in a program and if you see it later as a counter, this will result in an inaccurate computation. The arithmetic average or mean is simply the sum of the items divided by the number of items. Line 300 performs this calculation.

```
300 M=S/X      'mean
```

Lines 310 through 350 compute the standard deviation; line 360 computes the variance; line 370 computes the coefficient of variation.

```
310 S=0
320 FOR I=1 TO X
330 S=S+(H(I)=M)^2
340 NEXT I
350 D=SQR(S/(X-1))      'standard deviation
360 V=D*D               'variance
370 CV=(D/M)*100        'coefficient of variation
```

The complete program to include the statements necessary to output the desired computations is shown here:

```
100 INPUT "NUMBER OF HOMES SURVEYED ",X
110 DIM H(X)
120 PRINT"ENTER NUMBER OF OCCUPANTS"
130 FOR I=1 TO X
140 PRINT"HOUSEHOLD #";I;"=";
150 LOCATE ,18
160 INPUT "  ",H(I)
170 NEXT I
180 PRINT "ANY DATA ELEMENT ENTERED INCORRECTLY -Y/N "
190 A$=INKEY$:IF A$="N" THEN 250
200 IF A$<> "Y" THEN 190
210 INPUT "WHICH HOUSEHOLD DO YOU WISH TO CHANGE ",C
220 INPUT "ENTER NEW VALUE ",H(C)
230 PRINT "MORE CORRECTIONS -Y/N "
240 GOTO 190
250 REM start computations
```

```
260 S=0
270 FOR I=1 TO X
280 S=S+H(I)
290 NEXT I
300 M=S/X        'mean
310 S=0
320 FOR I=1 TO X
330 S=S+(H(I)-M)^2
340 NEXT I
350 D=SQR(S/(X-1))      'standard deviation
360 V=D*D               'variance
370 CV=(D/M)*100        'coefficient of variation
380 CLS
390 PRINT "RESULTS BASED UPON SURVEY OF ";X;" HOUSEHOLDS"
400 PRINT
410 PRINT "MEAN= ";M
420 PRINT "STANDARD DEVIATION = ";D
430 PRINT "VARIANCE= ";V
440 PRINT "COEFFICIENT OF VARIATION= ";CV
```

The result from the execution of the previously developed program follows. Here, 10 households were surveyed and the data elements 3, 2, 7, 1, 4, 6, 2, 1, 4, and 2 were entered into the program to obtain the noted results.

```
RESULTS BASED UPON SURVEY OF 10 HOUSEHOLDS

MEAN= 3.2
STANDARD DEVIATION= 2.043961
VARIANCE= 4.177778
COEFFICIENT OF VARIATION= 63.87379
Ok
```

Sorting

To conclude this discussion of arrays, look at how you can sort data items by using a very simple and easy to implement technique known as the bubble sort. This is an exchange type of sort, where you can bring items into an ordered sequence by exchanging the positions of items that are out of order. To see how this sort works, examine a list of numbers, such as

27   18   71   43   22

Begin the sort by first looking at the initial two data elements, 27 and 18. Because they are out of order, you must transpose them, so the list of numbers becomes:

18   27   71   43   22

Next, compare the second and third numbers. Since they are not out of order, you do not need to transpose them. The next pair of data elements, 71 and 43, are out of order, so you will have to transpose them, resulting in the list:

18   27   43   71   22

When the last two data elements are transposed, the list becomes:

18   27   43   22   71

Note that the largest value in the list was moved to the end of the list. After one compare-and-exchange pass the list order has improved, but it is not completely in order. You will need to use two more compare-and-exchange passes, first switching 43 and 22 and then switching 27 and 22, to get the list in order sequence. You can write a program segment using arrays to perform this type of sorting procedure by using the following program statements:

LIST
```
100 INPUT "DATA ELEMENTS TO BE SORTED ";N
110 DIM A(N)
120 PRINT "ENTER THE VALUE OF EACH ELEMENT IN ANY ORDER"
130 FOR I=1 TO N
140 INPUT "";A(I)
150 NEXT I
160 FLAG=0
170 FOR I=1 TO N-1
180 IF A(I)<=A(I+1) THEN 230
190 TEMP=A(I)
200 A(I)=A(I+1)
210 A(I+1)=TEMP
220 FLAG=1
230 NEXT I
240 IF FLAG=1 THEN 160
250 FOR I=1 TO N
260 PRINT A(I);
270 NEXT I
Ok
```

After the data elements are entered, the variable FLAG is set to 0 in line 160. This variable will be used to determine whether any exchanges resulted from a compare-and-exchange pass. When an exchange occurred, the FLAG variable will be set to 1 in line 220. At the completion of the pass, the value of FLAG will be 1 if an exchange occurred and the program will continue its compare-and-exchange passes until it does not make an exchange during a pass. This will signify that the data items are in sequence. Line 180 compares the Ith and I+1 data elements. If they are out of order, lines 190 and 210 will exchange them. The variable TEMP used in lines 190 and 210 is a dummy variable that is used when A(I) is exchanged with A(I+1). The use of this variable permits the program to set the value of A(I+1) to the previous value of A(I). Although a dummy variable was used to permit the interchange of values, you could simplify programming by using the SWAP statement, whose format is

format: SWAP var_1, var_2

This statement provides a convenient mechanism to exchange the values of two variables. If you anticipate converting your program to run on a machine whose BASIC language does not contain a SWAP statement, you should use a dummy variable for data exchange. Otherwise, the SWAP statement will enable you to replace three statements by that statement. Thus, the statement

```
190 SWAP A(I),A(I+1)
```

would replace lines 190 through 210 in the previous example. The execution of this bubble sort program with 15 data values follows:

```
RUN
DATA ELEMENTS TO BE SORTED ? 15
ENTER THE VALUE OF EACH ELEMENT IN ANY ORDER
? 165
? 231
? 2
? 12
? 43
? 198
? 321
? 777
? 317
? 1
? 128
? 587
? 912
? 326
? 876
 1 2 12 43 128 165 198 231 317 321 326 587 777 876 912
Ok
```

To sort in descending sequence instead of ascending sequence can be accomplished by changing line 180, as follows:

```
180 IF (I)>=A(I+1) THEN 230
```

The result of executing this one character change to the preceding program with five sample data elements follows. It would be a simple matter to incorporate both ascending and descending sorting into a routine, selecting the sorting method to perform based on user input or the status of a variable within the program:

```
RUN
DATA ELEMENTS TO BE SORTED ? 5
ENTER THE VALUE OF EACH ELEMENT IN ANY ORDER
? 21
? 1
? 43
? 12
? 37
 43 37 21 12 1
Ok
```

Formatted Display and Printing

Both interpretive BASIC and QuickBASIC contain two statements you can use to output a list of items to the printer or to the display according to a predefined format. The LPRINT USING statement provides the capability to print strings or numbers in a specified format on the printer. The PRINT USING statement provides the same capability for output on the display.

PRINT USING Statement

The format of the PRINT USING statement is

format: PRINT USING var$;exprlist[;]

Here, the string variable, *var$*, contains the formatting characters that define the fields and formats of strings or numbers in the list of expressions to be printed on the screen. When this statement is executed, each specification in the format string (*var$*) is extracted and examined. If the specification calls for a string or a numeric value, the list of expressions will be examined for a corresponding expression. If the specification calls for the display of a string constant embedded in the format string, that string constant will be printed. Each expression in the list of expressions will be printed on the display according to its corresponding specification in the format string. However, if the expression and specification are not of the same type, an error will result and the program will terminate. Thus, string specifications in the format must be used to print string expressions, whereas numeric specifications must be used to print numeric expressions.

Table 11.1 lists the numeric and string formatting characters that can be used to format string and numeric fields. To examine the use of these special characters, create and execute several program segments. Several simple examples will be presented first, and additional formatting characters will gradually be incorporated to illustrate the numerous formatting variations you can develop.

By using the pound (#) and decimal point (.) characters, you can specify integer or floating point formats for the display of numeric information. Suppose you wish to print the values of the variables A and B, allocating six positions to the left of the decimal point and two positions to the right of the decimal point for A and five integer positions for the variable B. Further suppose you wish to separate the printing of the value of each variable by two character positions. The print image you then wish to use would be

####.## #####

	Character	Use
Table 11.1 Numeric and String Formatting Characters	**Numeric**	
	#	Represents each digit position
	.	Represents the decimal point location
	+	Causes the sign of the number to be displayed
	−	Causes negative numbers to be printed with a trailing minus sign
	**	Causes leading spaces to be asterisk filled
	$$	Causes a dollar sign to be floated to the left of the formatted number
	**$	Causes leading spaces to be asterisk filled and the dollar sign to float to the left of the formatted number
	,	Causes a comma to be printed to the left of every third digit to the left of the decimal point
	^ ^ ^ ^	When placed after the digit position characters, it specifies exponential format
	_	Underscore causes the next character to be output as a literal character
	String fields	Causes the first character in the given string to be printed
	!	
	\n spaces\	Causes 2+n characters from the string to be printed
	&	Causes the string to be output exactly as input

Your PRINT USING statement would then become

```
PRINT USING "####.##  #####";A,B
```

The execution of the following two program lines illustrates the result obtained from incorporating the image within the string variable to represent the format to be followed:

```
100 A=1473.12:B=1056
110 PRINT USING "####.##  #####";A,B
RUN
1473.12  1056
Ok
```

Note that the execution of line 110 causes the display of the value of the variable labeled A to occur in columns 1 through 7. Suppose you wish the value of A to be displayed starting at column 11. You could change line 110 as follows:

```
110 PRINT USING "            ####.##  #####";A,B
```

Here, you simply changed the image to reflect your desire to have 10 spaces prior to printing the value of the first variable in the list. Although you could continue to add blanks into the image to shift the beginning of the display of the value of variable A further to the right, it is very easy to make a mistake in entering a large number of blank characters. A far easier method is to use a LOCATE statement prior to the PRINT USING statement to position the cursor to the location where you want the first image to occur. Thus, the pair of statements

```
105 LOCATE 10,11
110 PRINT USING "####.##  #####";A,B
```

would first locate the cursor at row 10, column 11, and then commence displaying the values of A and B according to the format contained in the string. Now suppose you wish to display the value of A commencing in column 11 and B in column 41. You could insert an appropriate number of blanks in the format between the two variables or you could use two PRINT USING statements linked together by a semicolon (;) at the end of the first statement. Here, the semicolon signifies that printing should occur on the same line. Thus, consider the execution results of the following program segment.

```
LIST
10 A=1234.56
20 B=9876
30 LOCATE 10,11
40 PRINT USING "####.##";A;
50 LOCATE 10,41
60 PRINT USING "#####";B
Ok
RUN
        1234.56                        9876
Ok
```

Here, the LOCATE statement in line 30 positions the cursor to row 10, column 11. The PRINT USING statement in line 40 displays the value of A according to the format in the string of that statement. The LOCATE statement in line 50 moves the cursor to column 41 of row 10, where the following PRINT USING statement will display the value of B according to the format in the string of this statement.

The format in the formatting string will be repeated if additional variables are in the list of expressions that you wish to display in the same format. This is illustrated by the following example.

```
LIST
110 PRINT USING "####.##";-555,111,9222,-777
RUN
-555.00  111.009222.00-777.00
Ok
```

When you use one format string for multiple displays of a sequence of values, you should insert spaces at the end of the format string. This will separate the printed values on the line, as illustrated by the next example:

```
LIST
110 PRINT USING "####.##    ";-555,111,9222,-777
RUN
-555.00    111.00    9222.00    -777.00
Ok
```

Now that you have some idea concerning how you can position formatted data, return to your initial formatting example to ascertain what happens if the value of the variable to be displayed exceeds the specified field size. Change the values of A and B as follows:

```
100 A=12345.6789:B=-987654321
110 PRINT USING "####.##  #####";A,B
RUN
%12345.68  %-987654400
Ok
```

Note that a percent sign (%) was printed in front of each number. This serves to indicate that the value of a variable overflowed or underflowed the format.

For the variable labeled A, note that five positions to the left of the decimal point were printed even though only four positions were in the field image. Unlike other BASICs, AT BASIC will automatically extend the print image; however, it will also print the percent sign (%) to indicate an overflow or underflow occurred. Also note that the decimal portion of A was rounded from .6789 to .68 on the printout.

The largest stored integer value is seven digits, so considerable rounding will occur when the value of B is displayed; however, note that the integer image is also automatically expanded by BASIC. When you work with extremely large or small numbers, you should convert those numbers to double precision prior to their output.

The next example shows how this can increase the accuracy of the integer part of the number to be displayed. Note that unless you add additional positions to the fractional part of an image, the fractional accuracy will not improve.

```
100 A#=12345.6789:B#=-987654321
110 PRINT USING "####.##  #####";A#,B#
RUN
%12345.68  %-987654321
Ok
```

Plus and Minus Format Characters

You can use a plus sign at either the beginning or the end of a format string. The use of this sign will result in the sign of the number (plus or minus) being displayed before or after the number. The next two examples illustrate the use of this format character:

```
LIST
100 A=106.42:B=73
110 PRINT USING "+####.##  #####+";A,B
Ok
RUN
 +106.42    73+
Ok

LIST
100 A=-51.81:B=-77.77:C=8.7:D=-.1
110 PRINT USING "+####.##    ";A,B,C,D
Ok
RUN
 -51.81     -77.77     +8.70     -0.10
Ok
```

In the second example, note that if the format string specifies that a digit is to precede the decimal point, the digit will always be printed, even if zero in value. Thus, although D was assigned the value −.1 it was displayed as −0.10 due to the format image used.

You can use a minus sign at the end of a format field to cause negative numbers to be displayed with a trailing minus sign. This is shown by the next two examples:

```
LIST
100 A=-51.81:B=-77.77:C=8.7:D=-.1
110 PRINT USING "####.##-   ";A,B,C,D
Ok
RUN
 51.81-    77.77-    8.70    0.10-
Ok

LIST
100 A=-51.81:B=-77.77:C=8.7:D=-.1
110 PRINT USING "A= ####.## B= ####.## C= ####.## D= ####.##";A,B,C,D
RUN
A=  -51.81 B=  -77.77 C=    8.70 D=   -0.10
```

Note that the second example included four strings (A=, B=, C=, and D=). These strings were placed within the string variable used to define the formats used in displaying the variables in the list of expressions. You can incorporate strings within any string variable used to define formatted output. The feature provides a mechanism to label formatted output. The execution of the following program segment illustrates how you can use this capability more fully:

```
LIST
100 INPUT "ENTER FEDERAL STATE AND LOCAL TAX RATES ";F,S,L
110 INPUT "ENTER YIELD OF TAX FREE SECURITY ";Y
120 CTAX=F+(1-F)*(S+L)
```

```
125 TEY=Y/(1-CTAX)
130 PRINT
140 PRINT USING "TAX EQUIVALENT YIELD = ##.#### ";TEY
150 PRINT "BASED UPON"
160 PRINT USING "TAX RATES OF .## FEDERAL .## STATE AND .## LOCAL";F,S,L
Ok
```
RUN
```
ENTER FEDERAL STATE AND LOCAL TAX RATES ? .50,.06,.02
ENTER YIELD OF TAX FREE SECURITY ? .12

TAX EQUIVALENT YIELD = 0.2609
BASED UPON
TAX RATES OF .50 FEDERAL .06 STATE AND .02 LOCAL
Ok
```

Double-Asterisk Format Characters

You can use a double asterisk at the beginning of a formatted numeric field to fill all leading spaces in that field with asterisks. When you use a double asterisk, the double stars (**) also specify two additional digit positions. Thus, **###.## defines a numeric field of eight character positions, which will display a number between −9999.99 and 99999.99 without an overflow or underflow notation and will fill any leading spaces in the field with asterisks. The next example illustrates the use of this pair of formatting characters:

```
100 A=12345.67 :B=999: C=-.51 :D=-5.1
110 PRINT USING "**####.## ";A,B,C,D
```
RUN
```
*12345.67 ***999.00 ****-0.51 ****-5.10
Ok
```

Double Dollar-Sign Format Characters

Another pair of characters you can use at the beginning of a numeric field is the double dollar sign ($$). The double dollar sign causes a dollar sign to be floated to the left of the formatted number. Like the double asterisk, the double dollar sign specifies two additional digit positions; however, one of the positions will be used to print the dollar sign. Thus, the format $$###.## can be used to display a maximum value of 9999.99 without an overflow occurring. If you have negative numbers in a field prefixed by the double dollar sign, the negative sign will appear before the floated dollar sign. You can also use a trailing minus sign to print negative values to the right of the displayed number. The following examples illustrate several uses of the double dollar sign in numeric fields:

```
100 A=12345.67 :B=999: C=-.51 :D=-5.1
110 PRINT USING "$$####.## ";A,B,C,D
```
RUN
```
$12345.67    $999.00     -$0.51     -$5.10
Ok
```
LIST
```
100 A=12345.67 :B=999: C=-.51 :D=-5.1
110 PRINT USING "$$####.##-";A,B,C,D
```
RUN

```
$12345.67    $999.00      $0.51-   $5.10-
Ok
```

LIST
```
10 X$="GILBERT HELD"
20 PAY=87.75
30 LOCATE 15,5
40 PRINT "PAY TO THE ORDER OF ";X$;
50 X=LEN(X$)+5
60 LOCATE 15,X+20
70 PRINT USING " EXACTLY $$########.##";PAY
Ok
```
RUN
```
PAY TO THE ORDER OF GILBERT HELD EXACTLY $87.75
Ok
```

Double-Asterisk Single Dollar-Sign Format Characters

You can combine the effect of the double asterisk and double dollar sign by using the three-character combination **$ at the beginning of a numeric format field. This three-character sequence fills leading spaces with asterisks and prints the dollar sign to the left of the number. When used in a numeric field format, this three-character sequence specifies three digit positions, one of which will be used to display the dollar sign. The following example illustrates the use of this three-character sequence within numeric format fields:

```
100 A=10.53 :B=987.65 :C=-102.45
110 PRINT USING "**$########.## ";A,B,C
RUN
*******$10.53 ******$987.65 ******-$102.45
Ok

100 A=10.53 :B=987.6499 :C=-102.45
110 PRINT USING "**$########.##-";A,B,C
RUN
********10.53 *******$987.65 *******$102.45-
Ok
```

Note that the largest numeric value that can be displayed without an overflow by the previous examples is 99999999.99, because one position will always be used to display the dollar sign.

Comma Format Character

You can use a comma to the left of the decimal point in numeric format fields to automatically generate a comma to the left of every third digit to the left of the decimal point. The comma itself signifies an additional digit position within the numeric format field. Thus, the format #####,.## could be used to display a variable with a maximum value of 999999.99 without creating an overflow. This format would result in the number being displayed as 999,999.99. One example of the use of the comma in numeric field format is

LIST

```
100 NATDEBT#=123456789098765.4#
110 PRINT USING "NATIONAL DEBT #################,.##";NATDEBT#
Ok
```
RUN
```
NATIONAL DEBT 123,456,789,098,765.40
Ok
```

You can combine the three character sequence **$ with the comma preceding the decimal point in a numeric field format. This combination enables you to obtain the display of variables in financial notation used most commonly in printing checks. The following example shows the use of this combination of formatting characters:

LIST
```
100 NETPAY=1873.42
110 PRINT USING "PAY EXACTLY **$#######,.##";NETPAY
Ok
```
RUN
```
PAY EXACTLY *****$1,873.42
Ok
```

Underscore Format Character

The underscore character can also be used in a numeric field format. When used, it will result in the following character being displayed as a literal character. The following examples illustrate the use of the underscore in numeric field formats as well as the use of some conventional characters in the print image:

LIST
```
100 A=37.5:B=9.8:C=-153.14
110 PRINT USING " _!####.## ";A,B,C
120 PRINT USING " A####.## ";A,B,C
130 PRINT USING " %####.## ";A,B,C
140 PRINT USING " !####.## ";A,B,C
Ok
```
RUN
```
 !  37.50   !   9.80   !-153.14
 A  37.50   A   9.80   A-153.14
 %  37.50   %   9.80   %-153.14

Type mismatch in 140
Ok
```

Note that the underscore character in line 110 resulted in the exclamation point being printed at the beginning of each of the print fields resulting from the execution of that line. In lines 120 and 130, the characters A and percent (%) were used without an underscore prefix, and they were displayed in the beginning of each field. This shows that you can avoid using the underscore character many times when you desire to print a literal.

There are, however, some characters such as the exclamation point that must be prefixed by a literal or a type mismatch error will occur. This is because such characters are themselves format specifier characters. This is shown by the execution of line 140. Thus, when in doubt use the underscore character to prefix the literal you wish to display.

Caret Format Characters

The last special character to be covered in formatted numeric fields is the caret (^). In formatted numeric fields you can use four carets (^ ^ ^ ^) after the digit position to specify exponential notation. The four carets provide a display image for the exponent E±nn or D±nn to be printed. When four carets are used, the significant digits (mantissa) of the number will be displayed left justified and the exponent will be adjusted accordingly.

An example of the use of this format specifier is shown here:

LIST
```
100 A=14325467#: B=-98765432#
110 PRINT USING "A= ##.###^ ^ ^ ^";A
120 PRINT USING "B=###.#######^ ^ ^ ^";B
Ok
```
RUN
```
A= 1.433E+07
B=-98.7654300E+06
Ok
```

Note that one digit position will be used to the left of the decimal point to print a space or minus sign unless a leading or trailing + or − is specified.

Unlike the diversity of numeric formatting characters, there are only three string formatting characters you must master.

Exclamation Format Character

The exclamation character (!) in a string field format specifies that only the first character in a given string should be displayed. The use of this formatting character is illustrated in the following example:

```
100 A$="GILBERT"
110 B$="HELD"
120 PRINT USING "INITIALS !.!.";A$,B$
```
RUN
```
INITIALS G.H.
Ok
```

Backslash Format Character

The backslash character, which specifies integer division in arithmetic operations, can be employed as a pair of formatting characters to specify the display of a number of characters from a string. If typed without a space between the pair of characters, two characters will be displayed from the string starting at the left. If n spaces are enclosed by the backslashes, 2+n characters will be displayed from the string. The use of this string format specifier is shown in the following example:

LIST
```
100 A$="GILBERT"
110 B$="BEVERLY"
120 PRINT USING "\ \+\ \ ";A$,B$
140 PRINT USING "\ \ ";A$
Ok
```
RUN

```
GIL+BEVE
GIL
Ok
```

Ampersand Sign Format Character

The last string format specifier is the ampersand sign (&) character. The use of this character in a string field format specifies that the field will be of variable length. That is, the string to be displayed will be output exactly as it is stored in memory. This is shown by the following example:

LIST
```
100 A$="GILBERT"
110 B$="BEVERLY"
120 PRINT USING "PLEASE PAY YOUR DUES &";A$
140 PRINT USING "OR WE WILL RUB OUT YOUR &";B$
Ok
```
RUN
```
PLEASE PAY YOUR DUES GILBERT
OR WE WILL RUB OUT YOUR BEVERLY
Ok
```

A portion of a program previously developed for a lease versus purchase analysis will be used to show the effectiveness of combining the LOCATE and PRINT USING statements to obtain a professional display of computational results that is suitable for a report. In this example, lines 20 and 30 were used to generate values so the program segment could be executed with data for illustrative purposes. The statements used to generate the display follow:

```
10 CLS
20 C2=150000!:EX=10000:T=.5:FYE=5000:B=150000!:T1=.1:C3=15000:S=30000
30 TADJ=50000!:NCOST=100000!
40 LOCATE 2,27
50 PRINT"NET COST OF OWNERSHIP"
60 LOCATE 4,10
70 PRINT USING"PURCHASE PRICE                              ##########.##";C2
80 LOCATE 6,10
90 PRINT"LESS ADJUSTMENTS"
100 LOCATE 8,10
110 PRINT USING"FIRST YEAR EXPENSING  ########.##";EX
120 LOCATE 9,10
130 PRINT USING"TIMES TAX RATE                .##  = ########.##";T,FYE
140 LOCATE 11,10
150 PRINT"INVESTMENT TAX CREDIT"
160 LOCATE 12,10
170 PRINT USING"BASE                  ########.##";B
180 LOCATE 13,10
190 PRINT USING"TIMES ITC RATE                #.### = ########.##";T1,C3
200 LOCATE 15,10
210 PRINT USING"PRESENT VALUE OF CASH FLOWS    ###########.##";S
220 LOCATE 17,10
230 PRINT USING"TOTAL ADJUSTMENTS              ###########.##";TADJ
```

```
240 LOCATE 19,10
250 PRINT USING"NET PRESENT VALUE COST OF OWNERSHIP        ##############";NCOST
```

Note that the PRINT USING statements in the program segment contained many strings that were used to label the resulting output and specify how computation results occurred. This is illustrated by the execution of the program segment.

```
              NET COST OF OWNERSHIP
    PURCHASE PRICE=                             150000.00
    LESS ADJUSTMENTS
    FIRST YEAR EXPENSING      10000.00
    TIMES TAX RATE                0.50  =    5000.00
    INVESTMENT TAX CREDIT
    BASE                     150000.00
    TIMES ITC RATE                0.100 =   15000.00
    PRESENT VALUE OF CASH FLOWS            30000.00
    TOTAL ADJUSTMENTS                      50000.00
    NET PRESENT VALUE COST OF OWNERSHIP=        100000.00
    Ok
```

LPRINT USING Statement

The LPRINT USING statement provides the capability to print formatted data on the printer. The format of this statement is

format: LPRINT USING *var$;exprlist*[;]

The LPRINT USING statement functions similarly to the PRINT USING statement, except that formatted output is directed to the printer instead of the display. All formatting characters applicable to the PRINT USING statement can be used in exactly the same manner with this statement.

Date and Time Processing

Included in both interpretive BASIC and QuickBASIC are date and time statements and functions. As statements, they permit you to set the date and time internally from within a program or in a direct mode operation. When used as a function, they provide a mechanism to retrieve the current date or time.

DATE$ Statement and Function

When DATE$ is used as a statement, you can set the date in the computer to the value indicated. The format of this statement is

format: DATE$=*var$*

Here, the string variable may be in any one of the following forms:

mm-dd-yy
mm/dd/yy
mm-dd-yyyy
mm/dd/yyyy

The year (yy or yyyy) must be in the range 1980 to 2099. If only two digits are used, then the year is assumed to be 19yy. If only one digit is used for the year, a zero will be automatically appended to make it into two digits. If only one digit is used for the month or day, a leading zero (0) will be assigned in front of the digit.

When DATE$ is used as a function, you can retrieve the current date. Here, the format is

format: *var*$=DATE$

where the function will retrieve a 10-character string, since the year will always be stored internally as yyyy regardless of the method used to set the date. The following example illustrates how you can set and retrieve the date under program control:

```
Ok
LIST
100 DATE$="10/20/85"
110 X$=DATE$:PRINT X$
120 DATE$="6-18-1985"
130 PRINT DATE$
140 DATE$="4-4-85"
150 PRINT DATE$
Ok
RUN
10-20-1985
06-18-1985
04-04-1985
Ok
```

Because DATE$ is a string function, you must develop a string manipulation and numeric conversion routine if you wish to use the numeric value of the date in a program. With the date stored internally as:

m	m	X	d	d	X	y	y	y	y

where X denotes the position of the delimiter [dash (–) or slash (/)]. As an example, if you wish to obtain the numeric value of the month, you must extract the fourth and fifth characters from the DATE$ string and convert that extracted two-character sequence into a numeric value. You can use the MID$ function to return the desired part of the DATE$ string and then use the VAL function to return the numerical value of the part you extracted. The following example illustrates the use of these two functions.

```
100 DATE$="6/17/85"
110 DAY$=MID$(DATE$,4,2) 'get 2 characters, beginning at 4th character
120 DAY=VAL(DAY$) 'convert to numeric value
130 PRINT "DAY IS ";DAY
140 TOGO=30-DAY 'now we can use it in a numeric computation
150 PRINT TOGO;" DAYS TILL PAYDAY"
RUN
DAY IS 17
 13 DAYS TILL PAYDAY
Ok
```

In this example, note that, although the date was set as 6/17/85, the day is stored internally in the fourth and fifth character positions of the string. Thus, you have to use the MID$ function to extract two characters, starting at the fourth character position in DATE$.

TIME$ Statement and Function

Similar to DATE$, TIME$ can be used as a statement or as a function. When used as a statement, it provides the ability to set the current time. The format for use in a statement is

format: TIME$=*var$*

Here, the string variable can be provided in any one of the following forms:

hh	Sets the hour (0 to 23); minutes and seconds initialized to 00 (double zero)
hh:mm	Sets both the hour and minutes; minutes must be in the range of 0 to 59; seconds are initialized to 00 (double zero)
hh:mm:ss	Sets the hour, minutes, and seconds; seconds must be in the range 0 to 59

No matter the form used to set the time, it will be stored internally as an eight-character string. The storage positions include the two field delimiter characters, as indicated:

h h : m m : s s

To retrieve the time, use TIME$ as a function. The format when used as a function is

format: *var$*=TIME$

The time will be returned as an eight-character string of the form hh:mm:ss. To manipulate the time as a numeric quantity will require you to extract the hours, minutes, and seconds from the string and convert them to numeric values. The following program segment illustrates how you can use the TIME$ statement and function to determine the amount of time required to execute a program loop of 10,000 iterations.

```
LIST
100 TIME$="00"              'initialize clock to zero
110 FOR I=1 TO 10000  :NEXT I
120 X$=TIME$
130 HR$=MID$(X$,1,2)        'get hours
140 HR=VAL(HR$)
150 MM$=MID$(X$,4,2)        'get minutes
160 MM=VAL(MM$)
170 SS$=MID$(X$,7,2)        'get seconds
180 SS=VAL(SS$)
190 PRINT "ELAPSED TIME =";HR;":";MM;":";SS
Ok
RUN
ELAPSED TIME = 0 : 0 : 12
Ok
```

Subroutine Interrupts and Event Trapping

One of the most useful features of both interpretive BASIC and QuickBASIC is the ability to suspend program execution to service an external interrupt before you resume execution of the program. In comparison to other microcomputer-based systems that require programming at the assembly language level to obtain this capability, each version of BASIC covered in this book contains several subroutine statements that allow you to process interrupts in the BASIC language. The general form of these statements is

$$\text{format: ON } \textit{event} \text{ GOSUB} \begin{Bmatrix} \textit{line} \\ \textit{label}^1 \end{Bmatrix}$$

where the event is caused by communications, function or cursor control key, light pen, or joystick activity. The line is the beginning line number of a BASIC subroutine that the program will branch to when the appropriate event occurs. If you are using QuickBASIC, you can specify either a line number or label as the branch location. For the branch to occur, the subroutine interrupt statement must be activated. This can be accomplished by the use of a series of BASIC statements that activates their associated subroutine interrupts. Similarly, a series of statements are contained in BASIC that can be used to deactivate subroutine interrupts. The use of these statements governs the ability of a program to respond to certain events that may or may not occur while the program is executed. In discussing subroutine interrupts, attention will be focused on function and cursor control keys, the light pen, and the joystick buttons.

Function and Cursor Control Keys

The format of the subroutine interrupt that establishes a program line number for BASIC to branch to when the specified key is pressed is

$$\text{format: ON KEY } (\textit{exprnm}) \text{GOSUB} \begin{Bmatrix} \textit{line} \\ \textit{label}^1 \end{Bmatrix}$$

The numeric expression, *exprnm*, must be in the range of 1 to 31 and indicates the key to be trapped as follows:

1–10	Function keys F1 to F10
11	Cursor up
12	Cursor left
13	Cursor right
14	Cursor down
15–25	Keys defined by the form KEY n,CHR\$(shift)+CHR\$(*scan code*)
30	The F11 function key[2]
31	The F12 function key[2]

To activate the subroutine requires a KEY(*exprnm*)ON statement to be executed in the program. Once such a statement is executed, the indicated function and cursor

[1]Applicable only to QuickBASIC.
[2]Applicable to the 101-key keyboard only.

control key subroutine interrupt will cause the program to branch to the indicated line or label if the specified key is pressed. Thus, the KEY(*exprnm*)ON statement activates the subroutine interrupt, whereas the ON KEY(*exprnm*)GOSUB line or GOSUB label statement causes the actual interrupt to occur. You can disable trapping of the specified key by using 0 as the line number in the ON KEY statement.

BASIC contains three KEY statements whose formats are

```
format: KEY(exprnm)ON
format: KEY(exprnm)OFF
format: KEY(exprnm)STOP
```

Similar to the ON KEY statement, the numeric expression must be in the range of 1 to 31 and indicates the specific function, cursor control key, or specially defined key to be operated on. Once a KEY(*exprnm*)ON statement is executed, every time BASIC attempts to execute a new statement, it will check to see if the specified key was pressed. If it was, the program will perform a subroutine interrupt to the line number specified in the ON KEY statement.

The KEY(*exprnm*)OFF statement disables event trapping and a subroutine interrupt will not occur even if the event takes place.

The KEY(*exprnm*)STOP statement can be used to temporarily suspend event trapping, since the event will be remembered and a subsequent KEY(*exprnm*)ON statement will cause the subroutine interrupt to take place based on the first key pressed after the KEY(*exprnm*)STOP statement was executed. Thus, the KEY(*exprnm*)STOP statement enables you to suspend event trapping to process the results obtained from servicing one subroutine interrupt without a second event being able to disrupt your processing action. When the actual subroutine branch occurs, an automatic KEY(*exprnm*)STOP is generated by BASIC to preclude recursive traps. In addition, the RETURN from the subroutine will automatically cause a KEY(*exprnm*)ON to be executed, unless a KEY(*exprnm*)OFF was performed inside the interrupt routine. Thus, you will normally use a KEY(*exprnm*)STOP statement outside of the subroutine if you wish to perform additional processing after the RETURN but prior to allowing additional interrupts to be processed. The following program segment illustrates the use of several KEY(*exprnm*) and ON KEY(*exprnm*) statements.

```
4000 KEY OFF
4010 LOCATE 25,10
4020 PRINT "F1=SORT F2=PRINT REPORT"
4030 KEY(1) ON
4040 KEY(2) ON
4050 ON KEY(1) GOSUB 5000
4060 ON KEY(2) GOSUB 6000
4070 REM continue processing
  .
  .
  .
5000 REM sort routine
5010 KEY(1) OFF:KEY(2) OFF
  .
  .
  .
```

```
5990 RETURN
6000 REM print report routine
6010 KEY(1) OFF:KEY(2) OFF
  .
  .
  .
6990 RETURN
```

In this example, the F1 and F2 keys are used to invoke a sort routine (F1) and a report printing routine (F2). Note that after the sort keys are turned off (line 4000) the message F1=SORT F2=PRINT REPORT is displayed on the 25th line to inform the operator of the use of these keys. Lines 4030 and 4040 activate the subroutine interrupts in lines 4050 and 4060. In each subroutine, both KEY(1) and KEY(2) are purposely turned off to prevent the operator from interrupting the invocation of one subroutine by pressing another of the activated keys. Now, modify and execute the preceding example to see how you can associate a key with predefined functions that will be invoked when the appropriate key is pressed. First, add a continuous loop to the program segment to represent the processing of an application. This loop is accomplished by the statement in line 4080. Next, add two PRINT statements, one in line 5020 and one in line 6020 that will be executed when the appropriate function keys are pressed. Thus, once the program is executed, pressing the F1 function key will cause a subroutine interrupt to line 5000, while pressing F2 will cause a subroutine interrupt to line 6000. Note that the RETURN statements in lines 5990 and 6990 were changed to RETURN 4030. Thus, once the subroutine is completed, the function keys are again enabled. The listing of this program segment follows.

LIST
```
4000 KEY OFF
4010 LOCATE 25,10
4020 PRINT "F1=SORT F2=PRINT REPORT"
4030 KEY(1) ON
4040 KEY(2) ON
4050 ON KEY(1) GOSUB 5000
4060 ON KEY(2) GOSUB 6000
4070 REM continue processing
4080 GOTO 4080
5000 REM sort routine
5010 KEY(1) OFF:KEY(2) OFF
5020 PRINT "F1 KEY GETS US HERE"
5990 RETURN 4030
6000 REM print report routine
6010 KEY(1) OFF:KEY(2) OFF
6020 PRINT "F2 KEY GETS US HERE"
6990 RETURN 4030
Ok
```

Now, run the program. First the soft keys will be turned off, and the message telling you the new meaning of the F1 and F2 keys will be displayed on the twenty-fifth line of the screen. Then, nothing will happen as the program goes into an infinite loop in line 4080. If you press the F1 or F2 keys, subroutine interrupt will occur to line 5000 or 6000, depending on the key that was pressed. If you typed this program into your computer and pressed the F1 key, the message F1 KEY GETS US HERE will be displayed, because we added line 5020 to the program to visually ascertain that pressing that key will cause a subroutine interrupt to line 5000. Similarly, the message F2 KEY GETS US HERE will be displayed when the F2 key is pressed. The execution of this program followed by pressing the F1 and F2 keys in the sequence F1, F2, F2, F1, is shown here:

```
RUN

F1 KEY GETS US HERE
F2 KEY GETS US HERE
F2 KEY GETS US HERE
F1 KEY GETS US HERE

     F1=SORT F2=PRINT REPORT
```

As shown, subroutine interrupts provide the ability to greatly simplify operator interaction with the PC AT. You can write a program that could perform assorted functions based on the operator pressing certain keys that have been predefined to result in subroutine interrupts to the appropriate statements to perform those functions.

Time

You can use the TIMER function in BASIC in conjunction with the ON-GOSUB statement to effect an event trap based on a transpired period of time. Examples of time trapping can include allocating a period of time for persons to respond to questions or using event trapping to update the time display on a user's screen.

Similar to key trapping, there are three TIMER statements associated with time related trapping whose formats are

```
format: TIMER ON
format: TIMER OFF
format: TIMER STOP
```

The TIMER ON statement enables TIMER event trapping; TIMER OFF disables TIMER event trapping. The TIMER STOP statement suspends TIMER event trapping. However, BASIC continues to detect the event, resulting in a subsequent TIMER ON statement causing a branch to immediately occur to the event if the event occurred during the time it was suspended.

To illustrate the use of event trapping by time, consider the following program segment:

```
1 ON TIMER(1) GOSUB 100
2 TIMER ON
3 GOTO 3
100 ROW=CSRLIN
101 COL=POS(0)
102 LOCATE 25,1
103 PRINT TIME$
105 LOCATE ROW,COL
106 RETURN
```

In line 1 the TIMER function has a value of 1 second, in effect causing a branch to the subroutine located at line 100 to occur once every second after the TIMER ON statement in line 2 is executed. Line 3 simply causes an infinite loop to illustrate that the time event trapping routine will work even when a program is processing information.

Assuming you want your subroutine to display the time in the lower left corner of the display, you must reposition the cursor. To ensure that this does not adversely affect the main program, first obtain the column and row of the cursor in lines 100 and 101 prior to using the LOCATE statement in line 102 to reposition the cursor to display the time. Once the time is displayed use the LOCATE statement in line 105 to reposition the cursor in its original location.

12 // Data File Operations

This chapter focuses on the use of BASIC to perform data file operations. Once again, the chapter collectively refers to QBASIC and QuickBASIC as QuickBASIC to denote the common statements in both versions of this language. After giving an overview of the types of files supported by interpretive BASIC and QuickBASIC, the chapter discusses the operation and use of file-related statements. Once you have reviewed a group of file-related statements, you will create several short but practical programs to demonstrate BASIC language file-processing techniques.

File Structures

Interpretive BASIC supports two types of files: sequential files and random-access files, whereas QuickBASIC adds support for binary file processing. Sequential files, as the name implies, contain data that can only be accessed or written sequentially. Data recorded onto sequential files is stored as ASCII characters, so you can use a word processor or text editor to view or modify the contents of this type of file. You can have sequential files on cassette or disk; hence, all versions of interpretive BASIC support sequential file operations. Cassette BASIC supports sequential operations on cassette, whereas disk and Advanced BASIC support sequential operations on both cassette and diskette. There is no cassette port on the AT and compatible computers, so the coverage of data file operations focuses on disk storage.

Random file access provides the capability to read information from a file or write information to the file without regard for the location of the information. In random-access processing, you will use a pointer that will specify the location from which information is to be read from a file or where it is to be written onto a file. Because only disk storage provides you with the capability to use random-access processing, random-access files are only applicable to disk and advanced interpretive BASIC.

Binary files, which are only supported in QuickBASIC, provide a third method to read or write file information when using that language. Binary files are treated as an unformatted sequence of bytes with access to data similar to random access but with reading and writing of data occurring on a byte-by-byte basis.

File Concepts

A file contains blocks of data known as *records*. Each record may contain one or more fields and each field in turn may contain one or more characters. The field normally represents one distinct piece of information, such as a name, address, telephone number, and so on. Thus, you can view a file as representing a collection of information that may reside on disk. Figure 12.1 illustrates the file structure of a file that could contain information for a program to generate mailing labels. Note that if this is a sequential file, you must read $record_1$ through $record_{i-1}$ to access $record_i$. If this file were a random-access file, you could use a pointer to point directly to $record_i$ to read the information contained on that record directly.

The five fields represent one logical record. When data is actually stored on a disk, it is stored as a physical record. The amount of data stored on one such record will depend on the format you use to output data to the file. Although the file structure in Figure 12.1 shows fields of equal length, in actuality, fields in a sequential file can differ in length between records, which permits each record in a file to have a different length as long as the number of fields in each record remains the same. The key to this capability is the use of field delimiters, such as commas between strings, between numerics, and between a string and a numeric, spaces between two numerics, and the use of a carriage return line feed (CR-LF) sequence to terminate a record. These field delimiters enable you to read a record and have BASIC automatically assign the contents of each field to the list of field names you included in the statement used to read it.

File Numbers

I/O operations performed in BASIC require a file number. This is a unique number that will be associated with the actual file you wish to read data from or write data onto. The file number provides a physical path between subsequent file I/O statements and the file you wish to access. This path is established by the OPEN statement, which is covered later in this chapter. The file number can be a number, variable, or expression. In interpretive BASIC, its value must be equal to or greater than 1 and less than or equal to the maximum number of files permitted to be open at one time in the version of BASIC you are using.

Cassette BASIC permits a maximum of four open files, whereas disk, Advanced BASIC, and GW-BASIC permit a maximum of three open files in the default mode. You can increase the maximum number of open files permitted in disk, Advanced, and GW-BASIC by invoking what is known as the F option in an interpretive BASIC command. The format of this optional parameter is

/F:*files*

where $1 = <files <= 15$.

File MAIL.DAT

	Field$_1$	Field$_2$	Field$_3$	Field$_4$	Field$_5$
Record$_1$	Name$_1$	Address$_1$	City$_1$	State$_1$	Zip$_1$
	⋮	⋮	⋮	⋮	⋮
Record$_N$	Name$_N$	Address$_N$	City$_N$	State$_N$	Zip$_N$

Figure 12.1 Typical File Structure.

When you bring up disk, Advanced, or GW-BASIC, you use the F option to specify the number of OPEN files your program requires that exceed three because, when omitted, the number of files the program can have OPEN at one time defaults to that value. If you require five files, your interpretive BASIC commands would be either of the following:

BASIC/F:5
BASICA/F:5

Because each sequential file requires 188 bytes of memory and random-access files require a minimum of 316 bytes, you should ensure that you do not specify more files in the interpretive BASIC command than necessary. Otherwise, you will remove memory from use by the program that is reserved for files you are not using.

In QuickBASIC the file number can be any integer between 1 and 255 without requiring you to use an option in the command line. In addition to this greater file number flexibility, QuickBASIC contains a unique FREEFILE function that can be used to obtain the next available file number. This function is examined later in the chapter.

Physical and Logical Devices

If you do not have a second diskette drive, in BASIC you can refer to logical device B by using the device identifier B:. When you do so, on executing the first statement in your program that references logical device B, DOS will issue the following prompt:

```
Insert diskette for drive B: and strike
any key when ready
```

Once you insert the appropriate diskette into physical drive A and strike any key on the keyboard, the program will perform its activity that referenced logical drive B on physical drive A.

If your computer is later expanded to include two diskette drives, you will then have two physical drives. Thereafter, any reference in a program statement to logical device B will automatically cause DOS to perform the appropriate action on the diskette in physical drive B.

This chapter includes several examples that illustrate the use of drive B. From the preceding, it should be noted that the actions of these statements will occur on physical drive A unless your computer is expanded to two diskette drives.

Sequential File Statements and Functions

OPEN Statement

The OPEN statement must be used before you insert any I/O statements in a program, because OPEN establishes a path to the file that will be used by subsequent file reference statements. The format of this statement for sequential file operations is

```
format: OPEN filespec[FOR mode₁]AS;[#]filenum
```

where $mode_1$ is

OUTPUT   to specify sequential output mode
INPUT   to specify sequential input mode
APPEND   to specify sequential output mode where output will be added to the end of the file; if the file does not exist, the file will be created and data will be treated as in the OUTPUT mode

The file number *filenum* must be less than or equal to 3 if you are using interpretive BASIC. If the /F option was in the BASIC command, the file number must be less than or equal to 15 and cannot exceed the number used in the /F option. As previously mentioned, file numbers between 1 and 255 are permitted in QuickBASIC. When working with tree structured directories, you can include a path to the file in the file specification because, if omitted, the current directory will be used. Some examples of the use of this statement and the operational result follow:

Statement Structure	Operational Result
100 OPEN "B:HISTORY.DAT" FOR OUTPUT AS #3	Permits output to the file named HISTORY with the extension DAT in the current directory on the diskette in drive B, using file number 3
200 OPEN "JAN.DAT" FOR INPUT AS #2	Permits input from the file named JAN with the extension DAT in the current directory on the diskette in the current drive using file number 2
300 OPEN "C:\SALES\DATA" FOR OUTPUT AS#1	Permits output to the file named DATA in the directory called SALES in drive C, using file number 1
400 OPEN "FEB.DAT" FOR APPEND AS # 1	Permits the adding of data to the file named FEB with the extension DAT in the current directory on the current drive, using file number 1

You may wish to control the operational mode of data flow within your program, so BASIC provides an alternate format of this statement, whose format is

format: OPEN *mode₂*, [#] *filenum*, *filespec*[LEN=*reclen*]

where *mode₂* is a string expression whose first character indicates the I/O operation as follows:

O   specifies sequential output mode
I   specifies sequential input mode

If a record length (*reclen*) is not specified, BASIC will use a default record length of 128 bytes. Two examples of this statement and their operational result follow.

Statement Structure	Operational Result
100 OPEN "1", #2, "B:JAN.DAT"	Permits input from the file named JAN with extension DAT on the diskette in drive B, using file number 2.
200 OPEN "O", #1, "C:\SALES\DATA"	Permits output to the file named DATA in the directory called SALES on drive C, using file number 1

To see how you can use this second format of the OPEN statement to control data flow within a program, consider the following program segment:

```
10 IF X<5 THEN A$="O" ELSE A$="I"
20 OPEN A$, #1, "JAN.DAT"
```

In the preceding example, when X is less than 5, the file JAN with the extension DAT will be opened for output. Note that this will destroy any existing data on the file if the file already exists. If X is not less than 5, the file will be opened for input. When you open a file for input, if the file does not exist, a File not found error will result.

When you process sequential files, you must execute an OPEN statement prior to using any of the following statements or the INPUT$ function: PRINT#, WRITE#, PRINT# USING, INPUT#, LINE INPUT#, and INPUT$.

FREEFILE Function

As previously mentioned, QuickBASIC contains a FREEFILE function that you can use for the dynamic assignment of file numbers. The format of this function is

format$_Q$: FREEFILE

When used in a QuickBASIC statement, FREEFILE returns the next available file number as an integer. The following program segment illustrates the use of this function in QuickBASIC. In this example the function would return a value of 2, because that would be the next available file number:

```
OPEN "JAN.DAT" FOR INPUT AS #1
FILENUM=FREEFILE
OPEN "FEB.DAT" FOR OUTPUT AS #FILENUM
```

CLOSE Statement

Once you have concluded your file operations, you may wish to terminate the path between your program and a particular file or files. You can use the CLOSE statement to conclude I/O to a device or file. The format of this statement is

format: CLOSE[[#]filenum[,[#]filenum] . . .]

When used without specifying any file numbers, this statement closes all devices and files that were previously opened. If you specify one or more file numbers, only those specified are closed. Examples of the use of this statement and the operational result follow:

Statement Structure	Operational Result
`100 CLOSE`	Closes all open devices and files
`200 CLOSE #1,#3,#5`	Closes the files and devices associated with file numbers 1, 3, and 5
`300 CLOSE #2,#4`	Closes the files and devices associated with file numbers 2 and 4

Once the CLOSE statement is executed, the association between a particular file or device and its file number will terminate. If the device or file was opened for sequential output, the contents of the information in the file buffer will be written to the file or device prior to the association terminating.

Because the execution of the END statement or the BASIC commands NEW, RESET, or SYSTEM will close all open files and devices automatically, a logical question is why would you use this statement in place of the END statement or a command that performs the same function?

First, the CLOSE statement performs the function within a program. You can place it in your program to ensure files are closed without having to worry about a program reaching an END statement or the operator keying in a BASIC command. Second, suppose you require access to a large number of files within your program. The default value of the number of files that can be opened at any one time in interpretive BASIC is three, so what happens if you require access to four or more files? You could use the /F option in the interpretive BASIC command to permit up to 15 files to be open at any instant in time. Because each sequential file uses a buffer of 128 bytes, you may either run out of program memory as you open additional files or you could reach the maximum number of 15 files permitted to be open. In such situations, the CLOSE statement enables you to terminate the path between one or more file numbers and specified devices or files after you performed operations on each file. This enables you to reuse the file number to OPEN another device or file or you can reopen the previously closed device or file if you require access to it later in the program. Thus, the CLOSE statement enables you to conserve program memory and to access an almost infinite number of files from a program, although you can only have 15 such files opened at one time. The following program segment illustrates the use of the CLOSE statement:

LIST
```
100 OPEN "JAN.DAT" FOR INPUT AS #1
110 OPEN "FEB.DAT" FOR INPUT AS #2
120 OPEN "MAR.DAT" FOR INPUT AS #3
    .
    .
    .
500 CLOSE #1, #2, #3
510 OPEN "APR.DAT" FOR INPUT AS #1
520 OPEN "MAY.DAT" FOR INPUT AS #2
530 OPEN "JUN.DAT" FOR INPUT AS #3
```

In this example, due to memory limitations you may wish to only have three data files opened at any one time. Thus, after you close file numbers 1 through 3, you can reopen them to three new files and continue processing.

Now, examine the format and uses of each of the statements and functions requiring the OPEN statement to write data onto and read data from files. Once this discussion is complete, you will be able to create several programs that demonstrate sequential file processing.

PRINT# Statement

The PRINT# statement provides the capability to write data sequentially onto a file. The format of this statement is

format: `PRINT#filenum,exprlist[;]`

where `filenum` is the file number that was used when the file was opened for data output and `exprlist` is a list of string and/or numeric expressions that will be written onto the file. If an optional semicolon is included at the end of the statement, the execution of a subsequent PRINT# statement will add output to a record. When a semicolon is omitted, a CR-LF is generated, which terminates the record.

The PRINT# statement functions the same as a PRINT statement, with the exception that data is written to a file instead of being displayed on the screen. When you use the PRINT# statement to write data to a file, you must be careful in your selection of delimiters used to separate each expression in the list of expressions contained in the statement. This is because different delimiters result in a different amount of blanks inserted between print fields. You can see this from the following example, in which you will use the normal PRINT statement, because it will provide a screen display of the image of data written to a file using the PRINT# statement:

```
100 READ A,B,C
110 DATA 1,3,5
120 PRINT A,B,C
130 PRINT A;B;C
RUN
 1               3               5
 1  3  5
Ok
```

In the preceding example, note that the commas used as delimiters between variables result in extra blanks being inserted between print fields. Because the same image of the data displayed on the screen with a PRINT statement is written to a file using a PRINT# statement, the blanks between print fields will be written to the file. Thus, the PRINT# statement does not compress data on the file.

To reduce the amount of required file space necessary to store data, you should use semicolons as delimiters when you have numeric expressions in your list. Because there is always at least one blank space between numeric expressions written to a file using semicolons as a separator, that space will serve to distinguish each numeric expression as a distinct entity when you input them from the file to the computer with an appropriate INPUT statement. The data written to sequential files is in sequential order, which means that the following statements:

```
100 PRINT #1,A
110 PRINT #1,B
120 PRINT #1,C
```

perform the same function as the statement

```
100 PRINT #1,A,B,C
```

Thus, in sequential file operations, you must ensure that the program stores data in the same sequence that you will use for the retrieval of data.

When strings are written to a file, you may use semicolons to separate them from other string expressions in the list of expressions as well as to conserve file space when the data is written onto a file. Furthermore, you must insert the appropriate delimiter into the file; otherwise, two separate strings would be written to the file as one interconnected string. Thus, the following program segment:

LIST
```
10 OPEN "MAILLIST.DAT" FOR OUTPUT AS #1
D20 NAMEL$="HELD"
30 NAMEF$="GILBERT"
40 PRINT #1 NAMEL$;NAMEF$
```

would write the interconnected string HELDGILBERT to the file. If you later attempt to read this record, you would have no way to read the data as two separate strings that represent a last and first name field. You can correct this situation by one of several methods that can be used to insert the appropriate delimiter into a file. The most obvious method to add the required delimiters is by inserting them into the PRINT# statement as indicated here:

```
40 PRINT #1 NAMEL$;",";NAMEF$
```

The execution of this statement would cause the following data image to be written to the file:

```
HELD,GILBERT
```

This results in two distinct fields separated by a comma. The information in the record now can be read back into the computer as two distinct strings, each representing one field of information.

A second method that can be used to generate a required delimiter between strings is obtained by concatenation of each odd numbered string in a sequence of strings, with a string representing a delimiter, as illustrated here:

```
35 DELIMIT$=","
40 PRINT NAMEL$+DELIMIT$;NAMEF$
```

In line 40, the concatenation of the comma to the first string will result in the comma serving as a separator that will distinguish two separate strings for later input. Now that you can add the appropriate delimiter, a logical question is what do you do when one string naturally contains an embedded comma? For example, suppose you wish to write the string ANAME$ to a file where

```
ANAME$="HELD,GILBERT"
```

Note that you cannot use NAME$; it is a reserved word. The statement

```
PRINT #1,ANAME$
```

would write the following data image to the file:

```
HELD,GILBERT
```

When you attempt later to read the record from the file, your string variable used in an INPUT# statement will only read information from the record until the delimiter is reached. This will result in the string HELD being extracted from the record instead of both the last and first names as well as the comma used in the string. To write the string to the file so it will be read back as one sequence, you surround the string with double quotation marks. You can use the CHR$ function, which converts an ASCII code to its character equivalent. Here, you would use the value 34 (see Appendix A), which would result in the one character string of a double quotation mark being written to the file each time a CHR$(34) function is encountered in the statement. Your previous statement would then be rewritten as follows:

```
PRINT #1 CHR$(34);ANAME$;CHR$(34)
```

The execution of this statement would cause the following data image to be written into the file:

```
"HELD,GILBERT"
```

Because the information contained in a pair of double quotation signs is treated as one string, this will solve your problem of unintentionally reading only a portion of a string previously written to a file.

String processing can be a very valuable tool in storing information in an efficient manner. By concatenating each field with a string variable containing a comma and then concatenating the result to the previous field, you can construct one string of variable length containing a last name, first name, middle initial, address, and so on, with each field separated from the next field by a comma. Once you read a string, you could develop a short subroutine that could easily break each part of the resulting stored string into its various components. Starting with a null string, you would then search the length of the retrieved string for a comma. Each character that is not a comma would be concatenated with the null string until a comma is encountered. Then, the appropriate string variable would be assigned the value of the concatenated string, that string would be set to a null value, and the search would resume for a second comma or the end of the string. By storing each data record on a file as one string, you can optimize your storage capacity.

When you mix both strings and numerics in a PRINT# statement, you must also insert appropriate delimiters into the PRINT# statement or you may obtain an error when you attempt to retrieve the stored data. To illustrate this point, consider the following example:

```
100 A$="GIL HELD"
110 YOB=1943
120 PRINT #1 A$;YOB
```

After executing these statements, the data would be stored sequentially as one string, as indicated here:

```
GIL HELD 1943
```

If you later attempt to retrieve the stored information using the statement

```
INPUT #1,A$,YOB
```

the entire string GIL HELD 1943 would be assigned to A$ and an Input Past end error would occur, because there would be no data on the file to assign to YOB. If you used a literal comma as a string delimiter in the PRINT# statement as follows:

```
120 PRINT #1,A$;",";YOB
```

the data would have to be written to the file as

```
GIL HELD, 1943
```

Then, the INPUT# statement would correctly assign GIL HELD to A$ and 1943 to YOB.

WRITE# Statement

Another mechanism that provides the capability to write data onto a sequential file is the WRITE# statement. The format of this statement is

format: WRITE# *filenum,exprlist*

The format and the operational result of the WRITE# statement are similar to the PRINT# statement; however, several important differences result from the execution of these two statements. First, the WRITE# statement automatically inserts commas between items as they are written to a sequential file and delimits strings with quotation marks. Thus, whereas it is necessary to put explicit delimiters in the list of expressions to use the PRINT# statement, you can avoid this requirement by using the WRITE# statement. The PRINT# statement functions like all PRINT-related statements by placing a blank character in front of positive numbers as they are written to a file. This serves as an automatic separator between items written to a file, printed, or placed on the screen using one of the appropriate PRINT statements. Because the WRITE# statement automatically inserts commas between items, no blank character is required in front of a positive number. After all items in the list of expressions are written, a carriage return/line feed sequence will be generated to the file. The following use of the WRITE$ statement:

```
10 NAMEL$="HELD"
20 NAMEF$="GILBERT"
30 YOB=1943
40 WRITE #1 NAMEL$,NAMEF$,YOB
```

would write this to the file:

```
"HELD","GILBERT",1943
```

Now, consider the following example:

```
100 READ A,B,C,D$
110 DATA 1,3,5,IMAGE
120 WRITE #1 A,B,C,D$
```

The execution of this program segment preceded by the appropriate OPEN statement would write the following to the file:

```
1,3,5,"IMAGE"
```

In developing programs in BASIC that use sequential files, you will normally prefer the WRITE# statement over the PRINT# statement. This is because it is easier to use the WRITE# statement to write data to a sequential file that a subsequent INPUT# statement can read.

PRINT# USING Statement

With the PRINT# USING statement, you can write to a file using a specified format. The PRINT# USING statement functions similarly to the PRINT USING and LPRINT USING statements. The only difference among the three statements is that the PRINT USING statement displays strings or numbers on the screen and the LPRINT USING statement causes data to be printed in a specified format, whereas the PRINT# USING statement writes the data image specified by the format of the statement onto a file. The format of the PRINT# USING statement is

```
format: PRINT#filenum,USING var$; exprlist [;]
```

The string variable following the keyword USING contains the formatting characters that define the field and format of strings or numbers that will be written onto the file. The use of these formatting characters was previously described in Chapter 11.

One of the primary uses of the PRINT# USING statement is to generate reports onto a disk instead of a printer, enabling you to distribute reports on diskette for later printing at different locations. A "file dump" program would then read the file and dump its image onto a printer, producing a hardcopy of the report. Several examples using this statement follow:

```
100 A=3.71
110 B=4.978
120 PRINT#1,USING "#.## #.####";A,B
```

result in the image

```
3.71 4.9780
```

being written onto the file opened with file number 1.

Changing the elements of line 120 to

```
120 PRINT#1, USING ".## #.####";A,B
```

results in the print image

```
%3.71 4.9780
```

being written onto the file. The percent sign (%) in front of the first number indicates that the number to be printed is larger than the specified number field.

INPUT# Statement

The INPUT# statement provides you with the capability to read data items previously written to a sequential file. As data items are read, they will be assigned to program variables, so you can use those data items within your program. The format of this statement is

```
format: INPUT# filenum,var[,var] . . .
```

The file number in the statement must be the number previously used when the file was opened for input. Unlike the conventional BASIC INPUT statement, no prompt message will be generated, nor will a question mark be printed when the INPUT# statement is executed.

When an INPUT# statement is executed, a type comparison is performed between the variable names in the statement and the type of data on the record to be read. If they do not match, a Type mismatch error will result. This is illustrated by the following example where it is assumed each record in the file contains three fields providing quantity-on-hand, cost, and an item description. The first two fields are numeric; the third field is a string. Suppose our INPUT# statement used to read information from the file is as follows:

```
100 INPUT#1,QTY,COST,ITEM
```

The third variable was entered as a numeric type, so a Type mismatch error would occur. You can correct this by modifying your statement changing ITEM to ITEM$. Thus,

```
100 INPUT#1,QTY,COST,ITEM$
```

would have three variable names that match the type of data in the file.

If you are reading numeric values from the file, all leading spaces, carriage return, and line-feed characters will be ignored. The first character encountered that is not a space, carriage return, or line feed is assumed by BASIC to be the start of a number. Each number of the file is considered to be terminated when a space, carriage return, line feed, or comma is encountered. When a string variable is specified in the INPUT# statement, BASIC will scan the record for a string. Again, leading spaces, commas, carriage returns, and line feeds will be ignored. The first character encountered that is not a space, comma, carriage return, or line feed will be assumed to be the start of the string. When the first character of the string is a double quotation mark ("), BASIC will assign all characters on the record between this quotation mark and a second quotation mark to the string variable in the INPUT# statement. This "quoted" string may not include a double quotation mark within the string, because it would cause BASIC to misinterpret where the string ends.

When the first character in the string is not a quotation mark, the string is an "unquoted" string. Unquoted strings are terminated when a comma, carriage return, or line feed is encountered as data is read from a file record. For both "quoted" and "unquoted" strings, the maximum string length that can be read is 255 characters in interpretive BASIC and 32,767 characters in QuickBASIC. The examples in Table 12.1 illustrate the resulting values of variables used in an INPUT# statement based on the indicated record information stored in the file.

The sequential file actually read by the INPUT# statement depends on the file specification used in the OPEN statement that contains the matching file number used in the INPUT# statement. Although you will normally specify the diskette drive (**A:** or **B:**) or fixed disk (**C:** or **D:**) in the OPEN statement, you could specify the keyboard (**KYBD:**). Such a specification would result in the INPUT# statement reading data directly from the keyboard. The communications adapter is treated similarly to other devices, so you can use the INPUT# statement to read a sequential data stream from that device, using the device address COMX: where X would be the communications port number.

Table 12.1
INPUT# Statement
Variables

INPUT# Statement	Record Information	Variable Assignments
100 Input#,A,B	105.7 2089	A = 105.7
		B = 2089
100 INPUT#A,B	105.7,2089	A = 105.7
		B = 2089
100 INPUT#1,N$,X$,X	MACON,GA,25	N$ = "MACON"
		X$ = "GA"
		X = 25
100 INPUT#1,N$,X	"MACON,GA",25	N$ = "MACON,GA"
		X = 25
100 INPUT#1,N$,X	"MACON,GA"25	N$ = "MACON,GA"
		X = 25

INPUT$ Function

The INPUT$ function provides you with the capability to read a string of specified length from a file or from the keyboard. The format of this function is

    format: INPUT$(exprnm[,[#] filenum])

The numeric expression in the format defines the number of characters that will be returned when the function is invoked. The file number used in the function must be within the ranges previously discussed for disk file operations.

The following example illustrates the use of the INPUT$ function:

LIST
```
100 OPEN "KYBD:" FOR INPUT AS #1
110 X$=INPUT$(30,#1)
120 PRINT X$
```
RUN
```
LET'S ENTER THIRTY CHARACTERS A
Ok
```

When the INPUT$ function is executed, no characters will be displayed on the screen. If you wish to display the characters you entered, you should follow this function call by a PRINT statement as indicated in the previous example.

In line 110, 30 characters are read from the keyboard and assigned to the string variable X$. The PRINT statement in line 120 echoes the characters previously input to the screen. When the INPUT$ function requests data from the keyboard no prompt message or prompt question mark (?) is generated. Therefore, it is good programming practice to prefix this statement with a PRINT statement that prompts the user for the required data.

The INPUT$ statement will read all characters up to the specified length of the string requested, including special control characters, with the exception of the Ctrl + Break, which will interrupt program execution. This ability to read strings regardless of their content makes this function valuable for reading ASCII codes that would otherwise be interpreted by the BASIC Editor as a request to perform a specific function. Thus, you could use this function to enter a backspace character from the keyboard into your program. When the INPUT$ function requests data from the keyboard, the function call will be automatically completed when the required number of characters are entered, alleviating the necessity of pressing the Enter key to terminate input. The following examples illustrate the use of this function and its operational result.

Function Structure	Operational Result
`100 X$ = INPUT$(50,#1)`	Reads a string of 50 characters and assigns them to the string variable X$
`100 Y$ = INPUT$(30,#2)`	Reads a string of 30 characters from file number 2 and assigns them to the string variable Y$

In the next example, you will use the INPUT$ function to read one character from the keyboard. This is similar to the INKEY$ variable, with the exception that program execution will be suspended while the INPUT$ function awaits a key to be pressed. In comparison, the INKEY$ variable will read the keyboard state at the time the variable is encountered. Thus,

```
100 OPEN "KYBD:" FOR INPUT AS #1
110 X$=INPUT$(1,#1)
120 IF X$="E" THEN END ELSE 500
 .
 .
 .
500 REM program continues
```

is the equivalent of

```
100 X$=INKEY$
110 IF X$="E" THEN END
120 IF X$="" THEN 100 ELSE 500
 .
 .
 .
500 REM Program continues
```

LINE INPUT# Statement

The LINE INPUT# statement provides the capability to read an entire line up to a CR-LF sequence of characters from a file. The format of this statement is

format: `LINE INPUT#filenum,string`

When used in sequential file processing, this statement causes all information to be read without regard to any delimiters except the carriage return line-feed sequence. The string read to include the carriage return line-feed sequence will be assigned as one entity to a string variable specified in the statement. The next execution of a LINE INPUT# statement will continue reading data from the file until the next carriage return line-feed sequence is encountered. This statement provides the ability to read programs stored in ASCII format. Each LINE INPUT# statement reads an entire line of information stored on a file, so this statement is very useful to input data from an ASCII file that you wish to transfer through the communications adapter to another computer.

The LINE INPUT# statement is useful if you previously created a file according to a particular format and now wish to examine its contents. Suppose you generated a report on a file using PRINT USING# statements. The following program segment would "dump" the formatted file to the printer:

```
100 OPEN "REPORT.DAT" FOR INPUT AS #1
110 LINE INPUT#1,X$
120 PRINT X$
130 GOTO 110
```

In the preceding example, what happens when you branch back to line 110 after you previously read the last record in the file? This will cause an Input past end error, which occurs when you attempt to read past the end-of-file mark. To avoid this error, you must use the EOF function to detect the occurrence of the end-of-file mark. When you detect the end-of-file mark, you will branch to a statement and avoid executing the input statement that would cause an Input past end error to occur. Let's examine the EOF function and then modify the file dump program to eliminate the Input past end error.

EOF Function

The EOF function provides the capability to test for an end-of-file condition. The format of this function is

format: *varnm*=EOF(*filenum*)

The EOF function returns one of two values, depending on whether or not the end-of-file mark has been reached on the specified file. A −1 (true) will be returned if the end-of-file mark is reached; a 0 (zero) will be returned if the end-of-file mark has not been reached. Attempting to read past the end-of-file will cause an error, so you should prefix each file INPUT statement in a program with an end-of-file test. Thus, your file dump program should be modified as indicated here:

```
100 OPEN "REPORT.DAT" FOR INPUT AS #1
105 IF EOF(1) THEN 140
110 LINE INPUT#1,X$
120 PRINT X$
130 GOTO 105
140 CLOSE #1
```

There are three additional functions that can be used in sequential file operations—the LOC, LOF, and FILEATTR functions. The first two are applicable to both interpretive BASIC and QuickBASIC; the third is applicable only to QuickBASIC.

LOC Function

The LOC function returns the number of physical records that were read from or written onto a file since it was opened. The format of this function is

format: *varnm*=LOC (*filenum*)

The number of physical records in a file is a function of the format you employ to record data on the file. In the following example, the numbers 1 to 512 were recorded first in the file named JUNK.BAS, which created 19 records of information, because a semicolon(;) was used after the variable 1 in line 105. The next example removed the semicolon, which resulted in spaces being placed between the numbers. Here, the number of physical records required to record the same data increased to 27:

```
LIST
100 OPEN "B:JUNK.BAS" FOR OUTPUT AS #1
105 FOR I=1 TO 512:PRINT#1,I;:NEXT I
106 PRINT "RECORD#=";LOC(1)
140 CLOSE #1
Ok
RUN
RECORD#= 19
Ok
105 FOR I=1 TO 512:PRINT#1,I:NEXT I
RUN
RECORD#= 27
Ok
```

Sequential files can be opened in only one mode at a time, so you cannot easily update or delete information in such files. To change a piece of information previously written to such a file, you must read the file until you locate the information you wish to change or delete. Then, you must obtain the location of the record you wish to update or delete. Then, you must obtain the location of the record you wish to update or delete and close the file. After you reopen the file, you will read information from the old file onto a new file until you reach the point where you wish to update or delete a record. If you wish to update the record, you will INPUT the changes from the keyboard and skip the information on the old file, writing the new information and all remaining information from the old file into the new file. If you wish to delete the record, you will simply transfer all information from the old file to the new file with the exception of the record you wish to delete. To accomplish this file manipulation, you must keep track of the physical records or the number of fields of the logical records you have processed until you reach the appropriate point where you wish to delete or modify information. Because working on a physical record basis requires you to know the number of bytes written to a file to form the record, it will be far easier to keep track of the number of fields of data you have processed. You will see how to do this when sequential file processing is discussed in the next section of this chapter.

LOF Function

The LOF function returns the length of the file in bytes. The format of this function is

    format: *varnm*=LOF(*filenum*)

You can use this function to determine the number of sectors on a diskette that a file occupies as shown by the following program segment:

```
LIST
100 OPEN "B:JUNK.BAS" FOR OUTPUT AS #1
105 FOR I=1 TO 512:PRINT#1,I:NEXT I
106 PRINT "RECORD#=";LOC(1)
107 X=LOF(1)
```

```
108 S=INT((X/512)+.5)
110 PRINT "FILE OCCUPIES ";S;" SECTORS"
140 CLOSE #1
Ok
```
RUN
```
RECORD#= 27
FILE OCCUPIES 14 SECTORS
Ok
```

FILEATTR Function

The FILEATTR function, which is only applicable to QuickBASIC, returns the number assigned by the operating system to a previously opened file and a number that indicates the mode in which the file was opened—input, output, append, binary, or random. The format of this function is

format$_Q$: FILEATTR(*filenum*, *attribute*)

where *filenum* is an integer variable whose value is between 1 and 255; the *attribute* can be set to 1 or 2. When *attribute* is set to 1, the function returns a value that defines the mode of an open file as indicated in Table 12.2.

Sequential File Processing

Now that file I/O statements and functions relevant to sequential files have been reviewed, try to use these statements and functions as you construct a series of programs.

In each of the following examples, certain file-related processing steps will be used to create a sequential file and to access the data on that file. As a minimum, you should consider the following steps to ensure correct sequential file processing:

1. Prior to writing data onto a file in output or append operations, ensure that the file is open.
2. Write data onto a file using the PRINT#, WRITE#, or PRINT# USING statements. Remember that the PRINT# and PRINT# USING statements do not automatically write field delimiters to the file.
3. If the file you are writing to previously existed and was not opened in the append mode, existing data on that file will be destroyed.
4. To access data on a file created by your program or opened by the program for output, you must close the file and reopen it for input.
5. Read data from sequential files using the INPUT# or LINE INPUT# statements.
6. To avoid an Input past end error when you are reading data from a file, use the EOF function to test for the end-of-file mark.

Returned Value	Open File Mode
1	input
2	output
4	random
8	append
32	binary

Table 12.2
Values That Define
the Mode of an
Open File

Suppose you wish to create a personal telephone directory and store the names and telephone numbers of your business associates and friends on a diskette. First you plan to develop a program module that will input the appropriate information from the keyboard and write that information onto a diskette. Next, you expect to develop a retrieval module that will search the diskette file by name and retrieve the appropriate person's telephone number. You will periodically change information previously placed in the file, so you will develop two additional program modules that will add information to the diskette or modify and delete information already on the diskette. You will also develop two program modules that will add new names and telephone numbers to your file and provide you with a hardcopy listing of the directory.

After you examine and perfect each of these modules, you will combine them into one program and add a menu to provide the capability of selecting any of the desired functions.

Telephone Directory Example

The following program module creates a sequential file named TELLIST from information input from the keyboard:

```
100 OPEN "B:TELLIST.DAT" FOR OUTPUT AS #1
110 CLS
120 PRINT "TELEPHONE DIRECTORY CREATION - ENTER 0 TO EXIT"
130 INPUT "LAST NAME";N$
140 IF N$="0" THEN 190
150 INPUT "INITIAL(S)";I$
160 INPUT "TELEPHONE NUMBER";T$
170 WRITE#1,N$,I$,T$
180 GOTO 120
190 CLOSE#1
Ok
```

Note that the WRITE# statement was used in line 170 instead of a PRINT# statement, because the former automatically inserts commas between items. IF the PRINT# statement was used, line 170 would be rewritten as

```
170 PRINT#1,N$;",",I$;",",T$
```

In addition, the WRITE# statement will automatically delimit strings with quotation marks, which is compatible to other BASICs. Now, try executing this program module and enter several names and telephone numbers as follows:

```
TELEPHONE DIRECTORY CREATION - ENTER 0 TO EXIT
LAST NAME? UNGER
INITIAL(S)? F.U.
TELEPHONE NUMBER? 444-4444
TELEPHONE DIRECTORY CREATION - ENTER 0 TO EXIT
LAST NAME? ROBERTSON
INITIAL(S)? X.Z.
TELEPHONE NUMBER? 111-1111
TELEPHONE DIRECTORY CREATION - ENTER 0 TO EXIT
LAST NAME? MAXWELL
INITIAL(S)? S
```

```
TELEPHONE NUMBER? 999-9999
TELEPHONE DIRECTORY CREATION - ENTER 0 TO EXIT
LAST NAME?  HELD
INITIAL(S) G.X.
TELEPHONE NUMBER?  000-0011
TELEPHONE DIRECTORY CREATION - ENTER 0 TO EXIT
LAST NAME?  0
Ok
```

Now that the initial data has been entered, you should develop a retrieval module:

```
200 CLS
210 PRINT "TELEPHONE DIRECTORY RETRIEVAL"
220 OPEN "B:TELLIST.DAT" FOR INPUT AS #1
230 INPUT "ENTER LAST NAME";NAMEL$
240 IF EOF(1) THEN 340
250 INPUT#1,N$,I$,T$
260 IF NAMEL$<>N$ THEN 240
270 PRINT N$,I$,T$
280 PRINT "ANOTHER SEARCH Y/N"
290 A$=INKEY$
300 IF A$="N" THEN 360
310 IF A$<>"Y" THEN 290
320 CLOSE#1 :CLEAR
330 GOTO 220
340 PRINT "NAME NOT ON DIRECTORY"
350 GOTO 280
360 CLOSE#1
Ok
```

In the telephone directory retrieval example, note that the end-of-file mark is tested for in line 240. If you encounter the end of the file, the name you are searching for is not in the directory, and program control will branch to line 340 and print the appropriate message on the display.

If you have successfully found the telephone number in the directory, you can specify to the program module whether you wish to make another search. Data stored on sequential files is placed in the order it was written to the file, so you must reposition your pointer to the beginning of the file unless you created the file in alphabetical order and search for names in alphabetical order. This was not done here, so you must first CLOSE the file and then reopen it to reread the file from the beginning. This mechanism is equivalent to a RESTORE# statement that is available in some BASICs but is unfortunately missing from both interpretive BASIC and QuickBASIC. The execution of this program module for the retrieval of the telephone numbers of several persons follows:

```
TELEPHONE DIRECTORY RETRIEVAL
ENTER LAST NAME? ROBERTSON
ROBERTSON    X.Z.         111-1111
ANOTHER SEARCH Y/N
ENTER LAST NAME? HOPKINS
NAME NOT ON DIRECTORY
ANOTHER SEARCH Y/N
```

```
ENTER LAST NAME? HELD
HELD         G.X.        000-0011
ANOTHER SEARCH Y/N
Ok
```

Suppose you wish to add new information to the directory in a previously created sequential file. You must open the file in the APPEND mode and use this program module:

```
400 CLS
410 PRINT "DIRECTORY ADDITION"
420 OPEN "B:TELLIST.DAT" FOR APPEND AS #1
430 INPUT "LAST NAME";N$
440 INPUT "INITIAL(S)";I$
450 INPUT "TELEPHONE NUMBER";T$
460 WRITE #1,N$,I$,T$
470 PRINT "ENTER C TO CONTINUE E TO EXIT"
480 A$=INKEY$
490 IF A$="C" THEN 430
500 IF A$="E" THEN 510 ELSE 480
510 CLOSE#1
```

Now, add several names to the telephone directory. The execution of the program segment and the addition of three persons to the directory is shown here:

```
DIRECTORY ADDITION
LAST NAME? HERMAN
INITIAL(S)? Q.B.
TELEPHONE NUMBER? WE6-1212
ENTER C TO CONTINUE E TO EXIT
LAST NAME? ZORBA
INITIAL(S) G.
TELEPHONE NUMBER?  555-5555
ENTER C TO CONTINUE E TO EXIT
LAST NAME? XRAY
INITIAL(S)? A.U.
TELEPHONE NUMBER? 765-4321
ENTER C TO CONTINUE E TO EXIT
Ok
```

Now examine how you can modify or delete information previously entered in a sequential file. Such files can only be opened for one mode of operation, so you must first access the information you wish to modify or delete and obtain its position in the file. After obtaining the new information, if you wish to modify previously entered data you must then CLOSE the file and again read the information one field at a time, transferring the information to a new file until you reach the position where the information changed. At that point, you will WRITE the modified field or fields of information from memory onto the new file, skip the old field or fields of information, and continue writing the remaining fields from the old file onto the new file until you reach the end of the file. At this point, you will erase the old file and rename the new file, using the old filename. If you wish to delete one or more fields of information, you would follow the same procedure; however, you would skip the fields you wish to delete instead of writing those fields from memory onto the file when you modify a sequential file. This program module follows:

```
600 CLS
610 OPEN "B:TELLIST.DAT" FOR INPUT AS #1
620 OPEN "B:TEMP.DAT" FOR OUTPUT AS #2
630 PRINT "MODIFY/DELETE SECTION"
640 INPUT "ENTER LAST NAME ",LNAME$
650 FCOUNT=0
660 IF EOF(1) THEN 760
670 INPUT#1,N$,I$,T$
680 FCOUNT=FCOUNT+1        'physical record position
690 IF N$<>LNAME$ THEN 660
700 PRINT "FOR:";LNAME$;",";I$;" TELEPHONE# IS: ";T$
710 INPUT "DO YOU WISH TO (M)ODIFY OR (D)ELETE INFORMATION ";A$
720 IF A$<>"M" AND A$<>"D" THEN 710
730 IF A$="D" THEN 820
740 INPUT "ENTER NEW TELEPHONE# ";TEL$
750 GOTO 820
760 PRINT "NAME NOT ON DIRECTORY"
770 CLOSE
780 INPUT "(A)NOTHER TRY OR (E)XIT ";B$
790 IF B$<>"A" AND B$<>"E" THEN 780
800 IF B$="A" THEN 610
810 IF B$="E" THEN 990
820 CLOSE#1
830 OPEN "B:TELLIST.DAT" FOR INPUT AS #1
840 FOR I=1 TO FCOUNT-1    'read up to prior physical record to be changed
850 INPUT#1,N$,I$,T$
860 WRITE#2,N$,I$,T$
870 NEXT I
880 INPUT#1,N$,I$,T$       'read the record to be modified/deleted
890 IF A$="D" THEN 910     'if delete do not write in file
900 WRITE#2,LNAME$,I$,TEL$ 'if to be modified put new information in file
910 IF EOF(1) THEN 950     'get
920 INPUT#1,N$,I$,T$       'remainder
930 WRITE#2,N$,I$,T$       'of
940 GOTO 910              'file
950 CLOSE
960 KILL "B:TELLIST.DAT"
970 NAME "B:TEMP.DAT" AS "B:TELLIST.DAT"
980 GOTO 780
990 CLOSE
```

The execution of this program segment showing the results of asking for a name not in the directory is illustrated in the following:

```
MODIFY/DELETE SECTION
ENTER LAST NAME HOPKINS
NAME NOT ON DIRECTORY
(A)NOTHER TRY OR (E)XIT ? A
MODIFY/DELETE SECTION
```

```
ENTER LAST NAME ROBERTSON
FOR:ROBERTSON,X.Z. TELEPHONE# IS: 111-1111
DO YOU WISH TO (M)ODIFY OR (D)ELETE INFORMATION ? M
ENTER NEW TELEPHONE# ? 000-0000
(A)NOTHER TRY OR (E)XIT ? A
MODIFY/DELETE SECTION
ENTER LAST NAME ROBERTSON
FOR:ROBERTSON,X.Z.  TELEPHONE# IS: 000-0000
DO YOU WISH TO (M)ODIFY OR (D)ELETE INFORMATION ? D
(A)NOTHER TRY OR (E)XIT ? A
MODIFY/DELETE SECTION
ENTER LAST NAME ROBERTSON
NAME NOT ON DIRECTORY
(A)NOTHER TRY OR (E)XIT ? E
```

Changing a telephone number and deleting a person from the directory is illustrated in this short sample. To improve operational efficiency, if you change or delete many pieces of information at one time, you should first place all change and deletion requests into arrays in memory. Then, you can sort the requests and perform all disk I/O operations at one time.

Now, you can combine each of the preceding modules into one program and add an appropriate menu to permit the operator to select the specific function he or she wishes to perform.

If you are using interpretive BASIC and forgot to save each of the program segments using the A option, you can reload each segment and save it with that option. This will enable you to merge all of the segments together to facilitate constructing one program from the previous modules. The completed program listing follows:

```
5 CLS
10 PRINT "WELCOME TO THE TELEPHONE DIRECTORY PROGRAM"
20 PRINT "YOU MAY ACCESS THE FOLLOWING FUNCTIONS BY"
30 PRINT "ENTERING THE APPROPRIATE NUMBER WHEN ASKED"
40 PRINT "   ENTER 1 TO CREATE INITIAL DIRECTORY"
50 PRINT "   ENTER 2 TO RETRIEVE INFORMATION"
60 PRINT "   ENTER 3 TO ADD NEW NAMES TO DIRECTORY"
70 PRINT "   ENTER 4 TO MODIFY/DELETE ENTRIES ON DIRECTORY"
75 PRINT "   ENTER 5 TO EXIT THIS PROGRAM"
80 INPUT " ****** ENTER YOUR CHOICE ****** ",C
90 ON C GOTO 100,200,400,600,1010
92 PRINT " READ THE DIRECTIONS--ENTER 1, 2, 3, OR 4"
94 GOTO 80
100 OPEN "B:TELLIST.DAT" FOR OUTPUT AS #1
110 CLS
120 PRINT "TELEPHONE DIRECTORY CREATION--ENTER 0 TO EXIT"
130 INPUT "LAST NAME";N$
140 IF N$="0" THEN 190
150 INPUT "INITIAL(S)";I$
160 INPUT "TELEPHONE NUMBER";T$
170 WRITE#1,N$,I$,T$
180 GOTO 120
190 CLOSE#1
```

```
195 GOTO 5
200 CLS
210 PRINT "TELEPHONE DIRECTORY RETRIEVAL"
220 OPEN "B:TELLIST.DAT" FOR INPUT AS #1
230 INPUT "ENTER LAST NAME";NAMEL$
240 IF EOF(1) THEN 340
250 INPUT#1,N$,I$,T$
260 IF NAMEL$<>N$ THEN 240
270 PRINT N$,I$,T$
280 PRINT "ANOTHER SEARCH Y/N"
290 A$=INKEY$
300 IF A$="N" THEN 360
310 IF A$<>"Y" THEN 290
320 CLOSE#1 :CLEAR
330 GOTO 220
340 PRINT "NAME NOT IN DIRECTORY"
350 GOTO 280
360 CLOSE#1
370 GOTO 5
400 CLS
410 PRINT "DIRECTORY ADDITION"
420 OPEN "B:TELLIST.DAT" FOR APPEND AS #1
430 INPUT "LAST NAME";N$
440 INPUT "INITIAL(S)";I$
450 INPUT "TELEPHONE NUMBER";T$
460 WRITE #1,N$,I$,T$
470 PRINT "ENTER C TO CONTINUE OR E TO EXIT"
480 A$=INKEY$
490 IF A$="C" THEN 430
500 IF A$="E" THEN 510 ELSE 480
510 CLOSE#1
520 GOTO 5
600 CLS
610 OPEN "B:TELLIST.DAT" FOR INPUT AS #1
620 OPEN "B:TEMP.DAT" FOR OUTPUT AS #2
630 PRINT "MODIFY/DELETE SECTION"
640 INPUT "ENTER LAST NAME ",LNAME$
650 FCOUNT=0
660 IF EOF(1) THEN 760
670 INPUT#1,N$,I$,T$
680 FCOUNT=FCOUNT+1          'physical record position
690 IF N$<>LNAME$ THEN 660
700 PRINT "FOR:";LNAME$;",";I$;" TELEPHONE# IS: ";T$
710 INPUT "DO YOU WISH TO (M)ODIFY OR (D)ELETE INFORMATION ";A$
720 IF A$<>"M" AND A$<>"D" THEN 710
730 IF A$="D" THEN 820
740 INPUT "ENTER NEW TELEPHONE# ";TEL$
750 GOTO 820
760 PRINT "NAME NOT ON DIRECTORY"
770 CLOSE
```

```
780 INPUT "(A)NOTHER TRY OR (E)XIT ";B$
790 IF B$<>"A" AND B$<>"E" THEN 780
800 IF B$="A" THEN 610
810 IF B$="E" THEN 990
820 CLOSE#1
830 OPEN "B:TELLIST.DAT" FOR INPUT AS #1
840 FOR I=1 TO FCOUNT-1      'read up to prior physical record to be changed
850 INPUT#1,N$,I$,T$
860 WRITE#2,N$,I$,T$
870 NEXT I
880 INPUT#1,N$,I$,T$         'read the record to be modified/deleted
890 IF A$="D" THEN 910       'if delete do not write on file
900 WRITE#2,LNAME$,I$,TEL$   'if to be modified put new information on file
910 IF EOF(1) THEN 950       'get
920 INPUT#1,N$,I$,T$         'remainder
930 WRITE#2,N$,I$,T$         'of
940 GOTO 910                 'file
950 CLOSE
960 KILL "B:TELLIST.DAT"
970 NAME "B:TEMP.DAT" AS "B:TELLIST.DAT"
980 GOTO 780
990 CLOSE
1000 GOTO 5
1010 END
```

The initial menu displayed on program execution is

```
WELCOME TO THE TELEPHONE DIRECTORY PROGRAM
YOU MAY ACCESS THE FOLLOWING FUNCTIONS BY
ENTERING THE APPROPRIATE NUMBER WHEN ASKED
    ENTER 1 TO CREATE INITIAL DIRECTORY
    ENTER 2 TO RETRIEVE INFORMATION
    ENTER 3 TO ADD NEW NAMES TO DIRECTORY
    ENTER 4 TO MODIFY/DELETE ENTRIES ON DIRECTORY
    ENTER 5 TO EXIT THIS PROGRAM
****** ENTER YOUR CHOICE ******
```

While the program can be made more efficient by sorting entries in alphabetical order and storing change and modification information in memory until all entries are completed prior to changing the directory file, this program should provide a mechanism to implement a practical and useful program to operate on your PC AT or compatible.

Random File Overview

In comparison to sequential file processing, the use of random files offers several distinct advantages. Due to the nature of random files, data can be accessed randomly from any location on the file without having to read all prior information as required with sequential files. This random accessibility is due to data being stored on disk in distinct units of information called records. Here, a logical record is the exact same size as a physical record, and each record in the file holds the same amount of information. This content is defined in terms of characters when the file is created and the amount of information that can be stored in one record is referred to as the *record length*.

Each record in a random file is identified by a unique number that specifies its absolute location in the file. Thus, if you know the record number, you can immediately locate the record on the file. The smallest random file will consist of one record. Such files will automatically expand as records are added; however, they will not shrink. Thus, to remove unwanted records from random files and shrink the size of the file, you must copy the records that are to be preserved onto a new random file.

A second major advantage of random files is the ability to perform both input and output on the same random file. This enables you to easily update data on the file without having to resort to multiple file operations, as explained in the review of sequential file processing.

A third advantage of random files is one of storage space. Sequential files are stored as ASCII characters, whereas random files can be stored in packed binary format. In most cases, the packed binary format will require less file space than an equivalent sequential file.

Similar to sequential file processing, there is a series of steps you must consider to perform operations on random files. These program steps are listed here:

1. Open the file for random access prior to performing any file reference operations.
2. If you are using interpretive BASIC, use the FIELD statement to allocate space in the random buffer for all variables that will be written onto or read from a random file. If you are using QuickBASIC, you can define your record through the use of a TYPE .. END TYPE statement. With the TYPE statement you can use a composite data type that mixes string and numeric elements, which eliminates the necessity of performing the actions listed in step 3.
3. Prior to writing to the random file when you are using interpretive BASIC, the LSET or RSET statements must be used to first place the data to be written to the file into the random buffer. The random buffer can only contain string variables, so use the MKI$, MKS$ or MKD$ function to convert any integer, single-precision, or double-precision variable to a string if you wish to write data to the file. If you are using QuickBASIC and define a record by using a TYPE .. END TYPE statement, you can skip using the previously mentioned statements and functions. If you use the FIELD statement in QuickBASIC, you can use the previously mentioned statements and functions as well as the MKL$ function, which is unique to QuickBASIC and which converts a long integer to a string value.
4. To record data on the random file, you must use the PUT statement to move data from the random buffer to the random file.
5. To access data in the random file, use the GET statement to first move the desired record from the random file into the random buffer. The buffer only operates on strings when you are using interpretive BASIC; numeric values must be converted back to their appropriate numeric type by using the CVI, CVS, or CVD function. If you are using QuickBASIC and have defined records using the TYPE .. END TYPE statement, you need not convert strings to numeric data. However, if you use the FIELD statement in QuickBASIC, you must convert strings to numeric data. In doing so you can use the CVI, CVS, or CVD function as well as the CVL function, unique to QuickBASIC.

Random File Statements and Functions

Before you examine random file processing, review the statements and functions associated with such files. The statements covered in this section include OPEN, CLOSE, FIELD, GET, LSET, RESET, and PUT that are applicable to both interpretive BASIC and QuickBASIC, as well as the TYPE . . END TYPE statement unique to QuickBASIC. The functions are CVD, CVI, CVS, LOC, LOF, MKD$, MKI$, and MKS$, as well as the MKL$ and CVL functions unique to QuickBASIC.

OPEN Statement

Similar to sequential file processing, you must also open all random access files prior to their first reference within a program. Each record in a random file holds the same amount of information and the record number is used as the pointer to access records randomly, so you must specify the record length in the OPEN statement. When working with tree-structured directories, you can include a path in the file specification. If a directory is omitted, the current directory is assumed for use. The format of this statement is

format: OPEN *filespec* AS[#] *filenum*[LEN=*reclen*]

Both output to and input from a random file can occur for the same file, so the mode specifier used in sequential file operations can be omitted. The record length (*reclen*) is an integer expression that sets the record length of the random file. Its value can range from 1 to 32,767, and, if not specified, a default value of 128 bytes is used. The following examples illustrate the operational result of several versions of this statement.

Statement Structure	Operational Result
100 OPEN"JAN.DAT"AS#1 LEN=32	Opens the file JAN.DAT in the default directory on the diskette in the default drive as a random file with a record length of 32
200 OPEN"B:JAN.DAT"AS#1	Opens the file JAN.DAT on the diskette in drive B as a random file; the record length is the default value of 128
300 OPEN"C:\SALES\DATA"AS#1 LEN=40	Opens the file named DATA in the SALES directory on drive C as a random file with a record length of 40

CLOSE Statement

The CLOSE statement in random file processing has the same format and use as in sequential file processing. The execution of such a statement causes I/O to a random file to conclude.

FIELD Statement

The FIELD statement must be used in random file processing to allocate space in the random buffer for all variables that will be written onto or read from a random file.

Thus, it must follow an OPEN statement but precede a GET or PUT statement. The format of this statement is

format: FIELD[#]*filenum,width* AS *var$*[,*width* AS *var$*] . . .

where *filenum* is the file number under which the file was previously opened; *width* is a numeric expression that specifies the number of character positions that will be allocated to the string variable (*var$*); and *var$* is a string variable that will be used for random file access.

The following examples illustrate the operational result of several versions of this statement that could be used in a BASIC program.

Statement Structure	Operational Result
100 FIELD#1,10 AS N$,20 AS Y$	Allocates the first 10 positions (bytes) in the random file buffer for file number 1 to the string variable N$ and the next 20 positions to Y$.
200 FIELD#2,15 AS TAX$, 15 AS PAY$	Allocates the first 15 positions (bytes) in the random file buffer for file number 2 to the string variable TAX$ and the next 15 positions to PAY$

The FIELD statement allocates space but does not actually place any data into the random file buffer. The actual placement of data into the buffer results from the execution of an LSET or RSET statement.

You can execute any number of FIELD statements with the same file number, and each such statement will serve to redefine the buffer from the first character position. This capability will enable you to manipulate the extraction of data stored on a random file or to be written onto a random file. You can see one effect of this technique of containing multiple FIELD statements in a program by examining Figure 12.2. Here, the first FIELD statement defines a name and address field consisting of 30 bytes per record. The second FIELD statement redefines the buffer. Here, the previous name field of 10 bytes is broken into three fields consisting of a last name (LNAME$) and two initial fields (IN1$ and IN2$). Once you use a variable name in a field statement, you should normally exclude that name from later use in an INPUT or LET statement with that variable name on the left side of the equality sign. This is because defining a variable name in a FIELD statement makes it point to the correct place in a random file and

Statement 100 FIELD#1,10 AS ANAME$,20 AS ADD$

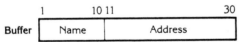

Statement 200 FIELD#1,8 AS LNAME$,1 AS IN1$,1 AS IN2$,10 ADD$

Figure 12.2   Redefining the Random Buffer.

the use of that variable in another BASIC statement could remove it from functioning as a field specifier.

Type . . END TYPE Block Statement

When you are using QuickBASIC, the TYPE . . END TYPE block statement is an alternative to the FIELD statement to define the fields within a record. The use of this block statement simplifies defining, writing to, and retrieving data from random file records. This simplicity becomes noteworthy as this block statement is used and compared to the FIELD statement, which requires functions to convert strings to numeric values and numeric values to strings. The format of the TYPE . . END TYPE block statement is

```
format_Q: TYPE name
             varname AS typename
             .
             .
             .
          END TYPE
```

The name assigned to the TYPE keyword identifies the user-defined type. The *varname* identifies the name of each field, whereas the *typename* can be INTEGER, LONG, SINGLE, DOUBLE, or STRING*n.

To master the use of the TYPE . . END TYPE block statement, you can develop a few examples using this QuickBASIC statement. The FIELD statement that allocated 10 bytes to the string variable N$ and 20 bytes to Y$ could be replaced by the following TYPE . . END TYPE block statement.

```
TYPE Stringrecord
   N$ AS STRING*10
   Y$ AS STRING*20
END TYPE
```

Now suppose you wanted to code fields to record the age, sex, and salary of employees where you wish to encode the person's age as a two-character integer, his or her sex as a one-character string, and the salary as a five-character number. If you used a FIELD statement to define the lengths of the buffers, it might be coded as follows:

```
FIELD#1, 2 AS AGE$, 1 AS SEX$, 5 AS SALARY$
```

If you used the TYPE . . END TYPE block statement, you only have to consider the length of strings, as illustrated by the following record definition, which is equivalent to the FIELD statement just coded:

```
TYPE Example
   Age AS INTEGER
   Sex AS STRING*1
   Salary AS SINGLE
END TYPE
```

As you compare the prior FIELD statement to the equivalent TYPE . . END TYPE block statement, note that each name in the FIELD statement that represents a record's field must be encoded as a string, with the number of positions explicitly defined. In comparison, each variable name in the TYPE . . END TYPE block statement that defines a field within a record is created following QuickBASIC variable naming rules and, with the exception of strings, does not require you to define the number of positions associated with each variable. As you examine additional random file statements and functions, the simplicity associated with the use of the TYPE . . END TYPE block statement in comparison to the use of the FIELD statement will become more apparent.

LSET and RSET Statements

LSET and RSET provide the capability to move data from the computer's memory into a random file buffer prior to executing a PUT statement. The formats of these statements are

format: LSET *var$=var$*₁
format: RSET *var$=var$*₁

Here, LSET left justifies the specified string variable $var\$_1$; RSET performs a right justification function. The string variable, $var\$$, on the left-hand side of the equality sign must be previously defined in a FIELD statement. If $var\$_1$ requires fewer bytes than were specified for the string variable, $var\$$, spaces will be added to pad the extra positions. If $var\$_1$ contains more bytes than were specified for the string variable, $var\$$, the extra characters are dropped from the right of $var\$_1$. Note that both LSET and RSET only operate on strings. Thus, if you wish to place numeric value into the random buffer, you must first convert those values to strings. You can perform this operation on numeric data through the use of the "make" functions, MKI$, MKS$, and MKD$ and, if you are using QuickBASIC, the MKL$ function that converts numeric type values to string type values. The use of the MKI$ and MK$ functions is illustrated in Figure 12.3.

```
100 FIELD #1,5 AS JCODE$,7 AS VALUE$
110 X$=MKI$(10412)
120 LSET JCODE$=X$
130 Y$=MKS$(137.52)
140 LSET VALUE$=X$
```

If you use the QuickBASIC TYPE . . END TYPE block statement in place of a FIELD statement to define the fields of the record, you do not have to worry about left or right justification of data within a field. Thus, you can eliminate the use of the LSET and RSET statements when you use the QuickBASIC TYPE . . END TYPE block statement.

Make String Functions

MKI$ converts an integer into a two-byte string, whereas MKS$ converts a single-precision number into a four-byte string. Thus, although numeric values are shown in

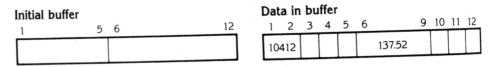

Figure 12.3   Operational Result of LSET Statement.

the input buffer in Figure 12.3, they are actually strings of 2 and 4 bytes in length. The MKD\$ function converts a double-precision number into an 8-byte string. If you are using QuickBASIC, a fourth "make string" function is available—MKL\$. MKL\$ is used to convert a long-integer value to a 4-byte string. The formats of these four functions are

format: *var\$=MKI\$(integer expr)*
format: *var\$=MKS\$(single-precision expr)*
format: *var\$=MKD\$(double-precision expr)*
format$_Q$: *var\$=MKL\$(long-integer expr)*

Because "make string" functions are used to convert numeric expressions to strings that can be stored based on the strings defined in a FIELD statement, these functions are unnecessary when your record fields are defined in QuickBASIC using a TYPE . . END TYPE block statement. Thus, the use of the TYPE . . END TYPE block statement eliminates both string justification and string conversion, which are required when a FIELD statement is used for defining record fields.

PUT Statement

The PUT statement provides you with the capability to write a record previously entered into the random buffer onto a random file. In examining the use of the PUT statement, the example here first uses the FIELD statement applicable to both interpretive BASIC and QuickBASIC to define a record. This will be followed by an example of a PUT statement when the TYPE . . END TYPE block statement that is only applicable to QuickBASIC is used to define the fields within a record.

When a FIELD statement is used to define the fields in a record, you must first use the OPEN and FIELD statements and one or more LSET or RSET statements prior to using the PUT statement in a program. The format of this statement is

format: PUT[#] *filenum[,recnum]*

where *filenum* is the file number under which the file was OPENed and *recnum* is the record number of the record to be written onto the file from the random buffer.

The record number specifies the position in the file that the contents of the random buffer will be written to and must be in the range 1 to 16 million. If the record number is omitted, the random buffer contents will be written to the file using the next available record number after the last PUT statement.

The following program segment illustrates the use of the PUT statement when a FIELD statement was used to define the fields in a record. Note that you must first open the file and define the fields of the random buffer prior to using the PUT statement.

```
100 OPEN "B:XRAY.DAT" FOR RANDOM AS #1 LEN=85
110 FIELD #1,30 AS FIRMNAME$,30 AS ADDRESS$,5 AS ZIP$,10 AS BALANCE$,10 AS LMT$
115 RECORD%=1
120 PRINT "data entry section. . enter x for FirmName to exit"
130 INPUT "FirmName= ",FIRM$
140 IF LEFT$(FIRM$,1)="x" GOTO 500
150 INPUT "Address= ",ADD$
160 INPUT "Zip= ",ZIP
170 INPUT "Balance= ",BALANCE
180 INPUT "Credit Limit= ",CLMIT
```

```
190 LSET FIRMNAME$=FIRM$
200 LSET ADDRESS$=ADD$
210 LSET ZIP$=MKS$(ZIP)
220 LSET BALANCE$=MKS$(BALANCE)
230 LSET LMT$=MKS$(CLMIT)
250 PUT#1,RECORD%
260 RECORD%=RECORD%+1
270 GOTO 120
500 CLOSE
```

In line 100 the file XRAY.DAT is opened as a random file on drive B with each record having a length of 85 bytes. The FIELD statement in line 110 defines five fields and the number of bytes assigned to each field. To associate a record number with each PUT statement, line 115 sets the first number assigned to the integer variable RECORD% to 1. If you omitted a record number from the PUT statement, BASIC assigns a value of 1 from the first time the statement is executed and increments the record value by 1 for each subsequent PUT.

Lines 130 and 150 through 180 prompt the user to enter information concerning a firm's name, address, ZIP code, account balance, and credit limit. In line 140 the first character in the firm's name is compared to lowercase X, resulting in a branch to line 500 when the values are equal. Lines 190 to 230 use the LSET function to left justify each field entry, whereas the PUT statement in line 250 writes the contents of the random file buffer as record RECORD%. Next, the record number is incremented by 1 in line 260, and the program branches back to line 120.

One of the more interesting aspects of the previous program segment is the fact that ZIP is entered as a numeric and converted to a string using the MKS$ function instead of treating it as an integer and using the MKI$ function. This was done because the largest integer you can have in BASIC is 32,767, while ZIP codes can exceed that value. If you are using QuickBASIC, you could specify ZIP as a long integer and then use the MKL$ function for conversion to a string.

Now examine the use of the QuickBASIC TYPE .. END TYPE statement block to perform the same random file operation as performed using a FIELD statement. The coding is

```
TYPE Custcredit
        FirmName AS STRING * 30
        Address AS STRING * 30
        Zip AS INTEGER
        Balance AS SINGLE
        Creditlimit AS SINGLE
END TYPE
DIM Rec AS Custcredit
I = 1'record number
OPEN "B:XRAY.DAT" FOR RANDOM AS #1 LEN = LEN(Rec)
start:
PRINT "data entry section . . enter x for Firmname to exit"
INPUT "Firmname= ", Rec.FirmName
IF LEFT$(Rec.FirmName, 1) = "x" GOTO loopend:
INPUT "Address= ", Rec.Address
INPUT "Zip= ", Rec.Zip
```

```
INPUT "Balance= ", Rec.Balance
INPUT "Credit limit=", Rec.Creditlimit
PUT #1, I, Rec
I = I + 1
GOTO start:
loopend:
CLOSE #1
```

In the TYPE . . END TYPE example, the name Custcredit is assigned to the user-defined type that contains five variable names. Next, the program uses a version of the DIM statement to declare the variable Rec as a record variable whose format was defined through the use of the TYPE . . END TYPE statement block. Note that the OPEN statement defines the length of the record as LEN(Rec). You can do this because the LEN function can be used to calculate the length of the variable (Rec) created to hold each record. Also note that after this is accomplished the user can simply input data, assigning the input to its field within the variable Rec, denoting this by specifying the record variable name followed by a decimal point and the field name. Once the appropriate data elements are entered, the PUT statement simply places the data from the variable Rec to the file. Thus, in QuickBASIC you can also use the following format for the PUT statement:

format$_Q$: PUT[#] filenum[,recnum][,var]

In the second format, which is only applicable to QuickBASIC, you can write the contents of a variable to a file similar to the manner in which the contents of Rec were written to the file XRAY.DAT previously. However, you can only use this format when you replace the use of a FIELD statement by the use of a TYPE . . END TYPE block statement, because the FIELD statement requires the contents of the random file buffer to be written to the file.

GET Statement

The GET statement is the complement of the PUT statement, because its execution causes a record to be read from a random file into a random buffer. Prior to using this statement in a program, you must OPEN the file and use a FIELD statement or, if you are using QuickBASIC, a TYPE . . END TYPE block statement, to define the fields in the random buffer. The format of this statement is

format: GET[#] filenum[,recnum]

where filenum is the file number under which the file was opened and recnum is the record number of the random file to be read into the random buffer. The record number range must be 1 to 16 million.

If the record number is omitted from the statement, the next record after the previous GET statement will be read into the buffer. The following program segment illustrates the use of this statement.

```
100 OPEN "B:XRAY.DAT" FOR RANDOM AS #1 LEN=85
110 FIELD #1,30 AS FIRMNAME$,30 AS ADDRESS$,5 AS ZIP$,10 AS BALANCE$,10 AS LMT$
120 GET #1
125 IF EOF(1) THEN 200
130 ZIP=CVS(ZIP$)
```

```
140 BALANCE=CVS(BALANCE$)
150 CLIMIT=CVS(LMT$)
160 PRINT FIRMNAME$;ADDRESS$;ZIP;BALANCE;CLIMIT
170 GOTO 120
200 CLOSE
```

This example illustrates the coding required to read the random file XRAY.DAT, previously created. Note that the code specified GET without a record number, which causes the first record in the file to be retrieved the first time that statement is executed. After testing for the end-of-file mark with the EOF function in line 125, the program converts the strings from the random buffer back to their numeric values, in this example using the CVS functions, because the original file storage example used single-precision numerics for ZIP, BALANCE, and CLIMIT.

If you used the TYPE .. END TYPE block statement, you could omit the string-to-numeric conversion, because records are written directly from variables and retrieved directly to variables without a random access buffer that requires data storage as strings.

Convert to Numeric Functions

As previously discussed, when you are using a FIELD statement, information is stored and retrieved as data strings. Thus, you must convert string variable types to numeric variable types if you wish to perform numeric operations. Interpretive BASIC supports three convert-to-numeric functions; QuickBASIC adds a fourth function. The formats for the convert-to-numeric functions are

```
format: varnm=CVI(2-byte string)
format: varnm=CVS(4-byte string)
format: varnm=CVD(8-byte string)
format_Q: varnm=CVL(4-byte string)
```

LOC Function

When used with random files, the LOC function returns the record number of the last record that was read from or written onto a random file. You can use this function to obtain the current record number, or you can use the function in a statement for testing purposes. Thus,

```
100 X=LOC(1)
```

returns the record number of the last record read or written onto a random file and assigns that number to the variable X. The statements

```
100 IF LOC(1)=20 THEN 120
110 PUT #2,LOC(1)
120 REM continue processing
```

could be used to skip record 20 when you are placing data of file number 2.

LOF Function

The LOF function is the same for both sequential and random file processing. That is, it returns the number of bytes allocated to the file.

Random File Processing

This section develops an "on-line charge authorization" program to illustrate random file processing techniques.

Suppose the credit department of a store wishes to develop an automated system that will access a customer's account number as sales are made in different departments of the store. This system will consist of a program that will verify that the customer has not exceeded his or her credit limit. For simplicity, assume that each customer record has the following format:

account number	credit limit	charges to date

Suppose account numbers vary from 40001 to 40100. Because using these account numbers as record numbers would waste a great amount of file space, you can transpose them into a range of record numbers more acceptable for random file processing. This transformation can be accomplished by subtracting 40000 from each account number. By doing so, you will use the record number as a transformed account number and for data storage purposes your record format then becomes

credit limit	charges to date

Now examine the BASIC statements necessary to perform the various processing functions you might require—such as file initialization, credit authorization, credit limit changes, and status report generation.

Your main menu segment might then be constructed as follows. Note that your option choice is assigned to the variable labeled AOPTION (because OPTION is a reserved word).

```
100 OPEN "B:CREDIT.DAT" AS #1 LEN=20
110 FIELD #1,10 AS CL$,10 AS C$
120 PRINT "CREDIT AUTHORIZATION OPTIONS"
130 PRINT "  1  FILE INITIALIZATION"
140 PRINT "  2  CREDIT AUTHORIZATION"
150 PRINT "  3  CREDIT LIMIT CHANGE"
160 PRINT "  4  STATUS REPORT"
170 PRINT "  5  EXIT PROGRAM"
180 INPUT "***ENTER OPTION DESIRED*** ",AOPTION
190 IF AOPTION >=1 OR AOPTION <=5 THEN 220
200 PRINT "OPTION NUMBER INVALID"
210 GOTO 180
220 ON AOPTION GOSUB 300,500,700,900,1010
230 GOTO 120
```

Again for simplicity, assume each individual account number has the same initial limit. Because the charge balance will be zero, your program module will initialize the credit limit field of each record to a constant and the charges to date field to zero. The following statements perform this function:

```
230 GOTO 120
300 INPUT "IS THIS THE END OF THE MONTH -Y/N ";A$
310 IF A$ <>"Y" THEN RETURN
```

```
320 INPUT "ENTER CREDIT LIMIT ASSIGNMENT ",CREDIT
330 CREDIT$=MKS$(CREDIT)
340 LSET CL$=CREDIT$
350 CHARGE=0!
360 CHARGE$=MKS$(CHARGE)
370 LSET C$=CHARGE$
380 FOR RECN%=1 TO 100
390 PUT#1,RECN%
400 NEXT RECN%
410 RETURN
```

In this program segment, you must convert numeric values to string values prior to placing such entries in the random buffer. This is accomplished by using the MKS$ function. You could also combine several pairs of statements. As an example, lines 330 and 340 could be replaced by the statement LSET CL$ = MKS$(CREDIT).

For the file authorization segment, you will first accept the account number and pending charge from the keyboard. Then, you will transpose the charge number into a valid record number and retrieve the credit limit and charges-to-date for that account. If the pending charge plus the charges-to-date do not exceed the credit limit, you will authorize the charge and update the charges-to-date field. Otherwise, the pending charge will not be approved and the charges-to-date field will not be modified. The statements required to perform these functions are

```
500 INPUT "ACCOUNT NUMBER ";ACCT
510 IF ACCT>=40001! AND ACCT<=40100! THEN 540
520 PRINT "INVALID ACCOUNT NUMBER"
530 RETURN
540 INPUT "AMOUNT OF PENDING CHARGE ";AMT
550 RECN%=INT(ACCT-40000!)
560 GET#1,RECN%
570 CL=CVS(CL$)    'convert to numeric
580 C=CVS(C$)      'ditto
590 NAMT=AMT+C
600 IF NAMT<=CL THEN 625
605 PRINT "********************"
610 PRINT "CHARGE NOT AUTHORIZED"
615 PRINT "********************"
620 RETURN
625 PRINT "********************"
630 PRINT "CHARGE IS AUTHORIZED"
635 PRINT "********************"
640 LSET C$=MKS$(NAMT)    'update
650 PUT#1,RECN%           'charge-to-date
660 RETURN
```

Now, examine the program segment necessary to change the credit limit. Here, you will once again first accept the account number and transform it into an acceptable record number. Then you will retrieve the current credit limit and ask the operator to enter its new value. Then, you will update the record, changing the value of the credit limit. The following statements perform this function:

```
700 INPUT "ENTER ACCOUNT NUMBER ";ACCT
710 IF ACCT>=40001! AND ACCT<=40100! THEN 740
720 PRINT "INVALID ACCOUNT NUMBER"
730 RETURN
740 RECN%=INT(ACCT-40000!)
750 GET#1,RECN%
760 CL=CVS(CL$)
770 PRINT "FOR ACCOUNT# ";ACCT;" CREDIT LIMIT IS ";CL
780 INPUT "ENTER NEW CREDIT LIMIT ";CL
790 CL$=MKS$(CL)
800 PUT#1,RECN%
810 RETURN
```

Although you have a random file, you will process the file sequentially as you generate a status report that will list each account number, credit limit, and charges-to-date, as well as print summary statistics. The next program segment shows the statements necessary to perform this function:

```
900 CSUM=0 :CTD=0
910 LPRINT "ACCOUNT #  CREDIT LIMIT  MONTHLY CHARGES TO DATE"
920 FOR RECN%=1 TO 100
930 GET#1,RECN%
940 CSUM=CSUM+CVS(CL$)
950 CTD=CTD+CVS(C$)
960 ACCT=40000!+RECN%
970 LPRINT USING"######  ########,.##   ########,.##";ACCT,CVS(CL$),CVS(C$)
980 NEXT RECN%
990 LPRINT USING"TOTALS  #########,.##  #########,.##";CSUM,CTD
1000 RETURN
```

To provide a mechanism for an orderly exit from the program, you can include both a CLOSE and an END statement in line 1010, as follows:

```
1010 CLOSE:END
```

Thus, when the operator desires to exit from the program, the file will be closed automatically.

Now, run the program just created and use one or more program options in each program execution. First, initialize the credit limit of all accounts to $500. The execution of the appropriate program option is

RUN
```
CREDIT AUTHORIZATION OPTIONS
   1  FILE INITIALIZATION
   2  CREDIT AUTHORIZATION
   3  CREDIT LIMIT CHANGE
   4  STATUS REPORT
   5  EXIT PROGRAM
***ENTER OPTION DESIRED*** 1
IS THIS THE END OF THE MONTH -Y\N ? Y
ENTER CREDIT LIMIT ASSIGNMENT 500.00
CREDIT AUTHORIZATION OPTIONS
   1  FILE INITIALIZATION
```

```
     2  CREDIT AUTHORIZATION
     3  CREDIT LIMIT CHANGE
     4  STATUS REPORT
     5  EXIT PROGRAM
***ENTER OPTION DESIRED*** 5
Ok
```

Suppose after lunch this busy credit authorization center gets a call from the widget department that a customer with account number 40005 desires to charge the purchase of a widget costing $600. You now run the program again and find out that the charge is not authorized, as indicated by the next portion of the display shown here:

```
RUN
CREDIT AUTHORIZATION OPTIONS
     1  FILE INITIALIZATION
     2  CREDIT AUTHORIZATION
     3  CREDIT LIMIT CHANGE
     4  STATUS REPORT
     5  EXIT PROGRAM
***ENTER OPTION DESIRED*** 2
ACCOUNT NUMBER ? 40005
AMOUNT OF PENDING CHARGE ? 600
*********************
CHARGE NOT AUTHORIZED
*********************
CREDIT AUTHORIZATION OPTIONS
     1  FILE INITIALIZATION
     2  CREDIT AUTHORIZATION
     3  CREDIT LIMIT CHANGE
     4  STATUS REPORT
     5  EXIT PROGRAM
***ENTER OPTION DESIRED*** 5
Ok
```

The widget salesperson knows the customer and can vouch for his bank balance, so you call your manager, who proceeds to raise the credit limit of the customer's account to $700. Now, when you enter option 3, the charge is authorized as shown here:

```
***ENTER OPTION DESIRED*** 3
ENTER ACCOUNT NUMBER ? 40005
FOR ACCOUNT# 40005 CREDIT LIMIT IS 500
ENTER NEW CREDIT LIMIT ? 700
CREDIT AUTHORIZATION OPTIONS
     1  FILE INITIALIZATION
     2  CREDIT AUTHORIZATION
     3  CREDIT LIMIT CHANGE
     4  STATUS REPORT
     5  EXIT PROGRAM
***ENTER OPTION DESIRED*** 2
ACCOUNT NUMBER ? 40005
```

```
AMOUNT OF PENDING CHARGE ? 600
********************
CHARGE IS AUTHORIZED
********************
```

To illustrate the result of selecting option 4, you have changed line number 920 so that RECN% will vary from 1 to 10 instead of 1 to 100. The execution of this option that provides a report summary for the first 10 account numbers follows:

ACCOUNT #	CREDIT LIMIT	MONTHLY CHARGES TO DATE
40001	500.00	0.00
40002	500.00	0.00
40003	500.00	0.00
40004	500.00	0.00
40005	500.00	600.00
40006	500.00	0.00
40007	500.00	0.00
40008	500.00	0.00
40009	500.00	0.00
40010	500.00	0.00
TOTALS	5,000.00	600.00

File Error Conditions to Consider

There are a number of file error conditions you must consider in developing a program that manipulates files. Foremost among these conditions are Disk full (error number 61), Too many files (error number 67), and Disk not Ready (error number 71). You can use the error-handling procedures discussed in Chapter 11 to develop error-handling routines to check for such conditions and display corrective messages to the computer operator. Thus, on detection of error number 71, you could inform the operator that he or she either forgot to close the diskette drive door or failed to put the diskette in the drive.

Appendix C lists BASIC error numbers and their associated messages and meanings.

Appendix A
ASCII Code Representation

All the ASCII codes in decimal and their associated characters are listed here. The column labeled "Control character" lists the standard interpretations of ASCII codes 0 through 31 when they are used for control functions or data communications control. In addition to these 32 characters, ASCII code 127 is normally used as a pad or time fill character in asynchronous communications and should be disregarded when received by the PC AT, or one may receive a series of little houses on the display, because ASCII 127 is the graphic symbol △. To do this, one can simply test for this character and not display it when it is encountered.

ASCII value	Character	Control character	ASCII value	Character
000	(null)	NUL	032	(space)
001	☺	SOH	033	!
002	●	STX	034	"
003	♥	ETX	035	#
004	♦	EOT	036	$
005	♣	ENQ	037	%
006	♠	ACK	038	&
007	(beep)	BEL	039	'
008	(backspace)	BS	040	(
009	(tab)	HT	041	)
010	(line feed)	LF	042	*
011	(home)	VT	043	+
012	(form feed)	FF	044	,
013	(carriage return)	CR	045	-
014	♫	SO	046	.
015	☼	SI	047	/
016	►	DLE	048	0
017	◄	DC1	049	1
018	↕	DC2	050	2
019	!!	DC3	051	3

ASCII value	Character	Control character	ASCII value	Character
020	¶	DC4	052	4
021	§	NAK	053	5
022	▬	SYN	054	6
023	↨	ETB	055	7
024	↑	CAN	056	8
025	↓	EM	057	9
026	→	SUB	058	:
027	←	ESC	059	;
028	(cursor right)	FS	060	<
029	(cursor left)	GS	061	=
030	(cursor up)	RS	062	>
031	(cursor down)	US	063	?

ASCII value	Character	ASCII value	Character
064	@	106	j
065	A	107	k
066	B	108	l
067	C	109	m
068	D	110	n
069	E	111	o
070	F	112	p
071	G	113	q
072	H	114	r
073	I	115	s
074	J	116	t
075	K	117	u
076	L	118	v
077	M	119	w
078	N	120	x
079	O	121	y
080	P	122	z
081	Q	123	{
082	R	124	¦
083	S	125	}
084	T	126	~
085	U	127	⌂
086	V	128	Ç
087	W	129	ü
088	X	130	é
089	Y	131	â
090	Z	132	ä
091	[	133	à
092	\	134	å
093	]	135	ç
094	∧	136	ê
095	—	137	ë
096	'	138	è
097	a	139	ï
098	b	140	î
099	c	141	ì
100	d	142	Ä
101	e	143	Å
102	f	144	É
103	g	145	æ
104	h	146	Æ
105	i	147	ô

ASCII value	Character	ASCII value	Character
148	ö	202	╩
149	ò	203	╦
150	û	204	╠
151	ù	205	═
152	ÿ	206	╬
153	Ö	207	╧
154	Ü	208	╨
155	¢	209	╤
156	£	210	╥
157	¥	211	╙
158	Pts	212	╘
159	ƒ	213	╒
160	á	214	╓
161	í	215	╫
162	ó	216	╪
163	ú	217	┘
164	ñ	218	┌
165	Ñ	219	█
166	ª	220	▄
167	º	221	▌
168	¿	222	▐
169	⌐	223	▀
170	¬	224	α
171	½	225	β
172	¼	226	Γ
173	¡	227	π
174	«	228	Σ
175	»	229	σ
176	░	230	μ
177	▒	231	τ
178	▓	232	Φ
179	│	233	Θ
180	┤	234	Ω
181	╡	235	δ
182	╢	236	∞
183	╖	237	Ø
184	╕	238	∈
185	╣	239	∩
186	║	240	≡
187	╗	241	±
188	╝	242	≥
189	╜	243	≤
190	╛	244	⌠
191	┐	245	⌡
192	└	246	÷
193	┴	247	≈
194	┬	248	°
195	├	249	•
196	─	250	·
197	┼	251	√
198	╞	252	ⁿ
199	╟	253	²
200	╚	254	■
201	╔	255	(blank 'FF')

Appendix B
Extended Character Codes

Certain keys and key combinations are not represented in standard ASCII code on the IBM AT. For such keys and key combinations, an extended code will be returned when the INKEY$ variable is used in a BASIC program. A null character (ASCII code 000) will be returned as the first character of a two-character string; the second character will contain the code that defines the extended character.

To determine if an extended character code was received by INKEY$, you must then examine the second character to determine the actual key pressed as illustrated by the following program segment:

```
100 A$=INKEY$:IF A$=""THEN 100          'cycle until key pressed
110 IF LEN(A$)=1 THEN 200                'not extended code
120 IF VAL(RIGHT$(A$,1))=71 THEN 150     'Home pressed
130 IF VAL(RIGHT$(A$,1))=72 THEN 160     'cursor Up pressed
.
.
.
```

The decimal values of the ASCII codes for the second character of the AT's extended codes and the keys associated with those codes follow:

Second Code	Meaning
3	NUL (null character)
15	← (shift tab)
16–25	Alt Q, W, E, R, T, Y, U, I, O, P
30–38	Alt A, S, D, F, G, H, J, K, L
44–50	Alt Z, X, C, V, B, N, M
59–68	Function keys F1–F10 (when disabled as soft keys)
71	Home
72	Home
73	PgUp
75	PgUp
77	PgDn
79	End
80	End
81	PgDn
82	Ins
83	Del
84–93	F11–F20 (uppercase F1–F10)

Second Code	Meaning
94–103	F21–F30 (Ctrl F1–F10)
104–113	F31–F40 (Alt F1–F10)
114	PrtSc
115	Ctrl-PgUp (previous word)
116	Ctrl-PgDn (next word)
117	Ctrl-End
118	Ctrl-PgDn
119	Ctrl-Home
120–131	Alt 1, 2, 3, 4, 5, 6, 7, 8, 9, 0, -, =
132	Ctrl-PgUp

Appendix C
BASIC ERROR MESSAGES

Number	Message
1	NEXT without FOR[1]
2	Syntax error
3	RETURN without GOSUB
4	Out of data
5	Illegal function call
6	Overflow
7	Out of memory
8	Undefined line number[1]
9	Subscript out of range
10	Duplicate definition
11	Division by zero
12	Illegal direct[1]
13	Type mismatch
14	Out of string space
15	String too long[1]
16	String formula too complex
17	Can't continue[1]
18	Undefined user function[1]
19	No RESUME
20	RESUME without error
22	Missing operand[1]
23	Line buffer overflow[1]
24	Device timeout
25	Device fault
26	FOR without NEXT[1]
27	Out of paper
29	WHILE without WEND
30	WEND without WHILE[1]
39	CASE ELSE expected[2]

Number	Message
40	Variable required[2]
50	FIELD overflow
51	Internal error
52	Bad file number
53	File not found
54	Bad file mode
55	File already open
56	FIELD statement active[2]
57	Device I/O error
58	File already exists
59	Bad record length[2]
61	Disk full
62	Input past end
63	Bad record number
64	Bad file name
66	Direct statement in file[1]
67	Too many files
68	Device unavailable
69	Communications buffer overflow
70	Disk write protect[1]/permission denied[2]
71	Disk not ready
72	Disk media error
73	Advanced feature unavailable
74	Rename across disks
75	Path/file access error
76	Path not found
—	Unprintable error
—	Incorrect DOS version

[1]Applicable to interpretive BASIC only.
[2]Applicable to QuickBASIC only.

Index